GW00372300

READER'S DIGEST

Gentle Baby Care

How to Nurture Your Baby the Safe, Natural Way

JULIA GOODWIN

THE READERS DIGEST ASSOCIATION, INC.

Pleasantville, New York/Montreal

To Simon, who held the fort brilliantly!

A Reader's Digest Book

Text copyright © Julia Goodwin 1997
Illustrations © Nicola Smee 1997

First published in the United Kingdom in 1997 by Ebury Press

Library of Congress Cataloging in Publication Data

Goodwin, Julia
Gentle baby care: how to nurture your baby the safe, natural way / Julia Goodwin
p. cm.
Includes index.
ISBN 0–7621–0024–9
1. Infants — Care. 2. Infants — Health and hygiene. I. Title.
RJ61.657 1998
649'.122 — dc21
97-17881
CIP

Designed by Lovelock & Co.

Printed and bound in Portugal

Contents

ACKNOWLEDGMENTS

I would like to thank Friends of the Earth, the London Food Commission, and the Women's Environmental Network for their information. I would like to acknowledge *The Parents' Green Guide* by Brigid McConville (Pandora) for the help it provided. I would also like to thank Ione Brown, who helped me enormously with the research on Chapter Four, and Karen Heavey, who did likewise on Chapters Two and Three. Finally, thanks to Dr. Sue Bower for her comments on the manuscript.

Introduction

If you've just had, or are about to have, a baby—congratulations. You are embarking on an exciting journey that will last for the rest of your life. The fun and satisfaction are impossible to describe until you experience them—but the responsibility can be awesome.

Today's parents have access to more information than any previous generation. But all that knowledge—from books, magazines, television and radio programs, and Internet sites—can be overwhelming. If we were to read every piece of relevant information on bringing up children, there would be no time left to actually do the job.

In this book I have tried to cover all the important issues—including the environmental ones—likely to be encountered during your baby's earliest days and later on in childhood. These range from how to avoid food additives to safe bathing and natural remedies for minor ailments.

More generally, this book discusses how to make your home a healthier place. It offers tips on natural furnishings, advice on indoor pollutants and danger zones around the house. Outdoor life is not overlooked; you'll find advice on dealing with insect and animal bites, pest control, and sun protection as well.

My goal is to paint a balanced picture, offering reasonable suggestions on ways to bring up children as naturally as possible in an increasingly artificial environment. However, we can take advantage of technological advances. Washing machines, dishwashers, the choice of convenience foods and health products now widely available—these have freed parents from many of the chores associated with caring for babies and small children that our parents and grandparents endured.

Easy-wash, easy-care children's clothes, disposable diapers, convenience baby foods, and infant formula have all made life easier for many parents. But we now know more about the possible disadvantages of some of these products than we did 10 or 20 years ago. There is also a multimillion-dollar baby product market running advertising campaigns to persuade us that our baby needs all these things and more. The truth is—he really doesn't.

Be aware of the tremendous power of baby product advertising and the way it is placed in publications you trust to give you honest information on baby care. Don't be taken in by it. For example, if you feel a sling and a convertible stroller will be the best ways of transporting your baby, don't buy a luxury buggy as well.

Make the best decisions you can in the light of the information you have. Don't worry if he has a jar of baby food twice a week or you've used a bath product that has given him a skin rash.

There is no such thing as a perfect parent. And who would want to have one if there were? Your baby will love you without reservation even if you do make an occasional mistake. Enjoy bringing him up and getting to know him.

N.B. I have referred to your baby as "he" throughout this book. I did so purely to make it easier for you to avoid confusion about whether I am referring to the baby or the mother.

CHAPTER ONE

Feeding Your Baby

We are what we eat. The way you choose to feed your baby will undoubtedly influence not only his own adult eating habits but also his long-term health. Babies who enjoy varied diets with plenty of fresh foods will grow accustomed to these flavors. On the other hand, babies reared largely on processed and synthetic foods will become accustomed to artificial tastes and textures, and will accept them as natural.

We know that too many of today's teenagers consume convenience foods and carbonated drinks in large quantities. By getting your baby into good eating habits early, you will make it easier for him to choose wisely as he grows up—baked potatoes instead of fries, salad instead of canned vegetables, fruit juice instead of sugar-laden soft drinks. And of course his health will benefit too. A recent survey of 5,000 children revealed that 10-year-old boys are 17 percent fatter and 10-year-old girls are 6 percent fatter than their counterparts were 20 years ago. Heart disease, cancer, and, for girls, osteoporosis, are all linked to diet. Getting your baby into good eating habits will give him the best possible start in life.

Breast-feeding

Women have been breast-feeding babies for millions of years. All the research shows that it is the safest and healthiest way to feed a baby. Breast milk needs no preparation, and its unique makeup can never be copied in formula.

Although breast-feeding is completely natural, it is a technique that has to be learned. Many women are tempted to give up if they experience difficulties. In North America more than half the mothers breast-feed their babies to begin with, but within four months three-quarters of them have switched to bottle-feeding.

Not being able to see the amount of milk your baby is taking in can lead to anxiety about whether he is getting enough. Mothers need a lot of support and encouragement during the first six weeks when breast-feeding is becoming established. You have to ignore housework, learn to make cooking simple, and concentrate on resting and eating well to build up your energy and your milk supply. All this can be very difficult indeed if you are alone, especially if you have other small children who are also demanding your time and attention.

Breast-feeding gives your baby the very best start in life. You will also grow to really enjoy feeding him and to experience great satisfaction in the knowledge that you are providing from within your own body everything he needs to grow and develop.

WHY BREAST IS BEST FOR YOUR BABY

A breast-fed baby is protected against:

- Infection. Proteins in breast milk called immunoglobulins, or antibodies, help to fight the bacteria that cause respiratory and urinary infections, ear trouble, and stomach upsets (gastroenteritis). Protection against infection can continue for at least two years after breast-feeding stops.

- SIDS. Statistics show that breast-fed babies are far less likely to be victims of crib death (sudden infant death syndrome, SIDS), the biggest killer of healthy children during the first year of life.

- Allergies. Eczema, asthma, and other allergy-related conditions are far more common in bottle-fed babies.

- Constipation. Breast-fed babies' stools contain more water, making bowel movement easier.

- Obesity. Breast milk is perfectly tailored to your baby's needs, so he is less likely to overfeed.

- Childhood diabetes and cancers. There is a lower incidence of these conditions among breast-fed babies than among those who are bottle-fed.

- Dental problems. Breast-fed babies have less tooth decay when they are older.

WHY BREAST IS BEST FOR YOU

If you breast-feed it is more likely that you will:

- Be protected against ovarian cancer and early breast cancer.

- Be unable to conceive. Although high levels of prolactin help to block ovulation, you should consider family planning if you want to delay or avoid pregnancy.

- Save time. Breast milk arrives at just the right temperature, ready for your baby to drink. And you don't have to be concerned about time-consuming cleaning of bottles and nipples.

- Save money. Breast-feeding costs nothing, although you will need to make sure you eat a healthy and balanced diet. Bottle-feeding is relatively expensive.

- Help protect the environment. The infant formula market uses vast quantities of steel each year to produce formula milk containers. Breast milk comes in its own package!

COLOSTRUM

As soon as possible after your baby is born, you should put him to the breast. This is when his sucking reflex is strongest, and the stimulation of your breast will help to promote a good milk supply. For the first two days, your breasts will produce colostrum, a thick, creamy substance that is rich in antibodies. Even if you feed your baby for only a few days, the colostrum will help protect him against infection.

Colostrum is a high-density, low-volume milk. Your baby needs only a small quantity. It contains more protein and fat-soluble vitamins than mature breast milk, but less fat and fewer carbohydrates, and water-soluble vitamins. It also has more cholesterol than mature milk. It is perfect for a newborn baby's digestive system.

WHEN THE MILK COMES IN

Three or four days after the birth, the colostrum you produce will start to change to mature milk. This is referred to as the milk coming in, and your breasts may feel uncomfortably full. Your physician will encourage you to put your baby to the breast as often as the baby wishes, since the more he sucks, the more stimulation the breasts receive to make more milk. Sucking also stimulates the production of the hormone oxytocin, which pushes the milk through the milk ducts and into the nipples, producing a strong, tingly sensation known as the letdown reflex. As the baby

BENEFITS OF BREAST MILK

Human breast milk is made up of water, proteins, carbohydrates, minerals, fats, vitamins, hormones, and enzymes like any other milk. But it is the unique combination of these substances that makes it the best, most natural source of nutrition for your baby. Here are some of the components that produce breast milk's special qualities:

- Protein (lactoferrin). The low protein content of breast milk is suited to a baby's immature kidneys. Formulas have a higher concentration of protein. Lactoferrin also helps your baby to absorb iron, and it stops bacteria from developing in the bowel.

- Casein. When milk enters a baby's stomach, it is turned into curds and whey. The curds made from the milk protein casein pass more easily through the baby's digestive system than bulky formula curds.

- Cholesterol. Breast milk contains cholestrol, which plays an important part in the development of the nervous system. It is also thought that exposing a baby to cholesterol early reduces the harmful effects later on.

- Fatty acids (long-chain polyunsaturated fatty acids, LCPs). These help a baby's brain to develop.

- Interferon. This protein, which is passed into breast milk directly from the mother, helps build up the baby's resistance to viral infection.

feeds, he also stimulates the production of prolactin, which encourages the breasts to make more milk for the next feed.

Breast milk is perfectly tailored to your baby's needs. The watery foremilk quenches his thirst, while the creamier hindmilk, which the breast produces after the first few minutes of sucking, provides nutrients and satisfies the baby's hunger. Nevertheless, all babies lose weight during their first week of life. They pass meconium, a thick black substance, for the first 24 hours before starting to digest breast milk or formula. At first, the meconium and urine they pass is not compensated for by the amount of food that they take in. Large babies lose more weight than small ones. The average weight loss is between 4 and 7 ounces (113 to 198g).

HOW TO BREAST-FEED

There are many different positions in which you can breast-feed your baby successfully. The key is to find one that is comfortable for you and easy for him to "latch on," or take the nipple and the surrounding dark area, called the areola,

into his mouth. Imagine a piece of Velcro attached to your baby's bottom lip and the opposite piece attached one inch below the base of your nipple. You need to match the two together. If he is latched on properly, you will see more of the areola above his top lip than his bottom one. His nose and chin will be touching your breast. When he is in the right position, he can use his tongue and jaws to squeeze milk into the nipple. He should be facing you, chest to chest, and should not need to turn or twist to feed. If he is not in the right position, he will end up chewing on the nipple, causing pain and possible bleeding. To remove your baby from the breast, gently insert your little finger into the corner of his mouth and push the nipple out of his mouth.

BE COMFORTABLE

Make yourself as comfortable as you can to breast-feed and have everything you need at hand before you start, so that the feeding will not be interrupted. Many mothers breast-feed sitting on a firm chair with a pillow in the small of the back—remember

HELPING YOURSELF

- If your breasts feel uncomfortably full, try to sit in a warm bath or stand in the shower before a nursing. That can help the letdown reflex and your milk will start to flow before your baby latches on and starts to suck.

- Ease any throbbing by putting cold, wet washcloths on your breasts.

- If your nipples become cracked or sore, try to expose them to the air as much as possible to speed up healing.

- If you use breast pads in your bra to absorb extra, leaking milk, change them frequently so that your nipples do not remain wet and soggy.

- The early days of breast-feeding can be difficult, so try to persevere. By six weeks breast-feeding should be fully established, and your breasts will be providing the right amount of milk.

to position the pillow first. A chair with arms lets you rest your arms. Others prefer to breast-feed lying on their side with their head supported by a pillow. Choose the best position for you. A towel or clean cloth diaper is useful to mop up any milk he brings up. You may find that breast-feeding makes you thirsty. This is nature's way of getting you to take more liquid, so have a glass of water within reach.

HOW OFTEN TO FEED

Many small babies eat every couple of hours, and there may be periods when your baby seems to be continually at the breast. Generally, breast-fed babies eat more frequently than bottle-fed ones because they are able to digest the milk so well. As your baby gets bigger, he may settle into a regular pattern, which may be more frequent than the classic every-four-hour feedings that the old textbooks used to recommend.

If your baby seems dissatisfied when he is feeding, you may worry that you are not producing enough milk. This is extremely rare. The World Health Organization (WHO) estimates that only 2 in every 100 women are unable to produce enough milk to feed their babies. To make sure your baby is getting enough:

- Try to take a good rest each day, eat lots of fresh foods, and drink plenty of fluids. Cereal, fruit, a sandwich, glass of milk, or cheese or peanut butter on toast are quick, healthy snacks. Many women find their milk supply gets low in the late afternoon and early evening; so snack then.

- Ask someone to verify that your baby is taking a big mouthful of breast, including the areola. Sometimes you can think you have a poor supply when in fact your baby is not positioned properly. Listen for a glugging sound as he begins to nurse.

BREAST-FEEDING A BIGGER BABY
Babies go through growth spurts, often at six weeks and again at three months. At these times you may feel uneasy that your calm, settled, contented baby has become fussy and may seem dissatisfied. The solution is to increase the frequency of feeding to allow the extra sucking to stimulate more milk production. As long as you let your baby feed more often, he should settle back into a more reliable pattern within a few days.

NIGHT FEEDING
At first, your baby will not be able to distinguish night from day, so you will need to encourage him to have his longest sleep at night. Keep night feedings low-key and he will go back to sleep more quickly:

- Don't turn on the lights.

- Don't be tempted to play with him or distract his attention from feeding.

- You may want to take him into bed with you to feed. This is safe, as long as you are not taking drugs or alcohol. Make sure he does not overheat and that his head is not covered by your bedclothes, and put him back in his crib after feeding and changing him.

- Your baby is unlikely to sleep through the night until he is at least three months old, so you must rest during the day to make up for the night waking.

HOW LONG TO BREAST-FEED

Breast-feeding for even a few days provides your baby with valuable antibodies to fight infection. Studies have shown that babies can enjoy the health benefits for as long as 2 years if they are breast-fed for 14 weeks (see "Why breast is best for your baby," p.9). Some women breast-feed for a year or more because they find it such a rewarding, economical, and enjoyable experience. It's really up to you and your circumstances.

After about six months, your baby will start to take solid food, and his dependence on breast milk as a source of nourishment will gradually decrease (see "Solid Foods," p.28).

When babies are able to sit unsupported, some of them become so interested in the world around them that they don't like the time they spend breast-feeding. These babies resist turning their back on all the activity. (With a bottle of training cup, they can sit and watch and drink all at the same time.) If your baby frequently stops in the middle of a feeding, arches his back and cranes his head around to see what's going on, then he is sending you a signal that weaning is not that far away.

On the other hand, some older babies love the snuggling closeness that comes with breast-feeding. They prefer to continue to nurse (if possible) even if they also drink other liquids from a cup.

GOING BACK TO WORK

It is possible to combine breast-feeding with paid employment, but you need to plan ahead so that your arrangement suits you, your baby, your spouse, the baby's sitter, and your employer.

You can decide to express milk at home, which your sitter can then feed to your baby in a bottle, or you may decide to switch to formula during the daytime and breast-feed in the mornings and evenings only. Many mothers who return to work will choose to continue the morning and evening feedings because they value these special times of closeness at the beginning and at the end of the day.

If your baby is more than six months old, you can introduce a cup with a feeding spout rather than a bottle. But if you plan

WHEN TO ASK FOR HELP

Ask your your baby's doctor for help if:

- Nursing is painful from beginning to end.

- Your nipples bleed.

- Your breasts become hard, swollen, reddened, and tender after your milk has come in.

- Your baby seems restless and dissatisfied at the breast.

- Your baby takes longer than 40 minutes to feed at each breast.

- Your baby feeds more than 10 times in 24 hours after he is a week old.

- Your baby eats fewer than three times in the first 24 hours or fewer than six times a day after that.

- Your baby has not regained his birthweight by the time he is 10 days old.

to switch to a bottle or organize bottle-feedings for him during the day, you need to get him accustomed to it first:

- Touch your baby's lips with the nipple and encourage him to take the bottle. (Some are shaped like your nipples; see "Choosing a nipple," p.24.)

- Offer the milk from a small spoon. Some breast-fed babies who are reluctant to switch to a bottle will happily sip from a spoon.

- Ask your spouse to give your baby the bottle. Your baby will not expect a breast-feeding from him.

- Offer the bottle when he is not too hungry, so he won't be frustrated by being fed in an unfamiliar way.

- Your supply of breast milk will start to reduce once you start bottle-feeding with formula.

EXPRESSING YOUR MILK

If you plan to express your own milk, you will need to get a hand or electric pump.

Expressed breast milk will keep for up to 48 hours in the refrigerator and up to a month in the freezer. It can be left in warm water for four hours at room temperature. Store expressed milk in clean baby bottles (see "Keeping bottles clean," p.22).

Thaw frozen breast milk by putting the container in a bowl of warm water. Don't use a microwave; it will heat the milk unevenly, which could scald your baby's mouth.

BREAST-FEEDING AND THE ENVIRONMENT

Breast-feeding is best for the environment as well as for your baby. You may worry that today's polluted environment has affected the purity of your milk, and there have been reports about very small amounts of dangerous chemicals, called dioxins, found in breast milk. But the benefits of breast-feeding far outweigh the risks.

The use of chemicals in our industries over the past 50 years has produced a certain amount of toxic waste, which has entered all our bodies and which your baby will have been exposed to as he developed in the womb whether you breast- or bottle-feed him. Recent reports suggest that these levels are now falling, and the baby-food industry is closely monitored by the government and the water quality closely checked.

BREAST-FEEDING AND HIV

The human immunodeficiency virus (HIV) can be transmitted through breast milk. If you are HIV-positive, it is recommended that you do not breast-feed. If you are unsure about your risk of HIV, get tested before you breast-feed.

YOUR FEELINGS

You may be overwhelmed by the powerful emotions that breast-feeding stirs in you. You may find that it cements the bond between you and your baby in a unique and fulfilling way. Or you may feel slightly embarrassed about breast-feeding in public or aware that your spouse is jealous of the intimate attention your baby is receiving, and these thoughts can override any sense of contentment.

Each woman's situation is different, and you have to weigh the benefits of this natural way of feeding your baby against any possible disadvantages. If you decide that breast-feeding is not for you, or if you want to stop before your baby is ready for a cup, bottle-feeding is the only alternative.

Once you have made the decision to switch to bottle-feeding, you may feel guilty. However, you should remember that each day of breast-feeding has given your baby extra protection against infections and illnesses, because you have passed on your antibodies to him in your breast milk. You may also find that your energy level rises once you stop breast-feeding. And if you feel positive, your baby will undoubtedly benefit too.

Bottle-feeding

More than three-quarters of the babies born in North America each year are bottle-fed by the time they are four months old. Your baby will be in very good company if you choose this method of feeding him. You may decide to bottle-feed straight from birth, or you may want to switch over after breast-feeding your baby for a few days, weeks, or months.

YOUR BREASTS

If you bottle-feed from the start, your breasts may feel uncomfortably full for the first few days. But since your baby will not be stimulating them to make milk by sucking, this feeling of fullness will soon disappear. Wearing a firm support bra day and night for a few days may help.

When changing over from breast-feeding to bottle-feeding:

• Cut down gradually, replacing one breast-feeding every two days with a bottle, or add an ounce or two of formula to each breast-feeding session. This will let your breasts start reducing their milk supply.

• Your breasts may become engorged. Relieve the discomfort by expressing by hand a small amount of breast milk, but not too much or you will stimulate them to make even more milk.

• If your breasts feel hot, if you develop a red mark on one, or if you start to run a temperature, you may have developed mastitis, caused by a blocked milk duct.

Apply hot packs to your breasts and make an appointment with your physician, for you may need antibiotics.

CHOOSING FORMULA

Experts agree that formula, usually based on cow's milk, is not, and never can be, exactly the same as breast milk. Originally intended for calves, which have big bodies and small brains, cow's milk has had to go through many stages of processing to be made suitable for human babies, who have small bodies and big brains. Protein and salt levels have been modified, and iron has been added during the process. The two main types of formula are:

• Whey-dominant. Usually labeled as a first milk or as suitable from birth, this formula has extra whey protein added to it to make it more similar to breast milk. Whey is watery and easier for a baby to digest than casein.

• Casein-based. Slightly higher in protein than the whey formula, this mixture takes longer to digest. It is sold as a "follow-on" milk, designed to satisfy "hungrier" babies. In fact, there's no conclusive evidence to support this. Both types of milk are suitable for babies from birth.

- Most formulas contain long-chain polyunsaturated fatty acids (LCPs), which are known to be vital in promoting brain growth in babies. These are closest to breast milk. Check the label to be sure your formula is rich in LCPs.

THE RIGHT FORMULA

- Your baby may go through a restless period in the early evening, and you may think he is not satisfied. Some mothers consider adding solids, but there is no need to: this behavior is common for both breast- and bottle-fed babies. They settle down as they grow older.

- A formula that does not suit your baby may cause such symptoms as vomiting, stomach cramps, or a rash or other allergic reactions. If your baby is gaining weight at about 8 ounces (224g) a week and is not showing any of these symptoms, his food is fine. If you are not happy with the formula you are using, consult with your baby's doctor before changing.

- Soy-based formulas are available for babies who are allergic to cow's milk formula, but you should always check with your baby's doctor before changing. There may be other drawbacks to using

ESSENTIAL EQUIPMENT

You will need:

- Six to eight 8-ounce (240-ml) bottles. Some types are for use with plastic disposable liners, which collapse as the milk is sucked out, preventing your baby from swallowing too much air when he sucks. A bottle includes a nipple (see Choosing a nipple on page 24); a cap to protect the nipple when it is not in use; a ring which screws on to fasten the nipple to the bottle.

- Two bottle brushes.

- A sterilizing system or a dishwasher.

- A measuring cup with a lid.

- Plastic knife and spoon.

soy milk, since some babies are allergic to it.

- Apart from breast milk, infant formula is the only food suitable for your baby until he is at least six months old. Goat's milk and condensed milk are not suitable foods for young babies.

- It is best to continue formula for 9 to 12 months.

- In an emergency, if you run out of formula, try boiled sugar water until you can get to the store.

MAKING UP FORMULA

- Follow the manufacturer's instructions on the container exactly. Never be tempted to add extra powder or concentrate because your baby seems hungry. The highly concentrated formula would put a strain on his kidneys, which are too immature to cope, and would give him a great thirst as well.

- Never add sugar or powdered baby food. If you think your baby is hungry, consult his doctor.

- Either pour the boiled water straight into the cleaned bottle or mix the water and powder or concentrate together in a measuring cup first. If you use a measuring cup, it must be cleaned thoroughly before each use (see "Keeping bottles clean," p.22).

- If you use powdered formula, always use the scoop provided by the manufacturer and always make sure the powder is loose in the scoop. If you pack it down too much, you will make the milk far too concentrated.

- Level off the scoop with a sterilized knife.

- Shake or stir in the powder well to dissolve it completely.

- It is usually easier to make up a day's worth of food at one time. Store the freshly made-up formula in the bottles with the caps on for 24 hours in the refrigerator.

- To reheat formula, stand it in hot water for several minutes. You can check the temperature by shaking a few drops of formula on your wrist before giving the bottle to your baby.

- Don't heat formula in a microwave, which might produce hot spots in the formula that could scald your baby's mouth.

KEEPING BOTTLES CLEAN

Bottle-feeding requires scrupulous hygiene so always wash your hands before you begin. All sorts of bacteria thrive in warm milk; so you must thoroughly clean the bottles, nipples, knives, measuring cups, and spoons you use to make up the formula. Hand wash to remove milk residue and then a full-cycle wash through a dishwasher is sufficient. If you don't have a dishwasher, you will need to clean the equipment in one of two ways.

- Steaming. The simplest way to sterilize is with an electric steam sterilizer, which stands on the kitchen counter. You can buy special models designed for use in a microwave.

- Boiling. This is a useful method when you have to make up an extra feeding

unexpectedly, but it is very time-consuming. You need to boil all equipment for 15 minutes, making sure no air bubbles are trapped.

When you hand-wash the equipment, use hot, soapy water. Glass bottles can be washed in the dishwasher. Clean inside the bottles with a bottle brush, taking extra care to remove any traces of milk or powder from the bottom and the neck. Turn nipples inside out and hold them under running water. Verify that the hole is not blocked.

As an extra precaution, rub ordinary household salt around the turned-out inside to remove any traces of milk or powder. (Be sure to wash off all traces of salt.) Drain clean equipment on a paper towel.

HOW MUCH AND WHEN

- A rough guide is 2 ounces (60ml) of formula per pound of body weight each day, but babies are individuals and their appetites vary. Your baby's appetite will soon show you how much he needs.

- Don't expect him to consume the same amount of food as your friend's baby, even if they are the same age. And don't be surprised if he is hungrier on some days than others.

- A newborn baby will need six to eight small feedings a day. Since formula takes longer than breast milk to digest, bottle-fed babies usually need feeding less frequently. He will probably take about 3–3½ ounces (90–105ml) at each feeding.

- Try to feed your baby whenever he seems hungry. You will soon recognize the distinctive cry that announces that he feels empty. You are likely to settle into a routine much more rapidly if he learns that his hunger will be quickly satisfied.

- Babies need to learn to give the right signals, of course. A newborn baby has never experienced hunger pangs before, as he was fed continuously in the womb through the umbilical cord. Be prepared for a few false alarms as he becomes familiar with all the new sensations in his body.

- Gradually, he will reduce the number of feedings but drink more at each one, until he is taking 7 ounces (210ml) of milk five or six times during each 24-hour period.

- Even if you start weaning at six months, he should still have at least four 7–ounce (210–ml) bottles of formula until he is a year old.

HOW TO BOTTLE-FEED

- Make sure you are in a comfortable position, with your back supported and feet flat on the floor, and have everything at hand before you start.

- Support your baby's head in the crook of your arm, above the level of his stomach.

- Test the temperature of the formula with a couple of drops on the inside of your wrist or inner forearm. It should feel warm but not hot.

- To keep your baby from swallowing too much air (he will inevitably swallow some), tilt the bottle so that the nipple is full.

- Put the baby upright at your shoulder, support his head, and burp him from time to time by rubbing or gently patting his back to release trapped air.

CHOOSING A NIPPLE

Whichever nipple you use, always make sure there is an adequate milk flow before feeding: turn the bottle upside down and check to see that two or three drops of milk are released each second. If the milk flows faster than this, the hole may have become too large. If it does not flow, the nipple may be blocked with a small particle of formula.

In either case, you should replace the nipple. Silicone nipples last up to a year; the rubber or latex ones begin to deteriorate after four weeks of use. Throw any type away as soon as it stops working properly.

- The universal nipple is the standard type that has been sold for many years. A cross-cut hole is better for formula flow than a pinhole.

- You must use a wide-based nipple with a wide-mouthed bottle. As your baby sucks, the nipple moves in and out of his mouth.

- An orthodontic, or natural-shaped, nipple is designed to encourage proper development of your baby's jaw and palate. The nipple hole must point toward the roof of your baby's mouth, spraying the milk upward.

- Your baby will usually turn his head away when he has had enough. Don't force him to finish the milk or formula.

- Throw away leftover milk or formula, as well as any bottles of milk that have been warmed up and not used within 20 minutes—bacteria may grow due to the warming process.

- A bottle-fed baby may need additional drinks of water (see "What about water?," p.26), particularly on a hot day.

ENJOY THOSE FEEDINGS

Feeding your baby can be an enjoyable, intimate experience. If you are not worrying about how much formula he is getting because you can see exactly how much he takes, it should be possible to relax and make this a special time together.

Cuddle your baby in your lap and enjoy looking into his eyes and talking quietly to him as he savors the experience. Don't be tempted to let too many other people take over unless you want them to. One of the main advantages of bottle-feeding is that your spouse can feed the baby too. This will help your husband feel fully involved and will allow you to get some rest. Many couples take turns feeding their baby at night.

BANISH GUILT

You may feel guilty about choosing to bottle-feed your baby. Or if you had problems breast-feeding and decided to change methods, you may experience a sense of failure.

Don't blame yourself—trying to live up to perfection is not good for you or your baby. One of the first lessons you learn as a mother is that bringing up children is not an easy task.

Try to remember that years from now, when you are watching your teenage son or daughter playing in a soccer game, whether you breast- or bottle-fed will then seem completely irrelevant.

You are a good mother if you provide love, security, and encouragement for your growing baby, in addition to meeting his physical needs. Don't waste precious time and energy fretting if you have to modify your plans slightly. Enjoy these months – they won't come again.

What about water?

Water is an essential part of a balanced diet. Babies lose more water through their kidneys and skin than adults do. And spells of sickness and diarrhea, more common in babies, can also lead to dehydration.

Breast-fed babies do not need any extra water because breast milk can adapt to quench their thirst, even in hot weather. But if your baby is bottle-fed or is starting to consume solids and less breast milk, you will need to offer him water.

KEEPING IT PURE

• Older houses built before 1986 may still have lead water pipes. Ask a plumber to check yours. Lead has been linked to nerve damage, mental impairment, and anemia in children. Slow lead poisoning does not necessarily show any immediate symptoms.

• Run the faucet for a few minutes before use to flush out any lead and reduce concentration levels.

• In some agricultural areas, nitrates have spread into the water supply from contamination by nitrogen fertilizers. Heavily farmed areas can be affected. Nitrates make it more difficult for babies to absorb oxygen and have been linked to other illnesses. Boiling water can actually increase the concentration of nitrates. Use bottled water if necessary. City water is checked for nitrates, but if you have well or spring water, you need to get it tested.

• Pesticide residues are sometimes found in drinking water. Filtering (see page 27) can remove some, or use bottled water instead of tap water. However, bottled water is an expensive option and uses a lot of energy to produce.

Chlorine is added to the public (city) water supply in most parts of the U.S. and Canada. While this is probably necessary because chlorine helps control harmful bacteria in the water supply system, chlorine has been linked to health problems.

Although it is added to water in tiny amounts, we absorb chlorine into our system when we drink it. Even bathing or showering in chlorinated water allows it to enter our bodies—in fact we absorb more chlorine through the pores of our skin during a five-minute shower than we would get from drinking 10 glasses of water.

Water companies constantly monitor the quality of the water they pump, and if they detect harmful bacteria in higher amounts than their standard, they sometimes "flush" the water system with higher-than-normal amounts of chlorine to control the bacteria. So if you can smell chlorine when you fill a glass with hot water, it's best not to drink it or bathe in it. (See "Ways with water," right.)

The heaviest chlorination is found in areas where the public water supply comes from reservoirs or other surface water. If your public water comes from wells, it will probably contain less chlorine. Inexpensive water filters that use granulated charcoal will remove chlorine. It's a good idea to have your water tested for bacteria, chlorine, and pesticides once a year. And if you use a filter, remember to change it at the recommended intervals.

WAYS WITH WATER

- Water filters can be connected to your faucets and shower heads to provide safe washing water and to filter all drinking water automatically. They remove chlorine, aluminum, lead, pesticides, and lime, which causes mineral deposits.

- Bottled water can be given as an alternative to tap water, but it should still be boiled and cooled until your baby is six months old. Check with your baby's doctor about which type is suitable.

HELPING THE WATER SUPPLY

- Write to your local paper and to your government representatives about water pollution. Become active in an environmental organization that works to combat pollution.

- It's a good idea to check the quality of your tap water once a year. Call your local health department for information about testing.

- If conserving water is key in your area, you can save water by bathing your baby every other night and giving him a sponge bath on alternate nights. And you can use less water for bathing.

- Use a cup for brushing his teeth rather than leaving a faucet running, which wastes about a gallon (3.8L) of water.

- As your child grows bigger, teach him to take showers instead of tub baths and to turn off faucets when washing or cleaning teeth.

Solid Foods

Babies usually don't need solids until 9 to 12 months, but many parents begin feeding their babies one or two solid foods as early as 6 months. By this time his digestive system will have matured enough to cope with more-complex foods. But milk will be his major source of nourishment until he is at least 9 months old (young babies are unable to eat enough solid food to meet their nutritional requirements). It is important to introduce one food at a time so that you can monitor allergic reactions and your baby's preferences. Over time, encourage him to develop a taste for a variety of foods to get him used to different flavors and textures.

Only the bare essentials are covered in the following pages. For further information on feeding your child a healthy, balanced diet, *The Healthy Baby Meal Planner* (Fireside paperbacks, $15.00) by children's food expert Annabel Karmel is highly recommended.

ESSENTIAL EQUIPMENT

You will need:

- An absorbent bib with a soft fastening. Leave the stiff plastic catch-all types until later.

- A plastic bowl and shallow plastic spoon. Plastic won't hold the heat, and shallow bowls and spoons make it easier for your baby to learn to feed himself.

- A large plastic mat or plenty of newspaper to put under your baby's highchair. Eating solids is a messy business!

- A blender or mini food mill for preparing home-cooked foods.

WHEN TO START

It is important not to hurry your baby on to solids before he is ready. If you think your baby needs to start solids before four months, or if he was born prematurely, your baby's doctor can advise you. The baby will still need at least four 7–8-ounce (210–240-ml) bottles of milk until he is six to nine months old (there are 60 calories in 3 ounces [90ml] of milk). Consider introducing solids after six months if:

- Your baby shows an interest in your food.

- He starts waking again for a night feeding after a period of sleeping through.

- He seems dissatisfied after being breast- or bottle-fed.

Introducing solids

Choose a time of day when you can relax and your baby is not usually fussy or starving. He may be frustrated if he expects to be fed milk and is presented with something completely new. So give him some of his regular food first to take the edge off his appetite but not to fill him up. Seat him securely in his baby seat or stroller and offer a teaspoon of baby rice mixed with expressed breast milk, formula, or cooled, boiled water. Let your baby suck the food off the spoon; don't push it into his mouth. If your baby likes it, offer a second and a third spoonful, and then introduce it at another meal. Remember, he's not accustomed to using a spoon, so not much food will go into his mouth. It is important to introduce one food at a time so that you can monitor allergic reactions and preferences. After a few days, try introducing some puréed vegetable or fruit with the rice. Be prepared for a variety of reactions. Some babies spit out the food or make faces. Others may turn their heads or even start to cry. If your baby is not interested, don't force him. Wait a few days and then try again.

PREPARING MEALS

- First solid foods must be puréed or mashed until they are completely smooth.

- Root vegetables can be boiled, steamed, or baked before being puréed or mashed.

- Make sure all fruit and vegetables are fresh. Some people prefer organically

FIRST SOLID FOODS (FROM SIX MONTHS)

Give the following:
- Baby rice cereal.
- Puréed carrot and potato.
- Well-mashed banana.
- Ready-made baby foods.

Avoid these:
- Red meat, fish, and chicken—too difficult to digest.
- Wheat cereals—contain gluten, which can cause an allergy.
- Bread—contains gluten, which can cause an allergy.
- Cow's milk—risk of allergy.
- Yogurt—risk of allergy.
- Eggs—risk of allergy.
- Nuts—risk of allergy.
- Added salt—kidneys cannot process it.
- Added sugar—risk of obesity and tooth decay in the future.
- Unpasteurized honey—risk of botulism, a form of food poisoning.
- Popcorn—risk of choking.
- Hot dogs—risk of choking.

grown ones from a local producer; remember to wash them thoroughly.

READY-MADE MEALS

All mothers have days when life is so busy that they open a jar of commercial baby food for convenience. Don't worry—it will do your baby no harm and can save you the stress of quickly trying to prepare food for a hungry, crying baby.

However, commercial baby foods are not ideal to give your baby on a regular basis.

ALLERGY WATCH

You will find it easier to discover if your baby is allergic to certain foods if you introduce new tastes one by one. Allergic reactions include:

- Skin rash.
- Red bottom.
- Wheeziness.
- Vomiting.
- Diarrhea.
- Swollen stomach.

If you have a history of eczema or allergy in your family, be particularly careful about introducing new foods. Some experts believe it is best to wait until five months before offering fruits because young babies find it difficult to cope with the fructose (sugar) in them.

Many babies also show an intolerance to wheat products, so it is important to choose gluten-free foods. Celiac disease is an extreme allergic reaction to gluten in wheat, rye, oats, and barley.

Intolerance to cow's milk, which affects about 2 percent of babies under a year, can be due to a reaction to the protein in the milk or an inability to digest the lactose (sugar) also present.

A severe reaction, such as swelling and difficulty in breathing, is rare (anaphylactic shock). Vomiting or a rash usually occurs 12 to 18 hours after exposure, making it difficult to detect which food was responsible.

Nuts and eggs are also common causes of allergy.

Reports have shown that added water and thickeners are used to bulk out the contents of jars and cans, and so some products fail to meet nutritional standards. Some meat-based baby foods may contain as little as 20 percent meat, and some foods have a lot of sugar in them.

Modified starch is widely used in the baby-food industry as a low-cost bulking agent. It is made from cornstarch. Some research shows that babies who eat it are unable to absorb carbohydrates properly, and they may have overly loose stools as a result.

If you would not want to eat only canned foods, why expect your baby to do so? Encourage him to enjoy fresh foods, and he will start to take part in family meals much sooner and be ready to experiment with a wide variety of tastes.

Finally, remember that the baby-food manufacturers want you to buy these products. Don't be taken in by that gorgeous picture of a big-eyed, adorable baby eating the latest jar of processed food. It has been specially designed to make you want to rush out and buy it for your baby. Your baby will be just as adorable if you feed him homemade fresh food!

DOS AND DON'TS

- If you have a freezer, cook in batches and freeze the food in mini portions, using an ice cube tray or specially made plastic baby-food tray.

- Thaw and reheat food thoroughly. Let it cool to lukewarm before offering it to your baby.

- Wash your baby's bowl and spoon in hot, soapy water. Continue thoroughly cleaning bottles and nipples.

- If you use convenience baby food, store in the refrigerator what's left in the jar for no longer than 48 hours.

- Don't use cow's milk to mix food to the right consistency until your baby is at least six months old.

- Use a low-tech hand crank baby-food mill to purée cooked vegetables. These mills are inexpensive and easy to use and clean. Made of plastic, they use a simple metal blade to do their work. Just fill the inner

cavity with the cooked food, insert the blade-bowl unit, and crank the handle as you push down on the bowl unit. The puréed food is pushed into the bowl through a sieve.

ADDING MORE SOLIDS (SIX TO NINE MONTHS)

Once your baby is enjoying his first solid foods three times a day, start to increase the amount and introduce more variety. The consistency should still be puréed.

Foods to try:
- Peas, corn, cabbage, broccoli, cauliflower, spinach, zucchini, turnips.
- Lean red meat.
- Chicken.
- Split lentils.
- Cultured yogurt.
- Apricots, peaches, stewed apples.
- Cheddar cheese, cottage cheese.

Foods to avoid:
- Wheat—risk of allergy to the gluten.
- Eggs—risk of allergy.
- Nuts—risk of allergy and choking.
- Soft cheeses—risk of listeriosis, an often fatal disease that develops from food infected with the bacterium *Listeria monocytogenes.*
- Added salt or sugar.
- Too many convenience foods.
- Unpasteurized honey—risk of botulism, a type of food poisoning.
- Hot, spicy foods.
- Hot dogs—high fat and risk of choking.

EXPANDING THE MENU (ABOUT NINE MONTHS)

At about nine months of age, your baby's maturing digestive system will not be so sensitive to certain allergy-causing foods, such as wheat, and he may want to feed himself. You should never leave him alone to eat, especially with finger foods, as he may choke.

Foods to try:
- Wheat-based foods—pasta, breadsticks, low-sugar zwieback, and toast.
- Cereals.
- Hard-boiled egg yolk.
- Lean red meat.

- Cultured yogurt.
- Fruits.

Foods to avoid:
- Nuts—some experts believe nuts in any form should not be given until about 18 months because of the risk of allergy, but others say that nut pastes can be used earlier than this. Check with your baby's doctor. Whole nuts should not be given until your child is five years old because of the risk of choking.
- Egg white.
- Added salt or sugar.

During the first two years of life, the brain grows faster than at any other time, making essential connections between the cells that cannot be reproduced later. Imagine a tree with large and small branches, twigs, leaves, and veins on each leaf. Each part of this structure has to connect to the next part. Iron is an essential part of your baby's diet. It guarantees that all these connections are properly made. By six months, your baby's iron stores will be depleted, so you should make sure he eats plenty of iron-rich foods to help his brain and central nervous system grow and develop as well as they possibly can. Foods rich in iron include red meat, green vegetables, dried apricots, and egg yolk. Vitamin C helps your baby absorb iron and can be found in potatoes and green vegetables.

FAMILY EATING

From nine months, your baby can start eating family meals. He can sit in his highchair pulled close to the table and enjoy more or less the same foods as the rest of the family. He will want to feed himself and must be allowed to make a mess. Chop up his food for him, then let him use his fingers or a spoon. The more independent you let him be, the sooner he will master the art of feeding himself with minimal mess. If you make a big issue of it, he is likely to give up trying. You may want to buy a bowl that sticks to the surface it is put on, which makes it harder (but not impossible) for your baby to turn it upside down. A large plastic bib with sleeves for him to wear while eating is also a wise investment. Your baby may be more or less fully weaned, but milk should be an important part of his diet until he is at least five years old.

VEGETARIAN BABIES

If you don't want your baby to eat meat, make sure he is getting enough protein from legumes, grains, and dairy products.

You need to be careful about iron too. Formula and follow-on milks contain extra iron, but if you are still breast-feeding, ask your baby's doctor for advice.

Vegan mothers need to ask for special advice on grain milks, soy products, and ways to avoid iron deficiency.

MILK QUOTA

Until your baby is a year old, he should have formula or breast milk as his main drink, although you can use small quantities of cow's milk in cooking from six months. After 12 months, he can be given cow's milk instead, but he still needs 12 ounces (360ml) of milk each day, including what he gets on cereal and in cooked dishes. By this age, he should be able to drink milk from a cup, with breast- or bottle-feedings as a comfort before bedtime if he doesn't want to give them up.

You can give 2-percent milk once your baby reaches two years old, but children under the age of five should not drink skim milk because it is too low in fat, calories, and other nutrients essential for a growing child.

OTHER DRINKS

If you want to give extra drinks, offer water. Until your baby is six months old, it should be boiled and cooled. Avoid carbonated waters. Fruit juice and powdered drink mixes and juice boxes contain a lot of sugar (sucrose, dextrose, maltose and fructose), so always check labels. Even well diluted, they can damage your baby's growing teeth, particularly if given in a bottle or as the last thing at night. They also contain lots of preservatives, additives, and colorings, so avoid them for babies under one. An occasional drink of juice diluted with six parts water will do no harm, but you may find that once he has tasted it, he may refuse to drink water.

GROWING UP WITH GOOD FOOD

Many toddlers prefer lots of small meals to three big ones. Unless there is a serious physical or psychological problem, most children will eat what they need to. Write down what your child actually consumes each day, and you will probably find it's a lot more than you thought.

- Avoid making food a battleground by trying to force him to eat. Continue to offer a varied diet, with plenty of chances for him to try out new tastes. If he leaves something or seems uninterested, calmly remove the plate saying, "Not hungry today? Never mind, we'll try again tomorrow." There is plenty of time later on for him to establish regular eating habits.

- If you resent the effort you put into preparing food that is left uneaten, concentrate on healthy, easy-to-prepare snacks such as vegetables and breadsticks with cheese dip or fruit chunks and yogurt. Baked beans and sandwiches on whole-wheat bread cut into small squares are also quick, nutritious snacks.

A SWEET PROBLEM

If you want to give sweet things, choose fruit.

You can always choose snacks such as low-fat crackers or corn chips if you are out shopping and want to give your child a treat, but avoid popcorn and nuts.

KEEP IT NATURAL

As your baby grows bigger, aim to give him a varied, balanced diet. If you don't rely too heavily on one particular food, you won't be too worried by a new food scare. And if you prepare as much of the food yourself as carefully as you can, you are less likely to risk contamination from faulty processing, packaging, or storage.

Read the labels on packaging. The longer the list, the more the food has been processed. All ingredients should be listed in order of quantity, starting with the largest amount. If the list starts with an artificial ingredient, don't buy the product.

Natural additives can include chemicals derived from insects and wood. If you want to avoid these too, buy a speciality book explaining what the names of such products actually mean. Studies show that many westerners eat more than 8 pounds (4kg) of preservatives a year.

PESTICIDES

• Buy local produce whenever you can. It will have a shorter journey to your dinner table, and if it's organically grown, you will be supporting a worthwhile initiative. We still don't know how harmful crop sprays may be in the long term, although some of the most lethal have now been withdrawn. But there have been no long-term studies on what happens to a person's health after a whole lifetime of exposure to pesticides, nor do we know how the mixture of pesticides an individual is exposed to may affect the human body.

• Organic foods often cost more than chemically-grown items because their production is more labor-intensive. Buying organic foods helps to create a bigger market for them which will serve to drive prices down. If your supermarket does not stock organic foods, urge the store manager to keep a selection, or shop somewhere that does.

- Don't be put off by misshapen apples and carrots. The perfect specimens found in our supermarkets have been chemically treated to achieve that result.

- You will find that organically grown fruit and vegetables taste much better, even if they don't look so appealing.

- More than 100 pesticides leave residues in our food, and some organic farmers claim that it is difficult to grow pesticide-free food in some places because the soil, water, and atmosphere have all been contaminated.

MEATY ADVICE

It is wise to resist giving hamburgers and sausages to your children very often. Choose only lean meat; some chemical residues accumulate in the fat. Also, avoid eating any of an an animal's vital organs where these residues are concentrated. If you do cook ground beef, make sure the juices run clear and the meat is not pink.

FOOD IRRADIATION

Irradiation exposes food to gamma rays from a radioactive source so it stays "fresh" longer. It kills bacteria and insects in raw foods such as grain, meats and poultry and can make some vegetables last longer.

- Some states have banned the sale of irradiated foods.

- Irradiated foods can still spoil. Irradiation is not a substitute for refrigeration and safe handling.

- Irradiation can destroy some vitamins in food.

- Since 1966 the US Food and Drug Administration (FDA) has required that irradiated foods be labeled as such. In 1986 a mandatory logo was added to this labeling requirement. Look for the logo—a circle above two petals, surrounded by a broken circle—if you want to avoid irradiated foods.

- Health Canada has approved irradiation of potatoes, onions, wheat, flour, and spices.

FOOD COVERS

Do not cover cheese or meat with plastic wrap that contains plasticizers. The plasticisers can migrate into the food, and they have been linked to cancer. Fatty foods are particularly susceptible to absorbing these harmful substances. Use wax paper, foil, or hard plastic containers with lids, or buy clear wrap without plasticizers.

COOL IT!

Safe food handling is especially important where babies are concerned because their immune systems are not yet fully developed. To cool food for your baby, cool if *fast* in the refrigerator. This does not give bacteria time to develop. Cooking destroys harmful organisms, but if food is allowed to cool down *slowly* dangerous bacteria can start to grow on it.

Soups and stews can be allowed to drop just below the boiling point before refrigeration, but other foods should be refrigerated immediately after cooking.

For the same reasons, do not defrost frozen food at room temperature. Ahead of time, place it in the refrigerator to defrost slowly. This keeps the food below the temperature at which harmful bacteria can develop, and the food will taste better, too. Rapid defrosting releases the food's natural moisture and makes it less nutritious.

Buy a refrigerator thermometer to make sure your refrigerator works at 36 deg. F. (0 deg. C.) or colder. The freezer should run at 0 deg. F. (–32 deg. C.).

Uncooked egg yolks can carry harmful bacteria. It is best not to give your baby (or your family) soft-boiled or fried eggs with runny yolks. Scramble eggs or make omelets so that the yolk is thoroughly cooked—this kills any bacteria. Remember that egg whites are a perfect protein source for you and your baby.

When buying fish or shellfish, make sure they come from waters that are certified as clean. Shellfish tend to store pollutants from the food they eat. If you find that any of your local waters are closed to fishing or shellfishing, support a group that is working to get them cleaned up.

CHAPTER TWO

Clothing Your Baby

Dressing your baby has never been easier. Gone are cumbersome and fussy dresses, jackets and bootees that require hand-washing and ironing. Today we have easy-care one-piece suits and socks and bootees that can be thrown into the washing machine and don't need an iron anywhere near them.

The choice of styles is tremendous. But don't feel you have to compete and make your child into a fashion plate. He will be perfectly happy in clothes that have been passed on from friends and family or bought at a "good-as-new" sale. Baby clothes are usually outgrown before they are worn out. You can conserve natural resources—and cut down on expenditure—by using secondhand outfits at least some of the time.

Be careful about fabrics. Some synthetic

materials make it difficult for your baby's skin to breathe. Try to stick to cottons and natural fibers whenever you can, especially for undershirts and other items that will lie next to your baby's skin. To make diapering easier, look for easy-to-open closures (hook-and-loop and snaps) at the leg area.

DIAPERS

Before disposable diapers were introduced in the mid-1960s, cloth diapers were the only ones available. Diaper pails, sterilizing solutions, and a clothesline of diapers drying in the breeze were part of everyday life for new mothers, even when a washing machine may not have been. Laundering cloth diapers was a time-consuming, messy process. Disposables have revolutionized diaper-changing, and the diaper pail and clothesline have been replaced by the diaper box and trash can. Today statistics show that most new parents choose disposables.

But there are other options, which include diaper-laundering services. Many parents are unaware of them, because the small companies that offer them have to compete with paper manufacturers with huge advertising budgets devoted to promoting disposables. Hospitals and pediatricians as well as local governments—which are ultimately responsible for disposing of diaper waste—could all play a greater part in helping parents make an informed choice about the kind of diapers they use.

DISPOSABLES

Disposable diapers are very convenient. They are widely available and easy to use; and once they are soiled, there is no messy scraping or soaking. You simply throw them away. For busy parents with many demands on their time, they are an attractive option. Understandably, disposables are generally preferred by babysitters and day-care centers.

Disposable diapers are available in different sizes according to weight and are anatomically designed for girls and boys, with the bulk of the padding placed appropriately for each.

What's in a disposable?

Most disposable diapers contain:

- Fluffed wood pulp. Manufacturing wood pulp is harmful to the environment because the valued ancient woodlands are cleared to produce the pulp and replaced by young foresting.

- At least two different kinds of plastic produced from nonrenewable crude oil resources. Some brands contain biodegradable plastic, but this requires certain conditions to biodegrade properly which are not always provided by landfill sites.

- Absorbent gel. This is used in the fluffed wood pulp to improve the absorbency of the diaper. Sometimes the gel escapes and sticks to the baby's skin. It is believed to be non-toxic, but little is known about any long-term effects.

Their effect on the environment

Disposable diapers are not environmentally friendly or natural:

- Huge quantities of wood pulp and plastic are used in their manufacture and despite their name, disposable diapers are not fully biodegradable. Some parts decompose in a few years; others survive indefinitely.

- Disposable diapers add to household waste and take up space in landfills. As the wood pulp decays, it produces carbon dioxide and methane, both greenhouse gases.

- You can help by lobbying diaper manufacturers to invest in more research on how to make their products completely biodegradable.

The cost of disposables

- Using disposable diapers costs a lot more than using cloth diapers, even when you take into account the cost of buying cloth diapers, the cost of electricity and washing products, and the wear and tear on the washing machine and dryer.

- If paper training pants or "pull-ups" are used during toilet training, disposables become an even more expensive option.

- Getting rid of disposables increases the cost of the waste disposal for communities.

CUTTING BACK

If you are uneasy about the high cost to the environment but don't want to abandon disposables altogether, you can significantly cut back on disposables by using fabric diapers (see below) some of the time, perhaps for the first couple of months when you are more tied to the home. Alternatively, use disposables only when you are traveling or out of the house.

CLOTH DIAPERS

With the advantage of being both cheaper and more environmentally friendly than disposables, cloth diapers are even more cost-effective

if you plan to have more than one child. Reusable diapers use fewer resources and produce less waste and pollution. If you have a washing machine, they are simple to clean once you establish a routine of soaking, rinsing, and washing.

According to one study, washing a baby's diapers at home may save up to five times the energy consumed by using disposables.

FITTED REUSABLE DIAPERS

For parents of wriggly babies daunted by the prospect of folding and pinning cloth diapers, there are number of fitted reusable diapers available. These fit like disposable diapers and come either as all-in-one designs or two-part systems with washable pads and waterproof overpants. Prices vary. They tend to be more expensive than traditional cloth diapers but are quicker and easier to use.

DIAPER SERVICES

If you are committed to using an environmentally friendly system of diapers, you will find that a service provides a convenient alternative to washing dirty diapers at home. These companies pick up your dirty diapers at the same time they deliver a clean supply. They usually offer a choice of reusable diapers which the customer either buys or rents.

THE BARE NECESSITIES

- Three dozen cloth diapers—as cloth diapers have to be rinsed, soaked, washed, and dried, you will need at least three dozen to make sure you always have a daily supply of clean ones. The most convenient ones are prefolded.

- Cotton squares—very absorbent, but bulky on newborns. They are also handy as general-purpose nursery cloths.

- Disposable one-way diaper liners to help keep your baby's skin dry and prevent diaper rash.

- Diaper pins or plastic fasteners to secure cloth diapers.

- Elasticized or tie-on plastic pants to prevent leaks. These should not fit too tightly

- Disposable diaper booster pads can be used as an option inside cloth diapers for greater absorbency.

WASHING DIAPERS

To help prevent your baby from developing diaper rash, it is important to wash diapers thoroughly. With a supply of 3 dozen diapers, you should have enough to wash them every other day when you have accumulated a full load. You will need two pails with lids, one filled with soaking solution for dirty diapers and another for wet ones. There are many commercial soaking solutions available. Alternatively, and just as effectively, mix:

- 2–3 tablespoons (30–45ml) white distilled vinegar or 1 tablespoon domestic borax or 5 drops (15ml) tea tree oil

- 1 gallon (4L) water

Method

1 Prepare fresh soaking solution every day.
2 Rinse off dirty diapers in the toilet before soaking in sterilizing solution as indicated on the container. Wet diapers do not need to be rinsed first.
3 Wearing rubber gloves, wring out diapers. Wash them on the hot-water cycle. Avoid biological detergents that can irritate sensitive skin. Commercial fabric conditioners make diapers less absorbent; try adding half a cup of vinegar to the final rinse instead. There is no need to boil diapers; just use the hot-water wash.
4 Dry diapers. The sun will dry and bleach diapers effectively. In bad weather dry on a clothes rack or tumble-dry in the dryer.

Some brands of reusable diapers have their own special care instructions. Always check the label before washing.

HOW TO CHANGE A DIAPER

Make sure you have everything at hand before you start. You will need:

- A changing pad or folded towel.

- A clean diaper.

- A plastic bag for dirty disposable diaper. Recycling supermarket bags is cheaper and more ecofriendly than using perfumed diaper bags.

- Warm water and cotton balls for wiping your baby's bottom.

- Barrier cream (optional).

1 Undo diaper and carefully wipe his bottom with the clean front portion, holding his feet safely out of the way with one hand.
2 Clean diaper area with cotton balls and water. Make sure you wipe a girl's bottom from front to back to avoid spreading bacteria into her vagina. There is no need to clean inside the lips of the vulva. If you are changing a boy's diaper, clean around the scrotum and penis, but don't pull back his foreskin if he is not circumcised.
3 Dry diaper area well.
4 Slide a clean diaper under his bottom, apply barrier cream if used, and fasten the diaper.

YOUR BABY'S STOOLS

At some point during his first 24 hours, your newborn baby will pass a greenish black, tarlike substance called meconium, which filled his intestines in the womb. When he has excreted all the meconium, your baby's stools will become dark yellow.

Once feeding is established, he will probably dirty his diaper after each feeding. A breast-fed baby's stools will become a mustard yellow color with a loose consistency. The contents of a bottle-fed baby's diaper are likely to be firmer and greenish gray. The color and consistency of your baby's stools may vary from day to day, especially once he starts eating solids, when they will also become smellier.

DOS AND DON'TS ON DIAPERING

- Change your baby's diaper in a warm, draft-free place whenever possible.

- Always use a diaper pin (never a safety pin). A diaper pin has a large round safety head that houses the pinpoint more securely. And it won't poke your baby as he moves around.

- When pinning cloth diapers, be sure to place your hand between the baby and the diaper to avoid sticking him accidentally. The pins become dull after a few weeks. Buy new ones.

- If you are using a disposable diaper on

your baby, first be certain that your hands are free of lotion or powder, which could interfere with the adhesive on the self-stick tabs.

- If you don't have room for a traditional changing table in his room you can use the top of a waist-high bureau that is at least 3 feet (90cm) wide and 18 to 24 inches (45–61cm) deep. You can keep diapering supplies in the top drawer and his clothes in the other drawers.

- As babies become more wiggly, changing them on the floor may be safest and easiest.

- When traveling or shopping, look for pull-down changing tables in restrooms. Never leave your baby unattended.

HELPING YOURSELF

- To prevent leaks, make sure that your baby's penis is pointing downward before you fasten the diaper.

- Boys often urinate when you take off their diaper. To minimize the spray effect, place a tissue or cloth over his penis when you change him.

- If your baby is still feeding during the night, let him feed first even if he has a dirty diaper. If he is hungry, he won't appreciate having to wait for his milk while you change him, and he will probably dirty his diaper during the feeding anyway.

- Never leave your baby unattended on a changing table or bed.

DIAPER RASH

Diaper rash is caused by bacteria or yeast in the baby's feces breaking down urine in the diaper and releasing ammonia that irritates and burns the skin. A mild case of diaper rash may appear as small red spots on your baby's bottom. In severe cases, blisters appear and the skin becomes inflamed and sometimes infected. To prevent diaper rash from developing:

- Always change a dirty diaper as soon as possible.

- Change wet diapers regularly, even superabsorbent disposable ones, because bacteria, not moisture, cause diaper rash.

- Wash or wipe and dry your baby's bottom at each change.

- Make sure that cloth diapers are thoroughly washed and dried.

Treatment

If your baby develops diaper rash:

- Use a diaper rash cream to soothe the affected area. Zinc oxide cream is effective, or try marigold ointment (calendula).

- Avoid using soap, wipes, or other products containing perfume or alcohol; they sting.

- Stop using plastic pants. They prevent urine from evaporating and may aggravate the condition.

- Let air dry the skin by leaving his diaper off for 15 minutes, if possible, after each change.

- Use barrier cream to reduce the skin's contact with urine or try a natural treatment such as calendula (pot marigold) cream or chamomile and lavender. Add one drop of each essence to a bowl of warm water. Then dip cotton wool into the solution and wipe your baby's bottom with it.

- Change his diaper more frequently.

Other causes

- Allergy. Diaper rash can sometimes be a reaction to something that your baby has eaten and hasn't digested properly, or a new type of laundry detergent, or cream or lotion put on his skin.

- Heat rash. Small blisters appear in the diaper area and on the body. Leave off plastic pants, dress your baby in lighter clothing, and use fewer blankets.

- Yeast. A spotty rash starting around the anus and spreading to the buttocks and inner thighs, caused by a yeast infection. Always consult baby's doctor.

- Inflamed and broken skin folds of thigh and groin due to prolonged wetness or caked talcum powder causing irritation. Make sure you dry this area thoroughly and avoid using talcum powder.

First clothes

It is tempting to buy a lot of outfits for your baby before he is born. But you will probably need only the basics, since clothes are often given as gifts or as hand-me-downs from parents of older babies. Babies grow very quickly, so it is not worth splurging on a selection of outfits for your newborn,

especially since he'll probably be sick on your favorite one as soon as you put it on him.

CLOTHING PRIORITIES

Comfort and practicality are the most important considerations when you are choosing clothes for your baby. However stylish the outfit, he will be miserable if it irritates his skin or it is difficult to put on and take off.

- Clothes must be machine washable. You will have neither the time nor the energy to do a lot of hand-washing.

- Look for soft natural fabrics, such as brushed cotton or cotton fleece, which won't irritate your baby's delicate skin.

- Easy-fastening, accessible openings will allow you to change his diaper without undressing him.

- One-piece suits that fasten under the crotch help to keep the diaper in place and are warmer than undershirts.

- You will find it easier to dress your baby if his clothes open down the front.

- Many babies hate having clothes pulled tightly over their head, so make certain that you look for clothes that have wide-neck openings.

- Check that socks, tights, and bootees are big enough. If they fit too tightly, they can damage the delicate bones in your baby's feet.

NEWBORN BASICS

- 6 undershirts
- 6 sleepsuits/all-in-one suits
- 2 knitted cardigans
- 1 seasonal hat
- 1 pair mittens
- 2 pairs bootees
- 2 pairs socks
- 1 all-in-one snow suit (for winter babies)
- 1 close-knit shawl or blanket

For the first six months or so, your baby will be quite happy wearing the same clothes in the day and at night.

- Open, lacy knits are unsuitable for babies, since small fingers can get caught in the holes.

- Long gowns that close at the bottom can make it very easy to change a newborn baby.

SECONDHAND CLOTHES

Baby clothes are often outgrown before they are outworn, so if you are on a tight budget, it is worth keeping an eye on the classified ads in your local paper for secondhand clothes and notices of garage sales. Local mother and baby groups sometimes hold clothes and equipment sales. Consignment shops that specialize in baby clothes are becoming increasingly popular and widespread. They offer worthwhile bargains.

FABRICS

Natural fibers

Comfortable and hard-wearing, natural fibers are made from renewable resources and are recyclable, so they have less impact on the environment.

- Cotton is widely used in baby clothes. Unlike wool, it rarely irritates sensitive skin. Choose garments made from 100-percent cotton wherever possible. Cotton is often blended with synthetics like polyester, so check the label carefully.

- Clothes made of cotton jersey, brushed cotton, corduroy, and cotton fleece are both soft and warm. Pure cotton underwear lets sweat evaporate and will help prevent your baby from overheating.

- Wool is a popular choice for baby knitwear, but it can often irritate the skin and is best worn as an outer layer only.

- The delicate nature of other natural fibers such as linen and silk means that they are unsuitable for baby clothes.

Synthetic fibers

Largely produced from oil, a nonrenewable resource, synthetics are often cheaper and easier to care for than natural fibers. But they are not a good choice for baby clothes, since they don't let sweat escape and dry as efficiently. Sweat can lead to irritation between the folds of skin and increase the risk of overheating. Some synthetic fibers are also more flammable. Synthetic fibers include polyester, and acrylic.

Synthetic blends such as polyester and cotton are more comfortable to wear and still retain many of the good properties of 100-percent cotton.

Fabric finishes

Fabrics, particularly cottons and cotton blends, are often treated with finishes to make them crease-resistant or fire-retardant, or to prevent shrinkage. The most commonly used finishes are resins, such as formaldehyde polymers, which can irritate sensitive skins. New baby clothes should always be washed before wearing to minimize any risk of irritation or allergic reaction from these chemicals. Other finishes include starches, which are used to stiffen fabrics such as denim and some other types of cotton. These usually wash out well.

DRESSING YOUR NEWBORN

Getting clothes on and off a small baby can be a struggle. Many babies hate being naked, and dressing and undressing them is made trickier by their flailing limbs and large, floppy heads. Your baby may cry when you change his clothes. Try to keep calm and handle him gently but firmly. If your movements are clumsy or tentative, he will become more agitated and the process will take longer. Don't change him unless you really have to. For changing your baby with the minimum of fuss:

- Always take his clothes off in a warm room. Babies lose body heat very quickly, and he will be more miserable if he is chilly or in a draft.

- When putting his undershirt on, roll it up and stretch the neck hole as wide possible so you don't have to tug it over his head.

- Roll up the sleeves and stretch the cuffs before feeding his arms through.

- Talk to him reassuringly while you dress and undress him, so he can concentrate on your voice.

OVERHEATING

It is important that babies are kept warm, but it is also essential to guard against overheating, which may be a factor in crib death.

If he is warmly dressed because he has been outside, take off your baby's outdoor clothes when you bring him into the house even if he has fallen asleep in his buggy. Sleeping in direct sunlight or next to a hot radiator will also cause overheating. If he is in a bouncy cradle indoors with a room temperature of 68°F (20°C), your baby should be warm enough in three layers of clothing: an undershirt, all-in-one suit, and a light blanket or cardigan.

CLOTHES FOR OLDER BABIES

As your baby grows, the clothes he wears will be subjected to rougher treatment and will have to be harder-wearing than his first garments. He will also need a more varied wardrobe; for example, when you are trying to establish a bedtime routine, you may find it helpful to change him into nightclothes. When he starts eating solids, his clothes won't escape the mess, however large the bib, so it's important that they can withstand repeated washing. And when your baby begins crawling, he will need clothes that allow him to move freely and that protect his arms and legs, especially his knees. It makes sense to buy clothes on the large side so that there is some room for growth. But be sure that they are not so big and baggy that they interfere with crawling or his first unsteady steps.

IN THE WASH

From the day that you bring your baby home it will seem as though the washing machine is constantly running. Diapers that leak before you have the chance to change them and milk that's brought up on a regular basis mean the laundry basket is always full. You may not have given your washing powder or liquid much thought until now, but certain formulas are unsuitable for baby clothes because some of the chemical ingredients can irritate sensitive skin. These are:

- enzymes

- chlorine bleaches

- perfumes

- optical brighteners (chemicals that make white fabrics appear whiter).

These substances are used in biological and enzyme formulas and they are also sometimes found in combined detergents and conditioners. To minimize the risk of washing agents irritating your baby's skin, use nonbiological formulas, pure soap flakes, or products designed for people who have sensitive skin. If you hand-wash your baby's clothes, always be sure to rinse them thoroughly, because some detergent residues are capable of causing skin irritation. Running washed clothes through an extra rinse cycle can help prevent this.

the market that are also usually gentler on the skin.

- Run your washing machine only when you have a full load. It helps cut your electricity bills, saves water, and minimizes phosphate pollution.

- Wash lightly soiled clothes on a short wash cycle rather than a long water-and-energy-wasting hot wash.

- Tumble-drying consumes a lot of electricity. It is best to run only full loads.

Dry cleaning

Dry-cleaned clothes are not suitable for babies. Not only are they impractical—dry cleaning is expensive, and babies are not fussy about where they bring up milk—the process involves harsh solvents, which give off powerful fumes and are highly toxic.

The most commonly used dry-cleaning solvent is perchloroethylene (represented by the letter P in a circle on some labels). It has been identified as a probable carcinogen and is an organo-chlorine, one of a group of

HELPING THE ENVIRONMENT

- Phosphates in cleaning agents, such as washing powder and liquids, upset the ecological balance of the environment. In rivers and lakes where phosphate levels are high, the algae that feed on them become so prolific that fish and other aquatic life cannot survive. There are a number of phosphate-free alternatives on chemical compounds that deplete the ozone layer and whose manufacture and disposal causes toxic waste.

FIRST SHOES

Socks and bootees are all that your baby needs until he starts walking. Because the bones in his feet are easily damaged, anything that covers his feet (from socks to bedclothes) must allow movement.

Once your child is steady on his feet and walking outdoors, he will need a pair of real shoes. Take him to a shoe store where the staff is trained to fit children's shoes. The clerk will verify that he is able to walk without curling his toes and then will measure the length and width of his feet. When your child tries on a pair of shoes, encourage him to walk around the store so the fit can be checked properly. The clerk should also check the shoes when the baby is standing still, to make sure his feet are not restricted in any way.

FOOTWEAR PRIORITIES

When buying a pair of shoes for your toddler, look for:

- A sturdy and hard-wearing design, never sandals. Leather is the most durable material and allows the skin to breathe, so the feet do not get too sweaty.

- Fastenings should be adjustable and hold the shoe securely on the foot. Avoid laces, which tend to come undone; buckles and Velcro are quicker and easier to fasten.

- Nonslip, flexible soles. Avoid shoes with rubber strips over the toes; they may trip children who don't pick up their feet.

GOOD FOOT CARE

- Shoes are for outdoors. Encourage your child to go barefoot on safe, nonslip surfaces as it strengthens the muscles needed for walking.

- Keep toenails short; cut straight across the top of the nail.

- Shoes mold to the wearer's feet, so do not use secondhand shoes for a baby learning to walk.

CHAPTER THREE

Bathing and Bedtime

A regular routine that starts with a bath or wash and ends with a goodnight kiss will help your baby learn what to expect at the end of the day. It will also encourage him to settle down in the evenings, thereby improving his and your chances of getting a good night's sleep.

both of you. It may be frightening to begin with—holding a slippery, wriggly newborn with one hand. But as your baby grows older, he's likely to revel in the feel of warm water and will splash and play happily while you gently wipe away the day's dirt and grime.

Bathtime

Bathtime can be an enjoyable experience for

NEWBORN SKIN

Newborn skin is very thin and delicate. In the womb a baby's skin is protected by a creamy substance called vernix, which prevents it from becoming waterlogged with the amniotic fluid surrounding him. At birth there may be some vernix left on your baby's skin. This will continue to protect and moisturize the skin before being reabsorbed.

During the first weeks of your baby's life, his skin will continue to thicken and

SPONGE BATHING

Very young babies don't need to be bathed every day. Two or three times a week is fine. Some newborns hate being undressed and immersed in water. If your baby is upset by bathing, you can wash him just as well by sponge bathing.

For this you will need:

- A bowl of warm water.

- A small dish of cooled, boiled water for his eyes.

- A soft towel, preferably with a hood.

- Cotton balls.

- A diaper and a change of clothes.

Babies lose heat very quickly, so before you start, make sure the room is warm and that there are no drafts.

- Undress your baby, leaving his diaper on, and wrap him in the towel.

- Clean his face with damp cotton balls. Then with a fresh ball, moistened with cooled, boiled water, clean one eye, starting at the top of the nose and wiping out to avoid spreading any infection such as "sticky eye" or conjunctivitis. Do the same for the other eye with a new moistened cotton ball.

- Wipe your baby's head, hands, and feet. Leave his diaper area until last and be sure to clean in all the creases at the top of the thigh. Wash only half at a time and keep the other half covered with a towel.

- Finish by dressing your baby in a clean diaper and a change of clothes.

harden. It may also become dry and flaky, but it's not necessary to treat it with special baby bath and moisturizing creams. Recent research suggests that these products have little effect and that it is better not to interfere with the skin's natural hardening processes.

BATHING YOUNG BABIES

For the first few months, your baby will be too small for a normal-size bathtub, so you will need a baby-size tub with a nonslip surface where he will be safe and secure. Place the small tub on a surface at hip height, or on a special stand if possible, to protect yourself from back strain. Be careful to hold him securely, as soapy, wet babies are very slippery.

You can bathe him in the kitchen or bathroom sink. But be certain that both faucets are turned firmly off before you put him in. You may also need to tie a cloth around the hot faucet, so that it will not burn your baby if he accidentally touches it.

SAFETY FIRST

Always remember that even a few inches of water can be dangerous. Follow these guidelines to keep your baby safe from harm:

- Make sure that the room is warm enough. About 75° F (24° C) is ideal.

- Keep the bath shallow, 2–3 inches (5–8cm) of water is plenty.

- The bathwater should be no hotter than 85° F (29° C). Always add cold water first and top up with hot. A floating bath thermometer is helpful until you get used to the feel of the water. Then you will be able to test it with your elbow or the inside of your wrist (not your hand, which is less sensitive).

- Make sure that you have everything ready before you start.

- NEVER leave your baby unattended, even for a second to answer the phone. Wrap him up and take him with you.

- Place a towel or a sponge in the bottom of the tub to soften its surface and help prevent head bumps.

INTO THE WATER

- When the bath is ready, undress your baby and clean his diaper area before wrapping him in a towel.

- Wipe his face and ears with damp cotton balls. It is easier to wash his head before he goes in the bathtub. So tuck his body under your arm (the "football carry"), support his head with your hand, lean over the bath, rinse his hair, and pat it dry (see "Hair care," p.62).

- Once he is in the baby tub, make sure his head and shoulders are supported at all times. Hold him gently but firmly at the top of his arm farthest away from you so that his shoulders are supported by your forearm across his back: if he feels insecure or slips under the water even for just a second, he will be frightened and may balk at bathing for some time.

- Use as few bath toiletries as possible on your baby's skin (see "Baby toiletries," pp.63–8). Soap has a very drying effect and, as noted before, can make the baby slippery and hard to hold. Bath preparations that you add to the water are less harsh, especially hypoallergenic ones, and are easier to manage.

BATHING OLDER BABIES

Between three and six months, your baby will outgrow the baby tub and be ready to move into a normal tub. But the steep sides can appear daunting from a baby's perspective. To help him get used to it, try putting him in his baby tub inside the big tub before making the transition. There are a variety of baby bath seats available, from shaped foam pads to specially designed plastic models.

When your baby is able to sit up unsupported, he will take a much more active part in bathtime. Not only will

he enjoy splashing around, he will also start to amuse himself with toys. Plastic ducks, boats, water mills, and other more sophisticated bath toys are great fun. However, a sponge, a clean empty plastic shampoo bottle minus the lid or a plastic mug can be just as entertaining. If he has an older sibling, sharing a bath will save time and water. Why not get in and join him yourself from time to time?

BATHROOM HAZARDS

Now that your baby is much more curious about his environment, you will have to be even more vigilant about safety in the bathroom:

- Although he is older, don't use more than 4–5 inches (10–13 cm) of water in the tub. Never leave your baby unattended in the tub, nor with an older sibling, especially if he is under five. A child can drown in less than 3 inches (8cm) of water. If you have to leave the room, take your children with you.

- Use a nonslip mat and a bath seat in the tub.

- Check the water temperature before you put him in. Set your water heater to less than 120° F (49° C) so that even if the hot water is run by mistake it won't result in a serious scald.

- Turn faucets off tightly and cover them with a cloth to prevent scalding.

- Make sure that adult toiletries, perfumes, cosmetics, cleaning supplies, and medicines are safely out of reach. These products cause many of the poisonings that take place in the home.

- Discourage boisterous play. Standing up unsupported and jumping could result in a fall.

- Don't drain the tub while your baby is still in it. The noise and the sensation of the water draining away may frighten him.

BATHING A TODDLER

Boisterous toddlers need close supervision at bathtime to prevent them from slipping or trying to climb out of the tub. Turning on the faucets and emptying bottles of shampoo and bubble bath are also favorite pastimes, so be on your guard and never leave your child unattended.

At this age, he may insist on doing things by himself. At bathtime you can encourage this independent streak by showing him how to wash himself with his own special sponge or washcloth.

CLEANING TEETH

As soon as your baby cuts his first teeth at about six months, make cleaning his teeth part of the daily routine. Looking after your child's baby teeth is an investment for the future: serious decay in first teeth can affect the development of second teeth. At first you will simply be getting him used to the idea, so it's not important how long you spend doing it.

- Use a minuscule amount of baby toothpaste on a soft, small-headed baby toothbrush, clean finger, or piece of sterile gauze.

- Rub his teeth gently.

- Clean the gums even where there are no teeth as this will get rid of bacteria, providing a healthy environment when the teeth come through.

- Rinse the brush in cooled, boiled water if your baby is under six months old and gently clean around the inside of his mouth.

HAIR CARE

Until your baby is about 12 weeks old, you can simply rinse his hair with clean water or use water with a little bath lotion dissolved in it.

To wash a young baby's hair:

- Wrap him a towel.

- Using the "football carry" (see "Into the water," p.59), hold him close to the tub or sink and gently wet his head with your hand.

- If you are using bath lotion, dip a washcloth in clean water and rinse off any lather.

- Dry your baby's head carefully with a soft towel.

To wash an older baby's hair, use a mild, nonsting shampoo once or twice a week. (Between washings, just rinse his hair with clean water.) Use only one application of shampoo, making sure to rinse his hair thoroughly. Take care not to get shampoo or water in his eyes. Not all babies enjoy having their hair washed. You can make the process less stressful for your child by:

- Keeping hair washing to a minimum. Avoid doing it when he has his bath, so that it doesn't spoil his fun.

- Rinsing his hair with a wet cloth instead of pouring water over his head, which may frighten him.

- Using a hair shield that fits around the hairline like a halo to prevent water and shampoo from running down onto his face.

- Letting him pour water on his head himself as part of a game.

If none of these measures help, stop. Leave it for a week or so and then try washing your baby's hair again. Meanwhile, you can keep his hair reasonably clean with a sponge and a damp brush.

- He will probably try to grab the toothbrush while you're doing it, so give him one of his own.

- Try to clean his teeth twice a day, once after breakfast and once before bed, as part of his routine.

- With reluctant toddlers, make a game out of teeth brushing by pretending the toothbrush is a train, or something similar.

- When he is old enough to brush his teeth himself, you will need to check his handiwork and finish it off for him.

Baby toiletries

In any supermarket or pharmacy there is a bewildering choice of baby toiletries, from soaps, shampoos, and bath lotions to talcs, moisturizers, and barrier creams. Not all of them are essential or even desirable. The safest and cheapest method of keeping a young baby clean is to use plain water with mild soap on dirty areas. Baby lotion or a barrier cream may be useful under diapers.

THE CASE AGAINST TOILETRIES

- Products that are highly perfumed, produce lots of bubbles, or contain known allergens, such as lanolin, may cause a skin reaction. If your baby's skin is easily irritated, it's important to test any new bath or skin-care products. Dab a little on a small area of skin on his forearm and leave for 24 to 48 hours. If the area turns red or swells up, do not use the product.

- Natural odors provide a newborn baby with important information about his environment. He recognizes his mother by smell, which also helps him to target the breast when he is hungry. Strong synthetic fragrances are undesirable because they interfere with these subtle messages.

- Overexposure to chemicals can affect the development of your baby's immune system. Keeping toiletries to a minimum is a way of limiting his exposure to potentially harmful substances.

WHAT'S AVAILABLE

Soaps

Soap is a strong defatting agent, which means it takes the natural oils and fats out of the skin. It has an acid-alkali (pH) balance of nine, whereas human skin has a pH balance of between five and six. It's best to avoid using it altogether during the first six weeks of your baby's life, when his skin is at its most delicate. Even when he is older, soap should be used sparingly. Mild baby soap or hypoallergenic varieties are less likely to dry or irritate his skin.

Bath lotions and gels

- An alternative to soap, most lotions are perfumed and produce bubbles when a capful is poured into the bath. They should be avoided.

- For babies with very dry skin or eczema, lotions are available that will help to moisturize and soothe the skin. Some are lanolin-based; others use mineral oil or soya oil. They are more expensive, but if your baby suffers from a chronic skin problem, they may be worth trying.

But many kinds can cause skin rashes and dryness. Ask your baby's doctor for advice.

- Bath lotions and gels can break down the surface of the water, allowing it to enter the vagina and possibly cause bladder infections.

- They can make the bath tub very slippery.

- Some leave a greasy residue, so the bathtub and any bath toys will need to be cleaned regularly.

- Rubber bath mats will deteriorate more quickly.

Baby oils

Usually mineral-oil-based and derived from petrochemicals, these preparations can be added to the bath to moisturize very dry skin, but they can also block pores. Natural oils such as sweet almond oil and ordinary olive oil make effective moisturizers (see "Cradle cap," p.123). In most cases, no oil is necessary at all.

Shampoos

Choose a mild, non sting shampoo or an all-in-one shampoo and conditioner specially formulated for babies.

Moisturizers

Many babies develop dry skin. Ordinary soap, hot water, and highly perfumed or colored toiletries have a drying effect. So where possible choose hypoallergenic and fragrance-free products. There are many specially formulated baby skin creams on the market to soothe and moisturize dry skin.

However, less expensive and equally effective alternatives are available:

- Aqueous cream is both soothing and moisturizing. It is cheaper than other alternatives and is available by prescription if your baby has a skin problem. It can also be used as a substitute for soap, although it does not lather.

- Eucerin cream.

- Paraffin-based creams such as Diprobase.

- Essential oils such as sweet almond oil.

Talcum powders

Although your own mother probably remembers sprinkling you with baby powder after a bath, it's not necessary, and it can make your baby's skin very dry. If you do use talcum powder, make sure you apply it from your hand rather than shaking it directly onto your baby, to prevent him from inhaling the very fine dust. Check that the powder does not cake in the deep creases at the top of his thighs, where it would irritate his skin.

Baby lotions

Applied with cotton balls or your hands, baby lotion can be used to clean the diaper area. However, on a very young baby it is better to use pure water.

Barrier creams

The acid in your baby's urine and feces can irritate his skin, causing diaper rash (see "Diaper rash," p.48). Such preparations as zinc cream form a barrier that helps protect your baby's skin, especially at night when he's usually in the same diaper for an extended period of time.

Baby wipes

Although convenient for cleaning, baby wipes may contain strong ingredients, including preservative, alcohol, and fragrance, and they are expensive. Some brands are suitable for wiping hands and faces as well. If you feel that wipes are necessary, look for brands free of chemicals. However:

- Ordinary water and cotton balls is just as effective for cleaning your baby's bottom.

- A damp cloth stored in a plastic bag can be used to wipe his hands and face when you're out.

NATURE CARE

Herbal remedies and essential oils have been used for thousands of years in bathing and skin-care preparations. A number of companies produce high quality natural cosmetics, including baby-care products. Many operate environmentally friendly manufacturing and retailing policies by avoiding unnecessary packaging and using refillable, recyclable containers.

- Many of these products contain plant extracts with natural cleansing or healing properties. Plants with moisturizing or soothing properties include aloe vera, pot marigold (calendula), chamomile, and jojoba. However, even these may irritate some babies' skin. Stop use at the first sign of irritation.

- They are easily absorbed by the skin. (Products containing petroleum-derived substances such as mineral oil can block the skin's pores).

- Since they contain fewer detergents, preservatives, and emulsifiers, they are less likely to irritate sensitive skin.

- Add two or three drops of Bach Rescue Remedy or a chamomile tea bag to the bathwater to help relieve dry skin.

ANIMAL TESTING

It is not always easy to establish which products are cruelty-free, since some manufacturers do not label their products clearly or do make confusing statements. "This product has not been tested on animals" can mean that the finished product has not been tested on animals, but the ingredients may have been. A growing number of companies now test their products by using cell cultures in test tubes and other non-animal-based techniques.

In addition, many of the ingredients in cosmetics and toiletries are derived from animals. These include collagen, stearic acid, gelatin, and tallow.

PRODUCT LABELING

If your baby has sensitive skin, or you are concerned about his exposure to chemicals that may cause an allergic reaction, try to choose products that list their ingredients. Legislation in the USA and Canada regulates the sale and labeling of food, drugs, cosmetics, and other products. Generally, manufacturers are required to provide a complete list of ingredients on the product label in descending order of quantity. The most common ingredients in toiletries are:

- Water (often listed as aqua).

- Fragrance. If your baby's skin reacts to a product, the most likely cause is perfume found in it. Try a hypoallergenic or odor-free (fragrance-free) alternative.

READING THE LABEL

Common terms used in product labeling include:

- Hypoallergenic—excludes substances most likely to cause an allergic reaction, but still is not allergy-proof.

- Fragrance-free—may contain a single fragrance, often to mask the smell of other ingredients.

- Unperfumed—contains no perfume at all.

- pH-balanced—a pH value close to that of human skin (about pH5.5).

- Color

- Surfactants. These are chemical compounds used to make products dissolve in water and foam. Without surfactants shampoo would not lather, bath lotion would not dissolve, and bubble bath would not bubble.

- Preservatives. These inhibit the growth of bacteria and mold to make sure that a product does not deteriorate during its shelf life. Preservatives are required by law if the product has a shelf life of less than 30 months. They are also a common cause of allergy.

Bedtime

The amount of sleep your baby needs and his sleeping patterns are unique to him. Some babies settle quickly into regular routines, sleeping through the night after only a few weeks. Others resist napping during the day and rarely have an unbroken night until they are school age. If you have a wakeful baby, you may worry that he isn't getting enough sleep, but as long as he is happy and healthy, you can be sure that he is, although you won't be.

NEWBORN SLEEPING PATTERNS

For the first six weeks or so, your baby may sleep up to 18 hours a day. Newborn babies are unable to distinguish day from night, so instead of being active by day and sleeping at night, they will sleep and wake right around the clock.

During this time, sleeping and feeding are very closely connected (see "Breast-feeding," pp.8–18). The amount he sleeps will be determined by how big he is and how often he needs to be fed. As a rule, the lower his birthweight, the more often he needs to eat. Premature babies tend to sleep more than those born full-term, you may even have to wake your baby every three hours or so to feed him. How you feed your baby may also affect his sleep patterns. As breast milk is more easily digested than formula, a breast-fed baby may wake more frequently for food than one who is bottle-fed.

WHAT WILL WAKE HIM?

Your newborn baby will probably fall asleep immediately after feeding. He will sleep quite deeply and be oblivious to most external stimuli. Because his respiratory system won't have matured fully, he may grunt, snuffle, or even sneeze when he is asleep. These noises are perfectly normal, and he will soon grow out of them. When he wakes, it will probably be due to:

- Hunger.
- His being too hot or too cold.
- A dirty diaper.
- Gas.

Once his physical needs have been met, and with a little cuddling and comforting, your newborn will fall asleep again quite quickly. If he has trouble settling, swaddling may help.

SWADDLING

Some newborns sleep better when they are swaddled, possibly because it mimics the constraining sensations of being in the womb. Wrapping your baby gently but firmly in a shawl, thin blanket, or flannel sheet will make him feel secure, keep him warm, and provide reassuring physical contact with something soft. A baby will often jerk and twitch before falling asleep. Swaddling prevents these involuntary movements from keeping him awake.

To swaddle your baby, follow the illustration above or ask your baby's doctor to show you how.

HEALTHY SLEEPING

Research shows that overheating my be a contributory factor in crib death (SIDS). To prevent your baby from becoming too hot:

- Place him on his back to sleep—this helps protect from crib death.

- Keep his room at a steady temperature, 65°F (18°C) is ideal.

- Avoid using too many covers. A sheet and two or three blankets is adequate for a room temperature of 65°F (18°C).

- Quilts and pillows should not be given to babies under 12 months.

- Use the Feet to Foot method of making the bed so that your baby's head is always uncovered. Position your baby with his feet at the foot of the bed. Turn the top sheet down, away from his head, over the top edge of the blankets and tuck them in around the mattress edges so that he can't wriggle down underneath the bedding.

- Make sure that crib bumpers are fastened securely.

WHOSE BEDROOM?

While your baby needs night feedings, it is often easier to have him in your room close to the bed so that when he wakes or needs feeding you can attend to him with a minimum of disturbance. A crib that can be adjusted so your baby's mattress is level with your bed may be useful since it means he can sleep next to you without actually sharing your bed (see also "Your baby's bed," pp.143–5).

Some parents find that they don't sleep soundly with the baby in their room, as they are awakened by every whimper and snuffle. In these circumstances it is probably more relaxing if your baby sleeps in a separate room.

SHARING YOUR BED

If you are breast-feeding, you may prefer to bring him into bed with you and feed him lying down in case either of you falls asleep. But sharing a bed with your baby is not widely recommended. In many cultures, however, babies always sleep with their parents. A common fear is that you may inadvertently crush or smother your child when you turn over in the night. This won't happen in normal circumstances; you will instinctively compensate for this tiny extra body when you move in your sleep.

However, recent research suggests that bed-sharing should be avoided if either parent has:

- Drunk alcohol prior to sleeping.
- Taken illegal drugs or sleeping pills.
- Is a smoker.

For most parents it is easier to settle for one approach or the other. Letting your baby sleep with you sometimes and at others insisting that he sleep in his own bed will confuse him and disrupt any sleep routines that you may be trying to establish.

The advantages:
- Greater intimacy with your baby.
- Convenient for feeding.
- Baby may wake less.
- More likely to settle quickly.

The disadvantages:
- A difficult habit to break.

- As your baby grows, it is less comfortable for you.
- It limits your privacy.
- It may keep you from relaxing—worrying about rolling onto your baby
- Being with your child day and night might leave you feeling that you have no physical or emotional space to yourself.

A BEDTIME ROUTINE

Lack of sleep and broken nights are facts of life for the parents of a young baby. It is unlikely that your baby will stop his night feedings before his weight reaches 12 pounds (5kg) (usually between three and five months). The fact is, he really needs to be fed frequently in order to sustain his rapid growth rate.

There is little you can do to make your baby drop his night feeding—he'll enjoy the comfort aspect of it too. But once he does start to sleep through the night, a bedtime routine will help your baby fall asleep and settle down again if he wakes up later in the night.

To establish good sleeping habits, you must first help your newborn baby differentiate between night and day by:

- Stimulating him while he is awake during the day.

- Putting him in a room other than his bedroom for his daytime naps.

- Darkening his room at bedtime.

- Keeping the night feedings as quiet and peaceful as possible—resist the temptation to play with him.

- Introducing a bedtime routine during his first few weeks of life. He will eventually learn that this sequence of events signals bedtime, helping him to make the

HELPING YOUR BABY TO SETTLE HIMSELF

As he grows older, it is important to follow the same bedtime routine each night if you want him to fall asleep by himself:

- Don't overstimulate him with loud or boisterous play in the hour or so before bed.

- Decide on a realistic bedtime. If you want him in bed by 6:30 PM and he only starts to feel sleepy about 8, you will have difficulty.

- Give him his last feeding, but don't allow him to fall asleep.

- Settle him in his crib with his favorite toys and comfort object if he has one.

- Say goodnight to him and leave the room without waiting to see if he settles.

- Avoid patting, rocking, or singing him to sleep. You will be putting him to sleep rather than letting him fall asleep on his own.

- Leave the door slightly ajar so that he can hear what is going on in the rest of the house. Loud music or noisy conversation may keep him awake, but a low level of background, or white, noise is reassuring for him.

- If he cries, wait five minutes before going back to him. Many tired babies cry for a few minutes before they sleep.

transition from waking to sleeping. At first, this routine will be very simple: bathing or washing your baby, changing him into his nightclothes, feeding him and putting him in his crib in his dark bedroom. As he grows, you can develop his routine by including looking at a book together before saying good-night to the rest of the family.

DAYTIME NAPS

Most babies have their wakeful times during the day. For some, it may be the middle of the morning; for others, it is late afternoon. Now that he is taking notice of his surroundings, it is important to provide him with stimulation: play with him and talk to him, enjoy plenty of physical contact with him and offer him a change of scene by taking him out for a walk in a buggy or a baby sling. He will also enjoy watching you carry out your chores if you put him in a baby seat or prop him up in his buggy and move him around the house with you.

As he grows, these wakeful periods will get longer, and if you are fortunate, by the time he is three or four months old, he may have settled into a daytime routine of mid-morning and early afternoon naps.

Sleep problems

Up to six months, the sleep problem is yours, not his, for your baby will sleep for as long as his body tells him to. This may not be long enough for you, but he has no control over his body functions and he will be kept awake by only hunger, discomfort, or illness. After about six weeks, he will become more wakeful and alert, but his sleeping and feeding habits will still be closely linked, so he will probably fall asleep after being fed and wake before his next feeding time.

Babies can start having sleep problems at about nine months. By then your child is aware of his surroundings and is able to keep himself awake. Although he may be sleepy during his last feeding, he probably won't fall asleep at the breast or on the bottle.

WHY WON'T HE SETTLE?

- He doesn't want to miss out on the activity around him.

A SLEEP PROGRAM

Coping with a baby who fights sleep at bedtime or regularly wakes in the night and won't settle is exhausting and stressful for you and your child, and affects family life. Once your baby is six months old, you can try to settle him by following a sleep program. Sleep programs are a tried-and-tested method of dealing with these problems, but both you and your spouse have to be committed to introducing one. Many parents have been successful in just a few days.

- Dedicate a week to introduce a sleep program, preferably when you have no other nighttime commitments.

- On the first night, settle your child in his crib and leave the room. If he cries, go back after a couple of minutes and settle him by patting or stroking him, but don't pick him up.

- Leave the room, and if he cries, leave him for a few minutes longer before returning and calming him.

- Repeat the procedure as many times as it takes for your baby to fall asleep, leaving a slightly longer interval each time.

- On subsequent nights, follow the same routine. Consistency is crucial. If you relent and pick him up, you will have to start all over again.

You may find it distressing to leave your child to cry even for a short period, but a sleep program is usually very effective, so it's worth persevering. It may take about 10 days before your baby learns to fall asleep by himself. Expect occasional relapses. For example, changes to his routine, teething, or illness will probably disrupt your baby's sleep pattern. If this happens, reintroducing the sleep program will usually reestablish his regular sleep routine.

- He doesn't want to be separated from you.

- He is overtired—he may be physically exhausted but is too anxious and tense to relax enough to fall asleep.

- He is unwell.

With a fretful baby who won't settle at bedtime, the temptation is to put him to sleep by holding him, rocking him, or walking around with him until he falls asleep in your arms. Although this may work in the end, your baby will learn to rely on you to put him to sleep. When he wakes in the night, he will need you to settle him again, so it's important that he learn to go to sleep by himself (see "Helping your baby to settle himself," p.73).

NIGHT WAKING

If your baby wakes in the night, he may simply be uncomfortable:

- Verify that he's neither too hot nor too cold. Feel the back of his neck rather than his hands, which may be cool if they are outside the blanket.

- Check to see whether his diaper needs changing.

- If he has stopped night feeding, don't offer him milk to put him back to sleep. He might start to associate night waking with feeding.

Even if he seems wide awake, avoid playing with him. Speak to him softly, pat his back or stroke his head until he is calm, and then quietly leave the room.

Health problems, such as ear or chest infections, may prevent your baby from sleeping. If your settled baby suddenly starts to sleep badly, or if he has been unwell and his sleep patterns don't return to normal after a few days, a visit to the doctor will establish whether the problem has a physiological cause.

FINALLY SETTLED

When your baby has established a proper sleep pattern, try to disrupt it as little as possible:

- Avoid altering naptimes or bedtime to compensate for lost sleep. A later bedtime is no guarantee that your baby will sleep later in the morning. He may simply wake up tired and fussy at the usual time.

- A catnap late in the afternoon may keep him going well beyond his normal bedtime.

- Don't drop his afternoon nap too soon. He will get overtired and overwrought, which can make it difficult to get him to sleep in the evening.

Crying and Comfort

Crying is the only way your baby has of communicating his physical and emotional needs. Some babies cry more than others, but all cry for a reason. Unless your baby is seriously ill, he will not keep it to himself. You can give comfort by tuning into his needs and understanding what he wants.

Crying

Earlier generations of parents were discouraged from comforting a crying baby for fear of spoiling him, but we now understand that a young crying baby is not trying to be manipulative. Research has shown that if you respond quickly to your baby's cries during the first six months, he is more likely to be settled and contented by his first birthday.

FIRST THREE MONTHS

A baby's body undergoes major changes to adapt to life outside the womb during his first three months. He is establishing feeding, sleeping, and waking patterns, and many of his vital organs are still maturing. So it's hardly surprising that your baby sometimes seems frustrated and miserable.

- Some experts believe that crying spells in the first year coincide with periods of rapid brain and nervous development at 5, 8, 12, 19, 26, 37, and 46 weeks. These are critical times, which researchers have compared to a kind of rebirth.

- About six weeks tends to be the peak age for crying, when on average most babies cry for up to two hours a day, though some may cry for as many as four hours in any 24-hour period.

- These crying spells can be especially disturbing for a mother who returns to work at six weeks. It is easy to believe that the separation is the only cause of the crying.

- Crying spells tend to diminish at about four months. By the end of his first year, your baby will probably cry only half as much as he did during his first three months.

- External factors may influence the amount that your baby cries. If he was born after a long or difficult labor, he may cry more and sleep less than a child who had a less traumatic birth.

- A baby can also be very sensitive to his mother's moods. If you are depressed or anxious, you may find that your baby becomes unsettled and cries more frequently.

COLIC

Colic is a muscular spasm in the wall of the intestines. A baby under three months old who has regular crying spells in the early evening, developing into screaming fits, may be suffering from colic, particularly if he keeps drawing up his legs and appears to be uncomfortable.

Colic is not really an illness, but more a pattern of behavior. There are many theories as to its cause, including overfeeding, trapped gas in the digestive tract, and tension.

Over-the-counter colic remedies are sometimes helpful, but avoid brands containing alcohol. Cuddling, rocking or gently massaging your baby's abdomen (see "Baby massage," pp.84–9) can be just as effective. Keeping a baby upright after feeding or allowing afternoon naps sitting in a sling or baby seat may also help.

Although colic causes a great deal of distress (for both parent and baby), most babies will outgrow it by the time they are four months old (see "Colic," pp.100–102).

Comforting

Often you will know instinctively why your baby is crying and how to comfort him. Sometimes he will stop as soon as you pick him up. At other times, however, you may be at a loss to calm him, which can be very distressing for both of you. The following are some of the possible causes:

DECODING HIS CRIES

As you get to know your baby, you will learn to decode these cries and be able to comfort and console him more effectively.

- A regular, monotonous cry may mean that he is hungry.

- A sharp intake of breath followed by a shrill scream is unmistakably caused by pain.

- Intermittent whimpering and grumbling lets you know that he is tired and nearly ready for sleep.

Hunger
Hunger is the most common cause of crying in very young babies. Feeding your baby on demand is the only effective way of dealing with it. Delaying tactics, such as offering a pacifier or giving him boiled water instead of milk, will only frustrate him further and probably make him cry more furiously.

Discomfort

He may be too hot or too cold. Ideally he should be kept in a room with a constant temperature of 68°F (18–20°C). The best way to check his body temperature is to feel the back of his neck or his stomach. If he feels hot or sweaty, remove a layer of bedding or clothing. If he is chilly, add another layer. A wet or dirty diaper may also make him miserable, so check and change him regularly. If your baby has a cold, a blocked or runny nose may prevent him from feeding and sleeping properly and make him fussier than usual. Use a bulb syringe to clear his nose.

Tiredness

A very common cause of crying, but one which is not always easy to spot. Trying to comfort a tired baby by picking him up and cuddling him may make him more miserable, not less. He may simply want to be put to bed and left to fall asleep on his own.

Shock or fear

A newborn baby is very sensitive to external stimuli. Bright lights, loud noises, and sudden movements will startle and upset him, as will boisterous play or rough handling. He may also cry if he feels physically insecure. Always hold him gently but firmly so he doesn't feel as though you are about to drop him.

Being undressed

Newborn babies don't like being naked. It makes them feel vulnerable, and they dislike having their skin exposed to the air. When you are undressing your baby at bathtime or whenever you are changing his clothes, leave his shirt on for as long as possible. And then when you do take it off, be sure to drape a soft towel across his body.

Pain

If your baby feels pain, his crying will have a shrill, urgent note that will start your adrenaline pumping. The cause may be bathwater that's too hot or an accidental prick with a diaper pin, or he may have a more serious injury. A painful condition, such as colic or an ear infection, may make him cry inconsolably. If you suspect that your baby is ill, you should seek medical help.

Lack of physical contact

Your baby may cry simply because he needs physical reassurance from you. The most natural response to a baby's cries is to pick him up and cuddle him. In many cultures, babies are held and carried in slings most of the time. Hold him close to your body or with his chest and body pressed against your shoulder and walk around with him. If neither of these positions soothes him, try cradling his head and neck in the crook of your left arm so that he is facing out, with your left hand supporting his body and your right hand holding him between his legs.

Carrying him around in a sling is an alternative way of keeping him close to your body and has the advantage of leaving your hands free. Graduate to a backpack when he's older. Most babies love "kangaroo care," or skin-to-skin contact with their mother or father. Try giving him a massage (see "Baby massage," pp.84–89). Don't let your newborn baby cry for long periods. He will become distraught, and it will take you much longer to comfort him if you let him become too distressed.

Boredom

As your baby grows older and becomes more aware of and interested in his surroundings, if he is left on his own with nothing to distract him, he will probably cry to attract your attention. Make sure he has plenty to look at when he is alone. Mobiles (see "Homemade toys," p.158), pictures, activity centers, or a few favorite toys will keep him amused when he is awake in his crib. Prop him up in his buggy or put him in a bouncy chair and let him watch what you are doing.

Separation anxiety

About the age of six months, your baby may start to cling to you physically and emotionally. He may become very distressed if he is separated from you, crying even if you are out of sight for only a few moments. Separation anxiety often goes hand-in-hand with a fear of strangers, and he may even become shy with familiar adults. This can be a very trying stage for parents, and it needs careful handling.

Try to get your baby used to the idea of being left with other people, starting with very short periods of no longer than 20 minutes. It's important that he understands that when you go out, you will always come back. Avoid slipping away without his noticing. He will be distressed if he suddenly finds you are gone and will cry and cling to you even more the next time you try to leave him.

Oh dear, what can the matter be...

Even the most contented and settled babies have crying spells. If your baby won't stop crying and you have eliminated all possible physical causes, try:

- Repetitive movement. Try walking around with him, rocking him in your arms or in his buggy, patting him on the back or on his behind, or even dancing with him.

- Sound. Playing music or turning on the television or radio can have a soothing effect, provided it is not too loud or strident. But remember that television is a poor babysitter and television-watching is a hard habit to break. Some babies respond to white noise, such as the low hum of a vacuum cleaner or washing machine.

Tapes of the sounds a baby hears in the womb are worth trying with your newborn.

- A change of scene. Distract your baby with a short shopping trip or a walk.

- Motion. Going for a ride in the car will sometimes calm a crying baby. The gentle vibration and noise of the engine seems to have a soporific effect.

- A squeaky toy or rattle. Something brightly colored that makes a noise can sometimes distract a baby.

- Talking or singing to him softly. Long before he has any comprehension of what you are saying, your baby will find your voice soothing and reassuring.

Frustration

Older babies can become very frustrated if they are trying unsuccessfully to complete a task—for example, to reach a toy or to sit up. Often you can help them to achieve their objective and the tears will stop.

AT YOUR WITS' END

Most parents have to cope with episodes of inconsolable crying during their baby's first year. Trying to pacify a baby who will not stop screaming when you have tried every tactic you know can leave you feeling exhausted, desperate, and even violent. The strength of these negative feelings can be frightening, but they are completely normal.

- If you are very stressed, your baby will probably pick up on your tension and respond by becoming even more upset. In these situations, the safest thing for both of you is to let someone else take over for a while so that you can calm down, preferably out of earshot of your crying baby. If you are by yourself, put him down in his crib, go out of the room, and shut the door. He won't come to any harm if you let him scream for a little while. You can hear if he stops, and go back to check on him.

- Living with a baby who cries excessively is an enormous strain and very demoralizing. Parents who feel that they are not coping should seek outside help. Some persistently miserable babies respond well to massage (see pages 84–9). Support groups (see Useful Addresses) have hotlines and offer advice and information on crying and comforting. Your doctor or baby's doctor should also be able put you in touch with support or self-help groups.

- Whatever advice is offered by outsiders, never underestimate the power of your own intuition. As your baby grows, you will learn through instinct and experience how best to comfort him. Parents of criers should take heart from the results of a recent study, which showed that, although mothers' efforts to soothe their babies did not always stop their crying, they did prevent it from escalating into inconsolable screaming.

COMFORT HABITS

The significant adults in a baby's life, his mother, father, and any other regular carers, provide him with the emotional and physical attention that he needs to feel secure and loved. Comfort habits contribute to your baby's well-being by providing him with another source of reassurance when he feels anxious or vulnerable. They help him to become more independent and develop his inner resources, and as long as he doesn't become over-reliant on them, you should not discourage them. A happy, well-adjusted child will abandon his comfort habits in his own good time.

Sucking

This is the most common of all comfort habits and one that often develops at a very early age. Babies are born with a sucking reflex to make sure they feed. As soon as he is able to find his mouth with his hands, your baby may suck his fingers or thumb for comfort.

Cuddlies

Older babies often develop an attachment to a special item such as a stuffed toy or blanket that they may suck, stroke, or simply cuddle. It will accompany them everywhere, and they may need to have it with them before they fall asleep. The cuddly's familiar smell and feel is very important, and usually the grubbier it is, the better. It can be invaluable in helping a baby settle in a strange place.

Keep a spare cuddly in case the original gets lost or irreparably damaged. If your baby has a special cloth, cut it in half and put the spare away somewhere safe in case of an emergency.

Baby massage

In many Third World cultures, babies have almost constant physical contact with the adults who take care of them. They may be swaddled and carried around on their mothers' backs or cradled by other family members until they learn to crawl. This period of physical closeness helps the baby adjust to his new environment outside the womb and strengthens the bond between

PACIFIERS

There is some evidence to suggest that excessive use of pacifiers may delay normal speech development, but professionals are generally agreed that they are harmless if used only at bedtime and when the baby is distressed. Parents are sometimes concerned that pacifiers may affect the development of their baby's teeth. But many dentists believe that they cause fewer problems than thumb-sucking, especially if the pacifier is orthodontically designed.

Pros:
- Very effective at soothing some babies.

- If he is given a pacifier at night when he wakes up, he can suck himself back to sleep.

- Babies who suck pacifiers rarely suck their thumbs.

- Adults can control pacifier use.

Cons:
- They can be difficult to give up.

- If he has a pacifier at night, he may not be able to find it when he wakes.

- Difficult to keep clean once your baby learns how to put it in and take it out.

- Giving your baby a pacifier whenever he cries means that you are dealing with the symptom, not the cause.

- With a pacifier in his mouth, your baby can't explore other objects with his mouth, which is a natural part of his development.

Pacifier safety
- Clean pacifiers with other feeding equipment during his first year.

- Don't attach them to his clothing. Strings and ribbons are dangerous.

- Check pacifiers regularly. Throw away any that have deteriorated.

- Never let your baby use a bottle of juice as a pacifier. It will cause tooth decay, and he may choke on the liquid if he falls asleep with it in his mouth.

parent and child. In these societies, massage is often a traditional part of newborn care. It is seen as a natural expression of love for the child and has important health benefits, stimulating the baby's immature immune and circulatory system.

PHYSICAL CONTACT

In the 20th century, babies in the developed world have become physically separated from their parents. From the 1920s to the mid-1960s, child-care theory was parent-centered. Great emphasis was placed on establishing routines, and mothers were discouraged from handling their babies. It was common practice for babies to be taken away immediately after the birth to be cleaned and checked before the mother could hold her child or put him to the breast. Bottle-feeding was promoted over breast-feeding; demand feeding, kissing, and cuddling the baby were frowned on for fear they would spoil the child.

Child-care experts now acknowledge the importance of close physical contact to a baby's emotional and physical development. Mothers are expected to feed on demand and are encouraged to hold and cuddle their babies freely.

Massage can play an important part in this early bonding process, providing parent and child with vital skin-to-skin contact in a mutually relaxing situation.

THE BENEFITS OF MASSAGE

For you:
- Helps you get to know your baby and gain confidence in handling him.

- Gives fathers a chance to bond with their babies.

- It is relaxing and soothing for both the giver and the baby.

For your baby:
- Fulfills your baby's need for tactile stimulation.

- Has a calming effect if he is anxious or miserable.

- Promotes sleep.

- Helps digestion and circulation.

- Moisturizes dry skin.

- Is good for coordination and mobility.

- May boost immune system and circulation.

- May reduce colic, constipation, diarrhea, coughs, colds, and irritability.

WHEN TO START

You can begin massaging your baby from birth. Many babies enjoy just having their head and back stroked to start with. If your baby is happy without clothes, you can use a little oil on your hands and massage him naked. If not, stroking him with his clothes on will be just as soothing. At around two months, your baby will probably start to enjoy being naked, and you will be able massage him more fully.

MASSAGE OILS

Plant-derived base oils like grapeseed, sweet almond, or coconut oil are the most suitable for baby massage. Many commercial baby oils are mineral oils. These are not easily absorbed by the skin and tend to block the pores, whereas organic oils let the skin breathe. Perfumed products and essential oils should not be used on young babies. Essential oils can be used only if diluted in the base massage oil—three drops of essential oil to four tablespoons of base oil. And only certain oils that have healing and soothing properties are suitable for young babies— English lavender, tea tree, and rose.

SAFETY FIRST

- Keep massage oil away from your baby's eyes, nose, and mouth.

- Don't massage your baby if he is unwell.

- Stop the massage if he cries or seems upset. Try again another time.

- Wait for 48 hours before massaging after an immunization and avoid the site of the injection.

- Massage can aggravate skin conditions, so get advice from your doctor if your baby has eczema (see pages 123–126).

PREPARING TO MASSAGE

- Make sure that the room is warm and free of drafts. Small babies lose heat very quickly, and your baby will not enjoy being massaged if he feels chilly.

- The best place to massage him is on a soft, clean, cotton surface like a towel placed on the floor.

- You can also lay him on your lap, but make sure your back is well supported.

- Wash and warm your hands, and remove any jewelry to avoid scratching or bruising your baby's delicate skin.

- Choose a time when your baby is neither too full nor hungry.

GIVING A MASSAGE

- Begin by undressing your baby (leaving his diaper in place) and placing him on the towel on his back facing you. If he is not comfortable without his clothes on, leave his shirt on to start with.

- During the massage, maintain eye contact with your baby and talk to him quietly. Keep one hand on him at all times to reassure him.

- Put enough oil on your hands so that they glide smoothly over your baby's skin, but not so much that he becomes slippery.

- A five-minute session is probably enough to start with. You can extend the massage time when you become more attuned to his body and he begins to relax and enjoy the experience.

- When you have finished the massage, wrap your baby in the towel and cuddle him before dressing him.

Head

You don't need to use oil to massage your baby's head. Using alternate hands, start by stroking his head from his forehead to the nape of his neck. Then stroke down his cheeks to his chin, taking care to avoid his eyes. Finally, holding his head gently between your hands, use your thumbs to stroke out from above his nose toward his temples.

Chest and abdomen

Using clockwise circular motions, working out from his navel, run your hands over his chest up to his shoulders and down the sides of his body.

Arms

Stroke your baby's arm down from shoulder to wrist, then gently holding his hand in yours, run your other hand up his arm from wrist to shoulder. Massage the palm of his hand with your thumb and gently stroke his fingers. Repeat with his other arm.

Legs and feet

Support his heel in the palm of your hand.

Massage down your baby's leg from thigh to ankle, using long, sweeping strokes. Stroke the sole of his foot from heel to toe, then stroke each toe individually. Massage the sole of his foot with your thumb, using circular motions. Repeat with his other leg.

Back

Gently turn your baby over and stroke down his back from his shoulders to the base of his spine. It is extremely important that you don't put any pressure on the spine itself. Using plenty of oil, pull his leg, hand over hand, through your palms. Repeat with his other leg.

Chapter Four

Your Healthy Baby

Healthy babies are happy babies. So if your baby suffers an illness in his first months, it can be very worrying, even if it's just an ordinary common cold. Many parents are concerned about giving their babies strong medicine unnecessarily. If you prefer a natural approach to health care, you can arrange for it effectively in conjunction with treatment from your doctor.

Recognizing illness

From the beginning, you will want to be on the alert for signs that your baby is ill. After some experience you will become attuned to be alerted immediately to any changes in behavior or appearance. Signs that may indicate your baby is unwell include:

- A temperature above 102°F (38.8°C)—a sign of infection.

- Floppy limbs.

- Shallow rapid breathing, fighting for breath, or wheezing when breathing.

- Vomiting and/or diarrhea.

- Passing less urine than normal or blood in his diaper.

- An unusual or different cry.

- Irritable, clingy, or whiny behavior.

- Drowsiness or sleeping more than usual.

- Taking less food than usual.

- Looking paler than usual.

- A rash.

- Glazed, red, or sunken eyes.

As you get used to your baby, you will learn whether his symptoms warrant just an extra dose of tender loving care, another day of observation, an immediate visit to the doctor, or an emergency dash to the hospital. However, if you're in any doubt, always call your physician for advice.

YOUR BABY'S DOCTOR

A good physician will support you not just when your baby is ill but with every aspect of his health care. So you'll find you spend a lot of time at your doctor's office during your baby's first year.

Before seeing your baby's doctor, it's a good idea to make a list of questions or problems you want to talk about. It can be easy to be intimidated by a busy professional, but it is very important that you understand the advice you are being given and the reasons for the treatment. Don't be afraid to question the doctor or ask about any alternatives. However, remain reasonable and willing to listen. It is in the best interests of you and your baby to maintain a good relationship with your baby's doctor.

Many doctors are happy to consider natural alternatives, provided the baby's health is not being put at risk.

Other resources
Many hospitals will often schedule a public health nurse home visit the first week after your baby is born. The public health nurse can answer many questions about feeding, bathing, and dressing him as well as

recognizing illness. In some areas public health departments also have well baby clinics, and some have telephone hotlines for advice.

Parenting classes before or after your baby is born can be very helpful. The classes cover all aspects of baby care and provide an opportunity to meet other parents. Recognizing illness and distinguishing mild

from severe problems is always a part of the curriculum. These helpful classes are available without charge.

Examining your baby

A crying, distressed baby is very difficult for the doctor to examine, especially after the age of about six months, when your baby is much more aware of what's going

CARING FOR A SICK BABY

When babies are ill, they instinctively turn to the person they know best for comfort. You can do a lot to help your baby feel better, but it's most important to give him plenty of cuddling and tender loving care.

- Encourage your baby to rest. Sleep is one of nature's greatest healers, allowing the body to concentrate all its energies into fighting off an illness. Babies who aren't given enough time to rest and recuperate are likely to be sick more often.

- Babies remain quiet or fall asleep when

they are unwell, but they are most at ease if their mothers are nearby. Carry a young baby in a sling or let an older one sleep near you during the day. You may want to sleep in his room or stay with him until he falls asleep at night.

- Weather permitting, take your baby out for a walk in a sling or buggy so he can sleep and you get a break. It will not harm him to go out in the car or buggy, even if he has a temperature. A change of scene and fresh air will do you both good.

on around him. You can make things easier for yourself, your baby, and the baby's doctor by being as calm as possible. If you are apprehensive, your baby will pick up any tension. If you show confidence and trust in your doctor, so will your baby. Keep the baby on your knee if possible and if he clings to you, resist your instinct to cuddle him tight. Relax so he'll know there's nothing to be afraid of.

Complementary medicine for babies

Complementary medicine, such as herbalism and homeopathy, is becoming increasingly popular with parents who are looking for safe remedies to help their children get better naturally. Young children require the gentlest of medicines. And since the best natural therapies are safe, mild treatments, many are suitable even for tiny babies. They not only treat the symptoms, they can stimulate the body's own natural healing powers and reduce the possibility of relapse. And many parents find that when they go to see a

practitioner of complementary medicine, the opportunity to talk in depth about their baby's problem to someone who really seems to listen and care is as therapeutic for them as the treatment is for their baby.

However, it is important to remember that babies and children can become very ill very quickly. Natural remedies, however effective, do not usually give instant results and they may not be effective in certain situations. For acute illnesses and in emergencies it is essential to get medical help from your baby's doctor.

COMPLEMENTARY THERAPIES

The following therapies offer simple and safe treatments for common ailments in babies. This is a very brief guide, so in order to obtain more information about each therapy, you will need to refer to a book that deals with that particular subject in some detail. Most natural health stores and good bookstores carry a selection of books about complementary medicine. Unless you are absolutely sure about a treatment, take your baby to your baby's doctor or a trusted, qualified practitioner for advice first, since there are many natural substances and treatments that may not be suitable and can even be dangerous for your baby.

Aromatherapy

Aromatherapy uses essential oils extracted from tiny glands in flowers, stems, herbs, fruits, and trees to treat a variety of conditions as well as to maintain good health and emotional well-being. It provides a holistic, noninvasive treatment, most commonly through massage, although inhalers, vaporizers, and compresses are other aromatherapy treatments. For babies, the oils need to be extremely well diluted and can be added to the bath, used in a vaporizer or as a massage oil. The safest essential oils for babies during their first year are chamomile, lavender, fennel, dill, rose, and sweet orange. Tea tree, which is generally recommended for problem skin and is very strong-smelling, is also suitable but you may prefer not to use it because of the smell.

Bach Flower Remedies

These remedies use the reported healing power of flowers to treat mental and emotional problems. Color, scent, and touch all contribute to the powerful effect of flowers, and it is these qualities that Dr. Edward Bach developed in the 1930s into a system of healing used all over the world. There are 38 Bach remedies to choose from, and all are safe to use for any age. Some of the remedies are related to personality types, for example, to treat an oversensitive, fearful baby. Others are used in a specific situation, for example, to calm a baby after an accident. By treating psychological problems, the remedies may also promote healing of physical symptoms. To choose a remedy, you have to be able to assess your baby's state of mind and match it to the right flower essence.

Herbalism

Herbs and plants have been used for healing since the earliest times in all cultures. Today many of the drugs used in orthodox medicine were first derived from plants and still are. There are thousands of herbs and plants, each with different properties that have a definite action on a particular body system. Some, such as the lemon, have an antibacterial action. Others, such as the pot marigold (calendula), are antiseptic. Some, such as chamomile, have relaxant and antispasmodic properties. Only the gentlest and safest herbal remedies are recommended for babies and are best given as an infusion, which is made by pouring boiling water over the herb and leaving it to steep for a few minutes. Herbalists use all the therapeutic parts of a plant—flowers, leaves, roots, bark, wood, and berries—as they believe it is the plant as a whole that has a medicinal effect. Never make a plant medication without checking with an expert or reliable reference book. Some plants, such as foxglove, are both therapeutic and poisonous.

Homeopathy

Homeopathy is based on the principle of "like cures like." Its origins go back to the fourth century BC, to the Greek physician Hippocrates. But it was the 19th-century German doctor Samuel Hahnemann who developed the idea into the treatment we know today.

A remedy using animal, vegetable, or mineral substances is prescribed in a very small dose that is known to induce (if used at full strength) symptoms similar to those of the illness the person is experiencing. This arouses the immune system to overcome the sickness and restore health. The correct remedy can be selected only after careful assessment of the baby or child's mental, emotional, and physical symptoms by a qualified practitioner. However, there are standard remedies, such as chamomile for teething.

Massage

Massage is another ancient therapy, and as well as being good for a baby emotionally, it can be used for treating many conditions from colic to teething pains. A gentle massage is comforting for babies, and the physical contact benefits both baby and parent. Stroking relaxes and tones the muscles, promotes healthy blood circulation, and is good for the skin. Massage needs to be gentle but firm, using simple strokes, and is completely safe (see "Baby massage," pp.84–89).

Common health concerns

As a new parent, it is natural to feel extremely anxious if your baby shows any sign of appearing unwell. With experience you will become more capable of recognizing illness. Some conditions, like jaundice, may seem frightening, but they are common in new babies and will not last long. By following the advice in this section, you can help to minimize distress, although you must seek medical advice as indicated.

NEWBORN JAUNDICE

In the first few days after birth, many babies develop a yellow tinge to their skin—an indication they have newborn or neonatal jaundice. Usually harmless, neonatal jaundice is caused by a buildup in the blood of a yellow pigment, called bilirubin. This is produced by the normal breakdown of red blood cells in the body, which can't be processed properly by the newborn's immature liver. About the third or fourth day, his skin takes on a yellowish tinge. But within a week or two, as the liver matures, the jaundice clears up naturally. In rare, severe cases convulsions or brain damage may occur.

If a blood sample reveals that the bilirubin level is high, your baby will need extra fluids to wash out the excess bilirubin and phototherapy to dissolve the yellow pigmentation in the skin.

While jaundice isn't usually a serious problem, it can be very distressing for a new mother trying to get breast-feeding established. Jaundice can cause babies to be drowsy and uninterested in feeding at a vulnerable time when frequent sucking is essential to stimulate milk production.

What you can do
- Breast-feed your baby. Your breast milk is the best medicine he can have. Studies have shown that breast milk is better than water or formula for helping babies get rid of neonatal jaundice quickly.

- Make sure he is fed often so he gets the fluid and calories he needs to flush out the excess bilirubin in his blood. Regular feedings will also boost your milk supply.

- If he's being given phototherapy treatment, don't feel you can't disturb him when he's due for a feeding. And don't feel pressured to get his feeding over with quickly so he can get back under the lights.

CIRCUMCISION

The surgical removal of the foreskin—the fold of skin that covers and protects the glans (head) of the penis—circumcision is a fairly common practice, and is also carried out for religious or cultural purposes. It is rarely actually necessary for medical reasons.

If you are choosing to raise your baby in a natural way, you may not wish to have him circumcised. But you must maintain good hygiene and teach him how to clean the area himself when the time comes, usually at about 24 months. It is not necessary to retract the foreskin until the skin slides back easily (18 to 24 months) to clean the area. Ask your doctor to show you how it should be done. If you choose circumcision, have the operation done under local anesthetic by a doctor.

Growth and development progress

It is natural for you to be concerned about your baby's growth and development—you want him to be happy and healthy.

The trouble begins, however, when you start to compare him to other babies. Each baby develops at his own pace. As an example, you may notice that some babies are interested in touching and manipulating objects with their hands. These babies are developing their small muscles. Because they don't spend much time practicing rolling over, pulling themselves, etc., they will likely walk later than other babies—but they will be adept with their hands. Similarly, the babies that have been actively working on their gross arm and leg muscles will likely walk early but be less adept with their hands.

It is an axiom of child development that there is a "wide range of normal." It is normal to walk at 9 months—and just as normal at 18 months. During the first two years your baby will be hard at work. What he accomplishes first is, to a large extent, his choice. The end result— walking, talking, and feeding himself—is the same.

WHAT YOU CAN DO

- Don't constantly compare your baby to others. Take him for his well-baby visits and don't be afraid to express any concerns to his doctor. Let the doctor tell you why he or she is satisfied with your baby's development. If the baby's doctor is satisfied, you should be too.

- Keep changing the objects a young baby looks at, and later on, touches and manipulates. Babies like faces and brightly coloured patterns.

- Talk and sing to him frequently. Avoid baby talk.

- "Read" stories to him. Turn the pages and let him look at colorful pages.

- Play games like peek-a-boo with him. A game such as this will help him learn that something is there even if he can't see it.

- Stay close but let your baby have some time to learn to entertain himself.

CRIB DEATH (SUDDEN INFANT DEATH SYNDROME—SIDS)

Sudden infant death syndrome (SIDS)—the unexplained death of an apparently healthy baby—is the biggest fear of all new parents. Although it occurs rarely, usually in the first six months of life, it is the biggest killer of children under a year old. No one yet knows exactly what causes it. But by taking the recommended precautions, you can significantly lower the risks.

What you can do

- Put your baby on his back to sleep. Evidence has shown that this is the safest position to sleep in, as it prevents babies from burying their faces in the mattress and becoming overheated. Lying face down can cause the upper airways to become obstructed too. Don't worry that your baby may choke in this position. Even babies born at 34 weeks have a well-developed gag reflex, which means they will cough to prevent milk from going down into their lungs. It is also advisable to put your baby to sleep with his feet touching the bottom of the crib so he cannot wriggle down under the covers.

- Make sure your baby doesn't overheat (see p.52 and "Healthy sleeping," p.71). Keep the room temperature at 65–68°F (18–20°C) and no hotter. Do not let your baby wear a cap indoors. Don't throw an extra blanket over the crib at night if you have left the central heating on, as babies sleeping in a warm room with too many clothes or blankets may be vulnerable. You will know if your baby is too hot if he is sweating, has damp hair, or is restless. If he is hot, remove a layer of bedding. Remove caps and extra clothing as soon as you go indoors, even if it means waking your baby.

- Never let your baby sleep with an electric blanket, next to a radiator, heater, or fire, or in direct sunshine. Quilts, comforters, sheepskins, and pillows may carry a risk of overheating. The Foundation for the Study of Sudden Infant Death Syndrome provides the following guidelines to the amount of bedding your baby needs, assuming that he is wearing an undershirt, diaper, and sleepsuit. If the room or air temperature is 60°F (16°C), cover him with a sheet plus three or four layers of light baby blankets; at 65°F (18°C), use a sheet plus two or three layers of light baby blankets; at 70°F (21°C), use only a sheet plus one blanket; at 75°F (24°C), use only a sheet. Remember, a folded blanket counts as two blankets. A baby in a heavy-footed sleepsuit needs fewer blankets.

- Don't smoke and don't allow your baby to be exposed to tobacco smoke. All researchers agree that smoking is one of the main contributors to crib death: if both parents smoke, the risk of crib death is five times higher than if neither parent smokes. Smoking during pregnancy also increases the risk of babies being born prematurely or with breathing problems that can make them more vulnerable to crib death.

- Breast-feed your baby (see "Breast-feeding," p.8). The natural way to feed your baby has clear advantages: breast-feeding even for a short while reduces the likelihood of infections that may affect breathing. If he does get an infection, a breast-fed baby's airways are less likely to be as congested as a bottle-fed baby's. Because a breast-fed baby is more likely to sleep close to you and wake more frequently than a bottle-fed baby, you may be more attuned to his breathing patterns and be able to pick up any difficulties.

- Sleep in the same room as your baby or use a listening system. For the first six months when your baby is most vulnerable, keep his crib in your bedroom. A New Zealand study published in The British Medical Association publication *The Lancet* in 1996 showed that babies who share the same sleeping room as one or more adults have a lower risk of crib death than babies who sleep alone (see "Whose bedroom," p.71).

- Contact your baby's doctor if your baby seems unwell. Many crib death babies have been shown to have had minor respiratory infections. If your baby is under six months old and has a temperature of 100°F (38°C) for more than two hours, call his doctor. If he doesn't improve, or seems to get worse, contact his doctor again, even if it is the same day or night (see "Fever," p.110).

COLIC

When an otherwise healthy baby cries regularly and inconsolably for no obvious reason during his first three months, colic is usually the cause, especially if he keeps drawing his legs up over his stomach. Feeding may stop the crying, but only temporarily. No one yet knows the cause of colic or how to cure it, but this muscle spasm in the intestine is thought to be linked to the baby's immature digestive system. Possible culprits include gas pains, cow's milk in the formula, tense mothers, and parents who smoke.

What you can do

- Check your baby's feeding position to make sure he's not taking in too much air. Feed him in an upright position and don't lay him down immediately afterward. Burp him halfway through as well as when he's finished. If you're bottle-feeding, experiment with a nipple with a hole of a different size. Some new nipples have a milk flow that is too fast. Older babies may need a bigger hole to increase the flow.

- Try to relax when you're feeding—use the breathing exercises you learned at prenatal classes if you find it difficult. Sensitive babies can pick up the nervous tension of an anxious mother.

- If you are breast-feeding, consider your diet. For example, try cutting out dairy products, spicy or garlicky foods, and

caffeine for a few days to see if that improves the colic. Feeding small amounts more often, rather than large amounts all at once, may be easier on your baby's digestion.

- A colicky baby may want to suck your finger, a pacifier, or a bottle of tepid water rather than take in extra formula that he is not digesting properly.

- Don't smoke and don't allow smoking in your home. Researchers have found that nicotine transferred into the mother's milk can upset a baby, as can tobacco smoke.

- Try holding your baby in different positions when he's crying. You could also try rocking, or walking with him.

- A warm bath followed by a massage, concentrating on the abdomen, may ease the pain (see "Baby massage," pp.84–89).

If nothing helps, you can only reassure yourself that the colic will eventually subside, usually when your baby is about three months old. However, if he seems ill between bouts of colic and is not gaining weight, take him to his doctor.

• Over-the-counter products are available to help break down any large air bubbles and can be given before feeding. Consult your baby's doctor before using these.

A natural remedy

Homemade "gripe water" can be made by simmering one teaspoon of dill or fennel seeds in one pint of water for 10 minutes. Strain and cool, then give sips to the baby on a spoon. Chamomile to be effective in relieving infantile colic. Mix one teaspoon of dried herbs in a cup of boiling water. Cool and give to your baby—up to three cups a day.

IMMUNIZATION

Immunization is designed to protect both individual children and the community from infectious or contagious diseases that can cause serious illness and death. These illnesses are measles, mumps, rubella (German measles),

whooping cough, polio, tetanus, diphtheria, hemophilus influenza Type B (HIB), which is one of the causes of childhood meningitis, varicella (chicken pox), and hepatitis. Immunization is becoming a dilemma for parents who want to do the best for their baby but are concerned about the possible side effects of the vaccines. But as a general rule of thumb, it is better to have your baby immunized than face the risk of contracting the disease.

HOW DO VACCINES WORK?

Some vaccines work by giving a healthy child a mild form of an infectious disease. This stimulates the body to produce antibodies against the germ without causing the disease, allowing the baby's body to recognize the "foreign" bacteria or virus and develop an immunity that will fight off the disease if he is exposed to it later on. Sometimes the effects of the vaccine wear off, so a booster is required later.

What are the risks?

Doubts about vaccines have arisen because a very few formerly healthy children have become chronically ill or gone into anaphylactic shock (a severe allergic reaction) after immunization. The measles vaccine has been associated inconclusively with autism and Crohn's disease, a disorder of the bowel. However, serious side effects from immunization are very rare, and recent research has shown that the risks of harmful effects from the diseases themselves, which can include blindness, deafness, paralysis, brain damage, or death, are far greater.

How is it done?

Your child will receive several sets of vaccines during his first five years, starting shortly after birth. Most are injected, apart from polio which can be given by drops placed on your baby's tongue. However, if he is unwell beforehand—say, he has temperature of 102°F (38.8°C) or other signs of illness—immunization may be postponed. Most children suffer no reactions to the vaccines, but possible mild side effects can include a raised temperature, soreness at the injection site, a rash, and irritability.

Reasons which may cause you not to have your child immunized are:

- If he has had a severe reaction to a previous injection.

- If he has had a severe allergic reaction to eggs (in this case, MMR—measles, mumps and rubella vaccination—may not be given).

- If your child is being treated for a serious, malignant disease like cancer. In this case, immunization may be delayed.

TEETHING

The level of teething discomfort varies greatly among babies, but most will show signs of suffering as their new teeth push through their sensitive gums. Your baby may become irritable and cry more if his gums are sore. He may also become clingy and wakeful at night, and dribble and develop sore red skin around his mouth and cheeks.

What you can do

- Chewing can bring relief. Give your baby something firm to chew on. A teething ring cooled in the refrigerator can be effective.

- Teething gels containing antiseptic and analgesics may be recommended for occasional use in babies over four months. Infant acetaminophen relieves severe discomfort.

- Rubbing his gums with your clean finger can also help.

- The homeopathic remedy chamomile, available as teething granules, can give effective relief and is a natural alternative to anesthetic teething gels.

- Never assume that if your baby is unwell, it is due to teething. Fever, diarrhea, vomiting, and ear infections are not symptoms of teething, so always consult your baby's doctor.

A natural remedy

Chamomile is a remedy for soothing sore gums. Add one drop of chamomile to 4 ounces of cold water and stir. Dip a cotton swab in the solution and gently rub your baby's gums. Store in the refrigerator for up to 24 hours.

DENTAL CARE

By the age of 2½ years, your child is likely to have all his baby teeth. These teeth are precious; though they are not permanent, they need careful looking after. They will be needed for eating for several years, and they reserve the space for permanent teeth to come into.
By caring for them properly, you are establishing good habits that will last a lifetime.

What you can do

- Start brushing the teeth morning and night as soon as they come through (see "Cleaning teeth," p.61).

- Use a fluoride toothpaste. Toothpaste helps remove sugar, food, plaque, and bacteria from the mouth. Fluoride strengthens the developing enamel that surrounds teeth, making it more resistant to decay.

- Sugary drinks and food are teeth's worst enemy. Offer water and non-sweet snacks between meals.

- Don't give your baby juice in a bottle. Sucking on a nipple keeps the teeth constantly bathed in juice and is known to cause tooth decay. Never put the baby to bed with a bottle. As soon as he's able, encourage the use of a trainer cup for all drinks.

- Look out for hidden sugars in food and drinks. Dextrose, fructose, glucose, maltose, and lactose are sugars that will rot the teeth. Be especially careful with pure fruit juice; it should be very well diluted for babies and children.

- Continue breast-feeding. One of the best contributors to good jaw alignment, which helps prevent dental decay later on, is a baby's sucking action on the breast.

Common childhood illnesses

All babies are susceptible to certain illnesses, as their immune systems do not contain enough antibodies to fight off infections. If your baby is ill, keep him with you or his babysitter during the day so you can check on him frequently. At night you may want to sleep in the same room. Ask your spouse to take turns if the illness lasts more than a night or two, since you will need some uninterrupted sleep to cope with looking after a sick baby.

Babies can become ill quite quickly, developing a fever and sometimes getting very lethargic. If this happens, it is reassuring to think that each illness helps to build up resistance for the future.

INFECTIONS

Breast-feeding your baby will help ward off infections during the first few months, but it's only a matter of time before he gets a cold or other infection. Most infections don't give cause for concern unless they are accompanied by a high fever (see "Fever," pp.110, 112). Tender loving care and time are the greatest healers. However, you will probably need to consult a doctor for any minor infections, especially if your baby is under six months.

Infections are caused by viruses or by bacteria. A virus attacks the body by invading a cell, where it replicates itself many times. Each of the new copies then finds its own host cell and repeats the process. Bacteria live in and on the body, and many don't cause disease. In fact, some are beneficial, but harmful bacteria cause disease when they are present in large quantities. Antibiotics are your baby's doctor's biggest weapon against bacteria, but unfortunately they have no effect on viral infections.

COLDS

The most frequent ailment of babies and toddlers, colds are caused by viruses that infect the lining of the nose, sinuses, ears, throat, and bronchi in the lungs. Typical symptoms are a runny nose, sneezing, sore throat, and cough. There is no cure for the cold, but there is a selection of remedies you can use to make your baby more comfortable. If you are worried about your baby, or if he is unable to take food, seek medical advice.

PREVENTING INFECTION

Even a healthy baby is likely to catch a cold during the first year, but you can reduce the likelihood of your baby picking up an infection.

- Breast-feed for as long as possible. One of its many benefits is that it helps protect the baby from infections. Breast milk destroys harmful bacteria and contains antibodies passed from the mother that protect the baby from viral infections. Breast-fed babies are less likely to suffer respiratory and urinary infections, ear infections, and gastroenteritis. If a breast-fed baby does pick up an intestinal bug, he will recover more quickly than a bottle-fed baby because he is able to continue feeding, while a bottle-fed baby may not be able to tolerate formula.

- Give your baby a healthy diet. Eating fresh, natural foods that provide all the essential nutrients will help him to be more resistant to infection (see p.28).

- Don't smoke and don't allow smoking in your home. Studies show that babies exposed to cigarette smoke have a much higher incidence of ear infections, bronchitis, and sinus infections.

- Where possible, try to keep your baby away from anyone with an infectious or contagious illness.

- Keep your baby's environment clean. Carefully clean feeding equipment for the first six months And when your baby starts putting things in his mouth, keep his toys clean.

What you can do

- Keep him comfortably warm, but not too hot. Taking him out for a walk in the fresh air may help to relieve his symptoms and distract him from his discomfort.

- If his nose is red and sore, a dab of petroleum jelly will protect it. If you prefer a natural remedy, try calendula or chamomile cream.

- For a stuffy nose in a young baby, use a bulb syringe to clean the nose. A few drops of salt water can loosen extra mucus. (Make sterile salt water by adding 1 tablespoon of table salt to 1 pint of boiling water. Cool to room temperature.) Apply to nostrils with an eye dropper.

- Offer plenty of drinks—cooled, boiled water, well-diluted pure fruit juice, or breast milk—in small amounts frequently, to prevent dehydration.

- If your baby is over three months, you can try using a vaporizer to help clear his breathing passages.

- Place a pillow **under** the mattress at the head end. Raising the head of his mattress slightly can help prevent a blocked-up nose at night.

- Don't be tempted to dose your baby with infant acetaminophen every time he has a cold. Save it for when he really needs it, for example, when he has a fever (see "Fever," pp.110, 112).

A natural remedy

Add three drops of eucalyptus oil to a bowl of steaming hot water and leave near your baby's crib but out of his reach. The vapor will help relieve his symptoms.

COUGHS

A cough is the body's natural way of clearing excess mucus and phlegm from the breathing passages. However, if your baby has a dry, tickly cough, it is usually caused by inflammation in the throat and lungs, and may be a reaction to irritants in the atmosphere.

If your baby is eating and sleeping well, there is usually no cause for concern, but coughs can sometimes be a symptom of a more serious problem. If the cough lingers and your baby also sounds wheezy, it may be due to a more serious problem, such as asthma or pneumonia. If the cough comes on suddenly and persistently, your baby may have swallowed something that has become lodged in an airway. With either type of cough, seek medical advice.

What you can do
- Your baby's cough may sound distressing, but it is actually serving an important purpose by clearing the airways. A "productive" cough brings up mucus and phlegm, and reduces the number of germs moving toward the lungs. This type of cough should not be treated with a suppressant medicine, which would prevent the cough from serving its protective purpose. However, if you feel you want to help nature take its course, you might use an expectorant medicine designed to loosen the secretions so they can be coughed up more quickly and easily. Some doctors doubt whether children's cough medicines have any effect except for making parents feel they are doing something to relieve their child's discomfort. A baby under a year old with a productive cough should be seen by a doctor.

- Some foods increase the production of mucus and encourage a cough to linger. Cow's milk, cheese, sugar, and bananas should be avoided during and for a week or two after a cold or cough.

- Give your baby plenty of drinks such as water and diluted juice to soothe his throat and help loosen the mucus.

- Don't expose him to the cold without proper clothing. Becoming chilled can make a cough worse, and cold air hitting his airways will aggravate the cough. Drape a blanket loosely over his head when you take him outside.

- Don't allow smoking in your home. Cigarette, pipe, and cigar smoke will aggravate his cough.

A natural remedy
A teaspoon of pasteurized honey and a teaspoon of freshly squeezed lemon juice in a cup of cooled, boiled water may help.

FEVER

Parents don't usually need a thermometer to tell if their baby has a fever. Instinct and a hand on the forehead are enough to alert them that their child is not well. However, if you're unsure, or you'd prefer to know how high it is, a forehead indicator strip or a thermometer held in the armpit will give you a rough indication. An accurate temperature can be obtained only using a rectal thermometer, but this invasive method is seldom necessary.

A baby's normal temperature is between 98° (37°C) and 99.5° (37.5°C). Anything above is considered a fever. However, the degree of the fever doesn't necessarily match the severity of the illness. Other signs of fever include flushed cheeks, fast heartbeat, faster breathing, and sweating.

A high temperature or fever is usually an indication that the baby has an infection and the body is trying to combat the bacteria or virus causing it. Although it doesn't necessarily indicate a serious illness, babies under six months should always be seen by a doctor. Symptoms that indicate the need for immediate medical attention include lethargy, persistent vomiting, drowsiness, lack of appetite, inconsolable or weak crying, not taking food.

Fortunately, most babies with a fever quickly respond to treatment with infant

HOW TO REDUCE A FEVER

- Make sure your baby is not overdressed, and remove blankets, leaving only a sheet.

- Open a window to let in cool air. but avoid cold drafts in winter. Chilling can actually increase a fever.

- Give extra fluids to prevent dehydration—breast milk or cool water will help.

- A lukewarm bath may help, but don't put him in a cold bath—he will hate it and may start to shiver, which will send his temperature back up. Alternatively, sponge him with tepid water.

- Give infant acetaminophen following the dosage instructions on the label.

MENINGITIS

A high fever is one symptom of meningitis, an infection of the membranes lining the outer surface of the brain. Both viral and bacterial meningitis are potentially fatal, especially in babies, and urgent medical attention is essential. Each year, there are a number of reported cases of bacterial meningitis, but the figure is now falling because of the success of the HIB vaccine.

The most common types of bacterial meningitis are meningococcal, pneumococcal, and hemophilus influenzal type B (HIB).

The germs that cause bacterial meningitis are very common and live in the back of the throat. People can carry them for weeks without becoming ill. Only rarely do they overcome the body's defenses and cause meningitis. Recognizing the symptoms could mean the difference between life and death. Meningitis may develop quickly within a few hours.

If your baby has a fever and any of the following symptoms, you should seek help immediately:

- High-pitched, moaning cry.

- Persistent vomiting.

- Increasing drowsiness.

- An aversion to bright light.

- Purple-red rash or bruises. These can occur anywhere on the body and are due to blood poisoning.

- Stiff neck.

- Bulging fontanels, the soft areas on a baby's skull before the skull bones fuse together.

Not all these symptoms may appear together.

Meningitis test
If your child develops a rash anywhere on the body, press the spots or bruises with a glass or your finger. If they do not turn white, see your doctor immediatly.

acetaminophen, increased fluids, and cooling down.

Febrile convulsions

It is important to reduce a fever over 102°F (38.8°C) quickly, since some children between the ages of six months and five years are prone to febrile convulsions. These occur as the result of a sudden rapid rise in temperature, which irritates the brain, causing the child to become unconscious; his body becomes rigid and his limbs jerk. If your baby has a convulsion, when it is over—usually after a minute or two—cool him down and call the doctor. Fortunately, though very frightening for the parent, these episodes do not cause any lasting harm. Low-grade fevers that do not cause the baby much discomfort do not need any therapy except extra fluids.

CROUP

Croup, signified by a harsh, barking cough with labored breathing, can follow a cold, or it may begin without warning. It is caused by an acute viral infection of the throat and windpipe, resulting in inflammation of the airways. The cough is caused by the irritation. Viral croup most commonly affects babies, and although it can sound quite frightening, it is usually only a mild illness that may last for a few days. It must be distinguished from bacterial croup, infection of the larynx, which can be more serious. Both kinds of attack usually occur at night. And if a child has great trouble breathing, large swings in temperature, refuses drinks, has trouble making any sound when crying, and is obviously distressed, you should seek medical help immediately.

What you can do

• During an attack of croup, try to calm your baby. If he is frightened and crying, it will aggravate the croup. Breast-feeding may help, or you can try cuddling and carrying him or looking at books together.

- Steam treatment is the most effective method of clearing his breathing passages. Sit with him in the bathroom, close the door and windows, and run hot water into the bathtub with the plug in, or turn on the shower. Alternatively, a cool mist vaporizer may help.

- Offer cold drinks to reduce inflammation.

- At mealtimes, when he's not having an attack, breast-feed or bottle feed him and give him well-puréed foods to minimize the risk of choking.

- If he has a fever, give him infant acetaminophen to help bring his temperature down.

- If you can't ease your baby's symptoms, call a doctor.

EARACHE

One of the most common childhood complaints, earache is usually caused by a viral or a bacterial infection. If after a cold, your baby becomes hot, miserable, crying, and clingy, particularly at night, vomits, and keeps pulling at his ear or his face, you can suspect otitis media; inflammation of the middle ear. It is a painful condition caused by a buildup of fluid trapped in the middle ear that presses against the eardrum and is worse when lying down. Sometimes the pressure causes the eardrum to burst and the fluid leaks out, which often relieves the pain. Ear infections are diagnosed with an otoscope (an eardrum-viewing instrument). So you must take your baby to the doctor, who will probably prescribe antibiotics, even though the infection may be caused by a virus (see "Antibiotics," pp.126–127). Chronic or recurrent otitis media can cause damage to the ear cavity or bones within it, leading to permanent hearing loss.

Even if your baby makes a quick recovery, it is essential to complete the course of antibiotics or the infection is likely to return. Have your baby's ears checked a couple of weeks later to make sure the fluid has completely cleared.

Earache can also be caused by inflammation of the outer ear canal (otitis externa) or by poking something into the ear, tonsillitis, or an injury to the ear. If your baby's ear drains, seek medical care.

What you can do

- Give infant acetaminophen to ease the pain.

- Wrap a warm hot-water bottle in a soft towel and cuddle your baby with it against his ear.

- Avoid exposure to cold winds.

A natural remedy

Put a cotton ball soaked in slightly warm (not hot) olive oil into the ear. Make sure the cotton ball is big enough that it cannot go all the way inside. Don't put anything in the ear if it is draining.

STICKY EYE

Soon after birth many babies get a yellow discharge in one or both eyes caused by a blocked tear duct. The tears can't drain properly and accumulate in the eye in a sticky pus. Though the eyes aren't sore, the pus may stick the eyelids together when the baby is asleep. There is also a risk that the discharge may become infected. Blocked tear ducts almost always clear themselves by the first 12 months.

REDUCING THE RISK OF EAR INFECTIONS

Ear infections tend to recur and can lead to future problems such as glue ear or hearing loss. These measures may help lessen susceptibility to ear infection:

- Breast-feed for as long as possible. Breast-fed babies have fewer ear infections due to the protective effects of breast milk.

- Babies with food allergies, particularly to dairy products, may be more likely to get ear infections. Dairy products encourage the production of mucus that can cause a buildup of fluid in the middle ear. If you are bottle-feeding, check with your doctor about soya or goat's milk.

- The doctor may prescribe a decongestant to clear the mucus.

What you can do

- Wipe the pus away frequently with plain water and cotton balls. Wipe from the inside of the eye out and use a separate cotton ball for each eye.

- With scrupulously clean fingers and very short nails, gently massage the tear ducts in the inside corner of your baby's eyes. Done regularly several times a day, this can help to clear the ducts. If they haven't cleared themselves after six months, consult the baby's doctor.

CONJUCTIVITIS

A red, sore, or itchy eye and inner eyelid with a greenish yellow discharge in older babies usually indicates conjunctivitis, an infection of the delicate lining covering the outer eye and inner eyelid. Your baby is likely to rub his eyes, spreading infection.

What you can do

- See his doctor to verify that it is not due to an injury.

- Clean away the discharge from the eye with a cotton ball soaked in a half teaspoon of salt dissolved in a cup of cooled, boiled water. Use a new piece for each eye and wipe as before.

- If you are still breast-feeding, use a little freshly expressed milk to bathe the eyes. The breast milk helps kill bacteria.

- Conjunctivitis is highly contagious, so always wash your hands after treating your baby and use a separate washcloth and towel for him. Change the sheet on his mattress every day.

- After three days see your baby's doctor. He may prescribe antibiotic treatment to clear the infection.

A natural remedy

To soothe sore or red eyes, make a solution with five drops of tincture of eyebright (from a health-food store) and one cup of cooled, boiled water. Soak a cotton ball in it and wipe his eyes as described above, using a new piece for each eye.

VOMITING

All young babies regularly bring up a little of their food. Called spitting up, it is nothing to be concerned about as long as the baby is healthy, feeding well, and gaining weight. Babies may also spit up if they take in too much air when they feed and regurgitate milk along with the gas. Bottle-fed babies who bring up a lot of milk after every feeding may be intolerant of the formula, and you may need to change to another formula after consultation your baby's doctor.

Vomiting, when the contents of the stomach are brought up forcefully, is usually triggered by toxins caused by an infection such as gastroenteritis. But it can also be a symptom of ear and throat infections as well as more serious illnesses including pneumonia, and meningitis.

Vomiting isn't usually serious and passes within a few hours, though it may be followed by diarrhea. Dehydration—loss of body fluids—is the biggest worry and in the most severe cases can cause death. If your baby is vomiting persistently, it is essential to see a doctor to find the cause. Medical conditions that may be responsible include pyloric stenosis, hiatus hernia, and celiac disease.

Another possible cause of vomiting in older babies is accidental poisoning from medicines, household chemicals, or plants. If you suspect your baby has swallowed something toxic, you should seek urgent medical attention. Call the Poison Control Center for immediate advice, especially if the nearest hospital is more than 15 minutes away.

What you can do

- Vomiting is unpleasant and frightening for a baby, so he'll need lots of tender loving care. Vomiting can be exhausting, so let him lie down and rest afterward.

VOMITING
– WHEN TO GET HELP

- If the vomiting has lasted for more than 24 hours.

- If there are signs of dehydration: a dry mouth and lips, sunken fontanels, infrequent urination or dark concentrated urine, sunken eyes, drowsiness, lethargy.

- If the vomiting follows a fall or head injury.

- If the vomiting is accompanied by other symptoms.

- If you are breast-feeding, continue to feed him if he wants to eat, but don't give him formula milk. Cow's milk is likely to make him vomit again. If you are bottle-feeding, offer your baby clear fluids for 24 hours (see oral rehydration). Contact the doctor if the child can't keep it down.

- Offer cooled, boiled water, a little at a time—try a few teaspoonfuls every 10 to 15 minutes. Keep offering it to prevent your baby from becoming dehydrated. Get help if theere are signs of dehydration.

- You can also give him an oral rehydration remedy available from the drugstore. This comes in two forms: (1) a powder that dissolves in water and (2) a premixed liquid. Each form replaces the correct balance of salts and sugars lost by vomiting and helps prevent dehydration. Offer either form frequently in small amounts from a teaspoon. For older babies, freeze the solution in popsicle molds that can be sucked.

- Don't give him solid food or formula until the vomiting has subsided for 24 hours, and then only bland, puréed food.

A natural remedy
Ginger is an effective remedy. Give one teaspoon of fresh root ginger in one cup of boiled water. Strain, cool and add pasteurized honey or small amount of sugar.

DIARRHEA

The term diarrhea refers to the consistency of the stools rather than how frequently they are passed. The number of times babies move their bowels varies widely. Breast-fed babies may pass stools after every feeding, or there may be three or more days between movements. If your baby has diarrhea, his stools may be liquid, green, mucus-containing, foul-smelling, or blood-tinged. He may have a sore red rash around the anus.

Acute diarrhea

A sudden attack usually due to gastroenteritis, acute diarrhea is often the result of a viral infection, although food poisoning may be responsible. When the intestinal lining becomes infected, it is unable to absorb nutrients from food in the digestive process and allows it to pass through rapidly, resulting in watery stools more frequently than normal. If the infection also causes vomiting and fever, there is a risk of dehydration, particularly in a young baby, and in this situation medical attention is essential.

What you can do

- See or call the doctor if you are the least bit concerned, particularly if your baby shows signs of dehydration.

- Replace lost fluids with a rehydration solution (see "Vomiting," pp.116–117).

- Breast-fed babies can continue to feed as normal, since human milk is not irritating. Even if the baby vomits, his body will absorb some of the nutrients. Give bottle-fed babies a rehydration solution. If acute diarrhea lasts more than 12 to 18 hours, call the doctor.

- Don't withhold food unless your baby is vomiting as well. If he shows signs of wanting to eat, give him a little bit of bland food such as banana, mashed potato, rice, or oatmeal made with water. As he improves, slowly return to his normal diet, but be sure to save any dairy foods till last.

- Don't give your baby drugs to dry up the diarrhea. Diarrhea due to infection is part of the body's response to invading bugs and helps to flush them out of the bowel. These drugs slow down the action of the intestines and can in fact worsen the condition because the germs and infected fluid stagnate in the gut, protracting the course of the illness.

- Always wash your hands thoroughly after changing a diaper, to avoid spreading the infection.

Chronic diarrhea

When the condition persists in a mild form or comes and goes, it may be due to an uncommon medical condition such as cystic fibrosis or celiac disease (a wheat intolerance). In such conditions, your baby will have very pale, smelly stools that float and are difficult to flush away, indicating that the body is not digesting fat properly. The sweat of babies with cystic fibrosis is salty. Give your baby the kiss test—if he tastes salty, talk with his doctor. Or chronic diarrhea may be a result of an intolerance to dairy products or a side effect of antibiotics. Intususception, a condition where the bowel gets stuck within itself, causes diarrhea and the passage of blood in the stools as well as vomiting and colic.

What you can do

- Determine the cause. It is important to establish whether your baby is gaining weight normally. If he isn't, or is losing weight and appears unwell, see his doctor urgently. If the baby seems well, his diet may be causing the loose stools.

- If you think a food intolerance is responsible, try cutting out the suspect food for a week or so to see if there is any improvement. Then give your baby the food again to see if the diarrhea recurs. Consult your baby's doctor before making any major changes to his diet.

- Avoid high-fiber or whole foods such as raw vegetables, brown bread, and brown rice until your baby is older and better able to digest them.

- Note how much fruit juice your baby is drinking. Too much juice, particularly apple juice, can cause diarrhea. Always dilute fruit juice.

CONSTIPATION

If your baby is obviously suffering discomfort while straining to pass a stool, which is hard and pebblelike, he is constipated. However, he is not necessarily constipated if he moves his bowels infrequently, since frequency varies greatly between babies, depending on age and diet. Hard, dry stools that are difficult to pass are usually caused by insufficient fluids. Sometimes streaks of blood can be seen on the outside of the stool, caused by a tear in the lining of the rectum. This will be painful for your baby, making him reluctant to pass stools, exacerbating the problem.

What you can do
- Try to find the cause of the constipation. A likely cause could be a change in your baby's diet or the introduction of weaning foods or switching from breast- to bottle-feeding.

- Give your baby more fluids to drink, either water or well-diluted pure fruit juice. Very dilute prune juice is good for constipation.

- Avoid foods that may contribute to constipation, such as underripe bananas, dairy products, and eggs. Instead, offer more fresh fruit and vegetables that contain natural fiber.

- Don't use suppositories or laxatives except as a short-term solution and only if recommended by your baby's doctor.

Natural treatments
Extra fluid, especially water, is essential.

SAFETY FIRST

- Keep medicines out of reach, ideally in a locked medicine cabinet.

- Keep a list of emergency numbers by the phone: doctor, hospital, Poison Control Center, police, and 24-hour pharmacy.

- Attend a first-aid course to boost your confidence and skills in an emergency—the Red Cross runs specific ones for parents and babysitters.

Massage is the safest treatment for constipation in babies. Gently stroke your baby's lower abdomen in a clockwise direction (see "Baby massage," pp.84–89).

Allergies

Eczema and asthma are closely related allergic conditions. Babies with eczema are three times more likely to develop asthma than other children, and in 70 percent of cases there is a family history of allergic illnesses. Eczema, also known as dermatitis, affects some 15 percent of babies and young children, although fortunately most grow out of it as they get older. The number of children with asthma has doubled over the last 20 years, and it now affects about one in 10 children in North America, many of whom will also grow out of it.

ASTHMA

Symptoms, which include wheezing, coughing, and breathlessness, usually start to occur after the first year, though from six months babies can develop a persistent nighttime cough. Asthma may be caused by an allergic reaction to substances such as house dust mites, pollen, animal dander, or food. Asthma occurs when the sensitive linings of the airways in the lungs (bronchial tubes) are irritated, swell, and go into spasm, restricting air flow. The linings may then leak mucus, which clogs the air passages even more, making coughing and wheezing worse. Babies under a year may get bronchiolitis, which has symptoms similar to those of asthma but is caused by a viral infection. Any baby with a recurrent or chronic cough should be monitored for asthma.

If you suspect that your baby may have asthma or something similar, it is essential to take him to his doctor for a correct diagnosis. In young children a diagnosis of asthma may require several episodes of wheezing. Your baby may grow out of his symptoms, or they may be due to some other illness.

What you can do
If you feel your baby may be at risk of asthma, follow these guidelines to reduce his susceptibility:

- Breast-feed your baby for as long as possible. Bottle-fed babies are known to be more vulnerable to asthma.

- Don't allow anyone to smoke in your home.

- Try to reduce contact with common allergens such as house dust mites, feathers, molds, pollen, and pet fur, which can irritate the linings of the respiratory passages and trigger an attack (see "Eczema triggers," p.125 and "Indoor pollution," p.134).

- Try not to buy stuffed toys, since they harbor dust mites. If your baby must have a teddy bear or soft toy, kill the mites once a week by putting the toy in a plastic bag, leaving it in the freezer overnight, then defrosting it and washing it in a medium-hot wash.

- Diet can sometimes be a factor. Food additives, especially yellow dyes, sodium benzoate, and sulfates are a trigger. Ask your baby's doctor if you should try cutting out mucus-producing foods, especially dairy products such as cow's milk and cheese. Give foods that are easy to digest. Some babies are affected by refined sugar, while others react to food additives.

- If your child does develop asthma, he will usually need drugs to control the attacks. However, there are various natural therapies (such as aromatherapy, homeopathy, herbalism, or naturopathy) you can use at the same time to help prevent attacks from occurring. Take your child to an experienced practitioner of complementary medicine for advice after beginning conventional medical treatment.

A natural remedy

A thyme bath can benefit a wheezy baby. Make an infusion of 2–3 teaspoons of thyme in 1 pint (480ml) of boiling water. Let it stand for five minutes, then pour into the bathwater. Check the temperature of the water before putting the baby in the tub.

ECZEMA

Eczema is an itchy, sore-looking rash which may be red, dry, scaly, bleeding, or weepy. There are many forms of eczema, but the two types that usually affect babies are seborrheic dermatitis (cradle cap) and atopic eczema. The cause of the eczema can be very hard to pinpoint, but is thought to be triggered by allergens similar to those of asthma. There is no cure, though there are treatments that can alleviate the symptoms.

Cradle cap

Caused by overactivity of the sebaceous glands that lie at the root of the hair follicles, cradle cap can be mild, with just a few flaky patches on the top of the head, or severe, with a greasy thick yellow crust all over the scalp. Fortunately, it rarely distresses the baby and clears up by itself when the skin becomes drier naturally .

What you can do

- Massage a little olive oil into the scalp before bedtime to soften the patches. Wash your baby's hair the following morning, gently rubbing off loose scales. Never pick off the scales; that might cause a scalp infection.

- Always use a mild shampoo and rinse thoroughly.

A natural remedy

After washing the hair, rinse the scalp with a decoction of burdock root, which has been shown to have antibacterial, antiseptic, and antifungal properties. Place the burdock root in a saucepan, pour in water, bring to a boil, and simmer for 10–15 minutes before straining. Do not use an aluminum pan. Use 1 tablespoon of root to 1 pint (480ml) of water.

Atopic eczema

Atopic eczema often starts as irritating, dry,

The exact cause of eczema is not known, though complementary practitioners believe that childhood eczema is linked to the digestive system.

What you can do

•   Eczema is very irritating, and it will be hard to stop your baby from scratching, particularly at night. Keep his nails trimmed to minimize damage to his skin. Light cotton mittens will also help, but many babies hate wearing them

•   Use emollients, available on prescription, to keep the skin moist and soft. These can be creams or lotions to apply directly to the skin or liquids to add to the bath-water. They help prevent the dryness that can cause itching and further inflammation.

•   Avoid using soap or perfumed bubble baths.

•   Your doctor may prescribe a mild steroid cream. This should be used only for a very short time during a flare-up. Long-term use of strong steroids can cause side effects,

flaky patches on the face when a baby is between three and six months of age, although breast-feeding can delay its onset. A rash then spreads to the scalp, neck, skin creases, and diaper area. It also occurs on joints such as the backs of knees and around the elbows and ankles. The rash is intensely itchy, and the skin may be reddened, cracked, and thickened. Scratching can cause bleeding and infection.

ECZEMA TRIGGERS

- It is important to discover what triggers your baby's eczema. If you have a family history of allergy, it is wise to avoid food allergens for the first year. These include cow's milk, eggs, orange juice, and wheat. Food additives, colorings, and preservatives can also cause a reaction. If you suspect that certain foods may be triggering your baby's eczema, try cutting each one out for a week and noting any effects. However, consult a nutritionist before radically altering his diet on a long-term basis.

- Avoid irritants likely to inflame your baby's skin. Dress your baby in pure cotton clothes next to his skin and avoid wool and synthetic fibers in clothes and bedding. Biological washing powder, fabric conditioner, perfumed soap, bubble bath, and shampoo should be avoided.

- The house dust mite is another known culprit. (see "Indoor pollution," p.134). If you suspect your baby is reacting to dust, wash bedclothes frequently in a hot wash or use an allergy-proof cover on the mattress and quilt (if he is old enough for one). Don't put wool blankets on the crib. Remove furry toys from the bedroom or give them the freezer treatment (see "Asthma," p.121). Keep the bedroom cool and open the window daily to improve ventilation. Vacuum frequently, but not with your baby in the room. Damp-dust regularly. Get rid of dust-collecting clutter in his room.

- Furry pets may also produce an allergic reaction—they shed skin scales (dander) that are a strong irritant. If you have a cat or dog don't allow it in your baby's bedroom.

including skin damage. Mild steroids, like 0.5–1 percent hydrocortisone, will not cause skin damage on babies if applied as prescribed for short periods.

- Natural therapies have been shown to be very beneficial. Medical trials in Britain have found Chinese herbs to be very effective. Always see a professional practitioner before treating your baby.

A natural remedy
Two to three drops of Bach Flower Rescue Remedy (available at health-food stores) added to the bath may help.

Antibiotics

Parents are becoming increasingly anxious about the use of antibiotics, particularly if they are trying to bring up their baby in a safe and natural way. While there is no doubt that antibiotics, play a vital role in fighting life-threatening diseases such as meningitis and pneumonia, their inappropriate or repeated prescription is giving rising cause for concern among some medical experts and scientists. Antibiotics work by killing or stopping the growth of bacteria that cause infections. Though they may be effective in the short term, they have a number of side effects—such as nausea, diarrhea, yeast infection, and allergic reaction—and can even cause recurring bouts of the illness if used inappropriately. You can ask your doctor if antibiotics are necessary for mild infections.

CAUSES FOR CONCERN

- Antibiotics can appear to cure an illness in the short term, only for it to return later, possibly in a more virulent form. This creates a vicious circle of infection and antibiotic use. If doctors aren't sure about the cause of an illness, they often play safe and prescribe an antibiotic. They may also prescribe antibiotics unnecessarily for viral illnesses such as sore throats, colds, coughs, and some forms of chest infection, such as bronchiolitis.

- Overuse of antibiotics has meant that some infections that used to be easy to treat are now difficult to cure, for the bacteria responsible have become resistant to the drug by making genetic changes to themselves. Superbugs have developed that are resistant to four or more antibiotics, so the infections they cause are particularly difficult to treat.

- Antibiotics may kill not only harmful bacteria, but also the helpful bacteria that inhabit our bodies. This upsets the body's natural equilibrium and allows a new infection to develop. For example, yeast is a fungal infection that is usually kept in check by helpful bacteria but that often develops after a course of antibiotics. Some research has linked outbreaks of meningitis with overuse of antibiotics.

What you can do
- If an antibiotic is prescribed for your baby, tell the doctor you would prefer not to give one unless it is really necessary. Depending on the seriousness of the illness, he may suggest you wait for 24 hours or give you a prescription you can use later if your baby doesn't show signs of recovery.

- Give the antibiotics as prescribed and complete the course. Antibiotics kill off the most susceptible bacteria first, leaving the most resistant. If you stop halfway through the treatment, you leave behind the stronger bugs, which cause a recurrence of the symptoms.

- Give your baby acidophilus powder (available from health-food stores) daily during the course of the antibiotics. This may help to restore the normal bacteria in the gut that are killed by the antibiotics, reducing the risk of side effects such as diarrhea or overgrowth of yeast.

- If your baby's doctor doesn't feel urgent medical attention is required, try a natural remedy. They all work at boosting the body's immune system so it can do the healing work.

CHAPTER FIVE

The Natural Home

Home is where the memories of childhood are made. Once you have a baby, you will certainly spend more time in your home, and the nesting instinct that so many parents experience may inspire you to take a fresh look at where you live and to consider ways of adapting it to suit the needs of a growing family. You may decide to redecorate a spare room as a nursery, or you may feel you need to plan an extension or even a move.

Where you live

If you are considering moving somewhere more spacious to accommodate your growing family, you may want to weigh the relative benefits of town and country living.

IN TOWN

The advantages of living in a town or city can be:

- Good public transportation. As your child grows up and becomes independent, he will be able to get himself to and from school and friends.

- Access to parks where children can play safely. Most playgrounds are fenced in.

- Good access to sports and other recreational facilities.

- More social opportunities. Research has shown that mothers of young babies in towns are less isolated, and have more opportunities to mix socially at toddler groups and organized clubs.

The disadvantages are:

- Air pollution. Cars, the major source of air pollution, pump out a toxic cocktail of pollutants that can cause breathing difficulties, reduce resistance to infection, aggravate asthma, and even cause cancer. Babies and children are particularly vulnerable to pollution because they are growing. Their bodies are generally quicker to absorb substances and slower to eliminate them, according to environmental pressure group Friends of the Earth.

- Young children pushed in strollers along sidewalks next to busy roads are at face level with exhaust pipes that pump out the fumes.

- Busy roads also mean there is an increased danger of accidents.

- Lead pollution is undoubtedly higher in towns. Lead is a poisonous metal. Contact with it can lead to anemia, high blood pressure, and damage to the nervous system in young children. Low-level lead pollution can impair the mental development of babies and toddlers without symptoms.

IN THE COUNTRY

The advantages of living in the country are:

- Better air quality, although in the spring and summer there is a greater risk of hay fever due to higher levels of pollen.

- Fewer cars, so if you live in an isolated area, you may feel it is safer to allow your children to play unsupervised outside the home once they reach a certain age.

- If you want to live in a house built from natural materials from the local environment (see below), you will probably find a greater choice in a rural area.

- Closer contact with nature. Your children will see animals in the fields, crops growing, fruit on trees. They can enjoy walks with you in woodland areas.

- Larger yard. Generally, houses built in rural areas have more generous backyard space, which will be useful as your baby grows into a toddler and can enjoy sandboxes and slides.

The disadvantages are:

- Limited public transportation. Traditionally, country living conjures up a picture of healthy children. But recent evidence suggests otherwise, since children have to be driven to school and their friends are usually not nearby. The average child today walks much less than he did 10 years ago and travels more by car and bus. And it is country children particularly who have become more sedentary.

- Sports and other recreational facilities are often far away.

- Risk of being isolated with a new baby. Isolation of new mothers has been linked to postnatal depression, a serious condition that affects up to one in 10 women after the birth of a baby.

COUNTRY MATTERS

Once your baby is born, you may want to join in with the local activities in your area. So if there is a community center, it would be worth-while considering moving to where you will have easy access to it.

Some schools promote safe routes to school in association with the police department. Find out if this is happening in the area that interests you. If your baby is not yet born, this may sound a long way off. But those first four or five years will pass very rapidly, and you may find that once you have put down roots in a certain area, you may be loath to move on.

WHAT'S IN A HOUSE?

Traditional building materials, such as bricks, stone, and wood, provide a healthy framework in which to live and bring up your baby. But in our quest for comfort, we have introduced all sorts of chemicals into our homes with potentially serious consequences. The term "sick building syndrome" has been coined to describe a repeated illness caused by poor air circulation in the buildings in which the sufferers live or work.

Materials that provide cause for concern include:

- Hydrocarbons and other solvents. Commonly found in adhesives, paint strippers, and wood treatments, these poisons have been linked to birth defects when either the mother or the father has been exposed to them, according to environmental author Brigid McConville. Keep your baby and pets out of the house and away from the fumes if you are using solvents while redecorating your home. Turn off any open flames such as pilot lights (don't just blow them out!), and open all the doors and windows while you are doing it. Better yet, use a safer substance. Never put old paint strippers down the drain, as they upset the balance of the bacteria that decompose sewage. Always recycle hazardous chemicals.

- Wall insulation. Insulating exterior walls reduces heat loss and saves both energy and money. If you plan to use foam insulation, insist that the contractor or supplier give you written proof that the material is free of formaldehyde or other potentially harmful substances.

- Formaldehyde. This potent irritant is found in synthetic varnish, plywood glue, chipboard, hardboard, wallpaper, fabric, and carpet finishes. Formaldehyde seeps slowly out of the materials into the home. It can cause headaches, depression, and dizziness, as well as affecting the eyes, nose, throat, and lungs. Choose natural wood for your kitchen and bathroom cabinets and furniture.

- Asbestos. Known to cause lung cancer, asbestos is now banned as a building material. But if you are renovating an old home you may come across it. Contact your local public health department immediately if you suspect you have found asbestos.

- Plastics. The manufacturing process of plastics pollutes the environment, and some plastics, including PVC (polyvinyl chloride), pollute the atmosphere of your home once they are in place. When

BASIC SAFETY TIPS

- Contact your local consumer protection agency. This will be part of local, state, or provincial government. Tell them you have a young child and ask them to send you literature.

- Learn first aid and CPR (see p.170, "Life-saving techniques"). This will always be useful and may help you save your child's (or somebody else's) life.

- Be careful when buying or accepting used toys, baby chairs, or other items as gifts. They may have been made before current product safety laws were in force.

- As soon as your child is old enough, teach him how to use the phone to call for help. Most fire departments offer classes for children in fire safety. Make sure your house has at least two working smoke detectors.

houses catch fire, more people die from the effects of toxic fumes than from the fire itself. Don't buy plastic chairs and sofas.

- Paint. Modern paints are less toxic than the old-fashioned varieties, and the use of lead has been banned in Canada since 1976 and in the US since 1985. But if you move into an old home that has not been decorated since then, there may be traces of older, more dangerous, lead paint. Lead can impair children's mental ability, so don't sand down old paint while your baby is nearby. Make sure all paint is dry, the fumes have evaporated, and the room is fully aired before you allow your baby into a newly painted room. Paint manufacturers have been working toward less harmful products, such as lowering the content of volatile organic compounds (VOCs).

  You can use latex paints for baseboards and areas your baby is likely to come close to. Always recycle old paint properly. If your municpality does not operate a special chemical waste disposal service, wrap them up securely and take them to a hazardous waste disposal site.

- Wood treatments. Lindane and Dursban are sometimes used to kill termites and other woodworms. Both are toxic.

- Wood. If you want to help preserve the environment and reduce the destruction of the world's rain forests (100 acres are being cleared each minute), avoid buying new household furniture that uses tropical hardwoods like teak, mahogany, ramin, and iroko. Choose the faster-growing softwoods like pine, larch, and spruce.

- Ducted air heating. Some experts believe that as air is recirculated, dust and bacteria are simply breathed in again and again.

  Building contractors are now starting to introduce passive ventilation, a new system that puts drafts back into buildings. It brings fresh air from the outside into internal rooms, allowing fresh air into the atmosphere and stale air a means of escape. Heat recovery is another new system that can even out the heating in your home, transferring heat from a warm room into a colder one.

- Radon is a radioactive gas that may build up in basements. Always ask about radon before moving into a home. Radon-measuring kits are available at most hardware stores or health departments.

INDOOR POLLUTION

- Tobacco is one of the greatest indoor air pollutants. Smoking near your baby dramatically increases the risk of his contracting bronchitis, asthma, and pneumonia, or being a victim of crib death (see "Your Healthy Baby," pp.99 and 107). According to a study published in the *Journal of the American Medical Association* (March 1995), a baby is 23 times more likely to die from SIDS (sudden infant death syndrome) where more than 21 cigarettes are smoked each day. The study also concluded that the risk of SIDS increases when the mother smokes during pregnancy or when she is breast-feeding. Babies and children in households where parents smoke are

forced to inhale dangerous quantities of nicotine and carbon monoxide, making them passive smokers. Mothers who smoke while they are pregnant increase the chances of suffering a miscarriage and producing a low-birthweight baby. Your baby is twice as likely to develop childhood cancer if you smoke. Foresight, the British organization for the promotion of preconceptual care, recommends that both parents should stop smoking four months before trying to conceive a baby. Smoking damages sperm, which takes about 12 weeks to form. Remember, sperm is responsible for half of a baby's genetic makeup.

- Wood and coal fires can pollute the atmosphere if the flue is not adequate or regularly cleaned. Natural gas can also leak exhaust into the home if heaters are not installed correctly. Furnaces should be checked every fall before use.

- House dust mites live in the dust that accumulates in carpet, bedding, fabrics, and furniture. They thrive in warm, wet conditions, so use an exhaust fan in bathrooms, open windows and doors regularly, and try not to dry washing on radiators. Up to 2 million mites can live in one mattress. Each mite will lay 40 to 80 eggs and produce 20 fecal particles a day during its 10-week life span. These droppings, which are easily blown around and inhaled, are a major irritant for allergy sufferers (see "Allergies," p.121). Repair any sources of dampness, such as water leaks and condensation,

and make sure your clothes dryer is vented externally. Dust surfaces with a damp cloth and vacuum thoroughly (see "Vacuum cleaners," pp.136–137)

- Pets shed particles of skin and fur, called dander, which contain allergens produced by the animal's sweat glands that can cause asthma, eczema, and hay fever symptoms. Cat allergens, particularly, can remain in a house for

years after a cat has lived there. If you have a cat, encourage it to sleep on a special blanket in a basket, and wash its bedding regularly to limit the spread of its dander. Keep cats away from your baby's sleeping area.

Air ionizers and filters

Air filters help filter pollutants out of the air and ionizers clear the air by electrically charging the particles. Use them to help keep the atmosphere inside your home clear, but keep fresh air circulating by opening windows and doors whenever possible.

HOUSEHOLD APPLIANCES AND EQUIPMENT

More and more household appliances and equipment are being developed with the environment and our health in mind. CFCs (chlorofluorocarbons), which damage the earth's ozone layer, are no longer produced in or imported into the US or Canada. Their use will be phased out completely by the year 2002.

Furthermore, appliance manufacturers are now realizing that consumers are interested in saving energy. Refrigerators, freezers, washing machines, dishwashers, and stoves all vary tremendously in the amount of energy they consume. Choose a washing machine that uses less detergent and water than other brands and a refrigerator that has no CFCs in the insulating foam.

Refrigerators

When choosing a refrigerator, look for a model that uses hydrocarbons in the refrigeration circuit and the insulating foam. They do not contribute to ozone depletion, unlike traditional CFCs. The manufacturer should also supply an instruction manual on how to use the appliance in an environmentally friendly way.

Vacuum cleaners

Some vacuum cleaners are designed with high levels of filtration to recirculate less dust. High suction power and low levels of dust in the exhaust are important if you want to reduce the risk of spreading house dust mites around your home. Some manufacturers claim that certain models are more effective at reducing asthma symptoms, but no medical research has been conducted that proves this. Remember to change the dust bag regularly—look for a model with a self-sealing or sealed dust bag to minimize spreading house dust in the atmosphere during disposal.

Built-in central vacuum systems are found in some new houses and can be retrofitted in older houses. They exhaust dust safely outside the house, and are much quieter than portable vacuums.

SAVING ENERGY

One kilowatt of electricity provides roughly two hours of vacuuming, three gallons of hot water, or two hours of ironing. But its production also causes 10.1 grams of sulfur to be emitted into the air by power stations. This eventually falls as acid rain, affecting our health and damaging buildings and wildlife.

Save energy by:

- Not overheating your house. Young babies need to be kept warm, but many of us overheat our homes. Keep the temperature between 65°–68°F (18°–20°C)

- Using low-energy lightbulbs. These last for nearly a year and use 80% less energy than conventional bulbs. Turn off the lights when you leave a room.

- Keeping your hot-water temperature at a reasonable level with a thermostat—120°F (49°C) is best. Scalding hot water that needs a lot of cold water added is wasteful and a safety hazard to young children.

- Installing wall cavity insulation (see "What's in a house?," p.131).

- Buying low-energy appliances (see "Household appliance and equipment," p.136).

Cooking equipment

Choose stainless steel, cast iron, or enamel cookware rather than aluminum. Although they are more expensive, they are long-lasting and safer.

A pressure cooker is a good energy-saving investment. It lets you cook complete meals at once. And by steaming vegetables at the top of the pan, you can make sure your baby receives nutrients that are often destroyed by traditional boiling.

RECYCLE YOUR GARBAGE

- Our society produces a frightening amount of garbage. It is estimated that each of us creates up to 10 times our body weight in waste each year!

- Set up systems for recycling as much household waste as you can. With a new baby in the home, you may be buying new equipment, which will be heavily packaged. Now is a good time to organize separate receptacles for leftover food and vegetable peelings, glass bottles and jars, metal cans, and a box for paper and cardboard (nearly 30 percent of our trash is paper and cardboard). Municipalities, malls, and supermarkets provide collection points for bottles and cans, and many areas have curbside collection of recyclables.

- As your baby gets bigger and outgrows his clothes and toys, you can take them to thrift shops or have a garage sale. Worn-out clothing can also be recycled, and some places provide textile banks at collection points. As your child grows up, he will learn to conserve resources too if he sees you setting an example.

Car travel

When you travel with your baby by car, you must strap him securely into an approved car seat. The ones for infants are designed to face the rear. Now that you have a baby, you may need a car that's comfortable, roomy, and convenient for family traveling. A spacious trunk is vital to store your baby's buggy or stroller and all the other equipment you will need to travel with for the next few years. Hatchbacks provide easy access, and minivans have a third row of seats, some of which can convert to extra trunk space. If you plan to have more than one baby, extra seat capacity will be useful once you are ferrying small children and their friends to kindergarten and other activities. Car pooling also cuts down on pollution and helps to conserve gasoline.

LEAD-FREE GASOLINE

Lead-free gas reduces the amount of lead pollution in our atmosphere, and a catalytic converter, installed in all new cars, also helps reduce the amount of toxic material emitted from the exhaust. Try to choose a car that is economical to run and does not drink gas. Although diesel engines are efficient, they still produce toxic emissions and thus may not be your best choice.

IN THE CAR

Making sure your baby is safe when you travel in the car is vital. You need to have a car seat or a properly anchored carrier even before you bring him home from hospital. There is a wide variety of child restraints on the market.

SAFETY FIRST

When buying a car consider these points:

- Check for child safety locks on doors and windows, and avoid models with heavy sliding doors that could trap little hands. Look for sliding doors that will stay open, even on a hill. High passenger seats mean even babies can sit in their car seat and see out of the window This makes car travel more enjoyable for them.

- Many new vehicles are equipped with air bags that inflate in a collision to protect people in the front seats. Babies and small children have been killed by the force of the expanding air bag. Never put your baby or child in the front seat whether or not your car has an air bag. He is much safer properly secured in the rear seat.

- Rear-facing baby safety seat (birth to 20 lb/9 kg). This is a is a tub-shaped seat designed to face the rear. It may have handles that make it easy to transport your baby in and out of the car. You can also use it to sit him up in at home. It buckles into an adult safety belt and should be used only on the back seat. It faces backward so that in the event of an accident, any pressure is exerted against the baby's back rather than his pelvis, which is still too soft to protect the internal organs properly.

CHOOSING A CAR SEAT

When choosing which seat to buy, consider:

- Only those with a seal of approval as a car seat, not a baby carrier.
- How easy it is to adjust the harness.
- Whether the covers are machine washable.
- Whether the seat reclines.
- How well it supports your baby's head.

- Convertible infant seat (birth to 40 lb/18 kg). These are designed so a newborn can recline, and they can be adjusted to face forward when the baby reaches 20 lb (9 kg).

- Front-facing car seat (20–40 lb/9–18kg). Once your baby can sit unsupported, you can use a front-facing car seat also in the back seat of the car. Choose one with wings to provide head support. Many models can be adjusted into a reclining position, which is useful if your baby wants to sleep. These seats are generally high enough for him to see out of the window, and some have clip-on trays.

- Booster seat (40–60lb/18–27kg). These enable lap belts to be positioned properly on children who have outgrown car seats. Your child can look out of the window and is raised to a proper height to enable him to be properly restrained with an adult seat belt.

BUCKLE UP

Anchoring kits for children's car seats are sold by baby-care and automobile-parts suppliers.

If you are not sure what type of anchoring kit you need for your car seat, ask the clerk for advice about anchoring kits or contact one of the customer service hotlines run by manufacturers and car safety organizations.

If you don't feel happy about installing the seat yourself, you can get it installed professionally at a garage. To make sure your baby is properly strapped in:

- Make sure that the seat buckle is not resting on the metal frame.

- Shake the seat before you put your baby in it. If it moves more than 1 in (2.5cm), you need to tighten the straps.

- Adjust the harness before each car trip to accommodate what your child is wearing.

- Keep the harness buckle as low as possible, so the lap strap rests on your baby's hips and thighs, not his stomach.

- Use the child seat *every* time you put your child in the car, even for very short trips. Many adults and children are injured in accidents that happen during trips "just around the corner."

CAR POLLUTION

Cars are one of the major sources of air pollution in the world today. Many environmental organizations are campaigning for people to walk or cycle wherever and whenever it is safe to do so, and for more use to be made of public transportation.

There is a limited amount that you can do to avoid the effects of the pollution, but you can help. For example:

- Keeping informed about air quality.

- Whenever possible, leaving the car at home and asking family and friends to do the same.

- Becoming involved with organizations that lobby for clean air (see "Useful Addresses," p.188).

The nursery

When you first step into a baby-care store, you may be overwhelmed by the amount of equipment on display. Cribs, carry baskets, bouncy seats, highchairs, car seats, playpens, safety gates, rows of toys, clothes, and feeding accessories—all designed to look as appealing as possible—threaten to make a big dent in your bank balance and clutter up your home.

PLANNING AHEAD

Make sure you buy only the essentials by planning ahead:

- Ask friends and relatives with babies what they found most useful and which brands lasted well. (Remember, though, that parenting styles differ, and their preferences may not suit you and your baby.) As with most goods, the most expensive items of nursery equipment are not always the best.

- Find out which items were a complete waste of money. There are all sorts of unnecessary gadgets on the market; don't be pressured into buying them.

PREPARING THE NURSERY

It is helpful to have your baby's room ready before he is born. Setting up the nursery will also help you get ready for his arrival. It will be a useful place to store his clothes and equipment.

- You will need only the bare essentials—a chest of drawers for his clothes and diapers, a clean surface for baby lotions and toiletries, and a sturdy box or basket for toys.

- Try not to clutter up his room with too many ornaments and knickknacks. Although they look pretty, they serve little purpose, and your growing baby will not understand the difference between toys he is encouraged to play with and precious ornaments he can't touch.

- Clutter also increases the risk of accidents. As your baby becomes mobile, it is important to keep floors as clear as possible of furniture with sharp edges and too many toys. When he starts to pull himself up and "cruise" around the furniture, he will be able to grab all sorts of objects that you thought were safely out of reach.

- Painting the walls of his room rather than papering makes it easier to clean up as your baby grows older and grubby hands and crayons leave their marks. A wide choice of stencils and borders is available to use as decoration. And as your baby grows into a toddler, you can start to display his first works of art too.

- Some children are allergic to the chemicals in paints. If you are concerned, use water-based rather than solvent-based paints.

- Although a soft carpet looks appealing and comfortable for a baby to sit and play on, it is not the most practical choice. It will collect dust and house dust mites (see "Allergies," p.121 and "Indoor pollution," p.134). And the inevitable spill, such as baby lotion and formula, may be difficult to clean up. You may prefer to have cork or vinyl tiles, linoleum, or washable nonslip area rugs in your baby's nursery which are much easier to keep clean.

- Washable window shades will attract less dust than venetian blinds or curtains, and a natural wicker or wooden rocker with cushion seat and back is preferable to an upholstered one.

- Overhead lighting or adjustable spotlights are more practical than a lamp with a pretty shade, another dust collector. Make sure the light is not directly above your baby's crib where it will shine straight into his eyes.

- Your baby's room should stay at a constant temperature of about 68°F (20°C). During very cold weather you may need to make sure that the thermostat is set to maintain this temperature day and night. A room thermometer will tell how warm the baby's room is.

YOUR BABY'S BED

You will need something for your baby to sleep on. He won't be fussy as long as it is comfortable. It should also be secure, with a safety mattress that has air vents at the end where his head will be. A bassinet with a hood to keep out drafts and protect his eyes from direct light will be suitable, as will a baby buggy.

At about three months, you will need to move him into a crib. Some have adjustable bases so you can raise the mattress for ease of access and gradually lower it as he learns to pull himself up on the bars. Many cribs have a dropside mechanism, so you can lower one side to lift your baby in and out and change the bedding. (See also "Bedtime," p.69–77).

Cribs are expensive, and safety standards have improved in recent years. Some models convert into a child-sized bed which will last for a number of years.

BED LINEN CHECKLIST

All crib bedding should be flame-resistant:

- Cotton sheets. Fitted sheets are best.

- Cotton waffle-weave blankets – light, warm, and easy to layer.

SAFETY FIRST

- Make sure that the handles of a basket or carrier are robust and distribute your baby's weight evenly when it is picked up.

- Choose a crib with bars no more than 2½ in (6cm) apart. A larger gap is dangerous: your baby could get his head stuck between the bars, or his body could fall through and trap his head.

- Be sure that the mattress meets safety standards and that it fits snugly. A gap of more than 1½ in (4cm) is unsafe because your baby might trap his head between the mattress and the side of the crib. You need a mattress that is firm and smooth; it should mold to your baby's shape.

- Don't use a crib more than 15 years old. The spacing of the bars may be too wide, and old paint finishes and varnishes may not conform to current standards.

- Don't choose a dropside crib with a large screw or screws at the top. Such screws could catch your baby's clothing. In addition, you should make certain that as your baby grows bigger, he cannot operate the side himself.

- Make sure that the paint is nontoxic and that there are no decals on the inside where the baby can reach them.

- Adjust the layers of blankets to provide your baby with a constant temperature while he sleeps.

BABY MONITORS

Intercoms

Many parents find that a two-way intercom brings peace of mind. One unit is placed in the baby's room, and the other being fully portable, can be carried from room to room. Some models can be taken outdoors on a special belt clip. The monitor can be set to transmit your baby's every sound or just to pick up louder sounds like crying. Some even have a nursery light attachment on the unit in his room.

If this gives you the confidence to sit and watch TV without worrying that you might not hear your baby cry, it's a worthwhile investment. But you may prefer to keep your baby close to you, particularly in the first few months. It will probably be more comforting for him, as he has been used to background noise and the sound of your voice while he was in the womb. You will also be able to tune in to his sleep patterns and reactions more easily. However, remember that most couples need some time to themselves with the baby safely in his own room or space.

Breathing monitor

A baby breathing monitor is a sophisticated device with small sensors or pressure pads that are placed on the baby's stomach to detect the tiniest change in his breathing pattern. Parents should use one only under supervision and if the baby has a serious health problem or there is a history of SIDS (sudden infant death syndrome) in the family. If you need this device, you'll need to learn CPR (cardiopulmonary resuscitation). Usually a breathing monitor will not be necessary.

TRANSPORTING YOUR BABY

There are several ways of transporting your baby. You need to think carefully about your lifestyle and what type of equipment would suit it best before you part with your money. For example, if you live in an upstairs apartment, you may decide that a baby buggy is impractical and opt for a baby sling and foldaway stroller. On the other hand, if you expect to do a lot of walking, a sturdy buggy with high sides to protect your baby from wind and rain may be the best choice.

You can choose from:

- A buggy with detachable body. The carrier can be used separately, and the chassis folds for storage. Make sure that the handle is at a comfortable height for pushing and that you can carry the basket separately if you need to.

- A three-in-one stroller. This combines a buggy and a carrier with a stroller and will be adequate until your baby is at least two years old. Make sure that the stroller seat is adjustable, so that it can recline and be suitable for a young baby.

- An adjustable stroller. A lightweight, folding stroller which is easy to store and carry. You can buy a hood and cover to protect your baby from wind and rain. Check to see that the seat is wide enough to last as your baby grows and whether it will recline. You also need to find out at what age your baby can first go into it, as some are not strong enough to support the back and head of a newborn.

- A stroller. A basic one-position stroller is

a useful spare or extra to keep at the grandparents' house or in the trunk of the car. Ask whether you can buy a hood and cover to go with it.

TRANSPORT EXTRAS

- A shopping rack or tray that fits under a buggy or stroller seat can carry stuff more safely than a bag dangling from the handles.

- A school-style backback can also carry your purchases and baby supplies, leaving your hands free to guide the buggy or stroller

- In inclement weather, a hood and cover will protect your baby and keep him warm and dry.

- A light blanket will keep your baby's legs warm in cold weather.

- A cheesecloth net will protect your baby from insects in the summer.

- A canopy or parasol will protect him from the sun (see "Fun in the sun," pp.181–186).

- A front-pack baby sling. Useful for carrying your young baby inside and outside the house, leaving your hands free. He will love the warmth and security of being snuggled up to you. The head support can be removed once your baby gains head control. Pick one whose sling is easy to put on unaided and that sits at a comfortable level on your body. Any sling can cause back and shoulder ache when worn for long periods of time, particularly as your baby gets bigger.

- A backpack. Once your baby is about six months old, a backpack allows him to watch the world go by. Choose an adjustable model with padded shoulder straps and belt for comfort. It should also have an adjustable seat for baby's added comfort. Be careful of backpacks with bars below the baby's feet. As the baby grows, he may be able to push himself up and out of this type of backpack.

Safety straps
All forms of transportation should be

Buying a highchair

- Safety. The highchair must feel stable. As your baby grows, he will enjoy leaning over the side. The highchair must be strong enough to remain stable at all times. It must also have a seat belt. Check for gaps that could trap little fingers.

- Ease of use. Consider how easy it will be to lift your baby in and out of the chair and how easy it will be to clean. A removable plastic tray is useful; it should have a lip to stop pieces of food or the plate from dropping over the edge. You will have to clean the seat and legs regularly, too, as food is bound to spill.

- Comfort. Some chairs have padded seats, or you can buy a specially molded cushion that fits into the highchair seat for added comfort and security. This is particularly useful when you first start using the highchair and your baby is still small.

used with a seat belt once your baby is two months old, and tiny babies should always wear a belt if they are put in a reclining stroller. Get into the habit of using a belt on every outing, however short.

Sitting up

From about three weeks old, your baby will enjoy watching your movements for parts of the day. You can either use a baby safety seat (see "In the car," p.139) or a bouncy seat, which you can also rock. This will last your baby until he is about four months old, when you will need a more solid seat with better support.

NEVER put your baby's seat on a table or raised surface, and always strap him into his seat, even if you only plan to leave him in it for only a few seconds.

When your baby is about six months old, you can put him in a highchair. It's worth taking the time and trouble to buy one that you are happy with, as you will be using it several times each day until your baby is about two years old. Several types are available:

- Folding highchair. This folds flat like an ironing board and can be stored out of the way when not in use. It's useful if you are short of space, but it can be tedious to have to put it up each time you want to feed your baby. The legs are often widely splayed and can be a tripping hazard as you work around your baby.

- Convertible highchair. Often made of wood, this is the sturdiest and most comfortable highchair. Later it will convert to a low chair and table, so that when your baby gets to toddler stage, he can sit at it to eat or draw.

- Standard highchair. With wipe-clean surfaces and detachable tray, this usually has metal legs.

- Clip-on seat. This clips onto the table and is for babies who can sit up properly. The advantage is that your baby can sit up with the rest of the family at mealtime. It can be useful if you are out visiting, but you need to be sitting with your baby at all times, for the clip-on mechanism can work loose. You can only use them on sturdy tables. When you put your baby in the seat, his weight can tip the table over.

SECONDHAND EQUIPMENT

Buying baby equipment is expensive, and it can be tempting to buy cheaply through classified ads or yard sales. Secondhand shops can be a good source of baby furniture. You may also feel that you are conserving natural resources by reusing equipment. But safety experts warn that many children are injured each year in home accidents involving nursery equipment.

Hidden dangers include:

- No instructions.
- Worn hardware and safety straps.
- Hairline cracks.
- Designs that do not conform to current safety standards.

You need to consider whether a secondhand product under stress will really protect your child and how you are going to assemble a highchair or crib without instructions. You also have no way of knowing if the previous owners have used it properly, and there is no guarantee should anything go wrong.

Common problems with secondhand purchases are:

- Worn bearings on strollers that cause wheels to wobble.

- Brakes that have become worn and less efficient.

- Car seats need to be installed correctly to be effective. If there is an accident, your seat will not protect your baby unless it is properly anchored.

- Once a car seat has been in an accident, it will have incurred damage or stress and is no longer safe to use.

- A secondhand crib may be missing essential components that hold it together and it could collapse. It also may have too wide a space between its bars (see "Safety First," p.144 –145.)

- The wood may be cracked or split, and the paint may contain toxic substances.

- A crib mattress that is too small for your child's crib could lead to your child being suffocated in the gap around the edge.

- A safety gate (see "Keeping your baby safe," p.153,155) needs to be installed properly to do its job correctly. Otherwise, it is not worth having.

Buy new products if at all possible. Choose carefully and save money by avoiding unnecessary extra gadgets and gimmicks. If you purchase a car seat that will take you through several years and children and a crib that will convert into a bed, for example, it is possible to make your money go much further.

FLOOR TIME

Don't forget to allow your baby plenty of opportunity to lie fully stretched out on the floor. Put down a blanket or activity mat and a few toys and let him roll, kick, and try to push himself up. This will strengthen his muscles and help him develop the necessary skills for sitting and crawling. Some doctors are concerned that babies who spend too much time restricted in seats do not get a chance to learn these essential skills.

Safety at home

Babies are programmed to explore. From the moment of birth, your baby will start learning to coordinate his reflexes to make himself mobile. First, he will manage to lift his head, then he will start to reach out and grab at whatever looks interesting. Next, he will surprise you by rolling right over when you change his diaper.

Once he has learned to crawl, you will be amazed how much ground he covers in just a few seconds. Then, sometime around his first birthday, he will manage to pull himself up and cruise around the furniture. Your helpless baby is now a highly mobile toddler, and for the next few years, you will have to watch his every move to protect him from the many hidden dangers lurking in your home.

Accidents are the major cause of death for children from age one to five. Every year thousands of toddlers have to go to the hospital because of injuries caused by an accident in the home. Therefore, always make sure you take proper safety precautions.

IN THE KITCHEN

- Move all household cleaners and bleaches from the cabinet under the sink to a locked cupboard high up on the wall. You could reduce the amount of dangerous chemicals in your home by using bicarbonate of soda to clean sinks, refrigerator, plastic tops, and stove top. Use salt and boiling water to keep drains clean and half a cupful (120ml) of vinegar added to a bucket of water to clean cork, tile, or linoleum floors.

- Buy child safety locks and attach them to kitchen cabinets and drawers.

- Use the back burners on your stove and turn pot and pan handles inward. A stove guard gives added protection.

- Push appliances to the back of the counter and see that cords are out of reach. Unplug the toaster and any other electrical appliance when they are not in use, to ensure your child cannot turn them on accidentally.

- Put tablecloths away for a few years. A crawling baby can pull a cloth and the table contents onto his head.

- Keep plates, all utensils—especially knives—as well as cups of coffee and tea in the center of the table.

- Make sure your baby is strapped into his highchair before you dish up hot food to the rest of the family.

- Wrap any sharp objects before you put them in the trash can. Keep trash out of reach.

- Install safety locks on the refrigerator and freezer.

IN THE LIVING ROOM

- Use safety covers on all electric outlets so that your baby cannot push his fingers or toys into the holes.

- Keep a fireguard attached to the wall in front of an open fire.

- You will still need to keep your baby away from it: the guard itself can become very hot. Don't use a free-standing guard, which will be easy to pull over.

- Put several large colored stickers on sliding glass doors so your baby (and all others) will realize it is solid.

- Move your radio and TV out of reach.

- Remove any small or breakable ornaments and any household plants that may be poisonous.

- Put plastic safety corners on sharp-edged tabletops. Make sure your coffee table has smooth corners or put it away for a few years.

- Keep your baby's toys in a box (without a lid) at floor level so that he can reach them safely.

- Remove cabinet or units that could turn over if he tries to pull himself up or climb on them.

IN THE BATHROOM

- Keep all toiletries, cosmetics, and medicines in a locked bathroom cabinet.

- Use a nonslip bath mat for your baby's bath.

- Always run the cold water before the hot

KEEPING YOUR BABY SAFE

- You may consider buying a playpen. It should have a built-in floor so your baby cannot move it around. Traditional models are square and made from wood, although you can buy mesh-sided ones. A playpen may be useful if you have a spacious kitchen or living room and want to keep your baby safe while you are busy. Don't leave your baby in the playpen for long periods, and make sure he can see you and has toys to play with. If you decide to use a playpen, introduce it to him before he can move around so he can get used to it as a nice place to be, rather than a curtailment of his fun.

- A safety gate will stop your child from climbing the stairs or entering a room. Make sure it fits properly and can be operated by an adult, but not by a child. The safest models can be anchored to the wall. This may mark your wallpaper, but the peace of mind is worth it. Don't buy a model that you need to climb over; your baby will soon start trying to copy you.

- A buggy net is useful to place over the buggy or basket if there are cats around. This will prevent them from curling up on top of your baby. It will also protect your baby against insects.

water and check the water temperature with your elbow before putting your baby in the bath.

- If you are using a baby bath, you may find it safer to place it on the floor than on a surface from which your baby could slip and fall.

- Make sure your hot faucet does not leak. Bathe your baby with his head well away from the faucet. Tie a towel or dishcloth around the hot faucet if you are concerned that it may scald him.

- Never leave any child under five unattended in the bathroom. They can drown in just a few inches of water.

IN THE NURSERY

- Make sure all mobiles are hanging where your baby cannot reach and pull them down.

- Keep your diaper-changing equipment, and diaper bags, away from the side of the crib so that your baby cannot reach out and grab them. Never leave plastic bags in your baby's room.

- Buy flame-resistant nightwear for toddlers. Avoid dressing girls in long nighgowns once they are mobile since they are likely to trip and fall.

GENERAL SAFETY RULES

- Check any equipment you buy for the symbol guaranteeing that it conforms to latest safety standards.

- Move all furniture away from windows.

- Install at least two smoke alarms in your house and check the batteries every three months by pushing the test button.

- Install a carbon monoxide detector.

- Never carry or pass cups of hot liquids above a child's head.

- Never tie a pacifier around his neck as the ribbon could strangle him.

- Learn to use CPR (cardiopulmonary resuscitation). Classes are widely available.

- Don't use open-weave blankets that could trap little fingers.

- Never use a quilt or pillow with a baby under one year old, because of the risk of suffocation.

- Think hard before you buy a crib bumper. The tie ends must be cut short and tied securely to prevent them from coming undone and getting caught around your baby's neck or wrapped tightly around a finger.

- Never put your baby in his crib wearing a bib. Avoid any clothes with ribbons or cords that could pull tight around the neck.

- Never leave your baby, even for an instant, on the changing table. If you change your baby on the floor, rolling off his changing mat will not be so dangerous.

- Make sure that the crib is placed away from electrical outlets and shelves that your baby can reach once he learns to pull himself in his crib.

THE HALL AND STAIRS

- Install safety gates at the top and bottom of the stairs to prevent your child from climbing up or falling down the stairs.

- Be careful when you answer the front door. Never leave it open—your baby can crawl out in a matter of seconds.

- Avoid polished floors and loose rugs that your child could slip on.

- Make sure the telephone and telephone table are in a safe place.

- Always hold on to the banisters when you carry your baby up and down stairs.

- Be sure that your baby isn't able to get his head stuck between the banisters.

BABY WALKERS

Safety organizations have been campaigning for these to be banned. A walker is designed to let your child move around in an upright position before he has learned to walk. Tragedies have occurred when babies have tipped themselves into fires and down the stairs. Additionally, experts say that babies left in them for long periods don't get the chance to practice walking properly, delaying their development. Don't buy one.

Toys and play

Babies have an enormous amount to learn, and their natural curiosity, combined with proper stimulation and encouragement from you, will guarantee that they quickly start to discover how the world works.

STIMULATION

In addition to learning to control his own body and explore the world about him, your baby needs stimulation for another important reason. During his first three years, his brain will grow faster than at any other time. At birth his brain will weigh just 12 oz (336g), but by the age of three it will have grown to 3lb (1.4kg). At the same time, important connections are developing

TOY SAFETY FIRST

- Dangerous stuffing, sharp edges, eyes on wires or spikes, small parts that may come unattached and cause choking are all potentially lethal to small children.

- Do not buy a secondhand toy unless you can see an approved safety stamp.

- Never buy secondhand stuffed toys.

- Avoid stuffed toys with button eyes.

- Be sure that the toys of older children in the family are kept out of reach.

between the different brain cells. A baby who does not receive adequate stimulation may have difficulty making those connections, giving him a poor start in life.

THE MOST IMPORTANT TOY

Toy manufacturers are keen to promote a whole range of baby toys that claim to be educational and provide learning opportunities. And it is true that a few well-chosen toys can help your baby explore the world around him. But you are his most important toy. If you smile and talk to him, carry him around so that he is part of the family and can watch you during your daily routine, if you respond quickly to his needs, cuddle him, take him out and about, and point out what's going on, play peek-a-boo, and hand-clapping games — he will thrive.

CHOOSING TOYS

Before you buy your baby toys, consider these points:

- Try to see the toy from your baby's point of view. You may find a cuddly teddy bear appealing, but he would much prefer something designed for little hands to hold and manipulate.

- Although many baby toys are made in pastel colors, young babies find strong colors much more attractive.

- For the first year or so, your baby may prefer playing with the paper that his toys were wrapped in. He will also not know the difference between an expensive toy and a pile of empty plastic ice-cream cartons. Once he can sit up in the bathtub, give him a set of plastic cups and smooth-edged empty yogurt or margarine cartons to play with.

- Older babies may feel overwhelmed by too many bright toys. Choose natural wooden ones to get him used to more subtle colors.

Remember that everything is new and interesting to a baby. Leaves waving in the breeze, rain, birds, flowers are all fascinating—and free. Make sure he has the chance to look at the natural world around him and that you spare the time to point it out and talk about it.

AGE GUIDELINES

Many manufacturers try to give guidelines to the age range each toy is suitable for. Use the guidelines if you are not sure whether a toy is right for your baby, but don't be disappointed if he can't perform all the activities or if he doesn't show interest in the toys. Never give a child under the age of three anything small enough to be swallowed or stick in his throat. Choking accidents are a major cause of child fatalities. Each baby is an individual who will develop at a different rate. One baby may be quick to learn to pull levers and buttons, while another may enjoy looking in detail at pictures and exploring the texture of a soft toy. Here are some tried and tested toys:

HOMEMADE TOYS

- Mobile. String together pieces of silver foil and colored cardboard. Dry pasta pieces and shiny measuring cups will rattle together to make an interesting noise. Hang the mobile in the room where your baby sleeps. Secure it safely, well out of his reach.

- Rattle. Use a small plastic bottle filled with lentils. Always check to make sure the top is securely fastened.

- Large cardboard box. An older baby will love crawling into and out of a box.

- Give your baby a wooden spoon and a collection of pots and pans from the kitchen. Let him bang the pots to make different sounds.

- Peek-a-boo. At about 10 months, your baby will start to enjoy games where you hide a toy or a cup, covering it with a cloth, so he has to crawl to find it.

From birth

- Playmat provides a variety of activities. Your baby will enjoy lying on it for short periods of time long before he learns how to ring the bells and squeeze the squeakers.

- Rattle. Choose a soft rattle for a young baby. As he learns to manipulate it, he is bound to hit himself with it, and a hard plastic rattle could hurt.

- Baby gym. Your baby can lie underneath it and try to catch the balls and toys suspended above him. Colorful pictures at his eye level will provide something bright to focus on. Never leave the gym attached over the crib when you are not in the room or when your baby sleeps.

From three months

- Activity center. This attaches to the side of your baby's crib. It has a set of mirrors, balls, squeakers, and rattles that he can learn to manipulate.

- Soft ball, blocks. He will enjoy exploring the texture of these long before he can throw or stack them.

From six months

- Cloth or board books. This is the perfect time to introduce your baby to books. Choose ones with familiar themes that your baby will recognize—cats and dogs, not dinosaurs or dragons. Buy one or two bath books he can use in the tub.

- Stacking rings, blocks, cups. Your baby will enjoy knocking down the towers you build him long before he manages to construct one himself. He can also explore the different sizes and colors.

From one year

- Shape sorter. Your baby will enjoy pushing shapes through different-sized

TOY LIBRARIES

If you live in Canada, there may be a toy-lending library at your local public library. You can borrow safe toys in good condition for your baby to try out for a few weeks. The staff can give advice on which toy are suitable.

holes. He will also like to shake the sorter when it is full.

- Push-along toy. After your baby has learned to walk well, a push-along trolley or truck will encourage him. He will also enjoy putting his blocks and cups inside.

From 18 months
- A sit-and-ride toy will encourage coordination. Make sure he does not ride it near hazards.

- Simple lift-out puzzles with large, easy-to-handle pieces will develop his matching and concentration skills. Help him at first.

Your baby's development

During his first year, your baby will develop the following important skills:

- Language. He will learn to understand words long before he can speak. By about eight months he may be making noises that sound like *Dada* or *Mama*. By his first birthday, you should hear his first word, and he will acquire two or three new words each month. The *D* sound is the easiest to say, so it sounds as if your baby is saying *Daddy* before *Mommy*. It's nothing personal! A baby's language skills develop more quickly if adults speak to him using proper words and sentences, rather than baby language.

- Movement. During his first six months, he will learn to roll over and sit up. During his second six months, his coordination and muscle control advance so he can sit, crawl (8 months), bottom shuffle or cruise (10 months) around the furniture. Sometime between his first birthday and 18 months, your child will walk with confidence.

- Listening. His listening skills will become more finely attuned. By 12–16 weeks, he will be able to locate where a sound is coming from and will look to see it. Between six and eight months, he will respond to his own name.

- Hand-eye coordination. From five months, he will learn to use his hands and eyes together, so if he sees an object, he will be able to reach out and grasp it.

- Hand control. At first your baby will use his whole hand to pick something up. Then from eight months he will learn to use the palm of his hand and his fingers together; this is known as the palmar grip. Finally, by 15 months, he will manage to pick up small objects with just his thumb and index finger. This is known as the pincer grip.

- Two-handed play. From seven months he will learn to pass an object from one hand to the other.

- Visual tracking. At four weeks a baby recognizes his mother's face. At 12–20 weeks, he knows when things are familiar and looks at his hands. At 20–28 weeks, he can see 800 times better than he did at birth. By 9 and 10 months, your baby will be able to follow a rapidly moving object, and his vision will be almost as good as yours.

- Object permanence. At about seven months your baby will realize that if an object or person disappears from view, they still exist. He will therefore look for a toy if he drops it, for example. This often coincides with the begining of a clingy phase that peaks at about nine months, when he is anxious that you may not return once you leave his sight.

- Learning to remember. In the early weeks of life, babies act on reflexes. By two months, they start to replace these with voluntary actions. Until three months, they can do only one voluntary action at a time—reach for a rattle, but not cry at the same time. By six months old, babies can do two things at once.

HOW YOUR BABY GROWS

- Weight. This will have trebled by 12–14 months.

- Height. He will have grown by 10–12 inches (25–30cm) by his first birthday.

- Teeth. These start to appear from five to six months.

CHAPTER SIX

Outdoor Life

From the time your baby is a couple of weeks old, you will start to go out and about with him. From about three months, he will enjoy looking at the shapes and colors—trees waving in the breeze above him, cars rushing past, dogs and cats, people and flowers. And as he develops, you will find yourself looking at the world through new eyes when you see how ordinary, everyday objects look special to your baby.

TIME FOR A WALK

Going for a walk is not only important for your baby but for you as well, as you will benefit from the fresh air and exercise. Aim to get out twice a day whether it is just a quick visit to the park or a stroll to the stores. Looking at the same four walls is as monotonous for him as it is for you. Even when you are weeding the flower bed, wrap him up and take him outside in his carrier or stroller for a change of scenery.

In the yard

Your baby will love spending time in the backyard, and as a growing child, he will find fun and adventure there.

SAFETY OUTSIDE

Once your baby starts to crawl, you will need to be as vigilant about safety outdoors as you are inside the home. Gardening tools and machinery can cause serious injury if left lying around or in an unlocked shed. At this stage, your baby will be putting anything he comes across in his mouth—which is all part of his development but that may include poisonous plants and small stones.

Keep your child safe in the following ways:

- Never let him play unattended outdoors.

- Don't let him pick up earth; it may be contaminated with chemicals or animal droppings.

- Make sure that gates are locked and fences are secure.

- If you have a pool or pond, fence it off. Empty a wading pool immediately after use and, never leave your baby or toddler

DANGER—ON POISONS

- Vomiting and abdominal pain can be signs of poisoning. If your child has eaten a poisonous plant, first call 911 for an ambulance and then call the Poison Control Center in your area; the number is in the phone book. They will tell you what to do until the ambulance arrives.

- If your child swallows any chemicals, call 911 for the ambulance first, then your Poison Control Center. DO NOT try to make the child sick, and DO NOT give him anything to drink. Also some poisons work on the central nervous system, preventing breathing. So if he is unconscious, try to keep his airway open by tilting his head backward and pushing his chin up to lift his tongue clear.

in it unsupervised. Drowning is one of the most common accidents in the home among children under five.

- Keep all chemicals on a high shelf in a locked room or shed.

- Cover your baby's buggy with a safety net. It will keep curious cats off him and will also catch any leaves or debris that may get blown up on a breezy day.

- Never start your car without knowing exactly where your toddler is.

- Put any play equipment on a padded surface such as wood chips. Grass will wear away quickly.

- Teach your child not to eat berries.

- Pull up any poisonous plants. These include deadly nightshade, death cap fungus, laburnum, foxglove, and lily of the valley.

DOGS

If you have a dog, he should be trained to reduce the risk of biting. A normally docile animal can become frustrated if he is

FIRST AID KIT

Keep your first-aid equipment in a clean, dry container where you can easily find it. Keep a kit in the car, too, and take antiseptic wipes on outings to clean cuts and scrapes. You will need:

- nonstick sterile wound dressings
- triangular bandage to make a sling or secure a dressing
- gauze bandage to hold dressings in place
- surgical cotton
- calamine lotion or camomile cream for insect bites, stings, and sunburn
- assorted bandages
- scissors, tweezers, and safety pins
- antihistamine cream for stings
- tube of antiseptic cream
- arnica cream for bruises
- calendula cream (marigold) for cuts
- eucalyptus oil—insect repellant
- a card of emergency telephone numbers

continually mauled by a baby or toddler and may snap in irritation. Occasionally, dogs have been known to turn on small children causing serious injury. Encourage your baby to be interested in animals and to treat them with respect, kindness—and caution. Don't let him treat them like toys.

Be especially wary of dogs like German shepherds, Doberman pinschers, bull terriers, and Rottweilers. Teach your baby not to touch them or go near them, but try not to instill fear in him so that he panics whenever he sees one.

Children are at risk if they ingest dog and cat excrement. Children touching it

DANGER—ON RABIES

Rabies is a potentially fatal disease spread by the saliva of infected animals. It is endemic in many countries. If you or your baby is bitten by an animal, call the police so that they can determine whether or not the animal has rabies. The victim must undergo treatment right away.

may get nematode eggs on their fingers and swallow them. The eggs hatch in the gut, and the larvae migrate to the eyes, the liver, lung, and heart. The resultant disease toxocariasis is regarded as self-limiting (6 to 18 months) unless there is reinfection.

If you have a dog, clean up your own yard and worm him regularly. You should also scoop up his feces when you take him out for a walk.

CATS

Toxoplasmosis is a disease that can be acquired from handling cat feces (or eating undercooked meat. It may cause a mild infection or illness similar to glandular fever—sore throat, tiredness, and enlarged glands. Pregnant women, however, are at much more serious risk. Miscarriage, stillbirth, hydrocephalus, jaundice, and eye disorders may result. If you are pregnant, do not change a cat litter tray. Keep cat litter trays out of the reach of toddlers, and make sure you wash your hands before eating. Worm your cat every three months. Keep cats and dogs away from work surfaces and give them separate food and drink bowls.

ANIMAL BITES

Animals have sharp teeth that leave deep puncture wounds, injecting germs deep into the tissues. Cat bites can be a particular problem. If your baby or child is bitten:

- Stay calm. Bites are rarely serious, but if left untreated, they can become infected.

- Wash the wound thoroughly with soapy water to remove any blood, saliva, or dirt. Apply antiseptic cream and cover it with a clean dressing.

- Have the wound checked by a doctor. If it is deep, it may carry the risk of tetanus or infection. Your baby should be protected against tetanus once he has had his first two DTP shots (at two and four months).

- With a clean cloth press firmly on a serious wound to stem the bleeding. Dress it and take your baby to the hospital.

INSECT BITES AND STINGS

Your baby is likely to be stung or bitten by bees, hornets, ants, fleas, or mosquitoes. Insects breed most rapidly during hot, damp weather. If your baby is crawling, cover his legs so they are not in direct contact with the grass. Place a groundsheet on the grass for him to sit and play on. Once he is walking, keep him away from flower beds where bees gather, and don't give him fruit juice or sweet things that attract wasps.

What you can do

- Like animal bites, insect bites and stings should be cleaned with warm water and soap. Try to avoid soap containing detergent, perfume, or

other irritants (see "Baby toiletries," pp.63–68).

- After cleaning, rinse the wound in clean water and apply antiseptic cream.

Flea and mosquito bites
- Keep pets free of fleas and encourage them to sleep only in a special basket.

- Treat small numbers of bites with calamine lotion or mild cortisone cream. Badly bitten children should see a doctor.

Ticks
- Deer ticks and dog ticks carry several serious diseases. Make every effort to rid your yard of them. Dog ticks can be seen easily. But deer ticks are tiny—the size of a pinpoint. They carry serious disease. If you find a tick on your child, it is best to take him to a doctor or a hospital emergency room to have it removed.

- If you have to remove one yourself, grasp it firmly as close to the skin as possible— you do not want to leave the head buried in the skin. Use your fingers and pull it

straight out. Put antiseptic ointment on the wound immediately. For the next 24 hours, check the wound frequently. If redness develops next to the wound or in a ring around it, seek immediate medical treatment.

Ant bites
- Do not let your baby sit directly on the grass.

- Treat bites with bicarbonate of soda paste (bicarbonate of soda mixed and water).

Poison ivy, oak, and sumac
- Destroy any patches of stinging plants in your yard.

- Washing may spread the rash.

- Treat with calamine lotion.

Bee stings
- Most bee stings are not dangerous, but in a few cases anaphylactic shock sets in. Such a severe reaction requires urgent medical attention. Such a situation is likely to be when he is stung in the mouth or stung several times at once.

COLD COMPRESS

There are two types of cold compress you can make:

1 For one kind, soak a pad of cotton or towel in cold or ice water. Squeeze it out so it is wet but not dripping and place it on the injury.

- Replace or drip more water onto the pad after a few minutes. Continue cooling the area for 30 minutes.

- If necessary, keep the compress in place with a bandage. It may be uncomfortable for 2 to 3 minutes, but it will help.

2 For the other kind, put crushed ice in a plastic bag. Add a little salt to lower the melting temperature.

- Seal the bag and wrap it in a cloth.

- Place it on the injury and continue cooling for 30 minutes.

- If necessary, hold the pack in place with a bandage.

- You may be able to see the black stinger sticking out of the center of a white area of skin that is surrounded by a swollen red bump. Remove the stinger by scraping it out of the wound with a clean fingernail or the edge of a credit card. Do not try to grasp it with your fingers or tweezers because it will probably break. You will also squeeze more venom into the wound.

- Treat with bicarbonate of soda paste as for ant bites (see p.167), or use rubbing alcohol or a cold compress (see box).

- If there is an allergic reaction, severe swelling will occur very fast and spread. Apply a cold compress and call an ambulance.

- Stings in the mouth may cause swelling that can obstruct breathing. Give the child some crushed ice to suck and take him straight to the hospital emergency room, or call 911 for an ambulance.

- Multiple bee stings usually require urgent medical attention.

Wasp stings

- Wasp stings sometimes cause an allergic reaction, with severe swelling or shock similar to a bee sting.

- The puncture may contain a black stinger. Look at its direction and try to scrape it out—the edge of a credit card works well. If you try to pull it out with your fingers or a pair of tweezers it will probably break.

- Don't squeeze; you might push the poison deeper into the skin.

- Wasp stings contain alkali venom. After cleansing, dress the wound with vinegar or lemon juice; the acid will help to neutralize the venom. Avoid rubbing the skin.

- If there is a lot of swelling, use a cold compress (see p.168). Treat stings in the mouth as for bee stings in the mouth (see p.168).

- Multiple wasp stings require urgent medical attention.

SNAKE BITES

Familiarize yourself with the poisonous snakes in your area. If your child is bitten:

- Keep calm and reassure him. Fear can cause shock.

- Wash the bite with soap and water and remove any venom you can see.

- Cover the wound with a clean dressing and get medical help immediately.

- Sweating, vomiting, and diarrhea are all rare reactions, but be on the lookout for them.

- Seek urgent medical attention. Try to remember what the snake looked like.

SHOCK

Shock can result from a bite or sting if there is severe allergy, pain, or stress. Watch out for symptoms such as pale skin, restlessness, confusion, anxiety, quickened pulse and rapid breathing, and marked and spreading swelling.

What you can do

- Lay your child on his side and, if he is wounded, try to stem any bleeding by pressing on the wound (see below).

- Loosen clothing and cover the child with a light blanket. Don't offer a drink. Get medical help immediately or call an ambulance if the child is in distress.

HEAVY BLEEDING

If blood spurts from a wound, or the flow is heavy, or a moderate flow lasts for longer than a couple of minutes, you need to stem it so the blood can clot. At the same time, get someone to call 911 for an ambulance.

What you can do:

- Raise the injured part to reduce the amount of blood flowing to it.

- Place a pad of clean cloth over the wound. Press hard on it for 10 minutes. Or press with your fingers, drawing the edges of the cut firmly together.

- Bind the pad in place with a bandage. If the blood soaks through, place another pad over the top and maintain pressure.

- If something is embedded in the wound, raise the injured part and apply pressure around the object, not directly on it, which will push it in farther. Don't attempt to pull the object out or to clean the wound.

- Release the pressure for a moment and roll up a small piece of cloth. Then twist the roll into a doughnutlike ring.

- Place the tightly twisted ring around the embedded object, and bandage it in place. Don't bandage tightly over the wound.

Lifesaving techniques

If your baby or child is choking or stops breathing, you must call 911 for help immediately. Tell the emergency operator that your child is choking (or not breathing) and give your name and address clearly. It is difficult to stay calm in these circumstances, but you must try. Do not hang up the telephone—the operator may be able to tell you what you need to do while an ambulance is on its way to you.

Every parent without exception should take a course in cardiopulmonary resuscitation (CPR), so that if a real emergency happens, you will be able to save your baby's life. The course will teach you how to dislodge an obstruction to the airway (the Heimlich maneuver) and how to do CPR correctly. CPR courses are offered everywhere and take only a few hours to complete.

Choking accidents are common with babies and children, and parents should know how to deal with them safely and effectively. You must distinguish between choking (where the child is still breathing, perhaps with difficulty) and a situation wherein the child has stopped breathing and has no pulse (which requires prompt and skillful CPR).

Choking baby

- If your baby (up to one year old) is choking and coughing but still breathing, let him try to cough up whatever is obstructing his airway. Do not attempt to remove the obstruction with your fingers unless you can see it clearly.

- If that doesn't work, place him face down, straddling your arm, with his head lower than his trunk, so that your hand is firmly supporting his shoulders and chin. Do not put your hand over his face. With the heel of your other hand, strike him forcefully (but not too hard) between the shoulder blades *four times* (See illustration A, p.172). This may dislodge the obstruction.

- If not, support his head and turn him over, sandwiched between your arms, and lay him in your lap with his head still lower than his trunk. Draw an imaginary line between his nipples and place three of your fingers about a ½-inch (1.25cm) below that line. With your fingers, deliver four slow, firm thrusts (see illustration B, p.172).

- Repeat the back-thrust and chest-thrust maneuvers until the obstruction is dislodged, or until he becomes unconscious.

A

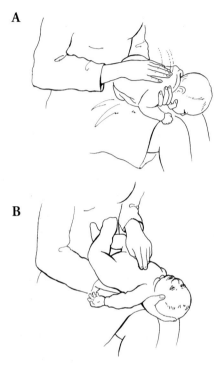

B

- If that happens, lay him on a flat, hard surface. Tilt his head back *slightly*, using a couple of fingers under his chin with your other hand on top of his head. What you are doing is putting his trachea (windpipe) in a straight line. Do not tilt a baby's head back too far or you can actually close the trachea. Place your

mouth over his nose and mouth and *gently* breathe out; just a puff of air is all that's needed. As you do this, keep your eye on his chest to see if your breath makes his chest rise. If not, reposition his head and try again.

WHEN TO USE CPR

First, you must establish that your child is truly unconscious. (Some babies breathe so shallowly that they seem to be unconscious—even if they are not.) Use the "look, listen and feel" method:

- Shake him gently or flick the soles of his feet

- Lay your cheek close to his mouth and look carefully for any chest movement that indicates breathing.

- Check for pulse. For a baby, feel for a brachial pulse located just above the elbow on the inside of the arm. For a child, feel for the carotid pulse on either side of the windpipe in the neck.

- Repeat the back blows and chest thrusts, then reposition him and try to breathe into his nose and mouth again. Repeat as necessary. If you are unable to find a brachial pulse and he is still not breathing, begin CPR. The brachial pulse is located just above the elbow on the inside of the arm.

Choking child

For a child between one year and eight years old, follow the same procedure as above but with the child lying on the floor instead of on your arm or lap. Instead of chest thrusts, you should use the heel of your hand placed just below the bottom of the child's rib cage, and direct your thrusts slightly upward, toward the child's head. If you are unable to find a carotid pulse and he is not breathing, begin CPR. The carotid pulse is found on both sides of the neck, just alongside the windpipe.

Streetwise

After the home, most accidents that happen to children occur in the street. Even a baby in a stroller can be at risk, because he will be out in front of you by about a yard. So be careful not to push him into the road while you are waiting to cross.

Heavy bags hung over the handles, can easily make the stroller tip over. When you stop, always put on the brake and never leave a child unattended. Do not tie a dog to your baby's buggy or stroller.

If you also have an older child, you need to hold his hand while you are walking along the sidewalk or walkway until you can trust him to hold the side of the buggy himself. You could invest in a pair of safety reins, although some toddlers hate wearing them. Or it might be safer to put both children in a double stroller.

CROSSING SAFELY

Teach your child how to cross the road as soon as possible. Each time you cross, explain to him what you are doing so that it becomes automatic.

- Find a safe place to cross, such as traffic lights, a pedestrian crossing, or a straight piece of road with no traffic visible in either direction.

- Stop at the curb. Look left, right, then left again, and listen for traffic.

- If traffic is coming, let it pass.

- Look left, right, then left again, and if the road is clear, walk—don't run—across it.

- Warn your child never to chase a ball into the street or to stand or play behind parked cars.

STRANGER DANGER

From an early age you need to talk to your child about keeping safe. Sadly, pedophiles may seem perfectly respectable, and about two-thirds of them are not strangers, but adults already known to the child. Pedophiles are good at making friends with children, and hang around playgrounds and parks where children are likely to be. Some find their victims through babysitting, and babies, who cannot tell you what has been going on, are particularly at risk. On the other hand, there are plenty of elderly people who love talking to babies and are completely harmless. But never leave your child alone with someone who offers to care for him, while you dash into a store, for example.

To protect your child:

- Check on anyone who is left in charge of your child. Talk, as well as write, to other people they have worked for.

- Explain to children the difference between safe and unsafe secrets. A secret about a birthday surprise is fine, but no one should ever ask them to keep kisses or touches secret.

- Never send anyone to pick up your child from a babysitter or nursery without warning the adult in charge and, once he is old enough to understand, warn the child himself.

- When he is older, arrange to have a family code-word. Tell him that if anyone else comes to pick him up, he or she will always know the code word. "No code, no go."

- Most pedophiles are not strangers. Your child must know that if anyone touches him in a confusing or frightening way he must tell you.

- Tell him to make a loud fuss if someone tries to touch or grab him. He should shout "No!," run away, and tell an adult. Practice yell, run, tell.

- For more information see Useful Addresses on pages 188–189.

Choosing a babysitter

It is important that you and your partner enjoy time together away from the responsibilities of caring for your baby. To do that, you need to choose a reliable babysitter.

- Get a personal recommendation. If you are new to an area, ask your baby's doctor for a good babysitter, or join a local babysitting circle.

- Don't employ anyone under 16. If you do use a teenager, check that she has access to an adult.

- Ask the babysitter to come to your house before your evening out so you can see

Playground safety

One of the favorite excursions for an older baby or toddler is a trip to the park or playground. Once your baby can sit upright, you can put him in one of the swings and push him gently to and fro.

Playgrounds usually have special areas for babies and toddlers. Keep to them, as older children play more boisterously. Watch out for children running behind the swings.

If there is a baby slide, your child will enjoy going down it, with you holding him firmly at all times. Check to see that the slide is made in one continuous piece with no jointed panels and that the surface beneath it is designed to cushion any falls.

how well she gets along with your child.

- Ask how much experience she has had and get names and addresses of other families she has worked for so you can contact them.

- Ask if she knows any first aid.

- Ask what she would do in an emergency.

- Explain how much you will pay.

- Explain how you want her to deal with any problems—for example, if your baby won't settle or wakes during the evening.

- On the evening itself, make sure you leave a number where you can be contacted and the number of the nearest hospital and your doctor.

- Trust your instincts. If you are not happy, use someone else.

Chemical sprays

The farming industry's use of chemical sprays to control insect pests and plant diseases has improved crop yields. But chemical residues are now found in much of our food, including meats, poultry, eggs, fruit, vegetables, grain, and milk. The water supply has been contaminated in many areas, particularly in agricultural regions. Government officials claim that the residues of these chemicals are too small to do any damage, but little is known about the long-term effects of even small doses.

PESTICIDES

- Some pesticides, which kill insects that eat and lay eggs in our food crops, have been linked to cancer in humans and animals. A few are believed to cause birth defects. As insects and other organisms develop resistance to chemicals, more powerful substances have been used, some of which are chemically related to nerve gases and other poisons. In humans, these substances can affect our immune system, thus lowering our ability to fight diseases.

- Amounts of pesticide residue on fruit crops vary dramatically. Some chemicals that have been banned in the USA and Canada are still used in countries that export their produce to North American markets. Individual pieces of fruit can have many times the "safe" average of the whole shipment. In these cases, eating a single apple or peach could take you over the acceptable level of intake.

- Environmental advocates believe that if supermarkets listed the chemicals used on crops next to their displays, consumers would be shocked into demanding stricter controls.

- Because chemical sprays are increasingly expensive, and because farmers are aware of public concern about farm chemicals, many growers are now using a system known as Integrated Pest Management (IPM). This combines minimal use of chemicals with old-fashioned organic growing methods. Some of the largest agribusiness companies are even switching to totally organic growing, which reduces their costs and makes their produce more appealing to the buying public.

- Consumers can encourage organic (non-chemical) agriculture by asking their supermarkets to carry organic produce that is safe to eat, by shopping at "green markets" run by regional small-farm groups, and by supporting organizations that lobby for tighter controls on farm chemicals.

FUNGICIDES

In 1990 the US Environmental Protection Agency threatened to ban a chemical called Alar when it found that lifetime consumption of treated produce could cause cancer in over four people per 100,000 exposed to it. It was used mainly on apples, but it was also used to treat other fruit and vegetable crops. The manufacturer of Alar promptly withdrew it from the market.

Children are thought to have a higher risk from many food chemicals than adults. Because of their smaller size, a serving of contaminated food has a greater effect. There is also plenty of time for chemicals to trigger cancer later in their lives. Even washing and peeling fruit does not offer complete protection, as many chemicals penetrate the flesh.

You can reduce the effect of chemicals on your child by:

• Washing and peeling any fruit you give him.

• Buying only organic fruit and vegetables. Because many more people are doing this, the price of organic produce is dropping. Weigh the slightly higher cost against the risk (and expense) of disease. Organic produce should still be washed, but you and your family can benefit from the nutrients that would be lost if you had to remove the peel.

• Growing your own vegetables when possible. Don't use any chemicals. You can grow a lot of vegetables in a very small space, even in pots and tubs on a deck or terrace.

• Buying bottled water. Pesticides and other chemicals have been found in public water and well water. Have your water tested to see whether it is pure.

• Avoiding farm fields when farmers are spraying crops.

• Supporting an organization that campaigns for fuller consumer disclosure and stricter limits on pesticide use.

STRAWBERRY SURPRISE

Over the past 10 years, strawberry growing in some areas has become much more intensive, partly due to the pesticide methyl bromide. It is used to treat the soil before planting and helps to produce firm-skinned, bright red strawberries. Although it doesn't leave harmful residues on the fruit, methyl bromide is a highly toxic chemical and very damaging to the ozone layer (see "Fun in the sun," pp.181–182). Its use has been phased out in The Netherlands because of concern over water contamination. Many European countries don't use it.

Methyl bromide is also used in the production of lettuce, celery, tomatoes, cucumbers, and mushrooms. In addition, it is used to fumigate soil, grains, nuts, and herbs, as well as containers, machinery, and processing facilities. Concern is so great that developed countries have agreed that the use of this chemical should be phased out by 2001. Environmental advocates argue that more urgent action needs to be taken.

What you can do
- Ask your supermarket for strawberries produced without methyl bromide.

- Join an organization lobbying against it.

Happy vacations

Vacations with babies and small children can be great fun but not necessarily relaxing. To have a successful vacation with a baby or toddler, you will need to accept that the limitations and extra work a baby brings do not disappear just because you have moved to a different part of the country or the world for a week or two.

BOOKING YOUR VACATION

Before you book, make sure that the destinations you are considering are truly baby-friendly. If the brochure does not provide enough detail, ask a travel agent to find out the following:

- Can a first-floor apartment or room be guaranteed? Anything above that level poses a risk if your child wanders out onto the balcony or staircase.

- Is there a nearby supply of diapers, baby toiletries, and baby formula or baby foods?

- Are cribs and highchairs provided?

- Is there a babysitting service? Who will be doing the babysitting? Some hotels offer qualified practical nurses; others rely on hotel staff.

- Are there any long flights of steps or steep hills where you cannot push a buggy?

- Will your room be well away from the nightlife, so your baby will not be disturbed?

- Is your room safely away from the swimming pool and main road?

- Is there a washing machine available?

- Is there somewhere to dispose of used diapers?

- Will you be able to make bottles of formula and baby meals safely?

TRAVELING WITH A BABY

Whatever method of travel you take, build plenty of breaks into your trip so you can feed and change your baby. Breast-feeding will be an asset, in this case, as the milk supply is ready to serve whenever he is hungry. Be sure to breast-feed or give him a bottle during takeoffs and landings. It will help keep his ears from popping.

Once your baby is about four months old, you might decide to vacation close to home until he is old enough to cope with longer journeys, as older babies and toddlers easily become restless and fussy.

Make sure you take hand luggage or have a bag handy that contains the following:

- Diapers.

- Formula in bottles, along with a few extra nipples.

- Baby food, spoons, bib.

- Extra set of clothes.

- A sweater or small baby blanket in case of air conditioning or drafts.

- Drinking cup and water or other drinks.

- Small toys and some books to "read" for an older baby.

SWIMMING POOLS

- In addition to drowning, swimming pools can pose another threat to small children if high levels of organochlorines are used to treat the water.

- Many pools use a salt treatment called sodium hypochlorite, which is much safer, although sore eyes can result if organochlorines are also added. If you want to take your baby swimming, find out how often the chlorine level is checked and what filter mechanisms are in place.

- Choose a pool that is regularly and well maintained.

- Young babies love swimming, and many pools have time allocated especially for mothers and babies. But don't take your baby swimming until he has completed his second polio immunization at four months.

Fun in the sun

It wasn't very long ago that parents were told that sunshine was good for their children and that a glowing tan was a sign of good health. To a great extent it still is. Sunlight not only evokes a sense of well-being, it also promotes activity in the skin's cells, which leaves people feeling full of energy. And sunlight stimulates our bodies to produce vitamin D, which is essential for strong bones and teeth.

COVER UP

Nowadays, though, we know that the sun's ultraviolet rays can cause great damage, especially to children:

- Sunburn increases the risk of skin cancer, which is now one of the fastest-growing cancers. The increase in cases in the past 25 years has been dramatic, and experts believe that today one bout of serious sunburn can put a child at risk of having skin cancer in later life.

- Malignant melanoma, the most

dangerous form of skin cancer, is linked with exposure to short bursts of strong sunlight, such as annual two-week vacations exposed to the sun.

- The thinning of the ozone layer is making the problem worse, say experts. Situated in the upper atmosphere, this layer of gases protects the earth by absorbing up to 99 percent of the sun's damaging ultraviolet rays.

- The continued use of CFC gases (chlorofluorocarbons) is having a devastating effect on the ozone layer. As

it breaks down, it allows more of the harmful rays to reach the earth. However, the good news is that CFCs are no longer present in new refrigerators and household appliances.

- In 1996 the ozone hole over the Antarctic measured twice the size of Europe. In the Northern Hemisphere the ozone layer has also been depleted, with substantial thinning over populated areas.

A HEALTHY TAN?

Children have thinner skin than adults, so they need more protection. Sunburn occurs when the small blood vessels under the skin dilate in an effort to protect it. The blood supply to the exposed area is increased, causing inflammation. The darker the skin, the more melanin is present to protect it. Fair skins can't produce melanin quickly enough, so a lobster-pink color is the result. Fair skins that have been wrapped up all winter are slowest to produce melanin. Red-haired children are most at risk.

Protecting your baby

- Keep a baby under six months out of strong sunlight. He can quickly overheat and dehydrate.

- In the summer stay inside between 11.00 AM and 3.00 PM when the rays are at their most intense. If you have to be out for part of that time, make sure you are in the shade and that your children wear protective clothing (see page 185).

- Put toys in the shade. Remember that the sun moves around during the day, so if you have a wading pool, change its position every couple of hours.

- Always use a parasol on your baby's buggy or stroller.

RAYS OF SUNSHINE

The sun's rays can penetrate shade and haze, and they can also be reflected off other surfaces. Less than half of them come from direct sunshine. The sun emits three types of rays:

- UVA rays reduce the elasticity of the skin and help to cause premature aging. They penetrate deeply, reaching the lower skin layers, causing the upper layers to thicken to protect them and eventually to look like leather.

- UVB rays cause freckling and sunburn. They are absorbed by the skin's top layers and stimulate the production of vitamin D and a protective pigment called melanin, which gives the skin its brown color. UVB rays are most intense at midday, in hot climates, and at high elevations. They were once thought to be more dangerous, but scientists now say that both UVA and UVB rays can cause skin cancer, including melanoma.

- UVC rays are the most damaging. These are the rays that the depleted ozone layer can no longer completely absorb.

- Gradually increase the amount of time your child spends in the sun. Don't let him stay out for longer than 20 minutes on the first day.

- The intensity of the sun's rays depend on where you are. Sand and sea, snow, high elevations and windy weather all intensify the effects of the sun. UV rays pass through water and are reflected off snow.

- Use a sunscreen or sunblock.

CHOOSING A SUNSCREEN

- Buy a sunscreen with a high sun protection factor SPF15 to 30 for sunscreens and SPF50 for sunblocks. The number indicates the extra protection the lotion gives against UVB rays above that provided by the child's own skin. So SPF15 means that if he wears this cream he can stay in the sun 15 times longer than he would be able to with no sunscreen lotion.

- Check the protection against UVA radiation. Most sunscreen manufacturers use a star rating system to indicate how much protection is offered.

- Some high-factor lotions can irritate a young child's skin, since they require higher concentrations of sunblocking chemicals. If you are in doubt, stick to SPF15 and re-apply it every 30 minutes. Products containing benzophenones and para-aminobenzoic acid (PABA) are known to cause allergic skin rashes. Lanolin can cause a reaction too.

- Sunscreens that contain zinc oxide and titanium dioxide, which are both natural chemicals, are the safest sunblocks to use on children.

- Some sunscreens leave a white film on the skin, so you can see where you have applied it and verify that no areas have been missed.

- Make sure you apply the sunscreen everywhere, including your child's feet, fingers, face, shoulders, and the back of his neck and knees. Pay particular attention to his nose and the tops of his ears.

- Re-apply it each time your child comes out of the water, even if the label claims that it is water-resistant.

- After applying sunscreen, wait 15–30 minutes for it to penetrate the skin before allowing your child into the sun.

- Store sunscreen creams and lotions out of the sun to prevent them from deteriorating. Buy new lotion each spring or summer.

TOO MUCH SUN

If your child has been in the sun for too long, he may suffer the following reactions:

PROTECTIVE CLOTHING

- Shorts, long-sleeve T-shirts, and cover-up swimwear in special fabrics offer extra protection. If weather permits, long pants will give the most protection.

- Give your child a cap with protective flaps at the sides and the back. The best ones also have a long visor thats acts as a mini-umbrella for your baby's face.

- Buy protective sunglasses. These are suitable for children from six months onward. Make sure they conform to safety standards. Don't be tempted to buy cheap sunglasses. These may enable your child to see in bright sunlight without blinking, but the sunlight will penetrate the lenses and burn the eyes behind the irises.

- If your child is wearing ordinary shorts and a T-shirt, remember that cotton offers less protection when it is damp, so you will still need to apply a sunscreen. Choose dark colors rather than light ones and avoid very stretchy and tight-fitting material, which offers less protection.

- Heat rash. Some babies and children develop a fine red rash in hot weather, either in or out of the sun. Treat it by taking your baby to a cooler room, bathing him in lukewarm water, and patting his skin until almost dry. Let him sleep in just a shirt and diaper so the rash is not irritated by clothes.

- Sunburn. Sometimes this becomes evident a few hours after the damage has been done. Cool the skin by patting it with a cloth that has been soaked in cool water. Use calamine lotion or a natural remedy such as aloe, marigold, or myrrh to soothe the skin and reduce inflammation. Fresh cucumber juice and dock leaves also ease pain. Give infant acetaminophen if he seems to be in pain. If blisters form, take him to a hospital emergency room. Do not break them.

- Heat stroke. If your child develops fever and seems unwell after being in the sun, he may have heatstroke. Give him plenty to drink, wrap him in a cool, damp sheet, and call the doctor or take him to a hospital emergency room.

Danger

Most cases of skin cancer are treatable if caught early enough. Freckles and moles are normal on children, but you should consult a dermatologist if they change shape or color, become inflamed, start to itch, or are present before he is six weeks old.

In the country

There are many practical ways of encouraging young children to take an interest in the country and outdoor life.

- Make your garden a pesticide-free zone. This will protect your child from chemical hazards and encourage local wildlife.

- Feed the birds in winter and provide nest boxes. Encourage your child to watch and recognize different species of birds. Give them bread crumbs, fruit, cheese, bacon scraps, cooked rice, and oatmeal. Provide water for them to drink and bathe in.

- If you live in a town or city, find out if

there are farming projects nearby. These teach young children about nature.

IN THE YEARS AHEAD

As your baby grows older, you can encourage him to take an interest in his environment and the issues surrounding it.

By following some of the advice in this book, you will have not only brought up your baby to be happy and healthy, you will also have helped the next generation to grow up to be concerned to protect and care for the world and its precious resources.

TEACHING YOUR CHILD TO BE A GOOD CITIZEN

- Leave livestock, crops, and machinery alone.
- Take your trash home.
- Help to keep all water clean.
- Protect wildlife, plants, and trees.
- Take special care on country roads.
- Make no unnecessary noise.
- Enjoy the countryside and respect its life and work, and the property of others.
- Guard against all risk of fire.
- Keep dogs under close control.
- Keep to public paths across farmland.
- Use gates and then re-fasten them. Do not climb over fences, hedges, and walls.

Useful Addresses

Pregnancy, birth and babycare

International Childbirth Education
Association, Inc.
PO Box 20048
Minneapolis, MN 55420
Phone: 612-854-8660
Fax: 612-854-8772
E-mail: info!icea.org
Web Site: http://www.icea.org/

LaLeche League International
1400 N. Meacham Road
Schaumburg, IL 60173-4048
Phone: 1-800-LA-LECHE
              847-519-7730
Fax: 847-519-0035
Web Site: ttp://www.lalecheleague.org/

ASPO/Lamaze (American Society for
Psychoprophylaxis in Obstetrics)
1200 19th Street NW, Suite 300
Washington, DC 20036
Phone: 1-800-368-4404
              202-857-100
Fax: 202-223-4579
E-mail: aspo@sba.com
Web Site: http://www.lamaze-
childbirth.com/

National Sudden Infant Death Syndrome
Resource Center
2070 Chain Bridge Road, Suite 450
Vienna, VA 22182
Phone: 703-821-8955
Fax: 703-821-2098
E-mail: circle1@ix.netcom.com
Web Site: http://www.circsol.com/SIDS/

National Foundation for Sleep and Related
Disorders in Children
4200 West Peterson, Suite 109
Chicago, IL 60646
Phone: 630-971-1086

Safety

National Highway Traffic Safety
Administrator Auto Safety Hotline

NHTSA
Office of the Administrator
NAO-10
400 7th Street SW
Washington, DC 2590
Phone: 1-888-327-4236
              202-366-0123 (main number)
E-mail: webmaster@nhtsa.dot.gov
Web Site: http://www.nhtsa.dot.gov/

National Child Safety Council
4065 Page Avenue
Jackson, MI 49204-1368
Phone: 1-800-222-1484
              517-674-6070
Fax: 517-764-3068

Health

Ask-A-Nurse Hotline (evenings and
weekends)
1-800-535-1111

National Institute for Child Health and
Human Development
Office of Research and Reporting
Building 31, Room 2A32

Bethesda, Maryland 20892
Phone: 301-496-5133
Web Site:
http://www.nih.gov/nichd/index/html

American Academy of Pediatrics
141 Northwest Point Boulevard
Elk Grove Village, Illinois 60007-1098
Phone: 847-228-5005
Fax: 947-228-5097
E-mail: kidsdocs@aap.org
Web Site: http://www.aap.org

American College of Osteopathic
Pediatricians
5550 Friendship Blvd., Suite 300
Chevy Chase, MD 20815
Phone: 301-968-2642
Fax: 301-968-4195

National Center for Homeopathy
801 North Fairfax Street, Ste. 306
Alexandria, VA 22314
Phone: 703-548-7790
Fax: 703-548-7792
E-mail: nchinfo@igc.apc.org
Web Site: http://www.homeopathic.org

American Association for Music Therapy
8455 Colesville Road
Suite 100
Silver Spring, MD 20910
Phone: 301-589-3300
Fax: 301-589-5175
E-mail: info@namt.com
Web Site: http://www.namt.com/namt

Sources for Flower Essences:

Flower Essence Society
PO Box 459
Nevada City, CA 95959
Phone: 1-800-736-9222
          916-265-9163
Fax: 916-265-0584
E-mail: info@flowersociety.org
Web Site: http://www.flowersociety.org/

Bach Flower Essences
Nelson Bach USA
Wilmington Technology Park
100 Research Drive
Wilmington, MA 01887
Education Line: 1-800-334-0843
Order Line: 1-800-314-BACH

International Association for Infant Massage
1720 Willow Creek Circle, Suite 516
Eugene, OR 97402
Phone: 541-431-6280
Fax: 541-485-7372

National Eczema Association
1221 SW Yamhill, No. 303
Portland, OR 97205
Phone: 503-228-4430
Fax: 503-273-8778

Meningitis Foundation of America
E-mail: support@musa.org
Web Site: http://www.musa.org/
(send questions on meningitis to e-mail
address noted above)

Food, Consumer and Environment

American Dietetic Association's Consumer
Nutrition Hotline 1-800-366-1655

Food and Drug Administration Center for
Food Safety and Applied Nutrition
Hotline: 1-800-FDA-4010
Web Site: http://www.fda.gov

U.S. Consumer Product Safety Commission
Washington, DC 20207
Phone: 301-504-0992 (main number)
Hotlines: 1-800-638-2772
          1-800-638-8270 (hearing
          impaired line)
E-mail: info@cpsc.gov
Web Site: http://www.cpsc.gov/

Consumer Information Center
U.S. General Services Administration
Washington, DC 20405
Phone: 202-501-1794
Fax: 202-501-4281
E mail: catalog.pueblo@gsa.gov
Web Site: http://www.pueblo.gsa.gov

Friends of the Earth
1025 Vermont Ave. NW, 3rd Floor
Washington, DC 20005
Phone: 202-783-7400
Fax: 202-783-8944
E-mail: FOE@foe.org
Web Site: http://www.foe.org/

Indoor Air Quality Information
Clearinghouse Hotline
1-800-438-4318
Fax: 202-484-1510
For more information write:
Indoor Air Quality
PO Box 37133
Washington, DC 20013-7133

Industry and Manufacture

American Chemical Society
1155 16th Street, NW
Washington, DC 20036
Phone: 202-872-4600
Fax: 202-872-4615
E-mail: webmaster@acs.org
Web Site: http://www.acs.org/

Auro Organic Paints
Sinan Natural Building Materials
Davis, CA 95617-0857
Phone: 916-753-3104
Web Site:
http://www.dcn.davis.ca.us/~sinan/auroinfo
.html

Toys

Toy Manufacturers of America Inc.
200 5th Avenue, Suite 740
New York, NY 10010
Phone: 212-675-3535
Fax: 212-633-1429

U.S. Toy Library Association
2530 Crawford Avenue, Suite 111
Evanston, IL 60201-4954
Phone: 847-864-3330
Fax: 847-864-3331
E-mail: FolioG@aol.com

Index

THE CINEMA 4D R8 HANDBOOK

THE CINEMA 4D R8 HANDBOOK

ADAM WATKINS

CHARLES RIVER MEDIA, INC.

Hingham, Massachusetts

Publisher: Jenifer Niles
Production: Publishers' Design and Production Services, Inc.
Cover Design: The Printed Image
Cover Image: Adam Watkins

CHARLES RIVER MEDIA, INC.
10 Downer Avenue
Hingham, Massachusetts 02043
781-740-0400
781-740-8816 (FAX)
info@charlesriver.com
www.charlesriver.com

This book is printed on acid-free paper.

Adam Watkins. *The Cinema 4D R8 Handbook*.
ISBN: 1-58450-216-9

Library of Congress Cataloging-in-Publication Data

Watkins, Adam.
   The Cinema 4D R8 handbook / Adam Watkins.— 2nd ed.
      p. cm.
   ISBN 1-58450-216-9 (pbk. w/ CD-ROM : alk. paper)
   1. Computer graphics.   2. Computer animation.   3. Three-dimensional
display systems.   4. Cinema 4D XL.   I. Title.
   T385.W37627 2003
   006.6'96—dc21
                          2003009112
Printed in the United States of America
03 7 6 5 4 3 2 First Edition

CHARLES RIVER MEDIA titles are available for site license or bulk purchase by institutions, user groups, corporations, etc. For additional information, please contact the Special Sales Department at 781-740-0400.

Requests for replacement of a defective CD-ROM must be accompanied by the original disc, your mailing address, telephone number, date of purchase and purchase price. Please state the nature of the problem, and send the information to CHARLES RIVER MEDIA, INC., 10 Downer Avenue, Hingham, Massachusetts 02043. CRM's sole obligation to the purchaser is to replace the disc, based on defective materials or faulty workmanship, but not on the operation or functionality of the product.

To my partner in crime, my walking companion,
my hot Friday night date, my best friend, my wife, Kirsten.

CONTENTS

CHAPTER 5 **UTILIZING THE POWER OF HYPERNURBS: MODELING ORGANIC FORMS FROM PRIMITIVES**   **147**

CHAPTER 6 **MATERIALS & TEXTURES**   **217**

PREFACE

WHY THIS BOOK?

With any software package, there are a number of benefits that arise from a fresh perspective on the tool and its uses. Maxon's Cinema 4D XL R8 is no exception. Despite its overall ease of use, C4D is also an incredibly powerful and diverse package. As such, its uses—and the methods of using it—are diverse. Not that any one method is the "right" way; in fact the flexibility of being able to achieve powerful projects in a variety of ways is part of the strength of C4D.

Exploring these paths is the primary function of this book. Included with your copy of C4D software is a set of manuals that provide a useful reference filled with definitions of all the tools. These manuals are great to have, and this book is not intended to replace the manuals. Instead, the book provides hands-on methods for analyzing the functions of C4D's many tools. The book takes a project-based approach that allows you to create impressive projects as you learn C4D's array of tools and functions

WHAT'S NEW?

Cinema 4D R8 is a major upgrade. There are updates to workflow, modeling tools, interface design, material construction, animation, character animation tools, and rendering. This multitude of new functions can be dizzying to get through. Some new functions are close to the old way of doing things, but just different enough to be confusing. This volume works with most of the new tools within C4D including:

- HyperNURBS Weighting
- Material Illumination construction for Radiosity functions

- HDRI (High-Dynamic Range Image) capabilities in materials and rendering
- The new Timeline with its new use of tracks and sequences
- The brand new F-Curve
- MOCCA (Character animation)
- Radiosity, GI (Global Illumination) and other hyper-realistic capabilities
- FlashEx (exporting your 3D to flash)
- Xpresso (the new visual expression creator)
- Many other updates and comparisons to old versions

Although there are far too many function and tools in C4D to cover all of them in this book, the core concepts are all here. All of the major tools for creating great 3D are covered to allow you to produce great work.

WHAT IS COVERED

In this book, all of the major areas of C4D and its uses are covered. Some light is also shed on many of the little understood and under-explored corners of the program. Beginning with the general tools and tool layout, you learn how to customize these tools so that you can create a work environment conducive to your workflow. However, it's important to note, this book doesn't attempt to cover every nook and cranny of this truly diverse package. There just isn't enough space to truly get to every part of the program; however, great care has been taken to explore nearly all of the most powerful and frequently used aspects.

Next, standard C4D workflow is covered; where to start, how to start, and when to finish. Then the real fun begins—the modeling tools within C4D. Modeling is covered, from primitive methods and NURBS, to object creation, polygon creation, and NURBS editing. Manufacturing modeling techniques and methods to model human forms are covered in detail along with the various other modeling methods (there are nearly as many modeling methods as there are 3D artists). Often a specific method really "clicks" with certain people, so with that in mind, some of the best modelers were invited to contribute a tutorial or two on their modeling paradigm. Thus, not only do we cover the modeling tools, but we analyze a variety of ways to use them, giving you a wide scope of potential methods to try and perfect.

After creating the shapes of our dreams, we put C4D's powerful texture capabilities to work. How do they work? When should they be used? What sorts of effects can be created with simple textures? How can we optimize textures to aid in quick renderings? Everything from creating textures from scratch, stylizing textures, and creating photorealistic textures, to using textures to denote geometry, and utilizing third-party textures to create truly dazzling effects is covered. We'll also look at the possibilities of procedural and bitmapped textures. Next, we'll learn how to create maps from photos or from scratch, and investigate mapping textures to surfaces and how to make them stick. In all, everything needed to take control over the look of your projects is covered.

After creating and texturing objects and projects, the all-important issues of cinematography and how to control the camera within C4D are explored. Stylized, realistic camera movement is covered as we review the tools included in C4D's camera capabilities. In the same chapter, we'll take a very careful look at the too often ignored areas of lighting and lighting theory by using lessons from the areas of photography and theatre. There is even a special section on the important role of lighting in creating photo-realistic or stylized scenes.

Moving along, we'll get into the complex and powerful animation tools contained in C4D. This section covers the timeline, space curves, tangents, and Beziers. C4D R8 has new improved tools to utilize within the timeline, so we'll explore how to use these tools and also look at when, where, and why to use them. How to organize projects is also explained, as this can make the difference between a project nightmare and an enjoyable experience.

Also included is an extensive section on character animation. C4D is not often recognized as a character animation powerhouse but with the new tools present in C4D v6, the possibilities have skyrocketed. In this section, we'll delve deeply into bones and the theory of movement, and explore how forward and inverse kinematics function, how to set FK and IK chains up, and how to use them to create a desired motion.

Toward the end of the book, we'll look at areas that truly lift C4D above the level of a mere 3D animation package: creating custom expressions, and analyzing ways to program small scripts to optimize and streamline the creation process. Through XPresso tutorials, you'll learn how to change the simple Graphic User Interface (GUI) of C4D into an under-the-hood custom-built power machine.

WHAT IS IN IT FOR YOU?

This book is best for beginners. It reviews all of the tools within C4D and explains how best to use them. Through intensive tutorials, you will learn ideas and techniques not covered in the manuals. You'll also learn about the theory and why things work the way they do—not so you can write your own 3D application, but because if you understand the theory behind the tool, you can better utilize the ideas within the tool.

This book is also great for intermediate users. There are lots of folks out there who have been using C4D for a while now. You have probably already gone through the tutorials contained within the manuals and have a fairly good grasp on how the tools work. This book will put new spins on the same tools, giving you a chance to see how the tools are used in ways you may not have tried. The tutorials in the latter half of the book are intense enough that they provide an excellent learning challenge if you have not mastered complex 3D ideas like modeling and animating human form. Especially if you have been using earlier versions of C4D, this volume will get you quickly up to speed with the new tools and functions.

Additionally, this book is great for advanced users. Those of you who are C4D experts and have delved deeply into the depths of digital domains will still find excellent information here. Have you ever thought it would be great if C4D just had a tool that would allow you to do *x*? Well, included here are tutorials by the programming wonder Donovan Keith and chapters on writing your own expressions with Xpresso as well as some in-depth analysis of making your own plug-ins. Even if you are not interested in programming as an advanced user, you can find out about some of the tricks various artists throughout the world have tweaked and mastered. And if you are comfortable and effective in C4D, hopefully, this volume will provide some further enhancing techniques. As an extra-special treat for advanced users, Naam (one of the true masters of C4D and co-creator of such C4D classics as the mime, and "The Joust") creates a pair of fantastic tutorials to share his expertise in character animation and show you how to use the new MOCCA toolset.

So young or old, novice or experienced, amateur or professional; enjoy this book. Hopefully it will provide you with tools, techniques, and tricks that will increase your C4D productivity and workflow.

ACKNOWLEDGMENTS

As always, thanks to Jenifer Niles for her opportunities, encouragement, and patience.

Thanks to my students at the University of the Incarnate Word (*www.cgauiw.com*). Your thoughtful questions keep me learning and moving forward.

Special thanks to Richard Clark for his great designs.

Thanks to Mom and Dad. Come play more—I have the time now!

Extra special thanks to Fish and Goose. My sanity depends on you two.

INTERFACE

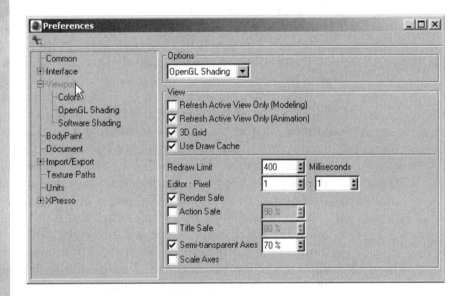

nterestingly enough, the interface of Cinema 4D R8 has a subjective mode to it. Completely customizable, the interface can be modified and optimized to fit you and your style of working. Before we learn how to customize the interface, let's look first at how the default interface is organized.

Upon opening C4D, you are presented with an interface that incorporates all major areas of the 3D creation process: modeling, texturing, lighting, cinematography, animation, and rendering.

THE MAIN WINDOW

Cinema 4D has a powerful collection of tools organized in a fairly intuitive format for general use. In this chapter, rather than go through the entire list of tools, we will look at groups of tools. The focus is on how tools are organized rather than on how they work. Later, we'll look at how each tool works in the context of a tutorial to learn both the practical and theoretical applications of the tools in C4D.

The C4D interface, or *Main window* (Figure 1.1), is organized into command palettes on three sides (top, left, and bottom) containing clusters of tools. These command palettes live most happily on a screen that is running at least 1024x768. However, if you have a smaller screen, you can still get to all the tools on a given palette. If you move your mouse up to the divider line separating palettes that contain tools out of the range of your screen, your mouse pointer will change to a small white pan hand (Figure 1.2). Click and drag (click-drag) to the left and right (for command palettes along the top) or up and down (for command palettes along the side) to scroll through the tools visible in the palettes. These visible tools also are completely customizable, but more on this later.

Managers

The command palettes surround the view panels and several *managers*. Managers are actually windows that represent program elements within C4D. Each of these separate managers is actually parallel to the other managers running at the same time. Thus, each manager can run independently, yet the changes made in one manager are quickly transferred to the other managers running at the same time. There are actually quite a few managers within C4D; so many in fact, that there is simply not enough room to display all

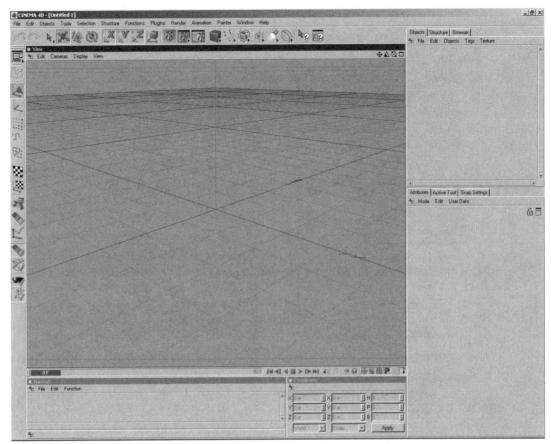

FIGURE 1.1   C4D Main window.

FIGURE 1.2   Pan hand.

of them at once. As a result, some of them are placed *beneath* other managers (Figure 1.3a and b). These "buried" managers can be easily accessed by simply clicking on the corresponding tab. When a tab is clicked, that manager is brought to the foreground. There are even some managers that aren't seen at all in the default main window—but more on these a little later.

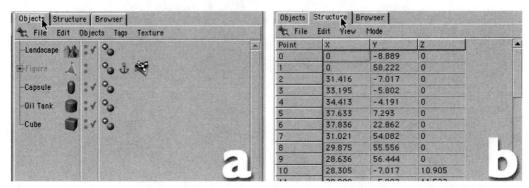

FIGURE 1.3   To conserve space, some managers are nested. (a) In this case, the Objects Manager is visible while the Structure Manager and Browser Manager are nested beneath. By clicking on one of the tabs of nested managers, that manager is then brought to the front (b).

Customizing Manager Size and Location

The managers share screen space with the view panel and the command palettes. The location and size of the managers is customizable. By moving your mouse to the edge of a manager (Figure 1.4), you can resize the manager to fit your needs. In some cases, you may want to make it smaller (e.g., if you need more space for the view panels), while at other times you'll need more space for the manager (e.g, if many tags are attached to objects within the Objects Manager). When the mouse pointer is over the edge of a manager, the pointer changes to a double arrow, indicating that C4D is ready to resize a window. Click-drag the double arrow, and you can resize the window within certain parameters.

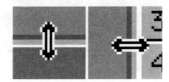

FIGURE 1.4   Resizing windows arrows; these allow you to give more screen space to a given manager or window.

The windows and managers within the interface are said to be *docked*. Notice that in the corner of the view panels and the various managers is a small Pin icon. This represents that this window (or manager) is temporarily pinned (or docked) at this location in the interface. If you don't like having it there, simply click on the Pin icon and drag the window to a more appropriate location. As you drag, you'll notice that a dark line appears near to your mouse pointer, indicating possible new locations to dock the window you are moving. Remember that by moving windows around in this way, you still maintain one monolithic overall windowed interface where you don't have any floating windows or palettes and everything is nested into its own spot.

Undocking Manager Windows

If you prefer to work with multiple floating windows (similar to those found in previous versions of C4D), you can *undock* windows or managers so that they float along the top of your interface. To do this, click and release the Pin icon and select Undock from the resultant pull-down menu (Figure 1.5). The result will be a new window that appears separate from the main interface.

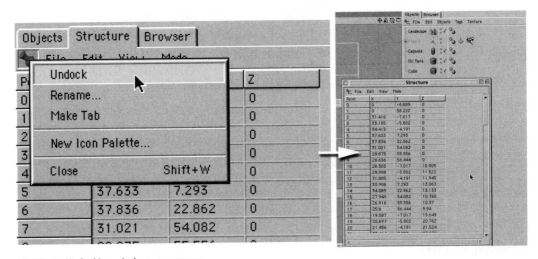

FIGURE 1.5 Undocking window or manager.

There are several important things to remember about undocking. First, after a window is undocked it can always be "docked" again. To do this, simply click-drag the Pin icon on the now undocked window to the new location where you wish to dock it. (A dark line will appear indicating the locations at which it can be docked.) When the window is redocked, the windows around it will resize to fit. Note that you can also dock directly to a group of managers represented by tabs. When you are click-dragging the Pin icon, simply move your mouse pointer over the Pin icon of a manager grouped with others in tabs. Your mouse pointer will change to a pointing hand. Upon mouse release, the window will be docked and tabbed in the group you have selected.

While we're at it, let's look at the other options that are part of the Pin pull-down menu.

- **Rename**—Self-explanatory method of renaming a manager if you so desire.
- **Make Tab**—When a manager is undocked, you can add other windows to the floating window. You can choose to tab this manager from the beginning.
- **New Icon Palette**—Using this tool, you can create a new floating window (which can be docked later) that contains a custom set of tools. To actually place tools in this new palette, you must use the Command Manager, which we'll look at later in this chapter.
- **New Group Window**—The term "group" as used here refers to more than one manager that shares a window. As we discussed earlier, you can swap between managers through tabs at the top of the *Group Window*. Creating a new Group Window allows you a new space to place multiple managers.
- **Close**—Closes the window or manager.

Depending on your working style, the managers you want available and prevalent will differ greatly. Some artists work with two monitors and have managers open everywhere because they have enough room. Other artists working with more restricted space may choose to group into tabs a large group of their managers, or even to hide some completely.

COMMAND PALETTES

In C4D, the pull-down menus are said to contain *commands*. Each of these commands performs different functions that allow you to work in and manipulate the digital 3D space. Along the top and left side of the default C4D interface are *command palettes* (Figure 1.6) These palettes are set up to allow you to reach often-used commands quickly.

FIGURE 1.6   Command palettes in default interface.

We won't look at what the default command palettes contain, because we'll be looking at all the tools over the course of the book. At this point, we will look at how to organize, alter, add, and subtract commands from the command palettes. This information fits well into the scope of this chapter but may be unclear to you this early in the reading. After you have read further chapters and have found a working pace and style that you like, you may wish to come back to this chapter to learn how to customize your workspace to accommodate your workflow.

Docking and Undocking Command Palettes

The command palettes that C4D has set up by default are docked within the interface. Like windows and managers, command palettes can be either docked or undocked. To undock a palette, simply right-click (COMMAND-click on a Mac) and select Undock.

Once these command palettes are undocked, you may dock them again. To do this, grab the command palette by clicking on the double line at the top of a vertical palette or the left end of a horizontal palette (Figure 1.7a) and drag it to where you wish it docked (Figure 1.7b). Similar to docking managers, a heavy black line will appear, indicating the possible docking positions as you near one (Figure 1.7c).

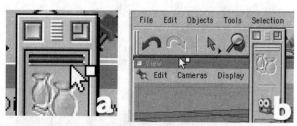

FIGURE 1.7   (a) "Docking handle" for vertical palettes. (b) Dark lines indicate potential docking locations. (c) The result of the redocked command palette.

Creating Command Palettes from Scratch

By default, there is only so much room available for the default command palettes. C4D seems to assume that you have a monitor that displays at least 1024x768. At that resolution, all the default command palettes are completely visible. However, you may have a bigger monitor or two monitors and would like to create additional palettes that contain your most-often-used commands or commands that aren't available by default. There are three ways to create a new command palette:

- Select Window>Layout>New Icon Palette
- In any extant command palette or manager, click on the Pin icon and select New Icon Palette from the resultant pull-down menu
- Right-mouse click (COMMAND-click on a single-button Mac mouse) anywhere within an extant palette and select New Icon Palette from the menu.

Adding Commands to Command Palettes

Notice that this new command palette is undocked and empty. To add commands to this palette, you must first activate the *Command Manager*. Click the Edit Palettes option at the top of the Command Manager to edit extant palettes. When this is selected, a big change comes over your interface. The Command Manager appears in the foreground and all the existing commands in existing command palettes are surrounded with blue boxes (Figure 1.8). C4D is letting you know it's ready to move tools.

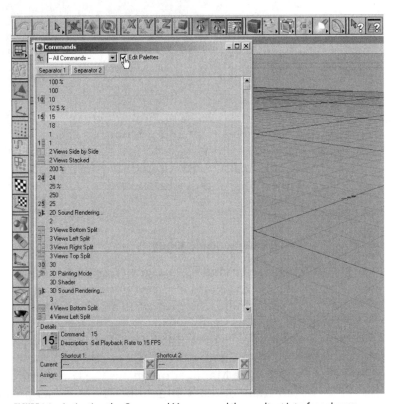

FIGURE 1.8   Activating the Command Manager and the resultant interface change.

Now, you can grab command icons from existing command palettes and place them into the new palette. When you attempt to place commands in a new command palette, note that the location to which you click-drag the command palette is very important. In the empty palette, the words "Empty Palette" appear within a sunken region (Figure 1.9). When you move new commands into this palette, the commands must be dropped within this sunken region. Trying to place them anywhere else will result in your mouse being substituted by the forbidden symbol. After the first command is placed within a new palette, subsequent commands can just be dropped next to existing commands.

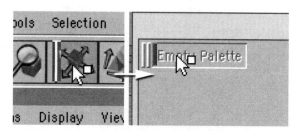

FIGURE 1.9 The "hot" drop zone of new command palettes.

There is another way to invoke the Command Manager: select Window>Command Manager. When the Command Manager emerges this way, note that the command palettes aren't automatically ready to be altered. If you use this method, you must click the Edit Palettes button at the top right corner of the Command Manager.

The Command Manager

The Command Manager is an incredibly versatile and powerful tool. We've already seen how, by activating it, we are able to shift commands. However, it is also important to note that within the Command Manager can be found a large list of commands that may not even be listed in existing command palettes. The Command Manager actually contains all the commands available in C4D. The Manager organizes the commands within C4D according to their primary function. There exists an embedded pop-down menu next to the Pin icon that allows you to display groups of commands. This includes the choice All Commands. No matter what groups of commands the Command Manager is displaying, you can add a command to any command palette. To do so, make sure that Edit Palettes is activated, and then simply click-drag the command from the Command Manager to the command palette of choice. Again, a dark line will indicate where C4D is planning to place the new command.

Additional Command Manager Capabilities

The Command Manager also provides the capability to alter keyboard shortcuts for any given command. When a command is clicked within the Command Manager, it will appear in the bottom section of the Command Manager, the Details section. If the command has a keyboard shortcut assigned to it, the shortcut will appear here under the Current input field (Figure 1.10a). If you wish to change the keyboard shortcut for the command, click the "x" button next to the shortcut and it will be erased (Figure 1.10b).

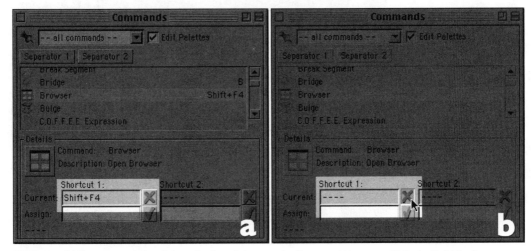

FIGURE 1.10   (a) If a command already has a keyboard shortcut, the Command Manager will display it. (b) Erasing assigned keyboard shortcuts.

To assign a keyboard shortcut, click in the Assign input field. You can now enter any keystroke or combination of keystrokes that will appear in the Current input field (Figure 1.11a). If this keystroke already is assigned to another command, you will be alerted immediately below the input field with an error message that tells you what the conflicting command is (Figure 1.11b). If you still wish to use that key combination for your tool rather than the default setting, first make sure that you erase it from the default command. To change the keyboard shortcut to something else, click again in the Assign input field and enter a new keystroke. When you are happy with the keyboard shortcut you have entered, click the green checkmark button next to the input field (Figure 1.11c). The keystroke will then appear in the Current input field.

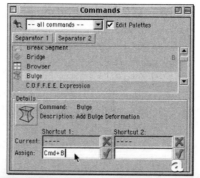

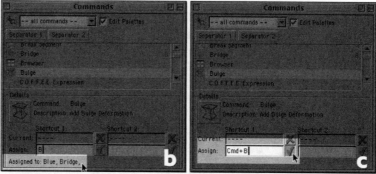

FIGURE 1.11   (a) To add a keyboard shortcut, select the Assign input field and enter the keystroke or combination of keystrokes you wish to assign. (b) Error indicating offending conflict of keyboard shortcuts. (c) Checkmark indicating you want C4D to remember the new keyboard shortcut assigned to a command.

Notice that there are two sets of input fields within the Details section. You can enter more than one set of keystrokes for any one command. Also note that when a new keyboard shortcut has been assigned, it not only shows up in the Current input field, it also shows up within the Command Manager above and in the pull-down menus of the general C4D interface (Figure 1.12). This is a perfect example of how C4D's managers are intertwined.

C4D only allows certain combinations of keystrokes to be short-cuts. These combinations include a single key, CTRL-key, SHIFT-key, and CTRL-SHIFT-key. There are also certain default keys (for example, "1" for the Camera Move tool). These default keyboard shortcuts are called C4D's *hotkeys*. Hotkeys are very powerful in their flexibility (they override all other tools that may be active). However, these hotkeys are off-limits to any other keyboard short-cut. It is also important to note that the manual suggests strongly that you not attempt to assign a shortcut that is typically used

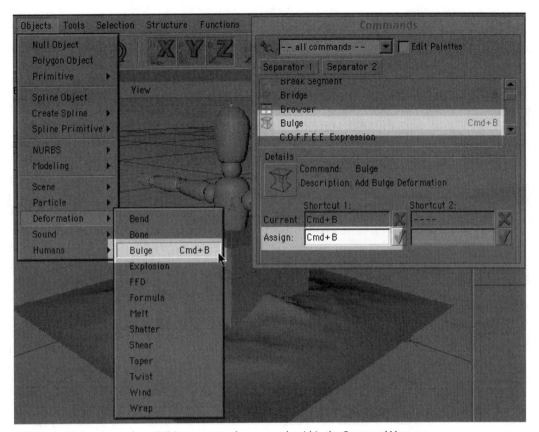

FIGURE 1.12   All the places where C4D incorporates changes made within the Command Manager.

by your operating system (e.g., CTRL-ALT-DELETE on a PC or OPTION-COMMAND-ESC on a Mac).

Back to the Command Palettes

Within your newly created palette, there is a slew of further customization that can be done. Right-mouse click (COMMAND-click) within any of the commands in the command palette and you'll be given a new pull-down collection of functions to optimize the look and function of the palette. These options include ways to fold or unfold commands (make nested groups of commands), make your commands appear as simple text, make your commands appear as text and icons, make your commands appear in rows or columns, change the number of rows or columns, delete commands, and change the size of the icons within the palette.

Because these are effectively described in the manual, we won't repeat them here.

Menu Manager

Besides being able to alter the command palettes, C4D allows you to even alter the pull-down menu's organization of commands. This allows you to create new menus and submenus. The *Menu Manager* works in much the same way as the Command Manager. With simple drag-and-drop methods you can move commands from one manager to another. Pull-down menus are the least efficient way of accessing commands, so we won't spend much time here discussing how to alter the extant menus. It is strongly suggested that you organize your most-used tools into appropriate command palettes and assign good, easy-to-remember keystrokes.

Saving a Custom Layout

So what happens when you have adjusted your layout just the way you want it? You want to be sure that you are able to access this same layout the next time you open C4D. You might also want to create a variety of layouts for different parts of your work process—one for modeling, one for animation, etc.... To save a custom layout that you have created, go to Window>Layout>Save Layout As.... This will allow you to save a layout file that you can call up at will. Similarly, you can use Window>Layout>Save as Default Layout to make your custom layout the layout that always is called up when you launch C4D.

C4D's Built-in Custom Layouts

In recognition of the large number of tools available, but not visible, in C4D, R8 includes several pre-built custom layouts. At the top of the left side, Command Palette is a new button (new to R8) that allows you to pick one of six custom layouts (Figure 1.13).

Preferences

There is one other location within C4D that allows for further customization of the interface's look and feel. This is within the Preferences dialog box. (In v7, this was called the General Settings.) To

FIGURE 1.13 You can access one of
several different pre-build layouts.

access the Preferences dialog, go to Edit>Preferences or use the keyboard shortcut of CTRL-E (COMMAND-E on a Mac). Most of the available settings within this dialog box are beyond what we need to alter, and this area is covered extensively in the manual. However, there are a few areas of import that we should look at.

When Preferences is first selected, you are given a dialog box with several areas listed to the left. The number of editable areas will vary depending on which modules you have in R8 (Figure 1.14). Of particular note are the Interface and Viewport sections.

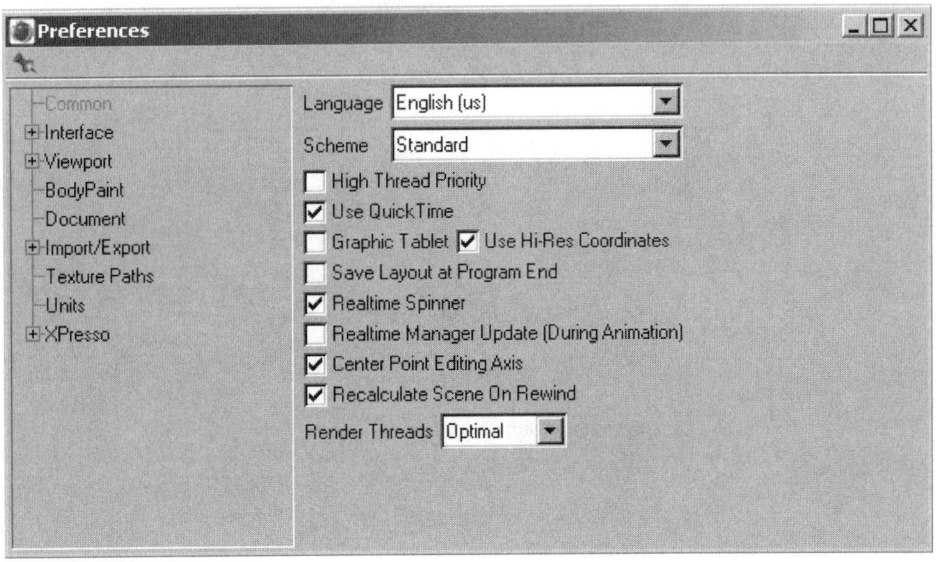

FIGURE 1.14 Preferences dialog box.

Interface

The Interface section and the Colors subsection allow you to make some changes to how the interface acts and looks. This is mostly a subjective matter, so we won't talk too much about it here; but if you don't like gray, for example, or you are working on a Mac when you are used to using a PC, you can come here and make it all change.

Viewport

Expanding the Viewport section provides some very useful tools. Just clicking the word Viewport will bring up a collection of options. Clicking the little cross next to Viewport will expand it to show other subsections that allow you to further work with your Viewports. Within the Viewport section you will find a collection of options that allow you to customize what sorts of visual interactivity and guides are included in your interface (Figure 1.15).

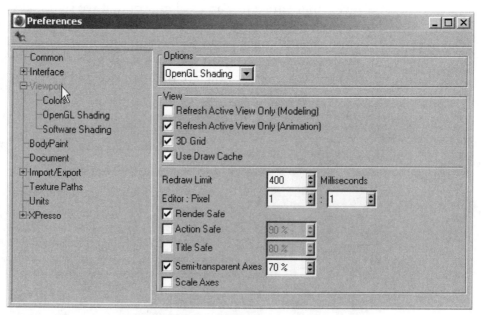

FIGURE 1.15   Viewport options within the Preferences dialog box.

Options

Perhaps the most important component of the Options section to be able to alter is the first one. By default, this is set to Software Shading. This means that C4D is using its software to show you the 3D world you are working in. Although this method is faster than most other software solutions, it really ignores a powerful part of your hardware—the video card. If you have any video card with 16mb of video memory or more, change this to OpenGL shading (more on this later).

Refresh Active View Only

When you have toggled views to more than one view panel, you can move an object in one view panel and instantly see it moved in the other view panels. This is because the Refresh Active View Only option is turned off by default. In most cases, it's important to be able to see how things are being positioned, rotated, and scaled within other views. However, when your projects get very large, this extra effort of drawing the changes immediately in four windows instead of one can contribute to a significant slowdown in your interface speed. If Refresh Active View Only is selected (as you may need to do with big scenes), C4D will wait to redraw the other view panels until after you have finished whatever function you are performing in the active window.

Render Safe

The Render Safe guides will never render, but they can help you in your workflow as you deal with issues of staging, framing, and virtual cinematography. What you see in the Editor or a view panel is not necessarily what will be seen in your final rendering. You may have your view panels set up to display very long or very tall windows. With Render Safe activated, you will be given some gray lines defining what will actually be shown when you render to the Picture Viewer (Figure 1.16).

Action Safe, Title Safe

What you see on a computer screen often is not what is seen on a television screen. TV screens often expand an image slightly and cut off the outside edge. By selecting the Action and/or Title Safe buttons, C4D will provide guides within the view panel to indicate the areas that you can be sure will be seen on a TV screen. See the Cinematography chapter (Chapter 14—Lighting and Camera Tools) for more information about these settings and their valuable uses.

FIGURE 1.16   Render, Action, and Title Safe guides.

Scale Axis, Semi-Transparent Axis

Scale Axis and Semi-Transparent Axis options will make much more sense when we begin modeling; however, suffice it to say that each object is displayed with a set of axes. These axes help you move an object along a given axis, and allow you to know how the object is oriented in digital space. With these two options, you can choose how the axes of objects are displayed when the object is selected, or when you are zooming in closer or further away from the object.

OpenGL

Once you have selected OpenGL shading in the Options drop-down menu of the Viewport section, you can alter the OpenGL settings. OpenGL is a technology that has been developed specifically to assist in quick rendering of 3D worlds. It is used heavily in games and can be of great benefit in 3D animation. OpenGL is hardware driven (driven by the video card), and is much faster than the software-driven alternative. Most upper-end computers have video cards that utilize hardware-driven OpenGL acceleration. If you are lucky enough to have significant hardware acceleration, the rest of the settings can assist in defining how you wish to use the extra horse-power. You'll need to read carefully the information included with your hardware to see if it actually supports the options listed in the OpenGL section of the Views tab.

View Panel

The space that takes up the most visual real estate is the large view panel (Figure 1.17). This view panel is your window into the digital world. Objects that you model will appear within this space. A good way to think of this window is the viewfinder of a camera that allows you to view objects and their relationships to other objects. As with an ordinary camera, there are several ways to adjust how this camera works.

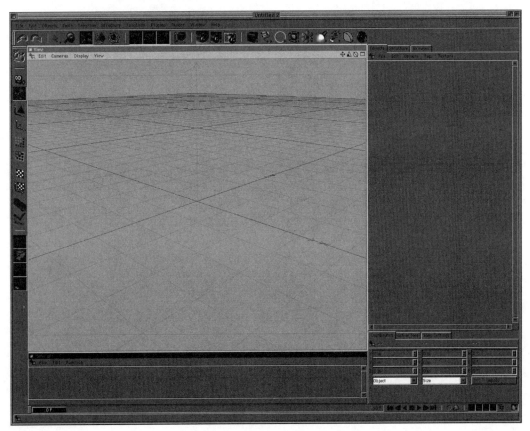

FIGURE 1.17   View panel window.

Remember those early math classes where you were given series of *coordinates* to allow you to plot points in a graph where *x* represented the horizontal and *y* represented the vertical? Well, a computer thinks of digital space in much the same way. However, since we are dealing in 3D, there are more than just two directions.

Using the *Euclidean Geometry Model,* the computer keeps track of digital space along three axis: the *x*-axis (horizontal), the *y*-axis (vertical), and the *z*-axis (depth). Therefore, the computer thinks of an object's location as a defined point within these three axes. This is an important thing to remember as we begin looking at maneuvering within the space and moving objects within the view panels. Whenever you start up C4D or open a new document, you'll see a guide in the middle of your view panel defining these three axes (Figure 1.18).

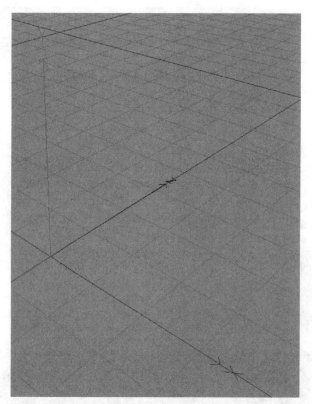

FIGURE 1.18   Axis-defining symbol present with new files.

Notice that the view panel has its own collection of pull-down menus as well as a set of four tools within the upper-right corner (Figure 1.19a). These four tools are important. They allow you (the camera person) to control where the virtual camera is, where it is pointing, and what "lens" you are using (Figure 1.19a).

These four tools function a bit differently from any other tools in C4D. For most tools in C4D, you select or activate the tool and then work with it within the view panels. However, to use these four tools, you must click-drag on the tool symbol itself.

The first of these four tools (Figure 1.19b), which looks like a cross with arrows on it, allows you to move the camera. Click-drag on that symbol and the camera will move up and down and right to left. Try it.

By simply click-dragging on this Camera Move tool, you are able to move in two directions—x and y, or up and down. If you are on a Mac, hold down the COMMAND button and click-drag on this tool and you will move the camera closer or further away. On a PC, CTRL-click-drag or right mouse-click-drag to get the same effect. By holding the "1" key down on your keyboard, you can also use this tool without having to click on the tool symbol. In other words, "1" is the keyboard shortcut for the Camera Move tool. When you hold the "1" down, the same rules apply—click-dragging moves the virtual camera up and down, and CTRL-click or right-click (COMMAND-click on a Mac) moves the camera in or out. Remember that this is always the tool to use when you wish to physically move the virtual camera you are looking through.

The second tool shown there is often misunderstood (Figure 1.19c). It's often referred to as the Camera Scale tool. This name is misleading; the tool is strictly a lens-zoom tool. Using this tool changes the focal length of the virtual lens. It does not actually move the camera any closer or further away from the object. The keyboard shortcut for this tool is "2."

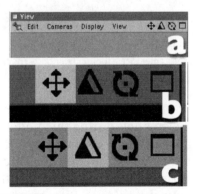

FIGURE 1.19   (a) View panel pull-down menus and tools. (b) Camera Move tool. (c) Camera Scale tool.

Below is an example of this. Figure 1.20a shows a cube at the default camera setting. Figure 1.20b shows the same cube when the Camera Scale tool has been click-dragged to the left. To get this kind of effect in the real world you would need a very short focal length, giving you a "fisheye" view in which the ideas of perspective are amplified and overexaggerated.

Conversely, Figure 1.20c shows the same cube with an extremely long focal length. To do this, the Camera Scale tool was click-dragged to the right. This is analogous to using an extreme telephoto lens. The result is an image with shallow, nearly nonexistent perspective.

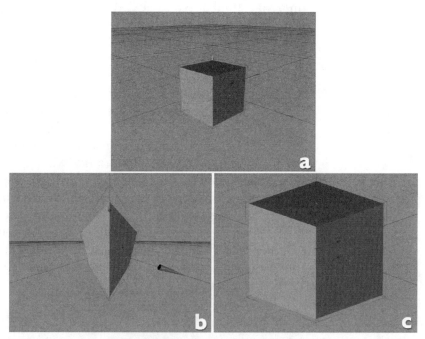

FIGURE 1.20   (a) Cube at default setting. (b) Fisheye result of very short focal length from using the Camera Scale tool. (c) Telephoto lens effect of using Camera Scale tool.

The secret here is to remember that when you work within the view panels during the modeling or animation process, you'll probably want to use a right-click-Camera Move tool (COMMAND-click-Camera Move tool on a Mac) to actually move the camera closer to your model, rather than the Camera Scale tool to change your style of lens. By moving the camera closer, you can maintain a constant focal length and work more accurately.

The next tool is called the Rotate Camera tool (Figure 1.21a). As the name implies, this tool allows you to rotate the camera around a given point. This "given point" is usually the center of whatever object is selected. When a new file is opened and an object does not exist, the camera stays focused on the (0,0,0) point, or the center of the digital universe.

This tool is accessible using the "3" key on your keyboard. Remember, this key must be held as you click-drag within the view panel. The Camera Rotate tool by default rotates the camera while it keeps the camera upright. However, by right-clicking (or COMMAND-clicking on a Mac) when you use this tool, you can give your virtual camera a "Dutch tilt" (Figure 1.21b).

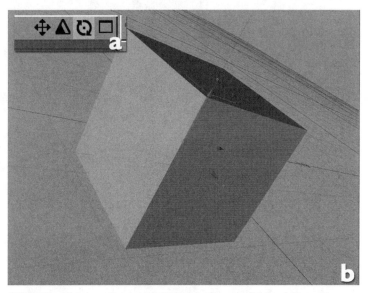

FIGURE 1.21   (a) Camera Rotate tool. (b) Dutch-tilt result of right-clicking with Camera Rotate tool.

The rightmost tool within the view panel is called the Toggle Active View tool (Figure 1.22a).

The default view that you get when you open a new document in C4D is one large view panel through which you are able to see the virtual world in perspective. Perspective is how our minds comprehend three-dimensional space on a two-dimensional plane. Real cameras capture reality in perspective and artists usually use perspective to portray reality in their works. However, this is not the only way to display the virtual digital space.

When the Toggle Active View tool is selected, the single view panel is suddenly divided into four panels that show the same space through four different cameras. This state of four views is called the *All-Views mode*. (Figure 1.22b).

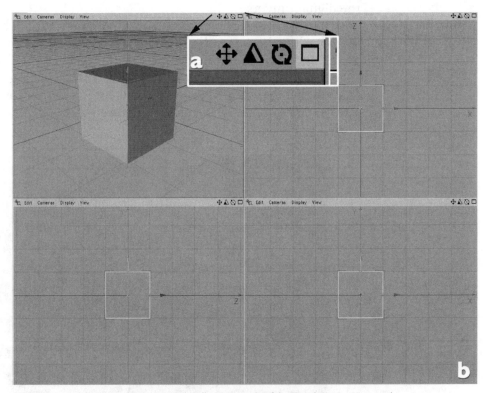

FIGURE 1.22   (a) Toggle Active View tool. (b) All-Views mode of the Toggle Active View tool.

Note that while you are in All-Views mode, each view panel has its own set of camera control tools and pull-down menus. Within each of these four view panels, you can use the Camera Move, Camera Scale, and Camera Rotate tools to move the camera through which you are viewing the scene in that view panel around. Note also that each view panel has its own Toggle Active View tool which, when it is clicked, expands that view to be the only view panel visible.

With any newly expanded view panel, you can again toggle back to All-Views mode by clicking the Toggle Active View tool (the keyboard shortcuts are PageUp and PageDown).

While you are in All-Views mode, only one view is "active" at a time. The other view panels will still refresh; however, when you do test renderings it's important to know which view panel is active. A view panel is active when you can see a thin blue line around it (Figure 1.23). Whenever you click inside a view panel or click along the upper area of the view panel (where the pull-down menus appear), you are activating that view panel. In essence, you are telling C4D that you are writing in this window.

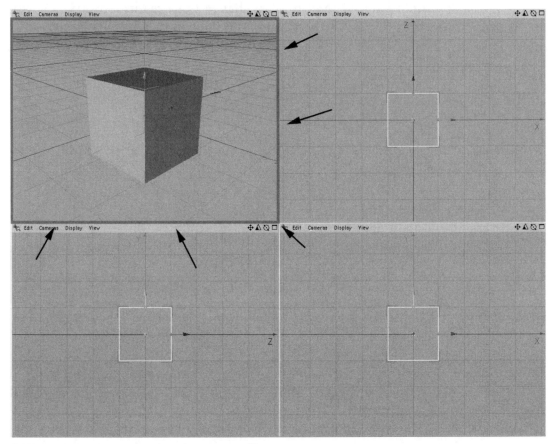

FIGURE 1.23   Active view panel, as shown by exaggerated line.

Finally, note that at the bottom left hand corner of the interface is an area that little bits of text flash up in. This is a real aid when you are first starting to use C4D as it helps you remember what the names are of tools within command palettes. As you move your mouse over any tool, the name of the tool or command will appear in this area. In the tutorials in this book, if you are having a hard time remembering which tool is being called for when it is called by name, be sure to take a look at this helpful area.

CONCLUSION

Now that we know how C4D is laid out and how its general tools are organized (and how to change this organization if we wish), let's look at how to make things happen in this newly understood view panel.

BEGINNING MODELING

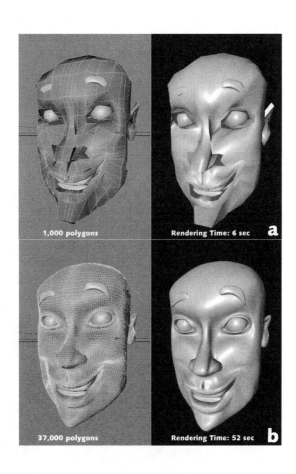

1,000 polygons

Rendering Time: 6 sec **a**

37,000 polygons

Rendering Time: 52 sec **b**

We've already looked at ways to manipulate our view in the 3D world. We've looked at perspective views and how to view the 3D world in the flat, non-interpretive formats of top, right, and front views, using forms of parallel projection. Now that we know how to look at the world, it's time to look at how to create within it.

3D is technically heavy and challenging. It also includes quite a bit of theory that is necessary to understand. Because of this, the first section of this chapter is dedicated to covering some of the basic ideas behind 3D object construction. Don't become discouraged as you read through the ethereal, abstract theory analysis, however. The second section of the chapter looks in-depth at how to realize the theory covered. The last part of the chapter takes all the theory, all the elementary how-to, and combines them to actually create.

3D Construction Theory

The most basic building block of 3D objects is the *point*. A point is analogous to the atom of our world. A point in 3D is visible in the Editor environment, yet it never renders (Figure 2.1). When a

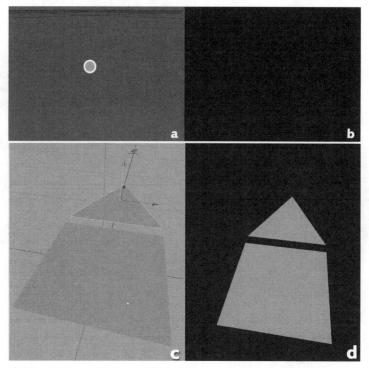

FIGURE 2.1   Point in (a) Editor and (b) Renderer. (c) Polygons can be three- or four-sided, and (d) visible in the Renderer.

group of three or four points are joined together, they are united by an edge. When three or four edges encompass a shape, they create a *polygon*. One way to think of a polygon—this collection of points (atoms) that now have a new structure as a group—is as the molecule of 3D objects. Polygons (polys) are either triangular or square (quadrangle) two-dimensional objects that are seen both in the Editor and in the *Renderer* (Figure 2.1). These polygons are paper-thin and rigid, i.e., a polygon can be altered in shape by moving the edges and points that make it, but the polygon itself cannot be "bent." When a large number of these rigid polygons are connected to one another and placed at small angles to one another, a curved shape can be created (Figure 2.2a-c).

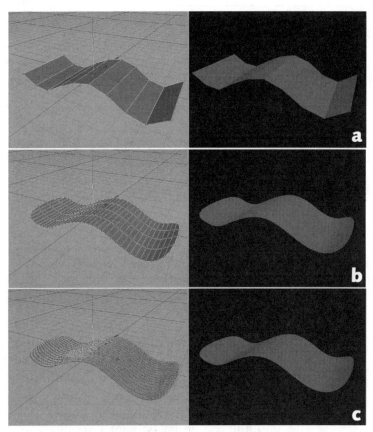

FIGURE 2.2   String of polygons collected to create a curve. The more polygons, the smaller the angles and the smoother the curves. (a) Shows the least number of polys, (b) shows a large number, and thus more curve to the surface, while (c) shows the greatest number.

When points are used to create a polygon, they are also referred to as a *vertex*. The idea is that this point is at the vertex of two or more edges. These vertices—and the edges that meet at them—can be altered (pushed and pulled in any direction) to change the shape of a polygon. Polygons also may "share" points and edges. For example, four or six points can create two polygons (Figure 2.3a). When two polygons share points, the result is a solid surface. If two adjacent polygons do not share two common points, there is technically no solid surface. The result can be shears, or holes, in a surface (Figure 2.3b).

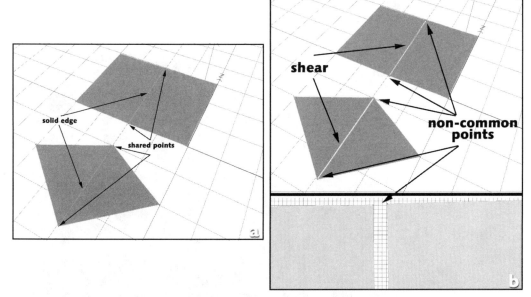

FIGURE 2.3 (a) Shared points to create a polygon. (b) If points are not common and are actually two closely-placed points, the result is two polygons that have a shear down the middle.

When several polygons are connected and enclose a three-dimensional space, they form a three-dimensional shape. For instance, Figure 2.4a shows a pyramid created with six triangular polygons placed together. Figure 2.4b shows a cube created with six square (quadrangle) polygons connected.

Three-dimensional shapes can contain both square (quadrangle) and triangular polygons. As discussed earlier, only collections of polygons can give the effect of a curved shape. The more polygons a curvilinear shape contains, the "smoother" the curves. For

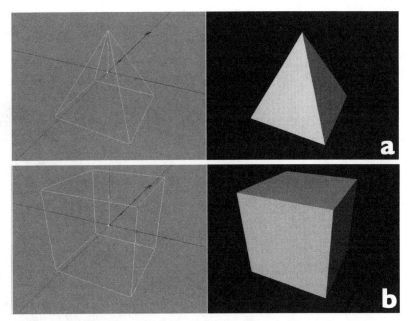

FIGURE 2.4   (a) Polygonal pyramid shown at left in Wireframe mode to see the polygon collection. The image at right shows the pyramid rendered. (b) Polygonal cube shown at left in Wireframe mode to see the polygon collection. The image at right shows the pyramid rendered.

an example of this, see Figures 2.5 (a, b, and c). Figure 2.5a shows a circular shape created with a small number of polygons. The result: an angular-looking ball. Figure 2.5b shows a similar spherical shape, but uses a few more polygons to create the shape; notice a much smoother form. Figure 2.5c shows a very large number of polygons creating the spherical form. This shape, of course, is the smoothest of the three.

The Concept of Poly-Count

The idea of polygons is central to almost all 3D modeling. As illustrated above, higher polygon counts (*poly-counts*) create smoother forms that are more pleasing and organic. However, the higher the polygon count, the more information your computer must keep track of. In a perfect world, your computer would not be limited or slowed by the number of polygons in your model or scene. However, as complex projects emerge and deal more and more with organic forms, the necessity of producing very rounded shapes

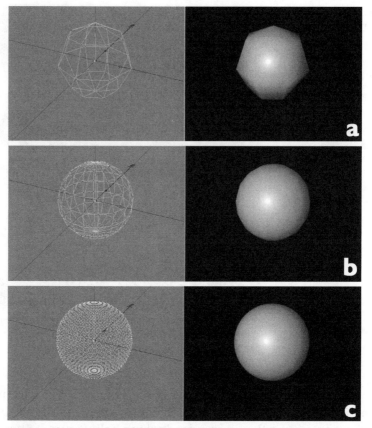

FIGURE 2.5   (a) A minimum number of polygons creates very angular shapes. (b) Increasing the number of polygons in a shape increases the curves. (c) The highest polygon counts create the smoothest shapes.

becomes increasingly important. As these rounded shapes become ever more rounded, the poly-count becomes so high that your computer simply cannot handle all the calculations fast enough to display them for you in the Editor (what you see through your View panel). Your *screen redraw time* (the time it takes your screen to "redraw" the information visible while you are in the Editor) can become painfully slow. In addition, C4D's usually speedy renderer can be crippled when it must contend with huge amounts of polygons (Figure 2.6). We'll talk much more about this later; however, it is important to note that even if you are working on broadcast-quality projects, keeping an eye on your poly-count will help maintain a snappy interface and smooth workflow.

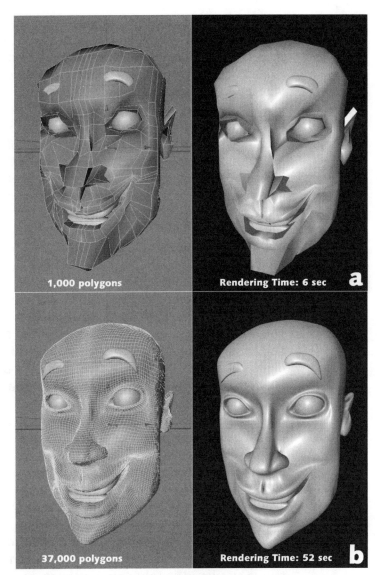

1,000 polygons

Rendering Time: 6 sec **a**

37,000 polygons

Rendering Time: 52 sec **b**

FIGURE 2.6   (a) The top image, using about 1,000 polygons, renders in less than 6 seconds. (b) However, the smooth (and consequently high poly-count) image, although better looking, takes 52 seconds to render.

NURBS

In addition to polygonal modeling, C4D provides a form of modeling that allows for tremendous flexibility: NURBS. NURBS (an acronym, singular and plural) stands for Non-Uniform Rational B-Splines.

NURBS objects are objects created by object generators. That is, they themselves have no inherent geometry; rather, they use other objects to create (or generate) a new object. A true team player, NURBS can make a pipe out of a circle, a vase out of a squiggle, a vine from a line and a profile, and a head from a cube.

In polygonal modeling, you actually work with the building blocks of 3D shapes—polygons. In NURBS objects, you alter the source objects (splines) that create the final NURBS object and C4D automatically calculates the final effect of the polygons that make up the NURBS object. This allows for a tremendous amount of flexibility. Very quickly—by merely altering a few parts of a constituent spline object—C4D can reorganize a large amount of polygons in the final NURBS object. This dynamic ability to change dramatically the shape of a 3D form is one of the huge benefits to NURBS-based modeling.

However, there are some drawbacks to this form of modeling. When you are using NURBS modeling, you rely heavily on C4D's interpretation of how the NURBS algorithms are functioning. If you are in control of the parameters of the NURBS object, this can be to your advantage. However, while an object is part of a NURBS object, you do not have control over the object on a polygon-by-polygon basis. This can be frustrating if you need to make minute changes to the model. This is not a fatal flaw, however, as NURBS objects can be changed into polygonal objects if need be. We'll look much more at the power of NURBS in the upcoming tutorials.

Splines

The primary building tools of most NURBS objects are *splines*. Splines contain points (or vertices) that still have no geometry of their own. These points define the shape (linear, curvy) of the lines between the points. Furthermore, the lines that connect these points also have no inherent geometry; the manual describes them as "infinitely thin." The idea is that splines will never render. They are simply a collection of points connected by lines that exist within three-dimensional space. The lines that connect these varying points in space create a shape referred to in C4D as interpolation. Although splines themselves have no geometry, they too can be used to create a wide variety of geometry. C4D has a diverse toolbox of spline creation operations. We'll talk much more about this later.

PRIMITIVES

The final type of object we'll discuss here is the collection of objects that C4D makes really well. These objects are *primitives*. Primitives are objects that C4D creates via mathematical formulas that create a shape based on determined values. Because of this dynamic mathematical nature, most primitives in C4D are said to be *parametric*, meaning the parameters of these primitive objects can be easily changed. What this also means is that although C4D uses polygons to display the objects in the Editor, primitives don't actually have any polygons of their own until rendered. The benefit of this is similar to NURBS objects; by altering the parameters, you can quickly get new shapes without having to alter the object at the polygonal level. The drawback is that you can only alter the shape according to C4D's parameter variables. There is a surprisingly large amount of possibilities in primitives. The best way to explore them is to create some and examine the possibilities.

PUTTING THE THEORY INTO PRACTICE

Creating Primitives

Before we get too far into the intricacies of primitives, it's worth while to mention one of the animator's best friends—the Undo function. If your interface is still set up in the default setting, you have a command palette across the top of your screen. This palette is broken up into five sections. These sections simply group the commands into clusters of similar tools. The first section with the two curved arrows contains the *Undo* and *Redo* commands. C4D has what is called a *non-destructive* workflow, meaning (in part) that multiple undos are possible. With non-destructive workflows, C4D keeps information on parts of models and the method used to create shapes as you work. By default, you have ten undo steps; you can change this by going to Edit>Preferences and then changing the Undo Depth setting listed in the Document area to your desired level of undos. Remember that all of these undos must be stored in your computer's memory—so if your computer doesn't have a large amount of available memory, keep this Undo Depth setting low.

The Undo and Redo commands are two of the most-used 3D commands. Every artist, no matter how accomplished, works through a series of refining and retrying. Keep the Undo and Redo buttons handy and know that there's no shame in undoing something just done. Indeed, many artists begin to develop cramps in their hands as they sit ready to hit the keyboard shortcuts for Undo (CTRL-Z) and Redo (CTRL-Y). As we work through the steps below, we won't look at how to undo and redo, as these are fairly common concepts to computer work. However, keep in mind that this tool is available.

Now, let's continue to explore the tools. In the fifth section of the command palette at the top of your default screen is an icon of a cube (Figure 2.7). This cube icon is the command function for creating a primitive cube. To use it, simply click it once. Immediately, a box will appear in the middle of your View Panel (Figure 2.7).

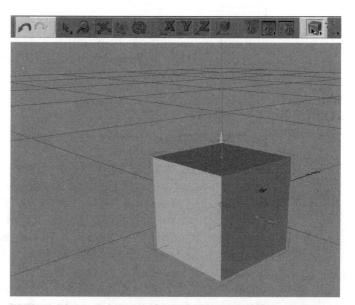

FIGURE 2.7 Primitive Cube icon at the top far right—just click to use. Also notice the Undo/Redo tools at the top far left, and the resultant primitive cube.

There are several important things to notice right away about the C4D interface upon the creation of the cube. The first, of course, is the existence of a cube in the middle of the Editor window. However, the placement of this cube is also very important to note. Notice that the cube has been placed at exactly the center of known 3D space; that is, the center of the cube is at (0,0,0) in the *xyz* Cartesian coordinate grids. This is an important idea to remember in C4D.

When you are placing any new objects, the default location is at (0,0,0). On the cube itself, notice the many visible tools available. The first visual tool is the red "corner pieces." These red corner pieces define the space which the 3D object takes up within digital space. These red corner pieces are not interactive, meaning that they are not functional tools to grab or alter. They are simply a visual communication tool between C4D and you.

Altering Parametric Primitives

The next things to notice are the orange dots on the top and two sides of the cube (Figure 2.8a). These are interactive, functioning tools that allow you to adjust the parameters of this parametric primitive. These orange dots are only present on parametric primitives—you'll not see them on NURBS- or polygonal-based objects. These parametric handles allow you to interactively change physical characteristics of the objects. This is actually a visual form of altering the mathematical variables described above that create the shape. To use these interactive handles, simple click and drag them. For instance, if you wish to make a cube wider, simply click on the orange dot on the side of the cube and drag out to the desired size (Figure 2.8b).

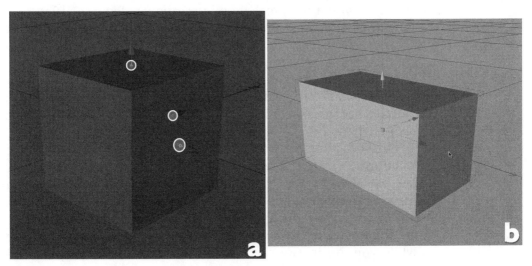

FIGURE 2.8   (a) Parametric Handles. (b) Altering Parametric Handles.

A little later, we'll discuss different ways of altering an object, including Object, Polygon and Object Axis, and Point modes. The real power of these parametric handles is that you can click-drag them no matter what mode or tool you actually have selected.

Parametric Primitives and the Objects Manager

While we're talking of parametric handles, notice what has appeared in the Objects Manager (Figure 2.9a). When you created the parametric cube, an icon with the word "Cube" appeared in the Objects Manager. The Objects Manager is a visual list of *all* objects present in a given scene. A lot of work can be done in the Objects Manager, and we'll be continually revisiting this manager.

Within the Objects Manager, you can change the names of objects. If you double-click on the word "Cube," you'll be presented with a new dialog box allowing you to rename this object if so desired (Figure 2.9b). In simple cases like this, it may seem unnecessary. However, as your projects become increasingly complex and the list of objects grows, having appropriately named objects becomes not only a nice help, but a necessity. It's suggested that you indeed spend time renaming your objects as you go.

Besides changing the name in the Objects Manager, you can alter the parameters of parametric primitives. Double-click on the cube icon and a new dialog box will appear (Figure 2.10a). For a cube, the parameters available to edit are limited. The first column allows you to change the size of the cube in each direction. The second column allows you to change the *segments* of the parametric primitive cube. The number of segments for a primitive cube is not very important while the cube is still a primitive. However, the number becomes very important in other functions that may be built off the cube.

The idea behind segments is that a primitive cube is constructed of six square (quadrangle) polygons. Each side is one polygon or one segment (Figure 2.10b). If the segment number is increased, then the number of polygons used to create one face of the cube is increased (Figure 2.10c). Note that while a parametric cube is a primitive, you can't see the number of segments along each side while you are in Gouraud shading (the default display mode in

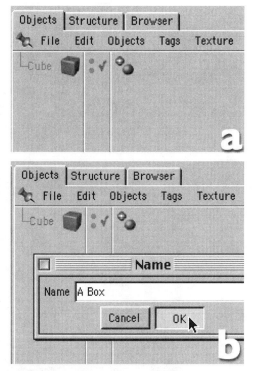

FIGURE 2.9   (a) Objects Manager. (b) By double-clicking on the name of the object within the Objects Manager, you can rename your objects as you go. This becomes important as projects become more complex.

C4D's View Panel). The primitive always renders as a simple flat side. However, if you change your Display setting for the View Panel to Wireframe, you can see the segments created. Larger numbers of segments allow for greater flexibility in future operations, but it also begins to slow your computer down as it attempts to keep track of the larger amount of polys.

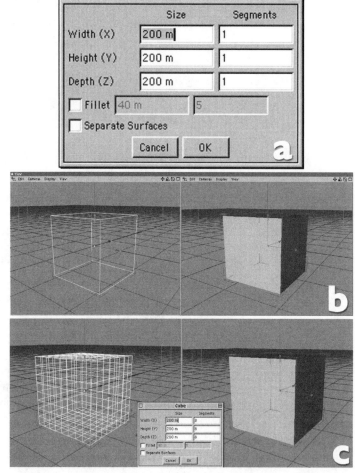

FIGURE 2.10 (a) Parameter Editing for Parametric Primitive Cube. (b) One segment = one polygon. (c) Multiple segments eventually lead to multiple polygons per face.

Fillets

Fillets are rounded sections or corners of shapes. Almost all of the primitives allow you to activate the Fillets option to make primitive forms less block and hard-edged (Figure 2.11a). This is where some of the power of primitives really begins to emerge. To create the rounded shape shown in Figure 2.11a, you would need to manually shift a great many polygons. However, with parametric primitives, you simply double-click on the blue primitive icon symbol

(Figure 2.11b) and activate the "Fillet" button within the dialog box. Then edit the values set in the input fields to change the depth of the rounded edge (Figure 2.11c).

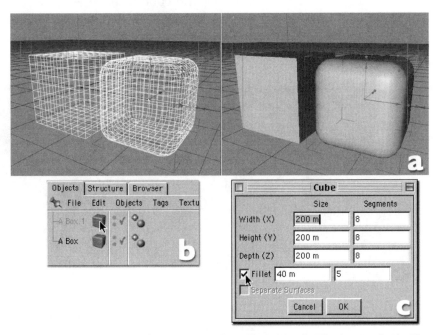

FIGURE 2.11   (a) Non-filleted and filleted primitive forms. (b) Activate the Fillet functions by double-clicking the topmost primitive icon symbol. (c) Fillet button and input fields activated to create the rounded shapes.

Notice that as soon as you activate the Fillet option in the primitive cube dialog box, new orange parameter-altering handles appear on the object. These handles can again be dynamically altered to effect the depth of the fillet on the corner. Up to now, altering the orange parameter handles could not be done by scaling the object. However, with the addition of these fillet parameter handles, you can see how parametric handles *reshape* a primitive rather than resize it. One other note about the primitive cube: there is also a check box to create a cube with Separate Surfaces. While your cube is still a primitive, this really doesn't have much bearing on your project in the Editor view or in a rendering. However, one of the ideas behind primitives is that you can "tell" an object to no longer be a primitive and simply be a collection of polygons (a form made of polygonal shapes rather than formed by a calculation). This is done by making the object *Editable* (Select Structure>Make Editable or use the keyboard shortcut "C"). If a cube without the Separate Surfaces box checked is made editable, the result is one shape where C4D understands all the segments to be connected together (Figure 2.12a). However, if the Separate Surfaces option is checked and then the cube is made editable, C4D understands this primitive to now be six (or however many segments you have enabled) separate polygons, i.e., it sees the cube as a group of unconnected polygons (Figure 2.12b).

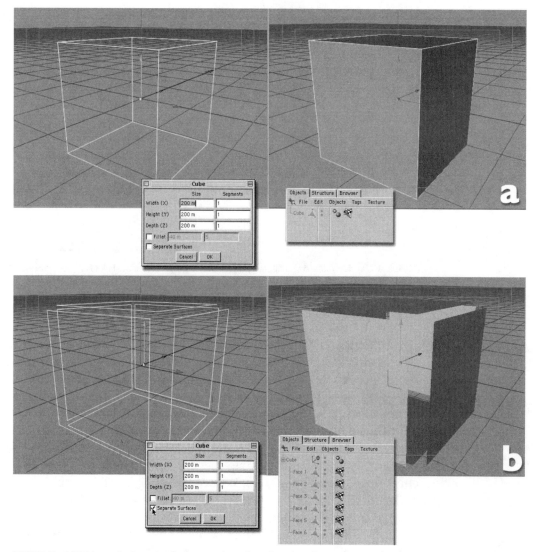

FIGURE 2.12   (a) Without the Separate Surfaces option selected, C4D understands editable cubes as a solid (although hollow) polygonal shape. (b) With the Separate Surfaces option selected, C4D makes a primitive cube editable into separate independent polygons.

Other Primitives

Some tools within command palettes contain other tools that are *folded* into the button. You can tell when other commands are folded by the small black triangle that appears at the bottom right hand of the command button (Figure 2.13).

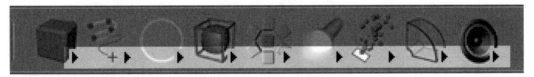

FIGURE 2.13   Nested or folded tools are often available within palettes. The little black triangle is the visual clue that there is more than meets the eye to that particular tool button.

The collection of primitive shapes that C4D creates is one example. These primitive shapes are actually nested (or folded) within the Primitive Cube command on the top command palette. If you click and hold on the Primitive Cube command button, a small subset of selections will appear showing you the other available primitives in C4D. To select a primitive, and thus place it within your scene (placed at (0,0,0) and listed in your Objects Manager), keep your mouse button clicked and move it over the desired form before releasing. Upon release, the primitive is placed.

It is also noteworthy that the primitive shapes available in C4D can also be accessed through the pull-down menu path of Objects>Primitive. The order in which they are listed is different from the order in which they are presented in the command palette. As this volume isn't a manual, we won't be going over each primitive and each of its specific eccentricities. In general, primitives are great to get shapes started, but are very quickly altered beyond all recognition. In fact, you can often tell a beginning animator by the plethora of primitive shapes in their scene.

CONCLUSION

So, let's move on. In Chapter 3, we will use primitives to begin building a room. We will use splines to create NURBS, and we will bring all the theory we have discussed together into concrete tutorials to put our theoretical discussion into practice.

3

PLAYING WITH PRIMITIVES

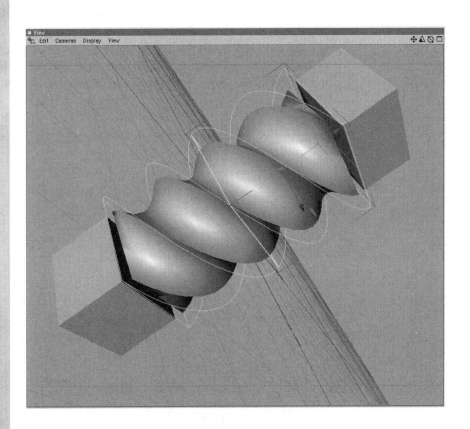

S
o now that we've gone over some of the definitions and theory of objects that can be created in C4D, let's look at actually creating things. There will be many steps to get there, but we'll use one tutorial at a time and soon, the room will be complete. In this chapter, we will use primitives to get things started.

Before we begin, let's look briefly at a few helpful reminders. In these chapters, the tools will be referred to by name. Sometimes it can be hard to remember what the names of all the tools are. C4D helps you do this in one of two ways. The first is to have C4D simply write the names of tools next to them in the interface. Right-click (Command-click on Mac) on any collection of tools or command palette in the interface. From the resultant pop-up menu, toggle the "Text" on (Figure 3.1a). This will result in each tool having its name displayed next to it (Figure 3.1b). The problem with doing this is that you begin to loose valuable screen real estate that you'll need for complex scenes. However, it is nice to have when getting started.

FIGURE 3.1   To display the names of tools next to their icons, right-click on a command palette and turn on the Text option.

The second aid that C4D provides is the hints or help that pop up at the bottom left of the screen. Watch that area as you move your mouse over any tool and you will see the name of that tool or command pop up.

TUTORIAL

3.1 CREATING AN INTERIOR—STEP ONE: PRIMITIVES

To begin with, let's create the floor of the room. To do this, we'll use the most basic solid building block of 3D—the Polygon Primitive. Note that we could also use the Plane Primitive, but by default, Plane Primitives are higher in poly-count, and as this floor is always going to lie flat, there really is no need to add unnecessary polygons. Add a Polygon Primitive to the scene by selecting the Add Polygon object from the command palette at the top (Figure 3.2a). The result should be a small square in the middle of the scene (Figure 3.2b).

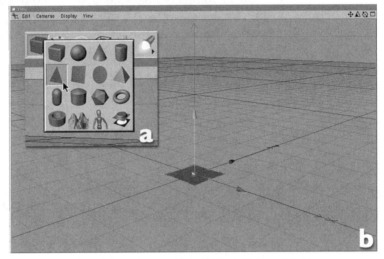

FIGURE 3.2   (a) Add Polygon Primitive object. (b) Placed Polygon Primitive.

The placement of this Polygon object is fine—it's sitting directly on the *z*- and *x*-axes. However, the size seems small. Select the Scale Active Element tool and click-drag anywhere in the scene to increase the size of the polygon. Watch your Coordinates Manager (in R8, it's right next to the Materials Manager at the bottom of your screen) as you drag to see how large you are making this polygon shape. Note that the Coordinates Manager has several columns and at the bottom of the columns, you can choose to change what is shown in the columns. Remember that "Size" is an absolute value while "Scale" is a value that is a multiple of the original default scale of "1." So be sure to look for the Size measurements when referring to how large an object is.

Although shape is completely relative in this instance, make this Polygon object about 1000m x 1000m. You may wish to simply enter these dimensions manually in the Coordinates Manager by entering 1000 in the X and Z input fields.

Press "H" on your keyboard to have your view panel display all objects present in your scene (which in this case is just the polygon).

For the walls, we could use a Plane, Polygon, or Cube Primitive. However, because we eventually will be having windows in the scene and will be able to see the relief of the window sill, a Cube Primitive would work best. Place a Cube Primitive in the scene by selecting the Add Cube object tool. A cube will be placed in the scene that will look very short. The reason for this is that half of the cube is sitting below the floor. Confirm this by toggling your view panels so that you can see the scene in orthographic top, front, and side views as well as the perspective view. In the bottom two view panels (right and front), you'll notice a square (the Cube object) dissected by a white line (the Polygon object). The first order of business then should be to move this cube so that it rests on the floor. Activate the Move Active Element tool by clicking it in the top command palette. Make sure that the Cube is the active object by checking your Objects Manager (the manager on the right edge of the UI) to see if it is in red. If so, simply click-drag anywhere within your bottom two view panels and move the cube up so that it sits level with the floor (Figure 3.3a).

Now we'll need to change this cube into a more suitable shape. With the cube still the active object, activate the Scale Active Element tool and click-drag on the red (x) directional handle of the cube until it is much thinner (Figure 3.3b). Scale it down in the x direction until the Coordinates Manager indicates it's about 20m thick (much too thick for a real wall, I know; the unit of measurement is actually of no import). Then we need to scale the wall to make it as long as the room. This time, instead of using the Scale Active Element tool, we'll use the Coordinates Manager. We know that the floor (and thus the room) is 1000m long in both the x and z directions. As we look at our cube, we can see that this is most likely to become the wall that runs along the z direction (blue). So, simply enter 1000m in the Z input field under the Size column and the cube will jump to that exact size (Figure 3.3c).

Now, we need to move the wall from the center of the room to the edge of the floor. We can do this in one of two ways:

1. Use the Move Active Element tool in the view panel that shows the top view (top right-hand view panel) and click-drag the red (x) directional handle until the wall is in place.
2. Use the Coordinates Manager. We know that the room is floor is 1000m long (because we entered that in the input field) and we

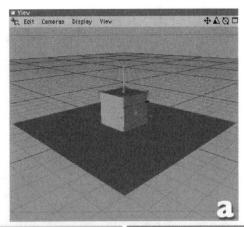

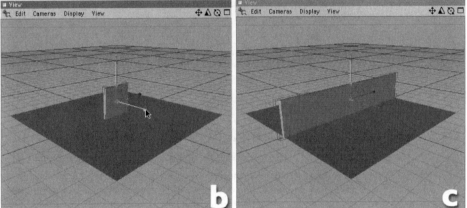

FIGURE 3.3   (a) Using the Move Active Element tool, we can quickly move the cube (soon to be a wall) level with the floor. (b) Using the Scale Active Element tool, we can turn a block into the beginning of a wall. (c) By using the Coordinates Manager, we can quickly alter the size of the wall to match the floor.

know that the floor's center is sitting at (0,0,0) (because we haven't moved it.) We also know that from the center of our digital universe to the edge of the floor in each direction is 500m. So we can use the Coordinates Manager to place the wall appropriately. It just so happens that the back end of the room is in the –x direction, so, under the Position column, enter –500 in the X input field (Figure 3.4a). The wall will jump over and be aligned just as you need it within your view panel (Figure 3.4b).

To create the other walls, we could use a similar process. Or, we could simply make copies of the wall already created and save ourselves several steps. With the cube selected, go to Edit>Copy or press CTRL/COMMAND-C. Then go to Edit>Paste or press CTRL/COMMAND-V.

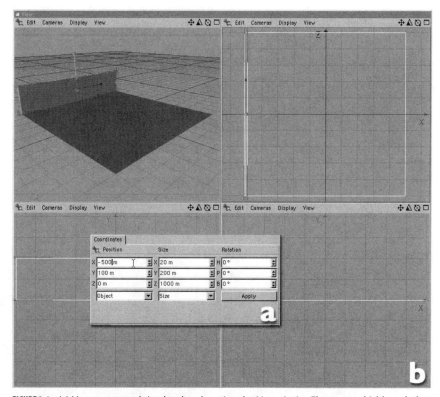

FIGURE 3.4   (a) Movement needn't take place by using the Move Active Element tool (although that is a good method); you can also enter the coordinates of a direction in the Coordinates Manager. (b) Result of Coordinates Manager alteration.

Just as a word processing application copies and pastes collections of words, C4D copies and pastes collections of polygons. You may not be able to tell that an object has been copied and pasted by just looking at the view panel; in fact, the scene should look just the same as it did before the copy/paste operation. The reason for this is that C4D pastes a copied element right back in the same location as it was copied from. This is so you don't have to waste time trying to track down what happened to your newly pasted element.

However, notice in the Objects Manager that a new cube has appeared. To keep it from being confused with the first cube, C4D has renamed it "Cube.1." Let's further refine the names by changing the labels for all the shapes thus far; to do this, simply double-click on the *name* of each object within the Objects Manager. A small dialog box will appear, allowing you to change the name of the object you selected. Let's change the name of the Polygon object to "Floor," the name of the first Cube to "Side Wall" and the newly created Cube to "Back Wall."

Now we need to rotate the new wall into position at the back of the room. You can do this with the Rotate Active Element tool or again with the Coordinates Manager. For this back wall, we'll first need to rotate the object 90° around its *y*-axis or 90° of its heading. If you are using the Rotate Active Element tool, simply click-drag on the green directional handle (*y*) until the wall is rotated. If you are using the Coordinates Manager, enter 90 in the H (H stands for "heading") input field of the Rotation column.

Now, you can use the Coordinates Manager to move the wall into place along the back wall by entering 0 in the X input field of the Position column and 500 in the Z input field (this moves the wall back to 0 along the *x*-axis, and moves it back 500m along the *z*-axis), or you can use the Move Active Element tool to manually move it back into position. Let's use the Move Active Element tool, but first let's look at some ways to enhance this tool's use.

SNAP SETTINGS

At the bottom right-hand corner of the interface is the Attributes Manager (new placement for R8). This manager allows you to control attributes of just about everything. But this powerful manager is not what we're looking for. There are two other tabs (Active Tool and Snap Settings) indicating areas that reside beneath the Attributes Manager. The Snap Settings tab is of particular interest in this case. If you've ever dealt with CADD or even used guides in Illustrator or Photoshop, you'll appreciate the value of this area. Snap Settings allows you to activate settings within C4D that cause objects to snap to centers, edges, points, or polygons. By default, this is turned off to permit movement without hindrance. However, in this case, where we are building an interior in which things need to line up, this ability to snap into position is heaven-sent.

Snap Settings is actually a very complex set of tools that luckily is explained in-depth in the manual. However, for our purposes it's important to mention a few things:

1. You must click the Enable Snapping checkbox to get things started.
2. If you are working in parallel projection view panels (top, front, right), then the Type is best set to Snap 2.5D. This allows objects to snap if they line up in the two dimensions present in that particular view but don't necessarily line up in the third dimension.

3. The Radius setting helps you determine the tolerance of the snap. Do you want things to snap if you are within an eighth of an inch on your screen or if you are within one half of an inch? This can be adjusted interactively.

4. All the other settings within this set of tools allow you to determine what sorts of things the object you are moving will snap to. In our case, we'll leave the settings as default, but make sure to check the Edge setting (Figure 3.5).

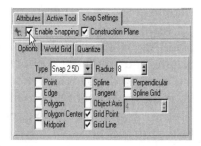

FIGURE 3.5   Snap Settings activated and set for this Tutorial.

5. Be aware that, although we won't talk much about them here, there are snap settings under the Quantize tab that allow you to establish snap parameters for rotations and scale.

So now, in the top right-hand-corner view panel (top view), use the Move Active Element tool and move the wall approximately to the middle edge of the floor. You should notice that the wall "snaps" into place indicating that the center of the wall has found the edge of the floor as well as the gridline that defines 0 along the *x*-axis. If you flip back to the Coordinates Manager, you'll find that the settings displayed are just as they should be. Be careful as you do this that you don't align the edge of the wall to the edge of the floor. Although this wouldn't be all bad, the side wall is set up with the center of the wall on the edge of the floor—so for consistency's sake, let's do the same for the back wall. You may need to use the Camera Move tool and right-click-drag or COMMAND-click-drag to zoom in a bit so you can ensure your wall is placed appropriately. Your scene thus far should appear similar to Figure 3.6.

Now that we've placed this wall, let's shorten it a bit so that we can set the nook in the wall later. You can do this in one of three ways. The first is to simply grab the orange parameter handle on the edge and *re-shape* the cube to be shorter. The second is to use the Scale Active Element tool and grab the blue *z*-directional handle and drag it smaller. The third way is to simply enter the new size into the Coordinates Manager.

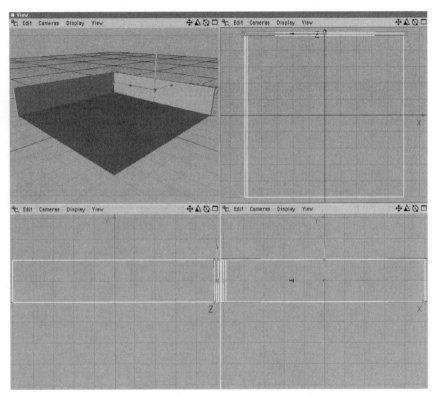

FIGURE 3.6 Scene with two walls, one placed via the Coordinates Manager, one placed with Snap Settings.

Note that at this point the object's axis is different from the digital world's axis. We need to shorten the wall in the world's *x* dimension. However, when the wall is active, note that it is the object's *z* dimension that is vital to us at this point. This occurred because we rotated the first wall. So, alter the side wall's length by entering 400 into the Z input field of the Size column. This will shorten the wall inward towards the center; you will be left with a short wall centered on the floor.

Use the Move Active Element tool to move this new shortened wall to the corner. The best place to do this is within the top view. With your Snap Settings still turned on, your wall should easily snap into place as shown in Figure 3.7. Zoom in to ensure that it has. When you build architectural digital models, it becomes very important that joints are made cleanly to avoid light leaks later.

Copy and paste this new wall and rename it "Wall 2." Resize its Z size to 300m. Next, move it to the other corner of the room for the niche. This little area of the room will still require walls that are the same thickness

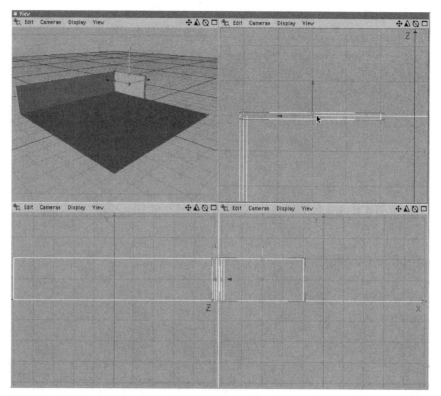

FIGURE 3.7 With Snap Settings still enabled, a quick arrangement of walls becomes possible.

as the other walls. So, to ensure consistency, simply copy and paste either of the back walls and rename it "Niche Wall 1." This time, we need to rotate the wall into a 45° angle. To do this, we'll explore some more benefits of the Coordinates Manager. If you copied one of the back walls, the H (heading) setting in the Rotation column should read 90°. C4D allows input fields to include mathematical formulae. In this case, we're going to want to rotate this new wall 45° from its current rotation state. Click on the H input field and simply enter "+ 45" and press Enter (Figure 3.8a). The input field will calculate this equation and Niche Wall 1 will add 45° to its current rotation value (Figure 3.8).

Now of course this wall is far too large for this nook. If you were designing this room, you could use the Scale Active Element tool to interactively find the appropriate length. For time's sake, let us assume we've already determined that a good length would be 125 meters. Enter "125" in the Z input field of the Size column for this Niche Wall 1. Zoom in on the top view so you're sure that you are getting clean joints, then,

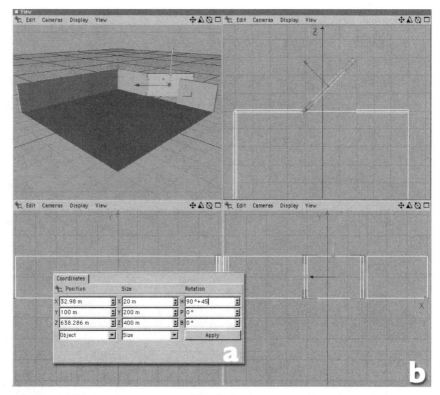

FIGURE 3.8   (a) The Coordinates Manager allows for the dynamic use of formulae to calculate any value. (b) Our project thus far.

using the Move Active Element tool, move the wall into position so the corners line up. Your Snap Settings should still be active so it should be easy to find where the corners meet.

Note that as these walls are moved, all movement should be done in the top view. You can use the perspective view to see what the model looks like, but it's often more accurate to do movement in the one view. This lets you make sure that all the walls stay rooted to the floor as they don't move at all in the *y* direction when you work in top view.

Copy and paste this wall and rename the new copy Niche Wall 2. In the H input field of the Rotation column enter +90 as the value to rotate the object into a mirror form of Niche Wall 1. The result will be an "X" of walls (Figure 3.9b).

Now you need to move this wall over to the other side of the "hole" in the wall. It's important to make sure this wall stays even (along the digital world's *y*-axis) with the original wall. To do this, we'll use some important tools.

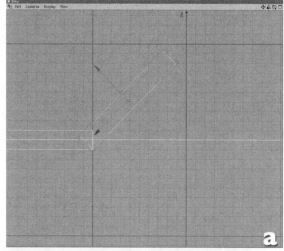

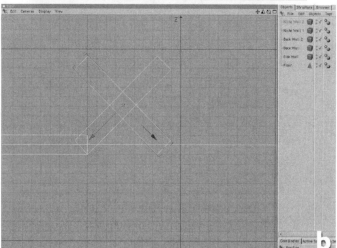

FIGURE 3.9 (a) Resized wall snapped into position. (b) Copied and rotated Niche Wall 2.

X-, Y-, AND Z-AXIS LOCK/UNLOCK AND USE WORLD COORDINATE SYSTEM

Next to the Move, Scale, and Rotate Active Element tools are four buttons with an X,Y,Z and a cube with directional handles on them (Figure 3.10a). The first three buttons are called the X-, Y-, and Z-Axis Lock/Unlock tools. They are there so that you can define the directions along which changes may be made. For instance, with the Move Active Element tool active, if you click (and thus lock) the X and Z buttons (Figure 3.10a), you will only be able to move the object up and down along the *y*-axis. The notable exception to this is when you use the directional handles which override the X- ,Y-, and Z-Axis Lock/Unlock tools.

The same thing happens for the Scale Active Element and the Rotate Active Element tools. Remember that the settings of these Lock/Unlock tools are relative to the Move/Scale/Rotate Active Element tool that is active. So, if you set only the Y to be unlocked in the Move Active Element tool, when you switch to the Rotate Active Element tool, all three axes will be unlocked. However, when you return to the Move Active Element tool, only the *y*-axis will be unlocked. Each of the tools remembers which axes are editable.

The Use World Coordinate System button allows you to define whether you are locking changes along the *object's* axis or the *world's* axis. Our wall here is a perfect example. By default, Use World Coordinate System is not depressed/selected. So if you lock the *y*- and *z*-axes with the idea that you'll move the new wall and keep it even with the first wall, you'll be frustrated. Upon click-dragging the wall, the *y*- and *z*-axes will be locked, but the wall will move in the direction of the wall's *x*-axis in a diagonal (Figure 3.10a).

However, if you click the Use World Coordinate System button (thus activating it), when you click-drag Niche Wall 2, it will remain even with

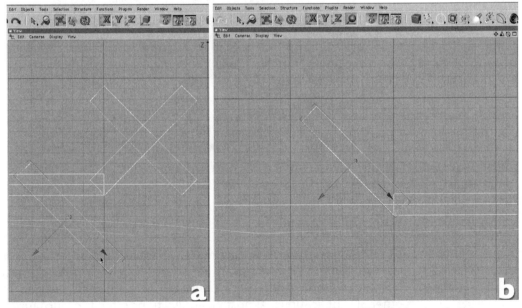

FIGURE 3.10   (a) When the X-, Y-, or Z-Axis Lock/Unlock buttons are depressed, an axis is editable; when the buttons are raised, the axes are not editable. When you use the object's coordinate system (Use World Coordinate System is deactivated) the object moves along the object's axis. (b) With Use World Coordinate System activated, objects will constrain according to the world's axis rather than an individual object's axis.

the first wall, as it will only be able to move along the *world's* x-axis (Figure 3.10b). Move the wall along the world's axis into position on the other side of the hole.

Copy and paste either of the niche walls and re-label this new wall "Niche Wall 3." Rotate it so it runs parallel with the other non-niche wall segments on this wall (use the Rotate Object Axis tool or enter 90 in the H input field of the Rotation column in the Coordinates Manager). Move the wall up so that it approximates the position in Figure 3.11 and increase the size (only along the object's z-axis) to also match the Figure. We want to make sure that both the inside and outside corners of this niche are "clean" so that we can use the outside later if desired.

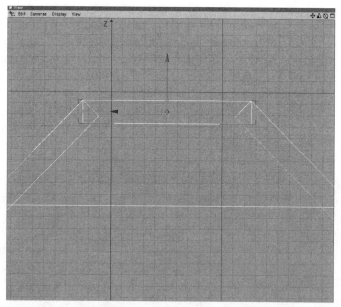

FIGURE 3.11   Last section of the niche created, rotated, and resized into place.

THE POWER OF GROUPS

Now that we've created several walls (in fact, all the walls we'll create for this exercise), let's look at how to alter them collectively. C4D allows for a powerful method of organizing objects that is a little different from most other 3D applications. Almost all applications offer a "group" function, but C4D's method doesn't simply group objects; it creates a *Null object* (an object with no geometry of its own) to become a parent of all the objects you've selected. Let's look at how this works.

As discussed earlier, many managers have their own collection of pull-down menus. The Objects Manager has an especially vital collection of tools located in the nested pull-down menus. Within the Objects Manager, go to Objects>Group. Initially it will seem as though nothing is happening; however, notice that your mouse pointer has turned into a small cross. This is C4D telling you that it's ready for you to show it what objects are to be grouped together. Just marquee (click-drag) around the objects you wish to group (in this case the niche walls) and a new object called Null Object will be created in your Objects Manager.

But perhaps more intuitive—and new to R8—is the ability to select more than one object. This allows you to use a slightly different workflow if you so desire. To use this new method, click the objects (Shift-click to add to that selection) you wish to group—in this case Niche Wall 1, Niche Wall 2, and Niche Wall 3. This will make multiple objects' names appear in red. Once you have the objects you wish to group selected, hit G on your keyboard and they will be grouped under a new Null object.

A small box with a plus in it now appears next to the Null object in your Objects Manager. The box indicates that this object has *children*. The idea behind the parent-child paradigm in C4D is that whatever change you make to a parent object is transferred to all the children of that object. However, the children also maintain some autonomy in that they can be altered independently of the other children of the parent. In this way, this parent-child method of grouping is much more powerful than traditional grouping strategies in other applications. If you click on the box with the plus sign, the parent will expand to show the children it contains. Notice that the children are indented and visually shown as children by the gray line which indicates the object they are connected to.

It should be noted that you needn't use the group function to make any object a child of another. In the Objects Manager, all you need to do is move (click-drag) an object over another object and release. You'll notice that when you do so, your mouse pointer will change to indicate that C4D knows you are trying to place an object as a child of another (Figure 3.12a). Children can become the parents of other objects and multi-leveled objects are possible (Figure 3.12b).

This Null object (the parent of the newly grouped niche walls) can be renamed by double-clicking on the name. Rename this group "Niche." Notice in the view panels that a Null object has its own directional handles (Figure 3.18). This means that the group (under the auspices of the parent object "Niche") can be moved, or resized.

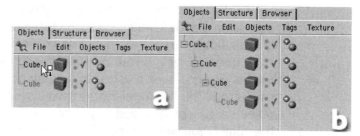

FIGURE 3.12   (a) When you make one object a child of another, C4D will let you know when it understands your intention by a change in the mouse pointer. (b) Children can become parents of other objects.

Now, look at Figure 3.13. It shows what your scene should look like at this point. There should be a parent object called Niche and the three Niche Walls should be the children of it.

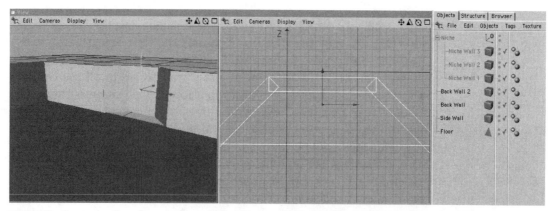

FIGURE 3.13   Grouped walls under a new group Niche. This group has its own manipulator handle.

Continue with this grouping strategy by grouping the other walls into a new group that you rename "Straight Walls." Now, you should have three objects in the Objects Manager—Niche, Straight Walls, and Floor. Another nice power of grouping is that you can group groups. Select the group Niche in the Objects Manager and then Shift-click the group Straight Walls; hit G on your keyboard and rename the new group "Walls."

USE OBJECT AXIS TOOL

As we've seen, each group has its own directional handles by virtue of the Null object acting as a parent. You've probably noticed by now that these directional handles actually can do more than just provide simple handles for altering objects. These handles are part of what is called the *object's axis*. The object axis is the point around which all alteration of the object takes place. Objects rotate around this axis; objects grow out or shrink in around this point. Up to now in our discussions, the default object axis (usually the center) has been fine and acceptable. However, there are situations where it is not only convenient but necessary to have the object's axis in a different location from the default center.

Consider this example: Figure 3.14a shows an arm modeled with all Cube primitives. The object axis for the group is situated somewhere near the geometric center of the collection of cubes—which in this case is near the elbow. This means that when the arm is rotated, it rotates around the elbow! Needless to say, this would make for one goofy moving character. To get the object axis at the elbow to where it needs to be, we need to move the object's axis. Up to this point we have been moving objects with the use of the Object tool (Figure 3.14b). The Object tool is by default activated when a new C4D file is open, as C4D assumes you'll want to be altering objects early in the process. But now, as we want to alter the object axis; we'll use the Use Object Axis tool located a few tools below the Object tool along the left-hand vertical command palette (Figure 3.14c).

Other than having the Use Object Axis tool depressed in the command palette along the left, there won't be any difference in the appearance of the interface. The only difference is that now, when you use the Move, Scale, or Rotate Active Element tools, the object's axis will move, scale or rotate, but the geometry itself will not. When you alter the object's axis, all the same rules we discussed earlier when you moved objects apply, e.g., movement can be restrained and snapped. In the case of the arm, you would use the Move Active Element tool to move the object's axis to the shoulder joint. After this adjustment, if you selected the Object tool again, the arm would rotate appropriately (Figure 3.14d).

This is an important tool to have available when you are dealing with objects that rotate at various points—for instance, doors rotate around hinges on the edge of the door, not in the center.

In our scene created thus far, we have a collection of walls that seem a bit short. The walls have all been grouped, and so we can alter the size of the group "Walls" and have all the walls resize together; however, the default object axis for this group is floating in air above the ground. The result is that when we click-drag the *y* directional handle for the group, the walls not only increase in height above the floor, they also drop farther through the floor. Now this isn't the end of the world, as the group

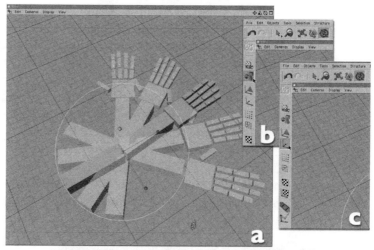

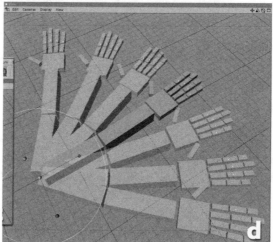

FIGURE 3.14   (a) Arm with inappropriately placed object axis results in objects rotating in ways they oughtn't. (b) The Object tool that is activated by default upon opening C4D. (c) In order to alter the point of rotation or the point of alteration (the object axis) we need to use the Use Object Axis tool. (d) When an object axis is placed appropriately, objects can be rotated or otherwise altered in better ways.

could simply be raised to meet the floor. However, as we were so careful to keep the walls on the floor, let's remedy the situation.

You can use the Use Object Axis tool and the Move Active Element tool to move the object axis down towards the floor. Or, you can simply enter 0 in the Y input field of the Position column in the Coordinates Manager. The result will be the axis lying right on the floor level. Now select the Object tool again and when the Scale Active Element tool is used to resize this wall group, all the walls "grow" from the ground.

Next, let's create a small table that will sit in the nook of the room that we've created. To do this, let's "hide" all unnecessary objects in the scene for now. To hide objects, simply click on the gray dots under the second column located beside the objects within the Object. There are two dots for each object. The top dot represents whether or not the object is visible in the Editor. The bottom dot is to determine whether the object is visible in the Renderer.

Note that when you click on the dot multiple times, there are actually three states: gray, green, and red. The default gray means that the object is visible. When you click the dot once it turns green; which also means that it is visible but goes one step further. When the dot is green it indicates that the Visibility setting is set to override the Visibility settings of parent objects. Clicking twice on the dot turns it red. When the top dot is red, the object is not visible in the Editor window. Furthermore, if you assign a parent object to be invisible, this translates down to the children of that parent, except when green dots are present. To see an example of this, click twice on the group Walls (turning the dot red). Suddenly only the floor is visible in your Editor window. However, when creating the table, it would be nice to see the niche walls for size reference, so expand the Walls group and click on the Niche group so that the dot appears green. The Niche group will be visible now (Figure 3.15), even though it is the child of a hidden object.

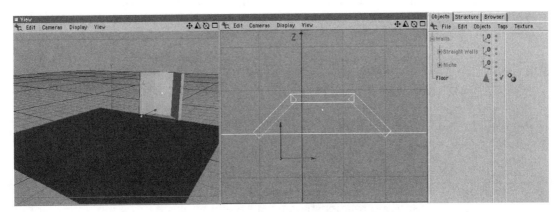

ON THE CD

FIGURE 3.15   When objects have green dots activated, they override any parent Visibility settings. See color version on CD-ROM if further clarification is needed.

Being able to hide objects not only helps by cutting out unnecessary visual clutter, but it allows your projects to become fairly large as you're working. Unless you have a fast computer with a lot of memory, your machine can quickly be reduced to a crawl as it attempts to draw all the objects present. By being able to hide objects (especially those with a high poly-count), you can speed your screen redraw speed and thus streamline your workflow.

TABLE CONSTRUCTION

Now let's build our table. For the tabletop, create a Cylinder object (click on Add Cylinder object in the top command palette nested below Add Cube object). This will place a tall Cylinder in the middle of the room halfway through the floor. Press "O" on your keyboard to zoom in immediately to frame the active object (in this case our newly created Cylinder) in the center of our view panel. You may want to activate various views and zoom in with the "O" key to get a variety of close-up viewpoints of the object. Now before we worry too much about the placement or size, let's round the corners off on this tabletop.

Double-click on the Cylinder *icon* (not the name) within the Objects Manager. In the resultant dialog box, click on the Fillet checkbox. Fillets are rounded edges. Don't worry about any of the values within this dialog box; we'll alter them visually and interactively through dialog boxes. Click OK to exit the dialog box. The Cylinder should now appear rounded at the edges (Figure 3.16a).

This may actually be too round. So, click-drag on the orange primitive control handle that sits on the side of the Cylinder where the curvature meets the side (Figure 3.16b). Click-drag this control handle until you have a slightly curved edge that looks good on a small, round table.

Now click-drag the orange control handle located at the top center of the shape to make the Cylinder shorter. It's often a good idea to actually click-drag in one window (such as the perspective window) but determine the appropriate amount of alteration by looking in the other windows. Now that you have the tabletop thin enough, it still is being cut in half by the floor. This, of course, is due to the object axis being located at the default (0,0,0) when the new primitive was created. Move the Cylinder up off the floor to determine that the shape and relative size are right for the room. Make sure you take plenty of time to view the shape and relationships from several angles by rotating your point of view in the perspective view panel and keeping the other view panels toggled open. Also, take a minute to rename this Cylinder to "Tabletop" in the Objects Manager.

Normally, you would want to create some underpinning structures. However, since such structures would be under the table, we'll use an

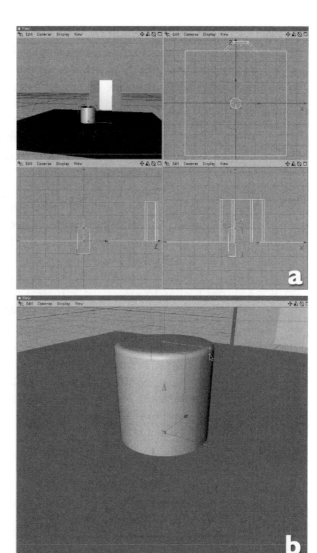

FIGURE 3.16   (a) Fillet enabled cylinder. (b) Orange control handles
allow for easy alteration of fillet radius. See color version on CD-ROM
if further clarification is needed.

old theatre adage, "If it ain't seen, don't build it." On a theatre set, the
most amazing sets seen by the audience often are a weird collection of
wood and steel left raw with measurements, stage notes, and chewing
gum on the back side. The reason is that since the audience never sees
the back side, there's no need to spend any time making it beautiful. In

3D, this is equally important; so often 3D artists spend incredible time creating objects in exquisite detail when half of the object is never seen, or the object is quickly panned by in the course of the animation. 3D is much too time intensive to spend time on non-essential model elements.

So, we'll skip directly to the wood skirt under the tabletop. Construct this by creating a new Tube object (a parametric primitive—thus available in the nested shapes beneath the cube button). After it is placed (Figure 3.17a) it will be much too large for our taste and the shape will be wrong. To correct this, let's begin by widening the hole in the middle by click-dragging on the orange control handle that controls the inner radius (Figure 3.17a). Resize the overall size of the object with the Scale Active Element tool and place it below the tabletop. You'll want to be sure that the Tabletop and this new shape line up in the *x* and *z* directions. If your Snap Settings are still enabled, this new object will snap into place. Another trick is to select the tabletop object, and in the Coordinates Manager, highlight and copy (CTRL/COMMAND-C) the value in the X Position input field. Then select the tube object and paste the value into the X Position input field for that shape. Repeat the process for the Y Position input field. This ensures that the centers of these two objects are in the same place. Note that when you resize the entire object in all directions, the relative proportions of the shape remain the same. Rename the object "Table Skirt" (Figure 3.17b).

DEFORMATION OBJECTS

To finish off the basic shape of the table, we need to build some legs. We could create graceful tapered legs in a variety of ways, but we'll use this opportunity to explore C4D's use of *Deformation objects*. In the far right of the top command palette are groups of tools that are essentially there to create elements (including objects, lights, cameras, and environments). One group of tools are those which appear orange. The orange tools are all Deformation objects; that is, objects that deform some other shapes. These Deformation objects have no geometry of their own, but when they are the child of an object, they deform the polygons of their parent. A good example will be the legs of the table.

First, create the geometry needed to deform by adding a Cube object. Resize the object so that it is tall and thin, as a table leg would be (Figure 3.18). For the proportions used in this tutorial, a cube that is 12m wide and 12m deep and 94m tall works out to be about the right size. Be

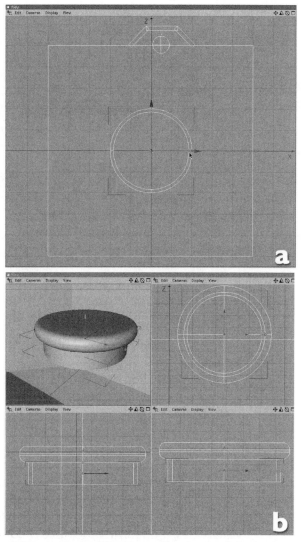

FIGURE 3.17   (a) Large tube object quickly altered with the interactive primitive control handles. (b) Resized and replaced table skirt.

sure to leave the leg in the middle of the room for now, although you'll need to raise it so that it is sitting on the floor of the room to get a good idea of its length compared with the table.

Now create a Taper Deformation by selecting Add Taper Deformation from the collection of Deformation objects in the top command

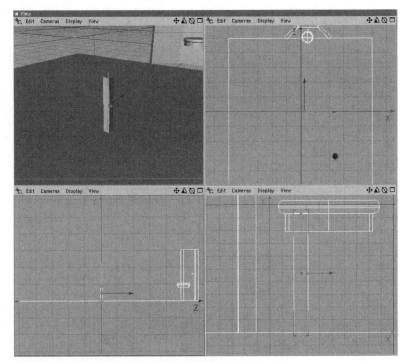

FIGURE 3.18   Resized leg ready for Deformation objects.

palette (Figure 3.19a) or by going to Objects>Deformation>Taper. A teal blue hollow box with orange control handles on it will now appear in the middle of the scene. Each Deformation object works a little differently, although most operate on this same visual convention to allow you to adjust the size and visually alter the settings of the Deformation object. (Some Deformation objects such as Shatter and Explode have no such visual clues, though.) In order for a Deformation object to actually affect a group of polygons—or any shape—it must be the child of the polygons it is to affect. So for the leg, place the Taper Deformation object beneath the Cube object by dragging and dropping it on the Cube object (Figure 3.19b).

Deformation objects can actually alter shapes in all sorts of ways in relation to this teal box. You can limit the power of the Deformation object with the Within the Box option (Figure 3.20a), where the Deformation object disregards polygons outside the box. The Limited option

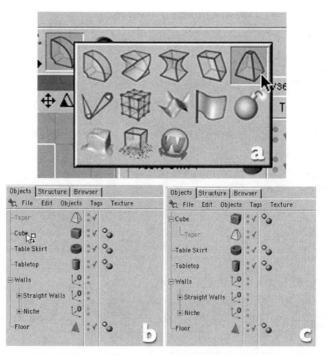

FIGURE 3.19   (a) Create a Taper Deformation object to taper the leg of the table. (b and c) To make the new Taper Deformation object have an effect on the cube, it must be placed as a child of the cube.

affects polygons within the box and the other polygons outside the box move to accommodate the movement of the polys within (Figure 3.20b). This is different from the Unlimited option in which the polygons act as though the Deformation object indeed surrounds the entire form (Figure 3.20c). All of these modes are available when the Deformation object's icon is double-clicked in the Objects Manager (Figure 3.20d).

The default setting for Deformation objects is Limited. Most people find it almost intuitive to resize the Deformation object so that it is slightly larger than the affected object. However, there are certainly cases where the other modes would be handy, such as in Figure 3.21 which shows a cube with two Deformation objects (one upside down) set in Within the Box mode to create a balustrade.

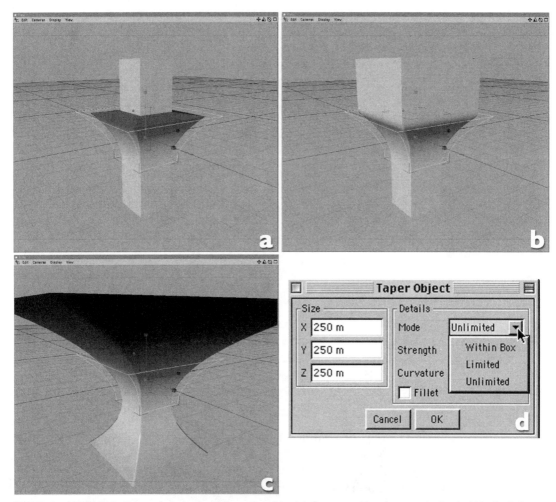

FIGURE 3.20 (a) Within the Box mode limits the Deformation object's influence to the polygons contained within the Deformation object. (b) Limited mode directly affects the polys within the box, but the other polys in the affected object move to accommodate the changes. (c) Unlimited mode affects all the polys of an affected shape as though the Deformation object were much larger than the affected object. (d) When the Deformation object's icon is double-clicked, a dialog box appears allowing you to define the mode.

Next, click-drag on the top orange dot of the Deformation object and make the top of the shape bigger so it tapers to the bottom (Figure 3.22). Now an interesting thing can be observed; notice that although the Deformation object is actually tapered in a curved line, the Cube object it is affecting still maintains straight edges. The reason for this is the nature of the segments or polygons that make up the Cube object. Double-click on the Cube icon in the Objects Manager and the resultant dialog box will display that the Cube object (by default) has one segment in

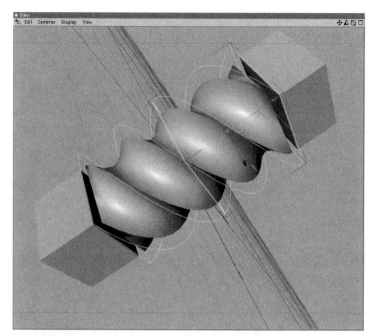

FIGURE 3.21   Two Deformation objects used together in Within the Box mode to create a complex shape.

the *x*, *y*, and *z* directions. Indeed, if the scene thus far were displayed in Wireframe mode, we would see that each side of the Cube object is just one segment (Figure 3.23a).

In order to get a curved taper for this leg, we need to allow the leg to have more polygons, and thus more places to bend. Change the Y setting from 0 to 20. The resultant Wireframe mode shows that the increased polys along the *y*-axis result in a rounded taper (Figure 3.23b). This is an important concept to remember for all Deformation objects. They are only as effective as the polygon topology they are affecting. Changes will still occur in low poly-count objects—they just won't be as smooth or rounded as in higher poly-count objects. Remember that the drawback to achieving smoother, rounder Deformation objects is that the resultant high poly-counts begin to slow your machine down. The smoother your shapes, the slower your screen redraw. Sometimes it is worth your time to experiment and adjust your poly-counts to give you the best look with the fewest number of polygons.

One of the most powerful aspects of Deformation objects is the ability to apply more than one Deformation object to one shape. Add a

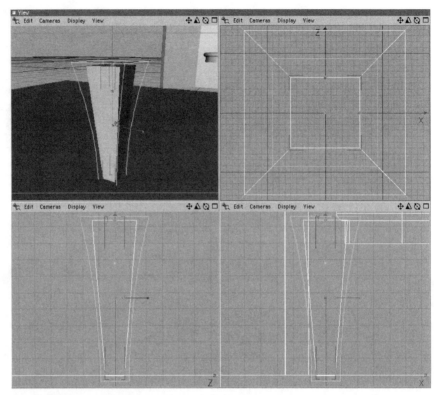

FIGURE 3.22 To use the Deformation object, click-drag it's orange control handles. See color version on CD-ROM if further clarification is needed.

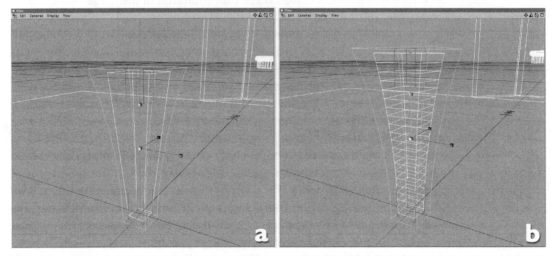

FIGURE 3.23 (a) Wireframe mode displays show the single segment sides of the Cube object that is to become our table leg; as such, the taper remains linear. (b) Increased segments along the *y*-axis creates more curvilinear tapers in our leg.

Twist Deformation object (Figure 3.24a) and resize it so that it is slightly larger than the leg thus far created. Make it a child of the Cube object and then click-drag the orange control handle (the primitive parameter handle) to twist our already tapered leg (Figure 3.24b).

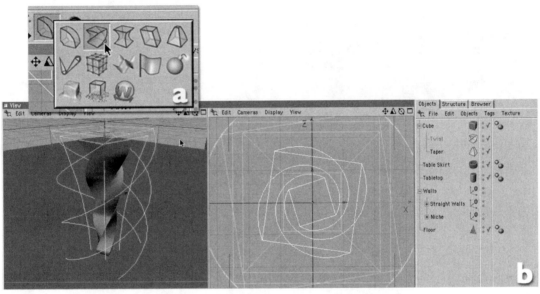

FIGURE 3.24   (a) Add a Twist Deformation object. (b) After making a child of the Cube object, twist away at the orange control handle to create a twisted leg. See color version on CD-ROM.

ON THE CD

Now move this newly tapered and twisted leg so that it sits beneath the tabletop as we've made it so far. Figure 3.25 shows the bottom of the table constructed of a Torus object, and several cylinders. Design the bottom as you'd like, but keep it all simple and made from primitives for now. When you have all the shapes built and laid into place, group (keystroke "G") all the shapes used to make this table together and call it "Table." Notice also in Figure 3.25 that the floor has been increased in size so that the floor lies beneath the table within the niche.

LAMPS

We have one last thing to model before we leave the realm of primitives. The sconces on the walls in our room contain shades that are made of primitive forms as well. These are made of one Cone object and two Torus objects (Figure 3.26). The Cone object is hollow because in the

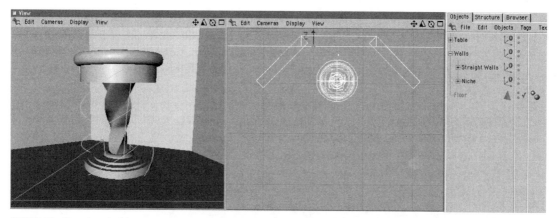

FIGURE 3.25 Completed table.

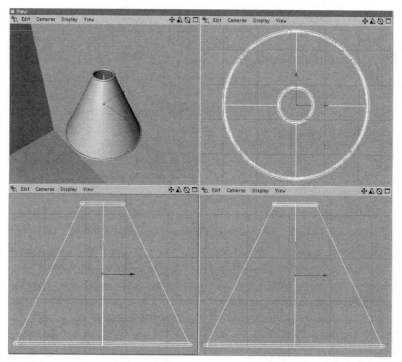

FIGURE 3.26 Lamp shades made of simple Cone object with Caps disabled and Top Radius enabled.

dialog box accessed by double-clicking on the Cone icon in the Objects Manager, Caps was unchecked. In this same dialog box, the Top Radius input field was changed to a non-zero value. Then by simply adjusting the control handles, the hollow Cone object can be altered to find an aesthetically pleasing shape. The Torus shapes were simply created and adjusted using the orange control handles to give a nice edge. When the shape is complete, group the Cone object and the two Torus shapes together and call it "Sconce Shade." For now, just place one Sconce Shade up on the wall. We'll be looking at other ways to duplicate forms later.

CONCLUSION

So there you have it, modeling with the help of primitives. You can see that we've barely gotten started, but with just primitive forms and a few simple deformers, we are able to create some interesting shapes. In Chapter 4, we will look at some more dynamic ways to create further complex forms. The best is yet to come.

4

GENERATORS (NURBS)

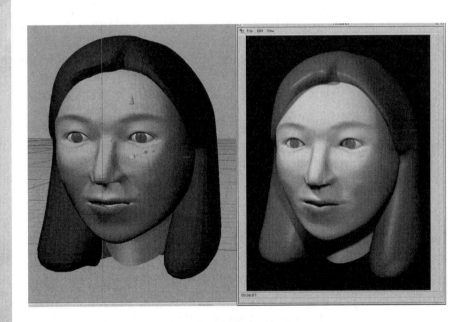

NON-DESTRUCTIVE MODELING

In Chapter 3, we covered modeling techniques for creating objects, including a wide variety of primitives. These primitives are created quickly and are immediately placed within the scene. This is a very intuitive form of modeling, but also in some ways very limiting. C4D includes a great collection of other modeling tools that expand the types of shapes possible and the freedom to continue to adjust these new shapes.

C4D has several techniques that make use of the idea of *generators*. Generators are objects that are created only through using other shapes or objects to create a new object with new geometry. However, objects used to create new forms via the generators still maintain their autonomy, so they can be altered when needed to change the form of the generator-based shape. This sort of freedom allows for smooth creation because changes are always possible.

In Chapter 3, we also touched upon one form of generator objects: Deformation objects. When we used the Twist Deformer for the pedestal of the table, the Deformation object itself had no geometry of its own; it was only able to manipulate the cube we placed within it. Such is the nature of almost all generator objects.

NURBS

The most common type of generator objects are NURBS. NURBS (singular or plural) actually is an acronym that stands for Non-Uniform Rational B-splines. The actual theory behind what this means exactly is complex and not particularly important except to note that its original conception was to find ways to accurately create curved surfaces. Although certainly not limited to curvilinear forms, NURBS do excel at making organic forms.

NURBS do not actually "contain" polygons. The idea is that through a collection of splines, a modeler can quickly create a variety of forms that are calculations of forms rather than actual groups of polygons. Usually, modeling is classified into polygon modeling and NURBS modeling. However, to assume that NURBS are polygon-independent is not entirely accurate, either. For although the forms are calculated free of polygonal information, when C4D gets ready to render a NURBS (or take the information you've given it and "paint" the picture), it must place polygons in the place of the NURBS form to "see" the shapes. Luckily, this all happens seamlessly behind the scenes and thus generally has no effect on your workflow. However, this bit of theory can become important in some advanced modeling or high memory-requirement projects.

Splines

The key building element of creating most NURBS objects are splines. Splines are not limited strictly to NURBS creation; in fact, they can be used for all sorts of things including animation paths and object organization within digital space. However, in this section we'll be focusing on splines' power as construction objects.

Splines have some interesting characteristics that are important to understand before they can be fully exploited as powerful modeling tools. First, splines are infinitely thin, appearing as lines that—although they are visible in the Editor—do not render; they are construction objects. The manual describes splines as "a sequence of vertices connected by lines, lying in 3D space." In other words, splines are a collection of points that you, the user, can alter to affect the line that joins these points together. These points are analogous to anchor points in vector-based applications, such as Illustrator. They are always editable and thus, the line is always changeable.

The nature of the line between the points can be straight or curved. The nature of the line is defined by the type of spline and the nature of the points that compose it. C4D provides for several ways to create splines. Mastery of how these splines are created and altered is vital to creating effective NURBS objects.

There are actually several methods of creating splines within C4D. The first method is to create an "Empty Spline" (Objects>Spline Object) and then fill this spline object with the spline information. A second and more common method is to use the nested collections of spline creation tools located in the top command palette (Figure 4.1). Because the nested spline creation tools shown in Figure 4.1 can do almost all the same things that creating an empty spline would do, we'll focus our attention on the nested tools.

Note that the tools shown here can be roughly grouped into two areas. The first two columns of tools have little brown dots on them that represent points or control vertices. The next five columns allow for the creation of Spline Primitives. Spline Primitives are similar to the primitives we talked of in Chapter 3; they are all splines that C4D makes very well and very quickly. They also all have collections of parameters that can be altered to dynamically and quickly change the shape of the spline primitive, as the spline is based upon a mathematical equation. A big difference between Spline Primitives and other primitives is that there are no interactive parametric handles for Spline Primitives. When you create a primitive circle spline, you won't get any orange handles. However you can still alter the primitive circle spline by double-clicking its *icon* in the Objects Manager.

FIGURE 4.1 Nested spline creation tools in the top command palette.

Each of these Spline Primitives has editable characteristics particular to their general shape. Some editable parameters are as simple as changing the radii of a circle while others become more complex, including things such as differences in number of pedals or cogs, thus changing the entire shape. Others become complex enough to take into account issues of three dimensions and do not become trapped in just two. Still others are complex enough to allow you to provide a mathematical formula to graph or even to allow you to create a collection of text splines. All are flexible, and you can change their settings at any time.

We'll look briefly at how one of the splines functions and how its different parameters can be used to create the spline shape you want. As we look at this circle spline primitive, there is one constant that we'll not talk much about: *Interpolation*. Interpolation is how C4D divides up the spline and how it connects the lines between the vertices. However, the change is not noticeable when you are just viewing the spline by itself; only in context of a spline being used within a generator object (such as a NURBS object) do changes in the interpolation really come into play (except for the notable exception of using the setting of "None"). So we'll hold off on discussion of the interpolation settings for Spline Primitives until we begin a more in-depth discussion of these splines in a construction sense.

Circle Spline Primitive

The circle spline is a much more diverse shape than a simple circle. By double-clicking the Circle icon in the Objects Manager, you can change the basic circle into a wide variety of shapes. Besides creating perfect circles (Figure 4.2a), the Circle Spline Primitive dialogue box also allows for the creation of Ellipses (Figure 4.2b) which allows you to define the differing width or height, and Rings (Figure 4.2c) which gives you the power to shift the size of the "hole" of the ring. You can even make an ellipse with a hole in the middle (Figure 4.2d).

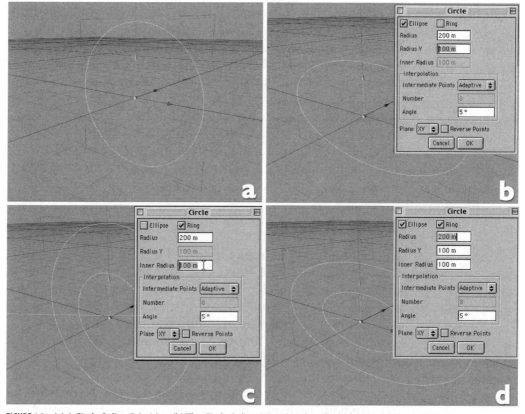

FIGURE 4.2   (a) A Circle Spline Primitive. (b) The Circle Spline Primitive also allows for the creation of ellipses. (c) Rings are quick and easy to create with the Circle Spline Primitive. (d) By activating both the Ring and Ellipse functions of the Circle Spline Primitive, you can create a flattened ring.

As is the case with all Spline Primitives, when you create a Circle Spline Primitive (done by clicking the Circle Spline Primitive tool) C4D will place the circle facing the view that is active. So if the top view is active, placing a Circle Spline Primitive will place a circle along the *xz* plane. If the front view is active, then the circle will be created along the *xy* plane. Other than rotating the circle into another orientation (if desired) you can also change the Plane setting within the dialogue box for the Circle Spline Primitive to change what plane it is lying along. The difference between these two methods is that rotating the Circle would cause the circle's *x*, *y*, and *z* axes to then not be lined up with the digital world, but changing the plane leaves the object's axes in alignment with the world's axis.

CREATING SPLINE CURVES

Although C4D's collection of spline primitives are indeed diverse and powerful, they don't make every shape you'd possibly need. Luckily, there is a second collection of tools that allows you to create any curve you'd like. Notice back in Figure 4.1 that there are two columns (6 tools total) of tools that allow you to create custom curves. All of these tools create spline curves as per your definition; however, they each use a slightly different methodology for creation. Each of these methods is simply a way of creating the spline using different interpolation or methods of joining vertices. Let's look a bit at how some of these spline creation tools work. We'll analyze them in the order that they appear in the command palette

Freehand Spline Curve

The first tool gives you the most freedom, but the least control. The Draw Freehand Spline Curves tool allows you to simply click and draw in one motion any curve you wish. To use this tool, select it and start to draw in your Editor. As soon as you release your mouse button with this tool, you are bumped out of the tool, a spline object appears in the Objects Manager, and C4D interprets your sketch by placing vertices.

The freedom comes from being able to simply "draw" the shape you want; the limitation in control comes from C4D deciding where to place your vertices. This may not seem like a big issue but revision is an important part of the 3D animation game, and you want to maintain all the control you can.

Notice that after drawing the shape, you don't have a simple white line defining the spline as we did with the primitives. Furthermore if you were to use the Move Active Element tool and try to move things, you'd find that nothing moves. This is because, after drawing a spline, you are automatically placed within Points mode. You can tell you're in Points mode by checking out the command palette along the left side of the screen (Figure 4.3).

FIGURE 4.3   After creating a spline, you will automatically be placed in Points mode allowing you to alter the spline just created.

The next four spline curve creation tools are all forms of creating curves that give you the change ability to define each vertex as you see fit. Each uses a slightly different method.

Bezier Spline Curve

Immediately below the Freehand Spline tool is the Draw Bezier Spline tool. If you come from a traditionally 2D graphic design background, this will be the most familiar. It functions very similarly to Adobe Illustrator's Pen tool. When the Draw Bezier Spline tool is selected, your mouse pointer changes to a symbol (Figure 4.4a). Unlike the Draw Freehand Spline tool which is exited as soon as the mouse button is released, the Draw Bezier Spline tool stays active until you select another tool, or "close" the spline by clicking on the first point created after adding points to your curve. Each time you click and release the mouse, a new vertex is placed.

While you are in the Draw Bezier Spline tool, if you simply click and immediately release, a vertex is placed with no visible bezier handles. By simply clicking and releasing several times, a jagged line can be created (Figure 4.4b). If you click and drag while you are in this tool, you'll be given a vertex, but the dragging part of the action will create bezier handles, making the curves easy to alter in the future (Figure 4.4c).

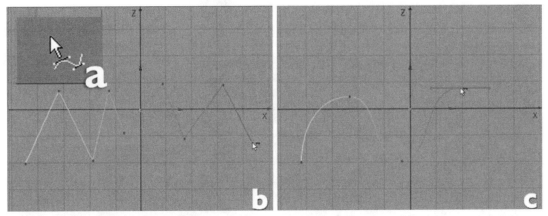

FIGURE 4.4 (a) When you are within any Draw Spline tool, the mouse pointer will indicate it by appearing like this. (b) Clicking and immediately releasing creates vertexes without curvilinear interpolation, thus giving you a straight line. (c) By clicking and dragging in the Draw Bezier Spline tool, you create vertices with bezier handles.

Note that closing a spline means that after creating a series of points, you return to the first point. When this is done, you are exited out of the Draw Bezier Spline tool. However, if you don't close the spline and don't select another tool, you'll remain within the tool. (For example, if you press the DELETE button on your keyboard, the last point drawn will be deleted rather than the entire spline.) In order to delete the spline, you must exit Points mode and enter Model mode or Object mode (Figure 4.5) and then hit DELETE. Note that while you are modeling, Model mode is preferable to Object mode.

FIGURE 4.5   You must exit out of the default Points mode you are in when you create splines in order to delete an entire spline. To do so, select either Object mode or Model mode.

B-Spline Curve

The Draw B-Spline tool is a way of creating very curvilinear forms. It's different from any of the other spline curve creation tools in that you are creating a set of vertices that the spline runs *between* rather than *through*. While you are within the Draw B-Spline tool, each time you click and release the mouse, the spline thus far will be drawn to that point (Figure 4.6a). When you click on the next position, however, the spline shifts from running through to the last point, to running beside it (Figure 4.6b). If the spline is open, the first point and last point will actually be on the spline's path (Figure 4.6c); but if the spline is closed, none of the spline will run through the points (Figure 4.6d). This is a great tool to use if you don't need exact curves, but are interested in making sure you have an extra smooth spline.

Cubic and Akima Spline Curves

When you using the Draw Cubic or Draw Akima Spline Curves tools, you simply click and release at points you wish the spline to

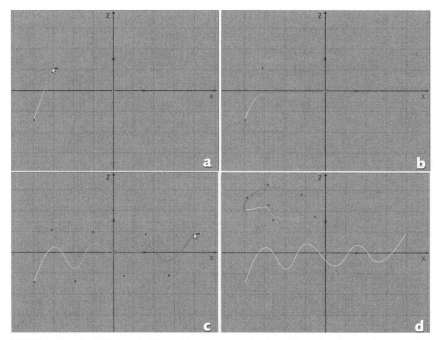

FIGURE 4.6 Creating B-Splines is different from other methods, as this tool creates vertices that the spline runs between rather than through. Still, it is a very powerful tool for creating nice smooth lines.

pass through. The spline passes through these points, rounding out the spline as it goes based upon the new information given. Both attempt to make a smooth spline. The biggest difference is that Cubic Splines will "overshoot" points in order to make a nice rounded curve (Figure 4.7a). The Draw Akima tool often is more accurate, but it can create undesirable effects (Figure 4.7b).

Editing Splines

The beauty of splines is that you're never locked into any part of them. What happens if you draw a spline with the Draw Akima Spline tool, but you don't like the sharp corners it gives you? What if you draw an open spline and later need it closed? What if you simply don't like the positions of the vertices created? What if the entire spline is simply too big? All of these things can be controlled with relative ease.

When a spline is created, a Spline object immediately appears in the Objects Manager. This spline can be renamed to whatever you'd

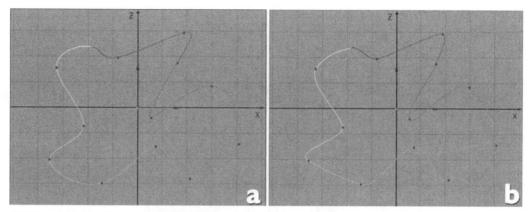

FIGURE 4.7   (a) Cubic Splines created with the Draw Cubic Spline tool creates nice rounded splines that emphasize round curves. (b) Akima Splines are often a bit more accurate, but you can end up with sharper corners.

like by double-clicking on the *word* "Spline." However, you can also change a variety of other settings by double-clicking the yellow "squiggly" *icon* located next to the word which opens the Spline dialog box (Figure 4.8a).

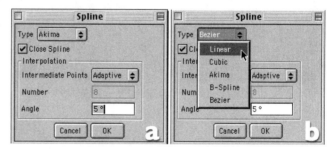

FIGURE 4.8   (a) The Spline dialogue box allows for a host of options to be changed. (b) The Type setting allows you to alter the type of interpolation for already-created splines, regardless of the Draw Spline tool that was used to create them.

The first noticeable power is the ability to change the style of interpolation labeled under the "Type" setting (Figure 4.8b). You can change the way the vertices are interpolated into a style as though you drew it with a different Draw Spline tool. Figure 4.9 shows the same curve with different types and the resultant splines.

Immediately below the Type setting is the ability to make the spline closed. So if you create an open spline by activating the Close Spline selection, C4D will close the spline off.

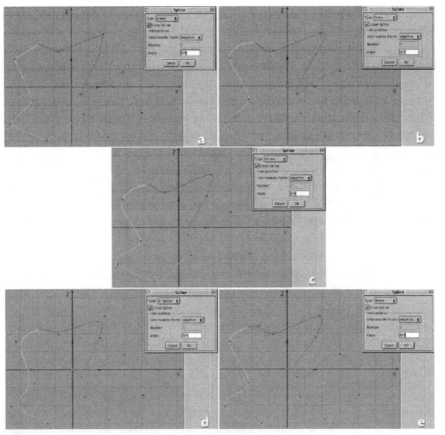

FIGURE 4.9   An identical collection of points can yield a variety of splines: (a) Linear, (b) Cubic, (c) Akima, (d) B-Spline, (e) Bezier.

When you create a spline, you are automatically defaulted into Points mode. This is no accident. Notice that when in Objects, Model, or Polygon modes, the spline (whether active or not) appears as a white line. It is only when you are in Points mode that you have the power to select the points or vertices that compose the spline and alter their position, rotation, or distance from one another. Furthermore, if there are is more than one spline within your scene, only the active spline will show its vertices, and thus only the active spline can be altered. To "activate" another spline for editing while you are still in Points mode, click on its name in the Objects Manager.

WORKING IN POINTS MODE

By being in Points mode, you can see all the points that make up the curve you've just drawn. To work with the points within Points mode, think of all alterations as two steps. First, click and release on the point you wish to alter (it will turn from brown to orange). Second, alter the point (move, rotate, scale). This may seem counterintuitive, but it is the way C4D works. The benefit to this is that you can select a point and then click anywhere within your view panel and affect the point. Points can be moved, scaled, or rotated, although usually most points are simply moved.

Remember that you can select more than one point. While you are in Points mode and with the Move, Scale, or Rotate Active Element tool active, you can select more than one point at a time by holding the SHIFT key down and selecting the additional point. Similarly, you can drop a point from a selection by continuing to hold the SHIFT button down and clicking an already selected point. There is another notable way to select points: by using the collection of Selection tools (Figure 4.10a).

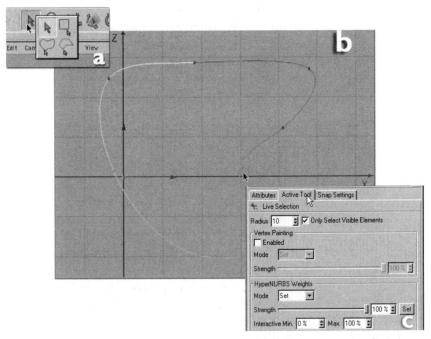

FIGURE 4.10   (a) Selection Tool. (b) Using the Live Selection tool is an intuitive process of painting a selection. (c) Active Tool Manager allows you to change the size of the Live Selection "brush."

This is actually a nested collection of four tools. The first is called the Live Selection tool and it allows you to "paint" a selection. Click (the mouse pointer will turn to a circle indicating the size of your brush) and drag over the points you wish to select. The selected points change color when they are selected (Figure 4.10b). You can add points of the active spline to the selection by holding the Shift key down and "painting" over the desired points or remove points from the selection by holding the CTRL (or COMMAND) key and painting over the tools you wish to remove.

You can control the size of the Live Selection brush in the Active Tool Manager (located beneath the Attributes Manager) at the bottom right-hand corner of the default C4D interface (Figure 4.10c). By increasing or decreasing the radius, the size of the circle indicating the Live Selections brush will increase or decrease accordingly. We'll talk much more about this Active Tool Manager later, as it is extremely useful in a variety of situations.

The other three tools—the Rectangle Selection, Free Selection, and Polygon Selection tools—are all other ways to select collections of points (and later polygons) by marqueeing (Figure 4.11a), drawing around (Figure 4.11b), or creating a selection by defining a shape, done by clicking on the corners of that shape (Figure 4.11c). Again, when you are finished with each of these selection tools, selected points will appear orange.

Once these points are selected, you can use the Move Active Element tool to move them around. The spline will reshape accordingly. Similarly, you can use the Rotate Active Element tool to rotate a group of points around the spline's axis or the Scale Active Element tool to scale the points out or in from the spline's axis.

Bezier Spline Alteration

Now an important thing to note here is that selecting any one point with a spline, using type Linear, Cubic, Akima, or B-Spline, activates a vertex by showing the orange dot in place of the brown. You can move this point directly and the spline will readjust according to the interpolation settings given it. However, bezier splines (splines created with the Draw Bezier Spline tool) have a noticeable difference. As we mentioned before, when you create a bezier spline, you could create a linear spline by clicking and releasing on a curvilinear spline with vertices that have bezier handles. You can still directly move the vertex, but these bezier handles (pre-

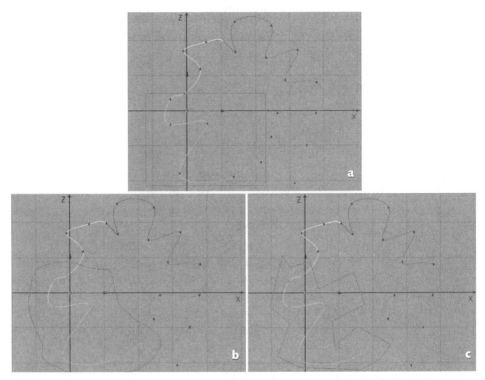

FIGURE 4.11   The other Selection tools are handy ways to select points with squares (a), freehand selections (b), or polygon shapes encompassing selections (c).

sented in purple) allow some extra control over the shape of your spline.

While you are in Points mode, you can select a point by clicking and releasing on it. If the spline is indeed a bezier spline, purple handles will appear. If you grab either of these bezier handles (the manual calls them "tangent handles") by clicking and dragging, you'll notice that the bezier handle opposite it will move as well. If you pull the handle outward, your curve will become longer. If you move the handles closer together, the curve becomes shorter. You can even click-drag a handle and drag it so short that it begins to lengthen in the opposite direction. When this happens, the spline develops a loop. One of the greatest benefits to bezier splines is the ability to create non-round vertices. By holding the Shift key down when you click-drag a handle, you can move one handle independently of the other. The result is an immediate shift from a smooth corner to a sharp corner. So, you could create a curve that was longer on one side of the vertex than the other. By Shift-dragging points you can create sharp corners as they would appear in teardrops or waves. You can create literally any shape with bezier splines. They are so powerful, in fact, that C4D uses these curves when it works with animation paths; but we'll talk more of this later.

General Spline Notes

There are a few important things to remember when you work with splines. The first is that nothing is permanent; you can change any point or any interpolation setting of a spline—so don't be overly concerned when you are roughing out a shape. The second is that splines, although they exist in 3D space, are still drawn in the limitations of your two-dimensional monitor. As such, it's very important that, in order to maintain control over the spline, you draw the spline in *any view but* the perspective view. When drawing and working with a spline and viewing the scene with a perspective camera, it becomes impossible (without spinning the object around repeatedly) to tell where the points are in relation to each other in all directions. If you draw in the perspective view, what appears to be a good-looking spline is actually a mess of points in all sorts of directions. Draw splines in front, top, or side views, then—if need be—move the points around, viewing their relative position in the perspective view.

NURBS

C4D's NURBS tools are shown in Figure 4.12a. These six tools are perhaps the most powerful modeling tools within the package. The first one shown there, HyperNURBS, is so powerful, in fact, that we'll be devoting all of Chapter 5 to it. The other NURBS tools shown are Extrude, Lathe, Loft, Sweep, and Bezier NURBS. Because much information on the other NURBS objects is provided in the manual, please refer to it for specific questions.

The key to NURBS tools is that, with the exception of the Bezier NURBS object, none has its own geometry. They are object generators, meaning that they create forms from other objects within C4D—namely, splines. When any NURBS is created, it will show up in the Object Manager, but there will be nothing but an object axis in the view panel to show that the NURBS object even exists. To give the NURBS object forms, you must tell it what splines it is allowed to use. This is done by making splines *children* of NURBS objects. To do this, in the Objects Manager, take a spline and "drop" it into a NURBS object (Figure 4.12b). We'll look at the specifics in the following explanations. First, we'll examine the Extrude NURBS tool.

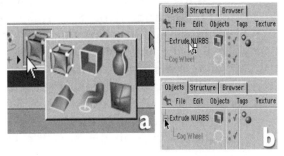

FIGURE 4.12   (a) The NURBS collection of tools. (b) To allow a NURBS object to know what spline it should use to build its forms, drop the spline into the NURBS object.

Extrude NURBS

Aptly named, the Extrude NURBS object allows you to extrude a profile along any direction. Imagine this tool as the simplest way to give three dimensions to two-dimensional splines. As an example, create a Text Spline Primitive and change the text it creates to your name.

If this were rendered, you would be left with a black screen because splines themselves have no geometry to render. Now create an Extrude NURBS object by selecting it from the top command palette, or by selecting Object>NURBS>Extrude NURBS. Again, if you were to render this scene at this point, you would still get a black screen as all you have are two objects with no relation to each other. Give them a relationship by dropping the Text Spline Primitive into the Extrude NURBS object.

Immediately, your text should have depth. You can change the size of this depth by double-clicking the Extrude NURBS *icon* in the Objects Manager. When you open the NURBS details, they will appear immediately below the Objects Manager in the Attributes Editor (this is new to R8). Notice that at the top of the Attributes Editor are several buttons: Basic, Coord., Object, and Caps. Clicking on these will display different attributes about the NURBS shape that you can edit. Also note that Shift-clicking on more than one of these buttons will open multiple attribute areas for editing.

Object Settings

With the Object button selected in the Attributes Editor, you have access to define some general issues of a NURBS object. The direction the Extrude NURBS extrudes by default is along the z-axis—this is referred to as "Movement." In the case of the text, you can see that the blue object axis handle (z) is indeed facing backwards and so this is just like what you want. However, it should be noted that if you have a spline facing the x- or y-axes, remember that you can change the direction along which the Extrude NURBS extrudes to match by changing the values in the Movement row to have the NURBS extrude in the direction (and for the distance) that you want.

Other important functions of this area of the Attributes Editor include the Isoparm Subdivision input field which allows you to define how many subdivisions will be shown when you are viewing your scene with Isoparm Display. The Isoparm Subdivision input box allows you to determine how many segments C4D includes as it extrudes the spline.

Caps and Details

Clicking on the Caps button in the Attribute Editor will allow you to define how this Extrude NURBS object's "ends" are treated. The Caps settings determine whether you have a hollow or solid extrusion. Selecting "No Cap" for both Start and End gives a hollow extrusion (Figure 4.13a), while setting just one to "No Cap" and leaving the other with Cap on obviously leaves an interestingly shaped mold (Figure 4.13b).

The Start and End settings also allow for much more diversity. For example, note that you can also set the Start and/or End to Fillet. This provides a bevel without a cap to the extrusion and gives you much more refined forms than simple straight back extrusions. To explore these rounding, let's place the Start setting at "Fillet Cap" and leave the End setting with just "Cap" (Figure 4.14).

As a result, you'll have a beveled collection of text. There are a wide variety of parameters that can be altered in this beveled look. When you select Fillet Cap, new settings (including Fillet Type)

FIGURE 4.13 Caps settings can determine whether you have a solid or hollow extrusion. (a) "No Cap" set for both Start and End gives a hollow, or "empty" extrusion. (b) "No Cap" set for Start and "Cap" set for End provides a solid extrusion.

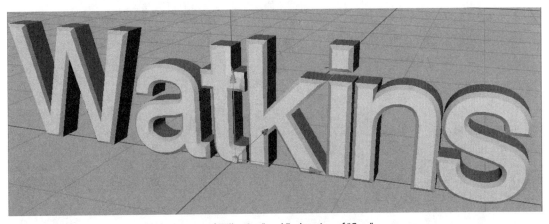

FIGURE 4.14 Our text thus far with Start setting of "Fillet Cap" and End setting of "Cap."

will become available that allow you to define how the bevel, or Fillet, works.

To discuss the Fillet Type and other related details, let's look first at the bottom half with all the checkboxes. Furthermore, to get a better idea of the changes we're going to make, the screen shots will be taken from a much closer angle. Notice that by default the "Hull Inwards" setting has been activated. The hull refers to the outermost area of the extruded splines. With this activated, the Extruded NURBS (or any NURBS using Caps, for that matter) provides the bevel you'd expect (Figure 4.15a) as the rounding comes outward and inward off the front of the extrusion. With Hull Inwards turned off, you get an interesting but odd extrusion and cap combination (Figure 4.15b).

The "Hole Inwards" setting only refers to splines that actually have "holes." For instance, in the word "Watkins" the only hole is the hole in the "a." With this deactivated, the holes act as the rest of the hull (Figure 4.15c); when it is activated, C4D pulls the rounding inward—which can create some odd effects (Figure 4.15d).

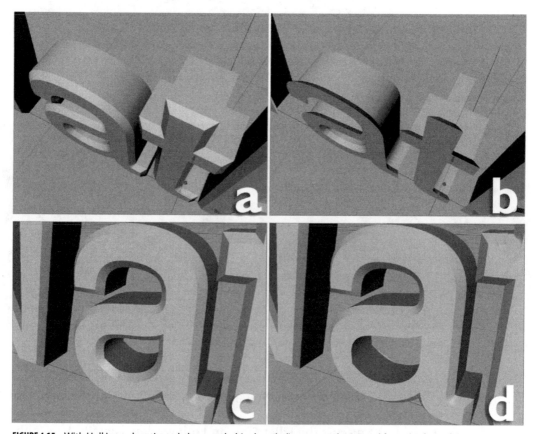

FIGURE 4.15 With Hull Inwards activated, the rounded (or beveled) cap extrudes inward from the face of the extrusion (a). With this deactivated, the extrusion increases in size off the face of the extrusion (a). Turning the Hole Inwards option on (c) or off (d) makes a big difference with splines that have a "hole."

When a spline is first extruded with regular caps, the extrusion goes straight back, leaving the overall look of the text and font the same (Figure 4.16a). However, sometimes confusingly, when "Fillet Cap" is selected, the spline seems to get "fatter"; almost as if someone turned on the "Bold" button for text (Figure 4.16b). The manual calls this "inflating." This inflation can be eliminated by activating the "Constrain Contour" setting. This keeps the overall hull the same size (Figure 4.16c). The drawback to using the Constrain Contour option is that if the radius of the rounding is too large and the hull isn't allowed to expand, you can get some odd overlaps where the cap is bigger than the bevel (Figure 4.16d).

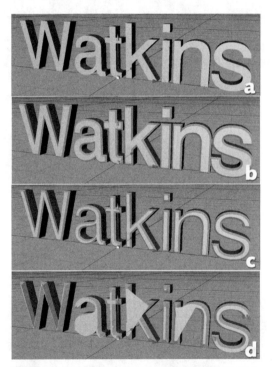

FIGURE 4.16   The Constrain Contour checkbox allows you to maintain the size of your outer hull.

The Regular Grid checkbox is really only applicable if you plan on bending, twisting, or otherwise distorting your text. The Regular Subdivision option has to do with establishing the polygon topology of the extrusions. By default, the extrusion is thought of in C4D as collections of triangular shapes. These work great unless the shape

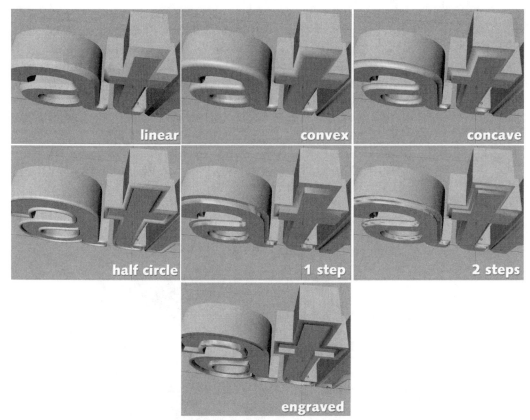

FIGURE 4.17 Examples of the different Fillet Cap settings. Note that all of these Fillet Cap settings maintain constant Start Steps and Start Radius settings.

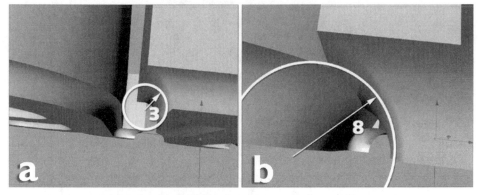

FIGURE 4.18 (a) With a Start Radius setting of 3, the depth of the rounding is much less than if the Start Radius setting were 8(b).

is bent in many places. When this happens, there sometimes appears to be some "shearing" or tearing where the triangles aren't able to bend appropriately in relationship to one another. By activating the Regular Subdivision checkbox, the extrusion is then built of quadrangles (rectangular shapes) with triangles only positioned on the edges. The higher the Regular Grid setting, the less shearing you'll see in such deformation situations. However, your polycount will increase correspondingly.

Fillet Type

The Fillet Type settings allow you to determine in what shape the filleted hull will appear. The easiest way to illustrate the different fillet options are through pictures of the Fillet Type settings results (Figure 4.17). However, before we go into the filleting options, we need to be sure that C4D has enough information to work with as it attempts to round the caps. Located within the Caps section of the NURBS Attribute Editor of the Extrude NURBS dialogue box are two input fields, called Steps, that are under Start and End. These let you determine how many steps C4D is to take to get from the edge of the extrusion to the edge of the rounding. With only one step, the beveling will always be in straight lines. If you increase the number of steps, you increase the smoothness possible in the rounding. In Figure 4.17, only the Start Steps setting is active.

Also note the Start Radius input field. Think of this value as determining a circle shape that determines the size of the rounding. Figure 4.18 shows two renderings of the extruded text with differing values for the Start Radius field and a superimposed circle to illustrate the idea.

HyperNURBS and NURBS in Practice

A method of modeling quickly gaining popularity in the 3D world is that of *subdivision modeling*. Also referred to as cage modeling, the basic idea is that you, the modeler, create a low-poly form which the 3D application subdivides into a more organic and high-poly form. The low-poly shape is called the cage, with the subdivided form being inside the cage. C4D—since v6—has had a nice implementation of this technology. R8 has added some new functions to HyperNURBS (that we'll talk about later in this chapter) that make its subdivision modeling one of the best in the industry.

A simple example using HyperNURBS (C4D's version) of subdivision is shown in Figure 4.19. Here, a simple cube (which acts as the cage) made up of six polygons is placed within a HyperNURBS object by making the cube a child of the HyperNURBS object (Figure 4.19a). Notice that the single polygon in each face is now subdivided (Figure 4.19b) to provide far more polygons, and hence more places to bend, ultimately creating a rounder shape.

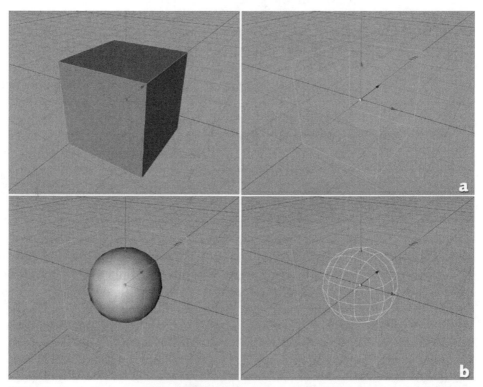

FIGURE 4.19 Simple illustration of HyperNURBS: (a) shows a simple six-sided cube, that when placed within a HyperNURBS object, (b) each side is subdivided and rounded.

There are several general rules about HyperNURBS that are important to remember. The first is that HyperNURBS can only affect one object or group of objects at a time. So in Figure 4.20a, even though all three cubes are children of the HyperNURBS object, only the first (the cube in the middle) has been subdivided. This problem is solved in Figure 4.20b as the three cubes have been grouped together and the Null object parent has been dropped into the HyperNURBS. C4D thinks of the Null object group as one object and rounds all the shapes contained therein.

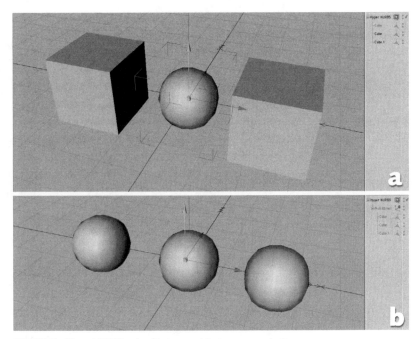

FIGURE 4.20   HyperNURBS only affects one object or group at a time.

The second rule is that HyperNURBS has attributes (available in the Attributes Editor accessible by double-clicking the HyperNURBS object within the Objects Manager) that allow you to define how many times to subdivide the contained polygons in both the Editor and the rendered (Raytracing) version (Figure 4.21). The benefit of this is that you can select a low number of subdivisions in the Editor to keep the interface snappy, but have a higher number of subdivisions (thus a smoother surface) when the object is rendered to the Picture Viewer (Figure 4.22).

The Raytracing subdivision settings are only in effect for renderings done to the Picture Viewer; simply rendering the active view panel will reveal a rendering using the settings in the Editor input panel.

This rounding of shapes is what makes HyperNURBS so powerful. However, it can also be hard to control. There are two ways to take control over the amount of curve your HyperNURBS shapes have. The first is the traditional method of proximity of polygons in the cage. Traditionally, HyperNURBS rounds edges according to how large each polygon is in relation to a connected neighboring

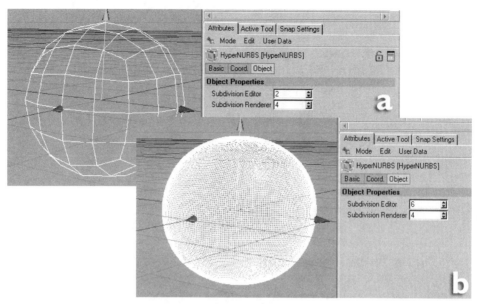

FIGURE 4.21 By increasing the Subdivision Editor value, the resulting HyperNURBS becomes increasingly rounded because it has an increasingly large amount of polygons.

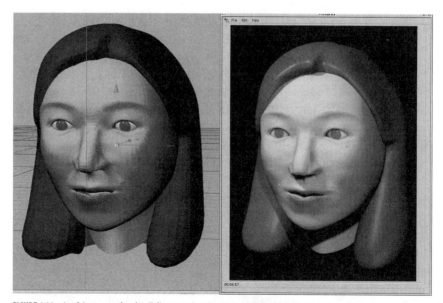

FIGURE 4.22 In this example, the Editor setting is set to "2," revealing a very blocky looking model, since the number of times C4D is subdividing each shape is fairly low. However, the Raytracing setting is set to 12, revealing a very smooth surface in the final rendering, as there are now many polygons where only a few were originally placed. Model by 3D I student Ya-Tsun Yang.

polygon at an angle to it. Thus, a cube with an original segment set-ting of "1" will make for a very round HyperNURBS object (Figure 4.23a). If you increase the number of segments the original form (the low-poly cage) has, the angles will become sharper as the rela-tive size of the polygons decreases (Figure 4.23b and c). If polygons are resized (Figure 4.23d), then the small polygons make for sharper corners as they appear on the right of Figure 4.23d com-pared with the corners on the left where the segments are further apart (larger relative polygons).

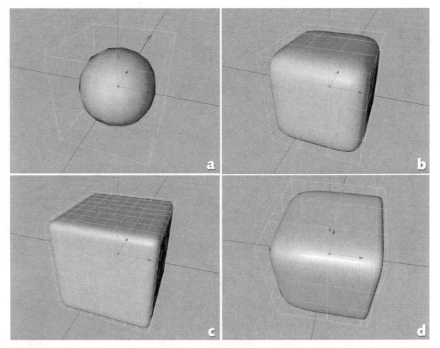

FIGURE 4.23   The further apart the segments are, the rounder the HyperNURBS.

A new method to controlling how round corners are within Hy-perNURBS objects is the ability to weight points, edges, or polygons. As we discussed earlier, a polygonal object consists of vertices (or points) connected by edges. When three or more edges connect, they form a polygon. When you place a polygonal object into a Hy-perNURBS object, the default weight of all elements is set at an un-intuitive 0. This means that the low-poly cage is simply rounding the form, but neither the edges, points, or faces are unduly pulling or pushing on the high-poly mesh within.

To work with HyperNURBS weighting, use the Selection tool (the arrow at the top left of the interface). When this tool is selected, you can see the editable attributes in the Active Tool Editor (in the bottom right of the interface, beneath the Attributes Editor shown in Figure 4.24). When activated, you will see that there is a section in the Active Tool Editor called HyperNURBS Weights.

You can add weights to polygons, edges, or points. Figure 4.24 shows a polygonal cube within a HyperNURBS. The Active Tool Editor shows the settings for the Selection Tool (which is active). Finally, notice that we are in Polygon mode, and one of the polygons of the cube is selected. The HyperNURBS Weights setting is at 0%.

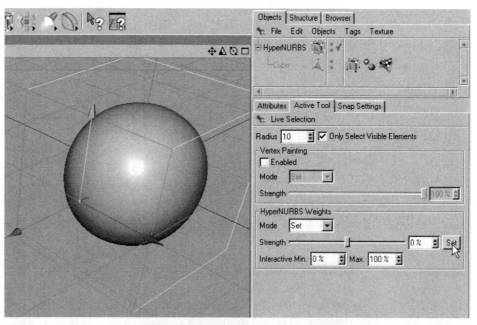

FIGURE 4.24   The default HyperNURBS Weights is 0%. With the Selection Tool active, you can change the weighting of polygons, edges, or points under the Active Tool settings.

There are a couple ways to use this method of weighting components. The simplest is to set the Strength setting to what you want to change the selected component's weight to, and hit the Set button. Figure 4.25 shows the same cube with the same polygon selected with a new HyperNURBS weight of 100%. Notice that now this polygon from the low-poly mesh acts like a super magnet, pulling all the polygons of the high-poly mesh to it, thus making the edge flat.

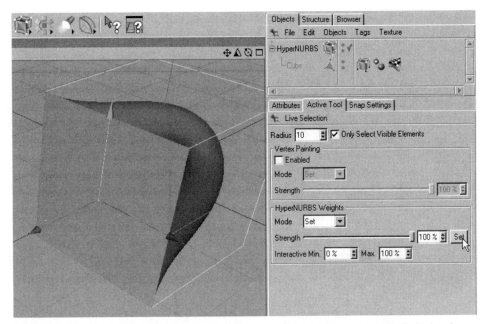

FIGURE 4.25 Setting the HyperNURBS weight of a polygon to 100% pulls all the polygons in the high-poly mesh flush to the low-poly surface.

Conversely, setting the HyperNURBS Weights setting to –100% and hitting the Set button, causes the low-poly mesh's selected polygon to repel the polygons of the high-poly mesh. Figure 4.26 shows the results.

This same technique works with varying results for edges (Figure 4.27a and b) when in Edge mode and points (Figure 4.28a and b) when in Points Mode.

The third general rule that it is important to understand is that only connected polygons are rounded. For example, Figure 4.29 shows a Cube Primitive that has "Separate Surfaces" activated. C4D sees each face of the cube as a separate object rather than seeing the collection of planes as connected parts of one object. The edge of each individual polygon is rounded, but not in relation to the other planes. So, polygons that are parts of different objects won't smooth into each other. In addition, if two polygons that are part of the same object don't share an edge, they will not blend into each other.

The final rule is that C4D works better with quadrangles than triangles. When you create low-poly meshes, try to stick to four-sided polygons rather than triangular polys.

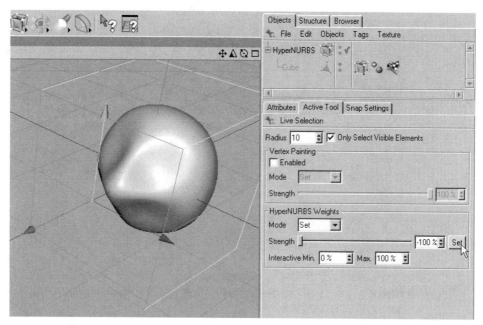

FIGURE 4.26 Turning the Strength to –100% pushes the high-poly mesh away from the selected component.

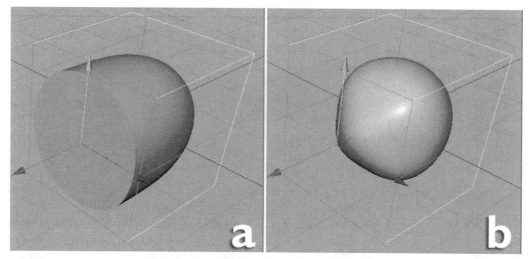

FIGURE 4.27 Using HyperNURBS Weights to weight all four edges. (a) Shows a weight of 100%; (b) Shows a weight of –100%.

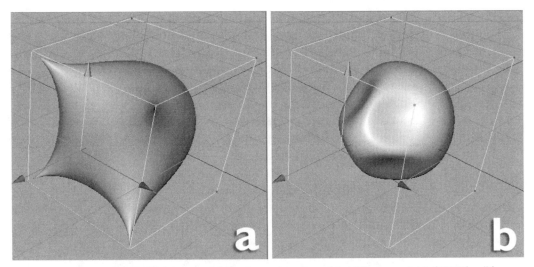

FIGURE 4.28   Using HyperNURBS Weights to weight the four points of one side. (a) Shows a weight of 100% for all four points; (b) Shows a weight of –100% for the same points.

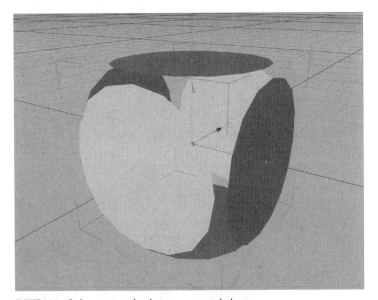

FIGURE 4.29   Only connected polygons are rounded.

HyperNURBS Methods

When working with HyperNURBS, you generally start out by working with a low-poly object—the cage. After some basic manipulation, you can drop the shape into a HyperNURBS and see the rounded shape. There are three main methods of creating the "cage" polygon form that you will later place within the Hyper-NURBS object. The first method, which we'll refer to as the Primitive Cage method entails altering a primitive form. This method involves creating a primitive shape like a cube or circle and extruding, twisting, or otherwise modifying the form to create a rough approximation of the desired form. When the form is placed within a HyperNURBS object, you are given a rounded version of the boxy approximation (Figure 4.30).

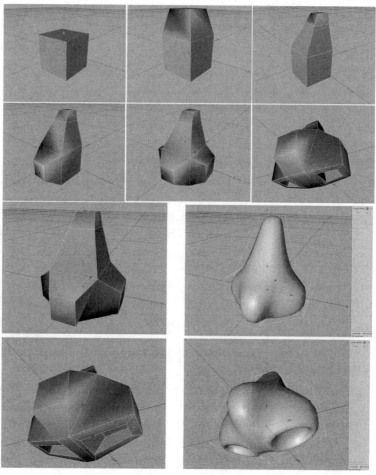

FIGURE 4.30   One method of working with HyperNURBS is to create the cage form by altering a primitive form, such as this cube. When the altered cube is placed within a HyperNURBS object, it becomes a much more organic-shaped nose.

The benefit of this method is that the polygons are already connected to each other. And creating new polygons is easy using Extrudes and Inner Extrudes (discussed below).

The second method is to build each polygon manually within a Polygon object and then place this polygon form into a Hyper-NURBS object. This allows ultimate control over the polygon topology, but takes longer, as each point must be constructed and moved, then combined with other points to create a polygon. However, using this careful process reveals amazing results. In later chapters, we will be spending quite a bit of time with this technique because it is so powerful.

VITAL HyperNURBS Tools

Beneath the Structure pull-down menu is a collection of incredibly powerful tools. Strictly speaking, these tools are not HyperNURBS tools; in actuality, they are polygon manipulation tools. However, they are indeed vital when you are working with forms planned for placement with a HyperNURBS object, as most HyperNURBS objects are constructed and edited by polygon-based objects.

Add Points

The Add Points tool allows you to create the building blocks of polygons. You may add points to any polygon-based object, including an empty polygon object (Objects>Polygon Object). When a Polygon object is first created it is completely empty without any geometry of its own. When the Polygon object is selected in the Objects Manager, you can select the Add Points tool (your mouse pointer will change to indicate you are within the Add Points tool) and add points to the form by holding the CTRL (or COMMAND) button down and clicking where you desire points. Make sure that you are in Points mode to see where you are placing the points. Now these points are fairly useless by themselves; without connecting them, there is no geometry to see or even place within a HyperNURBS object. This is where the Bridge and Create Polygon tools come in.

Bridge and Create Polygons

The Bridge and Create Polygon tools are both located beneath the Structure pull-down menu. They allow you to create polygons from extant points. The Bridge tool (also activated by hitting pressing "B" on the keyboard) allows you to "bridge" points together to form polys. To use this tool, you must first have points to work with. These points may have been created by you earlier with the Add Points tool, or they may be the existing points of a Polygon object; the Bridge tool works really well when you need to fill holes in a Polygon object. Imagine you have four points that you wish to create a polygon with; click on point #1 and drag to another (point #2) and release. This defines an "edge" to bridge from. Then click and drag from point #3 to point #4 to define the opposite edge to bridge to. Upon releasing your mouse, a polygon will be formed. This is a tool that needs more exploring. In later chapters, we will cover it in greater depth.

The Create Polygons tool works much the same way, except that, when using this tool, you want to click on each point (three or four) that you wish to make a polygon out of. You can click and drag from point to point or just click and release on a series of points, making sure that the last point clicked is the same as the first. This seems like a great deal of effort to create a polygon when one could simply be created by selected it from the Primitives list. The real power of these tools comes into play when you create a series of points which are then connected with either the Bridge or Create Polygons tools to make a form. When this form is dropped in a HyperNURBS object, your simple collection of points and polys becomes a complex form. In later chapter, we will build such a complex form by building up polygons from scratch.

The other tools we're going to talk about within the Structure pull-down menu, Extrude, Extrude Inner, and Knife, are primarily tools for use with the first method of Primitive Cage Creation. This method starts with a primitive form that is made editable (Structure>Make Editable). Although a primitive form will work within a HyperNURBS object, the only way to alter the polygons to utilize the Primitive Cage Creation method is to have a polygon-based form, which primitives are not. All of the tool explanations below will be built upon the idea of having a Cube Primitive that has been made editable.

Before we can get into these tools, it is important to understand a bit more about polygons. We've already talked about polygons having points and edges. Each polygon also has a front and a back that C4D keeps careful track of. A polygon's *normal* is the front of the polygon. C4D understands which side is the front and uses it extensively for several tools.

Extrude

The Extrude tool only works while you are in Polygon mode and a polygon-based form (not a primitive or NURBS) is active in the Objects Manager. What it does is take a selected polygon and extrude (or pull) it away from its location, in the direction of the polygon's normal. As it extrudes, it creates new polygons to fill in the spaces that would have been left if you had simply moved the polygon away from the rest of the form (Figure 4.31). The key to using this tool is to remember that every time you click-drag (even a little) and release, a new collection of polygons has been created. If no other tool is selected, the Extrude tool stays active, and subsequent mouse click-drags produce added extrusions. Often people end up with an intense group of extrusions because of errant mouse clicks. The best method is to use the Live Selection tool or the Move Active Element tool to select a polygon to extrude, and then switch to the Extrude tool to extrude that polygon.

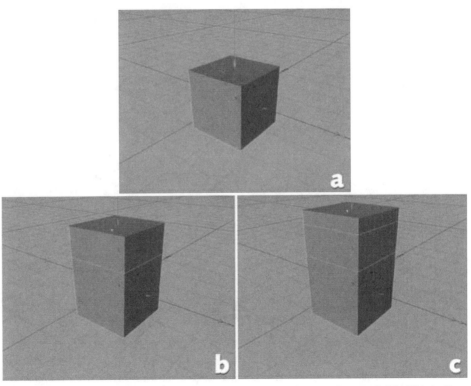

FIGURE 4.31   Extrusion process. (a) Begin by selecting a polygon or polygons to be extruded. (b) With the Extrude tool activated, click and drag to extrude that polygon away from the object. (c) Subsequent click and drags will continue to extrude.

When the Extrude tool is active, you can adjust several settings of that tool. You can adjust the tool's setting in the Active Tool Editor (bottom right corner of interface beneath the Attributes Editor). Perhaps the most important setting there is the last one. The Preserve Groups setting allows you to determine if a group of polygons will be extruded as a group (and thus it will not create polygons) between the extruded polys or extruded separately (Figure 4.32). The Maximum Angle and Variance settings go hand-in-hand with the Preserve Groups option as they determine if groups of polygons are to be extruded together (if the relative angle to each adjoining polygon is less than the value entered) or if they are to be extruded separately (if the relative angle of each adjoining polygon is more than the value entered). The Variance setting allows you to quickly create a variety of extrusions (with Preserve Groups deactivated) in a short amount of time (Figure 4.33). The Offset setting allows you to numerically determine the distance the polygons are extruded.

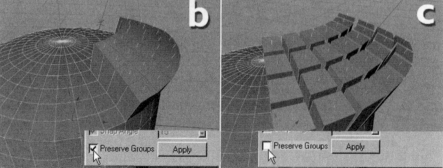

FIGURE 4.32 With a group of polygons selected, you can extrude (a) as a group, or (b) separately, as determined by (c) the Preserve Groups option in the Active Tools palette.

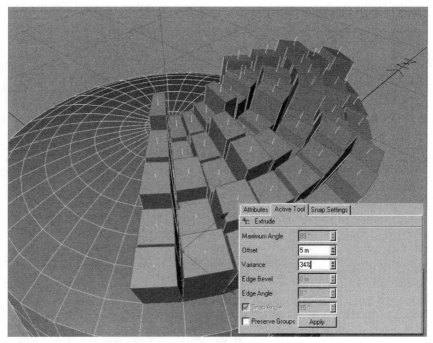

FIGURE 4.33 The Variance setting allows for quick extrusions of varying lengths.

New to R8 is the powerful and interesting ability to extrude edges as well. There was a time when you could only edit polygonal objects by moving points or moving polygons. The ability to manipulate edges is surprisingly powerful and you'll find it extremely useful when modeling complex human forms.

The ability to extrude edges means that you can create a new polygon that extrudes from the edge of a polygonal object (Figure 4.34a), or more importantly, you can create new rings of polygons (Figure 4.34b). When you are modeling human forms by creating rings around the eyes or mouth, this becomes an incredibly powerful tool. Much, much more on this later.

Extrude Inner

The Extrude Inner tool works much like the Extrude tool except that instead of extruding a selected polygon away from the object, it creates a new polygon that remains flat against the overall form (Figure 4.35). The same rules apply to the settings in the Active Tool Editor. The real strength of this tool comes from the ability to

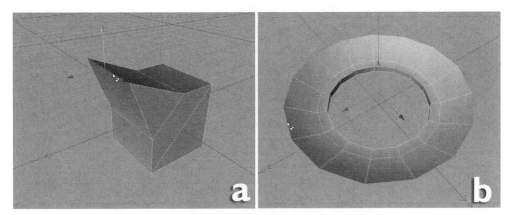

FIGURE 4.34 Extruding edges.

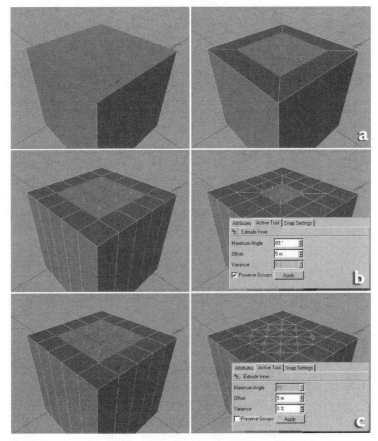

FIGURE 4.35 Extrude Inner (a) with simple polygon. (b) With multiple polygons selected, a group of new polys can be created along the face of the object, or (c) individual polygons can be created.

use it in combination with the Extrude tool. For instance, Figure 4.36 shows a cube which uses an Extrude Inner, followed immediately by an Extrude.

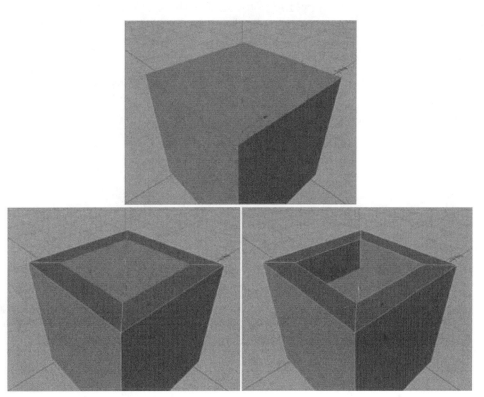

FIGURE 4.36   By using the Extrude Inner and then immediately using the Extrude, hollowed-out forms can be created easily.

Knife

The Knife tool is a great way to "cut" a polygon or collection of polys. If you have a form, let's say a primitive cube, that has been made editable and now has had a series of extrudes performed on it, you may find that you need an extra extrude that you forgot to insert. Or, perhaps you have a shape that is a good start, but you need more segments than you presently have. The Knife tool allows you to cut or subdivide polygons.

Figure 4.37 shows a simple editable cube (emphasis added on the image). Note that each face of the cube is composed of one polygon. The Knife tool can change this very easily. The simplest form of using the Knife tool is to select a polygon (in Polygon Mode) with the Live Selection tool (Figure 4.37a), and then activate the Knife tool, click-dragging to define the "cut" (Figure 4.37b). Holding the Shift key down constrains the angle to whatever setting is listed in the Constrain Angle dialogue box within the Active Tool palette. The result is shown in Figure 4.37c.

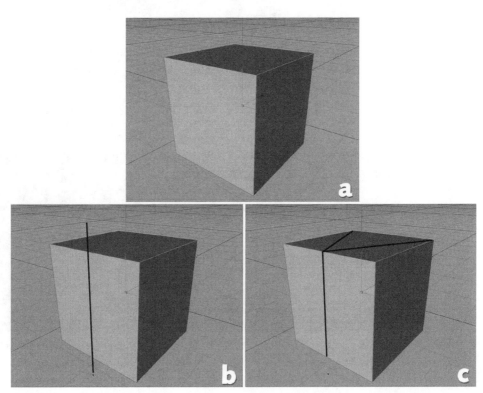

FIGURE 4.37 The Knife tool in action.

But, there is a drawback. Using the Knife tool in the way it is set up by default almost causes more problems than it solves. For example, notice that when it is only cutting one polygon, C4D must create triangles on the other faces to compensate for the split poly on one face. Another problem is that, while we are cutting in the perspective view, we've actually created a crooked cut that can be seen from a flat front view (Figure 4.38a). The trick to the Knife tool then, is to 1) make sure that all cuts are done from a flat on view (front, back, right, left, top, bottom) and 2) make sure that the default "Restrict to Selection" option is turned OFF when you are making cuts. This way, when a cut is made holding the Shift key down from an appropriate viewpoint, the Knife tool cuts completely through the object and keeps the cut straight (Figure 4.38b).

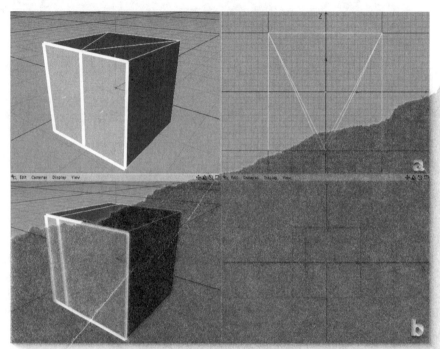

FIGURE 4.38   (a) When the default Restrict to Selection option is activated and the Knife tool is used in a perspective view panel, the results are uneven cuts that create triangles. (b) When you are cutting from a non-perspective view while holding the Shift key down, clean cuts that knife through the entire object can be made. (Emphasis added).

These tools may all seem useful enough, but what do they have to do with HyperNURBS? Well, for an example, if you create a HyperNURBS object and then take the cube created with an Extrude Inner followed by an Extrude—as shown in Figure 4.36—and make it a child of the HyperNURBS object, you would get the organic form shown in Figure 4.39. You can then, by selecting the cube within the HyperNURBS, continue to alter the blue cage form using the Extrude, Extrude Inner, and Knife tools, and the HyperNURBS object will continue to recalculate the curve, creating a complex form based on your simple changes.

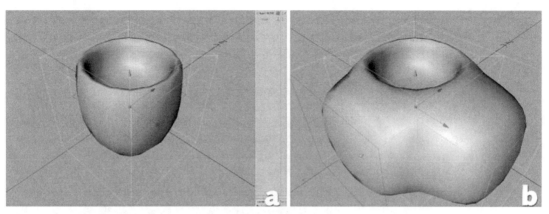

FIGURE 4.39 (a) Low polygon objects dropped in a HyperNURBS objects creates a rounded form. (b) You can continue to alter the form by altering the cage that was the original shape.

TUTORIAL

4.1 NURBS AND THE DINING ROOM

So now that we've talked for a long time about specific objects and some specific tools relating to NURBS, let's look at them in action. Open up the room that you created for Tutorial 3.1 (Figure 4.40). Notice that a few extra walls were have been added since we looked at it last. Do this on your version as well, using simple Cube Primitives.

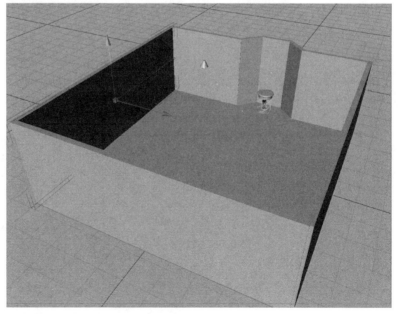

FIGURE 4.40 Our room with a few extra walls.

As this room is going to be a dining room, let's start off by building a dinner table. We could build the table all within the room setting, but it is often less confusing if you construct separate objects in separate files and merge them later. So for the table, make a new file (File>New). Notice that when you do this, your room file will seem to vanish. Actually, it is still open and can be accessed from the Window pull-down menu, so don't worry.

To start, we'll create the top of the table using an Extrude NURBS object. The table will be oval and we will create it by activating the "Top" View Panel and creating a Circle Spline Primitive. Double-click the circle's yellow icon in the Objects Manager and change the setting to create an ellipse that is only 100m wide for its *y* radius (Figure 4.41).

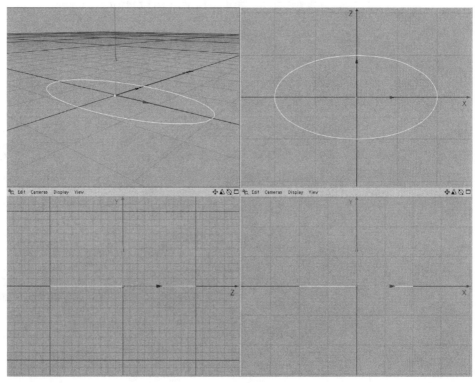

FIGURE 4.41   Creating the tabletop begins with a Circle Spline shaped to an Ellipse.

Now create an Extrude NURBS object and make the circle a child of the Extrude NURBS object. The first thing C4D will do is extrude the circle in the default *z* direction; unfortunately, this is equivalent of smearing the circle backwards rather than giving it any thickness upward. So, double-click the icon next to Extrude NURBS in the Objects Manager. In the Attributes Editor, make sure you are looking at the Object section of the Extrude NURBS attribute and adjust the Y Movement setting (the second value on the Movement row) to 7m (or whatever looks appropriate to you) and change the Z Movement setting (the last value on the Movement row) to 0. While you're at it, click the Caps button and create a bit of a lip to the top of the table by changing the End setting to Fillet Cap, as the top of the table in this case will be the "End" of the extrusion. Now further define the lip we are creating in the Details tab by selecting Concave from the Fillet Types pop-down menu, changing the End Steps setting to 8 to allow for a good curvature, and reducing the End Radius setting to 2. Upon clicking OK, you should be presented with a form much like Figure 4.42c. Now, with the Extrude NURBS object selected you may resize the entire object to fit your preference.

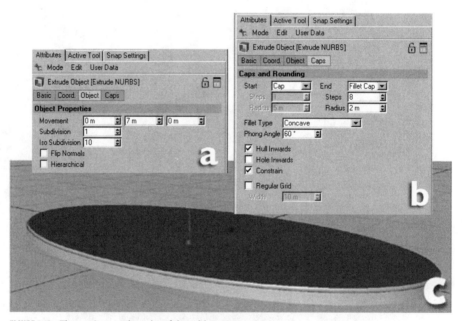

FIGURE 4.42 The settings and results of the tabletop extrusion.

To continue on with the style of the room, we'll use the same twisted pedestal legs we used for the niche table. To save time, jump to your Room file (via the Windows pull-down menu) and copy the central pedestal of the small table in the niche. To do this, select the Cube with deformers as children from the Objects Manager and copy it (Edit>Copy). Then go back to your table file via the Windows pull-down menu and paste the cube (Edit>Paste) (Figure 4.43). Note that this pastes not only the cube but the deformer objects that are the children of the cube.

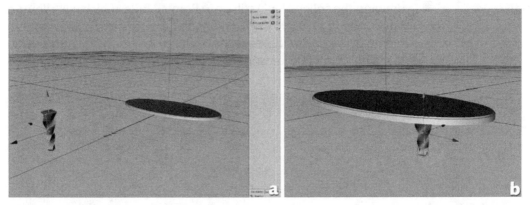

FIGURE 4.43   Paste the twisted cube into the table scene. It obviously pastes out of place and will need to be placed more appropriately into the scene.

To give the pedestal a base from which the smaller legs will sprout, create a Cylinder Primitive (Figure 4.44a). Open the Cylinder Primitive's attributes in the Attribute Editor by double-clicking the cylinder's icon in the Objects Manager. Change the Height Segments to "1" as we don't need any more than that, and reduce the Rotation Segments to "6" to create a six-sided block. Resize appropriately.

To create the legs at the bottom of the pedestal, we'll again use an Extrude NURBS object. First, we'll need to create the profile of the leg. To

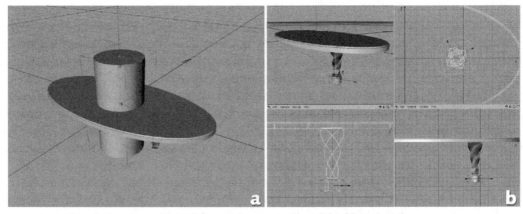

FIGURE 4.44   We create the block at the bottom of the pedestal by creating a Cylinder Primitive and then changing the settings to provide a six-sided block.

do so, make sure you are in a front or side view (non-perspective) and use one of the Draw Spline tools (the Draw Bezier Spline tool is used in Figure 4.45) and draw a rough outline of how you want your leg to look (Figure 4.45a). Remember to keep it rough because when you are done drawing the spline, you'll still be in Points Mode, which will allow you to select points and adjust them or their Bezier handles as needed. Remember the trick of holding the Shift key down to adjust one end of a Bezier handle while leaving the other end unaffected.

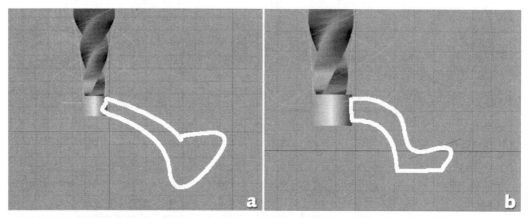

FIGURE 4.45 Roughly sketch the form in and make adjustments as needed to create the spline that will be used to create the bottom legs. (Emphasis Added).

To give the new leg thickness, create an Extrude NURBS object that the spline you've just created will be dropped into. To give this leg a little detail, make sure that the Fillet Cap is turned on for both the Start and End. Roughly match the settings to those shown in Figure 4.46.

Now as you've been building this leg, we haven't thought much about the location of any of the object axes. The problem is that when the Extrude NURBS was created, it was created it at (0,0,0), so that now, even though all the geometry is down at the bottom of the table, the leg's axis of rotation is up in the middle of the tabletop (Figure 4.47a). To fix this, select the Object Axis tool and move the axis down with the Move Active Element tool so that it is at the edge of the leg (Figure 4.47b). Placing it here makes it easy to rotate the leg into position around the block placed at the bottom of the table.

Rotate the leg into position at the bottom block at about 30° in the Heading (H in the Coordinates Manager). You may find that hiding the twisted pedestal (by clicking the top right gray dot next to the object in the Objects Manager until it turns red) helps you to see the necessary in-

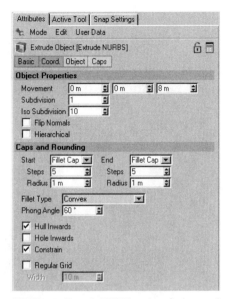

FIGURE 4.46 Extrude NURBS settings for bottom legs.

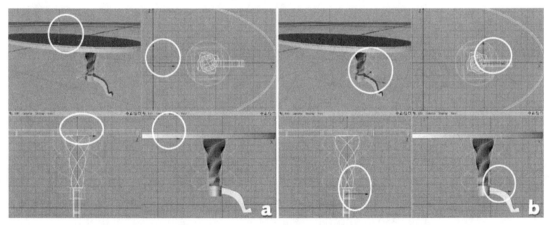

FIGURE 4.47 Make sure to realign the Object Axis for the new Extrude NURBS to be at the inside edge of the leg.

formation in the view panel. Copy and paste this leg twice and rotate each of these legs into position around the pedestal block.

Now hit "G" on your keyboard to group the three bottom legs, the block, and the twisted pedestal together. Copy and paste this and move it over into place on the other side of the table. Make sure that while you are moving it, you use the red *x* handle to ensure that the copy of the leg doesn't move up or down or in the *y* direction. Finally, be sure to group everything together and name it "Dinner Table."

Now select the Dinner Table object, copy it, and paste it into the Room file. The table will probably paste in sitting below the floor and probably at the wrong size. Visually move the table and resize it so that it appears to fit in the room (Figure 4.48). At this point, you may want to make adjustments to your room as well, so that it conforms to the table.

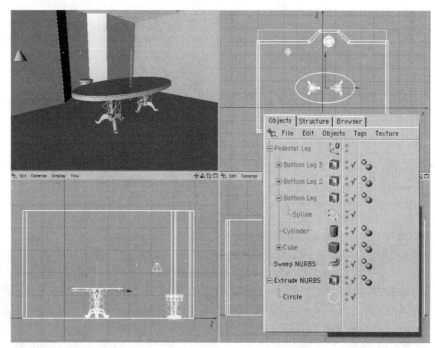

FIGURE 4.48 Our room thus far with the added table.

To explore some of the other NURBS objects, let's create a vase and flower to place on the table within the niche. Again, it is easier to create the vase in another file and then copy the new element into the room. So create a new file and, using one of the Draw Spline tools, create an outline for a vase in one of the non-perspective views (preferably Front, or Side Views—not Top (as drawing from the top would be setting up the scene to create a vase laying on its side). Make sure that you create a closed spline so that the vase has some thickness (Figure 4.49a). A single spline would make a paper-thin vase. Create a Lathe NURBS object and make the spline a child of it (Figure 4.49b).

There are several important things that should be mentioned about this Lathe NURBS object. First, the spline that was used to create it is a closed spline, thus creating an object with thickness. Second, it was

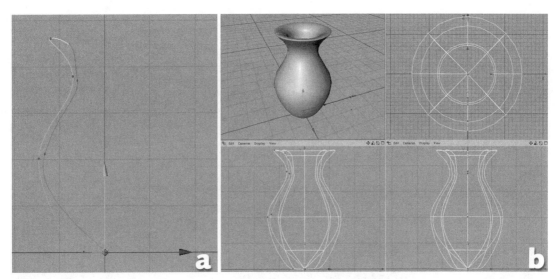

FIGURE 4.49 (a) The simple spline created with the Draw Bezier Spline tool. (b) The spline placed within the Lathe NURBS object and the resultant vase.

drawn with the understanding that the world's *y*-axis would be the center of the Lathe NURBS object. So the bottom of the vase (where the vase is closed) sits right on the *y*-axis, while the top (where the opening of the vase occurs) is placed away. The third issue is that the spline was not drawn in a perspective view panel; this is really a key to successfully creating splines for use in NURBS. By creating it in a side view, you can be sure that the spline is exactly flat, and thus will lathe appropriately. The beautiful thing about this is that now you can select the spline in the Objects Manager and, in Points Mode, shift the points of the spline to change the form of the vase. Take time to re-label the Lathe NURBS to "Vase."

To create a cartoonish flower, we'll use a Sweep NURBS object. So, we'll need a path spline (the spline to follow) and a contour spline (the cross-section that is following the path spline). Begin by using a Draw Spline tool to create a path for the flower stem (Figure 4.50a). Again, make sure to initially draw the spline in a side or front/back view. Then after the spline is drawn, you can go back in other views and shift the points around (Figure 4.50b).

Now that we have the path of the stem, we need to create the spline that will define the cross- section. Create a simple Circle Spline Primitive (our contour spline), small enough to be the cross-section of the stem you are creating—this is largely a visual subjective call at this point. Create a Sweep NURBS object and drop the path spline (probably called "Spline" at this point) and then the contour spline (Circle) into the Sweep

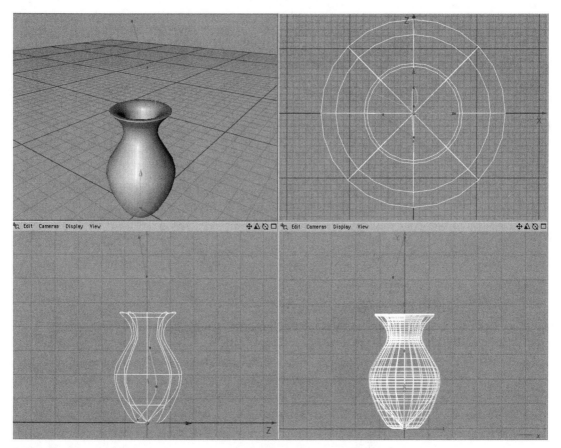

FIGURE 4.50 Create the path for the flower stem with a spline—here the Draw Cubic Spline tool was used.

NURBS object in the Objects Manager. You should get a result similar to Figure 4.51a. If you have a result similar to Figure 4.51b, where the stem is flat, you will need to change the Plane setting for the Circle Spline so that the Circle Spline knows what axis to extrude along. To do this (if you need to), double-click the Circle spline's icon in the Objects Manager, and in the resultant Attributes Editor, click the Object button and change the Plane setting until the stem is round.

We'll further refine the Sweep NURBS object by making the contour spline (Circle) taper off. To do this, double-click the Sweep NURBS icon in the Objects Manager and in the Attributes Editor, change the Scaling setting to 10% (these settings should be visible by default when the Sweep NURBS object is first double-clicked; if they are not, be sure to hit the Object button). This will cause the contour to be 10% of its original size when it reaches the end of the path (spline) (Figure 4.52).

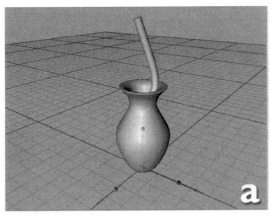

FIGURE 4.51   Initial Sweep NURBS object; (a) is correct, the incorrect object (b) is a result of the Circle spline being on an inappropriate plane.

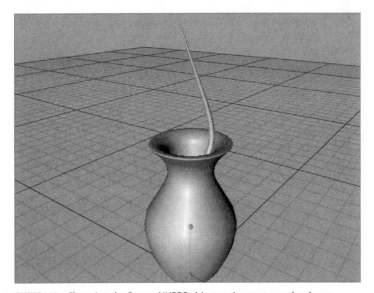

FIGURE 4.52   Changing the Sweep NURBS object options to taper the shape.

To create a couple of leaves, we'll use a Bezier NURBS object. Create a Bezier NURBS object (either from the tool palette on top of the UI, or using Objects>NURBS>Bezier NURBS) and move it a bit away from the vase and stem for now. Hit Press "O" on your keyboard to zoom in on the Bezier NURBS shape so that we can work with it. The leaf that we're going to build here will be gently curving overall, so we won't need a lot of subdivisions. However, down the middle of the leaf, we'll probably want a little crisper edge, so we'll need to adjust the Grid Points setting to allow for more rows of points. Double-click the Bezier NURBS icon in the Objects Manager and change the X Grid Points setting to "5" in the Attributes Editor. In the perspective view, make sure that the Display pull-down menu is set to X-Ray so that you can easily see the grid points.

Before we start shaping, we'll first want to organize our points to define areas of higher definition. Make sure that you are in Points mode and activate the Live Selection tool. "Paint" over each of the rows of points on either side of the center row (Figure 4.53a) by clicking and dragging the Live Selections "paintbrush circle" over the points. Then switch to the Scale Active Element tool and using the X restricted scale handle (the red box) click and drag to the left (Figure 4.53b). Scaling like this brings the two rows of points closer toward the middle.

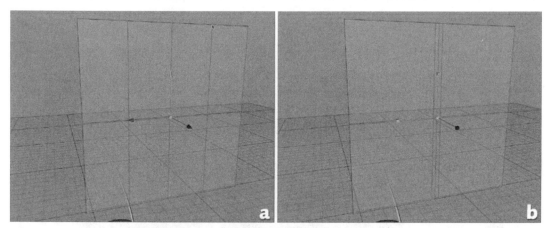

FIGURE 4.53   Preparing for shape altering by properly organizing the points.

Now, use the Live Selection tool to select the row of points down the middle. Move these points backward using the Move Active Element tool. Again, make sure to constrain your movement by using the manipulator handles (blue cone for the y direction) (Figure 4.54). Now that we have a middle trough, we can select each of the other points to form the outer edge into a leaf (Figure 4.55).

Now use the Object Axis tool to move the leaf's object axis to the bottom, then switch to Model mode or Object mode and move and scale the leaf into position on the stem. Copy and paste a few copies (Figure 4.56).

Repeat the same process for the daisy flower petal. The shape will be a bit different, but again make sure that the Object Axis for the Bezier NURBS is at the bottom center. This will become important as we create

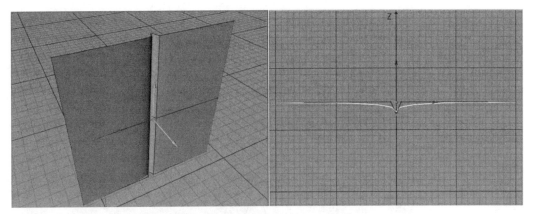

FIGURE 4.54   Creating a trough in the middle of the leaf.

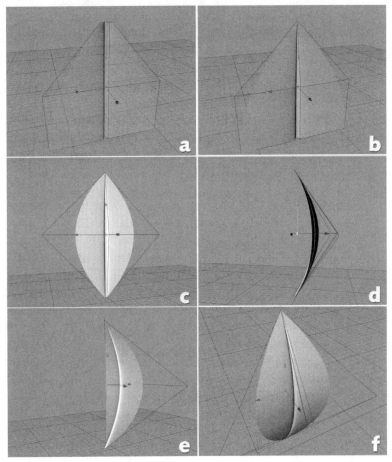

FIGURE 4.55   The rest of the leaf is formed by selecting and moving the remaining points into position to form a leaf shape.

FIGURE 4.56 Leaves in place.

an array in just a bit. Create a flattened Oil Tank Primitive and resize it so that it looks right for the center of the flower (Figure 4.57).

ARRAYS AND INSTANCES

An Array object is a tool that allows you to place one object within it, and C4D will duplicate and rotate *instances* of the object placed in the Array object. An instance is a powerful tool with 3D. The idea is that, to save on the amount of data to keep track of and to add flexibility, C4D can display the same object several times. This is different from a copy of an object; if you have 30 petals, C4D is displaying 30 petals, but if you have 30 instances of a petal, C4D is displaying one petal 30 times. This doesn't save you any rendering time, but does keep your data set—and thus your file size—smaller.

The petals of a flower are a perfect location to use an array. Create an Array object by selecting it from the top command palette (Figure 4.58a) or by going to Objects>Modeling>Array.

When an Array object is created, it appears in the Objects Manager, but no new geometry appears in the view panel. We are going to want our Array object to center around the flower center (our Oil Tank Primi-

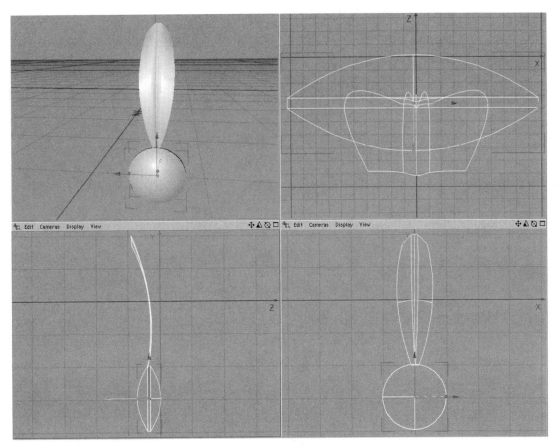

FIGURE 4.57   New flower petal with flower center made from Oil Tank Primitive.

tive), so use the Move Active Element tool to move the Array object to the middle of the Oil Tank Primitive (Figure 4.58b).

In order to let the Array object know which shape to "array," place the petal as a child of the Array object. The result will be somewhat weird (Figure 4.59a), as an Array object rotates and works with the object it is "'arraying'" by the object's z-axis, which in this case is the backside of the petal. To remedy this situation, first select the Array object and using the Rotate Active Element tool or the Coordinates Manager, rotate the object (90° in pitch) so that the petals are facing the correct direction (Figure 4.59b). What we now need to do is change the object axis of the petal, so that its y-axis is facing in towards the array. With the Object Axis

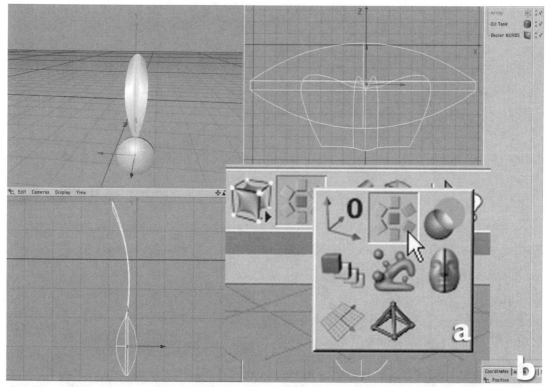

FIGURE 4.58   (a) An Array object. (b) Move the Array object into position within the middle of the flower center.

tool, and with the Bezier NURBS Object that is your petal selected in the Objects Manager, use the Rotate Active Element tool to rotate the petal's axis into position (Figure 4.59c).

By double-clicking the Array icon within the Objects Manager, you can shift the Radius setting in the Attributes Editor to bring the petals closer together. You can increase the number of copies to create a more dense collection of petals, or leave the number at the default 7 and instead copy and paste the Array object and rotate the Bezier NURBS for this new Array object so that the petals bend in at a slightly different angle. Repeat and you can get a fairly organic-looking flower with 24 petals visible, but with only 3 petals' worth of geometry (Figure 4.60). Group the Array objects and Oil Tank Primitive together and name the group "Flower." Move it into position at the top of the flower stem.

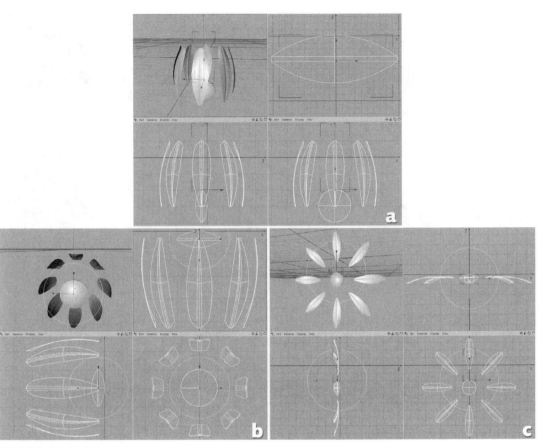

FIGURE 4.59   Manipulating the Array.

Group the flower, stem, and vase together and copy and paste the new group into the room (Figure 4.60). Resize as needed.

One thing that is often forgotten when people model rooms is that many rooms have crown molding around the top of the room. Furthermore, nearly every room has a floorboard that visually joins the floor to the wall. To create these pieces of trim around our room, we'll make use of a Loft NURBS object. The key here will be to create a cross-section of the trim that will act as a guiding "rib." Then we'll place each of these ribs at each corner of the room to guide the Loft NURBS in the direction it should be going.

FIGURE 4.60 Placed vase and flower.

Start out by drawing a spline in a non-perspective view (Figure 4.61c). Use a corner of the wall as a reference to see that the scale and relative point placement is appropriate. Again, if you are using a combination of smooth and angular splines, a Bezier spline is often the best choice.

By using the wall as a guide, we've kept the spline even on one side, but have created another problem. Since the wall is not at (0,0,0), the newly created spline's center is far away from the actual spline (Figure 4.61a). Correct the problem by using the Object Axis and Move Active Element tools to move the spline's axis so that it sits on the back end of the spline (Figure 4.61b). This will allow for easy placement and rotation of the spline later. Make sure that the axis is in line with the spline from a top view as well.

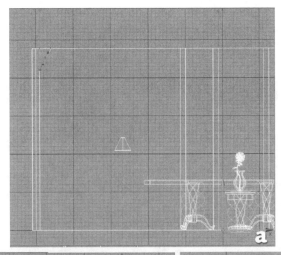

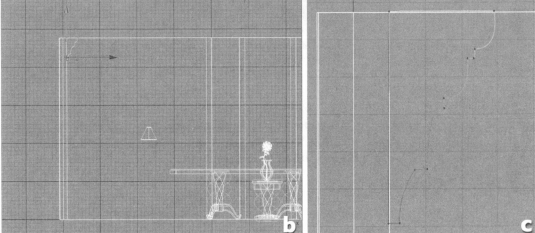

FIGURE 4.61   (a) When the Spline is created that will be the profile of your crown molding, notice that the spline's center of rotation is down at (0,0,0). (b) Make sure to move the spline's axis to sit on the back end to make for easy corner placement. (c) This is a close-up of a suggested shape.

Once the spline's axis is properly aligned, and you're sure that the spline is at a proper height, switch your attention to a top view. To make sure that the molding is at a constant width around the room, we need to make these spline guides in the corner that respect (or are conscious of) both walls. As such, we'll want to turn the spline 45° (Figure 4.62). This gives the soon-to-be-created Loft NURBS a good guide as it "lofts" between guiding splines. For this room, think of it as turning the spline so that it points toward the center of the room. Copy and paste this spline (the new copy will begin in the exact position as the old) and move this new spline into the next corner of the room (in this case we're moving clockwise). Make sure to once again rotate the spline to create a good corner guide.

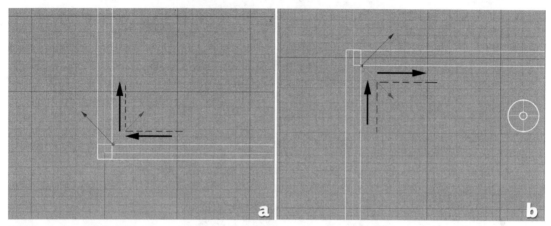

FIGURE 4.62 Rotating the spline 45° ensures that the Loft NURBS (anticipated in black) will have a good corner to turn.

Still in the Top View, continue to copy and paste each spline and move it into position around the room (Figure 4.63). In all cases, make sure to point each spline toward the center of the room. Figure 4.63 shows the potentially tricky area of the niche.

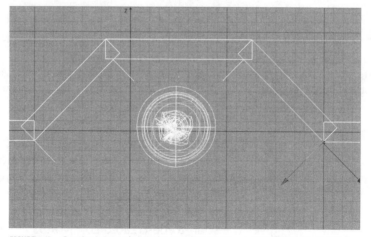

FIGURE 4.63 Continuing to place splines to be used in a Loft NURBS object. This is the placement in the niche.

The order of these copied and pasted splines is important. When the Loft NURBS is created, it will move from spline to spline in the order they are placed as children to create the form. If one spline gets out of place, you end up with the Loft NURBS jumping ahead to a spline, then doubling back to hit another. By copying, pasting, placing, rotating, then copying and pasting this new spline and repeating the process, you can ensure that your splines are all in the correct order. Continue to work around the room until you reach the last corner without a spline and fill it with a pasted spline (Figure 4.64).

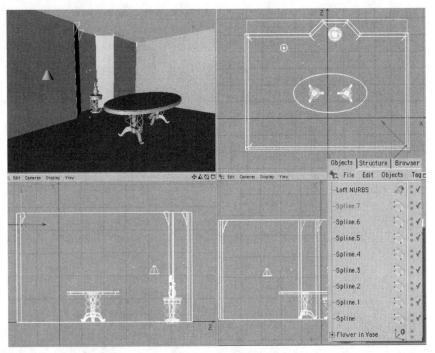

FIGURE 4.64 Make sure every corner is covered by one spline. Also be sure you understand which spline in the Objects Manager is which spline in the view panel—they must be placed in the Loft NURBS in the correct order.

Now take each of these splines and place them one at a time as children of a Loft NURBS object. Make sure to place them in the order that they lay in the room. For instance, in the example file, they are placed in a clockwise order. When they are all children, you'll find that the result is less than ideal (Figure 4.65a). NURBS in general are great ways to create organic forms. As such, the default Loft NURBS tries to create nice organic interpolation between splines. However, for architecture like this, we don't want organic interpolation—we need straight edges with sharp corners. To correct this, double-click the Loft NURBS icon and check the "Linear Interpolation" option in the Attributes Editor to get rid of the rounded connections. While you're at it, click the "Loop" option so that the Loft NURBS will continue to connect the last spline back to the first. (Figure 4.65b).

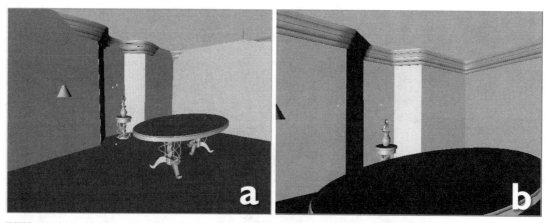

FIGURE 4.65   (a) Problematic original Loft NURBS using non-linear interpolation. (b) The Loft NURBS dialogue box with appropriate options checked.

Repeat this process for a floorboard (Figure 4.66).

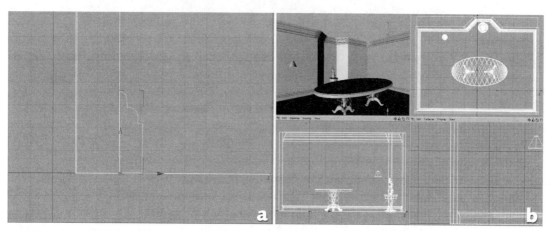

FIGURE 4.66   Floorboard created in the same method.

With these same techniques, doors and windows (Figure 4.67) can be constructed. Make sure that the windows actually have a pane of glass placed within them. The pane of glass will probably be a simple Polygon or Plane Primitive.

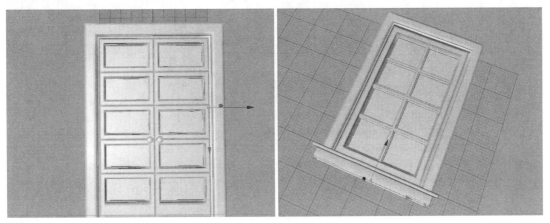

FIGURE 4.67   Doors and windows created with Loft NURBS and extrusions.

Next, you'll copy, paste, scale, and place your door and window into place within the room. The biggest obstacle is that there are doors and windows with no holes to place them in. To create the necessary holes, we will need to make use of Boolean Modeling.

BOOLEAN OBJECTS

Most search engines today allow for you to search for cougar –car; or bear +teddy –roosevelt. The first example tells the engine to "find sites to do with cougars, but not the car." The second tells it to "find sites about bears and teddy, but none that deal with roosevelt." Boolean modeling works the same way. You get to define "take this wall, but not the block set within in it, and show me the result."

Boolean objects are created from the top command palette (Figure 4.68a) or by going to Objects>Modeling>Boolean. The Boolean object it-self has no geometry, but rather generates forms from other objects placed as children within it. The first object is always referenced as "A" with the second being "B." If you double-click the Boolean icon in the Objects Manager, the attributes of the Boolean object are displayed in the Attributes Editor. Here you can change the function of the Boolean to perform the functions shown in Figure 4.68b.

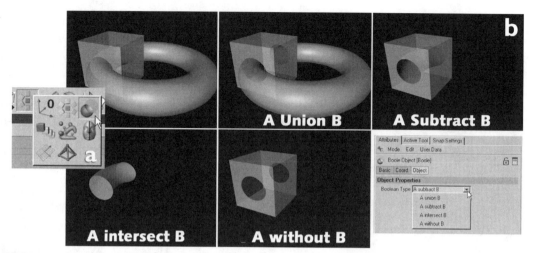

FIGURE 4.68 (a) Creating a Boolean object which itself contains no geometry. (b) The various functions of a Boolean object. These are renderings with a semi-transparent texture applied to see what's happening on the inside of the object.

For the holes where our windows and doors will go, the "A" will be the walls and the "B" will be cubes we create that are the same size as the door or window that will fill the hole. So for the window, first create a Cube Primitive that is the same width and height as the window you created earlier with Loft NURBS and at least as deep as the wall it will be cutting a hole in. Move it into place so that it completely intersects the wall (Figure 4.69).

Make sure you have a Boolean object created in your Objects Manager, and drop in (make it a child of the Boolean object) the Cube Primitive you're using as the hole object (B). Then find the wall for the niche shown in Figure 4.70 and drop it into the Boolean object as a child (A). Since A Subtract B is the default setting for Boolean objects, as soon as both objects are children of the Boolean object, the Primitive Cube (B) will disappear and the result will be a clean hole in the wall. Note that now your niche wall is part of a Boolean object, which you may want to rename something like "Niche Wall with Hole."

Repeat this process for the other niche walls and any other places that you'd like to place windows, and move pasted copies of the windows into the holes (Figure 4.71).

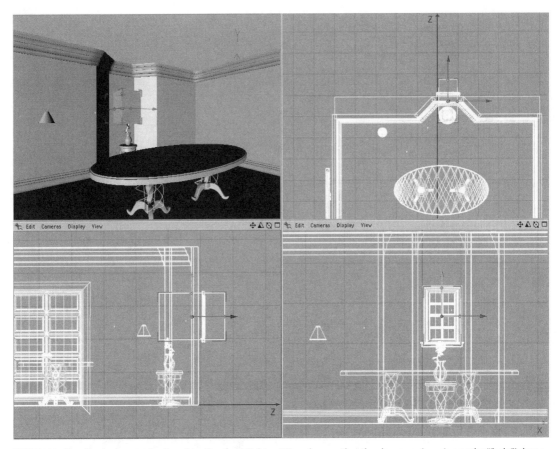

FIGURE 4.69   To effectively use a Boolean function for A Subtract B, make sure that the shape you're using as the "'hole'" shape completely penetrates the wall, and is the same size as the object that will be filling the hole.

Now, the doorway is a little more difficult. As before, create a Cube Primitive that is the appropriate size to cut a hole, however, this time we don't just need to cut a hold in the wall, but also in the floorboard. Boolean objects only work with two objects or two *groups*. You might think that if the floorboard, the wall, and the Cube Primitive were put in a Boolean object, all would be well. Unfortunately, the Boolean object would subtract the second shape from the first and completely ignore the third. To solve this problem, some grouping is needed.

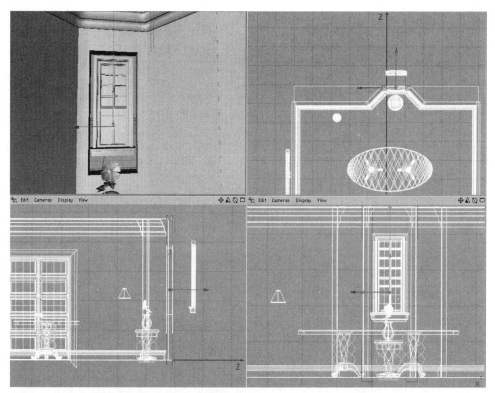

FIGURE 4.70 The results of the Boolean operation. You can see right through the hole to see the window sitting outside.

FIGURE 4.71 All the windows in place set within holes.

The Cube Primitive will remain by itself; however, group the side wall where the door will be with the floorboard. Then create a Boolean object, and make the Wall-Floorboard group and the Cube Primitive children of it (Figure 4.72).

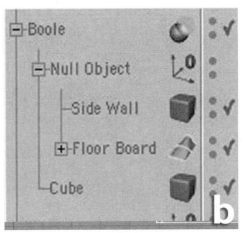

FIGURE 4.72   Compound cut made by grouping the wall and floorboard together before placing into the Boolean object.

The next thing we'll do is create the openings in the remaining walls. To do this, we'll use an Extrude NURBS as the object that will cut the hole. Begin by creating a nice spline in the shape of the opening. Remember to draw it in a non-perspective view, preferably the one perpendicular to the wall you are to cut from (Figure 4.73a). Create an Extrude NURBS object and make the newly drawn spline a child of it. Place the Extrude NURBS so that it intersects the appropriate wall (Figure 4.73b).

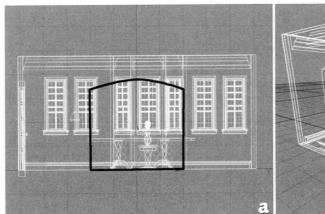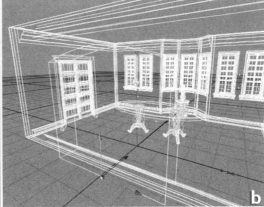

FIGURE 4.73   Preparing for cutting archway from wall.

Now, track down the wall you are going to cut from within your Objects Manager and move it close to the Extrude NURBS object that is to be the archway hole. We're going to cut this Extrude NURBS from the wall, but also we'll also need to cut it from the floorboard. But the floorboard is already tied up in another Boolean function. So what's to be done?

The trick is to use the already functioning Boolean object. We've looked at using a group to cut from, now we need to make sure that the object we're cutting is actually a group as well. Remove the Cube Primitive that is acting as the hole for the door from the Boolean object. Group the Cube Primitive and the Extrude NURBS together; you may want to label this new group "Holes." Now, take this Holes group and replace it within the Boolean object, taking extreme care to maintain the proper order. Now, take the wall that the arch is being cut from and make it a member of the Wall-Floorboard group, so C4D knows that it also should be subtracted from. This is fairly complex, so pay special attention to the Objects Manager shown in Figure 4.74. The key is to remember, in the Boolean's eyes, there are only two objects: the group that contains all the shapes being cut from (including both walls and the floorboard) and the group of holes (including the doorway hole and the archway hole).

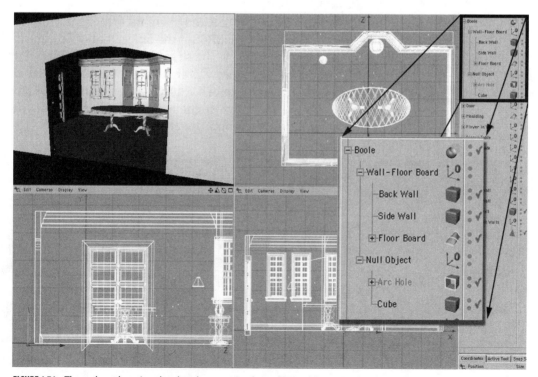

FIGURE 4.74 The arch cut by using the already extant Boolean object with appropriate grouping.

Copy and paste the Extrude NURBS that creates the archway and ro-tate it 90°. When the invisible Extrude NURBS is pasted, it will become visible, as this new copy is not within the Boolean object. Move this newly pasted Extrude NURBS into position inside the only unmolested wall. Resize it a bit smaller and then drop it into the "Holes" group of the Boolean object we've been working with. It then will cut from the floor-board. When the last wall is placed within the Wall-Floorboard group, it too will be subtracted from—giving a result similar to Figure 4.75.

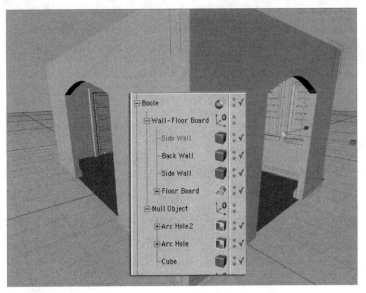

FIGURE 4.75   Arches cut, doorways functional, and window ready.

The remaining objects in the room are all built using techniques al-ready described. Figure 4.76 shows the room from a couple of different angles. The chairs are built almost entirely out of Cube Primitives except for the seat cushion, which is built with a Loft NURBS. The runner in the middle of the table is a simple Bezier NURBS that was carefully edited at a points level to curve down at the edge of the tables. The bowls are Lathe NURBS.

One problem you may notice is that when we look out the arches, we see the grid of the digital world. This will be a problem later when we render and these arches open up into black voids. A common theatre trick is to place "backing flats" in holes like this. A backing flat is a simple wall that denotes the rest of the house although none of it is really built. Figure 4.77 shows the results of some carefully placed backing flats.

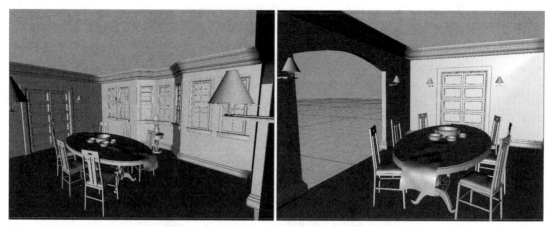

FIGURE 4.76 The room thus far with added objects—all built using techniques described to this point.

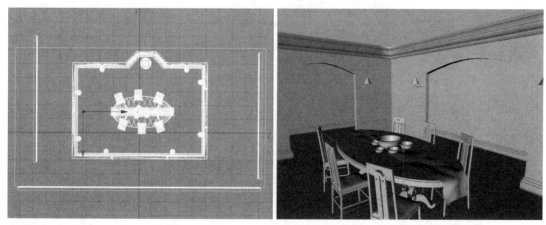

FIGURE 4.77 Backing flats.

CONCLUSION

And with that, we'll leave the realm of basic modeling. The coming chapters have some excellent tutorials on modeling organic forms such as human heads. There are other areas of C4D that enable other methods of modeling. However, if you master the techniques described here, you can create nearly every form imaginable.

UTILIZING THE POWER OF HYPERNURBS: MODELING ORGANIC FORMS FROM PRIMITIVES

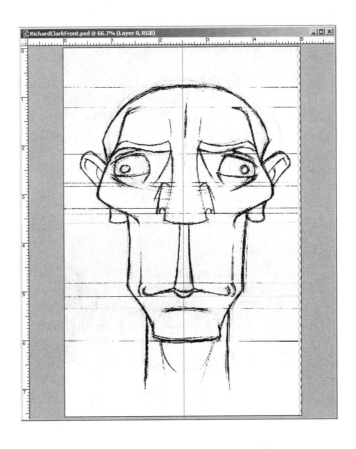

n Chapter 4, we looked at a lot of various modeling techniques dealing with NURBS. As discussed earlier, there are two major types of HyperNURBS modeling. The first deals with altering a primitive form within a HyperNURBS to create a much more complex shape. This chapter examines both techniques. First, in Tutorial 5.1, Anson Call will outline the method of creating organic faces through starting out with a large primitive and adding detail as needed. Later, in Tutorial 5.2, we will look at a method of building out to create our organic shapes.

TUTORIAL

5.1 PRIMITIVE BASED HYPERNURBS MODELING OF A HUMAN HEAD

By Anson Call (*ansaytor@mac.com*)

The following tutorial will show you how to make a head using Hyper-NURBS and assumes that you know the basics of the Cinema 4D XL Release 8 toolset. This version has the added functionality of the Edge Tool, which allows for enhanced manipulation of the HyperNURBS cage. If you are using a previous version, most Edge tool functions can be approximated using the Points tool.

Please remember that this example isn't the only right way to model a head, and that along the way there can be many deviations that you could take depending on your wants and needs. There are just some things we won't delve into, such as individual discretion on what particular features of the head should look like. That's up to you. Also, this tutorial assumes that you have some experience with C4D and its interface. If you don't understand what a HyperNURBS is, then you should first analyze Chapter 4 of this book or read through the HyperNURBS sections of the manual first. With that said, let's get started.

First, let's set up our HyperNURBS by creating a Cube Primitive (name it "Face") and a HyperNURBS object and placing the "Face" object as a child of the HyperNURBS in the Object Manager. Make sure that you make the "Face" object editable (Structure>Make Editable). Second, perform a subdivision on the cube (Structure>Subdivide).

Then, change to Points mode. Your project should look something like Figure 5.1.

Now select one half of the model's points using the Points tool and delete them, leaving the other half intact as shown in Figure 5.2. Then, in the Object Manager, take the half of the face still visible and place it as a

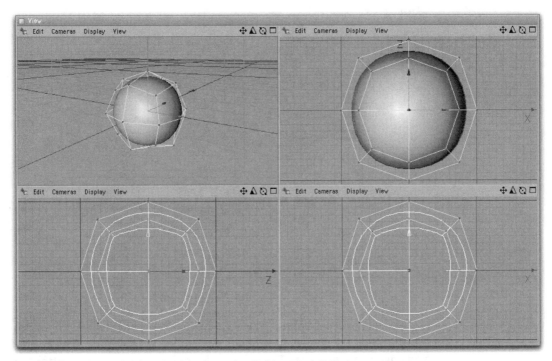

FIGURE 5.1   Getting started with a primitive cube made editable and subdivided.

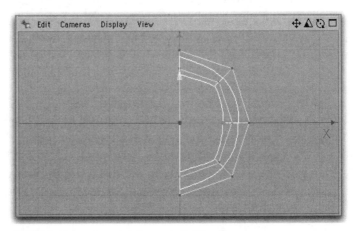

FIGURE 5.2   Delete the points for one half of the shape.

child of a Symmetry object which in turn will be a child of the Hyper-NURB object (Figure 5.3).

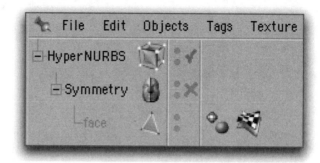

FIGURE 5.3   Take this half face, place it as a child of a Symmetry object, and then place the Symmetry object as a child of the HyperNURBS object.

Notice that there aren't many points on the model thus far. Remember that fewer points means fewer polygons, and the model is "lighter" and easier to work with. There'll be a lot more later, but remember that less is more in this case, and keep it as simple as possible. The next thing you need to do is to get a basic shape of the head you want. Do this while you alternate between the Point, Edge, and Polygon modes by clicking on their corresponding tool. To get the neck, select the polygons on the back side of the head and perform an Extrude function (Structure>Extrude), while in Polygon mode (Figure 5.4).

After you do this, you'll need to delete the inner polygon that was created when we did the extrusion (Figure 5.5) and set the inner points to zero on the x-axis (Figure 5.6). Remember that you can do this by selecting a point (one at a time) and entering 0 in the X Position input field of the Coordinates Manager, or by selecting both points, and using Edit Surface>Set Value to set the value of both points to X=0. Turn off the symmetry by clicking the green checkmark next to it as your visual needs dictate.

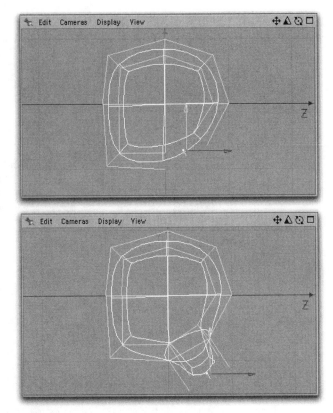

FIGURE 5.4   Getting started on the neck by extruding faces off the back of the head.

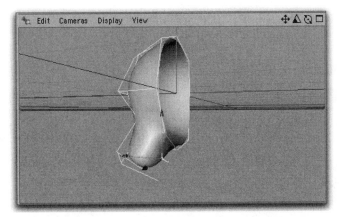

FIGURE 5.5   Select the face on the inside of the newly extruded neck and delete it to avoid pinching.

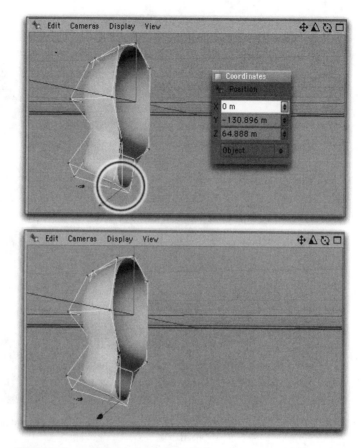

FIGURE 5.6 To avoid gaps in the neck, move the center points of the neck to **0** in the *x* direction.

Your basic head shape should look similar to Figure 5.7 once the Symmetry object is reactivated.

Now we'll need more points to work with. So, repeat the subdivision step listed above with the same settings. This should give you enough points to proceed (Figure 5.8).

At this point, you can do some more tweaking to the basic shape before we move on. Again, don't be afraid to turn the Symmetry object off and on as it will help you see your model better. It is important that you try to keep the points as evenly spaced as possible (avoid bunching them up) because this will help you avoid wrinkles.

Now let's perform a few knife cuts on our model to add points that will later assist us. Using the Knife tool will cut polygons in half where we determine it should be cut. To access the Knife tool, go to

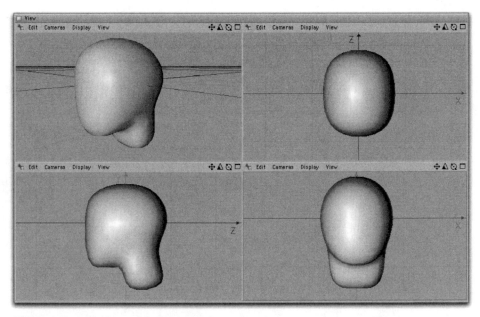

FIGURE 5.7   The basic shape of the head, complete with neck.

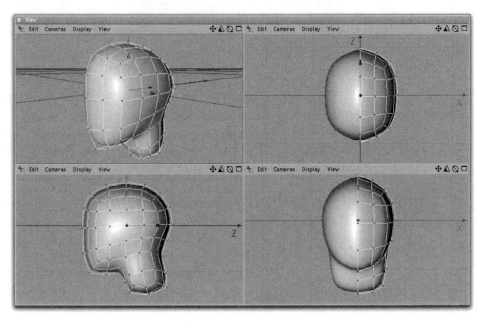

FIGURE 5.8   Added points and polygons through a subdivision command.

Structure>Knife or use the keyboard shortcut "K." Make sure that you're in Points mode at this point, so that you don't have to worry about some of the more detailed settings of the tool. Figure 5.9 shows where you should use the Knife tool; this will give us some extra geometry to use that will be needed when it comes time to work on the nose.

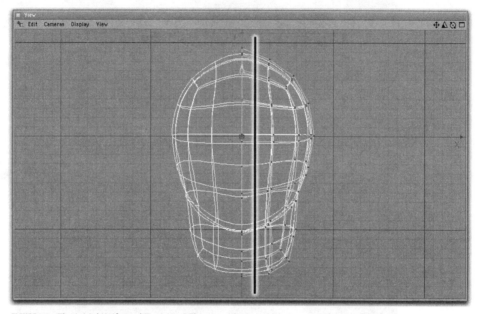

FIGURE 5.9 The initial Knife tool "incision." This provides needed geometry for the detailed nose region.

Repeat the process once more, using similar cuts like those shown in Figure 5.10.

Be sure to try and not cut diagonally through polygons. We want to keep four-sided polygons as much as possible. With these added knife cuts, we should have enough polygons to begin creating details of the face.

To make use of these new polygons, let's start with the nose. Select the polygons shown in Figure 5.11 and use the Extrude tool to extrude them twice (Figure 5.12 and 5.13).

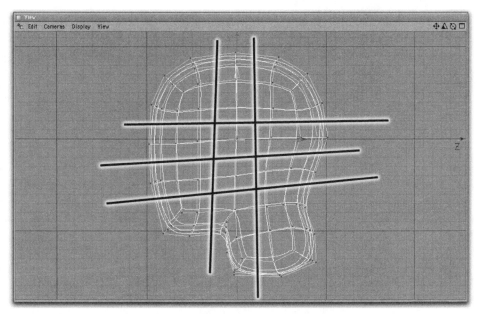

FIGURE 5.10   Additional knife cuts to provide for future needed geometry.

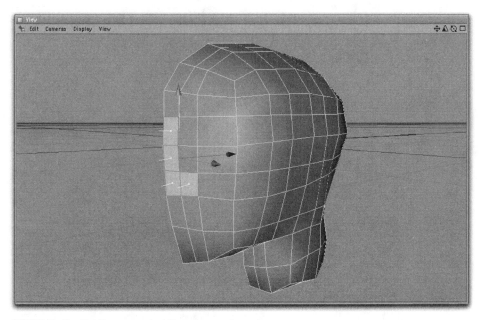

FIGURE 5.11   To start the nose, select the polygons shown here.

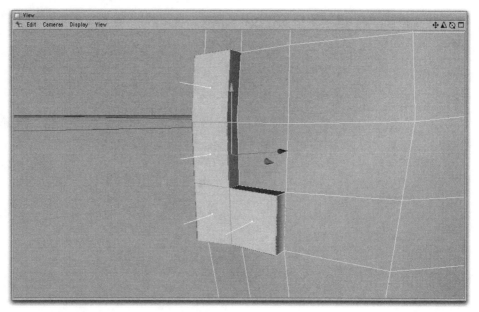

FIGURE 5.12 Using the Extrude tool (Structure>Extrude), drag out one small extrusion.

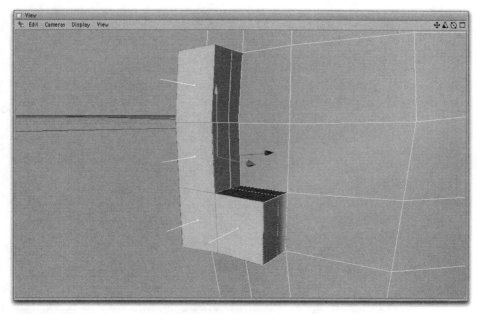

FIGURE 5.13 Still with the Extrude tool, drag out a second extrusion.

Similar to when we extruded for the neck, we've created polygons that can make puckers in our model as the HyperNURBS attempts to round the form. This occurs when we extrude any polygon that has points centered on the *x*-axis. To solve the problem, select the points along the inside of the nose and delete them (Figure 5.14).

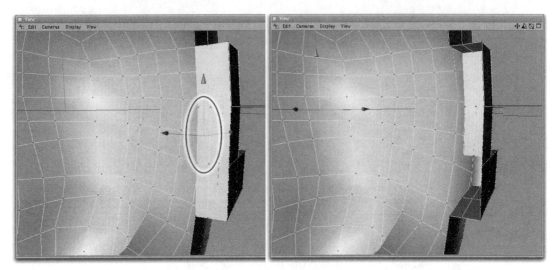

FIGURE 5.14   Avoid puckering along the center of the nose by deleting the points along the symmetry axis. This automatically removes the polygons associated with the deleted points.

You will have some points that have wandered off the *x*-axis. Remember that if the points wander away from the *x*-axis (the plane of symmetry), then you will end up with holes; and if they wander over the *x*-axis, you end up with overlapping folds. As it is important that the points that exist along the center of the head reside at exactly *x*=0, let's put any errant points back. Select a point and enter zero for the X input field of the Coordinates Manager. Do it for any point on the nose that needs it. You can tell by turning on Symmetry and locating any rips. If it has a rip, it's because a point or points does not have a value of zero for its *x* value. In fact, its not a bad idea to check all your points that would normally be on the *x*-axis.

Next, take some time to push and pull the points of the new extrusions into a more nose-like shape. Remember to activate the HyperNURBS object often so you can see the rounded version. When you are happy with the overall shape of the nose, start on the nostril. To form the nostril, switch to Polygon mode and we'll use several Extrude Inners (done with the Extrude Inner tool (Structure>Extrude Inner)) so that we have enough points to work with to get a clean edge to the nostril (Figure 5.15).

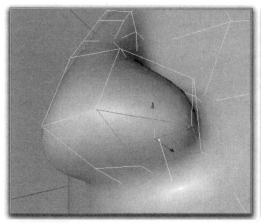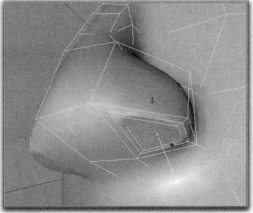

FIGURE 5.15   Using the Extrude Inner tool, extrude several times to create new collections of polygons for the nostril.

Once you have around three or four Extrude Inners, realign the points to make sure you have a good-sized innermost polygon, and then extrude upward into the nose (Figure 5.16).

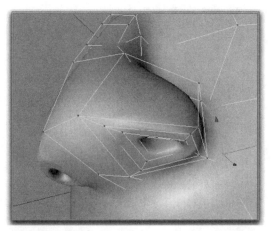

FIGURE 5.16   Once you have enough polygons for the nostril, use Extrude (not Extrude Inner) to extrude up into the nose to form the nostril.

Let's move on to the mouth. We need some more geometry and we could use our Knife tool as before. However, let's try a different technique using Extrude with the Edge tool. Switch to Edge mode and select the edges that rest near the mouth region (Figure 5.17) and press the 'd' key to start your extrude. Hold down the Control key while you drag the mouse. You should notice two sets of polylines forming above and below your original selection. This is a good way of adding geometry without using the Knife function.

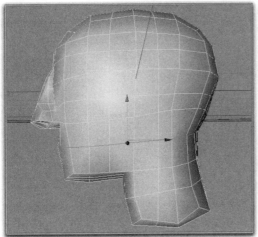 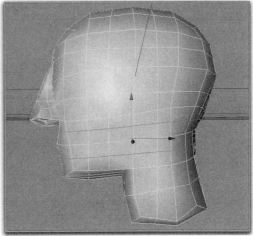

FIGURE 5.17 Extruding new geometry by extruding an edge.

Again, from this point, we'll create the added geometry for the mouth through a series of Extrude Inners (Figure 5.18). And just as before, the Extrude process will create some polygons close to the symmetry plane that will need to be deleted.

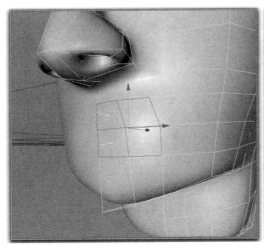 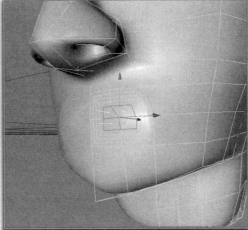

FIGURE 5.18 Using Extrude Inner to create new geometry for the mouth.

To clean things up, we'll need to select and delete the points shown in Figure 5.19.

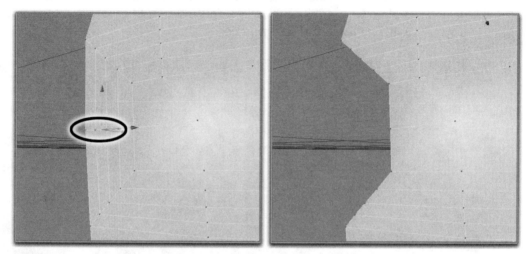

FIGURE 5.19 Cleaning up the extrusions by deleting points that form unnecessary polygons.

Finally, take all the points that are off-center and make sure that they line up with X=0. You can do this one at a time using the Coordinates Manager, or select all of them that should be centered and use Structure>Edit Surface>Set Value (Figure 5.20).

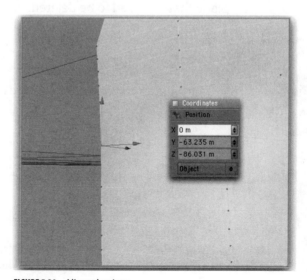

FIGURE 5.20 Aligned points.

Now that we have all the geometry we need to create the mouth, we can begin to form the oral cavity. An oral cavity is important to have later if the model is ever to be animated. Select the innermost four polygons (Figure 5.21) and using the Move Active Element tool, move them straight back into the head. Then resize these polygons to give a more cavernous shape to the mouth.

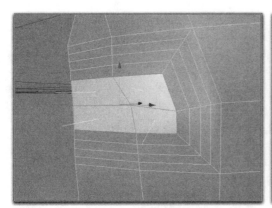 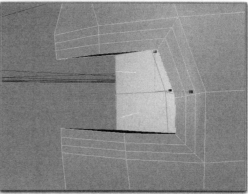

FIGURE 5.21   Creating the oral cavity by selecting and moving the innermost four polygons that make up the mouth.

With the oral cavity created, we can turn our attention to the lips. As we've done a series of Extrude Inners already, we have the polygons necessary to create the lip shapes. To do this, shift between Points, Edge, and Polygon modes and adjust the shape to better form the lips. The Edge tool can be particularly effective here in forming the lips. This is still a rough interpretation, so feel free to make any additional changes (Figure 5.22).

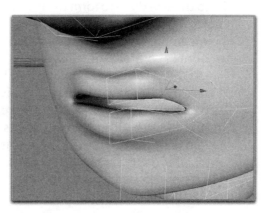

FIGURE 5.22   Create the rest of the mouth and lips by adjusting the edges, points, or polygons to give volume and shape.

Let's move on to the eyes. Again, we'll need some added polygons to accurately form this region. As before, we'll use a series of Extrude Inner (Figure 5.23). Before you do this, though, it is a good idea to pull in the corners (using the Points tool) as each successive inner extrude will inherit this shape. This is a time saver as we won't have to do as much refining later on.

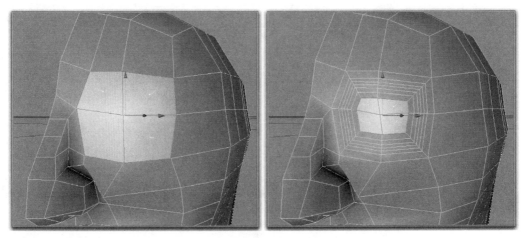

FIGURE 5.23 Creating geometry needed for the detail of the eye by using Extrude Inner.

When you have sufficient Extrude Inners, pull the last set of created polygons into the head to form the eye cavity. This process is very similar to the one done to form the mouth. However, the eye is probably the most complex part of the head (other than the ear) so you'll need more points in order to get enough geometry to give you the appropriate amount of control (Figure 5.24).

At this point, it is a good idea to bring in a sphere to use as an eye (Figure 5.25). Create a Sphere Primitive to help you get the shape you want as you form the eye. After the sphere is placed, continue to refine the eye by pushing and pulling points, edges, or polygons.

On to the ears: switch to Polygon mode and select the polygons that are in the general area of the ears. Once these are selected, go to Selection>Hide Unselected to hide the rest of the head. This way, you

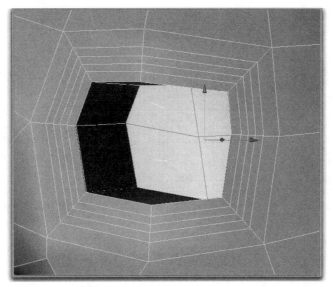

FIGURE 5.24   Creating the eye socket by moving the last collection of polygons into the head.

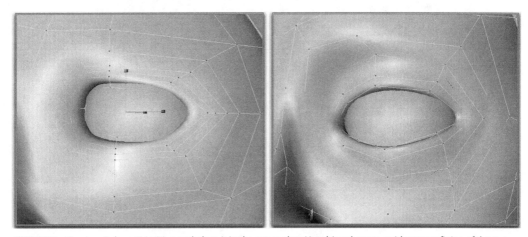

FIGURE 5.25   Create a Sphere Primitive and place it in the eye socket. Use this sphere to guide your refining of the eye. Refine using either points or edges.

can work unencumbered with the delicate and intricate parts of the ear (Figure 5.26).

To create the general shape of the ear, extrude the polygons, rotate them, and extrude them again. This produces a very nice starting collection of polygons in a very general shape of the ear (Figure 5.27).

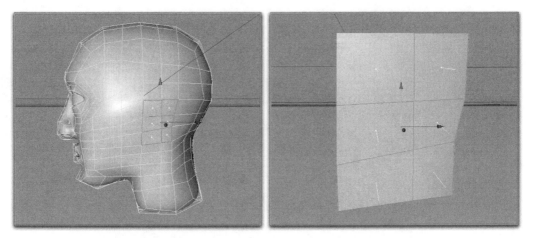

FIGURE 5.26 Focusing on the polygons that are to make the ear.

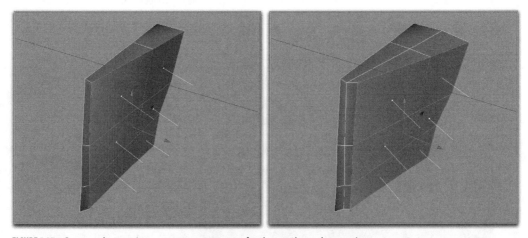

FIGURE 5.27 Start out by creating some extra geometry for the ear through extrusions.

Take the polygons thus far and rough out a general shape of the ear (Figure 5.28).

The inner area of the ear is a complex collection of curves. In order to model this, we need more geometry. Select the polygons for the inner section of the ear and create lots of Extrude Inners (Figure 5.29). Then select the polygons that form the overall inner ear area and use the Extrude tool to extrude inward.

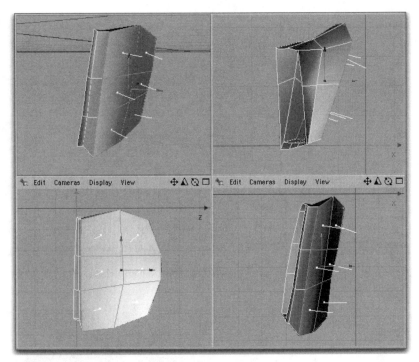

FIGURE 5.28   Roughing out the shape of the ear.

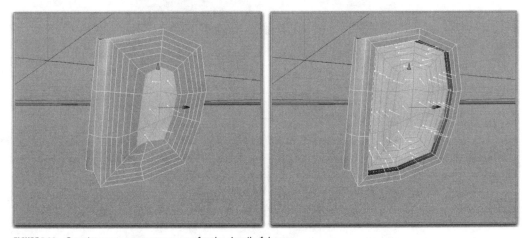

FIGURE 5.29   Creating new geometry to use for the detail of the ear.

Now refine the ear a bit using the various selection tools to get a bit more detailed ear (Figure 5.30).

Unhide the hidden polygons and you're left with a fairly general looking head (Figure 5.31). We've really done minimal work on the eyes,

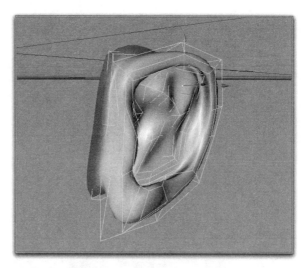

FIGURE 5.30 After pushing and pulling, you should have a rough ear shape.

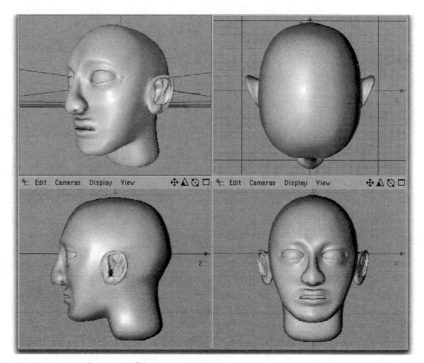

FIGURE 5.31 Rough version of the completed head.

ears, mouth, and nose, and much work should still be done in those areas. However, the groundwork has been done and you can refine those areas to get the shape you want (Figure 5.32).

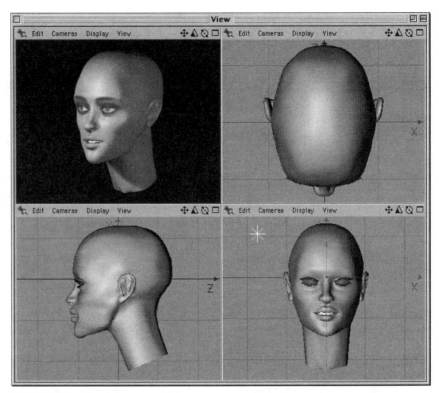

FIGURE 5.32   Final head after some refining.

5.2 ADDITIVE MODELING OF ORGANIC SHAPES

In Tutorial 5.1, Anson showed how to use HyperNURBS and Symmetry objects to take a general shape and refine down to details such as the nose, eyes, and mouth. In this tutorial, we will be taking a different approach to modeling a detailed head. Here we will start with very few polygons in one specific area (the eye) and build the entire head out from that point.

There are tutorials like this in many places for a variety of different programs. For this particular tutorial, we will not only be looking at how to build the head in the best possible circumstances (meaning the author knew exactly how many polygons to put where from the beginning), but we will look at what to do when you need more unexpected geometry, or when you find that you made a mistake in the process of earlier construction. The hope is to help you understand the *concepts*, not just the steps, so that you will be able to build your own organic shapes without having to follow someone's tutorial.

As always, the actual .c4d files for this tutorial are included on the CD-ROM (Tutorials>Chapter05>Tutorial 5.2). For this tutorial, multiple versions of the model are saved along the way for you to refer to. Also, remember that sometimes grayscale images can be hard to read. To make it easier, the background of the interface has been changed to black. But don't let it confuse you, it's the same C4D R8 interface. If the screenshots are unclear or you'd like a closer look, please check out the color versions of all images contained on the CD-ROM.

ON THE CD

Figure 5.33 shows the character we are going to build. The character is excellently designed by Richard Clark and he was careful in his design and subsequent character style sheet to carefully line up important parts of the face. Note that he has gone so far as to make sure that the top of the head, the eyes, the nose, ears, and chin are all lined up with horizontal lines drawn directly on his style sheet. A good sketch really makes a model much, much easier to construct. Take some good time to carefully design your characters and carefully provide yourself the kind of resource that will make your construction process simple.

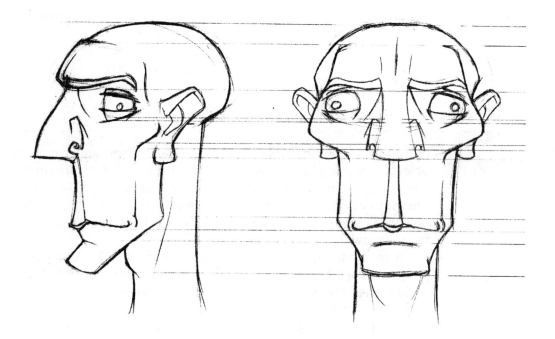

FIGURE 5.33 Character design and sketch by Richard Clark.

Once you have your character sketch digitized, you need to do a bit of preparation of the sketch. First, split the original sketch into two sections—a front sketch and a side sketch—and be sure to save each. Also verify that you have carefully centered the front sketch so that the middle of the image is truly the middle of the face. Often, creating a guide within Photoshop (Figure 5.34) can help ensure that you have equal amount of face on both sides of the image. Save the file and take careful note of how many *pixels* the image is (check this by choosing Image>Image Size in Photoshop). If you would prefer, you can just use the pre-prepared split versions, on the CD-ROM in Tutorials> Chapter05>Tutorial 5.2>Resource Shots.

ON THE CD

FIGURE 5.34   Split the character sketch into two segments and verify that the face is split perfectly down the middle.

ON THE CD

Before we really get into things, save the empty .c4d file you will be working in. This will provide a location for C4D to go to for important things such as these resource files. You may wish to transfer the Resource Shots folder from the CD-ROM to your save location.

Once you have both halves of the face saved as different files and have taken careful note of how large each is, in C4D we can configure our front and side views to use the images we created in Photoshop as guides. Within the Front View Panel, select Edit>Configure. This will allow you to set up how this view panel is going to function.

Within the Configure Viewport dialog box, notice the Background section. Here you can define a picture to permanently place in the background of this view panel. This image won't render, but will be available as a resource. Click the ... button and show C4D where the front view of the character is (remember, you can use the ones located on the CD-ROM). For the Front View Panel, after you have clicked the Show Picture check box, and have defined where the image is, change the Horizontal Size and Vertical Size input fields so that they match the number of pixels of the image. The prepared files on the CD-ROM had a front image that was 868 pixels by 1135 pixels. Notice in the screenshots shown in Figure 5.35 that these values were entered as meters. The reason you do this is to maintain proportions. The relative size is really irrelevant, but you do want to make sure that both your front and side views maintain the correct proportions for their width and height and their relative sizes to each other.

ON THE CD

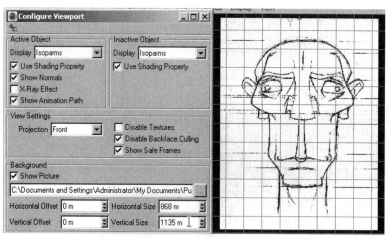

FIGURE 5.35 Configuring the Front View Panel.

Repeat this process for the Side View Panel, using the side image you've prepared or copied off the disc.

Once this is set up, you will notice that the Perspective View does not show either the front or side shots imported into the other view panels.

However, if you zoom in or out in either the Front or Side View Panels, you will zoom in or out on these resource images.

Once you are happy with your resource setup, create a sphere that will act as the eye. This will give us further resource information on where to start to create and modify our polygons around the eye. Remember as you resize and position the sphere that the actual sphere that is the eyeball is larger than what you actually see (Figure 5.36). Hide this sphere for now.

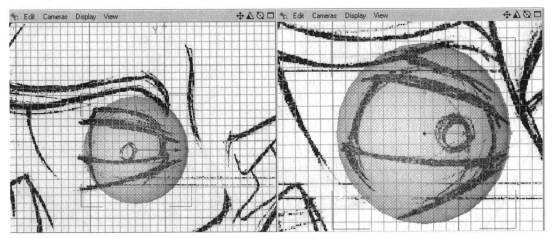

FIGURE 5.36   Creating a sphere to act as an eye resource.

Next, create two Symmetry objects. Remember that Symmetry objects will create a mirror image of an object. We want two of them so that we can have two eyeballs, and also so that the rest of the face that we are going to be constructing will be mirrored as well. This way, we only have to build half the face. Place the sphere created for the eyeball in one of the Symmetry objects.

In previous versions of C4D, to work with this additive modeling method—sometimes called point-by-point—we would need to start out by building rings of points. Now however, with the new Edge tools, this process is sped up considerably. Instead of building a ring of points, create a Tube Primitive (Figure 5.37). This will give us a built-in ring to work with. Position it appropriately around the eye. Place it in the second Symmetry object created earlier.

In the Attributes Editor (for the Tube), change the Rotation Segments to 12. If you have a particularly complex face, you can use more; or you can use less and add new rows of polygons later with methods we'll

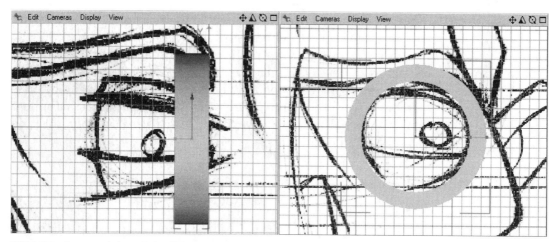

FIGURE 5.37 Create and place a Tube Object Primitive.

discuss. Twelve is a good number to start with. Also resize the middle hole of the tube so that it approximates the shape of the eye.

Next make the object Editable (hit "C"). For some reason, C4D, when it makes these Tubes editable, it makes the caps of the Tube separate objects. This means that if you grab an edge on the top of the shape and move it, it leaves behind the edge of the next polygon on the side. However, we need all of these polygons to be connected at their vertices and edge. To do this, simply select the entire Tube object (now a polygon object—no longer a primitive) and select Structure>Optimize. This will get rid of unused points, which in our case will fuse all of our edges together. Enter 10 in the Tolerance input field and hit OK.

Now we need to do some refining. Change to Points mode and choose the Live Selection tool. In the Active Tool Editor (nested beneath the Attributes Editor), turn off Only Select Visible Elements. For now, you want to be able to paint across points or edges and have it select the points or edges on the backside of the shape as well.

Now, in the Front View, use the Live Selection tool to paint pairs (actually you'll be painting (selecting) a group of four points when you count the points on the back side) of points and then move them so that they align to the inside of the eyelids (Figure 5.38).

In the Perspective View, adjust your foursome of points so that they curve appropriately around the eyeball (Figure 5.39a). Create a Hyper-NURBS object, and place the Symmetry object that is the parent of the Tube as a child of it (Figure 5.39b).

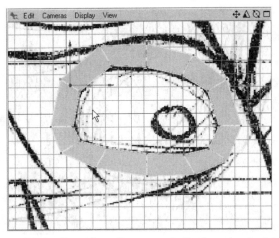

FIGURE 5.38   Front View adjustments of adjusting pairs of points.

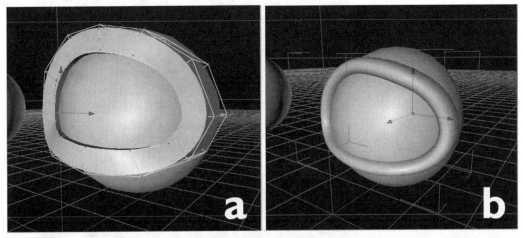

FIGURE 5.39   (a) Adjusting to the curve of the eye. (b) Symmetry object and Tube as children of a HyperNURBS object.

Select the polygons around the outside edge of the Tube (you'll need to switch to Polygon mode and use the Live Selection tool), and delete them (Figure 5.40).

Now switch to Edge mode and select the outside edges of the Tube object. You can do this one at a time, or you can select one edge, then right-click (Command-click), and select Edge Loop from the pop-down menu (Figure 5.41).

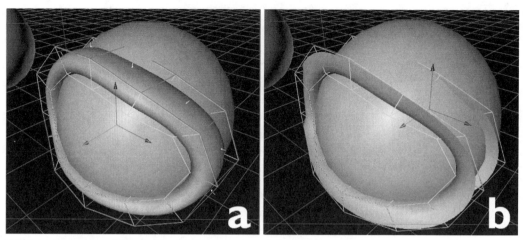

FIGURE 5.40   Selecting and deleting the outside edge of the Tube object.

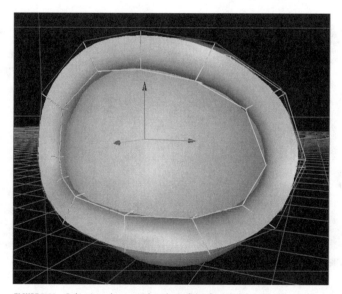

FIGURE 5.41   Selecting the outside edge of the front of the tube.

Next, we will use the Extrude Tool. We used this tool often in earlier tutorials, but in this case we are going to extrude an edge, not a face. So make sure you are still in Edge mode, and hit "D" on your keyboard, or select Structure>Extrude. There are many ways to use this tool. For now, we will let C4D do much of the work for us. In the Active Tool palette, change the settings to read like those in Figure 5.42 and hit Apply. The result, also shown in Figure 5.42, is a new edge ring offset of 20m. It extends out in all directions. This is essence has created a new ring of points and bridged all these new points to the old ones.

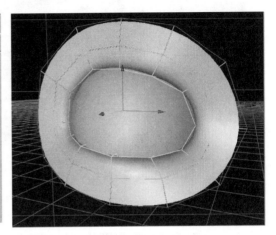

FIGURE 5.42   Using the Extrude tool

Now comes the time of refining. To refine things so that you can see how the polygons look in comparison to the resource image you've imported, you can do one of two things. First, you can create a material quickly that has Transparency activated. Apply this texture to your mesh and you will be able to see through it. Or, you can use Display>X-Ray from within each view panel. This will make whatever element is active see-through. Refine this collection of edges either by modifying where the edges lay (move and rotate) or by doing so in Points mode with the points (Figure 5.43).

Select the outside ring of edges again, and use the Extrude tool to create a new ring of polygons. Remember to refine either by points or edges. You will probably find—as things get increasingly complex— that you will want to manipulate things on a point-by-point level. Also, remember that you can turn the subdividing of the HyperNURBS off, by clicking the red check and turning it to an X. Then, turn it back on again. Sometimes, you will want to swap back and forth often to be able to see as many points as you can (Figure 5.44).

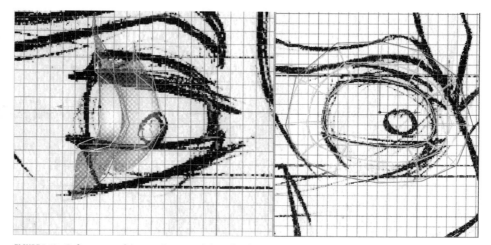

FIGURE 5.43 Refinement of the newly created ring of polygons.

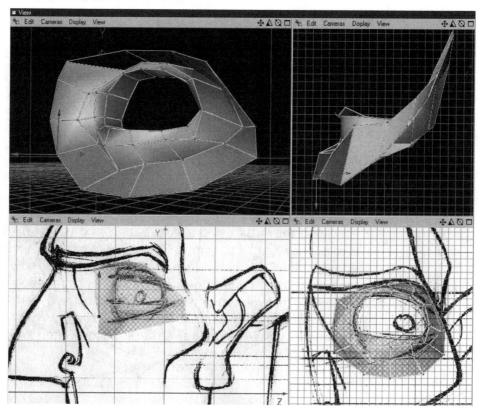

FIGURE 5.44 Continuing to build out and edit using Points mode.

EYE BAGS

Once you have extruded out so that you begin to create the bridge of the nose and the cheek bone, you can go back and add a bit of detail. In this case, we will want to add some detail around the bags of the eyes. To do this, be sure you are in Edge mode and select the edges that would be right under the bags of the eyes (Figure 5.45).

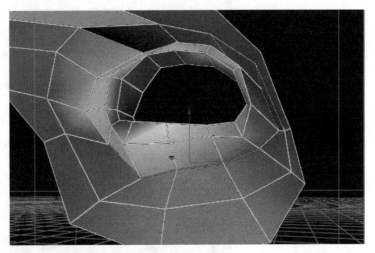

FIGURE 5.45   Adding further detail under the eyes.

Hit "D" on your keyboard to activate the Extrude tool. Click-drag to the right to extrude out a new collection of edges. Notice that when you do this, these new edges are also attached to new polygons (Figure 5.46a). Switch to the Move Active Element tool, and move this still-selected group of edges back into the head (Figure 5.46b). This will create a deep crease under the bags that will punch up the look.

Now to give the bag under the eye still more body, select the points that lay at the bottom of the bag and right above the row of points just made through the edge extrusion (Figure 5.47a) and pull them down over the crease (Figure 5.47b). The results of all of this should look something like Figure 5.48.

Continue to extrude our rings of edges. As you continue to extrude, you may find that when you hit the Apply button in the Active Tool, the default Offset value of 20m is not a good setting. As your model gets more complex, change this value to 0. Hit Apply. Your view panel will appear as though nothing has happened. However, immediately switch to

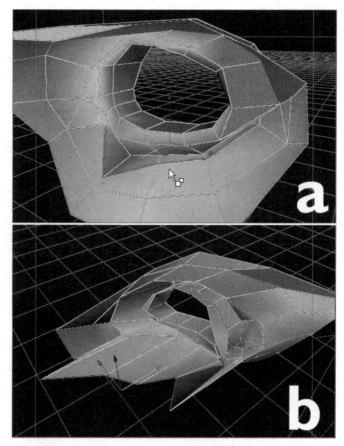

FIGURE 5.46 (a) Extruding new edges. (b) Moving the newly extruded edges back into the head to create crease along the face.

the Scale Active Element tool and scale out in all directions. You will see that the Extrude tool had extruded a new collection of edges, but that they were sitting right on top of the old ones. By resizing, you are moving them all away from their center.

Continue to update and tweak these new rings of polygons.

As time goes on, you may find that you need additional polygons. For instance, Figure 5.49 shows the face where there begins to be a very large gap right over the top of the eyebrow. Big gaps are not always bad, but if they get too big, you lose the power to add necessary detail. To cut this gap in half, we will use the Knife tool.

Change to Polygon mode and select the Knife tool (Structure>Knife). In the Active tool, turn off Restrict to Selection. Now click-drag through

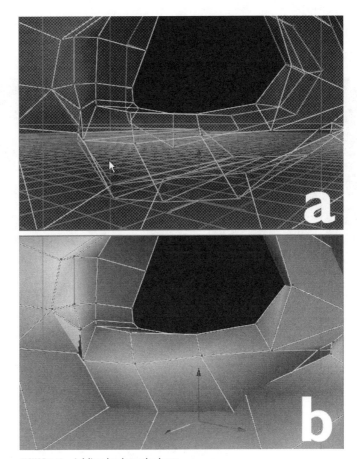

FIGURE 5.47   Adding body to the bags.

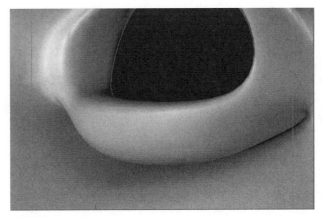

FIGURE 5.48   Rough bags completed.

the middle of the polygons you wish to cut (Figure 5.49). The result (Figure 5.49b) will be a new collection of edges.

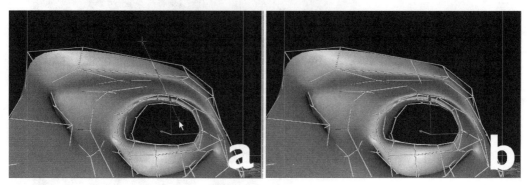

FIGURE 5.49 Adding polygons to an area using the Knife tool.

Continue to build out. Remember that you need to be building around the side of the head, down the cheek, up the brow and in toward the nose all at once. Tweak points often.

As you build, you will begin to get fairly close to the bridge of the nose. The following few steps show one method of constructing the nose.

NOSE

As you get close to the nose, take the innermost points and move them all toward the middle of the face (Figure 5.50). Don't worry about building the nose out yet, just get the front view correct.

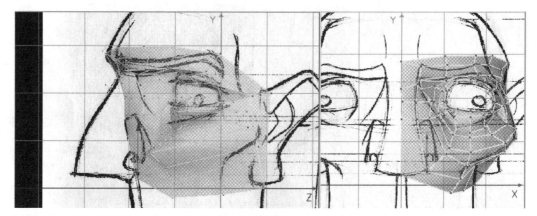

FIGURE 5.50 Getting started with the nose by covering up the nose hole.

To create the polygons that we are going to want for the nose, we will extrude this flat collection of nose polygons out. Select the polygons shown in Figure 5.51. With the Extrude tool, extrude out twice this collection of polygons (Figure 5.52).

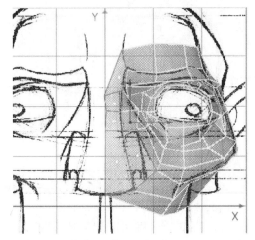

FIGURE 5.51   The key polygons for the nose construction.

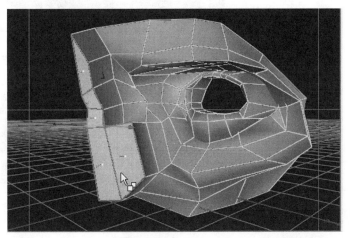

FIGURE 5.52   Extruding out the polygons to give us the necessary geometry.

Once you have these polygons extruded, you can begin to refine them a bit into the general shape of the nose (Figure 5.53).

Now something has happened as you've been extruding these polygons; you've created unwanted polygons along the axis of symmetry

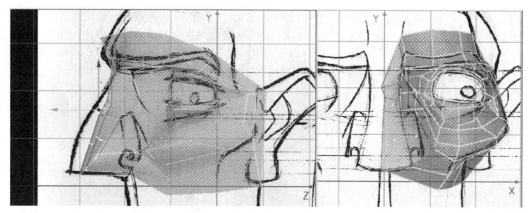

FIGURE 5.53 Refining the new polygons roughly into the shape of the nose.

(Figure 5.54). These polygons on the inside plane will cause the face to have a big split down the center if the HyperNURBS and Symmetry objects are both active. So take a moment and delete all the polygons that sit along the center *zy* plane (Figure 5.54).

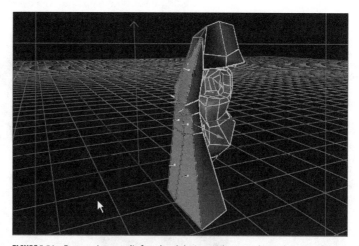

FIGURE 5.54 Preventing a split face by deleting polygons along the axis of symmetry.

Be sure and take time occasionally to turn the HyperNURBS back on to see the progress you have made. Note that in Figure 5.55, many of the points have been massaged into place to give us a profile very close to our resource image.

Before we move on to the nostrils, we need to do a bit more house-cleaning. As we have been constructing our face (one half of it, anyway),

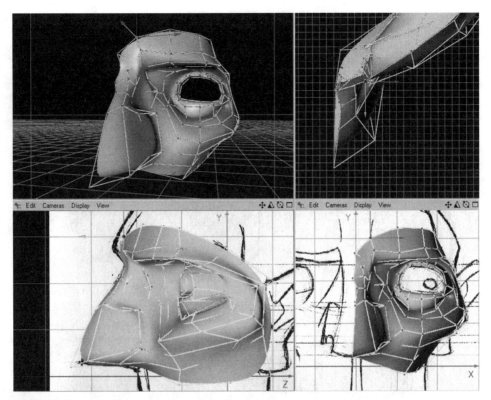

FIGURE 5.55   Nose thus far.

we have not had to worry too much about how the Symmetry object will work. But now that we have points right along the axis of symmetry, it will be important that they are lined up appropriately. Figure 5.56 shows a screenshot of how the points were at this point in the tutorial. In Points mode, select these points (only those that should be right in the middle of the face). To get them all to be at the center, we need to make sure that every point is an X=0. We could do this one at a time, or by selecting Structure>Edit Surface>Set Value. In the Set Value dialog box, change the X input field to Set, the value next to it to 0, and the Coordinates System to World. This will take all of these points and align them up exactly with X=0 in the World Coordinates system.

Now, when you turn your Symmetry object back on, you will have a clean area across the top of the nose.

Time for the nostrils. To create the nostrils, we will use polygons already in existence to fashion the holes we need. Because this character has an interesting set of nostrils, we want to give ourselves plenty of

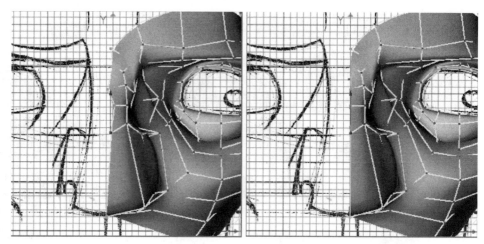

FIGURE 5.56 Before and after using the Set Value to get the center points right on center.

polygons to construct its shape. Figure 5.57 shows a suggested collection (*at least* two polygons large).

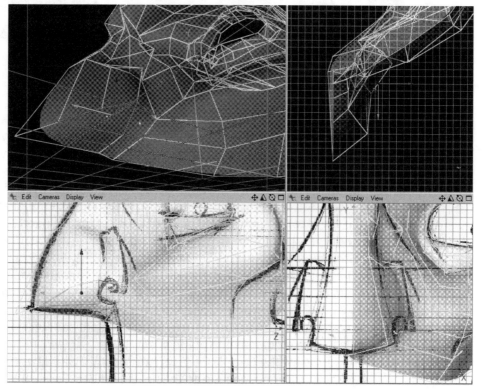

FIGURE 5.57 Selection for the nostrils.

Now, we want to use the Extrude Inner tool. This is very similar to the Extrude tool, except that the new polygons it creates are left at the same plane as the polygons they came from. Select Structure>Extrude Inner or hit "I" on your keyboard. Click-drag to the left to make a new collection of polygons slightly smaller than they were.

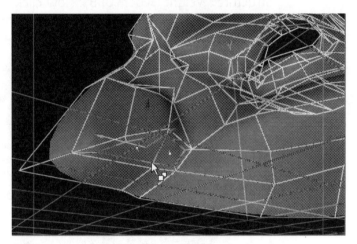

FIGURE 5.58   Extrude Inner to create new polygons for the nose.

Now with these polygons still selected, hit "D" on your keyboard and extrude up into the nose (Figure 5.59). Although these are rough nostrils, you have most of the geometry needed to give these nostrils the necessary detail.

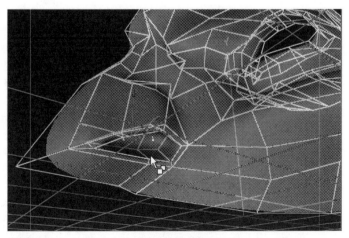

FIGURE 5.59   Extruding up to create actual nostril holes.

Move the points around to create the shape of the nostril you want. The shape of the edge of the nostril seems a bit soft here. Luckily, because of C4D's new Weighted HyperNURBS functions, we can alter this a bit.

Select the edges around the edge of the nostril (Figure 5.60). Select Structure>Weight HyperNURBS. Now click and drag anywhere in the scene and you will see the smoothed polygons of the nostril be drawn toward these edges.

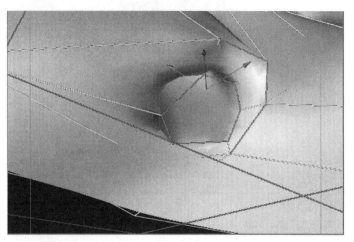

FIGURE 5.60   Weighting the nostril edges to make them more precise.

At this point, we need to pursue a brief tangent. In a perfect world, we would model away and always have just the right number of polygons all the time. Unfortunately, sometimes we don't. Figure 5.61 shows a collection of polygons across the side of the nose that cover a lot of surface area. On the one hand, it's nice to have lower poly counts as it is easier to edit this way. However, this particular nose has some detail around this part of the nose that we need to be able to get to. With the current large spread of polygons, we don't have the points necessary to do the sculpting we need.

To get the necessary polygons, we will use the Knife tool again. This time, carefully select the polygons you need to cut. Select the Knife tool ("K" on your keyboard), and make sure that the Active Tool has Restrict to Selection activated (as we only want to cut this collection of polygons). Now cut a diagonal line to give us a new row of edges.

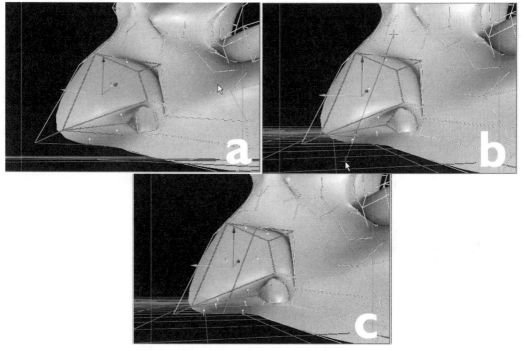

FIGURE 5.61   Adding new polygons with the Knife tool.

Now, still in the perfect world, this would magically give us the polygons we need. Unfortunately, knifing in this way can sometimes create some awkward puckers and tucks. Even if your model does not show the pucker shown in Figure 5.62, take a minute to review the next few steps as it is important to know how to correct such an anomaly.

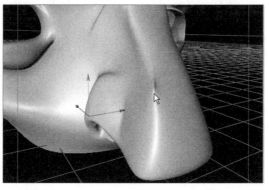

FIGURE 5.62   Pucker to be rid of.

This kind of pucker is often caused when a collection of polygons (usually more than four) meet at one point. When you are using all four-sided polygons, this is unusual, but with the Knife function just completed, some triangles were created. Figure 5.63a shows some of the offending triangles. It turns out that if you look at these two triangles (which share at least two common points), you can see that they could be restructured into one four-sided polygon. To do this, select the triangles and delete them (Figure 5.63b). Once deleted, make sure you are in Points mode and right-click (Command-click) and select Create Polygon. Now just click on each of the four points that surround your hole. A new polygon will be created in its place (Figure 5.63c).

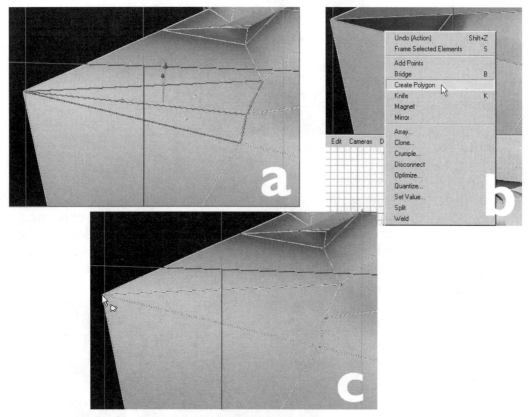

FIGURE 5.63   Fixing a pucker by getting rid of unnecessary triangles.

Adjust your new collections of points and edges to more closely match the three-dimensional shape of the nose.

Continue to select the outside ring (but not the edge along the center of the face) and extrude the edges (then resize them out) to provide
for new geometry (Figure 5.64). Remember to make sure that your new
polygon's points that are near the center of the face get reoriented back
to the center plane. Keep working out and down toward the mouth.

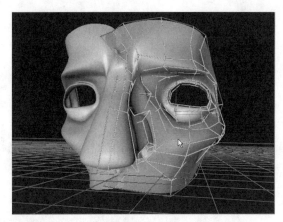

FIGURE 5.64   Continue to add geometry for the head by
extruding edges.

For now, build over the mouth as though there wasn't one. We will
go back and add the necessary geometry later. As you work, if you find
areas of insufficient geometry (Figure 5.65), use the Knife tool step we
talked about earlier to add some in. In Figure 5.65, you'll see this is important; as the polygons around the mouth here are too wide. The
mouth is an extremely complex area and we need the polygons to help

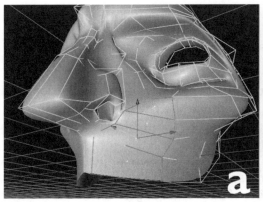 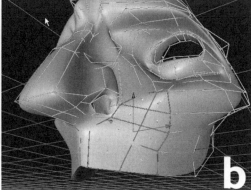

FIGURE 5.65   Adding geometry for the mouth area.

define the necessary curves. Figure 5.66 shows a "so far" shot. Extrude and adjust until you are about at this point.

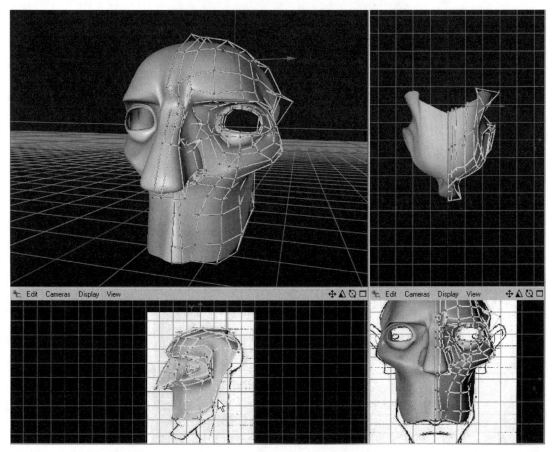

FIGURE 5.66   The head so far.

BACK OF THE HEAD

As you work around, you will reach a point where the collection of edges that are moving down and around the cheeks will come close to the edges that are moving up and over the head. Eventually, you'll need to start consolidating polygons.

Figure 5.67a shows just that point. When we reach it, we'll need to stop extruding rings and semi-rings and start extruding rows. Figure 5.67b shows the extruding of that row of edges. Notice that this leaves a hole, shown with the circle. To fill this hole, you can do one of three things: 1) You could use the Create Polygon tool (Structure>Create Polygon) and click on each of the three points of that hole. 2) You could use the Bridge tool (Structure>Bridge) and click and drag between the two collections of points on either side of the hole. 3) You could select the two open points of the hole, right-click and select Weld to have the points welded as one. In any case, make sure you close the hole up.

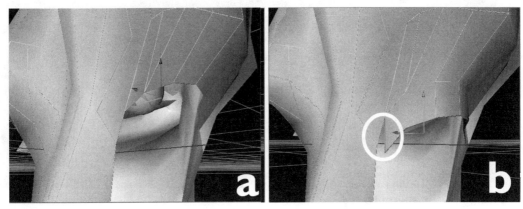

FIGURE 5.67   Attaching the converging collections of edges.

Continue extruding this row of edges down, patching up the holes as you go until your model looks similar to Figure 5.68.

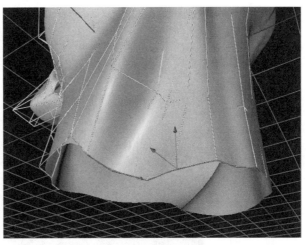

FIGURE 5.68   Building down the head to the neck.

As you build down the head, be sure to build in the beginning of the back of the jaw. Then, as the neck is completed, come to the edge of the jaw created thus far, and begin extruding just that edge up to create the bottom of the jaw and start to wrap up toward the mouth (Figure 5.69).

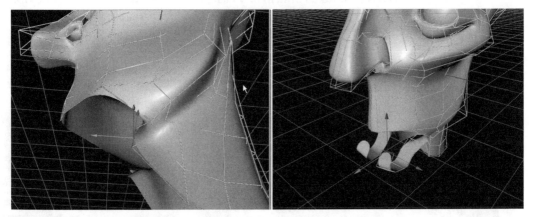

FIGURE 5.69 Constructing the jaw's general shape.

Build inward toward the axis of symmetry to close off the bottom of the jaw (Figure 5.70). Remember as you are creating these polygons, take a careful look at the Front and Side views, where you have source images to help you define the curves you are creating.

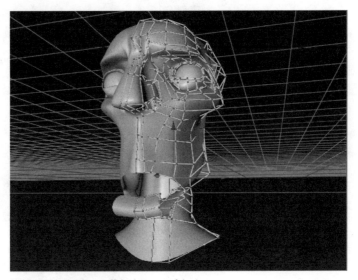

FIGURE 5.70 Finishing off the bottom of the jaw.

Once the bottom is done, start building up around the sides of the jaw and close off the space that will be the mouth. Figure 5.71 shows the right-click pop-down menu for two points that you will join together as the sides wrap up and around to meet the geometry already constructed down the side of the cheek.

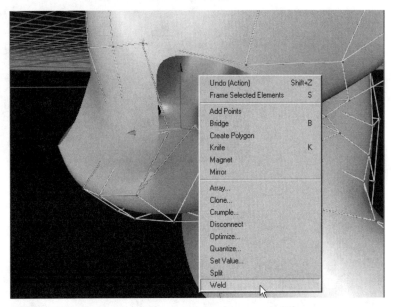

FIGURE 5.71   Welding points together as various edges come together.

Figure 5.72 shows the Figure thus far. Notice there's no mouth or ears quite yet—but their time will come. Remember to take careful note of how your geometry matches up with your source imagery.

To create the Adam's apple, select the polygon where this piece of anatomy would go and extrude it outward. Be sure to delete the newly created polygon on the axis of symmetry and put those points that should be centered at $x=0$. Finally, reshape to taste.

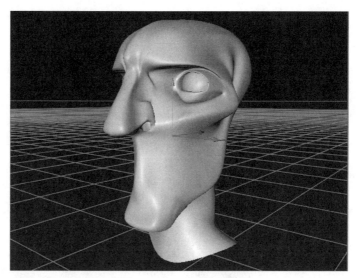

FIGURE 5.72 Figure thus far.

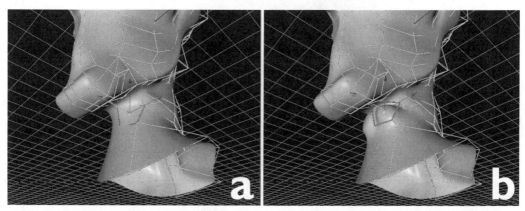

FIGURE 5.73 Creating the Adam's apple.

CLEANING UP IN PREPARATION FOR THE MOUTH

Every model will be a little different at this point. However, let's look at a potential problem spot on my model. Although you may not have the same problem on the same spot, you will probably have this sort of problem elsewhere, so it's worthwhile to find out how to fix it.

Figure 5.74 shows a collection of polygons around the mouth that is made up of a lot of unnecessary triangular polygons. As we are going to need some good solid four-side polys, this area will need to be rebuilt. Begin by deleting the offending polygons (Figure 5.74b).

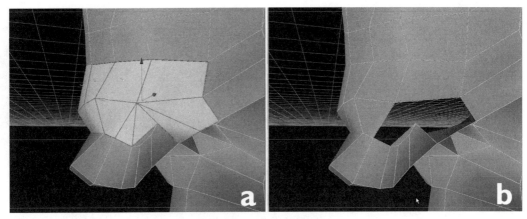

FIGURE 5.74   (a) Bad collection of polygons. (b) Problem polys deleted.

The best way to fill this will be with the Bridge tool. Make sure you are in Points mode and drag between pairs of points to create a new polygon that bridges the hole. Figure 5.75 shows one solution to the area. Notice that most of the new shapes are four-sided polygons.

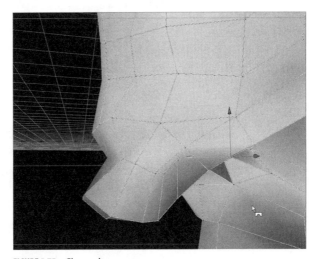

FIGURE 5.75   Cleaned up area.

MOUTH

To build the mouth, we will need some added geometry. Start by selecting the polygons that are in the general area of the mouth (Figure 5.76).

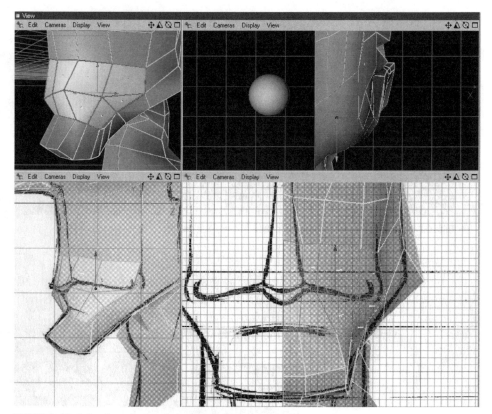

FIGURE 5.76 Defining the polygons that will become the mouth.

Now use the Extrude Inner ("I" on your keyboard), and create at least four extrusions (Figure 5.77). This gives us roughly the geometry we will need. However, there is much sculpting to be done.

As you have created these Extrude Inners, you also have created some unwanted polygons right in the middle of the face. Select these (Figure 5.78) and delete them.

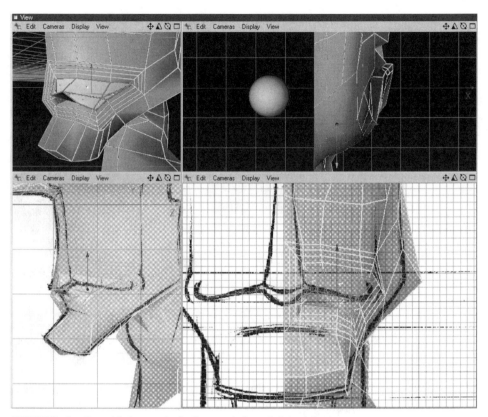

FIGURE 5.77   Creating added geometry for the mouth through Extrude Inners.

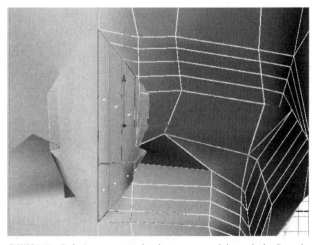

FIGURE 5.78   Deleting unwanted polygons created through the Extrude Inner functions.

Now, take all the points that are the closest to the *zy* plane or the axis of symmetry and get them at *x*=0 (select the points and use Structure>Edit Surface>Set Value). The results should appear similar to Figure 5.79.

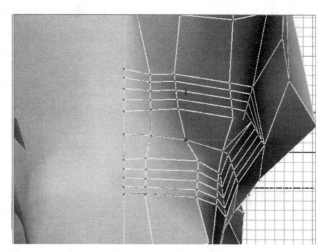

FIGURE 5.79   Aligned points.

Now begins the detailing, the massaging, and the shaping. Begin by creating the top lip (Figure 5.80). This can be done in Points mode by dragging points out into position.

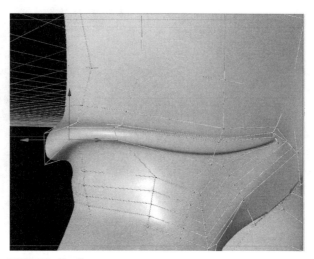

FIGURE 5.80   Top lip.

Before we get too far into the bottom lip, we will take some of the extant polygons and create the oral cavity. The oral cavity will be especially necessary if you ever plan on animating this character.

To create the oral cavity, in Polygon mode select the collections of polygons shown in Figure 5.81a. Use the Extrude tool to extrude these polygons back into the head (Figure 5.81b). Make this new collection of polygons larger with the Scale Active Element tool, then extrude again and make this third set smaller again. This will give you a nice cave of an orifice.

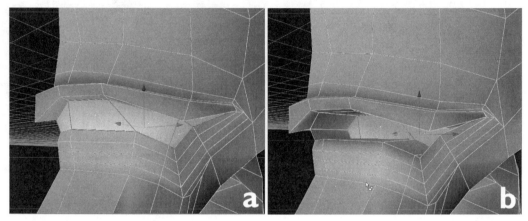

FIGURE 5.81   Starting to create the oral cavity.

Figure 5.82 shows a look at this cavity after the new polygons that were created on the axis of symmetry were deleted, the points on the axis of symmetry were moved to $x=0$, and the cavity was reshaped just slightly.

Now we'll create the bottom lip. Close the mouth by selecting the points that will be the top of the bottom lip and moving them up to meet the bottom of the top lip (Figure 5.83).

One nice thing to take advantage of here is C4D's ability to weight edges, and faces with the Structure>Weight HyperNURBS. Figure 5.84 shows the top edge of the top lip being selected (by Edges, of course) and then shaped by selecting Structure>Weight HyperNURBS and dragging a little sharper definition. Similarly Figure 5.85 shows the bottom lip's front polygons selected, followed by an identical Structure>Weight HyperNURBS to pull the subdivided polygons up closer to that collection of polygons.

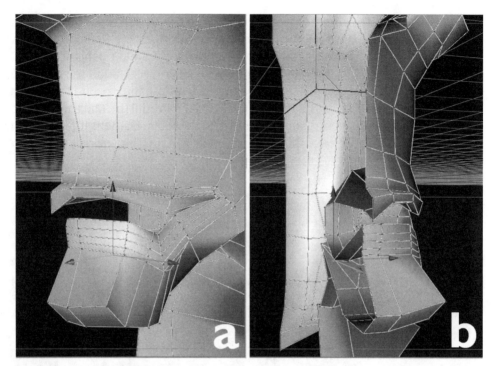

FIGURE 5.82 Finished oral cavity.

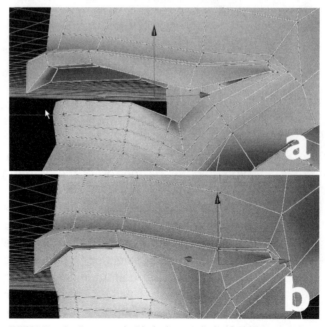

FIGURE 5.83 Getting started with the bottom lip by closing the mouth.

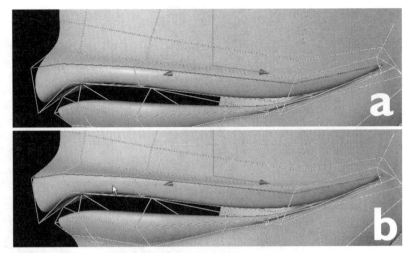

FIGURE 5.84 Adding definition to the top lip by weighting edges.

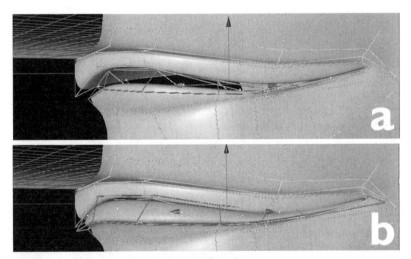

FIGURE 5.85 Adding definition to the lower lip by weighting the polygons.

ON THE CD

Finally, Figure 5.86 shows the model thus far with a finished mouth. If you have any questions on the structure of the face up to this point, take a look on the CD-ROM (Tutorials>Chapter05>Tutorial 5.2).

Before moving on to the ear, let's create the eyebrows. Figure 5.87 shows the polygons along the brow being selected. With the Extrude tool, these polygons are extruded out and then the points worked to get the smooth brows and shapes just right.

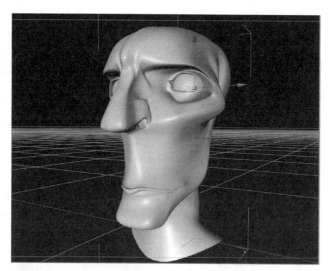

FIGURE 5.86   Figure getting ready for the ear.

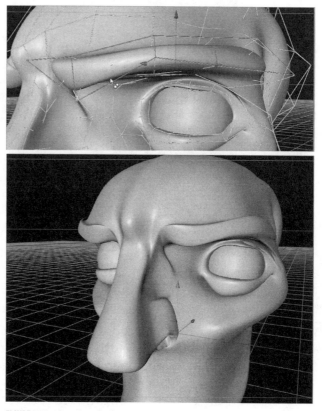

FIGURE 5.87   Creating the brow.

THE EAR

Now it's time to create the ear. There is an amazing amount of detail in those little sound catchers on the sides of our heads. Look closely at someone's ear; there is more detail in that ear than in the rest of the human head. Because of this, creating an ear can be a daunting task.

There are many different methods that can be used to create ears. There are several really strong techniques online for various 3D applications. After this chapter, hopefully you'll feel confident enough with polygonal modeling that you could interpret almost any 3D package's tutorials and apply them to C4D. There are about as many techniques out there as there are ears. In fact, almost every ear I've built has had some major variations in the techniques used.

Listed here is the technique finally settled on for the ear of our character. This character has a definitive ear that is a stylized simplification. This makes for some interesting challenges, as the shape is a bit unique, which means that traditional ear modeling methods may not necessarily apply.

To construct the ear, we will build it as a completely separate polygon mesh and then merge it into the completed head. For now, hide your completed head (click the top grey button next to your head object until it turns red). This will give you unfettered access to look at the resource image of the ear.

Create a Primitive Cube and rotate it so that it approximates Figure 5.88 (showing the Side view). What we are going to do is create the polygons for the biggest surface area of the ear, and then go in and add the curves at the top of the ear and the inside of the ear later.

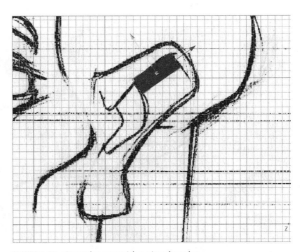

FIGURE 5.88   Start the ear with a simple cube.

Make the cube Editable, and then use the Extrude tool to extrude and rotate new polygons down to cover the area covered in Figure 5.89. You may choose to use more or fewer subdivisions if you would like.

FIGURE 5.89 Getting started with the ear by extruding the general shape out.

This isn't a bad start, but each segment of the ear only has four sides. Thus, it is very difficult to get the kind of rounding that is required in the curves of the ear. To add segments, we will look at some new possibilities for the Extrude tool. Start out by selecting the front edge of the shape (Figure 5.90a). Hit "D" on your keyboard to activate the Extrude tool. Hold the CTRL key down and click-drag to the right. Notice that what this does is create two new edges on either side of the selected collection of edges that follow a parallel path along the surface (Figure 5.90b).

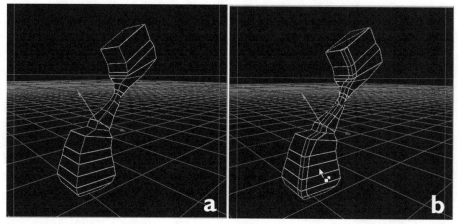

FIGURE 5.90 Adding necessary geometry with the Extrude tool.

Now you can switch to Points mode and begin moving this new collection of points around to put points along the front of the ear to allow
for appropriate rounding of the shape. Make sure you can see your
model in the Front and Side view so you can use the resources to reshape the points you have to match the sketch (Figure 6.9.1).

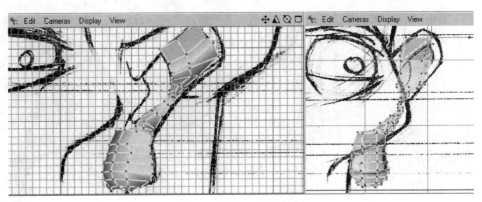

FIGURE 5.91   Adjusting new points to match general shape of the ear.

Now we can begin to add details such as the curves at the top of the
ear. In Polygon mode, select the polygons shown in Figure 5.92 and extrude them out to give you some added geometry.

Add another collection of extrusions for the front part of the top
curve. To be able to get the curve really defined, we need to create a bit
more geometry. Select the polygons shown in Figure 5.93 and extrude
them out (Figure 5.93b).

Now, to build the tight underside of the curve, we will use an Extrude
Inner. Select the polygons shown in Figure 5.94a and hit "I" on your keyboard to activate the Extrude Inner tool. Click-drag to the left and you
will get a new collection of polygons that become smaller but stay on
the surface of the original polygons (Figure 5.94b).

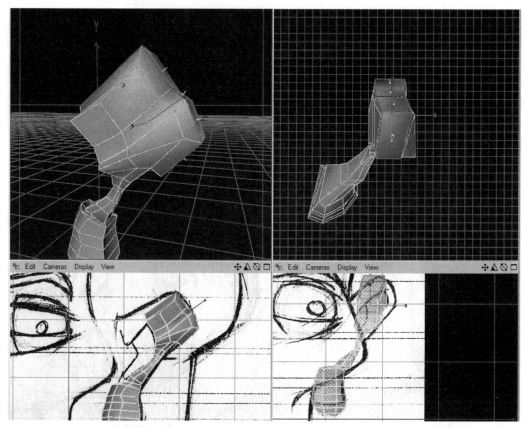

FIGURE 5.92   Adding top of ear with extrusions.

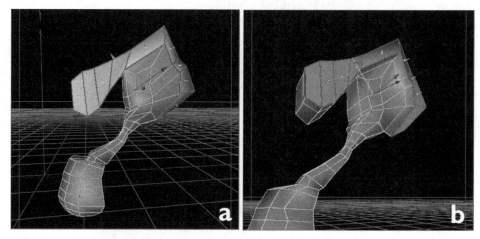

FIGURE 5.93   Continuing to build the top tight curves of the ear.

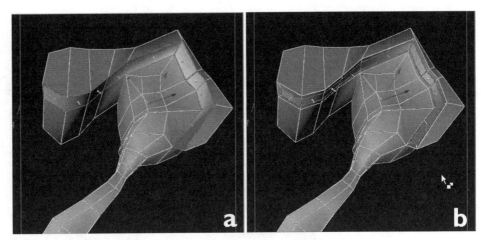

FIGURE 5.94   Using Extrude Inner to give us polygons for upper curves.

Now, it largely becomes an issue of tweaking points. Move your new geometry around to give you the shape you like. At some point, remember to place your ear into a new HyperNURBS object to get an idea of how things will round off. Figure 5.95 shows our progress thus far.

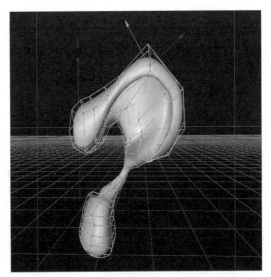

FIGURE 5.95   Ear thus far placed within a HyperNURBS object to create a subdivided round shape.

The next goal will be to close off our shape to make a large ring. Use extrusions to extrude up the front part of the ear to near the top (Figure 5.96). Modify the points of the new polygons as you go to shape the new form.

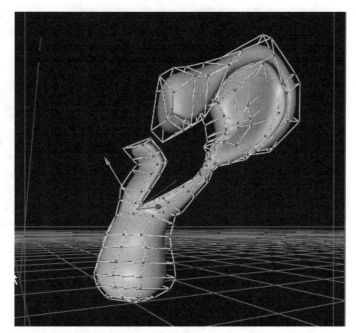

FIGURE 5.96   Starting to complete the ring of the ear.

Once you get close, take the polygons of the two edges of this ring and delete them. This will clear the way to bridge the two ends of the ring together (Figure 5.97).

Use the Bridge tool to bridge the hole together and close off the ring (Figure 5.98).

Now we need to create the inside of the ear. This will actually be a two-step process. First, we'll create the ear channel into the head and then the back side of the ear that actually connects into the head. To do this, select all the edges around the back side, inside edge of the ear (Figure 5.99). Hit "D" to activate the Extrude tool and again, hold the CTRL key down as you drag out a new row of edges. This will create a nice, small, thin row of polygons.

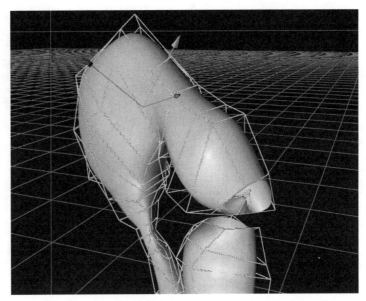

FIGURE 5.97   Deleting ends of the ear ring to allow us to close the shape off.

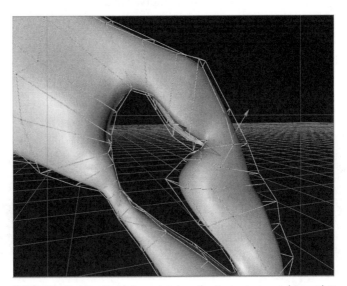

FIGURE 5.98   Results of bridging points together to create new polygons that close off the ear.

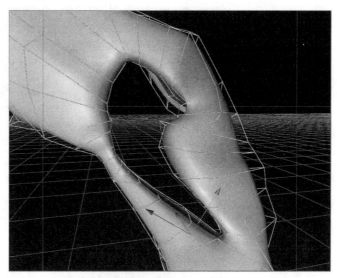

FIGURE 5.99 Creating new polygons to build canal and back side of the ear with.

Next, select these new polygons (Figure 5.100a), and extrude them back (Figure 5.100b). Notice that Figure 5.100 shows the results of several extrusions. The first two are right at the beginning to help define a sharp departure, and the third extrusion is longer to create long polygons.

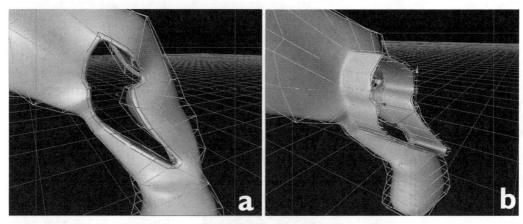

FIGURE 5.100 Using multiple extrusions to create the inside channel and outside edge of the ear.

Now delete those polygons that you were extruding (Figure 5.101a). This will create two independent edges. Take the inside ring of edges, and use the Scale Active Element tool to resize them smaller to create the ear canal (Figure 5.101b).

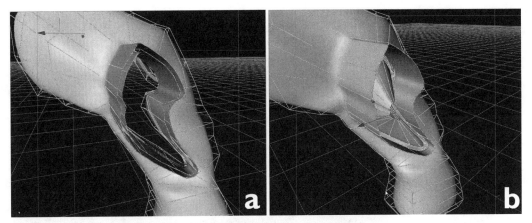

FIGURE 5.101   Delete the polygons, then select the inner edge ring and resize.

Now that the inside of the ear is done, and the back side looks pretty good, the only thing left is to refine the front side. Take a look at anyone's ear and you'll see that although there is a fairly sharp corner where the ear attaches to the head at the back of the ear, the front of the ear is really quite a subtle connection. As your model probably stands right now (Figure 5.102), there's a big ledge at the front of the ear, and the part that we are going to use to connect to the head. This will cause Shrek-like ears if not corrected. Our ears really have a fairly smooth transition into the head on the front part of the ear. Rework those points to get a smooth transition.

The only thing left now is connecting the ear to the head. To do this, we first need to make our ear mesh and our head mesh into one mesh. Figure 5.103a shows the Objects Manager of the tutorial file. Your names may vary. Select the Cube that is the ear, and then Shift-select the Tube that is the head. Select Functions>Connect. This will make a new polygonal shape (probably called "Cube") that C4D thinks of as one mesh. Take this new Cube and place it as a child of a new Symmetry object and place that Symmetry object as a child of a HyperNURBS object. Re-label this "Real Head." Make sure to hide the original ear and the original head objects so that they don't create extra versions of the geometry you want to work with (Figure 5.103b). From now on, we'll be working with this new Real Head object.

Now, we need to make room for the ear. Start by deleting the polygons around the area where the ear will connect to the head. Figure 5.104 shows the deleted areas from a view outside the head and one inside the head (you'll find it helpful at this point to deactivate both the

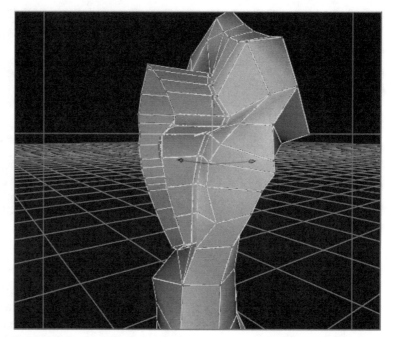

FIGURE 5.102   Front points that need to be adjusted to get the transition into the head correct.

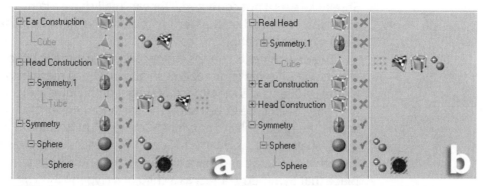

FIGURE 5.103   Making one mesh of the ear and head and placing the new mesh into its own Symmetry and HyperNURBS objects.

HyperNURBS object and the Symmetry objects by clicking their green checkmarks to red Xs in the Objects Manager).

Before we start combining polygons or building new polygons, we'll want to make the hole in the head a little closer to the shape of the ear. To do this, select the ring of edges that make up the hole in the head (Figure 5.105a). Use the Extrude tool to extrude a new ring of edges that

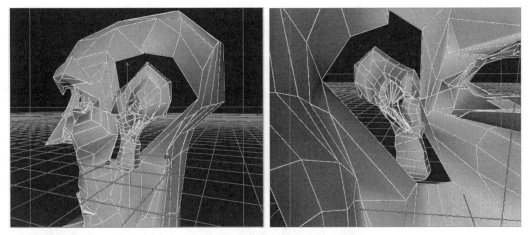

FIGURE 5.104   Deleting polygons to make room for the ear connection.

are scaled into a smaller hole (Figure 5.105b). Don't worry about making this hole exactly the same size as the ear, but the closer the better.

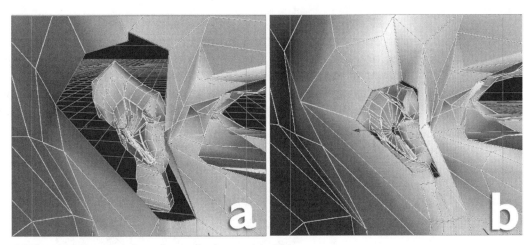

FIGURE 5.105   Tighten the hole up, close to the shape and size of the ear.

Now there's a slight problem; undoubtedly, the number of polygons you have on the outside edge of the ear is different than the number of polygons you have surrounding the hole in the head. This can be fixed by using the Bridge tool to bridge between pairs of polygons and remembering that you can build triangular polygons—in fact you will have to in order to close up the shape. As most of these polygons are behind the ear in an area that isn't seen much, this will be acceptable. Just be sure to not leave any holes (Figure 5.106).

FIGURE 5.106 Filling the hole by using the Bridge tool to create new polygons to bridge the head to the ear.

Finally, Figure 5.107 shows the outside of the ear.

One final note in preparing your model: As we have been building polygons for our form, there is a good chance that we built polygons that have their Normals reversed. Normals are the front sides of polygons (3D applications recognize absolute fronts and backs of polygons). If you have a group of polygons with their Normals facing outward and then one polygon with the Normal facing inward, you can have a number of strange problems when it comes to texturing and certain model-

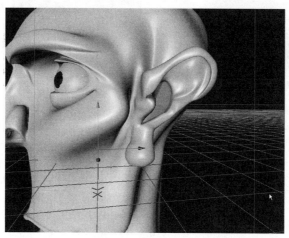

FIGURE 5.107 The finished attached ear.

ing situations. So before you are done, switch to Polygon mode and change your Live Selection tool to the Rectangle Selection variation. Make sure that the Active Tool settings has Only Select Visible Elements turned off, and marquee around the entire model. You will see some little yellow lines poking out of your head. Use Structure>Align Normals to tell C4D to find any backward polygons and make sure that they are facing the right direction. This seems like a strange piece of housekeeping, but it will keep things working as they should later in your texturing, lighting, animating, and rendering processes.

Make fine tuning as you see fit. Add another sphere for the strange pupils of the design and you're set (Figure 5.108).

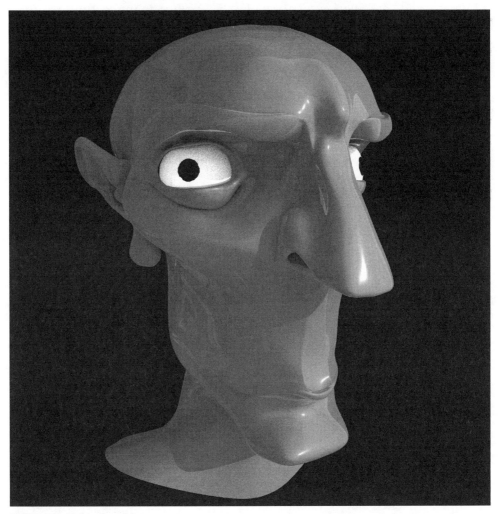

FIGURE 5.108   Finished model.

Tutorials like this are difficult to construct. There is an immense amount of tweaking that has to happen at various levels that is unique to the small decisions you make as you are building a shape. So, of course, this tweaking isn't covered in the course of the tutorial. But be sure that you go back and re-work, re-tweak, and refine your finished model until it has the shape and feel that you want.

CONCLUSION

Organic modeling using HyperNURBS and polygonal modeling techniques can be an incredibly rewarding experience. Once you have a good grasp of polygonal modeling techniques, there is really no shape that you cannot build.

6

MATERIALS & TEXTURES

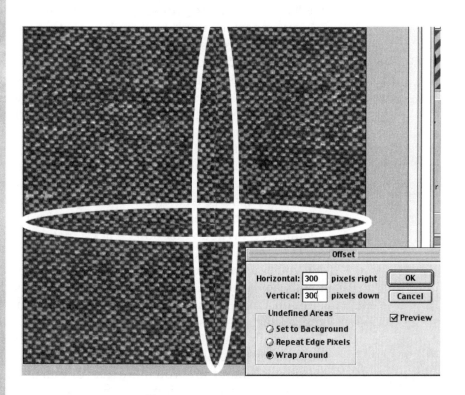

MATERIALS

When they are not in motion, there is very little that visually differentiates a bowling ball from a tennis ball, a pea from a beach ball, or a golf ball from a wicker ball. One of the things that does differentiate these different balls is texture. Textures are the visual clues that reference the tactile and visual qualities of a surface. Texture is everywhere and, without it, our real world would be a drab existence indeed.

3D is no different. If you've been following the tutorials, you're probably tired of looking at the same gray plastic-looking models. In this chapter, we're going to examine ways to spruce up our models, to give them color, dimension, tactile surfaces, reflective qualities; we'll even define the geometry of objects through texturing.

An important thing to note before we get started is that although "Texture" is the general catchphrase for surface qualities in 3D, each program handles the actual nomenclature a little differently. C4D uses the term "Material." A material is a collection of instructions that defines a surface. These materials are kept track of in the Materials Manager at the bottom of the interface. A new material can be created by selecting File>New Material within this Materials Manager. This new material will be represented by a little swatch that shows a sphere with an approximation of the material in its currently defined state. The Materials Manager stores all of the materials you have created for a given project.

Each of the instructions that define the material is called a "Parameter." When you double-click a material within the Materials Manager, a window called the Materials Editor will open, allowing you to alter these parameters (Figure 6.1). New to R8 is a more tightly integrated Attributes Editor. This means that if you click once on a material in the Materials Manager, you will be able to access all the same parameters in the Attributes Editor (Figure 6.2). This is really a nice function as it leaves you plenty of screen real estate, and is generally easier to access. Similarly, you can have the Attributes Editor show you more than one channel at a time, which makes for very quick editing of a material's channels.

There are parameters here that define the color; other parameters define how reflective the surface is, etc. When you have double-clicked a material and are working in the dialog box, by clicking on the name of a parameter, the Materials Editor will change to display the options available for editing that parameter. To activate a parameter, check the box next to the parameter's

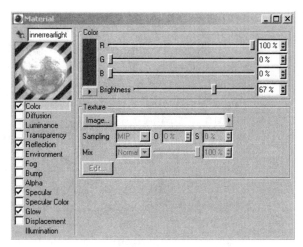

FIGURE 6.1   Double-clicking a material swatch in the Materials Manager will open a dialog box to edit the channels of the texture.

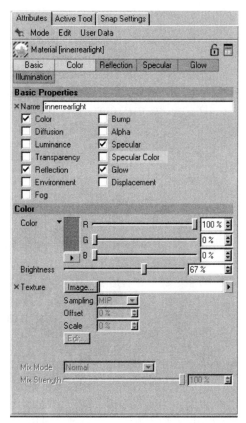

FIGURE 6.2   New to R8, single-clicking a Material opens its channels in the Attributes Editor.

name. In the Attributes Editor, you can activate parameters in the Basic section, and jump to each activated parameter by clicking (or Shift-clicking) its name at the top of the Attributes Editor.

Each parameter can be defined separately from the other parameters. However, a material takes into account all *active* parameters to create a final surface quality. An active parameter is checked within this Materials Editor. Often, a parameter will have two sections, a "Color" section and a "Texture" section. The idea here is that you can define a flat color in the Color section, or you can import a bit-mapped image or a procedural shader into the Texture section. The images brought into the Texture input fields are often referred to as "Texture Maps" as they tell C4D what to do where.

The best way to see how materials function is to see a material built from scratch and how the different parameters interact with each other. But before that, let us take a brief divergence into the realm of "Shaders."

SHADERS

Shaders are procedural textures, and thus are independent of pixel-based images. There are two different types of shaders: 3D and 2D. 3D shaders are incredibly powerful in that they are able to take into account the actual shape and mass of an object. In previous versions of C4D, there were a few 3D shaders available. Lately, BhodiNut's Smells Like Almonds (SLA) Volume Shaders have become available as well. SLA is an incredibly powerful collection of shaders. Effective manipulation of these shaders can make for astounding images.

Within the Materials Manager, you can create a new 2D, 3D or Volume Shade through the File pull-down menu. Select File>Shader or File>BhodiNut Volume and then pick from a variety of 3D shaders that C4D makes very well. When you've selected a 3D shader, it will show up in the Materials Manager like any other material. If you double-click on the shader in the Materials Manager, you'll be presented with a box different from typical Materials dialogue boxes. For a detailed description of how each of these 3D shaders work, refer to the manual. We won't cover them here, as 3D shaders tend to fall into the "canned-texture" look very easily. A canned texture is a texture someone else made and that everyone else is using. Typically, canned material on a reel is bad news and a real turnoff for employers. Although, by using the SLA shaders, you can create some truly unique, creative, and dynamic materials, the many veins of creation and alteration of these shaders is beyond the scope of this book, so we won't be covering them in depth here. But remember that they are there, and take a look at Web sites such as Deepshade *(www.maxon.net/deepshade)* for examples of how folks have used these shaders to create some great stuff.

TUTORIAL

6.1 Exploring the Powers of Materials

To explore the true power of materials, let's make one. Create a Sphere Primitive in an empty scene and create a new material by going to File>New Material within the Materials Editor. Save this file into its own folder somewhere on your hard drive. Now, go to Explorer or your Finder and go to the directory where you just saved this C4D file. In the same directory, create a new folder and call it "Tex"; you'll see why this is important in a minute

To apply a material to an object in C4D, you can either click-drag the material from the Materials Manager to the object within the view panel or onto the name of an object in the Objects Manager. When you do this, the Texture dialogue box will open to allow you to scale or change the mapping of the material on the object. For now just click OK, as we'll be discussing a lot of the options available here later. Once this is done, the Objects Manager will show a material has been applied, as a material icon will appear next to the object. Also, the view panel will attempt to make a rough approximation of the texture (assuming you are using Display>Gouraud Shading for that panel). Notice that the default settings of a new material are identical to the gray plastic; so there doesn't appear to be any immediate change in the view panel.

Double-click the new material within the Materials Manager to open the Materials Editor. (You could edit this material by selecting it once and editing the channels in the Attributes Editor, but for illustration's sake, its easier to show in the Materials Editor.) This Materials Editor is non-modal, which means you don't have to close it down every time you make a change to a material. Also notice that this Materials Editor can be "pinned" into position if you have the screen real estate with the Pin icon at the top left corner. Next to that is an input field allowing you to define the name of your texture.

By default, a new material is set to the same gray plastic that objects appear in by default. As such, the Color parameter and the Specular parameters are activated. This gives it the gray color selected in the Color section of the Color parameter and a bit of a sheen or highlight, which is what the Specular parameter activates. Just for an exercise, deactivate both the Color and Specular parameters so that there are no parameters active. The result is a pitch-black material. It's so black, in fact, that it completely obliterates any form we were once able to see (Figure 6.3).

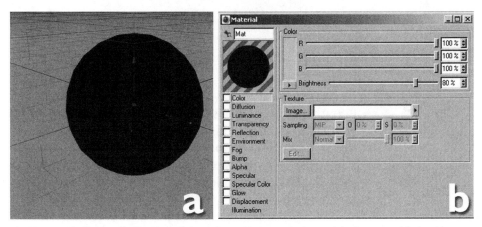

FIGURE 6.3 With all channels deactivated, the surface with the applied material appears as a black void.

COLOR PARAMETER

Now activate the Color parameter by checking the checkbox. Make certain that you are working with the Color parameter by verifying that it is highlighted in the list of parameters. The most basic power of colors is the ability to simply select a color using the sliders (R=Red, G=Green, B=Blue) or click the rectangular swatch and pick a color using your system's color picking system. As soon as you pick a color, you will see the color change in several places: in the "preview sphere" of the swatch within the Materials Editor, the preview sphere for the material in the Materials Manager, the material tag in the Objects Manager and finally, the actual geometry of the object the material is applied to in the view panel (Figure 6.4).

But there's much more that can be done with this Color parameter. Besides simply altering the overall color, you can place an image within the Texture input channel to define what the color will be. Simply click the Image…button within the Texture section of the Materials Editor. C4D will then prompt you to tell it what image to use. Go to the CD-ROM that came with this book and, in the folder Tutorials>Chapter06>Tutorial 6.1>Tex>, select the file called SphereColor.tif. C4D is very open in acceptable formats, it will accept, .jpg, .iff, .tiff, .tga, .bmp, .pict, and even

ON THE CD

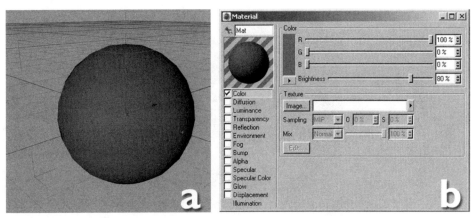

FIGURE 6.4 Our sphere with just the color channel activated. Be sure to check out this sequence of figures on the CD-ROM if you are confused about these sometimes ubiquitous gray-scale images.

Photoshop .psd. You can even import a .mov or .avi file as a moving texture. For this, we'll use a swatch of fabric scanned on a scanner that you just imported as SphereColor.tif (Figure 6.5a). When you select an image, C4D will immediately prompt you with the message shown in Figure 6.5b, telling you that the image is not in the appropriate "search path." The reason this appears is that C4D does not import the image file into the C4D file. Instead, it simply links to that particular image, which it will access when it comes time to render. C4D looks for these images at the same level directory as the C4D file is saved at. If it does not find the file there, it searches for a folder called "Tex," and looks in there; this is why we created the Tex folder a little earlier. So, when you attempt to import a file from some other directory, C4D recognizes it is not in its "search path" and politely asks if you'd like it to copy the image file there.

This has drawbacks and advantages. The advantage is that you can easily update the image outside of C4D and, when the C4D file using that image map is opened, all the materials using that image map will be updated. The drawback is that you must carefully keep track of these images. Don't throw them away once you've imported them into C4D.

If you click "Yes" on the message, you'll find that the Tex folder you created in the same directory as the C4D file you are working with has a new file, the image file you've imported. Although you really do not *need* to have a folder called Tex (you could just save all the texture images at the same level as the C4D file), it's really easiest to keep track of everything by gathering it into the Tex folder.

Once an image is selected, the name will appear in the Image… input field and all the preview spheres will show the result. Notice that

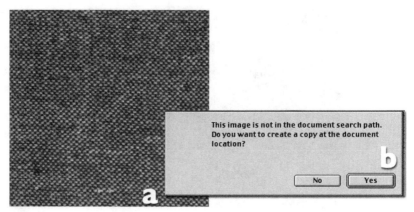

FIGURE 6.5   (a) Swatch to be used as a color image map. (b) Error message when you import an image file from an unexpected location.

when an image map is imported, it overrides the setting in the Color section of the parameter. The Mix section of the Color parameter allows you to mix the Color and Texture information. Assume that the Texture setting is the top layer of the material. If the Mix setting is set at Normal and 100%, then the top texture (the image) completely covers the bottom color. If you reduce the strength, the bottom color will be allowed to show through. This setting can also be set to "Add" the Color information's RGB values to the Texture setting, "Subtract" the Color information's RGB values from the Texture setting, or "Multiply" the values. In general, you will find that this type of color adding, subtracting, and multiplying is not the optimal way to work. For real control over texture image maps, make your color adjustments in Photoshop.

SEAMLESS MAPS

Notice that in the renderings where an image map has been used thus far, there is an ugly seam down the side of the sphere where the left edge and the right edge of the map are meeting up. These seams are very common when you are building materials from scratch. Luckily, with a little Photoshop help, these seams can quickly and easily be taken care of.

Begin by opening up the image map in Photoshop (in this case SphereColor.tif). Activate the Offset filter (Filter>Other>Offset) and set the Horizontal and Vertical settings to any arbitrary value. What this filter does is move the entire image off to the side or up and down. The real power comes from being able to "Wrap Around." This takes the part of the image that has been offset off the edge of the canvas and brings it in on the other side. What this means is that the edges of the canvas match perfectly and the seams are then in the middle where you can get at them (Figure 6.6). The amount you offset the image largely depends on the size of the image and is completely arbitrary. Just make sure that it is offset a good amount so that the seams are clearly in the middle and easy to alter.

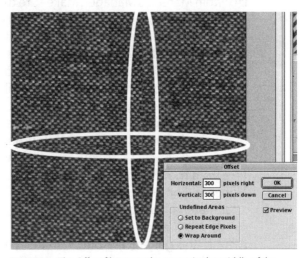

FIGURE 6.6   The Offset filter puts the seams in the middle of the scene to work out. Use the Rubber Stamp tool to lift parts of the texture map onto the seams. Be sure to run the Offset filter again to make sure you didn't create new seams in the process.

The trick then is to use the Rubber Stamp tool to work out the seams that are running down the middle of the map. Once you've worked them out, make sure to run the Offset filter once more to make sure you didn't inadvertently create new seams. Now your old seamed image map is replaced with your new and improved seamless map with no more lines.

It's important to make your color image map seamless early on. As we work through, we're actually going to build a lot of the other maps from this color map; so if the color map is seamed, the rest will be seamed as well. It just makes sense to do it right to begin with. You can close this sphere now. As brief a tutorial as this was, you have looked at all the basics of activating a channel, modifying it, and importing a texture image to use. In the next tutorial, we will get more in-depth with all the channels to make our room take flight.

6.2 GETTING STARTED WITH TEXTURING A ROOM

Open the room we've been working on in earlier tutorials. Using the basic parameters we've been discussing, we'll begin to put some color and life into our room.

Let's begin by putting some color on the walls. In the Materials Manager, create a new material (File>New Material). Double-click the material within Materials Manager. Make sure the Color parameter is activated: enter the Color parameters window by clicking on the word Color in the list of parameters. Let's make the walls of this dining room a light khaki color. Click on the rectangular color swatch and pick a nice tan (something around R=90%, G=83%, B=75%). For now, leave the other settings as they are. Label this material "Tan Walls." Now find the walls to your room within the Objects Manager; don't worry about the backing flats, just the walls. You may have them grouped together as part of a Boolean object, or they may be a list of walls grouped with other objects such as floorboards. Apply this texture to all the walls by click-dragging the texture from the Materials Manager to the objects or group in the Objects Manager. For now, just click OK for the Texture window that pops up after material application.

As you are applying these materials, take care that you don't apply them to too general a group. A material will be transferred down to include objects that are the children of any object, and you probably don't want tan windows with tan glass. Take some time to track down each wall and place the texture accordingly. Another shortcut you might want to use is the ability to copy a material from one object to another. By holding the CTRL (COMMAND) key down and click-and-dragging a material tag, you can copy the material to another object. After you have all the wall materials in place, take a moment to do a quick test rendering by clicking the Render Active View button.

Now there are obviously a lot of weird things in this room—no ceiling, no lighting except for the floodlight that sits above the camera view we're looking through, etc. But still, a scene should never look as flat as it is appearing here. To fix this problem, we'll need to adjust the bump of the material to give the walls a bit more interest.

Activate the Bump parameter by clicking the box next to its name in the Materials Editor. Also make sure that you can work with this newly activated Bump by clicking on the word Bump. Besides being able to import images in the Texture area, you can use some of the 2D shaders that C4D creates automatically. To do this for our bump, use the right triangular button at the end of the Image…input field, and select Turbulence from the list of 2D shaders. Turbulence is one of the best ways to give a slight variation to a surface. The Strength setting of the Bump parameter needn't be very high and shouldn't be very high; somewhere around 5-7% is fine. (Figure 6.7a). This gives the material just enough tactile properties so that the walls don't look so plastic-like. The next thing to do is adjust the Specular parameter to be more in line with a painted wall. The default setting for materials is a very plastic setting for the Specular parameter. A latex or oil painted wall would have a wide, flat specular highlight. Increase the Width setting, and decrease the Height setting (Figure 6.7c). Click Refresh and do a test rendering.

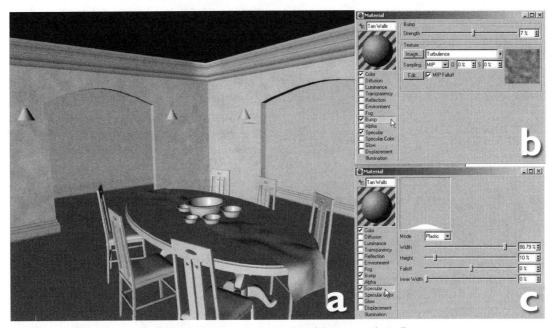

FIGURE 6.7   Adjusting the Bump and Specular parameters to give a bit of character to the walls.

The great thing about this texturing system, is that when we make a change in the Materials Editor the changes are communicated out to every place the material has been applied. If we wanted to make the room bright red, we only need to change the Color parameter of the material, and all the walls with that material applied would then be red.

Now that the material is looking better for the walls, let's place a material into the hall walls and make it a different color. Instead of having to worry about making a material from scratch and trying to match all the settings but the color, we'll duplicate this "Tan Walls" material. Make sure the Materials Manager is active by clicking on the material "Tan

Walls." Using the Edit pull-down menu *within the Materials Manager*, select Copy and then Paste. A new material will appear called "Tan Walls.1." If your Materials Editor is still open, that will become the material currently available for editing. Change the name of this new material to "Burgundy Walls" and change the Color parameter Settings to a burgundy color (R=39%, G=15%, B=18%). Now apply this new material to the backing flats; making the walls in the hall a dark burgundy (Figure 6.8.).

You may notice at this point that there are some problems with the scene as we've set it up. The materials on the walls seem to be different scales (they are) and the insides of the arches are white, rather than the tan of the rest of the wall. Not to worry, we'll fix these issues shortly.

Let's move on to the trim (floorboard and crown molding) in the room. Assuming that this is a painted wood, create a new material, call it "Trim," and change the Color parameter from the default gray to a white. Again, activate the Bump parameter and use Turbulence or Noise (an alternate 2D shader also available via the small triangle at the end of the Image…input field) at a very low strength to give a bit of tactile quality to the surface. Also, increase the Width, and reduce the Height of the Specular parameter. Find all the trim in your scene and apply the material to it (Figure 6.8.)

ON THE CD

FIGURE 6.8 Burgundy backing flats with white trim throughout the room. Even smooth painted wood should have a bit of bump to it. See color version on CD-ROM, if further clarification is needed.

Now let's turn our attention to the windows. We'll want the trim on the windows to match the molding and floorboard. But let's take a minute and look at how the parent-children relationship works with materials. Assuming you have each window grouped together, click-drag the "Trim" material onto each window group (Figure 6.9a). This will make the entire window (including the glass) have the wood trim material. Since we don't want this room to be quite so uniform, create a new material and name it "Glass." Glass is a really complex material and is largely a subjective call; however, almost all glass should have the Color, Transparency, Reflection, and Specular parameters activated.

We've talked about Color and Specular already. The Transparency channel allows you to define a surface as transparent or semi-transparent. Within the Transparency channel area, you can even assign a color to the transparency, making light that passes through the surface tinted. This also means that as you look through such a surface, objects on the other side will be tinted. Reducing the Brightness slider will make the surface increasingly opaque.

The Reflection parameter is also pretty self-explanatory. Activating this channel makes a material (and in turn a surface) reflective. You can see objects around a reflective surface in the surface. The color setting here allows you to give the reflection a tint. Reducing the Brightness slider makes the surface less reflective.

The Color and Transparency parameters often have a little bit of a gray-blue selected as the color. The Transparency setting can have 100% transparency, or you may wish to set the Transparency setting a little lower (around 85%) so you can see the pane better. The settings for the Reflection channel largely depends on what time of day you plan your scene in. During the day, glass has a fairly low amount of reflection on the inside of a house as the most powerful light source is outside (the sun). However, at night, when the most powerful source is your lamp on the table, the inside of the glass is highly reflective, making it difficult to see outside. Let's assume this scene is in the evening, so we will leave the reflective qualities quite high (80%). Finally, glass specular qualities are very broad and actually quite high. Some folks (if you are designing an older house where the glass has begun to wave) like to place Turbulence in the Bump channel. This is all up to you.

Now, apply this new glass material to the object (within your window group) representing the glass (Figure 6.9a). Notice that in Figure 6.9b, the "Trim" material is applied to the window as a whole and the rendering shows every object that is part of the window being that white trim —except the glass. This is because if a child has a material applied (as the glass planes do), this material overrides any parent object's material. This saves lots of time, as you only need to drop trim on 7 windows, and 14 panes of glass, rather than dropping trim on each piece of window trim, each transom, and each mullion.

FIGURE 6.9   Applying glass to the windows and trim to the window trim.

Now let's focus on a sconce. This sconce will be mostly metallic and will present an interesting group of challenges. For the base, let's create a chrome-like silver material. Create a new material and activate the Color, Reflection, Specular, and Specular Color parameters. Often chrome has a slight blue color with high (90%+) reflection. The key to making this metal believable will be in the Specular parameter. First, change the mode to Metal. Then, make the Width setting very thin (10%) but make the Height setting extremely high (150%). This gives our metal an intense, thin highlight.

Specular Color allows you to change the color of your specular highlight. This is especially useful for metals as the characteristic that visually sets many of them apart is a colored highlight. Change the Specular Color parameter to something with a little blue and you'll be set.

For the bars holding the shade up, let's use a brushed brass effect. For this effect, create a bump map in Photoshop that is a gray scale image. A simple method is to create Noise (Filter>Noise>Add Noise) (Figure 6.10a), then use extreme Motion Blur (Filter>Blur>Motion Blur) to smear the noise to the side (Figure 6.10b). Use the Offset technique to work out any seams and increase the contrast a bit (Figure 6.10c). Make sure to save it in a "Tex" folder within the same directory as your C4D room file.

Create a new material and activate the Color, Reflection, Bump, Specular, and Specular Color parameters. In the Color channel, give the material a goldish-brown color; for the Reflection channel, make the

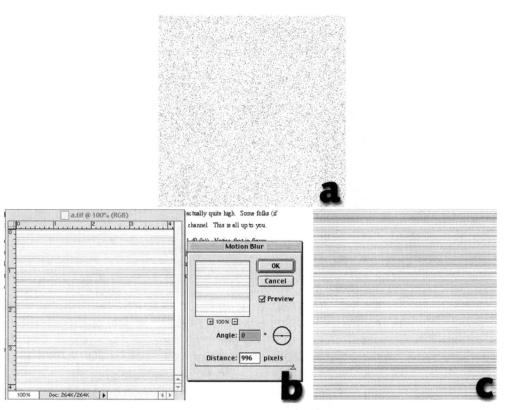

FIGURE 6.10   Creating a bump map from scratch to give the brass a brushed look.

color a yellow color so that the reflections in the surface are tinted yellow; in the Bump channel, import the just-created bump map in the the Texture Image…input field; for the Specular channel, adjust the parameter to Metal mode with a low Width setting and very high Height setting; finally for the Specular Color channel, change the color to a bright yellow. After applying the material to the sconces bars, the appearance should be something like Figure 6.11.

For the shade we'll make a pierced steel look. This way there will be interesting shadows and light cast immediately around the area when a light is put within it. Create a new material and name it "Pierced Stainless Steel." Again, as a metal, this should have a slight color (light blue for stainless steel) and a very high, thin Specular parameter with a bit of light blue color in the Specular Color parameter. Again, the Reflection parameter should be activated and kept at a fairly high setting. However, for this texture there will be a couple of specialties. The first we'll

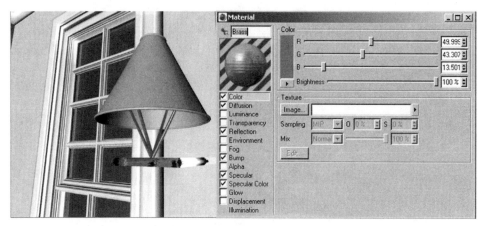

FIGURE 6.11 Finished brass material applied to the sconce.

activate is the Alpha parameter so that we can place an image map of the pierced pattern we wish to use (Figure 6.12a). An active Alpha channel makes certain parts of the material appear as though there was no geometry there. This is different from the Transparency, as the Transparency parameter makes things transparent like glass, meaning that you would be able to see the specular highlights on the surface. Alpha parameters render as though there was no geometry there. The really powerful part of this process is the ability to use Texture Image…maps like the one shown in Figure 6.12. This allows us to define parts of the material that will be see-through and other parts that will be opaque. It's like defining geometry with materials!

So, activate the Alpha parameter by checking its box, click the Image…button, and find the file Tutorials>Chapter06>Tutorial 6.2> Tex>alphachannelmesh.tif on the included CD-ROM. Again, tell C4D it is okay to make a copy of it in the appropriate directory when it asks. The Alpha map and its use in the Alpha parameter are shown in Figure 6.12.

ON THE CD

This surface would be hot and burnt from a light bulb inside. So, to give it that appearance, we'll use the Diffusion channel. Diffusion is a great parameter for creating grungy surfaces or adding a gentle layer of dirt or other scum to an object. As usual, a custom image would work best, but in a pinch, C4D includes some built in 2D shaders that work fine. For the Diffuse parameter, the Turbulence shader works great. Click the triangle button at the end of the Image…input field and select Shader>Turbulence. Up at the top right of the Materials Editor you'll see what parameters you wish this Diffusion to affect. Be sure Specular and Reflection are checked. Finally, apply this new material to the lamp

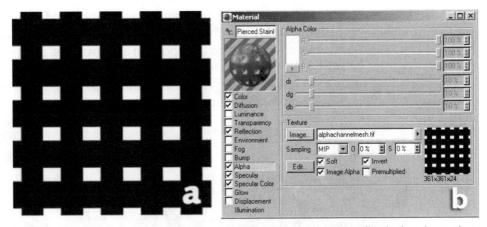

FIGURE 6.12   (a) A look at the Alpha channel map. The black will render, the white will make the polygons they cover disappear. (b) A look at the Alpha parameter settings when the map is imported.

shade. Figure 6.13 gives a quick look at what the light shade would do if a light were placed within the sconce (more on lighting in later chapters (Chapter 7).

FIGURE 6.13   Textured sconce.

Be sure to place these metal textures on all sconces in the room. Or, you can delete the other sconces, copy this textured sconce, and paste the textured version where you see fit.

The last set of simple materials includes a simple Color and Specular parameter-enabled material for the runner on the table. A simple green color for the flower stem and some simple flat colors for the flower. The only problem here was that the Bump parameter was activated for the flower center, and instead of importing a bit-mapped image, a Checkerboard shader was selected with a very high rate of repeat (Figure 6.14). Also in this last rendering are the doorknobs, textured with the brass material we built for the lamp (Figure 6.15).

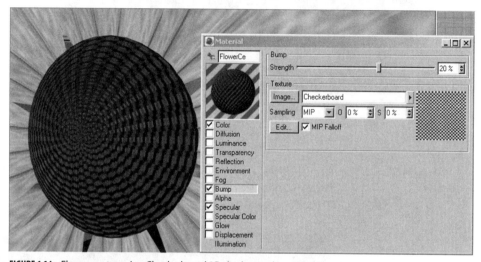

FIGURE 6.14   Flower center using Checkerboard 2D shader as a bump map.

FIGURE 6.15   Remaining simple textures.

There's still much to be textured here. However, much of good texturing has to do with mapping. In the next tutorial, we'll look at how C4D thinks of materials, how it applies the materials, and how we can further define how materials are placed across image surfaces. We'll look at other sources for texture maps and C4D-built materials and we'll finish texturing this room.

TUTORIAL

6.3 ADVANCED TEXTURING OF THE DINING ROOM

In the previous tutorials, we looked at how to create our own materials using some simple shaders. We also discovered how to create our own materials based upon scanned objects (including photographs). On the Web, there are numerous resources for texture image maps and pre-built shaders. Just enter "Textures" in any search engine and a multitude of entries will appear. One great source is *http://www.3dcafe.com,* which stores large collections of freely downloadable models and some images for use in materials. Take some time to explore these images, and grab the largest version of the image that you can. Once you have an image, you can use the image as a guide to build up your various maps. First, make sure that the downloaded image is seamless, using the Offset/Rubber Stamp technique described earlier in this chapter. This first seamless version will probably become your color map. Then you can create new layers within Photoshop to begin building up other image maps. The process shown in Figure 6.16 is building a final bump map by drawing over the color map and then deleting the color layer. Usually, you can create multiple texture image maps from one source image; but just remember to save each as a separate name.

In this case, we'll want to build the floor for our room from the color and bump map shown in Figure 6.16. Open your room file within C4D and create a new material called "Floor." Activate the Color, Diffusion, Reflection, Bump, Specular, and Specular Color parameters. In the Color parameter, bring in the file floorcolor.tif included on the CD-ROM (Tutorials>Chapter06>Tutorial 6.3>Tex>floorcolor.tif); or you can build one yourself and import that. In the Bump channel, import the image map floowbump.psd which is also included on the CD-ROM (Tutorials>Chapter06>Tutorial 6.3>Tex>floowbump.psd); or again, you can prepare one yourself to import. Within the Diffusion channel, use a low intensity version setting of Turbulence to give just a hint of dust. Keep the Reflection settings low (around 20%). Now apply this material to your floor object (Figure 6.17a).

ON THE CD

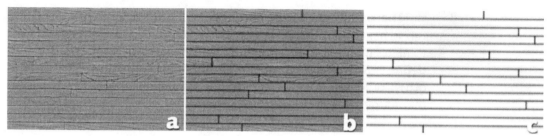

FIGURE 6.16 Building custom maps from stock images off the Web.

The problem is that as it looks now, the slats of the floor are about two feet wide. This is because of C4D's assumption that, by default, one copy of the material should cover the entire object. This is often a problem with floors. Luckily, this is very easy to correct. If you double-click the Texture tag within the Objects Manager, you can change the Length setting to make the scale of the texture more appropriate in the Attributes Editor. Often, it is a matter of trial and error to find the right size (or you can use the Texture tool to manually resize the material), but for this project, it turns out that 20% (for both the Length x and Length y) is about right (Figure 6.17b).

In addition to 3D Café (referred to above) and sites like it, there is a fantastic resource on the Web to get materials made especially for C4D to use or to study. *Deepshade* has a large collection of materials—created by many of the C4D masters around the world—that are free to download. The address is *http://www.maxon.net/deepshade*. Once you get into the "shaders," you can click on any material to get a closer look (Figure 6.16). If you find one you like, simply download the file (which downloads in a .sit format—you'll need Aladdin System's Stuffit Expander (also available via the "expander" link at *Deepshade*)). When the file has been downloaded and unstuffed, you'll notice that it is actually a C4D file and often in a "Tex" folder. To use these textures, simply take the entire folder (usually labeled by a number), including the C4D file and its "Tex" file, and put it in the "Tex" file for your project.

To actually use the material that you've downloaded, use the File>Load Materials pull-down menu within your Materials Manager. Select the C4D file of the downloaded material. C4D will then import all the materials connected to that file. Sometimes projects from *Deepshade* are one material, while other times the actual appearance is a result of several layers of materials. For the table and the wood on the chairs, we'll download and import *044 Dark Wood,* submitted by Phil 3D. Notice that the material is already unstuffed on the CD-ROM (Tutorials>Chapter06>Tutorial 6.3>Tex>dark wood).

ON THE CD

FIGURE 6.17   (a) Newly placed floor material. (b) Fixed floor with correct scale.

Once this material has been loaded, try to place this "Dark Wood" material on the Dinner Table group. This would make sense as the entire table is made of the same wood; however, because the polygon topology is so different over different parts of the table (very dense in the high curve areas, very few polygons in places like the top of the table), the textured results are less than desirable. This undesired result happens because of the default mapping (UVW Mapping). *Mapping* is the process of deciding how the material is applied to the surface. UVW mapping is an advanced and powerful method of looking at the object's UV coordinates (analogous to *x* and *y*) and stretching the material so that it is evenly distributed between the UVs. When you are creating models, C4D is also automatically creating UV coordinates. By default, it makes some educated guesses based on how close polygons are to each other. Unfortunately, in objects such as our table, some areas have very high polycounts while other areas have much lower. Therefore, in some places, the UVs are extremely close together so the material looks tightly mapped, while at others where the polymesh is less dense, the UVs are far from each other, making the material look very stretched.

The UVW mapping has attempted to wrap around the edge, while the top appears flat and painted. In situations such as this, it is important to texture each part of the table separately.

Let's start on the top. As the table has this huge surface area on the top, we need to pick a projection method that doesn't bunch up at the poles. The textures that do that best are Flat and Cubic. Move the Texture tag from the Dinner Table group to the Extrude NURBS form that comprises the tabletop. Double-click the tag to open it in the Attributes Editor and change the projection setting to Flat (Figure 6.18a).

There's a problem here. The material is being projected, but it's as though the projector is sitting on our window rather than projecting from above. We need to rotate the material to project downward. This sort of rotation from side projection to top projection is a rotation of Pitch. Open the Texture tag by double-clicking it in the Objects Manager. The mapping for the material will appear in the Attributes Editor. Enter 90° in the P input field.

Ah, that's looking better. However, there is still a problem; as the material is being projected downward, it ends up leaving streaks of color down the side of the tabletop. Therefore, a more appropriate projection would be Cubic, so that these sides of the tabletop would appear as wood as well (Figure 6.18b). Change the projection to Cubic for the tabletop.

For everything under the table, a different projection method will be needed for each part. To be able to control the projection separately, you'll need to apply the dark wood material to each part individually (do this by dragging the material from the Materials Manager to the object in the Objects Manager). The twisted cube that is the pedestal part works best with Cylindrical projection. The short legs (Extrude NURBS forms) are closest to a cube and so Cubic projection works for them (Figure 6.19).

Next, we'll turn our attention to the chairs. Repeat the same process for the wood parts of the chairs. Again, applying one material to the entire object will not produce the desired results, so you'll need to get specific. Apply the dark wood material to each part of the chair individually. Luckily, most of the chairs are cubic-based, so the projection choices are easy (Figure 6.20). The seat of the chair can be textured completely with

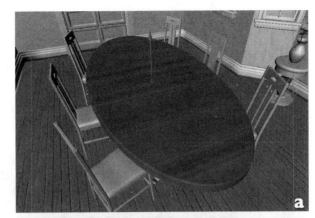

FIGURE 6.18   (a) Flat projection on just the tabletop. (b) Cubic projection ends up being most appropriate for the tabletop.

FIGURE 6.19   Completed textured table.

2D shaders. Create a new material and activate the Color and Bump channels and select a Shaders>Checkerboard shader for the Bump parameter. Edit the shader and select a high number of U and V Frequency settings. This creates a nice weaved material look. Finally, add the same dark wood material to the niche table.

FIGURE 6.20 Textured chairs and table.

You may want to take some quick test renderings to see how your woods are working together. You want your floor and table to still look good together even if they are different types of wood. If you find that you need to change the characteristics of one material or the other, simply open the material from the Materials Manager and make the adjustment there; every place the material is used will automatically be updated.

The door is a painted door and so it can be created entirely within C4D's Materials Editor; no image map is required. So create a new material, activate its Color channel, and color it as you wish. Also activate the Bump channel and put Turbulence in the Image…input field; be sure to turn the Strength setting down to around 5%.

Let us finish the room off by working with the vase. To do this, create a new file in Photoshop and paint the design and color you would like to see on the vase. (Remember that this map is going to wrap around the vase to paint accordingly, so use the Offset Filter but only in the Horizontal direction.) Work out the seam. As the vase is going to have a very porcelain feel, you don't need any image maps beyond the color map (Figure 6.21). If you would like, you can just use the file vasecolor.tif located on the CD-ROM (Tutorials>Chapter06>Tutorial 6.3>Tex>vasecolor.tif) instead.

FIGURE 6.21   A color map created from scratch in Photoshop.

Once your color map is complete, create a new material and bring this color map into the Color parameter. Adjust the Specular and Reflection channels to create a nice smooth surface and apply the texture to the vase. Make sure that the projection is Cylindrical so that the map will truly wrap around the vase (Figure 6.23a). You will also need to resize and move the material into position so that it "fits" the form it is designed to cover.

There are a couple of ways to resize the material. The first is to adjust the Length x and Length y of the placed material in the Attributes Editor (accessed by double-clicking the vase's Texture tag in Objects Manager). The second is a fairly intuitive tool called the Texture tool (Figure 6.22).

To use this tool, simply select an object in the Objects Manager and then activate the Texture tool from your side command palette. The object you have selected will have a sort of light blue mesh in the shape of the projection you are using for that object's material (i.e., a cylinder for Cylindrical projection, a cube for Cubic projection, etc.). You can then use the Move Active Element, Rotate Active Element, or Scale Active Element tool to move, rotate, or scale the texture across the surface of the object. This makes for very intuitive adjustments of textures. Figure 6.23 shows the cylindrically mapped vase with the Texture tool active.

FIGURE 6.22 The Texture tool.

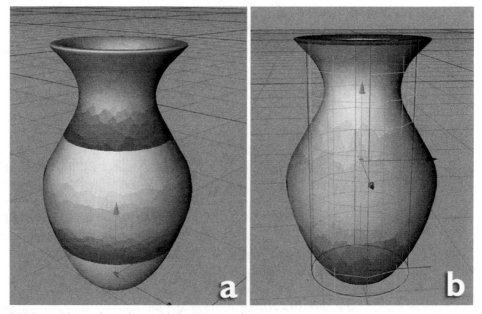

FIGURE 6.23 (a) Vase. (b) Final vase with the Texture tool active.

CONCLUSION

The possibilities for refining and creating textures and materials are nearly infinite. There are layers and layers of techniques that could be applied to these objects. An important thing to remember about effective materials is that they are largely dependent on the lighting. A bright green runner with a red light shining on it will appear dull and gray. Lighting and texturing go hand in hand. In Chapter 7, we will look at C4D's lighting tools; how to create lighting instruments, adjust them, and make them do things that mimic and defy the laws of light in the real world.

LIGHTING

nterestingly enough, the right lighting and the right camera can hide poor work, make mediocre work look good, and make good work look great. Conversely, the wrong lighting and camera work can reduce the best 3D modeling and texturing to shambles.

Like most of 3D, lighting and camera work have two distinct sides. One is the technical issue of understanding how the tools within C4D work. The other is knowing how to utilize those technical issues to create an aesthetic result. The aesthetics of good lighting will be touched on in this chapter. However, first we must understand how lighting and cameras work.

LIGHTING IN ACTION

There are lots of theories to good lighting. There are theories that photographers use which are different from what theatre set designers use, which are different from an interior designer's techniques. The overall solution is that there is no set formula for creating lighting. Every situation offers unique challenges and new solutions to different problems. In this chapter, we'll analyze a few lighting problems and look at some ways to go about solving them. These aren't the end-all answers of lighting, but they are a good place to start.

We'll start out by looking at the basic anatomy of a light object in C4D. Then we'll look at how to place, use, control, and edit lighting instruments in your scene.

Anatomy of a Light

This is Anatomy 101's cliff-notes. Because the manual covers each little part of the light objects in depth, we won't do that here. What we are going to look at are the core aspects that matter for most lighting situations.

Figure 7.1 shows a simple light object created from scratch. Notice that by default the light sits at (0,0,0) in digital space. Also notice that it is represented by a little puff-ball of lines. What this is attempting to show you is that the default light is an Omni light. This means that the light radiation that comes from this object starts from a point and emanates out in all (omni) directions. Notice also that in Figure 7.1, you can see the Attributes Editor for the light. Whenever you create a light or select it from the Objects Manager, the Attributes Editor will show you the attribute for that light.

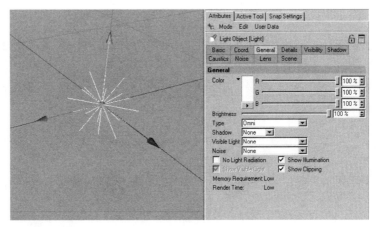

FIGURE 7.1   An Omni light as created by default.

There are several characteristics of this light worth noting. First, it casts no shadows. Second, it shoots off infinitely in all directions. To ensure that a light is casting shadows, simply turn on the kind of shadow you wish to use within the General section (Figure 7.2).

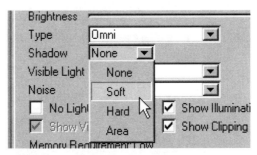

FIGURE 7.2   Making a light cast shadows.

To make a light so that it has decay or so that it does not shoot off forever and ever, jump to the Details tab and turn on the Falloff to any setting. Linear and Inverse falloff are easy to control and give the best results (Figure 7.3). As soon as you activate Falloff, you can enter Inner and Outer Distance values immediately beneath it. The Inner Distance indicates the distance that the light radiation is at full intensity. The Outer Distance value shows at what distance from the light the light radiation ends entirely.

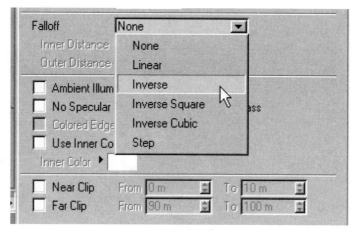

FIGURE 7.3 Activating Falloff for a light object.

As soon as you activate Falloff for a light, notice that in your view panel you now have new symbols added to your light. If your Inner Distance is set to a non-0 value, you will have a sphere that visually represents the distance (the smaller dark gray sphere). The larger white sphere indicates the Outer Distance. By click-dragging the orange control handles, you can visually alter these Inner and Outer Distance values (Figure 7.4).

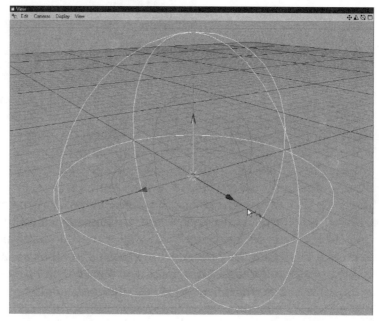

FIGURE 7.4 Visual indications of Inner and Outer Distances for Falloff values.

Note that this same technique can also be used if you are using Visible or Volumetric lighting (check the manual for more information on these lighting tools). Visible and Volumetric lights are lights where you can see not only the effects of the light radiation but the light itself. (Think of light streaming through the trees or through the window, or a spotlight on a smoky stage.) In the General section of the light's Attributes Editor, you can activate Visible or Volumetric light. In the Visibility section, you can control various aspects of the Visible or Volumetric light—including Inner and Outer Distance (Figure 7.5).

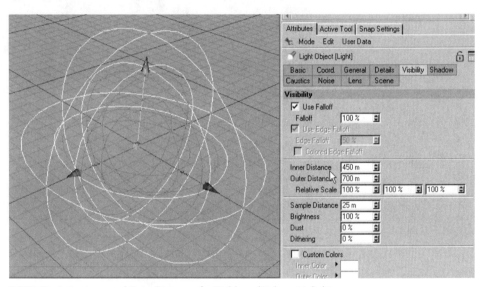

FIGURE 7.5   Active Inner and Outer Distances for Visible and Volumetric lights.

The nice thing about C4D's lighting is that you now also have a visible clue in your view panel that allows you to visually alter the Inner and Outer Distances for your Visible or Volumetric light. One problem is that with so many visual clues representing so many things, it becomes hard to know which sphere indicates which characteristic.

To overcome this problem, go back to the General section of the light's Attributes Editor and look toward the bottom of the Editor. Here you can turn off or on the ability to Show Visible Light or Show Illumination. This way, you can turn off the light's Radiation Falloff while you visually adjust the Visibility Falloff, and vice versa.

Any light object in C4D can be converted easily to another type of light. Figure 7.6 shows a Spot(Round) light. The type of light you have is dictated in the General section of the light's Attributes Editor. These spotlights allow you to point a light in a particular direction and give you much more control over all. Note that in Figure 7.6, you can see the Falloff value for the Radiation Falloff and the Visibility Falloff. You can change these visually within the Editor as well.

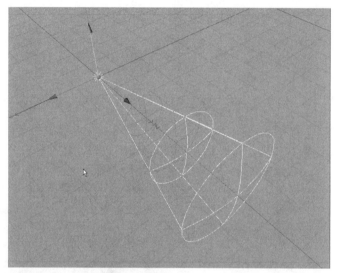

FIGURE 7.6 A spotlight with the same Radiation and Visibility Inner and Outer Distance Falloff values as the Omni light in Figure 7.5.

One other part of a light's anatomy that we should note is the ability to change the Inner and Outer angle (Figure 7.7). In the Details section of Spot(Round), Spot(Square), and several other types of lights, you can change the angle at which the light cone is to emanate. If the Inner and Outer angle are very close in value, the edge of the light as it shines on a surface will be very crisp. If the values are very different, the light edge will be quite soft (Figure 7.8).

This explains the basics of lighting. You'll notice that there are many other areas we have not talked about. Some of them we will cover in the tutorials below, and some just are not usually needed. Suffice it to say, C4D's lighting system is one of the best in the industry and you can do almost anything with it. New to R8 are such advances as the ability to allow a light to exclude objects that it is

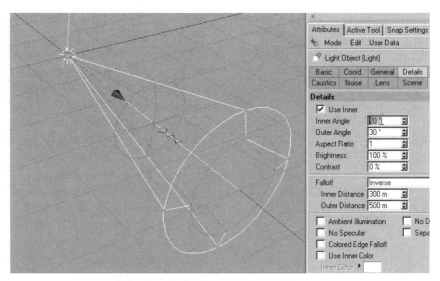

FIGURE 7.7   A Spot(Round) light with a non-0   Inner Angle.

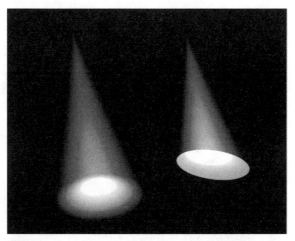

FIGURE 7.8   Comparison of two spotlights with close Inner and Outer angles and widely varied Inner and Outer angles. The light on the left is Inner Angle=5, Outer Angle=30. The light on the right is Inner Angle=28, Outer Angle=30.

illuminating (Figure 7.9) and to use post-rendering effects such as exaggerated highlights (Figure 7.10).

The multitude of options available in C4D could occupy a volume in itself. But what we've covered so far will get you started and allow you the power to begin lighting your scene.

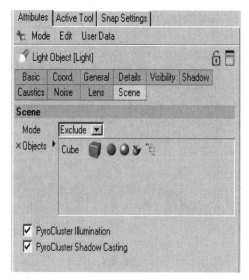

FIGURE 7.9 The ability to exclude objects from a lights radiation is new to R8.

FIGURE 7.10 A tangential new light feature is the ability to have a post-rendered highlight effect add pizzazz to your scene.

7.1 Nighttime Lighting for The Dining Room

When you are lighting a fairly complex model such as the room we've been modeling, it is often a good idea to do a few tests of your settings and light setups somewhere other than within your model. When you begin placing a variety of light sources in a model (especially if they are casting shadows or have any visible effects), your computer can become painfully slow as it tries to calculate all the new information. When you try to render, even with C4D's speedy renderer, you'll face a long wait. So, to create and refine the chandeliers that hang in this room (and light it), let's create them in a new C4D file.

Figure 7.11 shows the chandelier modeled; you can either model this yourself or just open the file Chandelier(NoLight).c4d (Tutorials> Chapter07>Tutorial 7.1>Chandelier(NoLight).c4d) from the CD-ROM. The screen shots show no materials, although the file on disk has some already built into it. Note that an interesting part of the overall lighting effect for this project will actually be the material. Sounds odd, but C4D (by default) does not calculate true translucency. You would think that by placing a Light object within this lamp and giving the glass part of the object a transparent material, the material would light up. However, the rendering engine is just not that sophisticated. There are some third party solutions to this problem. BhodiNuts's Smells Like Almonds have shaders that do illuminate if a light is set behind it; however, one drawback of the powerful SLA shader set is that it is are often fairly render-time intensive. So to save rendering time overall, we will just fake the illuminated surface.

ON THE CD

First, before we dive into the translucency issue, add a floor and a ceiling to this scene so you can get a rough idea of what will be going on as we work with the light. The distances don't have to be exact; we just need to add surfaces to see how the light is working within the chandelier. Also, if you have built the shape from scratch create a simple black metallic material and place it on all the rods or non-glass parts.

What we'll do now is first create a material for the glass parts of the chandelier that makes it look as though there is a light within it, and *then* actually add the Light object. Create a new material and apply it to the glass part of the chandelier. Activate the Color, Luminance, and Glow parameters. Making this glass shade look as though there is really a light behind it will be a combination of effective Luminance and Glow parameters manipulation.

Let us assume that the light source is a regular tungsten bulb. Let's also assume that it has a bit of a yellow tint to it (as most tungsten bulbs do). Within the Luminance and Color parameters, select a color that is a

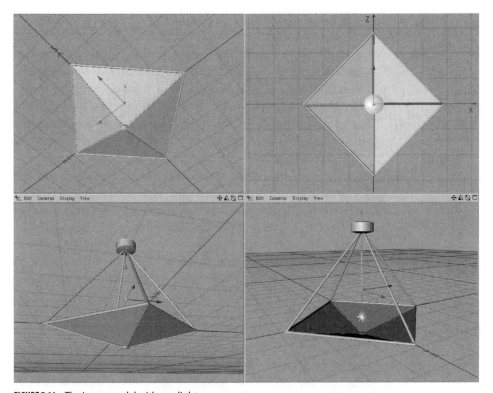

FIGURE 7.11 The Lamp model with one light.

very unsaturated cream (R=100, G = 96, B = 82, Brightness = 87). The Luminance parameter will give this glass its own light regardless of what lights are around it. This will help give the light its implied translucence.

In the Glow parameter, leave Use Material Color checked, but change the Inner Strength setting to 200% and set the Outer Strength setting to 150%. The radius setting is largely dependent on how big your chandelier is at this point, so take some renderings to find out. The idea is that you want a little bit of glow off the face of the glass, but not so much that the shade becomes a flaming ball. Apply this new material to the glass section of your lamp and take some test renderings at a variety of distances to see what you've got (Figure 7.12).

When you're happy with the translucency effect, it's time to add some actual light to the scene. It's a bit unsettling to see the renderings in Figure 7.12 and see this glowing lamp with no evidence of any light radiation on the floor or ceiling. Add a Light object to the scene and position it so that it sits within the shade. Light objects can be accessed in one of two ways. The first is via the pull-down menu Objects>Scene>Light. The

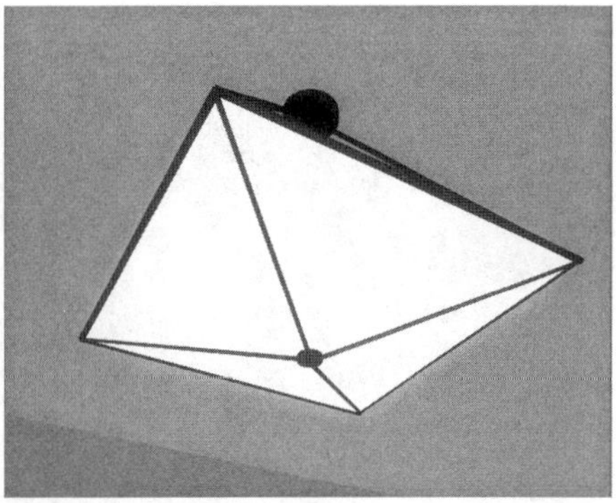

FIGURE 7.12   The Lamp object with a translucent material.

second, and the one that most people use, is to use the top command palette and click once on the tool that looks like a flashlight. As with everything else in C4D, a new object (such as this light) will be placed at (0,0,0); so you'll need to grab it from wherever it is and move it up into the chandelier with the Move Active Element tool.

As we probably will never be viewing this light source with our heads against the ceiling, we don't need to build anything else into the lamp geometry to "'support'" this new light object. Remember that all light objects in the C4D scene are (by default) invisible in the renderer. Yes, you can see the *effects* of the light, but there is no object in the rendered shot that is visible. This is no problem for this scene as the lamp object we are working with here will provide a visible object that the light will *appear* to come from, even though the actual light source and the lamp are two different objects.

Also add a couple of simple primitives on the floor to provide something to cast shadows. When you first apply the light and render (Figure 7.13), you can see that this is not a bad start. The ceiling is lit and so is the floor.

But when you really look at this, there are certainly some problems. First, there are no shadows anywhere. In the real world, when light from this one light source strikes a solid opaque surface, the light rays will be stopped, thus casting a shadow. To make a light object cast a shadow, double-click the Light's flashlight icon in the Objects Manager. This will open the light's attributes in the Attributes Editor. Click the General button and change the color of the light to a slight cream and change the Shadow setting to Soft Shadows (Figure 7.14).

Upon rendering, the ceiling looks great. The metal parts are casting shadows and the lamp truly appears to be hooked to the ceiling.

FIGURE 7.13   Placed light with no shadows.

FIGURE 7.14   Once shadows are activated for the light source, the ceiling looks better but still there are problems with the floor.

However, the objects on the floor have disappeared. The reason is that the shade of the lamp is blocking all the light, which creates a huge shadow that covers the floor. To fix this, we can either make the chandelier truly translucent so that light can pass through the surface, or we can let C4D know that it's supposed to let rays pass through those particular polygons. As we talked earlier about the drawbacks of working on a truly translucent surface, we'll just tell the lamp's glass parts not to cast shadows. We'll do this by adding a Compositing Tag to our glass (note that in v7 this was called a Render Tag).

Compositing Tags are added to objects by right-clicking (or COMMAND-clicking) on an object and selecting New Tag>Compositing Tag from the resultant pop-up-pull-down menu. When you add such a tag, the Tags attributes will be visible in the Attributes Manager allowing you to define some characteristics for the object that affect how it is rendered. By default, the Tag button of the Attributes Editor will be depressed; this is perfect as this gives us the options we're interested in. In this case, we want to deactivate the Cast Shadows option. This will allow light to pass unobstructed through the glass. Take some test renderings to see how well this has worked (Figure 7.15).

FIGURE 7.15   Renderings with shade no longer casting shadows.

Getting closer, however, the metal underpinnings of this shape are casting way too heavy a shadow on the floor. In reality, the light would be much diffused and would never cast that kind of a shadow. So, to keep these bottom metal underpinnings from casting shadows, repeat the process of adding a Compositing Tag to those objects or copy the Compositing Tag from the glass to these underpinnings by CTRL-click-dragging (or COMMAND-click-dragging) the tag. Take another rendering to make sure all's well (Figure 7.16).

Now that there is a fairly good lamp with a light here, group all the chandelier parts and the light together and name the group "Chandelier." As we are going to have a few of these in the room and they'll be the same, we'll create an instance of this Chandelier object instead of just copying and pasting the group. By creating instances of the chandelier, we are simply displaying the same chandelier more than once. If we make alterations to the original, the instances will reflect those changes. So, if we need to make adjustments to the intensity of the light or anything else, we only need to do it once (to the original) and the

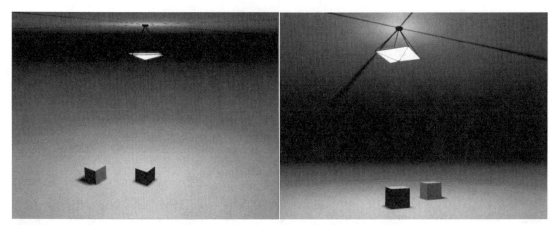

FIGURE 7.16 All shadows as they ought to be.

changes will automatically be updated to each instance. Create an instance from the top command palette (Figure 7.17) or by going to Objects>Modeling>Instance.

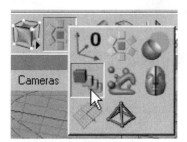

FIGURE 7.17 Creating an instance object.

Double-click on the Instance object icon and make sure that the object it is instancing is Chandelier (this is assuming you named your grouped chandelier "Chandelier"; the name is very important). When the Instance object is first created, it may not be properly aligned with the ceiling or the original Chandelier. Rename the Instance object to "Chandelier Instance" and move the instance into position, then copy and paste this instance and place it as well. Take a test rendering (Figure 7.18).

The renderings in Figure 7.18 show that we have three Chandeliers, and thus three light sources. By default, light sources cast a full intensity (100%) light in all directions for an infinite distance. Because of this default setting, and because we now have three such light sources in our

FIGURE 7.18   Three chandeliers, one the real thing, and two Instance objects.

scene, we have a scene that has "overexposed" areas everywhere. The floor appears washed out. We need to adjust the light Brightness and Falloff settings. Within the original Chandelier object (you won't be able to find a light object within any of the instances), double-click the light's icon to open the light's attributes in the Attributes Editor. Just as with materials, there are a multitude of editable attributes nested within several buttons. In past steps, we have been in the default General area where we can change things such as color and shadows. Now, we want to get a bit more in depth. Click the Details button and a new set of attributes will be displayed. Reduce the Brightness setting to 20%. Take a rendering to see the results (Figure 7.19).

FIGURE 7.19   Three light sources at 20%.

This seems a bit dark for three lights. The reason is that with chandeliers like these, there would not only be light from the light chandelier going down, but there would also be soft, diffused bounced light coming off the ceiling. R8 does support Radiosity—the rendering engine that allows for the calculation of bounced light—however, the rendering time is quite substantial. We will look at how to use some of the radiosity settings a little later, but for this tutorial, we will fake this bounce light. One way to do this is by using "Light Arrays."

When a light source is near something such as a light-colored ceiling, there exists quite a bit of wrapped, bounced light. Light radiation comes from more directions than just the light source because the radiation bounces off the other surfaces. So, the key then is to create light sources around the main light source that produce enough light to appear as though it were bounced. A light array is a collection of lights centered around a main light source that produces this non-intense bounced light. An easy way to create a light array is to create an Array object (Objects>Modeling>Array or use the top command palette show in Figure 7.20).

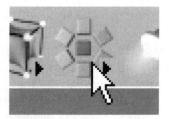

FIGURE 7.20 Creating an Array from the top command palette.

Copy and paste the main light and place this newly pasted light within the Array (as a child). Click on the Array to open its attributes in the Attributes Editor. Here you can tell the Array to make 12 copies. You'll need to find the best settings for the radius as dictated by your scene. They should be a short distance away from the main light source to provide that "wrap-around" quality (Figure 7.21). Now this light array needn't be shadow-casting or very intense, so open the light's attributes for the Light object within the Array, and change the Brightness setting to around 5% (in the Details section), and turn off the shadows (in the General section). Place this Array object in the Chandelier group so that there is an array present in all of the instances (Figure 7.22). Take a couple of renderings.

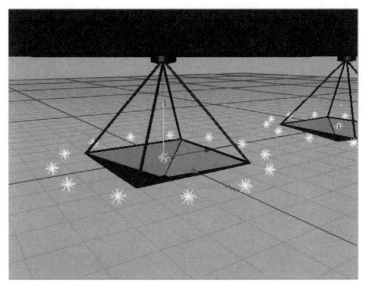

FIGURE 7.21   Create a light array with an Array object. Set the Radius setting of the Array object to spread the lights out just a bit from the center light.

FIGURE 7.22   Rendering using the Light Array.

There are some nice effects in Figure 7.22. First, there is more light overall. Second, the shadows everywhere are softer, as though the bounced light were softening them up. Too often, a beginner's 3D projects end up having black, opaque shadows. If you really look at most lights in most situations, you can always see the objects within the shadow—they are never truly black, never truly obliterating the surfaces they fall upon. These arrays help rendered shadows appear more "real."

But there's still a problem. The floor is lighter than the ceiling. Add a couple more planes to act as walls and you'll also see that the farther away the objects are from these lights, the brighter they seem. Interesting, but not at all how it works in the real world.

The problem is with our Falloff setting. All the lights we have placed so far have had the default Falloff setting of None. This Falloff setting resides in the Details section of a light's attributes.

This means that the lights we have created are shooting light radiation in all directions (Omni Lights) with no decay. The further from the light source we get, the wider the light radiation. So, the further we move from the light, the more these radiation rings begin to overlap. Of course, this is just the opposite of what should be happening. In the real world, light should be most intense on the ceiling, as it's the closest to the light sources, and the other walls and floor should be lighter the closer they are to the light and darker in the corners that are furthest from the light.

So how do we correct this? Well, C4D, as we discussed earlier, has settings that will allow you to define a falloff. That is, as the light radiation moves further from the light source, more and more of the radiation is "absorbed" into the objects in the scene or the radiation simply decays. C4D doesn't assume you want this, and so doesn't calculate it for you; rather, you get to manually define these regions. In both the main Light object and the Light object in the Array, change the Falloff setting in the Detail section to "Inverse." While you're there, notice that when you change the Falloff setting to anything but None, the two Inner Distance and Outer Distance input fields become active. This allows you to define at what distance your light's radiation should falloff.

For now, change the Inner Distance setting to something besides "0" (say Inner Distance=300m and Outer Distance=500m). The initial values are fairly arbitrary and can be altered easily in the view panel once they are activated.

Back in the Editor window, visually adjust the Inner Distance setting so that it clearly intersects the ceiling. This tells C4D that the light is to be at full intensity (whatever Brightness setting is assigned to the light) within this distance. So the ceiling is well lit. Then click-drag (again within the view panel) the Outer Distance setting out quite a ways. We want to make sure that there is light cast all over the room, but we also want to be sure that it is getting less intense as it travels. Make the Outer Distance setting further than the confines of the room. Repeat this process for the Array light; keep the Inner Distance setting tight, but really let the Outer Distance setting out quite a ways. Don't get too worried about these Inner Distance and Outer Distance rings quite yet as they will undoubtedly need to be altered once these lamps are copied into our room. Render to see what you've got (Figure 7.23).

FIGURE 7.23   Rendering reveals the light acting as it should. The darkest spots are the corners of the room and the areas furthest from the light. The lightest areas are right next to the light source.

To further emphasize the hotspot of the ceiling, add one more Light object. Up to this point, we have been using Omni lights, or lights that act like a light bulb. This time, we want a little tighter control over where the light shoots radiation. With this new light selected, in the Attributes Editor, click the General tab and change the Type to Spot(Round). Place it so that it faces up toward the ceiling. Only use about 40% intensity for this light (in the Details tab). It's there to augment, not to control the lighting setup. Make sure to place this new light within the group Chandelier so that this new light will be placed in all of the Chandelier instances as well (Figure 7.24).

Once you've got things working right in this mock room, group all the chandeliers together and Copy and Paste them into the Dining Room. You'll need to resize the group to match the Dining Room, and you'll need to position them as they need to be to match the shape of your room. Also take a minute to adjust your Inner and Outer Distance settings to match the size of your room. Take an initial rendering to see what you've got (Figure 7.25).

We're getting closer, but we're not quite finished yet. The Light Array does a good job of keeping shadows soft in a way consistent with bounced light, but that is almost exclusively from the ceiling. We need to remember that the walls and windows would bounce light as well. To fake this kind of bounced light over such a large distance, we'll use Area lights.

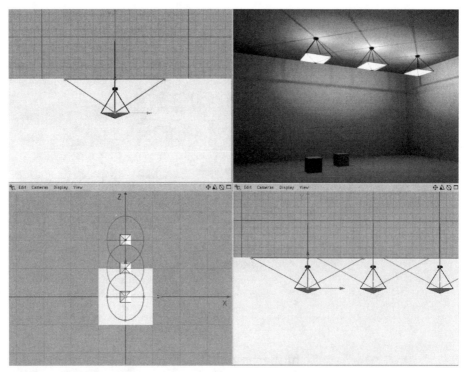

FIGURE 7.24   One last Spotlight to augment the hot spot of the ceiling.

ON THE CD

FIGURE 7.25   Chandeliers placed within the Dining Room scene. Be sure to check out these images in color on the CD-ROM in the Images folder.

Create a Light object and change its Type to Area (in the General tab of the Attributes Editor). Area lights are big walls of light. Take this wall of light and put it just in front of one of the walls of geometry in the Dining Room (Figure 7.26). You will want to make the wall of light slightly smaller than the real wall so that the edges of the Area light can help illuminate the corners. This means that you'll probably need to change the Aspect Ratio to around .5 within the Details tab of the Light Attributes Editor to make the Area light longer than it is tall.

The idea here is that the wall of light is emitting the radiation that would be bouncing off the walls. Make sure the color of the Area light is the same, or nearly the same, as your walls. In the Details part of the light, reduce the brightness to around 35%. Also, be sure and activate Falloff (Linear or Inverse is fine), and visually adjust the falloff to that it roughly matches Figure 7.26. Repeat the process for all the walls in the room. You needn't activate shadows for these Area lights, as their primary job will be to soften shadows in the room and brighten corners and dark spots (Figure 7.27).

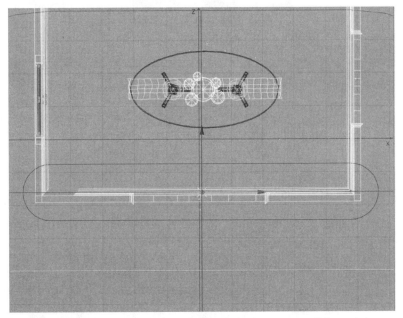

FIGURE 7.26   To further produce the image of bounced light, create Area lights and place them just in front of the walls.

FIGURE 7.27 Rendering with Area lights.

For the final touches, put small Omni lights in the sconces. Make sure that the Shadows option is turned on so we can see the result of the pierced steel material we have created. Make the Falloff setting for the sconces very small. We don't want these sconces to make a great deal of difference in the overall illumination; we just want to see that they are on (Figure 7.28).

ON THE CD

Remember that this completed file can be found on the CD-ROM (Tutorials>Chapter07>Tutorial 7.1), if you'd like to take a look at the exact settings of any of the lights used to create Figure 7.28. You may choose to alter things a bit to fit your taste. Night can be one of the most fun times to light as it is completely under artificial lighting circumstances. Experiment with the settings to get the effects just the way you want them.

FIGURE 7.28   Final rendering complete with bounced light.

7.2 DAYTIME LIGHTING FOR THE DINING ROOM

In the previous tutorial, we lit the scene as though it were late at night, the sun was down, and the light sources were all artificial. Daytime lighting will use some of the same techniques we've just described, but some new ones as well.

If this were during the daytime, the lights would probably be off. Therefore, make sure that your Glow parameter is turned off for the materials on the Chandeliers. Similarly, make sure to hide all the Light objects in the Chandeliers and Sconces in both the Editor and the Renderer (make sure both gray dots are selected red in the Objects Manager), and delete all Area lights used as bounce from the last tutorial as well. The bounce for this daytime scene will be totally different, so we'll want a clean lighting palette.

So if everything is turned off, you should have a fairly dark room. Let's light the scene as a midmorning scene and assume that the windows are facing toward the east. This will allow us to work with volumetric light as it streams into the room. As we are going to use volumetric light, we can't use the logical choice of a Distant Light setting to work as the sun. So, we'll use a Parallel (Square) Light object to create the sun just outside the window. Create a Light object and change its Type to Parallel(Square).

After you have the Parallel Light object created, make sure that you have Hard Shadows and Volumetric settings selected, and that the Inner Distance setting is more than 0 for both the Details tab and the Visible Light sections. We want to be able to control the actual light radiation and the visible light for this Light object.

Because this is the sun, also make the Brightness 200% in the Details tab and the Brightness in the Visible Light tab 150% (Figure 7.29). With the assumption that this is mid-morning, the light would still have a little bit of a yellow-orange tinge. Make sure this is set in the General tab under the Color setting.

With all that light at all that intensity, you'd think the room would just be completely full of light. Actually, the rendering should resemble Figure 7.30. The reason is that we only have the Parallel Light object as a light source. As the default raytracing rendering engine in C4D doesn't calculate bounced light, we get to fake it again.

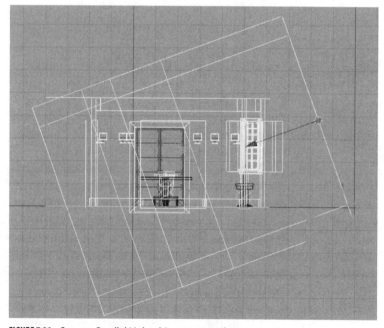

FIGURE 7.29 Set up a Parallel Light object to act as the sun.

FIGURE 7.30   Despite having a bright light with high intensity visible light, the result is still a dark room. This is because we have no bounced light.

At a time like this, where there are no other lights on in the room, the bounced light is incredibly important. It's actually more important than the light streaming into the room. This parallel light that we've built is a slow renderer (Volumetric lights always are), so for now, hide it in both the Editor and the Renderer. To speed things up, hide all the furniture as well so you don't have to wait for your computer to redraw it; you don't need it to render. Remember that to hide objects, click the top gray dots for each object in the Objects Manager.

Now with just your empty room, you can more quickly begin to plot out how the bounced light would behave and where it would illuminate. The first place the majority of the light streaming through the window would hit is the floor. To create this reflected light, create a Light object and make sure that it is an Area Light object; rename it "Floor Bounce." Because the floor is a polished wood, it would reflect light quite well, so make the Brightness of this bounced light quite high—around 200%. Also activate Soft Shadows (as this bounced light would create very diffuse shadows). Make sure that this Floor Bounce light has an Inner Distance setting, so that you can control where this light is at full intensity. Remember that these bounce lights are going to be the only true illumination in the room. Notice in test renderings that if the Area light is too close to the floor, it won't produce much radiation on it; you need to keep it off the floor a little bit so that it also illuminates the floor (Figure 7.31). Take lots of test renderings (adjusting the Inner and Outer falloff of the light between renderings) until you get a good image indicating bounced light (Figure 7.31).

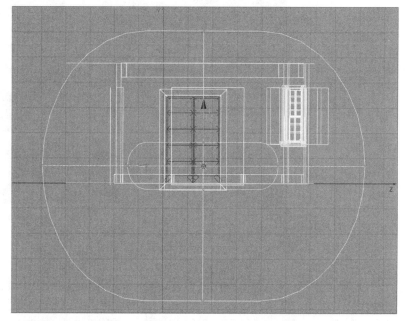

FIGURE 7.31 To create the Floor Bounce object, make sure your Area light is actually a short way above the floor.

The next largest source of bounced light would be the walls opposite the window. For the walls in this Dining Room, we need to actually make three Area lights—two for each side of the arch and one for the backing flat. Because the backing flat is a dark burgundy, we need to make sure that the Area light providing that bounced light is producing a red/pink color. Create three new Area lights and name two of them "OppWall Bounce1" and "OppWall Bounce2." Set the Brightness settings to only about 35% for both; as these walls are further from the light and are not as glossy, there is not as much bounce. Again, make sure that the Inner and Outer Distance settings are activated for both of these lights; again, the initial settings in the Attributes Editor can be any non-0 value as you'll need to visually adjust them in the view panel anyway. Maneu-

FIGURE 7.32 Leave the distance between the Inner and Outer distance settings large, so the bounce will be a very soft, very diffuse light.

ver the Inner Distance setting so that it barely kisses the wall and make the Outer Distance setting large to provide soft light to the scene. These Area lights needn't cover the whole wall; because the light from the window is streaming in and down, chances are they would only cover the bottom part. So keep these a bit shorter overall. The third Area light should be a bit higher—about 60%—because of its red color, and it should have the same Inner and Outer Distance settings. However, this time, change the color of the Area light to a pink color. Rename this light Red Bounce (Figure 7.33). Take a rendering to see how the bounce buildup is going (Figure 7.34).

To finish the room up, we need to make some very weak Area lights on the ceiling and the two side walls. The Brightness setting should only be around 15% and these do not need to cast shadows (Figure 7.35). (If you like, you could create a special Area light for the blue door that—of course—would be blue.)

When all the bounced light is in place, turn the Volumetric Parallel Light object back on to get the sun streaming through the windows again (Figure 7.36). If everything is set up right, the scene should actually

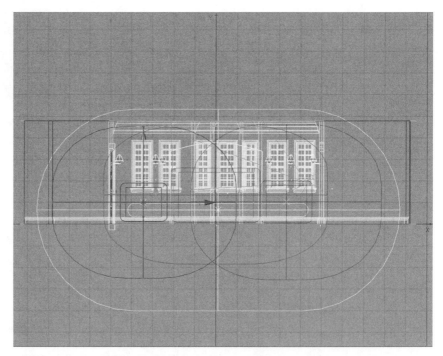

FIGURE 7.33 Creating back wall bounces.

ON THE CD

FIGURE 7.34 Rendering with back wall bounce. Notice the blush of color on the floor near the walls. Check these out in color on the CD-ROM.

FIGURE 7.35 Completed bounced light.

FIGURE 7.36 Final lighting all set together.

appear as though there were only one light— the streaming sunlight. All the bounce Area lights we've inserted should simply be reinforcing the idea that an extremely bright light is coming into the room. Unhide your furniture and give this daytime scene a final rendering (Figure 7.37).

FIGURE 7.37   Rendered with furniture unhidden.

TUTORIAL

7.3 ROMANTIC LIGHTING FOR THE DINING ROOM

We've now seen night and day. In both of the previous tutorials, we've looked at ways to make the scene believable, using Area lights to establish bounced light and light arrays to soften shadows. Now, we can have a little fun. Lighting for a romantic evening is always a favorite of students because there is so much that can be done. The real key to this type of lighting? Props.

It may seem odd, but oftentimes the best lighting isn't necessarily all in the lighting. Much of lighting is making sure the objects are present that make us believe the lighting layout. For a romantic setting, props are everything. Begin by creating some candlesticks (Figure 7.38). Then model the flame for the candle as well. Although we'll be looking at ways to trick the camera into thinking there's much more here than we are building, it's important that you actually have some geometry for the flame. Again, because the Dining Room is so large and cumbersome at this point, create your candles in a separate file. Your Editor will stay snappy and you'll be able to do test renderings much faster.

FIGURE 7.38   Modeled candlesticks.

Although we may not ever see this candle flame close-up, we can make a low-memory material that will help keep the flame realistic. Light a real candle and take a look at what's happening in the flame. The bottom of the flame (the hottest area) is blue. The flame then moves to a yellow-white as you move up the flame. To duplicate this, create a new material and activate the Color, Luminance, and Transparency parameters. In the Image…input channel in all of those parameters, select Gradient from the list of 2D shaders. Gradient will allow us to change the color of the image map across the surface of the flame geometry.

Click the Edit…button within each parameter and edit this gradient so that it is Axial at 270° from a dark blue to a light yellow. In other words, you should have this gradient in all three channels. Apply this new Flame texture to the Flame objects. By activating the Texture mode, you can scale and move the texture so that it is appropriate on the face of the candle (Figure 7.39). Later, we're going to put a lens effect on this flame that covers up most of what we've done here; however, because lens effects are post-rendering effects, they won't show up in any reflections in the scene. As we have a reflective table and reflective bowls, we need to have a working texture on the object.

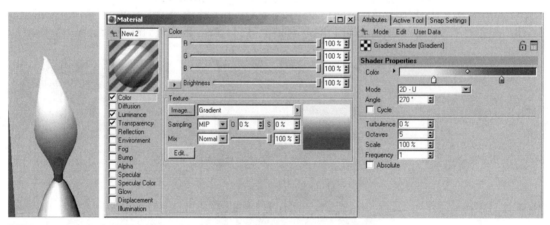

FIGURE 7.39 A roughed-out Flame texture.

Now that we have a good texture on the Flame object, we need to make the scene look as though it is actually emitting light. No matter what material you put on the object, it will never put forth any light radiation by itself (at least not using raytracing; it can in radiosity, but more on this later). Only Light objects will do this. A candle flame casts light in all directions. So the best choice would be an Omni light. Create a Light object and leave its Type as Omni. If we were only going to have one candle we'd want the shadows to be hard, but as we're going to have multiple candles—and thus multiple light sources—the shadows should have a less hard edge. So, set the shadows to soft. Also, candles have a soft orange light to them, so set the color to an amber-orange color (R=98.8%, G=75.7%, B=21%).

In the Details tab, set the brightness to about 60%. Set your Falloff setting to Inverse and make sure that your Inner Distance setting is more than 0. Back in the view panel, you want to verify that your Inner Distance setting is very small, probably no bigger than the flame itself. However, the Outer Distance setting should be very large. We want this light to degrade very slowly but have a fairly wide range. As a finishing touch, go to the Lens Effect tab for the light (in the Attributes Editor) and activate a Manual Glow setting. Deactivate "Use Light Parameters," as we want to define this glow manually. In the Glow Editor tab, set the Glow settings to Element 1, Type 4, Size 20%, R-2 and select a creamy yellow for the color. Leave the Ring setting inactive, but set the Beams setting to Element 1, Type 2, Size 30% (Figure 7.40). Hide all the other candlesticks so that you just have one candle with this new Point light and take a test rendering.

FIGURE 7.40   The Point light at the top of the flame can help give off the orange light of the scene, and the lens effect can help soften our Flame object.

This isn't a bad start. However, there are some problems. Because a Point Light object starts at a point, it is easy to quickly block its light radiation. This is just what's happened here. To correct the problem, first make sure that the Flame object has a Compositing tag that makes it not Cast or Accept shadows (set these options in the Attributes Editor for the

Compositing tag). Second, even if the Flame object doesn't cast shadows, because the light is so close to the top of the candle, the candle blocks the light downward. Thus, the entire bottom of the scene is totally dark. To get around this problem, we'll create another Light object. Make this object a Spot (Round) with Soft Shadows. Give it a light yellow color. In the Details tab, leave the Inner Angle setting at 0, but make the Outer Angle setting 175º. Make the Brightness setting only about 45%. Again, activate Inverse Falloff and verify that the Inner Distance setting is more than 0 so you can control it. Make sure the Spotlight object is pointing downward and move it a little bit above the top of the flame (Figure 7.41).

FIGURE 7.41   A Spotlight overcomes the problem of the Point light's radiation being blocked by the top of the candle.

We still need to deal with issues of bounce. For these candles, we'll want to make sure that whatever surface they are sitting on exudes a bit of light bounce. So create another Light object and make it an Area light. Hold off on making any color changes until we determine exactly where the lights will be placed. In the Details tab, we want this bounce to be very soft, so assign Inverse Falloff, but leave the Inner Distance setting at 0. Visually adjust the Outer Distance setting in the Editor to give off a slight bounce from the floor of your mini scene (Figure 7.42). Remember, the floor of this scene is acting as the tabletop will in the room scene.

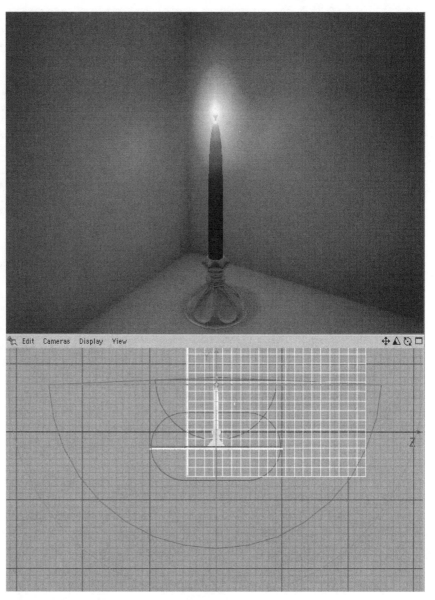

FIGURE 7.42 Finished candle lighting.

Group all three of these lights together and call it Flame. Make several instances of this flame and put them within each copy of the candles. This way, if there need to be adjustments when the group is rendered, it's a simple task. Show all your candles and take a rendering to see how they all work together (Figure 7.43).

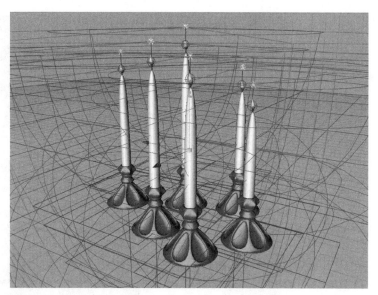

FIGURE 7.43 Group of candles.

Once you're happy with the effect of the candles, copy and paste them into the Room scene. At this point, make sure that these candles are the only light source. Undoubtedly, you'll need to resize the group of candles so that they fit in with the scale of the room (Figure 7.44). Furthermore, you'll probably need to increase the main light source's Outer falloff settings for the candles so that it extends past the walls. We want this light to give very soft light to almost every corner of the room (Figure 7.45).

Although, in theory, most of these walls would probably be giving off a little bit of bounced light, the amount would be almost negligible. The closest plane that would be providing bounced light is the table, but we've taken care of that with the Area lights at the bottom of the candle. Since they are sitting on the table, simply give a little bit of a red color to that Area bounce light and you're set. The only other area that would cause any noticeable bounce would be the ceiling. Create an Area Light object of very low Brightness (10%) and align it with the ceiling as we have done in the past (Figure 7.46). Make sure that its color is a slight amber color. Activate your sconces at a low brightness to give some more texture to the room (Figure 7.47). Add any other props you choose (wine glasses, roses, etc.), render, and you're done (Figure 7.48)

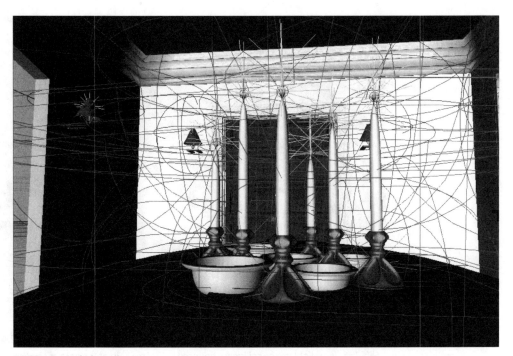

FIGURE 7.44 Scaled candles.

ON THE CD

FIGURE 7.45 Extended light source to give the room a nice glow. Check out the CD-ROM to see it in color.

FIGURE 7.46 Area light on the ceiling for bounced light. Area light at the base of candles.

FIGURE 7.47 Sconces turned on for added depth and texture.

FIGURE 7.48   Added props and the seduction is complete.

7.4 RADIOSITY RENDERING

Talking about radiosity rendering can take one of two forms: either a few paragraphs of description or volumes of discussion. As we just don't have room for a lengthy discussion of what exactly radiosity is, we'll concentrate here on what radiosity does. And because we don't have room to talk about every radiosity setting, we'll discuss the general things that need to happen to set up a radiosity for lighting.

Further, because—technically—radiosity is a rendering issue, we won't spend a huge amount of time talking about it here. What we will talk about is how to prepare a scene for radiosity-rendered images and what kinds of things to do to speed the traditionally slow process up.

What radiosity *does* is calculate bounced light. This is more important than you might think. Most renders do not calculate the way that light really bounces from surface to surface illuminating as it goes. You've seen in earlier tutorials how without bounced light, you need to take a lot of time carefully placing lights to produce the illusion of bounced light. Although being able to control exactly what light bounces where has its advantages, super-realistic renderings are fairly easily achieved using radiosity.

So why not use it all the time? Well, calculating bounced light on lots of surfaces is quite an achievement. Even the most advanced computer can be slowed to a crawl when trying to figure out how each photon of light bounces or reflects off each polygon.

The basic setup of a radiosity scene can be summarized with four key ideas:

1. Only place the light sources as they would really work in your scene. For instance, for a daytime scene where the light source is the sun outside, one parallel light will do it. This light needs to be carefully set up so that its falloff is appropriate and doesn't stop halfway through the room. The reasoning here is that you are letting C4D do all the "light thinking" for you.

2. Work with your materials. Notice that each material has an Illumination channel. It's the only channel that you cannot turn off or on. When you double-click a material, or single-click the material and work with it in the Attributes Editor, you can choose to have a surface Generate or Receive GI (global illumination) (Figure 7.49). Of course, shiny objects such as glossy floors will have a high value for Generate (200% or more), while matte surfaces like cloth will have a very low value (10%-20%). Do not have everything generating the same GI amounts, or the scene can end up looking stale and flat.

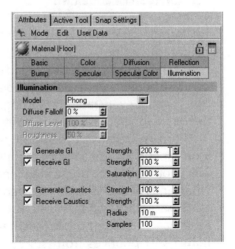

FIGURE 7.49   Generating or Receiving GI (global illumination).

3. Set up your Render Settings to use Radiosity (Figure 7.50). Notice that when you press the Render Settings button, there is an entire section for Radiosity. The manual give some nice textbook definitions of what each of the settings within this area does, so we won't cover them here. But do note that you can set your strength above 100%. Sometimes this is important to really punch up what you're trying to do. Note that the Accuracy setting can make a big difference in both the visual quality of your rendering and your rendering times. Higher Accuracy is, well, more accurate, and gives a nice rendering; but you also sacrifice lots of time (Figure 7.50).

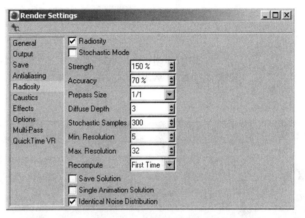

FIGURE 7.50   Render Settings and the Radiosity section.

4. Finally, optimize your scene. Objects with low amounts of polygons don't require a huge amount of accuracy. Using Compositing tags (right-click on an object and select New Tag>Compositing Tag), you can enable GI Accuracy for objects individually (Figure 7.51). By doing this, you save your precious processor cycles for the more complex objects in your scene.

True, it does take a while to get everything set up for radiosity. It takes even longer when you want to get careful optimization set up, such as specialized materials or per-object GI Accuracy. For still shots, optimizing your scene might not be worth the hassle. But especially if you are building animations that you plan to use GI for, you can cut your rendering times down to one-fourth of their original times by these simple optimization processes.

FIGURE 7.51 Setting up GI Accuracy for individual objects.

So although a radiosity scene takes time, the results can be hard to get any other way (Figure 7.52 and 7.53).

FIGURE 7.52 Rendering using Radiosity.

FIGURE 7.53   Rendering using Radiosity in Stochastic mode.

CONCLUSION

So we've looked at a whole slew of different lighting situations. Of course this is just the beginning. One of the most interesting parts of 3D is the lighting as each situation is different. Keep a keen eye out for what happens in the real world, and look for ways to emulate these phenomena.

ANIMATION BASICS

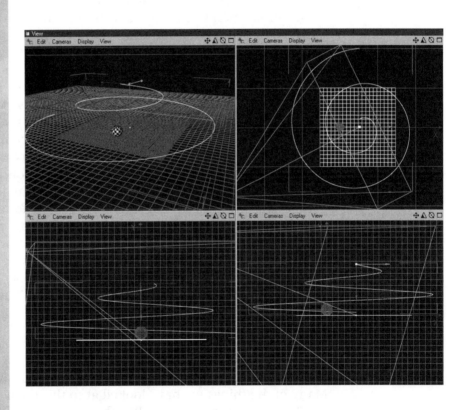

Animation is a relatively young art form, yet it still has a history. The art of drawing individual cels to create the illusion of motion continues to evolve and continues to excite. However, even with the continuing evolution, the basic tenets of animation have remained the same. Animation is composed of a series of still images, each slightly different from the last. When these are viewed in rapid succession (several each second), they give the illusion of movement.

This movement is hard to capture. Most animation runs between 24 and 30 frames per second; which means that even a short 2-minute animation has anywhere from 2800 to 3600 frames. So, as animation evolved and animation teams began to emerge, an artistic production line began to form. The master animator would draw the most important frames—the keyframes —of an animation (e.g., the character at the bottom of a jump, the top of a jump, and the landing) to sketch out the movement and the moments of most important action. Then the more junior animators would come in and draw all the "in-between" frames. These less experienced animators ironically ended up drawing most of the frames of an animation. You can still see this process at the end of many animations as the credits will display a group of "In-betweeners."

3D animation runs along this same idea. You are the master animator and establish the keyframes of the animation. The computer acts as the in-betweener and fills in all the frames in between. Animation then becomes the process of giving your computer enough information so that it knows how to accurately fill in those frames. C4D works at a standard 30 frames per second (fps); so establishing a simple move over 3 seconds could mean creating as few as two keyframes, while C4D creates the other 87 frames.

LOTS OF NEW THINGS

One of the things that R8 has really changed is the animation tools. Many of the things we have looked at to this point were the same in v7 as they are now in R8. But the animation tools have undergone a dramatic overhaul. Just about every part of C4D R8's animation tools is new and improved. As we go along, we will be highlighting some of the new improvements in C4D's animation implementation.

To cover how C4D works with animation and how you can exploit these tools to create fantastic movement, we will be completing a series of tutorials. These tutorials will demonstrate basic animations, and also provide you with a way at looking at many of the various functions and capabilities in action.

But before we get too far into the tutorials, let's look at some of the basic tools and how they are set up. After we have looked at where the tools are and what their major function is, we can then get going on the tutorials, where we will look at these tools in action.

Animation Toolbar

At the bottom of the main user interface is the Animation Toolbar (Figure 8.1). In some ways, this resembles a basic Timeline. It has some interesting capabilities that allow you to do things much quicker than any other animation interface within C4D. In fact, many simple animations can be completely controlled here with this collection of tools without having to get into any other of C4D's animation tools.

FIGURE 8.1   The Animation Toolbar.

The Animation Toolbar's left side is fairly straightforward. The blue rectangle (which we'll refer to as the Current Time Marker) shows where in time you are. When you move this Current Time Marker, the view panels above will redraw to show you what the state of your 3D world is at that point in time. The number within the Current Time Marker indicates exactly what frame you are on. You can move this Current Time Marker by clicking and dragging it to a new frame in time.

To the right of this are some buttons similar to those seen on a VCR. Notice that going out from the middle "Stop" button you can play forward (or backward), move forward (or backward) one frame, and jump to the end (or beginning). What these tools allow you to do is move through your animation, or to play your animation. One note about this—and we'll talk more about it later—when you hit the Play button, C4D will attempt to play *all* the frames as quickly as it can (this is the default setting). Unfortunately, as your scene gets more and more complex, it is harder and harder for C4D to be able to process all that information as quickly as it needs to. So the playback you see in your view panels will often end up being quite a bit slower than the animation actually will play when rendered. Don't rely on just playing the Animation Toolbar to define your timing. Be sure to use the Make Preview function (Render>Make Preview…) to have C4D create a quick editor rendering that shows you what your motion will really look like at full speed.

Next to the VCR controls is the Play Sound button. We have not talked much about importing sound into C4D so we won't spend a lot of time here, but this allows you to turn any imported sound on or off when playing back your animation.

The next three buttons—the Record Keyframe, Autokeying, and Selection Object—allow you to define when and how you are recording the all important keyframes. The most important button is the Record Keyframe button; when you press this button, the active object will have a keyframe recorded for it. We will revisit this in more detail in just a bit.

The Autokeying and Selection Object tools are interesting and can help create some quick animation, but can cause real problems if not used with care. For example, if Autokeying is on, once you have recorded a keyframe for an object, every time you move that object at any time in your animation, a new keyframe is automatically recorded. This may seem like a good idea, but when you get down to the nitty-gritty of refining your animation, new keyframes can end up all over the place as you slide your Current Time Marker around and adjust small things. You just lose too much control. For the exercises here, we won't be using the Autokeying function much.

The next five buttons indicate what types of keyframes you are going to record. By default, when you have an object selected and hit the Record Keyframe button, you record a Postion, Scale, Rotation, and Parameter keyframe (the last kind of keyframe that isn't activated is the PLA (point level animation)). This is because all of these are depressed in the Animation Toolbar. These look just like the Move, Scale, and Rotate Active Elements tools, so they are easy to distinguish.

So it is not necessarily a bad idea to record all of these keyframes. If you are not changing the rotation of an object, lots of keyframes don't really hurt your project. But they do give C4D a lot more to think about needlessly, and problems can occur when later you decide you want to define a bit more about the rotation of an object. If you have been recording rotation keyframes, the entire time you were working out the position of the object, you have already got a lot of information about how this object will turn that you have to go through and clear out. In addition, when it gets down to the time where you are plodding through individual keyframes to get that motion just right, a bunch of unnecessary keyframes can clutter up your Timeline. Although it takes a bit more forethought, it's usually worth it to deactivate the kinds of keyframes you do not wish to record.

Finally, the last button on the Animation Toolbar is the Options button. Click and hold this button to provide a few more options on how the Animation Toolbar works. The first three options—which relate to Interpolation—will be discussed much more later. Interpolation has to do with how C4D decides to create the frames between keyframes. This is really not the best place to control this, so we'll skip over it for now. The next two options—All Frames and Project—involve how quickly C4D is going to attempt to playback the animation. By turning All Frames off, when you play the animation using the VCR controls we talked about earlier, C4D will stay on track for time, rather than worrying about playing every frame. What this could mean is that you may only see one frame each second—or even one frame every two seconds— if your scene is that complex; but it will give you a more accurate view of the timing of your project.

Finally, all the numbers indicate at what frame rate you want C4D to attempt to play the animation. This is rather goofy as, if you can play back at the frame rate of your project, you might as well play it at that rate. If you cannot, you can decide whether to view it in slow motion —and see all the frames—or drop frames to play it closer to real time. So, there is not much need to mess with this area unless you are in very specialized situations where extremely high frame rates are required.

Timeline

The huge leap that C4D made from v5 to v6 was further refined in v7. But on R8, lots and lots of new things have emerged in the Timeline (Figure 8.2).

Notice that the Timeline has its own collection of pull-down menus. These are completely separate from the regular C4D pull-down menus and are very deep. We won't be covering all of them here, but through the course of the tutorials, we will visit many of them.

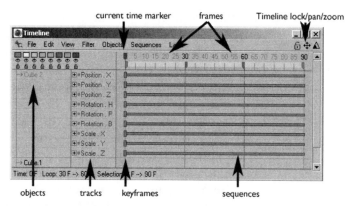

FIGURE 8.2   The Timeline in R8.

The Timeline can be broken down into several general areas. The first, of course, is the pull-down menus. Also of note as we're speaking of this is the ability to right-click (COMMAND-click on a Mac), to pull up new collections of pop-down menus. These are largely specialized menus and many of them are fairly redundant, but we will talk of these in the tutorials as well.

The next area contains the tools that help you organize your workspace. The layer system tools (Figure 8.3) allow you to assign objects, groups of objects, or even individual keyframes to a layer. The layers are defined by their color and can be hidden (the little eyeball icon) or locked (the padlock icon). This can be really helpful when your scene becomes complex, especially when it has a lot of moving elements.

FIGURE 8.3   Layer buttons.

To assign an element to a layer, just select it in the Timeline window and click on one of the color swatches. You can even have C4D show you all the elements assigned to a given layer by using the Layer pull-down menu in the Timeline. Here, there are a variety of options to allow you to toggle and select various layers.

Still moving across the top of the Timeline is a collection of three more icons that allow you to control what you see in the Timeline. The padlock icon allows you to show all the objects in the scene (when it is "unlocked") or only the objects that are animated (when it is "locked"). Similarly, the icon that looks like the Pan tool from the view panels works the same way as it does in the view panels. Just click and drag to pan across the Timeline. Also similar is how this tool works in the view panel; if you hold the "1" key on your keyboard and click-drag in the Timeline, you will also pan across your view. The focal length tool next to it allows you to zoom in and out of your Timeline. Again, just as in the view panel, hold the "2" down and click-drag to do the same thing. Or, you can hold "1" down and right-click-drag to get the same effect. This zooming in and out on the Timeline allows you to deal with keyframes that may happen in rapid succession to each other.

Now let's look at the areas below. On the far left is the list of objects or groups that you are animating or can animate. Immediately to the right is a column that will show what *Tracks* are activated. Think of animation tracks as animation characteristics. Each track represents something that is being animated (or changed over time). This can include position, rotation, and scale as well as things such as material, visibility, light falloff (for Light objects), type of light, or just about anything. In R8, there is nearly nothing out of reach in the animation process. When you record a keyframe in the Animation Toolbar, new tracks will automatically be created for you, for each of the active buttons you have depressed at the right of the Animation Toolbar.

However, you can also add specific tracks manually by right-clicking on an object in the Timeline. A pop-down menu will come up (Figure 8.4) that will allow you to add whatever track you wish to place animation on.

Now a track by itself actually contains no information. There is no movement or change associated with an empty track. However, tracks can be filled with *Sequences*. Sequences are collections of keyframes—and keyframes *do* define motion. Sequences are represented within the area of the Timeline that shows the keyframe ticks and actual keyframes. Sequences are represented with a bar. When you create a new sequence, by default it is the size of the Project's Settings (or how many frames are available in the scene—by default, 90). However, sequences can be longer or shorter than the project. In fact, there can be more than one sequence in any given track. This can be handy when you want to make sure that there is no movement between two keyframes (e.g., an object moves to a position, waits there for 3 seconds, and then moves again), or when you have a specific kind of movement defined by a collection of

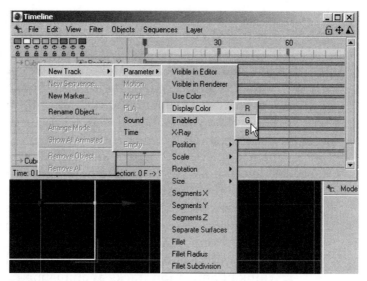

FIGURE 8.4 Activating animation tracks to objects.

keyframes. By limiting the sequence to fit that collection of key-frames, the sequence can be duplicated to other locations within the animation. This undoubtedly seems a bit ethereal and hypothetical at this point, it will make more sense in the tutorials.

A new thing that is really handy in R8 is how sequences now contain an extra bit of information in the Timeline. When a sequence contains two or more keyframes, a kind of mini-F-curve becomes available. In the tracks column, you will notice that tracks will have a little + sign. By expanding this, the sequences' F-curves will become visible beneath it (Figure 8.5). This might not seem important now, but when we begin to work with interpolation, it will be very handy.

Before we get into the tutorials, the last important thing to notice is that this main area where the sequences are shown has a couple of different shades of grays in the background. The lighter gray indicates the project's length—in this case, 90 frames. Also, right above the section that contains the sequences and keyframes are ticks that represent individual frames in the scene. Note that there is a blue pointer at the top that represents the Current Time Marker of the Timeline. By clicking and dragging this pointer, you can move to a different time that will be represented in the view panels. So, you can navigate through time either in the Animation Toolbar or the Timeline.

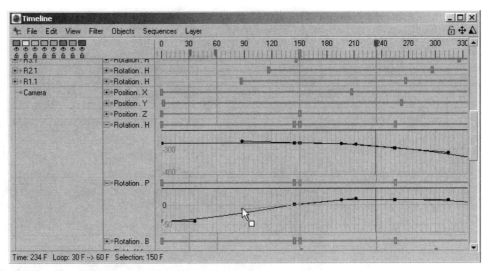

FIGURE 8.5   Mini F-curves available beneath sequences.

TUTORIAL

8.1 BOUNCING BALL

Yes, this is a basic movement. However, it will allow us the ability to look at how to create keyframes and edit them. Through the process of this tutorial, we will look at how to adjust timing, how to change the interpolation between keyframes, and how the basic animation tools work.

To start out, let's create the scene that we plan to animate. First, create a Floor object and a Sphere Primitive. By default, your sphere will be 200m, so enter 100m in the Coordinates Manager to move the sphere up so that it sits right on the floor.

We are going to use concepts that are basic to good animation, such as stretch-and-squash, among others. To use these most effectively for this ball, we will want ensure that the squashing is happening where the sphere meets the floor. To do this, we need to make the Sphere editable (hit "C" on your keyboard). This turns the primitive into a polygonal object so that we can adjust the object axis. Activate the Object Axis tool, and in the Coordinates Manager, change the Y value to 0. This will move the sphere's object axis so that it sits right at its base, where we want the sphere to stretch-and-squash from. Finally, create a quick material and place something like the Checkerboard into the Color channel. This will allow you to keep a closer eye on how your sphere is turned, placed, or stretched (Figure 8.6).

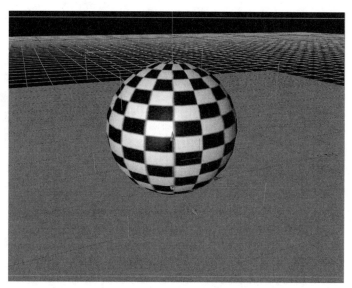

FIGURE 8.6 The setup.

One final note before we get started: when we have been building objects, the default tool has been the Model tool (on the tool palette to the left of the interface). However, when we get ready to animate, it is usually best to animate with the Object tool. So be sure and activate the Object tool. If you can't remember which tool is which, watch for the hints at the bottom-left corner of the interface.

Let's start by just getting our ball to travel a short distance over one second of time. One second is 30 frames, so we will need to place a position keyframe at frame 0 (to give the ball a starting reference) and another position keyframe at frame 30 (to give the ball an ending reference). Remember that all motion must have at least two keyframes.

Make sure that your Current Time Marker is at frame 0 in your Animation Toolbar. Still in the Animation Toolbar, turn off all the tracks except the position. Although we could record keyframes for everything else, there really is no need to do so and it will only complicate things later. Finally, click the Record Keyframe button (Figure 8.7).

Now move the Current Time Marker to frame 30. Move the ball so that it sits at X=500 (you can do this manually or by entering the value in the Coordinates Manager). Again, hit the Record Keyframe button.

Since you have given the sphere a time and position to start and a different time and position to end, you have created motion. Use the controls in the Animation Toolbar to rewind to the beginning of the

FIGURE 8.7   Recording the first keyframe of our simple motion.

animation and then play the animation. Your ball should smoothly slide across the floor over 30 frames.

Also notice that there is a new element in the view panel. The yellow dotted line you see is the path that your animation is taking. The little black dots on the line actually indicate each frame. At the end of the line will be two large yellow dots representing keyframes. These paths can provide a great idea of how your objects are moving.

But what we really want here is to be able to make the ball hop. To do this, we will add another keyframe that further refines the motion of this ball.

Move the Current Time Marker to frame 15. You should see in your view panel that the ball moves to about halfway between the two keyframes created. We want to refine this a bit and define this point as the highest point of the hop. Move the sphere so that it sits at X=300 and Y=150 and hit the Record Keyframe button. The results should look something like Figure 8.8.

Notice that the arc of the hop is defined with the yellow path. Also notice that the path isn't a symmetrical arc. Because gravity is going to

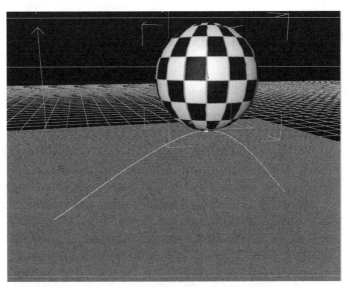

FIGURE 8.8   The hop starting to take shape with three keyframes.

catch up with the ball, most of the forward motion will take place right as it launches. To get an idea of what you have so far, play your animation using the controls in the Animation Toolbar.

So, the ball is hopping, more or less. It's moving in a basic arch. Let's give it a bit more character.

We'll want to make this ball look like it is propelling itself forward. To do this, we'll utilize some basic stretch-and-squash. We'll need to place some scale keyframes, so, in the Animation Toolbar, turn off the position tracks and turn on the scale track.

To make this jump a bit more believable, we want to allow the ball to squash, then stretch right before liftoff. But to make it convincing, we need to be sure the ball stays on the ground for the 15 frames it's going to take to do this. So to give us this extra time, we'll move the extant position keyframes over.

Open the Timeline by hitting Shift-F3 or Window>Timeline. Your Timeline should look like Figure 8.9a.

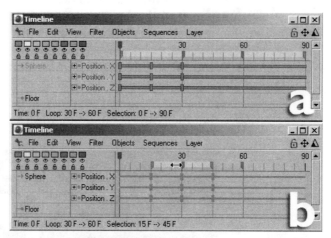

FIGURE 8.9 The Timeline thus far.

Marquee around the position keyframes for the sphere. A great deal happens just with this simple motion. First, the sequences are no longer highlighted in red, but rather the keyframes are. Second, there are new red markers in the frame ticks that indicate the beginning and end of the selected keyframes' range. Third, look at the bottom of the Timeline. Here you'll see where the Current Time Marker is, but more important, you will see "Selection: 0 F → 30 F." We knew this of course, but the line will provide us important information when we start moving this selection. Finally, notice that between the two red markers is a salmon-colored bar.

To move keyframes, you could just click and drag any of the selected keyframes; or simply click-drag this salmon bar. As you drag these keyframes, notice that the Selection information at the bottom of the Timeline updates to show the new location of your range of keyframes. Move the selection so that the hint line there reads "Selection: 15 F → 45 F."

What this does is make the sphere sit still for the first 15 frames. The ball will start moving at frame 15 when it sees its first keyframe and knows that it needs to get to a new position now at frame 30.

Now that we have the extra time, we can get to stretching and squashing.

Back in the Animation Toolbar, make sure the Current Time Marker is at 0 frames. Again, make sure that only the scale track button is activated and record a keyframe. This gives the sphere a size to start from.

Now move the Current Time Marker to frame 8. Switch to the Scale Active Element tool (or hit "T" on your keyboard). Scale the sphere down in the *y* direction until it is about half the height it usually is (around 100m). Because the ball will maintain a constant volume, if it squashes down in the *y* direction, it will need to squash out in the *x* and *z* directions. To expand in both directions but not in the *y*, lock the *y* direction in the top command palette. Make the ball bigger in the *x* and *z* direction until it is about 1.4 times the size. Again, record a keyframe (Figure 8.10).

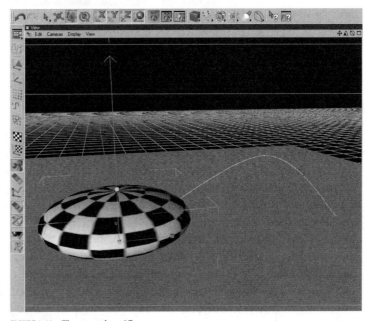

FIGURE 8.10   The squash at 8F.

Now for the stretch. Move the Current Time Marker to frame 15. Now we want to have the ball be taller than usual (around 300m) and thinner. So, use the Scale Active Element tool to stretch the sphere along its *y* axis to about 300m. Then, if you still have the *y* locked, you can click and drag anywhere to thin the sphere down to about 100m for the *x* and *z* measurements. Record a keyframe (Figure 8.11).

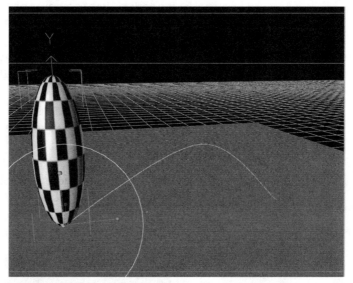

FIGURE 8.11   The stretch at frame 15.

You can drag the Current Time slider across the Animation Toolbar to scrub through the animation so far. You should see the sphere squashing and then stretching and leaving the ground just as it reaches the height of its stretch.

Next, we'll make the sphere squash again at the top of the jump. Although this is an oversimplification of good motion, for clarity's sake, we'll place this next scale keyframe at the same place in time as the position keyframe that defines the top of the jump. Hit CTRL-"G" to jump to the next keyframe for the active object. In this case, your Current Time Marker should jump to frame 30.

At frame 30, resize the sphere so that it is once again 200m in X,Y, and Z. Record a keyframe (Figure 8.12).

Now we will have the sphere stretch as it approaches impact with the floor. To do this, we'll move the point in time where the ball touches down and stretch the ball out. Hit CTRL-"G" to jump to the next keyframe for the ball, and you should jump to frame 45.

FIGURE 8.12   The squash back at frame 30.

At frame 45, we could manually adjust the scale to get the ball in the "stretch" position again. But for an illustration of the power of the Timeline, lets just copy a keyframe from the last time the sphere was stretched (back at frame 15). To do this, open the Timeline and select the Scale keyframes set at frame 15. Now hold the CTRL key down and drag the new keyframes it duplicates over to frame 45 (Figure 8.13). The view panel should update to show this new information.

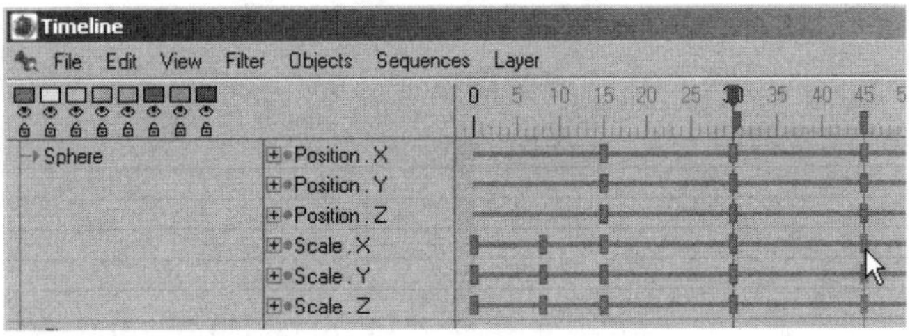

FIGURE 8.13   Duplicating keyframes to a new place in time.

To get the squash, we can do the same thing with the keyframes recorded at frame 8 and at frame 0. Select the Scale keyframes at frame 8 and CTRL-drag them to frame 53. Then CTRL-drag the keyframes at frame 0 to frame 60.

Scrub through your animation to get an idea of how the motion works so far.

Now we need to add some rotation keyframes to get the weight of the stretch-and-squash working a bit better. To prepare for this, in the Animation Toolbar turn off the scale track and turn on the rotation track. This lets C4D know that the keyframes we'll be recording should be rotation keyframes.

Move the Current Time Marker back to frame 8 where the sphere is at its lowest squash. We'll have the sphere start rotating to point in the direction its about to take off into at this time. So, we'll need to record our first keyframe here.

Hit CTRL-G to jump to frame 15 (the next keyframe for the sphere object) and using the Rotate Active Element tool, rotate the sphere forward to around 30 degrees (or you can enter 30 in the B input field of the Coordinates Manager). Record a keyframe (Figure 8.14).

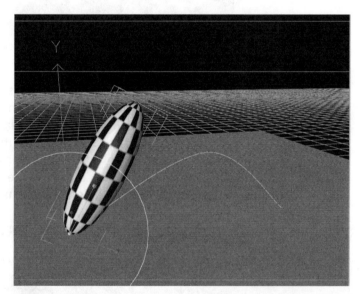

FIGURE 8.14 Creating the second keyframe of the rotation sequence.

In anticipation of its landing, the sphere will rotate its bottom for touchdown. So, jump to frame 30 (the next keyframe for sphere (hit CTRL-G)) and rotate the sphere back to 0 degrees. Record a keyframe.

Now move onto where the sphere hits the ground (frame 45) and rotate the sphere backward 30 degrees (B=0 in the Coordinates Manager) and record a keyframe here.

Finally, we need to get the sphere righted again, so hit CTRL-G to jump to frame 53 and rotate the sphere back to 0 degrees and record a keyframe.

Use the Animation Toolbar to get an idea of what we've got going so far. Depending on the speed of your computer, you will probably be able to get a good idea of how the motion is flowing in real time. But to make sure, let's create a quick preview.

Figure 8.15 shows the Make Preview button selected from the nested Render palette. Since we have only animated to frame 60, we only need to build a preview from frames 0-60. You can choose to build to a Quicktime or AVI. My personal preference is Quicktime as it allows me some more control in the player to look at things by frame than Windows Media Player does, but the choice is up to you.

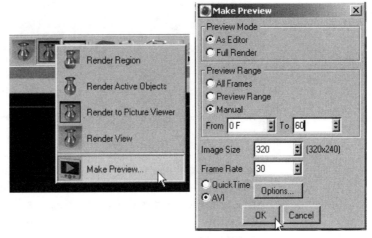

FIGURE 8.15   Creating a preview of the animation thus far.

In the bottom left-hand corner of your interface, you will be able to see a very quick progress bar as C4D creates the movie file. As soon as the preview is built, it will be opened in either Windows Media Player or Quicktime Player. Play it to see what the timing *really* is.

So, it's not bad, but still feels a bit like the ball is hopping in slow motion. Luckily, it's really quite easy to speed up a collection of keyframes. We'll do this in the Timeline.

Actually, there are several ways speed things up, but let's look at it one step at a time. The way that we are going to get the motion to happen faster is to make the time between keyframes less. In the spatial terms of the Timeline, this means that the keyframes need to be closer together. To do this, marquee around all the keyframes associated with the hop (from 0-60). As we saw earlier, this will place red markers at the front and rear of the selection and a salmon-colored bar will appear where the frame ticks are. To scale all these keyframes closer together, just click and drag the red marker at the end of the selection (the red marker at frame 60). You'll notice that as you drag this marker to the left, all the keyframes will squeeze proportionally together. Also notice that the hint line at the bottom of the Timeline will show the new range. For now, drag the keyframes together so that the entire selection happens from frame 0 to frame 45 (Figure 8.16).

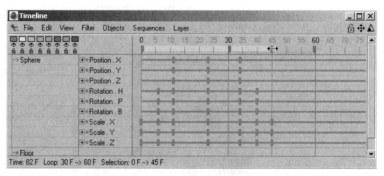

FIGURE 8.16 Speeding up timing by scaling keyframes closer together.

Now, we'll put in another hop. To do this, we won't need to manually record each of the keyframes again; instead, we'll duplicate the already extant keyframes and make the necessary adjustments.

We know that the sphere currently ends up at the same size and same rotation as when it started. So we don't need to copy that keyframe, but do marquee around all the keyframes for the sphere, except the first (Figure 8.17a). Hold the CTRL key down and drag the new keyframes this duplicates so that they sit from frame 51 to frame 90 (Figure 8.17b).

Now this is a good start, but if you take a look in your view panel and play the animation, you'll find the ball jumping back to (0,0,0) instead of staying where it lands and taking off from there. This is, of course, because we have moved the keyframes that define the position. So to get things to work right, we need to adjust the position keyframes.

Figure 8.18 shows what happens when the Position.X track is expanded in the Timeline. This gives a visual representation of the movement over time. You can see that the fourth keyframe (frame 56, one of those that was just duplicated) is back down to where the first keyframe is. This is why the sphere jumps back to the start.

What we need to happen is have the sphere stay still and not move between frames 34 and 56. We can manually define this in a couple of

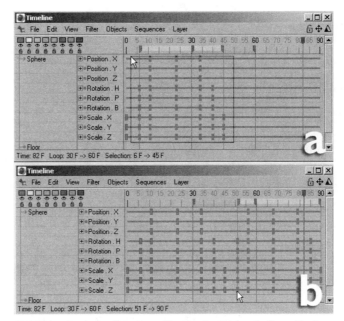

FIGURE 8.17   Setting up for a second hop by duplicating the first collection of keyframes.

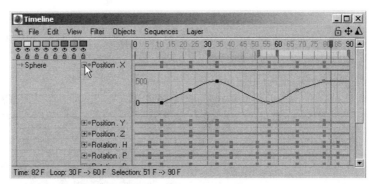

FIGURE 8.18   Expansion of the Position.X track to show where the keyframes define the motion to be.

steps. First, click on the point in the curve below the Position.X sequences (not the keyframe), as shown in Figure 8.19. Notice that when you do this, the Attributes Editor will give you information about this particular keyframe. The Attributes Editor shows us what Time the keyframe is at (34 F), and what Value is assigned (500m). Using this Attributes Editor, you can manually adjust the time or value of any keyframe. For now, the important thing is noticing that the value is 500m.

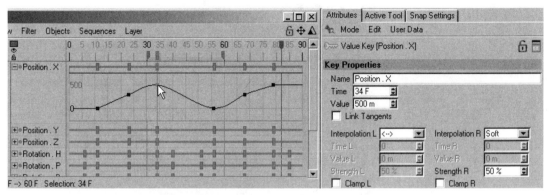

FIGURE 8.19 Finding out information on a keyframe in the Attributes Editor.

Now click on the curve point associated with the keyframe at frame 56. This will show you in the Attributes Editor that the Value is listed at 0 m. Change this value to 500m. You will see that the Timeline updates to reflect this new entry. Now what we need to do is add this 500m to the keyframes at frames 68 and 79. Just click on the curve points for each of these and enter +500 after whatever value is in the Value input field. This will make the keyframe at 68 a value of 800m, and frame 79 a value of 1000m.

The net result of this will be to make the sphere jump forward, do its stretch-and-squash and then jump again; this time jumping forward (Figure 8.20).

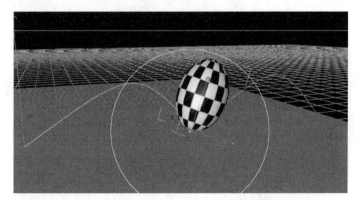

FIGURE 8.20 The double jump setup after adjusting the Position.X settings.

Now, if you look really carefully at the jump between frame 34 and 56, you'll notice that the sphere actually slides back just a little bit. This is corroborated in the Timeline by noticing that the curve beneath the

Position. X track actually shows a dip before it rises, even though frames 34 and 56 have the exact same value. So, why is this?

Well, by default C4D animates with a kind of soft interpolation. Interpolation refers to how C4D defines the frames in between keyframes. A soft interpolation means that it attempts to make the movement smooth so that you don't necessarily see where the keyframes occur. A hard interpolation would mean that each time an object reached a keyframe, there would be an abrupt change as it moved toward the next. Soft interpolation creates great smooth movement by looking ahead. It looks at where it is going to be at the next keyframe and alters its path to provide for smooth transitions.

To see this a bit better, open F-Curve Manager (Window>F-Curve Manager). Select the sphere from your Objects Manager. Immediately, the F-Curve Manager will be filled with a real mess of curvy lines. Each of these lines are indicating the F-Curves, or interpolation curves of the animation thus far for the sphere as represented by the position value along the *y* axis of the graph and time value along the *x* axis. To simplify things a bit, click on Position.X in the left column. The F-curves at the right will show only the interpolation curve for the *x* movement in your scene (Figure 8.21).

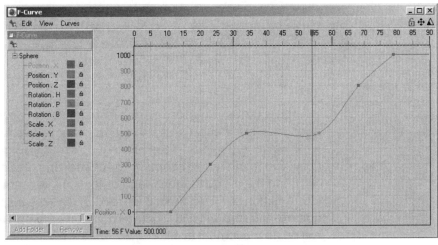

FIGURE 8.21   The F-Curve Manager showing the interpolation curve for Position. X.

Notice that the curve is indeed smooth, and that between frames 34 and 56, it dips the interpolation curve to allow for the coming sharp rise up to frame 68. What we need to do is make the interpolation between these two keyframes (34 and 56) straight, so that there is absolutely no movement.

To do this, marquee around the two keyframes at frame 34 and 56. They turn a slightly brighter shade of red; although the change is hard to see. Right-click on one of the two points and select Custom Tangents>Soft Interpolation. Immediately, the points will have Bezier handles that will allow us to manually define how the interpolation going in and out and between these two keyframes will function (Figure 8.22).

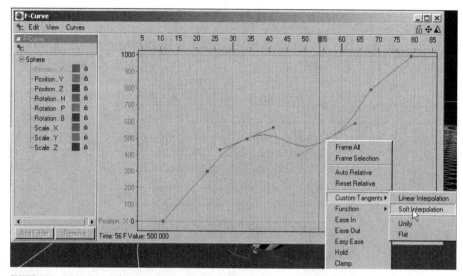

FIGURE 8.22 Activating Soft Interpolation for the tangents of the keyframes.

These tangents function similarly to any other Bezier curves in C4D. If you grab one handle and move it, the handle opposite it will move as well. However, holding the Shift key down as you grab a handle will allow you to move one handle without affecting the other side.

Bend the inside tangent handles for both keyframes to create a flat interpolation between them (Figure 8.23). This means that as the sphere goes from frame 34 to 56, the interpolation is completely flat and there will be no movement at all.

The ability to control these F-Curves is tremendously powerful. Let's say you want to have an object start out slow and end slow, but have a fairly fast movement in the middle. The F-Curve may look something like Figure 8.24. This was done by just placing a position keyframe at frame 0 and another at frame 90, then selecting both, right-clicking on the keyframes (in the F-Curve Manager) and selecting Custom Tangent>Soft

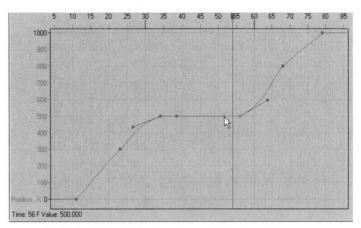

FIGURE 8.23   Flattening out the interpolation curve between keyframes.

Interpolation. Then finally, we selected each keyframe and selected Custom Tangent>Flat.

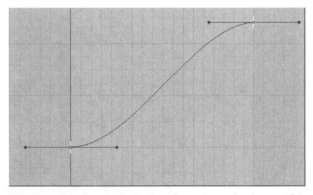

FIGURE 8.24   Creating nice easing into the motion and easing out of the motion with the F-Curve Manager.

Perhaps you want to have things move in a very mechanical fashion. If so, your F-Curve might look like Figure 8.25. Notice that there are no curves in this F-curve, because we don't want flowing movement. This was achieved by selecting extant keyframes and right-clicking on one and selecting Custom Tangent>Linear Interpolation from the pop-down menu.

Or, maybe you are animating a pogo stick as it bounced along, or a hard ball. In these cases, the F-Curve Manager might look something like Figure 8.26. This was done by selecting the keyframes at the top of the

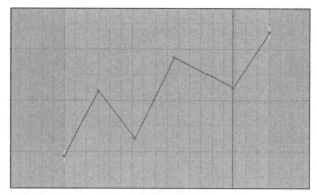

FIGURE 8.25 Very mechanical movement defined with linear interpolation.

hop, where the motion would be smooth and selecting Custom Tangent>Soft Interpolation and then selecting the keyframes at the bottom, where the object would just be touching and then abruptly lifting off again, and selecting Tangent>Linear Interpolation.

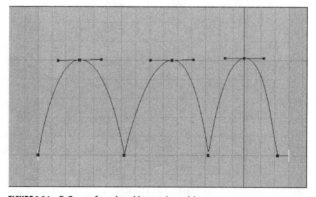

FIGURE 8.26 F-Curve for a hard bouncing object.

The power of the F-Curve Manager is considerable. It allows for what was referred to as Soft, Medium, and Hard Interpolation in C4D's past versions.

So there you have the bouncing ball. We have animated the position, scale, and rotation of an object. We've adjusted the placement of the individual keyframes and even altered the nature of the interpolation of how the frame function between the keyframes. We've covered quite a lot. If you like, take a look at the finished animation file on the CD-ROM (Tutorials>Chapter08).

ON THE CD

Remember that this tutorial is a very rough animation. The actual timing needs all sorts of tweaking, so feel free to become more comfortable with keyframes and how they work by tweaking your animation to create the kind of character you want the little ball to have.

But stay tuned for more information. There are many, many other functions of animation. In the next tutorial, we will look at a few more specialty animation tools available through C4D.

8.2 ADDITIONAL ANIMATION CAPABILITIES

TUTORIAL

So now that we've looked at the basic animation ideas, we can move on to some of C4D's more interesting but harder to understand animation tools. For this tutorial, we will continue to build on the setup we created for the previous tutorial.

There will need to be a few new things added to the setup. First, create a Target Camera and move the Camera.Target object so that it sits at about where the ball hits the floor between jumps (about X=500). Also make sure that you are looking through the Camera you just created by selecting Cameras>Scene Camera>Camera from within the Perspective view panel's pull-down menu.

Now for the new additions. The default length of projects in C4D is 90 frames, or about 3 seconds. The two hops we have thus far happen to be right around 90 frames. For this tutorial, among other things, we will have a camera that loops around a scene before the hop starts, and after the hop ends. To do this, we need more frames available in the scene.

To make a project longer—or to add more frames—go to Edit>Project Settings in the main interface or you can find the same pull-down combination in the Timeline. In the dialog box that pops up, simply change the Maximum value to the desired length—in this case, 200 F. Notice that when you do this, in the Timeline, the background of the sequence area will have a new area of a lighter gray background to define the new larger project length. However, note that the sequences that were created prior to this new project length definition remain at the length that they were when originally created. As we create new sequences from now on, the default length of these new sequences will be the 200 frames that is the length of the project. If you ever need more room in a given sequence, simply click the sequence and in the Attributes Editor, change the Right Border (or Left Border if you need more sequence to the left) to the desired length.

Next, we will move all the animation we have created thus far a little ways down the Timeline so that the action takes place in the middle of the project. The quickest way to do this is to select things by tracks (click on Position.X (which will in turn select all the Position tracks), then Shift-click Rotation.H (which will in turn select all the Rotation tracks), and then Shift-click the Scale. X track (which will select all the Scale tracks). By selecting the tracks, all the associated sequences, and thus keyframes, will be selected as well. Grab the handy salmon-colored bar at the top of the sequence section and move all of these selected keyframes so that the new hint line reads Selection: 60 F → 150 F.

Now we can start to animate the camera. Remember that in most cases a camera is just like any other object; it can be animated in its position, scale, or rotation. However, this camera is a bit different as it has a Camera.Target object associated with it. This means that the Camera object will always be pointed at the Camera.Target object, so you don't have control of the camera's rotation directly, only through the position of the Camera.Target object. This actually makes things a bit easier for us as it will allow us to stay focused on the scene as we move the camera around.

To animate the camera, we could just start putting keyframes at various locations as we positioned the camera into new places. However, let's look at some other techniques.

What we will do is create a spline that we will have the camera follow. This will mean that we only have to place two keyframes to get the camera to go around the scene several times. This will make for a much easier process than having to place lots of keyframes for each time the camera needs to change directions.

So the first thing we'll need is the spline that is the path we wish to have the camera follow. For a little bit of interest, let's use a Helix. You can create it by selecting it from the nested spline tools in the top palette or by selecting Objects>Spline Primitive>Helix.

The helix that is created is, of course, in the wrong place and turned the wrong way. In the Coordinates Manager, change the position to be X=500 and Y=850. Change the rotation to be B=90. As the Helix is selected, you will be able to see a whole slew of attributes for it in the Attributes Editor. Change the settings to be Start Radius=200m, End Radius=2000m, and Height = 800m. This should give you an interesting spiral that looks something like Figure 8.27.

This helix is going to define how the camera moves. The way that it will do this is through an expression. We are going to actually animate how an object interacts with an expression. To assign the expression,

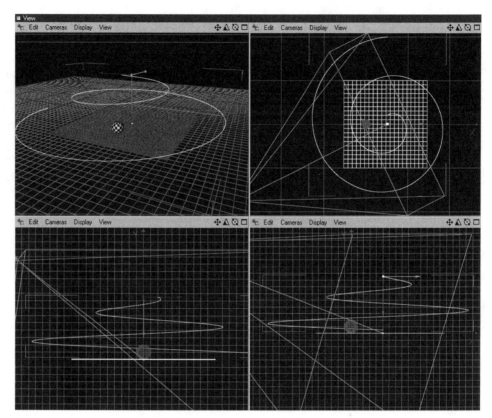

FIGURE 8.27   The Helix object in place and adjusted.

right-click the Camera object in the Objects Manager and select New Expression>Align to Spline Expression from the pop-down menu.

A new tag will appear after the Camera and when this Align to Spline Expression tag is selected, its attributes will appear in the Attributes Editor. To tell the camera what spline to align to, just drag the Helix object from the Objects Manager into the Attributes Editor into the Spline Path input field. Your camera will instantly snap to the beginning of the helix spline.

The problem is that if you play your animation, you will see your ball hopping through your camera view, but the camera doesn't move. To actually have the camera move along the spline over time, we need to look in the Timeline.

In the Timeline, notice that Camera actually has a small triangle next to it rather than the small circle that many of the other objects have. Click this triangle to expand Camera to include other animatable objects associated with the camera. The most important to us is the Tag: Align to Spline.

The Tag:Align to Spline currently has no tracks, sequences, or keyframes assigned to it. Right-click on the Tag: Align to Spline and select New Track>Parameter>Position from the pop-down menu (Figure 8.28). Suddenly a new Position track will appear in the tracks column and a blank sequence will appear in the sequence area. Now all we need to do is add keyframes to this sequence.

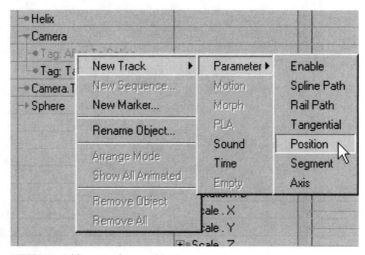

FIGURE 8.28   Adding a track to an object or expression.

To add keyframes to a sequence, CTRL-click on the sequence at the time you wish to add the keyframe. In this case, do so at frame 0. When you do this, a new keyframe will appear and the attributes of that keyframe will appear in the Attributes Editor. Take a look there and make sure that you indeed have the keyframe at Time=0 and that the Value=0%. To have motion, we of course need two keyframes, so we need to add the second. Do so at frame 200 by CTRL-clicking on that frame. As soon as the keyframe is created, change its Value to 100 in the Attributes Editor. This tells the camera to be at 0% along the spline at frame 0 and move along the spline to the end (100%) at frame 200.

Play your animation and you'll see that the camera moves along the spline over the 200 frames of the animation. Now here's where the power of this sort of animation comes in: select the helix in the Objects Manager and, in the Attributes Editor, change the attributes to be Start Radius=500m, End Radius=1500m, End Angle=360, and Height=1200m. Then, in the Coordinates Manager, change the position

Y=1250. As you change the attributes and position of the helix, the animation of the camera is automatically updated. Play the animation and see for yourself.

Now, for an extra touch, make sure that Tag: Align to Spline is selected in the Timeline and open the F-Curve Manager. Scale out and pan around until you can see the gray line that is the F-Curve for the Position track. Marquee around both of the keyframes, then right-click on one and select Custom Tangent>Soft Interpolation to get control over the tangent handles for these keyframes. Then, again, right-click on one of the keyframes and select Custom Tangent>Flat. This will flatten out the tangents, meaning that the motion along the spline will slowly get up to speed and then gently slide into place at the end (Figure 8.29).

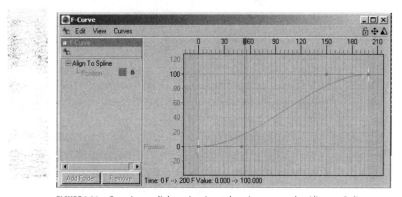

FIGURE 8.29   Creating a slick easing in and easing out to the Align to Spline.

So when you're happy with it all, add some lights to the scene and any other textures you might feel it needs. A good idea before rendering the animation is to create another preview to see if the timing is really what you want.

When you are sure the timing is right and you have the scene set up the way you want, you can prepare for rendering. To do this, open up the Render Settings either from its button in the top palette or from Render>Render Settings or with its keyboard shortcut CTRL-B. There are two areas here that need special attention. The first is the Output area. Within the Output area, you can determine how large you are going to render the project (320x240 is usually a good size for first round renderings). Also, in the Frame area, you can determine how many frames are going to be rendered. The default is the Current Frame, but when we are doing animations, we need more frames to be rendered—all of them, to be exact. So change the setting to All Frames. This will automatically update the input fields to the right to read 0 to 200 (Figure 8.30). Note that you can also manually adjust these settings to only be a small section of a large project if you wish.

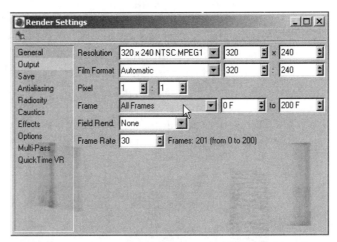

FIGURE 8.30 Setting up animation renderings must include a visit to the Output section of the Render Settings.

Next, go to the Save section. When you are rendering out an animation, C4D is rendering a sequence of stills that it can put together into a movie file. Because of this, you *must* give C4D a place to save these stills before it can put them all together into a movie. Making sure that you have Save Image checked, click on Path and give C4D a location to save the file to. The Format area allows you to decide how the renderings are to be saved. You can of course render them as a sequence of tiffs, but then you have to assemble the tiffs in a video editing package. Usually it is easiest to change this format to AVI Movie or Quicktime Movie. Then click the Options…button to define what codec you want to use. AVI Movie Big and AVI Movie Small are usually not good choices, as you surrender codec control to C4D. It's best if you decide how you want the files compressed (Figure 8.31).

Once you've got all of this set up, you can close the Render Settings window and hit the Render in Picture Viewer button in the top palette. Your Picture Viewer will open and display the frames that it is rendering (Figure 8.32). Notice that at the bottom of the Picture Viewer, there is a progress bar that shows how far along the rendering is for that frame, and what frame out of how many frames total, it is rendering.

This is a simple animation, so the rendering should be fairly speedy. But do notice that our little 200 frame animation means that C4D must render no less than 200 frames. It's easy to see how a complex animation

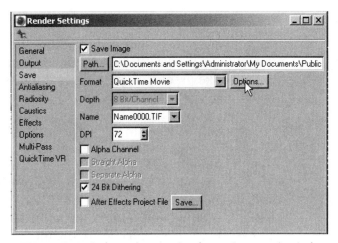

FIGURE 8.31   Preparing to render animation also requires some time in the Save section of the Render Settings.

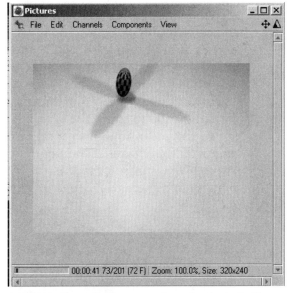

FIGURE 8.32   The rendering process of an animation in the Picture Viewer.

could end up taking a long time to get done. Because of this, its important to be sure about your motion before taking the time to render. Do
this by making previews of every clip before rendering.

CONCLUSION

So this covers the basics of animation. We have looked at most of the building blocks. We've analyzed how motion occurs, how C4D organizes keyframes, sequences, and tracks. We've even looked at animating expressions and how to take control of F-Curves to refine motion.

There is much still to be explored. The list of animatable characteristics is immense. You can animate almost anything, from the color of a light, to its intensity, to the material it is illuminating, to that material's bump height, to the shape of the object the material is applied to. So we have just scratched the surface. However, if you understand the core ideas of how animation works and how C4D allows you to get in and control the motion, you can work through any of the myriad of animation options.

In future chapters, we will look more at some of the more specialized animation capabilities. One of these is MOCCA. Naam has written an excellent chapter (Chapter 9) getting you up to speed on character animation. Still further on, we will learn more about how to get your files ready to render and the many things that you can do to get your animation-rendering style to be just as you want it. Finally, we'll look at Donovan Keith's chapter on Xpresso (Chapter 12) and how to use expressions to control motion within your scene. So there's much more animation and animation-related information still to come.

In the meantime, play with really giving this ball the kind of character that makes the animation interesting. Animate the lighting to give visual spice to the scene, and look at other ways to animate your camera to give extra drama to the shot. Experiment a lot and have fun.

CHARACTER ANIMATION IN CINEMA 4D AND MOCCA

by Naam

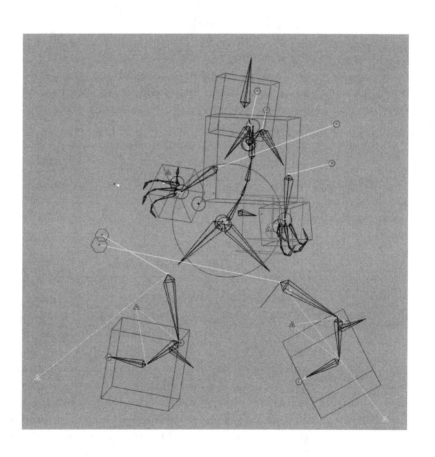

Character animation is, for a lot of people, the main reason for getting into 3D animation in the first place. The ability to actually make stories featuring impossible creatures and characters in dreamed-up settings—limited only by your own imagination—and then being able to present them in a smooth and maybe even photorealistic manner is a huge draw. It's a shame, then, that character animation is also one of the most intense and involved ways to use general-purpose 3D animation software. There is just an intrinsic difficulty in the way we perceive people in motion. The structure of bodies, the way they move, and the amount of subtle details we expect to see in a person in motion are astounding. Nevertheless, the results, if done right, can be just as astounding. Suddenly, that heap of textured polygons comes alive, and seems to really have a mind of its own!

Of course, this "coming alive" of a character is a joint effort of the modeling, setup, and animation parts of the process. A lack of effort in one part can have an adverse effect on both of the other parts. An inefficiently modeled or poorly designed character can't be set up properly, and bad animation can ruin the believability of an incredible character. The animation setup, however, tends to be the most technical step in the process, and maybe because of that, it's the step that people tend to have the most problems with. Make no mistake, however; setup is an art form in and of itself, taxing your creativity just as much as modeling and animation do. But there's so much involved in a good setup—and so many techniques that can be used—that people can be at a loss as to how to even begin setting up a character.

Because of this, we will mostly be focusing on the setup of characters in this and the next chapter. We hope to provide a solid workflow through the whole process, offering tricks and techniques to follow that can prevent mistakes from popping up and that will generally result in a flexible setup in the end. Of course, there are many ways to achieve an ideal setup, but as there is so much involved, it's really better to choose one way to work and highlight all the individual steps, than it is to browse through all the different ways in which you can approach the problem. We will also be concentrating on full body motion, with just a tad of facial control with the hope that you will be able to translate the workflow into a full facial method, as the techniques involved are much the same.

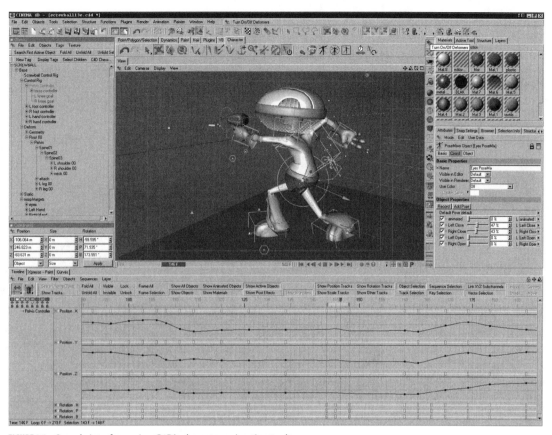

FIGURE 9.1   Sample interface using C4D's character animation tools.

CINEMA 4D

In the past, Cinema 4D wasn't really geared toward character animation. Sure, it was possible to use it for character animation, but it wasn't easy to do so because the program didn't offer a reliable workflow for the process. This changed with R8. Not only are there now quite a few character animation-specific tools on offer, but the general workflow of the program, the way you animate, the mere fact that you can animate anything, and the added muscle of Xpresso, all add up to a much more pleasurable and powerful experience when applying the program to character animation.

However, Cinema 4D remains a general purpose animation program, and as such, there still are quite a number of actions to go through before your character is ready to be animated. There are advantages to this, of course. For one thing, there really is nothing stopping you from designing the most ludicrous characters imaginable instead of, for example, being limited to a rig with two arms and two legs, however flexible this rig is. So, prepare for quite a workload if you want to take the process seriously.

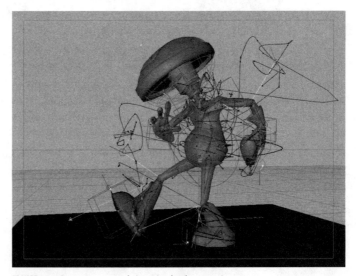

FIGURE 9.2 So many controls in a single character!

THE THINGS THAT MAKE OR BREAK A SETUP

You can say what you want about character animation, the structure you need for a human or animal character to move convincingly is intricate. There are just so many parts that should move in a semi-realistic character that it can easily seem to be too much to handle. Consider that even a three-fingered hand needs at least 15 bones! The trick with creating a good setup is, actually, the interface between you and the rig—not Cinema 4D's interface, but the interface you are creating yourself. This interface consists of the way you select and control the objects, the way these objects steer the character, and the way you create and change the animations.

First, we'll run by the various tools available, and examine their use (or non-use) for setting up and animating a character and its interface. Next, we'll make a fly-by of the complete workflow—from modeling to animation—and point out some general as well as Cinema 4D-specific rules of thumb that should help us get that ideal animatable character in shape. In Chapter 10, we'll put this knowledge to use by actually applying it to a specific character, and we'll describe the whole process step by step.

CORE CONCEPTS

But before we start out with the tools, let's just quickly discuss just a few basic topics that you need to be aware of.

IK vs FK

This is a age-old debate and really a matter of personal preference: should you animate via Forward Kinematics (FK) or Inverse Kinematics (IK)? The difference between the two is apparent. With FK, you are directly controlling the elements of the articulated structure yourself. With IK, however, you're guiding the way the structure should be posed by offering moving "targets" or "goals" for the structure to reach. As such, with IK you give away a decent amount of direct control to the computer, but gain the advantage of being able to precisely point out where, for example, a hand or foot should be placed. With FK, on the other hand, you'll have a hard time moving a hand to a specific place in the world, but you gain the advantage of animating the structure just how it would behave in real life. You have complete and utter control with FK as well, and, generally, motions will seem to be intrinsically natural.

This is really a matter of suiting the system to fit your needs. You can make the distinction to only apply IK when you need to be able to have the character "touch" the environment realistically, but there are people that, even in that case, still prefer to use FK. So it's up to you. We'll be providing a setup walkthrough in Chapter 10 that leads to a system that is mainly driven by IK in the end. However, well before halfway through this setup, you will already have created a character that can be animated by FK! So another advantage of FK is speed. If you just need a simple character to do something simple, quickly, there is really no need to provide it with a full setup.

HPB

Let's start out by stressing the importance of the HPB system for defining rotations. Since animating characters (especially when using FK) is all about rotating individual bones inside an articulated structure, it's good to have an eye for how this is happening internally (Figure 9.3).

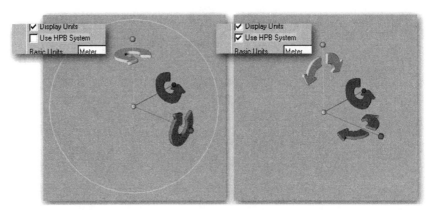

FIGURE 9.3 The difference in handling the Quaternion and HPB rotation axes.

Cinema 4D, like many 3D applications, is using three axes of rotation: Heading, Pitch and Bank. Even though you can animate these rotations by using the very intuitive Quaternion system (in other words, the yellow rotation circle in the viewer window) Cinema 4D records the rotations using HPB. This sometimes leads to woefully unexpected interpolation of rotations when playing back the animation, as the conversion from Quaternion to HPB isn't as straightforward as you might imagine. There's several ways a HPB system can rotate to lead to the same orientation of an object. To prevent these awkward interpolations from happening, you may want to animate using the HPB system, which gives you direct control over just the angles Cinema 4D uses internally. You should at least try it every once in a while—by turning on the option in the Units page of the General Preferences—especially if you have trouble with a certain recorded rotational movement. This will give you a feel for how HPB is dealing with your rotations. It's perfectly possible to animate using Quaternion, but it is a very good thing to at least know how the rotations work internally, especially when it comes to character animation.

THE TOOLS

Let's start out with the rundown of the tools on offer in Cinema 4D and the MOCCA module that concern character animation. A full explanation of how to use all the tools will not be provided, as that is already covered in the Cinema 4D and MOCCA manuals. Rather, we'll look at some of the strengths and weaknesses of the tools as far as full-blown character animation is concerned. Let's start by just highlighting some useful aspects of very common tools, as they have a big impact on the creation of a character interface.

Nulls and Splines

Most of the time, at least when working with IK or soft IK, you are bound to end up working with a lot of Null objects as controllers. Luckily, Nulls can have a shape, so they are both easily visible and easily selectable in the editor. A downside of these shapes is that they will always rotate around the center of the object. For feet controllers, for example, this may not be desirable. In these cases, you'll want a controller roughly the shape of the character's foot, which will rotate around the ball of the foot (or heel). To provide this, it pays to model a simple linear spline into a cube-like shape, and use that instead of a cube-shaped Null object. You could model a simple polygon cube as well, of course, but the beauty of splines is that they won't render or deform, and are still easily selectable (Figure 9.4).

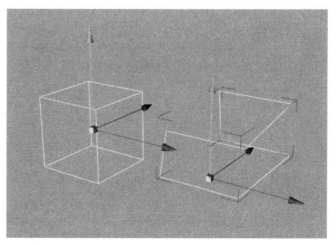

FIGURE 9.4   Spline controllers can be used if you need an arbitrary axis of rotation.

Selection Objects

Selecting objects in the Objects Manager can be a real drag, especially since, when creating an intricate character setup, the objects that you actually need to control the character can be all over the place. This is where Selection objects come in. These specialist objects add a lot of power to editor behavior. With the correct Selection object active, you can make sure that only the controller objects you need at that time will be selectable and recordable, greatly enhancing the power of the viewer window. With a good setup, editor display, and smart use of Selection objects, you don't really need the Objects Manager at all.

Configurable Timeline and Curve Manager

The Timeline has also been greatly enhanced in R8. Not only does it allow you to edit curves right in the Timeline itself and navigate easily by the means of the "1" and "2" hotkeys, but the way several types of workflow are now embedded ensures that it can be made to behave just as you need. You can either choose one of the automated behaviors (such as Show All, Show Animated, Show Active Object) or you can "lock" the Timeline, and load it up with just the objects you need for your animation.

The way you use the Timeline is absolutely up to you. For example, you can use Active Object mode (just showing the selected object in the Timeline). This allows the Timeline to be kept small and at the far bottom of the screen; all you need to do is check where the keyframes of the selected object(s) are and do any object selection in the editor window with the use of Selection objects. Some users may prefer to set up the Timeline with just the objects to be animated and do object selection in the Timeline's treeview. Once set up, you can also switch between any of the automatic modes and the setup mode without problems. A typical setup might, for example, have certain unselectable objects loaded in the custom Timeline, such as PoseMix objects for morphing and posing, while using the Active Object mode when animating the editor-selectable objects.

Much the same goes for the F-Curves Manager, which can either be set up manually or be left to automatically display the curves of the selected object. Some people will actually want to work with the F-Curves window exclusively. You don't have the handy top-down rows of objects and keyframes here, but the rest of the keyframe-editing behaviors that you can do in the Timeline can be done in the F-Curves Manager as well.

Display/Selection Filters

The Display and Selection filters add another layer of customization for your animation needs. Once you have a character fully boned and rigged, you may want to lose the bones being displayed scene-wide. For this you can use the Display filter. And if you drive your character with Null and Spline objects only and don't want to meddle with Selection objects, simply turn off the selection for anything other that Nulls and Splines in the Selection filter, and off you go!

IK

Although you have, with MOCCA, the far superior Soft IK system, that doesn't mean you should use that all the time. The old fashioned IK is very limited, but it still comes in handy for small, simple chains, and it calculates a lot quicker than Soft IK. It also comes, however, with quite a few handicaps, and you should adopt a certain workflow to make it work at all. We'll be having a closer look at the needed use in Chapter 10.

THE MOCCA TOOLSET

Next, let's look at the various tools available with the MOCCA module. Athough all of these tools are meant to empower your animation workflow, and most were specifically designed with character animation in mind, not all of them will be as useful as you might imagine when you are aiming for fully controllable rigs and characters.

Timewarp

Timewarp (Figure 9.5) is a small but very nice extra feature you get with MOCCA. It is implemented as a tool just as the Move, Rotate

FIGURE 9.5 The Timewarp tool.

and Scale tools, but you'll only discover its power once you hook it up to a hotkey. For example, you can assign it to the "`" key, which is next to the "1" key on the keyboard (the one which drives camera panning). It allows you to scrub in time by dragging in the editor. This simply means you don't need to travel to the scrubber bar or Timeline to change the current time; you can just stay in the editor, animating away. It really seems a minor addition, but once you get to know it a bit, you may find it to be indispensible.

The Bone Tool

FIGURE 9.6   The Bone Tool.

This may be a very good tool to set up your bones to start with, but once you want to make changes or add some extra features such as Null bones or Helper bones, it's better to avoid using it unless you know what you are doing. As a general rule of thumb, use the Bone tool just to make the first setup of your character, because placement of the joints is so incredibly easy with it. But once the initial setup has been made—and especially if you have already applied expressions and Soft IK—stay away from the Bone tool and use the regular Move and Rotate tools to make final adjustments.

Another downside of the Bone tool is that it has its own way of determining how the bones should be rotated around the z-axis (their banking). Most of the time, it does so neatly, but often enough you will find yourself having to change the banking of individual bones after leaving the Bone tool. And because HPB angles greatly influence motions in articulated structures, you may actually have to do just that.

Claude Bonet Tool vs Vertex Maps

FIGURE 9.7   Claude Bonet and Vertex maps.

Of course, Claude Bonet also creates Vertex maps, but it does so in a very different way to the "old" Vertex maps. So when we talk about Vertex maps, we're referring to the "old" ones.

The basics of Vertex maps themselves (e.g., how they are used by bones to decide how a mesh should be deformed) are explained in the Workflow section of this chapter. Here, we'll just concentrate on the workings of the two tools.

The main difference between Vertex maps and Claude Bonet is the interface. Both allow you to assign points (vertices) a certain "weight" in relation to a certain bone. With Vertex maps, this is a matter of making a point selection, assigning it a weight using the Set Vertex Weight command, naming the Vertex Map Tag, and using the same name in a Restriction Tag placed on a bone to tell it to use that Vertex Map for deformation. You can, conversely, use the Live Selection tool to paint the weights of the vertices more or less interactively. Claude Bonet, on the other hand, takes away the extra work of having to name maps and manually link maps to bones. This makes it much more intuitive to use. With the Claude Bonet tool active, you simply point out a bone in the Objects Manager, and paint on the mesh directly. You can hold the CTRL key to paint "negatively," in other words, subtract paint from the mesh. And there are some other useful options in the Active Tool Dialog, such as the ability to refer a bone to the Claude Bonet map of another bone, effectively making them share the same map.

So where Vertex maps force you to manually deal with the basics, Claude Bonet takes full control of the basics and lets you paint the Vertex maps in a very intuitive way. This is great, but it has some disadvantages. One of these is that there is no way for you to access the basics. For example, Claude Bonet weights aren't transferable from one object to another, whereas with Vertex maps, you can CTRL-drag the Vertex Map tags to another (identical) object, and the same points will automatically have the same weight. In short, Claude Bonet is less flexible and more character-specific, but a lot easier. Luckily, Vertex maps and Claude Bonet weights work just fine side by side. It is often advisable to use both types of weighting for different parts of your character. Vertex maps are, for example, ideal for parts that should be transferable between characters, or for bone structures that should be transferable, such as the hands.

Soft IK

FIGURE 9.8 Soft IK tools.

This has to be one of the strongest aspects of the whole MOCCA set. Basically, Soft IK is a kind of dynamics simulator especially built for rigging characters. As such, it should be used with great care, because it is easily overused. You shouldn't see this as a replacement of IK, but as an entirely different way to animate. Although it may be tempting to rig your whole character with Soft IK, there are some downsides to this. First, being a simulator, it takes quite some tweaking to get it to behave just as you need it to. In fact, you are actually allowing the computer to take over a lot of the more detailed control if you apply Soft IK. Second, it is quite CPU-intensive; an intricate Soft IK rig can really slow down the animation display in the editor. Third, some body parts are simply more easily steered manually or with an expression. For instance, it would be a waste of time to set up a hand to be steered by Soft IK.

As such, a number of the Soft IK commands soon lose some of their allure. The "Setup IK Chain" command, for instance, creates a Soft IK rig for the entire bones hierarchy, up into the tips of fingers even, adding goals to wherever a branch in the hierarchy ends. Although this is a good way to quickly get Soft IK tags and goal settings all over your rigs, you'll probably be removing half of the tags and a lot of the target objects before your rig is manageable. It may be just as easy to add Soft IK tags and target objects manually on a "need to have it" basis.

Notwithstanding these shortcomings, Soft IK is a marvelous way to interact with your character. Once it clicks with you, you'll be amazed by how easy is to do just what you want. It's much like handling a real-life puppet by attaching rubber bands to get limbs to bend this way and not that, and using springs to make limbs try to get back to their favorite positions (the so-called Rest Position and Rest Rotation (Figure 9.9)). With Soft IK, it's all about tweaking and tuning. The initial setup isn't that difficult, as it is pretty easy to figure out where you need to pull your skeleton to get the motion you want. But once you have that down, it's all about balancing the various forces acting on the rig, something that is actually quite natural to do.

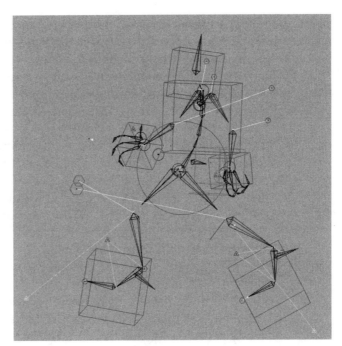

FIGURE 9.9   Soft IK controls skeletons by applying various forces onto the IK structures.

The main workhorses of the Soft IK system are the Rest and the Constraints settings. The Rest State settings allow you to provide the elements in a Soft IK chain with a preferred pose, so to speak. However hard you pull on the chain by other means, if you "let go," the chain will try to move back to its rest state. This, of course, depends on how strong you make this urge by tuning the Strength values.

The Constraints settings allow you to target other objects for positioning (Goal) or banking (UpVector). Simply put, a Goal setting is identical to the way regular IK works: the chain will try to reach that goal, bending where neccesary and allowed. The UpVector constraint will try to rotate the element around its *z* axis, only to point the +*y* axis (or the one you set here) roughly toward the targeted object. The beauty of these settings, as with the Rest settings, is how you can attenuate the force they exert on the whole chain by tuning the Strength setting. This way, you can add goals to make, for example, the knee point roughly toward a certain target, while having the foot always hit the target spot on, regardless of what the knee is doing.

Then there's the Anchor setting and its Strength setting. A Soft IK chain needs an anchor just as IK needs one. This is achieved by enabling the Anchor option in the Soft IK tag of the topmost bone in the chain. The anchored bone in the chain can still be moved around by hand (or animation). The Strength setting of this tag defines the rigidity of the whole Soft IK chain. Setting it to 100% will give you very rigid behavior of the chain—almost like direct IK, although it takes a bit more time to calculate. Setting the chain's strength to something lower, such as the default 30%, will leave more of the motion of the chain to Soft IK's dynamics and lead to more fluid behavior of the structure. This can look very nice without too much fuss, but isn't always wanted.

The Dynamics settings of the anchored tag are for the brave. You can simulate natural behavior—such as drag and gravity—with these, but again, they take control away from you. It's usually advisable to record animation first without using these settings, then turn them on afterwards to give the animation a bit of extra style. On the other hand, if you are a precise animator, you will have already provided for this with the animation itself. So in the end, the Dynamics options are mostly usable for real dynamic elements in your scene or on your character, but that isn't the focus of these chapters.

Let's just highlight some of the features that may bring you trouble.

Limits Settings

First, there are the Limits settings. Wisely, these are hidden by default. It's far easier to prevent elements from ever reaching these limits by both careful animation and decent weighting of rest states than it is to set these limits correctly and still have a manageable setup.

Then there's a setting called Force Position in the rest state part of the tag. This setting forces the elements to stay put, instead of (by default) allowing them to be pulled apart. It's not as dangerous a setting as the Limits are, but you still should use it with caution. When Force Position is set, objects further down the chain tend to be forced into rotations you may not expect, simply because they may be trying to rotate towards their targets, only to be pulled back by the Force Position option (Figure 9.10).

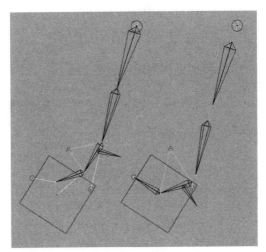

FIGURE 9.10   A Soft IK chain with Force Position turned on (left) and off (right).

Auto Redraw

FIGURE 9.11   Auto Redraw icon.

This option was built in as a necessity for Soft IK. Basically, it redraws the editor once every so-many seconds, so that the Soft IK simulation is kept "live" and effects of the various forces on the chain can be clearly seen. This should only be used when setting up and testing the rig; to use it in animation itself makes little sense, and it might even get in the way.

Bone Mirror

FIGURE 9.12   Bone Mirror Icon.

This handy tool allows you to only set up half of the rig (boning, weighting, and controlling) then copy this whole structure, including all the correct bone-weighting, Soft IK settings, and Controller objects, over to the other side. As such, it is a very handy workflow enhancer, even though you're bound to want to re-adjust the mirrored side just a bit.

Cappucino and KeyReducer

FIGURE 9.13 Cappucino icon.

Cappucino is a tool that allows you to do real-time recording of mouse movements. The main use of this is to get your timing spot on. Preferably, you won't use this on the object you want to animate itself, but use another "sketch" object (just a sphere) to "draw" out the timing of a move. Then, you use this motion-sketch to define the timing of the actual motion. You can, of course, use it directly on the objects, but that will only work in very peculiar instances, whereas as a tool for blocking out the timing of your animation, it's perfect! If you do use it directly on the object, be sure to use KeyReducer to reduce the keys, as Cappucino creates a single key per frame.

P2P

FIGURE 9.14 P2P icon.

This is an easy but limited tool. P2P stands for pose-to-pose. It allows you to build a library of poses (and, optionally, the geometrical shape) and animate between these. Although the concept of this library is great, it has one major shortcoming: you can only morph from one shape to the next. As such, it is not very useful for full-control character animation. For very simple animations, or for small parts of your character such as the hands, it may come in useful, especially as it is so easy to manage. It all really depends on the motion you are aiming for. If the main action of your character is full body motion, and you just need to have a few basic poses for the hands, it may be useful to do this via P2P. But as soon as you need a little extra control (for instance, you want to move the index finger in between poses) you are better off using another tool, such as the PoseMixer discussed below.

PoseMixer

FIGURE 9.15   PoseMixer icon.

The name may be misleading, as PoseMixer is actually a powerful morph tool that takes poses into account as well. This is one of the strongest of Cinema 4D's morphing tools (point-level animation or PLA, P2P, MoMix, and the old Morph Track) as it offers full control over the strength of each target and can actually do almost all the things that the other tools are, one-by-one, limited to.

However, there is a drawback that you'll need to live with: PoseMixer has to target actual existing structures in the scene. So if you want to use PoseMixer to morph a character's face between two shapes, you need at least three instances of the face present in your scene.

The first is the face that will be rendered, the "live" face, the one you will be changing with the PoseMixer object. The second is a (probably) hidden copy of the face that defines the face's "base" state, called "Default Pose" in PoseMixer. It needs this copy to figure out how much the target faces differ from the live face. It doesn't really matter what state this face is in (it could be, for example, its "angry" expression) as long as it is different from all your targets. But since this is the expression you will get when you set all sliders to zero, a neutral expression will be the most logical to use.

The third face PoseMixer will need in this example is the target face itself—a shape of the face you want to morph to. You can add as many target faces as you need, and interactively mix between those.

Another drawback of PoseMixer is that once you give control over a structure to PoseMixer, you can't directly control that structure yourself anymore. Luckily, you can work around this by controlling one of the targets of the PoseMixer object. Say you want to use a certain result of PoseMixer on a face, but need the brows to be just a tad higher, and don't have a target that does so. In that case, you can animate the brows of one of the targets to get that result. So actually the first mentioned drawback of needing existent targets in the scene can be turned into a huge benefit. Even better, PoseMixer can be "nested" inside itself so you can use one PoseMixer structure to morph from a second PoseMixer structure to a third.

MoMix

FIGURE 9.16 MoMix icon.

This is another pose-mixing tool, but with animated targets. The MoMix object allows you to mix between animated structures. So when you have animated a character walking and the same character running, you can mix between those animations via the MoMix object to create specialized sequences. The drawback is that, just as with PoseMix, to mix between two animations (say a walk and a run) you're going to need four instances of the character in your scene file: the actually animated (live) structure, an unanimated reference structure, a walking structure, and a running structure. So if the structure hangs together from expressions, having it evaluated three times per frame is going to tax the processor quite severely.

That said, MoMix has some powerful features that allow you to make long, basic animations with ease. It works by creating "actor" sequences to the object's two (or more) motion tracks. Each sequence can point to another animated structure by selecting the sequence in the Timeline and dragging the so-called Actor (the animated structure) from the Objects Manager into the Actor field of the Attributes Manager. The length of this sequence then defines how the motion will be time-stretched. So, if you have a walk that lasts a second and use an actor sequence of two seconds, the walk will be performed twice as slow. In line with this behavior, the loop settings of the actor sequence define how the original motion is looped. So if you need two steps of the same walk, just set the sequence to (soft) loop two times. Also, when sequences are placed overlapping each other on the two Motion Tracks, there will be an automatic transition between the two. Suffice to say, MoMix was mainly designed to work with baked or Motion Captured Actors. You can use it with fully rigged characters, but it will have a hard time updating in realtime. Most of the time, you'll be able to safely remove any expressions from the actors; as long as you take care they stay present and active on the live rig.

Workflow

Building, setting up, and animating a character can be divided into a few discrete steps. Of course, some of these steps have overlap and the general order can be mixed up a bit. You can, for example, choose to do any morph-target modeling after you have set up the rig completely, create a control rig before actually having created the skeleton, or create Vertex maps in the modeling phase. Nevertheless, the steps themselves remain discrete, and generally speaking, following them up one after the other creates a very efficient workflow. Also, it's a convenient way to explain, in order, all the intricacies of setting up a character.

In short, your workflow will consist of the following: design, modeling, texturing, boning, weighting, adding control, streamlining, and finally, animating. Texturing we can skip all together, as there is nothing here (other than making textures stick to a deforming surface) that is character animation-specific. The design step is completely up to you as well. Granted, there are a lot of things to keep in mind when designing a character, but these are all elements of the other steps. Once you know the limits and possibilities of Cinema 4D in each of these steps, you can easily embed these into the actual design of the character. There is really very little that you *can't* do, once you put your mind to it.

So, let's look at some aspects of design.

Modeling

Of course, modeling isn't the focus of this chapter, but there are some things to keep in mind when modeling a character for animation, so let's point some of these out.

Pose

It is common practice, when modeling a character for animation, to model it in a pose that would have the least amount of stretch to the skin. Arms pointing straight out to the sides, hands with the palms facing down, legs stretched and a bit spread, even a resting shape of the mouth. One reason for this is that it will be much easier to weight the vertexes for the simple reason that you will be able to reach them all. Another reason is that, by putting the joints in a position of little "tension" to the virtual skin, you'll have a much easier time getting the joints to bend smoothly and realistically.

In case of IK, it's best to model the character with slightly bent elbows and knees. It's easier to get (Soft) IK to point a joint in only one direction if it is already slightly bent like that, than it is to have it start out perfectly straight. This is not of too much concern, as you can always bone, weight, and activate the deformation in a joints-stretched pose and bend them before applying (Soft) IK. It's just that, if you do it like that, you're going to have a hard time if you need to get the skeleton back to its initial position.

Structure

From the early beginning of the character design, keep in mind what structure you are giving the character. Most often, you will want to base your model on HyperNURBS. The advantage of HyperNURBS is that you can deform the "cage" object, and have the resulting HyperNURBS be perfectly smoothed *after* the deformation. This looks a lot better than deforming the final (i.e., already smoothed) geometry. The thing is that, for this to be possible, the whole character's structure and skeleton needs to be inside a HyperNURBS object. This means that it's good practice to model each element of the character as a HyperNURBS element, or in other words, as a low-resolution Polygon object. This has further advantages when you think of weighting, as Polygon objects are the only type of objects that can be weighted effectively. Primitive objects don't let you access their vertexes for weighting, and neither do the various NURBS types. This is not to say that you should never use Primitives or NURBS objects, but you should use them with caution, and probably just for rigid parts of the character or clothing. Luckily, almost any shape can be made with a HyperNURBS, so you may want to convert some of the other type of objects you use to low-resolution Polygon objects, so that they will still look good (and deform well) inside the HyperNURBS structure.

If you want to use other types of geometry for detail on your character, and keep the object type intact, put some thought into how they should move with the character. For instance, it's perfectly okay to use a Sweep Nurbs as a shoelace, or a Lathe Nurbs for an eyeball, as they are easily animatable with point-level-animation on the source splines. But chances are that you'll want to keep this out of the bone's influence, and stick it onto the foot or into the skull by means of an expression.

Point Density

When modeling your Polygon cage, keep in mind at all times how the part of the character's body you are dealing with is going to be deformed. Joint areas should have enough geometry to have them deform smoothly, but other, largely undeformed, parts (like the lower leg or upper arm) can do with much less actual geometry. A good rule of thumb is to have at *least* three cross-sections for a joint: one for the parent bone, one for the child bone, and one to move smoothly in between (Figure 9.17).

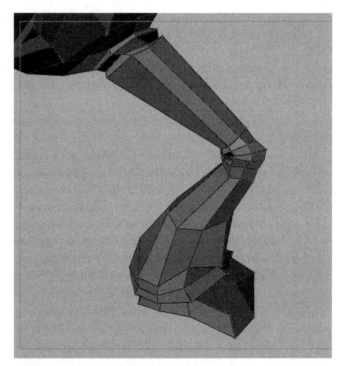

FIGURE 9.17   A mesh needs higher point density in the areas where it will be deforming the most.

Also, with one-way-only joints such as the knee and elbow, it is good practice to have a higher density of vertexes on the outside (e.g., the elbow or kneecap itself) and lesser density on the inside of the joint. That way, you will both provide enough geometry for really stretching the outside but not enough geometry to harm the inside of the bending area.

Symmetry

Symmetric modeling is a very powerful way to model—effectively, twice as fast. Keep in mind, though, that when you're animating, you may want to turn off generators for speedier editor feedback. The Symmetry object being a generator, this means that you'll only be seeing half your character in the view panel. So for the animation part of things, it's best to convert the Symmetry object to a full polygon cage. It's best to do this as late in the process as you possibly can, as keeping Symmetry active will mean that painting weightmaps will be twice as fast as well. However, for areas that you are going to morph—such as the face—keep in mind that it's dangerous to model morph targets in Symmetry and convert them to non-Symmetry objects later on. You may be messing up the point order of these objects (although this is not a given), resulting in an undesirable polygon explosion later down the line.

Boning

Boning, contrary to popular belief, is the process of putting Bone deformers into the shape of your character so that the character's mesh will actually deform with them. A complete hierarchy of a character's bones is also called a skeleton. Boning may be the easiest step in the whole process. After all, it's involves just putting bones in the proper places, and once you know the proper places, this rigging phase will be over quickly. In Chapter 10, we'll be looking at where those proper places are, but for now, here are a few bone-specific items.

Placement

Just a short word to debunk a popular belief: bones do not have to touch each other. You can safely pull bones away from the tip of their parent, and still have good deformation. This also means that you don't have to provide some bones, such as those leading from the pelvis to the hip, as the pelvis and hips will move in unison anyway.

Structure

Bones, just as other deformers, need a certain structure to work correctly. In short, they will deform any geometry they find in the parent of the first bone *and* in all of its children. So you can either group the bones together with your geometry on the same level of the hierarchy, or simply link them to the mesh directly. However, it also means that any geometry you link to the bones will be deformed as well. This is not a good idea as the mesh object will be both translated *and* deformed by the skeleton, leading to very unpleasant results.

There are a few ways around this shortcoming, however, if you need something to move with the bone rather than deform. You can always, by means of an Xpression, keep said object at the proper place, while keeping it well away from the deforming hierarchy. You can also make sure it's weighted so that none of the bones will actually influence it (Figure 9.18).

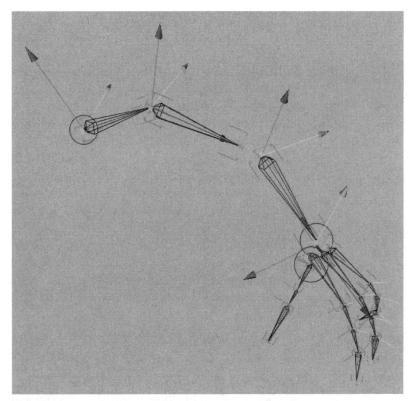

FIGURE 9.18 Carefully aligning bones in the same limb similarly keeps you out of trouble. Note that the hand has another alignment, which is consistent throughout all the finger bones.

Another thing to keep in mind when creating your skeleton is the rotation of your bones. If you are going to use FK or IK, the way the *x*- and *y*-axis are aligned will greatly influence the behavior of their rotation, and if you're going to use Soft IK, their alignment will depend on where you're wanting to apply and place UpVector Constraints. So, as a general rule we might simply say you'd better try to keep axes nicely aligned. For example, if you decide you want the *y*-axis of the lower arm to point straight to the back, try to get the *y*-axis of the upper arm and shoulder pointing the same way. This way you can either use the same UpVector Goal object with Soft IK, or have them bend in the exact same way when grabbing the same axes using FK. Preventing 90-degree angles in banking will simply make your rig more predictable. It also prevents gimbal lock. For areas such as the shoulder and legs, where you are dealing with 90- and 180-degree angles, use Null bones to "zero out" the rotations of the bones you will actually be animating.

Null Bones

New to Cinema 4D R8 is an option to turn bones into so-called Null bones. By enabling the checkbox in the bone's settings labeled Null, you are simply telling the bone not to have influence on the deformation, but still pass the deformation of its child objects onto the mesh. Were you to use any other object, such as a regular Null object, you'd have split up the bone chain, leading to the child objects to the Null having no influence over the mesh anymore.

So what are these Null bones good for? Well, actually, it's not unusual to need an extra set of axes between a bone and its parent. Be it to zero out the rotation, to prevent gimbal lock, or simply because you need a dedicated Anchor object for your IK structure, they come in pretty handy. However, note that the Bone Tool doesn't really like Null bones too much. It can add them and update them, and this is all fine, but it is good practice to only add the Null bones as the very latest step, when you're sure about their placement, because it's pretty hard to select and adjust them once they're there.

Function

There's a setting on each bone called "Function" that defines how the bone will actually deform the points. The higher you set this variable, the more rigid the mesh will appear: bends will be more concentrated in the actual joint area instead of along the length of a bone. It basically measures the distance from the bone to a point, and uses the function to diminish its influence to provide for smoothly bending deformations.

For characters, you will most probably want to use a Function of around 1/r^6. Keep in mind, though, that the Function for the whole skeleton is defined by the root bone's setting! So the topmost bone in the hierarchy (unless this is a Null bone) will define how the whole mesh will deform.

Helper Bones

Also known as Shaper bones, these aren't a specialized feature, just a handy trick. Sometimes you will discover that, even though you have properly weighted your mesh, not all of the mesh is moving along with the bones you assigned it to. This is where the previously mentioned Function setting comes in to ruin your day. Because it defines a relationship between the distance from the point to the bone and the strength of the bone's influence, you will run into trouble when you need to use a small bone for quite a good volume of mesh. When even turning the bone's strength way up doesn't help, you need a Helper bone. Simply add a single bone as a child of the said bone, make sure it refers to the same Vertex Map (be it via Claude Bonet or Vertex maps) and try again. By filling up the shape of the bit of mesh with a Helper bone or two, you'll see it will all come along just fine.

Weighting

Weighting is a somewhat misunderstood feature in Cinema 4D. Many users seem to think that they need to use it to define which points should go with which bone. It's actually completely the other way around: you use it to *exclude the other points* from being influenced!

Why this distinction? Well, consider once more the Function setting; this was what defined how much a point would be translated by a certain bone, providing smooth deformation all over the mesh. Even when, as a ludicrous example, you weight a vertex in the foot to a bone in the nostril, it would not come along because the bone is much too small and the distance much too great.

It is perfectly all right to use the same Vertex map for both hands, or fingers, or even legs, at the same time. The bones will be so far apart that the other bones completely take over. This makes for quite a time gain in weighting! You can weight the character with the mesh still being in symmetry phase, and simply point both sides of the skeleton to the same Vertex maps. Actually, in many cases, it's okay to, for example, use one single Vertex map for both upper and lower legs, and possibly even the feet. This all depends on the mesh and the placement of the bones, but it's a good thing to keep in mind as it can save a lot of time.

Control

Creating a way to control the skeleton can be an artform in itself. There's no real limit to how much you can automate in a rig. The most basic way of control is, of course, to simply grab the bones and control them by hand, one by one. Needless to say, this isn't the ideal way to animate. So you add IK to control the legs and have them firmly planted on the floor, and prevent them from going through it, possibly by making the toe roll automatically when the foot rotates. Then you go on doing much the same for the arms and spine, add automatic counter-rotation for the head, and finish off with keeping the pelvis centered over the legs at all time.

Well, of course, you could do all that, but you would actually be putting control over the character into the hands of the computer. The real art in controlling the character is in providing as much control as you can via as few controllers as possible. It's really best to stay with the basics at first, taking care that you have a good system for actually being able to simply move the foot around without having to mind the leg too much, before you start worrying about floor collision and toe roll. Handy as these automated behaviors are, it's really not that difficult to simply never move the foot beyond the floorplane by hand. So the focus on control in these chapters will be mainly on using (Soft) IK, Xpresso and PoseMixer to allow for flexible animation capabilities.

There is really little to tell about control without actually having something to apply it to, hence we'll keep it short here, and fully explain the basics and some advanced uses in Chapter 10.

Streamlining

Streamlining can also be thought of as part of control, but I've separated it, as it is the final step in the controlling stage. This step is all about structuring the character and scene in such a way that you can reach all of the controls with a minimum of fuss. This may sound as though it would only be of interest for larger productions (where scenes have to be handed from person to person) and have little impact on small personal projects. But when it comes to animating, there's already a lot you have to keep an eye on. Having to scour through the Object Manager to find the object you were supposed to animate simply stands in the way of creating a nice performance with your character.

This step, as does the control step, has a lot to do with your personal preference for workflow. Nevertheless, in Chapter 10, we'll be outlining some handy tricks and ideas about how you might go about it, such as trying to do away with the Objects Manager for controller selection.

Animation

Now let's discuss what animation is really is all about: the actual performance of the character. There is so much to tell about this that it would be unthinkable to try to describe it with a few lines in this and the next chapter. Technically, it isn't much different from animating other objects in Cinema 4D, as you're simply moving objects around and creating keyframes for them. But there are some general principles to keep in mind, as well as some Cinema 4D-specific ones that apply to the movement of characters as living entities. For all the ins and outs, there're plenty of character animation books around that can teach you those. In here, we'll just try to keep it short by summing up a few of the most basic ones.

The Fourth Dimension

As a general, all-encompassing rule, remember you are animating motion. You're not making pictures in motion, you're modeling the motion itself. In effect, you are modeling the fourth dimension. And this fourth dimension has its own lines, shapes, and texture. Just as interesting shapes in three dimensions can have a certain succession of rhythms, so does shape in the fourth. Slow, large, wide movements can flow into sudden jumps and stops. For example, a staccato run cycle can be followed by a long, low, stretched slide as the character comes to a stop. In short, the interesting part of any performance is the rhythm and timing.

Timing

The importance of timing is reflected in so many areas of the process that you actually can't lose sight of it. Timing defines mass and weight, thought, mood, dynamics, and the overall readability of the performance.

Of utmost essence is to make sure you are showing one thing at a time. If you show the character with several limbs doing several different things at the same time, the public will have a hard time deciding on which detail to focus. Make sure that the pose and motion of the whole character is focused on one action. Of course, there'll always be overlap in a sequence of motions and cases where two things have to take place at the same time, but each event should use at least a long enough bit of time for the audience to be able to "read" it properly before you offer them another event for their consideration.

Weight, Mass, and Dynamics

Remember, at all times, that your character has a certain weight. Even if he's floating in zero gravity, his body and limbs have a certain mass and this is influencing the way they move around. You should consider the whole character at one time. If a person sticks out his hand, for example, the rest of his body will have to compensate for the shift in the center of gravity this action creates. This can be very subtle, but it is an essential technique in creating a believable performance.

In locomotion, weight is the most obvious aspect. You can immediately see if a character seems "floaty" or stuck to earth. In a walk, you should take care that the back leg really seems to push the body off the ground and forward and that it catches itself with the forward leg, even though both feet can be on the ground at the same time. But also the mass of the character in locomotion should be taken care of. Making him come to a sudden stop, for example, will mean that he'll have to battle against the inertia of his body to keep from toppling over. But also in a stance, make sure that the pose of the character reflects the way the character is actually keeping himself upright.

Also, as a direct result of the fact that each part of the character has a certain mass, take dynamics into account, both on a large and small scale. If the character is on a platform that starts moving, he'll have to shift weight to compensate for the acceleration. If he is hit in the side and pushed over, his arms and legs will tend to stay behind. If he's coming to a sudden stop, smaller parts of the character will tend to overshoot.

Anticipation and Overshoot

Anticipation must be the most basic effect in the motion of living entities. In short, it's the effect of introducing a motion by making a character prepare for it. It's the crouch before a high jump, the backswing before a good kick. Or, to take a popular example, it's a character that leans in one direction, lifts one leg up and bends the arms, prior to actually running offscreen in the opposite direction. It's a very natural principle; for most motions you simply need some momentum and this momentum is created by an extra "swing" in the other direction.

The effect of using this in animation is so amazing that you sometimes actually don't need the motion itself anymore. In the running offscreen example, the run itself doesn't have to be any more than a little puff of dust floating where the character just was. Without the anticipation, though, you'll have a hard time figuring out which way the character went or if he maybe just disappeared from this world altogether.

As a general rule, the longer the anticipation is, the shorter the action itself can be because the audience will have had more time to be prepared for what is to follow.

At the other end of the spectrum is overshoot. Basically, it's another natural dynamic effect, this time at the end of an action. It can be used to explain to the audience what just happened exactly. In contrast to the run offscreen example above, consider the way Roadrunner always tends to enter the frame. From one moment to the next, he's simply there, waggling from overshoot.

Both anticipation and overshoot should be considered for each and every motion. However subtle or short, they help make the motion more convincing.

Arcs

A big danger that results from using IK or Soft IK to drive a character's rig is that you can lose sight of how limbs are actually supposed to move. You want the hand there, so you simply place the hand's

Goal there. But with moving characters, always consider the way the limb is built up of rotating bones. The result of this is that the various joints naturally move in arcs. You're able to move your hand in a straight line in real life, but only if you specifically decide to do so. It's simply not natural. If you drive (a part of) your skeleton with FK, this is less important, as arcs are an automatic result of the fact that you rotate bones one by one. But with IK, always try to arc your Goal objects' animation paths in a logical way.

Apart from it being more natural to arc the motions, it is actually visually more pleasing as well! Consider that in dance, everything you see is arcs in motion, so if you're aiming for impressive motion, try creating impressive arcs for the limbs to follow.

Thought and Reason

No matter what kind of character you are animating, even if it is an insect or robot, you should allow it to make up its mind. With characters, there is almost always some extra step involved in the usual chain of cause and effect, and that is the step of realization. Before a character reacts to a certain event, it'll need some time, however short, to decide to react, and to work out how to react. This isn't really an effect that you can point out or describe, but it is something to keep in mind at all times. It'll make the character really be there, alive and sentient in the scene. The audience needs to receive this hint of thought to be able to consider the character as an actual presence.

One step further, and you come to reason. When attempting a somewhat more involved performance, when you get closer to acting than to stunts, you need to know, even if just for yourself, why the character decides to act the way he does. Again, this is no exact science, and maybe it's just a way to get your creativity going, but if you know more about the background of a character, his inner workings, and the way he faces the world, it will shine through in the final performance, even if you can't really put your finger on what it is exactly.

TECHNICAL ASPECTS OF C4D IN CHARACTER ANIMATION

Those are the basics of the philosophy of animation itself. What about the more technical aspects, specifically when it comes to Cinema 4D?

Editor Speed

Because timing is everything, take every step necessary to get decent playback speed in the editor. Most of the time, this will involve disabling Generators, either globally or locally. But also keep the other options in mind: backface culling, hiding all but the character itself, or animating the character in a dedicated character-only scene, changing display modes, etc. Basically, any calculation you don't really need is best done without. It's perfectly normal to do some timing-sensitive motions by disabling deformers globally and switching on Box display so you can work with the bones only. It takes some getting used to, and can't be used for more detailed, geometry-sensitive motions, but for getting down the first timing of a shot, is it invaluable.

Editor Preview vs External Preview

Even if the editor preview speed within Cinema 4D seems smooth and fast, do not underestimate the power of an external preview. This means rendering the animation out, as editor, to a movie file. The "Make Preview" function is really a lifesaver here, especially when you start meddling with the somewhat more intricate and unresponsive characters. When watching a movie file externally, you can be sure that the timing is exact, down to the single frame, and as it is (probably) a rendered-out animation you are aiming for, it is good to check the animation with a preview before detailing motions. This is especially true when using Soft IK. Not only can Soft IK make the editor display a lot slower, the actual motion of the Soft IK skeleton depends on how many frames per second it is recalculating. You will notice that some elements of a Soft IK skeleton may seem to stay behind too much, but when rendering at full FPS, they move perfectly in unison. You need to develop an eye for effects such as these, and learn what motions in the editor to watch and what to ignore. Finally, make an occasional all-features-enabled preview render, as there is a lot that will only show up when everything is active.

Animation Process

As mentioned before, timing is everything in animation, so it's best to devise a workflow to first get the timing spot on before you start adding all kinds of detailed motion. You can imagine that having to change the timing on a fully posed character is going to be a lot more scrolling and selecting in the Timeline than when you only have to do this with three or four objects.

So keep it all simple in the beginning by first animating the main elements in the shot. For a walk cycle, that would be just the pelvis and feet, and for a talking bit, it might be the motions of the head and possibly the broadest gestures of the arms. Once you're satisfied with the timing of these broad motions, start refining these motions—perhaps adding spine motion and a head bob for a walk cycle, keep checking the timing, and start filling in the more detailed motions on the rest of the character.

To simplify this process, it may be a good idea to use several Selection objects—one with just the basic controllers, another with the more detailed controllers such as elbows and knees, and finally one for the things you should be touching last, such as the hands. Also keep in mind that you can make the same organization in the Timeline by coloring the more basic tracks differently from the more detailed ones.

Manual vs Automatic Keyframing

When working with selection objects, it is best to use automatic keyframing. This is because when doing a manual record while a Selection object is active, ALL objects in the Selection object will receive a keyframe, and this is rarely wanted. (This changes in R8.1, where you have an extra "Restrict Keyframe Recording" option that allows you to turn this feature off.)

Looping

If you want to loop say, a walk cycle, should you use the looping feature of Cinema 4D's sequences? Initially, this seems an ideal way to do it, as you only have to worry about animating the loop one time and let Cinema 4D worry about the rest. However, there are some advantages in doing it all by hand. Of course, you don't want to animate each step of the cycle, so "by hand" as used here means manually copying the keyframes that should loop a few times. As you will have tried to minimize the number of controller objects, this isn't too much of a problem, though the same could be said of editing the sequences to loop automatically. However, you are going to have a hard time animating into and out of a looping bit when you are using automatic looping. With manual looping, it is easy to change the keyframes that matter to smoothly move from a looping bit to another move (Figure 9.19).

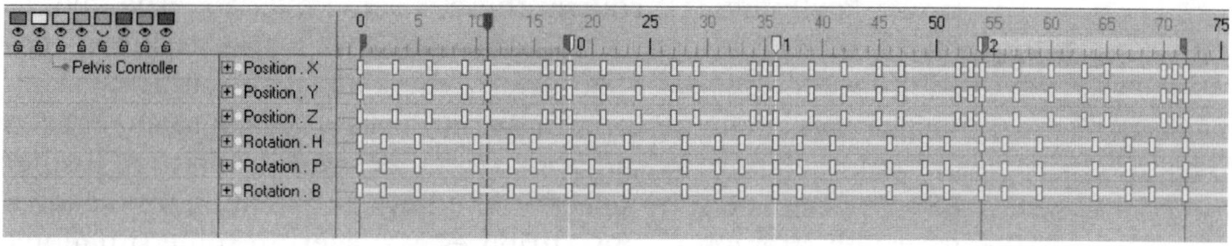

FIGURE 9.19 Manual looping in action. Note the use of markers.

Keyframe Interpolation

As mentioned earlier, the real essence of animation is the motion itself, and the absolute influence on these motions is the keyframe interpolation. And although you can use the default keyframe interpolation, it is really best to use a custom one that better fits your needs. Which interpolation type to use really depends on the way you work.

To change the interpolation type of the keyframes you are going to record, open up the Record submenu in the main Animation menu, set the interpolation type to Custom Interpolation, and open up the custom settings with the Edit Interpolation menu entry.

You may want to use different interpolations at different steps in the process of animation. You can, for example, when starting out with an animation, use step interpolation to get the overall timing spot on, since you don't need to worry about the possibly bad side-effects of interpolation then, which only tend to get in the way when blocking out the main motions. Later on, if you're ready for the next step, simply select all the keyframes and change the interpolation type, as well as the one you'll be using for recorded keys.

What kind of interpolation suits you best depends mostly on if you are an F-curves or a keyframe person.

Keyframes vs F-Curves

Of course, they work perfectly in unison, but there are, roughly, two ways to fine tune animation: keyframes and F-Curves. Some people choose to only use keyframes to refine the timing of motions, adding well-placed in-between keyframes to take care of ease in and ease out. Other people are far more at home with F-Curves to tune the way their keyframed parameters should behave in between keyframes. Of course, there is some overlap, especially as certain motions simply can only be done with F-Curves, but in general, these are the two main approaches at in-betweening.

For the keyframe enthusiasts, it is possibly best to choose the Soft interpolation type and link the tangents. You can then further refine in-betweens by selecting the keys and turning up or down their Soft strength in the Attributes Manager. In some situations, you may want to use the Fast and Slow interpolations though.

If you're determined to refine the motions using the F-Curves, it's best to choose the Custom interpolation type from the start—for both left and right—and leave the tangents unlinked. Newly created keys will be set with tangents like the Soft type, but you will immediately be able to grab the tangents and tweak the motion.

Clamp

A final option to mention is the Clamp option in the interpolation settings. This option compares the values of the neighboring keyframes, and if nearly the same, clamps the interpolation, preventing the overshoot effect of the default Soft interpolation. It's an extremely handy feature, but it can get in the way. For animating the position of the feet, for example, it's ideal, as it keeps them from sliding around, as long as the keyframes are nearly identical. But if you're animating subtle rotations somewhere, it's best to leave the option turned off, as it tends to create sudden jumps in the rotational values. Also, remember that this clamping is pretty easy to achieve manually. Either set both keyframes of the clamp to linear interpolation, or turn down their Soft strength to 0%.

CONCLUSION

That should about cover all the background information you need, and possibly even some that you don't need as of yet, to prepare you for the tutorial in Chapter 10. Here, we'll come across some more detailed and specific uses of the tools in Cinema 4D, so even if you don't plan to follow the tutorial step by step, we strongly suggest that you read through it anyway, as there are a lot of little tweaks and tricks described that you only come across when you actually start applying skeletons and control rigs to that heap of polygons that should be made to come alive.

10

CHARACTER SETUP: A COMPLETE WALKTHROUGH

by Naam

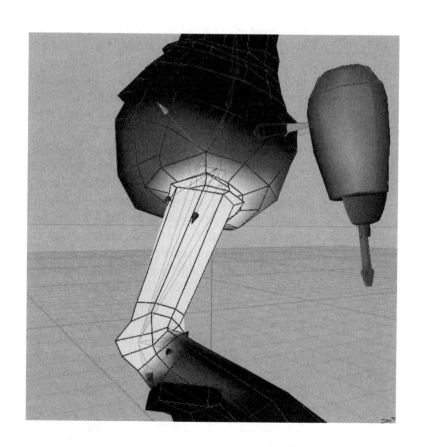

ON THE CD

So, you're up to speed now with the various tools available for making your character come alive using Cinema 4D and MOCCA. You know the pros and cons of them, you might even have the idea that you're ready to start working with them. The next step is, of course, to put all these ideas to good use. And what better way to explain that than to take a character and show precisely how it can be done? Note that as we work along, if you would like to see the .c4d files in process, be sure to check out the CD-ROM. The files are located in Tutorials>Chapter10.

THE CHARACTER

Meet Screwball (Figure 10.1), intergalactic screwdriving maniac extraordinaire. This is the character we'll be setting up in this chapter, as well as showing you how to animate. He has been designed to illustrate some of the challenges available when rigging a character. Hence, he's got some parts that should stay rigid, some parts that should clearly be deformable, and fully articulated hands. Also, he's got a screwdriver dangling from his belt which he should be able to grab and point at enemy screws. Luckily, the screwdriver is attached to his belt magnetically so this won't be too difficult.

As you can see, the character is completely nonrealistic. This gives us a lot of freedom in how we can make him deform and move. Nevertheless, with a (semi-)realistic character, the structures we'd be applying would be much the same; the weighting and tweaking would simply take extra effort and time before really fitting the degree of realism.

Although we'll be following the workflow mentioned in Chapter 9, we won't be covering modeling and animation itself as extensively as you might expect. Instead, we'll be concentrating on providing this character with a flexible rig.

Before you open the example files, there are a few extra elements in each scene that you may wonder about. Firstly, there's the lighting, floor, and sky. Though hidden, these objects provide for a nice rendering if you want to render out test animations. Furthermore, there is a system called "FlexCam" in place, which is an expression-driven camera system. Basically, it allows you to pan and rotate the editor camera without its behavior being dependent on the object selection. It does so by keeping a dedicated "point of interest" target up to date, moving it around when panning, but keeping it still when dollying (moving forward and backward) or

FIGURE 10.1   Screwball, intergalactic screwdriving maniac extraordinaire.

orbiting. If you run into trouble because this secret point of interest is at some distance from the actual point of interest, simply orbit about 90 degrees, and pan toward the correct point of interest, and it'll stay there until you move away again. Alternatively, simply re-move the whole system if you don't like it.

MODELING

ON THE CD

While modeling, the same outlines as described in Chapter 9 were followed. Have a look at file screwball_01_chaos.c4d (Tutorials> Chapter10) on the Cd-ROM if you want to investigate the model more closely. All joints should have enough resolution to make them bend smoothly, and almost all parts are HyperNURBS Polygon objects. There are just a few parts, such as some elements of the screwdriver itself, that are actually of another type (in this case Lathe Nurbs). As these parts will stay rigid anyway, this isn't much of a problem. We will see if we need to attach them to the mesh using an expression, but let's hope they'll automatically deform properly.

If you look at the Objects Manager of the model (Figure 10.2), you may be startled. It's very disorganized, with Objects scattered all over the place, sometimes grouped in symmetry, under HyperNURBS. Only the screwdriver seems to have a structure that may make any sense. So first, some cleanup needs to be done.

As mentioned, we will want to have the whole character (well, at *least* the HyperNURBS elements) grouped inside a single HyperNURBS to make it deform smoothly. But, we also need to consider that some of these elements—such as the helmet and screwdriver—shouldn't be deformed. This could be done in two ways. You can give each of the non-deformed elements their own HyperNURBS or apply a hierarchical structure that will allow you to deform just a subset of the polygon elements. We're going to use the latter, because then we can just hit the "Q" key on the keyboard if we want to turn off all HyperNURBS generation and animate in low resolution. We're keeping some of the symmetry objects active, as they may help in weighting the mesh later on.

Here's the structure we'll be using for boning and weighting (Figure 10.3). All the Polygon objects are tucked away, neat and tidy in groups, clearly named, even the tags are out of the way. With the clutter gone, it's much easier to see what the actual hierarchical structure of the character is going to be. We're still going to decide, later on, where to put the controllers for the character, but as you can see, there is already a root bone at the place where all of the bones will be put.

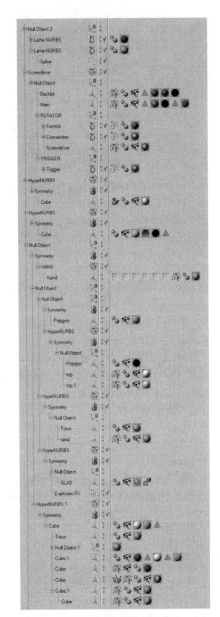

FIGURE 10.2   The Objects Manager can get quite cluttered when you're modeling.

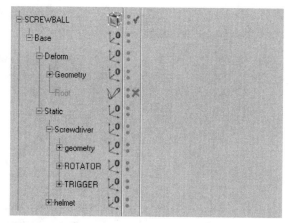

FIGURE 10.3   Cleaned out Objects Manager provides the all-important structural overview.

BONING

As we've discussed, we'll only be boning one half of the character. After we're done with that, and the weighting is done as well, we'll simply be copying one half, including all weighting, over to the other side.

Open the file screwball_02_boneready.c4d. Contrary to what the file name indicates, the root bone hasn't been placed yet. This root bone won't actually be animated. In fact, it will be nothing more than a Null bone, zeroing out the rotation of the pelvis bone. This will prevent ugly rotations and gimbal lock.

Before we start adding new bones, note the importance of the bones' actual names. Once we are weighting the character, we will want to point certain bones at the Claude Bonet Vertex maps of other bones. Having to do that from within a window that only shows a lot of objects called "Bone" won't be too much use then. (Figure 10.4). Also, we'll be making heavy use of Cinema 4D's Transfer command, which relies on the naming of objects. It's a good idea to give each and every bone a unique name, up until the knuckles of the hand, and to do this after creation of the skeleton. But if you don't mind having various bones receive the same name (such as "Spine" for all spine bones, or "Hand" for all hand bones) you may want to rename the bones as soon as they are created. Adding new bones with the Bone tool will name them like their parent, so this may save you some time.

FIGURE 10.4   The result of not naming properly.

So, to start out, add the root bone to the scene (just create a bone) and drag it to the correct place in the hierarchy. Check Figure 10.3 again if you need a hint on the hierarchical placement. Then position it just as the pelvis bone will be positioned. That is, it should be more or less in the center of gravity of the character, Z pointing in the direction that the spinal column will take, Y pointing backwards. Also, it needs to be in the dead center of the character, so when we mirror the substructures, they will be placed correctly. This is best achieved by using the Coordinates Manager. Simply set the X position to zero, and also zero out the heading. The length of the bone isn't terribly important, it will be turned into a Null anyway, but since you're at it, you may as well give it the length you want the pelvis bone to be.

This may seem like a lot of work just to add the first bone, but don't despair. It's important that this first one is aligned properly so the rest of the bones will then be aligned as they should.

Pelvis to Skull

Next, you need to create the actual pelvis bone. Usually, you can simply do this by CTRL-dragging the root unto itself in the Objects Manager, leaving you with both bones in the exact same position and rotation. You can turn the root into a Null bone now, and set the function of the pelvis to $1/r^6$.

Okay, now we're ready to enter the Bone tool. But first, be aware that switching between the Bone tool and the Move/Scale/Rotate tools can lead to trouble, as there is some automatic fixing going on. Hence, you best remember to fix the bones prior to each switch. Don't worry, you only need to make this step twice, once when entering the Bone tool, and once when exiting it (provided that everything goes okay in between, of course).

So, fix the bone structure (Right click on the root in the Objects Manager, then choose Fix Bones and click yes in the following dialog). Then enter the Bone tool. You may want to turn off deformers globally for speedier editor feedback.

The spine, neck, and skull bones all need to be in the same yz plane as the pelvis bone, so switch to the side view.

To create a new bone with the Bone tool, be sure you have selected its future parent, and CTRL-click at where you roughly think the end of the new bone should be. One bone gets added to the chain. Now, you can click and drag the yellow dots in the editor view to move the joints to their proper locations. You may also want to move a whole bone while keeping its parent and child joints moving along. To do this, simply click and drag the bone itself.

That is about all there is to it. Just keep adding bones like this until you arrive at the top of the skull. Have a look at Figure 10.5 if you need some hints for the actual placement. As you can see, there are three bones for the spine and two for the neck. Of course, one bone for the skull is more than enough. It really all depends on how the character has been modeled and how you want it to move.

Okay, now we'll branch off to the arms, and investigate some half-documented features.

Let's work on the left arm. It's best to start out in front view. The thing with the arms is that they need to be attached to the upper spine bone, but can't use the spine's endpoint as the pivot. So how can we do this with the Bone tool? Doesn't that keep all the joints nicely slotted together all the time? It does, but there are ways around that without switching to other tools.

You are probably already familiar with the "1", "2", and "3" hotkey buttons on your keyboard, which allow you to pan, dolly/zoom, and orbit the camera. Well, the "4", "5", and "6" hotkeys do the same with the active objects. It's just a temporary switch to the Move, Scale and Rotate tools.

With the upper spine bone selected, CTRL-click in the front view to create a new bone. With this bone selected, hold the "4"

FIGURE 10.5   The spine might look like this.

key on your keyboard and drag it away from the top of the spine. It is now a separate bone, and can further be moved with the Bone tool.

The pivot of the shoulder is very dependent on the character. Do keep in mind, especially when you are planning to do a full Soft IK setup, that you will want to rotate the shoulder rather than move it. You can skip the shoulder bone altogether and use the position of the upper arm to deform the shoulder, but it is really best to add a shoulder bone in most cases. In the case of Screwball, we want the shoulders to have a rather wide range of motion, so we should place the pivot at the right side of the spine (see Figure 10.6).

Now, you will want to utilize a Null bone here to zero out the rotation of the shoulder bone, to prevent unpredictable rotational behavior. To do this, first make sure that you're satisfied with the placement of the shoulder bone. Keep its tip close to the top of the shoulder. You may also want to apply a bit of rotation to the bone (using the "6" hotkey in the perspective view), so the y and x axes

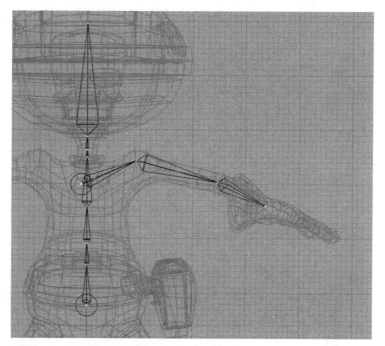

FIGURE 10.6 The setup of the left arm.

point back and up. Then, in the Active Tool Dialog, click on Add/Update Null Bone and you'll have your shoulder bone zeroed out inside its newly found parent. And now we can move on to the arm.

The Arm

There's actually nothing very special about the arm. You just follow the familiar steps to create the upper and lower arm. However, take care with the placement of the elbow; it should definitely be more to the back than to the front of the mesh.

It's common practice to actually have the lower arm be made up of two bones instead of one, one after the other. That way, you are providing the necessary flexibility for the wrist joint. After all, in real life, if you 'bank' or twist your wrist, it's actually your whole lower arm that gets twisted. But in case of Screwball, his huge gloves neatly cover his wrists, so there's nothing wrong with just using a straight elbow-to-wrist connection.

The Hand

Next, we'll create the hand. This is where things really get interesting, and it's in areas like this that you should be glad for a flexible tool such as the Bone tool. We're not going to look at boning a hand step by step, as it is a pretty straightforward affair, but here are some useful pointers.

First off, although you may feel your fingers are made up of three bones only, in animation you really shouldn't disregard the bones on the inside of your hand that lead toward the fingers. These add great extra control for the expressiveness of the hand. But if there are four bones in the inside of the hand—leading to Screwball's three fingers and one thumb—surely you will want to have an extra parent bone to move the whole hand in unison. This may or may not be a Null bone; it doesn't really matter as the various finger bones will easily pull along the hand perfectly. Next, consider that you may want to use a morphing system for the hand. If you are going to use Cinema 4D's PoseMixer, you will need yet another parent. Why? Well, PoseMixer works similar to a deformer, so it will influence its immediate parent and all the children. Hence, once PoseMixer is active, you won't be able to rotate the hand's parent bone anymore. (This is purely a reminder of what you may come across later on. For now, one parent for the hand, be it Null or not, is more than enough.)

Take care of the x- and y-axis orientations. Although the Bone tool seems to have its own way of aligning this, you don't want to have to re-rotate all these bones with the Rotate tool once you're done, even though sometimes there's really no way around it. As most of the hand bones should only be bent in one direction, choose one axis (x or y) to always point upwards or downwards, in each and every finger.

Try to keep the joints closer to the top of the hand than the bottom. If you check your own fingers, you'll notice that the bottom really deforms, while the top stays rather straight. This can be simulated (and overdone) by keeping the actual joints close to the top of the mesh. This, by the way, goes for all one-way-only joints in the body (fingers, elbows, and knees).

Keep in mind that once you created one finger (a string of four bones), it's much easier to simply CTRL-drag it in the Objects Manager and adjust it after that than it is to create a similar string three times in a row.

Three, not four? Yes, the thumb will require special treatment. As you know, you have opposable thumbs. It's really quite interesting to try to figure out how that works in real life and thus how the x and y axes should be oriented to get the best rotation. Fact is, here again you're probably better off with an extra Null bone as parent (again to zero out rotations). That way, you will have two distinct directions in which the thumb's first bone can get bent. But beware, if your main hand bone (the thumb's parent) is a null bone, DON'T use the Active Tool Manager's Add/Update Null Bone command, as it will actually update the main hand bone to be positioned at the thumb's place, which will ruin the layout of your carefully placed finger bones (all 12 of them).

Finally, as a general rule, let the final bone of each finger stick out of the top a bit. This simply helps deformation.

If you have really no idea where to begin, check out Figure 10.7 for some ideas. Note the angle of the thumb root.

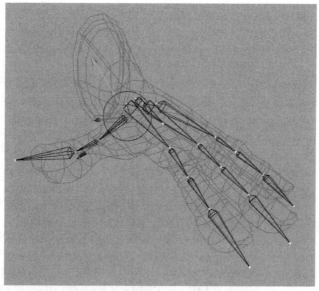

FIGURE 10.7   A reasonably good way to bone a hand. The thumb bone has been highlighted to show its preferred motion axes.

Now let's look at the leg.

The Leg

There isn't much that's special about the structure of the leg, either. We use a Null bone for the root (again, to zero out the upper leg's rotation), which is parented directly to the pelvis bone, and simply add bones for the upper and lower leg, the foot, and the toes. You may have noticed that Mr. Screwball doesn't really need any more definition in this area. The only things of real importance are the placement of ankle and toes joints. This particular character seems to need quite a high ankle, so the whole base of his leg will bend when he's moving his foot. The toes are going to be tricky, as the bit that looks like a shoe shouldn't be deformed too much while the foot should still roll over the floor easily. For now, it is enough to just put the structure as shown in Figure 10.8 in place, as these are all matters that will be resolved in the weighting phase, probably with the occasional fallback to an extra bit of boning.

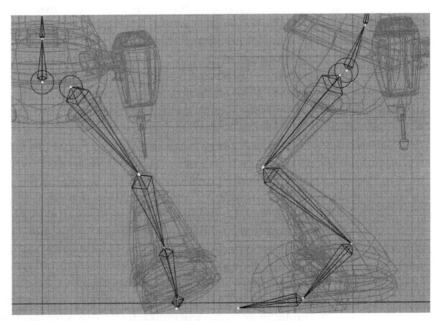

FIGURE 10.8 The bones of Mr. Screwball's leg from the front and side.

As for the foot bone itself, it's more or less standard to have it oriented from ankle to toes. However, that means we're probably going to need a helper bone for the heel.

As a last step, add an extra child to the pelvis bone, and stick it inside the little attachment mechanism that holds the screwdriver. That should be enough to rigidly move the little thing along with the deforming belt.

That's all for the bones. There may be some cleaning up to do, just to make sure that all the bones' axes are aligned properly. This final tweaking is best done with the Rotate tool in Object Axis mode. Remember to fix the skeleton before leaving the Bone tool. Then check the bones in trouble spots (such as shoulder, hand and fingers) to see that they have neat alignment of the axes, so rotating them on one axis or the other makes for a good, natural motion. Also, you my want to check the Coordinates Manager; sometimes the Bone tool's automated rotation causes weird rotational values (such as 180, 180, 0). Try to find better solutions for those as they may begin to haunt you once you start animating them. Also, try to keep banking at zero.

If you have any renaming to do, do it now as well. As previously explained, correct naming will be useful for weighting certain bones to others, and as that is the next phase, now's the time for some inventive naming.

WEIGHTING

Now we're going to weight the character's geometry to the bone structure we've just created. We'll be doing this mainly with the Claude Bonet tool, which will allow us to interactively paint the weights and see the mesh be deformed in near realtime. For the hands, though, we'll be using old fashioned Vertex maps. You may have noticed that there are already maps present on the hand object. This is because this hand actually came from another character and was then adjusted to look like a glove. Because the hand is such an intricate model—and it sometimes needs more bones than the rest of the skeleton put together—it's nice to be able to copy the model over from one character to the next, and, with Vertex maps, this is made easy. Claude Bonet maps need a bone structure present to remember the weighting, but Vertex maps don't.

If you're not too sure about the skeleton you created, load up the file screwball_03_halfboned.c4d; there you will find the character with the skeleton explained in the previous section.

We'll be moving about the skeleton while weighting, so it is a good idea to first record the pose it is in now. Okay, this pose is already recorded in the fixed state of the bones as well, but you don't want to keep unfixing and fixing the skeleton just to get back at the rest pose. Just select the root bone, call Select Children, and record a keyframe for the rotation of all bones. If you think you'll be moving the bones during weighting, just record a keyframe for position as well.

Before entering the Claude Bonet tool, you should remove the attachment group from the deformed hierarchy group. Claude Bonet has trouble with this group, because it is a couple of Lathe Nurbs and you won't be able to weigh them. To prevent trouble, drag it out of the Deform group in the Objects Manager.

Now enter the Claude Bonet tool. You'll see that the mesh of the character will turn grey. Also, any generators will be turned off, so you can only paint onto the actual Polygon objects themselves.

If the mesh is grey, it means that the currently selected bone does not have any Claude Bonet Vertex maps to consider. As such, it will deform the whole mesh, no questions asked (unless, of course, there is an old-fashioned Vertex map/Restriction combo going on). So before you start painting, it is good practice to first assign a completely empty Claude Bonet map to every bone you'll be weighting. To do so, just select the bone in the Objects Manager, set the strength slider in the Active Tool Dialog to zero, and click the Set Value button next to the slider. The mesh will now turn black, meaning that not a single point is weighted for that bone. If you do this for every bone, you'll make sure that, once you test out your weighting by rotating a bone, the child bones don't secretly effect or deform the mesh.

You could do this for the hand structure, but since we'll be weighting these bones another way, it's enough to simply disable all hands bones for now. Simply CTRL-click on the hand root's green check in the Objects Manager so it will be turned off—including all its child bones (Figure 10.9).

Weighting now is just a matter of selecting the bone in the Objects Manager, setting Claude Bonet's Strength slider to an appropriate value (usually around 10%-20%), painting in the editor, and watching your pristine black mesh turn slowly green where you paint it. Needless to say, the more green a vertex is, the more it will be weighted to the selected bone. If you want to turn down the weighting of a vertex, simply paint with the CTRL key pressed.

You can also see all the other bone's influence on the mesh in different vertex colors (if you didn't turn this option off in the Active Tool Dialog). Also, remember the "6" hotkey. Use it to rotate the bone and see the effect of your weighting, then keep painting

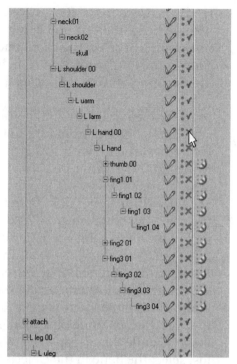

FIGURE 10.9 CTRL-click to disable an entire hierarchy of deformers.

the mesh in deformed state to fix the errors. The mesh will snap to the newly weighted state as soon as you let go of the mouse. To get the skeleton back in the rest pose, simply redraw the editor (hit "A" on your keyboard). Alternatively, you can globally disable animation altogether by deactivating it. That way, your test poses will stay in the editor until you enable animation again. To quickly get back to the test pose in this case, simply enable and disable the Animation switch.

To check the influence of your weighting on the final, Hyper-NURBS mesh, hit "Q" on the keyboard to enable the HyperNURBS object (which was automatically disabled when you entered Claude Bonet). You can still paint in this mode, but you won't be able to see the weighting displayed. When starting out painting a new bone, it's handy to first quickly set a group of points to 100% weighting, and weigh the bones in the overlap area more carefully. You can quickly do this by enabling the Paint Absolute option in the Active Tool Manager and setting the slider at 100%. Now your painting strokes will instantly turn your vertices green (or 'ungreen' by holding CTRL). Also note the Only Modify Visible Elements option in the Active Tool Dialog. Just turn this off if you want your brush to reach all vertices, even though they are at the back of the mesh.

Needless to say, you don't need to paint the weights on Null bones, since these won't be contributing to the deformation at all.

Now you can go ahead and do the weighting. It's really something that you can't apply any exact science on, it takes some experience to figure out what kind of Vertex Maps work best in which situations. It's a case of painting, rotating, painting, rotating, and painting again. But first take a look at a few trouble spots in the mesh of Screwball.

The Hip Joint

As you may have noticed, the hip joint of Screwball's upper leg bone is buried deep within the pelvis area. This means that, although the leg geometry itself can be made to rigidly follow the rotation of the bone, the area around where it attaches to the pelvis needs some careful weighting, allowing for a nice smooth falloff in the weighting values from the leg on out. Have a look at Figure 10.10 to see how this could be solved.

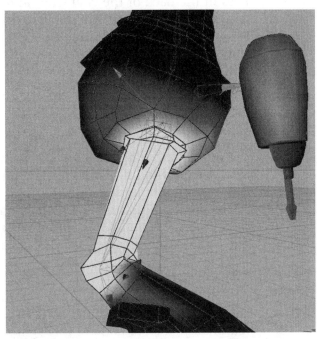

FIGURE 10.10 Careful weighting of the upper leg provides a smoothly deformed pelvis area.

The Knee and Elbow

In the knee and elbow area, you may be facing some difficulty getting the wrinkles to deform correctly. Because the actual geometry is so close to the bones themselves, painted vertices may seem to "flip" between states even when the weighting is only changed subtly. In cases such as this, it's a good idea to shorten the parent bone a bit. So when working on the knee, select the upper leg bone, and in the Attributes Manager, change the bone's length to about two-thirds of what it is currently. In this way, you'll be able to weigh much more precisely, as the vertices won't be so close to the upper leg bone object. But don't shorten the bone too much because that might cause it to lose its influence on the joint, leading to certain vertices "staying behind" when the skeleton is walking away, for example.

The Spine

Weighting the effect from the spine on the belly and torso is also one of the more difficult tasks. Keep in mind you don't need each bone to have a "band of influence" all around the character's torso. Rather, you could have the first spine bone only influence the vertices in the back of the character, and let the topmost spine bone and the pelvis bone battle it out over the belly vertices. Also, we will be providing an expression later on what will bend the spine smoothly, so the bend is spread out over all the bones of the spine. This means you're best off test-rotating all the spine bones, and not concentrating on one bending bone in particular.

The Ankle

The ankle and toe deformation really requires some attention to detail. There's a lot of overlapping geometry there. Remember you can turn off geometry in the Objects Manager to make the vertices easier to view. Also, you're probably going to have to adjust the bone placement and possibly remodel some of the vertices a bit to make this area deform properly. An extra Knife cut across the shin-flap object helps a lot. And if you're having trouble doing the heel, remember the concept of helper bones. Just select the foot bone, and, in the Move tool and in Object mode, CTRL-drag the little orange handle at the tip of the bone to create an extra bone. Keep it reasonably small, and place it roughly in the heel area of the foot. Give it some uninteresting name like "++", and use the Set Reference button in the Active Tool Dialog to point it at the Claude Bonet Vertex map of the foot bone. It is very important that you weigh this bone (either using Set Reference or through manual weighting), especially if you have shortened the upper leg bone, or else you will run into trouble. Have a look at Figure 10.11 for a hint on placement of this helper bone.

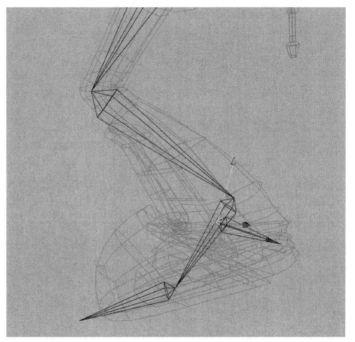

FIGURE 10.11   Add small helper bones to fill up parts of the mesh that should stay more or less rigid.

The Attachment

Remember that little bone used to deform the attachment? Well, we're going to be making special use of that. Because it is very probable that there still are vertices in the mesh that haven't been weighted completely—such as points that don't receive a 100% weight from any bone (you should try to prevent this from happening)—we're going to use this bone to drag those vertices along. By keeping a central bone completely unweighted (in other words, a bone that influences the whole mesh), you will prevent not-entirely-weighted vertices from staying behind if the skeleton is moved away from its origin. This is easy to do: just don't weight the bone. We could do this with the pelvis bone as well, but not with any other bone, as these may cause the "left behind" points to move around when the limbs are moving. So, if you have weighted the attachment bone when you were dealing out empty Claude Bonet tags in the beginning of the exercise, remove the map by clicking the Remove Paint (This Bone) function in the Active Tool Dialog.

The Hand

As mentioned earlier, we'll be using old-fashioned Vertex maps and Restrictions for the hand structure. As the Vertex maps are already applied to the model (it came from another character originally, remember?) this is simply a matter of adding Restriction tags to the various bones and filling in the names of the appropriate Vertex maps there.

First, have a look at the various Vertex maps. Hover the mouse over them to see the name pop up in Cinema 4D's Status Bar (bottom left of the UI) or the help bubble, or alternatively select them and check the name in the Attributes Manager. Note there is one Vertex map per finger, and not a single one per bone. We don't really need that here, but we do need the fingers to stay out of each other's influence, hence the choice for one map per finger. There's also one extra map for the whole hand. We'll be using this for the inner-hand bones.

First of all, enable the bones of the hands, if you disabled them in the previous weighting step. CTRL-click on the red X behind the hand's root bone in the Objects Manager to activate them all in a single click.

We're going to use Claude Bonet to weight the wrist area; in other words, the influence of the arm and hand bones on the glove. But we'd better not do this before we get the restrictions for the fingers sorted, or the finger bones will secretly influence the wrist area—and all the rest of the mesh as well. So let's start with that.

It's simple really. Select the first bone of a finger and add a Restriction tag to it. Next, fill in the name of the desired Vertex map using the Attributes Manager (in case of the index finger, this'd be "fing1", just as the bone names). You can then right-click the Vertex Map in the Objects Manager and select Copy Tag To Children to have each finger bone have the same tag applied. Do this for all four fingers, and you're practically done.

However, you'll need to check out the deformation. To do this in the most flexible way, it's a good idea to animate the whole hand into a certain pose (such as a fist), preferably in negative time. So move the timeslider back, enable AutoRecording for Rotation (and remember to disable it later on), optionally (if you want to make selections in the editor) set the Selection Filter to just Bones, and pose all the bones. It's really best not to miss a single bone—rotate them all. It's an even better idea to record two test poses, rather too many than too few.

You may notice now that, although the fingers deform correctly, the midsection of the hand receives some major Polygon stretching. Hence the Vertex map called "hand" comes into play. One by one, select the Restriction tag of each finger's first bone, and fill in "hand" in the second Restriction field. Now the hand should deform correctly.

The only thing left to do now is to take care of a good deformation of the wrist area. This can be done with Claude Bonet again, just the way it was described before. Have a look at Figure 10.12 to have an idea how to weight the area. Also, a slight error in modeling may pop up here, where the arm starts protruding through the glove if it gets bent too much. Simply remodel the arm a bit if this happens, just scale down the cluster of points at the end of the arm. There's a glove covering it, so no one will notice.

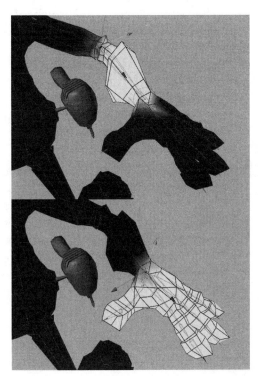

FIGURE 10.12   The weighting of the wrist.

Weighting really takes a lot of time, but once you have done this a few times, it'll become easier with every step. There's no real cure for this part of the job, except for hoping for an automatic weighting function in future C4D releases. But even then, you'll probably be spending just as much time trying to tweak the result of that.

ON THE CD

If you are curious for a possible result of this exercise, open the file screwball_04_halfweighted.c4d on the CD-ROM, in which all above weighting is applied.

CONTROL

Sadly, we're not done yet. We still need a way to control this skeleton. Of course, you could now mirror the limbs over to the other side, and animate the whole character simply by rotating all the bones by hand. But let's be ambitious and look at a few ways we can control this rig.

We will start out by applying old-fashioned IK to the legs and continue by adding a few controls for the more difficult parts of the character. Then, we'll finish off applying Soft IK to the arms as well, resulting in a very flexible, easy-to-control character.

IK for the Legs

For this exercise, we'll be building a rig using the pre-R8 IK tags to control the legs. As we will be mirroring the bone structures in the limb with all the IK applied, we'll keep the character half-boned for now.

The old IK was very limited and inflexible, but it still provided for enough control to apply it to basic situations such as the legs. There are some tricks which may seem silly at first, but which make the IK chain actually workable. For instance, the old IK system has a very hard time with situations it can't find a solution for. The chain seems to get "stuck" in these cases, and sometimes this makes for jittery animations. But by providing for a structure that has a margin for error built in, this old IK method is perfectly al right for most cases.

Open up the file screwball_04_halfweighted.c4d. First off, you still need to drag back the little attachment to the correct place in the hierarchy to have it move with the skeleton.

A little warning is warranted before we continue: quite a few of the steps that follow (contrary to the boning and weighting phase) require a certain order of execution. This is simply what happens once you start working with expressions and inter-object relationships. It's all too easy to disrupt the entire hierarchy by forgetting to turn options on or off. So pay close attention to your settings, remember to save before attempting activation of the structure you created, and use the Timeline to store the skeleton's state, so you can always step back and fix mistakes. We will revisit the recording of keyframes at crucial points.

We will be steering the leg with a controller that will pivot at the ball of the foot. You could also make it pivot at the heel; it's really a matter of preference. We choose the ball of the foot because, in general, a humanoid character will spend a lot more time on his toes than on his heels. (There are few occasions where you need a pivot at the heel, but quite a few people still prefer it anyway.) Start by creating a Null object, and call it something like "L foot controller." Use Cinema 4D's Transfer command to fix it to the location and rotation of the left toes bone. Create another Null object, call it "L ankle goal," Transfer it to the state of the foot bone, and parent it to the foot controller. This makes for a structure that will rotate around the ball of the foot, though the actual IK will work with the goal in the ankle position. For safety's sake, record the position and rotation of these Nulls.

Now we'll be creating the IK system for the leg itself. The leg's Null Bone will serve as IK anchor, so add an Anchor tag to this object. Next, add a "Kinematic" tag to the upper leg bone. The Kinematic tag makes sure that the object is included in the IK calculations. This is really all we need the tag to do. We won't be setting limits on the upper leg bone because we can just as easily prevent "illegal" rotations by careful animation, and setting limits would mean limiting the chain, probably to the extent of confusing the IK chain.

Now we come to the knee, which deserves a little extra attention. Remember the trouble that near-90 degree angles could generate? Well, here we have one. Try switching Cinema 4D to HPB system (in the preferences, on the Units page) so you are directly in control of the values that Cinema uses for animation. Now try to bend the lower leg bone exactly backward, so the foot touches the buttocks. It's not that easy, is it? This is a definite case of gimbal lock. And as we want to have the leg bend along one axis only (so the knee doesn't 'break'), we need an extra Null Bone in the knee to zero out the rotations of the lower leg bone.

Be sure to disable Animation; then go into the Bone tool. Select the lower leg bone and click Add/Update Null Bone and switch to Rotate, and to the Axis tool. Now, rotate the just created Null bone (rename it something like "00") so the x- or y-axis is pointing back to the buttocks along the upper leg bone. (Take care to keep the z-axis pointing where it was.) Select the lower leg bone and, using the Coordinates Manager, set its rotation to zero on all axes. That should take care of it. You can now rotate the lower leg bone along one axis only and it will bend just as a real leg would. Remember to record the rotation of the new bone and its child in the Timeline.

Now we can continue. Add a Kinematic Tag to the knee Null bone. This one we don't want to have rotate at all, so we need to fill in the limits. However, a few degrees of rotation will help the IK system to find a solution. So check the Coordinates Manager and fill in rotations a bit below and above the current orientation (usually 5 degrees extra space is enough). Turn on the limits on all axes. Also, set the damping to 100%.

Add a Kinematic Tag to the lower leg bone now. Again, set the limits, keep a few degrees of freedom on all axes. Of course, the direction in which the knee will bend (probably P) will have to have a lot of freedom, so rotate the leg to both the extreme bends and use the rotation values you see there for the appropriate axis in the Kinematic tag.

Finally, add a Kinematic tag to the foot bone. Leave the limits completely free again.

Now you will need to tell the foot bone to conform to the ankle goal you created previously. If you only do this using IK, the foot will not rotate like the goal does, but only attempt to move toward it. So we're going to add an extra, simple Xpresso tag to take care of that.

First, disable Expressions globally. Then add an IK Tag to the foot, and drag the ankle goal Null into the field in the Attributes Manager. Next, add an Xpresso expression. The Xpresso Editor should appear, allowing you to drag both the foot bone and the ankle goal into it. Using Xpresso, feed the ankle goal's global rotation to the foot bone's global rotation.

There's some importance to the order of the two expressions you just added, though: you will want to have the Xpresso expression evaluated after IK, because IK still influences the rotation of the foot bone. To do this, just take care the Xpresso tag is to the right of the IK expression tag. Have a look at Figure 10.13 for a screen capture of the expressions order, as well as the Xpresso structure used.

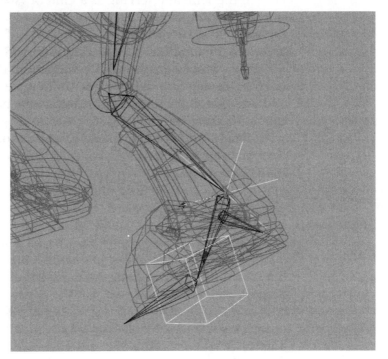

FIGURE 10.13   The expression order and structure on the IK leg.

So now we're ready to test out this structure. You may want to save now, because you simply don't know what can go wrong, and for expression-driven structures, there's rarely an undo.

Enable the global Expressions switch and look at what happens. If all is well, nothing will happen, meaning that the chain has no trouble whatsoever finding the solution for the leg's rest state. Now drag the foot controller object through the scene, rotate it, and note if the foot is accurately positioned and rotated. If it is not, you may want to loosen up the IK limits on both the knee bones a bit. Just provide for a few extra degrees of rotation. Also, if you find the upper leg bone getting in painful positions, don't worry. Select it and rotate it to "help" the IK chain find a better solution. You will be using the rotation of the upper leg bone as a way to point the knee in the direction you want. As such, it will have keyframes, making these painful bends a thing of the past. It's just that right now you are ignoring the animation in the Timeline for testing purposes; when you are actually animating him, the IK chain won't be allowed to wander off like this because there will be a recorded pose in the Timeline serving as a kind of "start-off" pose for the IK system to work with.

You may discover that, at certain poses of the legs, the geometry doesn't deform as you'd expect right now. Sadly, it will always be like that; some errors simply pop up later in the process. You'll just have to re-apply weighting to the trouble areas, possibly even adding some extra points to the geometry here and there to take care of the problems.

Remember, for somewhat speedier editor display, you can either turn off Generators globally, or turn off Screwball's Hyper-NURBS generator.

Mirroring IK

If you're satisfied with the workings of the leg, it's time to copy it over to the other side. We'll do this with the Bone Mirror function, but since this has been designed to work with Soft IK, we'll need to do some extra tweaking.

First, disable Expressions globally, and get all bones and controllers back into the default pose by enabling and then disabling animation. If you haven't already removed the Symmetry objects, do so now by selecting them and calling "Make Editable." Vertex maps will automatically be mirrored as well. Now, select both the Foot Controller and the root of the leg. You may want to select the shoulder root as well to copy over everything in one go. Call "Bone Mirror" from the MOCCA toolset. You may have noticed that in the example skeleton, many bones have an "L" prefix. This should now automatically be changed to "R" while mirroring by filling in "L" in the "Replace" and "R" in the "with" field. Include the space for safety and clean out the "Prefix" and "Suffix" fields. Use "Parent" as the origin, turn on all options at the right, and turn off Auto Find Center. Now, hit Mirror. Next, for safety's sake, record rotational keyframes on all the bones you just copied as well as positional keys on the Controller objects. Also it's a good idea to fix the bones right now (Figure 10.14).

Before you turn on expressions and animations again, you will have to adjust the expressions you just duplicated, to make them refer to the newly created Controller objects. Also, keep a close eye

FIGURE 10.14   The Bone Mirror settings.

on the Kinematics tag on the two knee joint bones. As they have been mirrored, some angles will be reversed. Just select the tags, compare the values to the values in the Coordinates Manager, and make the appropriate angles negative or positive.

As a final tweak, you may want to check the Vertex maps for the newly created leg. Mirror Bones duplicates the Vertex maps it finds to the other side of the model, effectively creating twice as many maps as you require (this is only because we decided to already use a single map for both sides of the body at the same time). This isn't too bad in itself, but Mirror Bones is known to sometimes "forget" a single object, leading to unwanted deformations. The safest way to be absolutely sure that the new bones refer to the same points as the old ones is to run by the bones one by one and use Set Reference in the Claude Bonet Active Tool Dialog to re-refer them to the maps on the old bones. Another way is to just look at your mesh and how it deforms, and in trouble spots, re-refer to the maps of the original bones.

Now, save, and turn the global switches back on. Test out your rig and tweak where necessary.

As you may also have noticed, and as we have already mentioned before, Cinema 4D's internal IK can be unpredictable. We did everything we could to make it behave properly, but still you will have to take care during animation, and fix problems by rotating the upper leg bone. This, of course is not ideal. Hence, we'll be replacing the IK system in the legs with an, albeit slower, Soft IK system shortly. First, though, let's add a few extra controls to make the rest of the character behave properly.

Placing the Helmet

You also might have noticed that the helmet object isn't moved along with the head right now. This is of course logical, as we chose not to deform it. We'll add a quick expression to have it move with the skull now though.

Just add a Null object to the scene, call it "helmet goal," parent it to the skull bone, and Transfer it to the global position and rotation of the helmet object. Now, add an Xpresso expression to the helmet group, create a node for both the helmet group and the goal object, and directly feed the goal's global position and rotation to the helmet node. Done.

The Torso Controller

So, let's see if we can add a bit of extra control to the spinal column. We'll want to control the bend of the whole spine by one object only. This object, called the Torso Controller, will have to move and rotate with the pelvis. So, add an extra Null object to the scene, call it Torso Controller, parent it to the Pelvis bone, and Transfer it to the last spine bone (in case of the example rig, this would be bone Spine03). Now add an Xpresso expression to the Torso Controller. You will need to create object nodes for all spine bones in this Xpression as well as two object nodes referencing the Controller object itself. Why two? Well, we will want to feed the rotation of the Torso Controller to all the spine bones, but after that happens, we'll need to place the Torso Controller at the end of the spine again. Because the spine will have been bent, the end of the spine will have moved, so the Controller needs to update its position.

Before linking the Xpression up, make sure that it is positioned and rotated exactly as the last spine bone. Now, have a look at Figure 10.15 for the way you should link up the various nodes. Luckily, the spine bones' various rotations in the example skeleton all have more or less the same rotation, so we can simply divide the total rotation by three. Sometimes, though, you may want to use different rotation per spine element.

An extra word of caution may be needed here. Remember how we talked about the difference between HPB and Quaternion rotation? Here is a place where you may have trouble with using Quaternion rotation. Because the Xpression measures the HPB values of the Torso Controller and Quaternion rotation converts to HPB in its own way, rotating the Torso Controller using the yellow circle may lead to the spine bending in an unpredictable manner once you rotate it to extreme angles. Simply switch to the HPB system of rotation if this is the case.

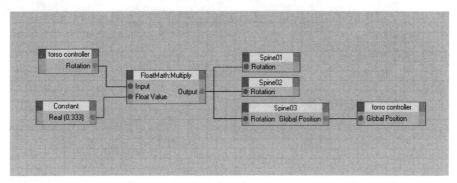

FIGURE 10.15   The Xpression for the Spine Controller object

Grabbing the Screwdriver

We still need to add a controller to control whether the Screwdriver is dangling from the belt, or is positioned in the hand. We'll be using a slider on the Screwdriver object itself to mix between two goal objects.

To make this work, you will need to create a new User Data slider in the Attributes Manager. Select the Screwdriver, and call Add User Data...; choose the interface type of your choice, but be sure to use a Percentage ranging from 0% to 100%. You will also need two goal objects in Screwball's rig. One can be parented to the small "attachment" bone, and use the Transferred location and rotation of the Screwdriver object. The other will have to be parented to the left hand bone. The placement and rotation of this one is best dealt with once the proper expression is in place.

Add an Xpresso expression to the Screwdriver object, and create object nodes for both of the goals and for the Screwdriver. Again, you will need the Screwdriver Object Node two times, once to get the User Data slider you just created and once to feed it the correct position and rotation.

Look at Figure 10.16 to learn about the way these nodes should be linked up.

This seems like a somewhat more involved expression, but the basics are pretty straightforward. Simply put, it measures the Percentage of the User Data slider and uses that to mix between the

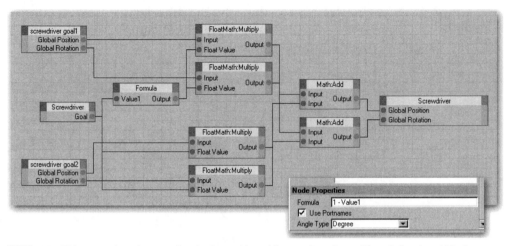

FIGURE 10.16 This expression takes care that the Screwdriver object can be animated from belt to hand. The inset shows the settings of the Formula Node.

global position and rotation of the two goal objects. Take some time to figure out how it works exactly, as it may serve you in the future.

Now you have a character that should be easily animatable. If you take care that the Selection Filter is set to just Nulls and Bones and the controller Null objects have a decent shape and size, you can simply start selecting bones and posing this version of Screwball without too much trouble.

Open the file screwball_05_IKed.c4d to see how the character looks and handles with all these controls in place. There are a few extra gimmicks implemented for the deformation of the belly and arms. Simply put, the rotation values of the Torso Controller and those of both lower arms are used to morph the upper body using a PoseMix object. This helps the wrinkle on top of Screwball's belly disappear when he bends backwards and it generates a tiny bit of muscle bulge for the biceps when the elbow gets bent. Have a look at the Xpression on the PoseMix object linked to the "body" geometry object to see how it works exactly.

Soft IK Legs

Now, let's re-address the legs to make them more predictable than they are with IK. We'll be using Soft IK for this, which is an entirely different take on the substance. If we "give" the leg to Soft IK, we'll need to control every aspect of the bones with it. Not that this is any problem; it is quite easy to control a structure such as a leg, up into the toes using Soft IK.

First, you're going to have to remove the IK tags and expressions from the current legs. Also, you may want to delete the right leg (the bones of that leg, that is) again. And finally, for Soft IK, we won't be needing the extra knee bone anymore, so you may want to remove this (remember to re-record keyframes if you do). Alternatively, you can load in the file screwball_05_pre_sIK.c4d, where everything is in place to start applying Soft IK.

We will be using a separate Soft IK system per leg instead of a single one for both of them. We do this because, were we to use the Pelvis as root for the Soft IK system, we'd be having to use it as root for an optional Soft IK system for the arms as well.

Before you start, disable Soft IK with the special MOCCA command. Now, take care that each bone in the left leg chain (including the root) has a Soft IK tag. You can do this in one of two ways.

First, you can use the Setup Chain command with the leg's root bone selected, which drops tags on all the bones, and automatically sets the rest positions and rotations. It also creates a tip effector on the end of each branch in the hierarchy it finds. This command needs a bit of cleanup, though, especially as we have the extra helper bone "++" in the heel. This bone doesn't need a Soft IK tag and the tip effector can be removed together with the goal it targets; just delete these two objects in the Objects Manager. The tip effector on the toe will come in handy and already is pointing a goal null, so we can leave it like that.

Second, some people may prefer to simply add all Soft IK elements by hand. If you do, or if you want to understand the automatically created chain better, note the following: the Soft IK tag on the root bone must have the Anchor option enabled. There also needs to be an extra object at the tip of the last bone in the chain; otherwise we'll never be able to rotate the last bone using Soft IK. So, if you're doing this by hand, add an extra Null object to roughly the tip of the last bone and give this one a Soft IK tag as well.

A Soft IK chain needs to know the rest state of the chain, i.e., the positions and rotations of all the objects in the default pose. The rest pose more or less "pulls" the chain back to a certain shape, so the Soft IK simulation isn't allowed to wander off too far. So be sure to call the function Set Rest Position and Set Rest Rotation with the root of the chain selected. Conversely, if you want to set a rest position or rotation on one element only, use the buttons inside the tag itself (Figure 10.17).

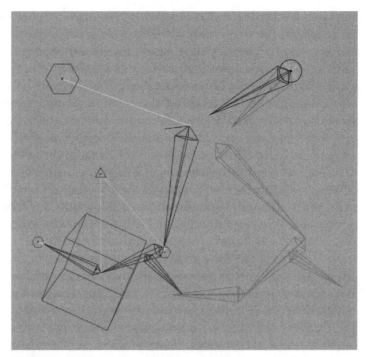

FIGURE 10.17 The rest position and rotation of a chain "remembers" a chain's rest pose.

Now that all the tags are in place, we will need to add some objects to influence the chain. If you added the chain automatically, there will already be a "L toes.Tip goal" Null object created that will pull on the end of the toes' bone. But of course, that is not enough. Let's create them, one by one.

First off, we'll need a Controller object for the ball of the foot (just as with regular IK). This object will both pull on the axis of the toes bone and contain all of the other Soft IK goals for the foot. Select the toes' bone, and call the function Add Root Goal. The created goal object will be our Foot Controller, so you may want to rename it. Also, if you create objects in this way, they will be placed as a child of the chain's root bone. This is not where you want it, so drag it out of the hierarchy.

Now, if you haven't used the "Setup Chain" command, select the toes' bone and use Add Tip Goal to create an object that pulls on the tip of the toes. Parent this object to the Foot Controller object. Finally, in the same manner, add a goal object for the heel by selecting the foot bone and adding a root goal. This null, too, should be placed inside the Foot Controller.

That's got all of the positioning goals present. Next, we want to make sure that the foot doesn't start banking when we don't want it to. For this to work, we need to use an Upvector goal. Such a goal tries to rotate the bone so that the +y axis is pointing towards the goal, but it will only influence the banking of the bone. You can optionally make it work on the -y, +x, or -x axis as well.

So, select the foot bone, and call the function Add UpVector. A new Null will be created at some distance from the foot bone. Drag this object inside the Foot Controller as well, and, for clarity's sake, move it closer to the foot. Take care to only drag it in its local yz plane by Shift-dragging the red x axis in the editor or else it will bank the foot bone out of its rest position.

We'll need the toes to have an UpVector target as well. For this, we can simply use the same null we just created (if toes and foot are oriented properly, that is). So select the Soft IK tag of the toes bone, find the UpVector field in the Attributes Manager, and drag and drop the Null inside.

Finally, we will need an extra goal for the knee joint to influence the way it bends. So, add a goal object to the root of the lower leg bone, using the same functions as above. This goal object is best left as a child of the leg's root (in this case the pelvis), and should be moved well away from the knee.

Now it is time to tweak the setup we just created. Tweaking Soft IK is essential and not really an exact science. Keep in mind that it's probably going to be impossible to tweak it so that the bones are in their exact rest pose, so if you need to change the bone's fixing state—or need to use the Bone tool—do so with Soft IK disabled.

For safety, record a position keyframe for all the goals you have created as well as a rotation keyframe for the Foot Controller. Next turn off animation globally (just so you can test without things popping back into their recorded state), make sure that expressions are enabled globally, and enable Soft IK. The leg will probably jump to a new position because the pull of the knee goal is too big.

Tweak the setup by selecting the various Soft IK tags and, in the Attributes Manager, changing the strength of the various goal fields. You will want to keep the Foot Controller objects' goal strengths at 100%, but the knee goal strength can be as low as 10%.

Another essential technique in creating a reliable chain is to fine-tune the Rest Rotation strength of the various tags. A few steps back, you have provided the whole leg with a rest state, and by tuning these parameters, you are defining to what extent the single elements should adhere to their rest state. It is really a matter of balancing the various strengths out. As you will observe, changing a Rest Rotation strength on one bone has an effect on the pose and motion of the whole chain. As a general rule of thumb, keep Rest Rotation low on joints such as the hip and foot as these should be able to rotate in any direction freely. The knee, though, should act a bit more limited, so increase the Rest Rotation strength on the lower leg bone more than on the others.

All in all, it's good to keep the Rest Rotations low, especially in flexible structures such as the leg. Try keeping them well below 50% if you can. When we reach the shoulder later on, you'll discover that that bone's rest rotation may actually be pretty high, as you only want the shoulder to move if you really stretch the arm a lot.

You may observe the leg being pulled apart completely, despite the Soft IK's rest position strength being on 100%. This isn't too bad if you are aiming for a bit of squash-and-stretch, but you may want to prevent this from happening. To do so, just enable the Force Position checkbox in all the Soft IK tags.

Again, remember to turn off the global Generators switch for speedier editor display. Also try out AutoRedraw to make your Soft IK leg update even though you are not touching it. You will notice that Soft IK, once set up correctly and tweaked to your liking, is a lot better than the IK system we implemented a few sections ago.

Mirroring Soft IK

Now that you have the left leg working well, it's time to mirror the setup over to the other side. This can be done in much the same way as with IK, with a few slight differences. Because the Bone Mirror function is specifically written for Soft IK, you don't need to select the controller objects anymore. Simply select the root of the chain, mirror it, and all controller objects will be mirrored along with it, and are placed in the correct place in the character's hierarchy. Also, you will find that the Soft IK Tags don't need any extra tweaking. You will, however, still need to take care of the correct keyframes on the chain and controller objects. And the Vertex maps issue still stands, just as it does with mirroring IK.

Open the file screwball_07_sIKlegs.c4d to inspect the result of all above actions.

A Few Extra Tips on Working with Soft IK

So, the Soft IK system looks like an incredibly flexible way to work with articulated structures. But, as with all systems, there are some quirks and behaviors that definitely take some getting used to.

To begin with, Soft IK is a simulation, and, if you have any experience with simulations, you will know that they can go wrong if not handled correctly. The same holds true for Soft IK. If you have been animating a character for a long time, you will probably, now and then, observe some limbs getting mangled because the Soft IK system has problems keeping up with your actions. This happens most notably when you are scrubbing through time in big steps or when the editor speed is too slow to cope with the frame rate of your animation. Joints may seem to break or limbs get twisted. If this happens, give the program some extra time to catch up with your actions (using AutoRedraw or repeated redraws of the viewer window). If all else fails, try to disable and enable Soft IK just momentarily to provide it with a new starting point for its calculations.

Also, you may find that specific bones get twisted when enabling Soft IK. This is because Soft IK uses its own system to measure and influence the rotation of the elements and some setups simply don't provide for this system. To solve this, you may actually have to fix some of the bones while they are in their Soft IK state. Although this can be dangerous and should only be applied on single bones at a time, sometimes it's the only way to get a mangled bit of your setup to work.

Soft IK works most predictably and rigidly when the anchor strengths are set to 100%. However, having the strength set so high also taxes your CPU a lot, sometimes even to the point of having useless editor feedback when you are playing the animation. Hence, if you have an intricate Soft IK setup, it is best to animate the rig with a lower anchor strength (the default 30% often does the trick just fine) and switch it back to 100% prior to rendering or preview rendering.

For the same reason, it may pay off in the long run to supply a non-deforming dummy character to work with, especially if you have a high-density, realistic character. A dummy character is built up of a split-apart version of the original mesh, so the pieces of mesh can move along with the bones directly instead of being deformed. By doing so, you can leave out the deformation step while animating, providing for much smoother editor feedback.

Working with a lot of Soft IK control can mean having the editor littered with control objects in the form of shaped Nulls. Remember that you can globally turn off the display of Null objects in the Display Filter menu item. The same goes for the various Soft IK specific lines running from the bones to the goals, though you'll need to turn these off in the tags themselves. Conversely, if the Soft IK is only applied to bones, you can turn off Bones display in the Display Filter and make the Soft IK indicators disappear along with it, thereby cleaning up editor display.

Soft IK for the Arms

After the above exercise, applying Soft IK to the arms should not be too much of a problem anymore. Let me just highlight the important aspects.

With the arms, do NOT use the Setup Chain command from the MOCCA menu or palette. Remember how that places tags on each and every object and creates tip effectors and goals on the end of each branch in the bone chain it finds? Keep in mind that our hand alone has sixteen bones and four fingers. You can see why you wouldn't want to use the automatic function here. In the case of the arms, you will probably want to use two "knee-type" constraints, one for the shoulder and one for the elbow. The shoulder constraint is best placed a short distance above the shoulder, and the elbow one to the back. Having two of these means that tweaking the system is somewhat more delicate. You will want the shoulder to only bend if you really start pulling on the hand. This is best achieved by finely balancing the Rest Rotation strengths between the shoulder bone and the rest of the bones.

For the hand, you will want to use one controller for position and rotation, just as with the foot. For this, you're going to need three constraints acting on what seems like one bone: one for the base of the hand (the wrist), one for the tip of the hand bone (which is, in fact, an extra Null placed at the end of the bone, just as with the toe tip) and an upvector constraint for the final axis of rotation. Simply parent the tip-of-bone goal and the upvector goal to the wrist goal and you'll have an easy-to-manage Hand Controller, pulling the whole arm and rotating the hand at the same time (Figure 10.18).

You could also opt to control the arm from the upper arm up only, so disregarding the shoulder. That way, you'll have more direct control over the bend of the shoulder itself.

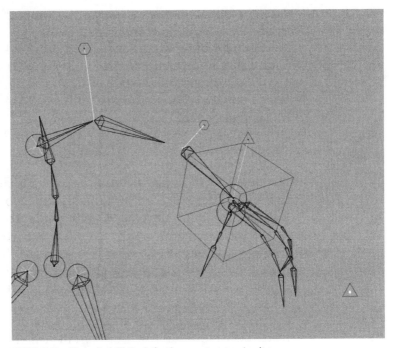

FIGURE 10.18   All the Soft IK Goals for the arm structure in place.

Follow the same steps as described for the leg's Soft IK to mirror the new arm over to the other side of the body. Keep a close eye on the Claude Bonet Vertex maps

Better Control of the Head

Finally, you'll want to add a more flexible Head Controller. Right now, you need to grab the skull bone and both neck bones directly and rotate them by hand. It would be better if you could control both the neck and the head with one single controller. For this to work, we'll remove one of the neck bones and actually put the neck and skull bone side by side in the hierarchy. Next, add a Target Expression on the single bone and point it at the skull bone. Now, if you move the skull around, the neck bone will automatically bend to point towards the base of the skull. This gives a far more flexible setup.

Keep in mind that you will have to re-record the safety keyframes we placed earlier, as well as probably fix the neck and skull bones again after you have applied the Target Expression.

And maybe a bit of re-weighting for the vertices in the neck is in order.

Have a look at file screwball_08_sIKall.c4d to see both the Soft IK arms and new skull control in action. For ease of use, there's a User Data slider on Screwball's root HyperNURBS object, with which you can change the strengths of all Soft IK chains at once.

STREAMLINING

The final step in setting up your character is streamlining the structure of the file. You may find this step to be overly precise for your taste, but having some controls of your character deeply embedded inside the—by now—quite elaborate structure you've built can slow the animation process down so much that attempting to animate a decent bit of acting can become difficult. Furthermore, if you do have a decent hierarchical structure, placing the character into a scene and moving it about—including animation—is going to become so much easier. Sadly, Soft IK-controlled structures don't react too well to having their parent scaled (even with the Object tool), so you will either have to build your characters to scale, scale the set, or, if all else fails, use an instance of your character, which you can scale, and hide the original.

Of course, you can take this step too far, so let's just look at the essentials, plus some extra organizational steps for you to pick from.

Separating the Controllers

Placing all controllers inside a dedicated group will help you to quickly find them, as well as, maybe, provide you with the ability to apply MoMix later in the process. This means, though, that you need a few extra control objects. Right now, the character is set up so that you still need to grab the pelvis and skull bone directly to animate them. Transferring this function to a dedicated set of control nulls allows you to put all controllers, with the exception of the fingers, into one separate control group.

Simply add an extra Null object called Pelvis Controller to the scene, Transfer it to the position and location of the pelvis bone, and use an Xpresso expression to feed its global matrix—or the global position and rotation—directly to the pelvis bone itself. Do the same with a new Null object called Skull Controller.

Now, with this in place, you can parent the Torso Controller directly to the Pelvis Controller, and the Skull Controller, in turn, directly to the Torso Controller. The Foot and Hand controllers will already be separated from your character if all is well, so that only leaves the knee, shoulder and elbow controllers. These can directly be linked to the Pelvis and Torso Controllers as well. Group all this into a Null object called "Controllers" or something similar, taking care to re-record the various controllers' positions and rotations in the process, and you're done. All controllers are neatly lined up, with almost no need anymore to open up the skeleton itself (Figure 10.19).

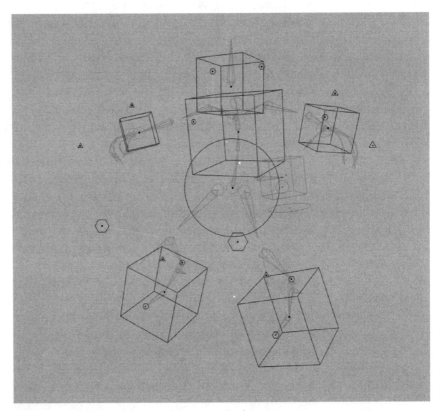

FIGURE 10.19   All objects of the control rig are now in place.

The Hands

We still need a bit of extra control for the hands. As mentioned previously, PoseMixer would be ideal to animate an intricate structure such as the hands, so let's put that into practice.

There's already a MorphTargets object group in the scene if you loaded one of the example scenes of the last few steps. This would be an ideal place to place the targets for both the hands. Sadly, you're going to have to use separate sets of targets for each hand, though you may make use here of the Mirror Bones function to copy targets from left to right (or, of course, vice versa).

First off, let's set up the basic structure. Inside the MorphTargets object group, put an extra Null object called "L hand targets" and transfer it to the position, rotation and scale of the left hand root bone. If you have not already done so, create an extra bone between the hand root and the various finger bones. PoseMixer, just as all deformers, will change the state of its parent object and all its children (excluding itself, of course) so you need this extra bone to still be able to control the rotation of the hand's base yourself.

Investigate the "live" hand skeleton. There should still be a "Screwdriver Goal" null object in there. You should be able to animate the precise location of the screwdriver with this, and as such, it shouldn't be influenced by the PoseMixer object. To allow for this, make sure that the goal object is the last child of the hand parent.

Next, CTRL-drag the second parent bone of the hand into the "L hand targets" group. Keep in mind that there are probably keyframes on this structure, so turn off the global Animation switch, and remove the keyframes after you have copied the hand skeleton into the targets group. Name this hand "default" and disable all the bones by CTRL-clicking on the green check of the parent bone in the Objects Manager.

Now, to allow for being able to still manually animate the screwdriver goal object we just talked about, *remove* it from the target hand you just created. Because it is the last child of its parent, PoseMixer will simply skip it because it can't find any similar child in the target shape.

Next, create a copy of the default hand, at the same level in the hierarchy, and call this one "Animated." This will be your "flexible" morph target, one that you can pose and shape to your liking during animation, for the simple reason that, sometimes, using just the basic shapes of the hands may not be enough for the most precise tasks. Now you can start making targets for the actual basic shapes, but you probably should only do those when you need them. (You may not need a left-handed fist in your animation, for example.)

You can of course roughly pose the hand targets into the poses you need, but you will probably want to see the effect on the mesh in realtime. To do this, simply add a PoseMixer object to the "live" hand, and, with it active in the Attributes Manager, drag the hand named "default" to the Default Pose field. For completeness, drag the "Animated" hand to the first PoseMixer slider, and create another pose. Here you drop the hand target structure you want to pose. If you now set this slider to maximum (keeping the others at zero, of course), set the Selection Filter so you can only select bones, hide the original hand skeleton and show the hand you want to define, you can start posing the target skeleton hand and see the result on the mesh in realtime (Figure 10.20).

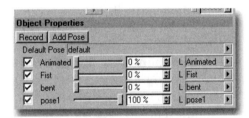

FIGURE 10.20   By keeping PoseMixer in a "solo" mode like this, you can interactively model the pose of the targets.

Try adding a few targets for the hand in this manner and watch what happens to the hand when you drag the PoseMixer sliders. This is going to be such a timesaver in animation.

For the most efficient PoseMixer targets, try to keep the poses as extreme as possible. Subtle poses as targets don't make too much sense, as you can already create these by simply using low values for the PoseMixer strength sliders.

To complete the control for the hands, do the same for the right hand. Remember you can use Bone Mirror to copy the left hand targets over to the right hand.

The Face

Although Screwball's face is barely visible behind his neatly tinted chrome-glazed helmet glass, you'll still want to be able to animate it now and then. Again, this is a perfect job for PoseMixer, since it works with geometry just as it does with pose data. Just follow much the same steps as you did for the hands, keeping in mind that the targets have to be linked to a parent that is, relatively, placed exactly like the parent of the live geometry, just as with the extra hand's parent.

Even though the eyes are both in the same Polygon object, it is perfectly possible to use separate targets for both eyes. PoseMixer will automatically discover which parts of the targets are actually different from the default geometry, and only morph those parts. So, in case of Screwball's eyes, it's best to make separate targets for closing the left eye and closing the right eye, and use two sliders to control both eyes independently of each other.

Screwball's mouth could be done with another PoseMixer structure as well, but it's actually designed to be influenced with a Spline Deformer. To make this work, you'll need two splines: one for the default shape and one for the deformed shape. This deformer spline can then be used to animate the lips, either with Point Level Animation or by using another PoseMixer morph. Of course, as that last option would more or less defeat the purpose of adding a Spline Deformer, use Point Level Animation only.

The Final Structure

Now all the controllers, morph targets and what-have-you needs to be easily transportable from scene to scene. To do so, simply place the morph target's group and the controller's group, as well as the selection object(s), inside the character's Base object group. As this Base is, in the example files at least, the direct child of the character's HyperNURBS object, the order of geometry, control group, and morph targets doesn't really matter. Do make sure to put a Stop tag on the MorphTargets group, though, as you don't want to waste precious CPU cycles on the HyperNURBS-smoothing of objects that you don't actually see (Figure 10.21).

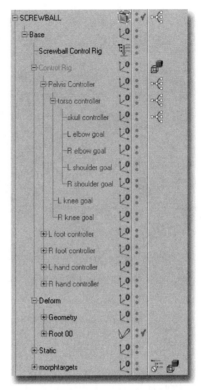

FIGURE 10.21   The final Objects Manager structure.

SOME FINAL TOUCHES

To make matters completely flexible, create a Selection Object, call it "screwball controls" or something like that, and drag all the controllers for the skeleton into it. You can leave out the UpVector and Bone-tip goals, as you won't actually be animating them. Now you can restrict editor selection and keyframe recording to just these controls by selecting it in the "Keyframe" submenu, which is also found as a popup-menu under the little red dot with the question mark.

Also, you may want to Lock the Timeline, so you can load objects into it manually. Do so for the Motion Mix objects as well as the Deformer Spline that controls the mouth. You may even want to add the Default Spline as you can further tweak the deformation of the mouth by animating this. Unlock the Timeline again and set it to the automated mode you like most, for example, Active Object. Now, by locking and unlocking the Timeline, you have direct access to the PoseMixer and Spline objects without needing to find them deep within the skeleton and geometry (Figure 10.22).

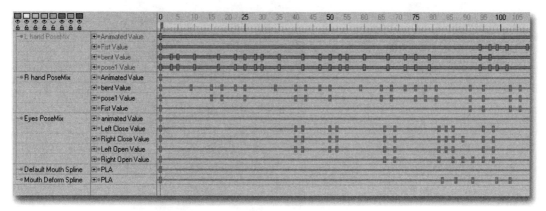

FIGURE 10.22 A manual (locked) Timeline with just the hard-to-select objects.

Remember that some of the controllers will need to have both position and rotation recorded, while others only need position or rotation. To prevent your having to continually switch between the various keyframing modes, give the tracks you won't be needing a dedicated hidden layer color. Simply keep one of your layers hidden at all times, select the offending tracks, and CTRL-click on the hidden layer's colored square to hide them from the visible Timeline. Sometimes you may have to show them again (because, for example, the previous/next keyframe commands are stuck on one of the hidden keys), but for the rest of it you can safely leave them alone.

Have a look at the scene file called screwball_09_streamlined.c4d. In here, all the streamlining steps have been implemented as have as the extra controls for animating the hands and the face. A few targets have already been defined, and the "default pose" keyframes have been moved back in time a bit, so this file is ready to be animated for real.

ANIMATION

So we finally get to the step where all the magic is supposed to happen. However, teaching the craft of animation is worthy of a complete book itself. It's a craft you can teach yourself, simply by experimenting a lot, observing what works and what does not, looking at people and animals in motion in the real world, and frame-stepping through movies or animations to get a feeling for the frame-by-frame differences that can occur.

Let's just walk through the creation of a simple walk cycle for Screwball in very rough steps, just to offer you a basic workflow to get your character in motion.

First, remember that we've put "storage" keyframes on Screwball's skeleton and rig. It's a good idea to keep these present in the file because you may need to do some extra tweaking of the rig, in which case you're bound to be needing the rest pose of all elements involved. However, as far as the control rig is concerned, it's best to keep them some frames back in negative time, as you will probably want to start the animation itself on frame 0. If you loaded the example file, the default pose keyframes are already placed at -6 frames. If not, or in your own scene, it is really only a matter of selecting all controller objects, moving back in time a bit (say to minus 6 frames), and manually recording a keyframe. Keep in mind that, because the sequences are continuous, these keyframes will influence the interpolation of the frames you will be dropping at frame zero.

Now, move back to frame zero, and, with the Selection object active, and automatic keyframing enabled on both position and rotation, roughly pose the character into his first step using the various controller objects. Even though you'll be animating from main controllers to the detailed ones, it's handy to at least have the whole character roughly in shape to start out with, arms hanging down.

A basic walk cycle is built up of six key poses, that can be an equal distance apart in time. The first one is the "step" pose, where one leg is extended forward, ready to hit the ground, and the other is extended backwards, still on the ground, pushing the body up and forward. Both knees can be stretched in this pose (this depends on the walking style you are aiming at), and the body is now in the highest position of all six key poses. Next is the "touchdown" pose, where the front foot has just caught the weight of the body, which is somewhat lower than in the previous pose, and the knee is bent. The back foot has done the pushing-off step, and is off the ground but still extended backward, even further than in the previous pose. The third pose is the "crossover" pose, where the foot that was just in front is carrying the entire weight of the character and is right beneath the pelvis. Keep the knee bent as well here. The other foot is just being moved over to the front; how this is done really depends on the character. Sometimes it goes straight under the pelvis; sometimes it can be swung around the body for a more comical effect. The next three steps are identical to the three just described, but with the roles of both feet reversed.

This rough start of the walk animation can be animated with just the three controllers for both the feet and the pelvis. Keep in mind—when animating this as a cycle (i.e., you aren't changing the position of the whole character in space)—that with each new pose, the foot that is touching the ground should travel more or less the same distance. Take a look at Figures 10.23 and 10.24 for an idea of the differences between the poses.

FIGURE 10.23   Side-view of a somewhat Wild-West style walk cycle for the Screwball character.

FIGURE 10.24   Front-view of a somewhat Wild-West style walk cycle for the Screwball character.

Now, try animating this yourself. The bulk of the animation can be done in the side view, adding the side-to-side motion later on.

Also, try to give the pelvis some forward and back motion: it's pushed forward just a little in the step and touchdown poses and can travel back in the crossover pose.

Remember to set the interpolation type before you start adding keyframes. You might want to use linked tangents and soft interpolation for now. Refinement can be done by turning the keyframes to custom interpolation later on.

Try to stick to just the six poses for now, lining up the keyframes of the various controllers. Once you have the basics of the animation down, and all axes of motion are recorded, you can go on tweaking the in-betweens by adding extra keyframes, though this is probably not even necessary for the walk cycle.

As long as you start animating in the side view only, you can use the pelvis's first three keyframes for the second three poses. This keeps the animation looping smoothly.

To provide for a decent looping animation in the editor as you are animating, decide on a length for the loop (say, 25 frames), set the preview area in the Timeline to just this length (remember to subtract one frame to prevent a "hiccup," so set the preview markers on 0 and 24 frames), set the Play mode to Preview Range, and, of course, Loop. You will have to manually copy the starting keyframes over to frame 25 each time you change them.

When you are satisfied with the speed of the feet and the motion of the legs, start adding some extra weight to the pelvis by slightly animating it side-to-side. In the crossover pose, it should really be over the foot that touches the ground, maybe even further to the side if you decided to do a real wide swing on the other foot. In the other two poses, it travels from one leg to the other.

If you like the weight, continue by animating a bit of hip-sway. You can overdo this to accentuate the Wild-West style walk pictured earlier. In any case, the hips should be rotated so that the side of the leg that is forward is also pointing forward. In the crossover pose, to really communicate the weight being over the "down" leg, tilt the pelvis so this side is higher than the other.

You may also want to add some extra rotation and side-to-side motion to the feet as they are in the air. To keep them from going through the floor due to the interpolation, keep the y curve (which is, after all, the height above the floor) flat as long as the foot touches the ground. You can easily do this by grabbing all the y-position keyframes where the foot is on the ground and setting the Soft interpolation strength to 0%.

After the basic leg motion has been done, you may want to refine it by animating the knee controllers (although keeping these unanimated, just placing them slightly apart on frame 0, usually is more than enough for a walk cycle). It's better to focus on the torso and arms next. Animate these so that they are countering the motion of the legs and hips. Keep in mind that the hands should really be moving in arcs, and, if you want, add a bit of "looseness" to them by rotating them backward when they are moving forward, and vice versa. The torso should purely counteract the pelvis, so when the pelvis tilts one way, the shoulders tilt the other way. Remember as well that the shoulders are actually where the arms are driven from (there are no IK goals in real life), so they should move forward and backward just as the arms are doing, by twisting the Torso Controller.

Once you've done this, start animating the head as well. You might want to give it a slight "bob" by tilting the nose up as the body moves down, and vice versa.

Further refinements may go into the motion of knees, elbows, and shoulders, and possibly the toes. And finally, add a bit of subtle motion to the fingers by animating the PoseMixer objects just a bit. Really keeping every part of a character alive is what sells his presence in the animation.

Have a look at the file screwbal_10_walking.c4d for a basic walk cycle adhering to the above mentioned method.

CONCLUSION

What happens next is up to you. Try copying the loop a few times and changing some of the motions slightly. Make him come to a stop or hit his head. Maybe make him grab his screwdriver by animating the User Data slider on the screwdriver. Tackle him. Try using the spline deformer to animate the face. Just keep on experimenting and see what animation does for you.

And of course, a lot of further improvements can be made to this setup as well. A simple Xpression to keep the Foot Controllers above the floor, for example, or a Target expression to animate the Head Controller independently of the pelvis and torso. The things we've added until now were basic, and should give you an idea of the amount of control you can apply.

Of course, you will want to apply the things you just learned onto your own character next. Well, that shouldn't be too much of a problem as all the tricks and techniques we offered, with maybe the exception of some character-specific notes (for the weighting, for example), are interchangable between different designs. So try to put it all to good use. Remember to keep it simple if you're not too sure of yourself yet. Animation itself doesn't suffer from simplicity, and even with a very simple character, the experience in building it up from scratch to finish is invaluable. Good luck!

11

CAMERAS AND RENDERING

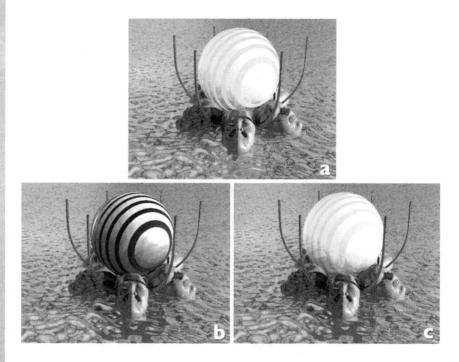

Wre've looked at modeling forms. We've looked at adding texture to these forms to create tactile-looking surfaces. We've looked at how to bring those polygons to life through the ideas of animation. The last step of 3D animation (that takes place within a 3D application, anyway) is rendering.

The reason that cameras are included in a chapter on rendering is that rendering is essentially the act of "seeing" the 3D world as you've created it in its final glory. The instrument through which you see this world is a virtual camera. Additionally, there are many effects attached to cameras that ultimately tie closely to the rendering process. So, because of this close relationship, we will look a bit at the anatomy of C4D's cameras, how they work, and how they tie into the rendering engines. Then, we will tear into the rendering capabilities of C4D.

CAMERA ANATOMY

Figure 11.1 shows a screenshot of a camera as it initially appears in C4D. There are actually a lot of things here that should look very similar to the visual clues that light objects give you. Basically, you have a symbol that represents where the camera resides in visual space and a pyramid that indicates the field of view for the camera. Around the edge of the camera's field of view are orange parameter handles that allow you to change the field of view, which means you can change the virtual lens on the camera to a wider angle or more of a zoom.

An important thing to note about the camera is that you can also change any of the settings for the camera in the Attributes Editor. Simple select the camera in the Objects Manager and its attributes will be available for numeric alterations (Figure 11.2). Notice that besides the ability to make the camera a non-Perspective camera, you can numerically define the Focal Length, Aperture Width, and Field of View for the Camera object.

To create a camera, simply click and hold the flashlight icon in the top command palette and select the camera icon from the nested tools (Figure 11.3). You can also create a camera with the pull-down menu Objects>Scene>Camera.

When a camera is created, a few things about it are different from when any other object is created in C4D. The first is that the position of the camera is not at the traditional (0,0,0) in space. Rather, the camera is placed at approximately the position of the

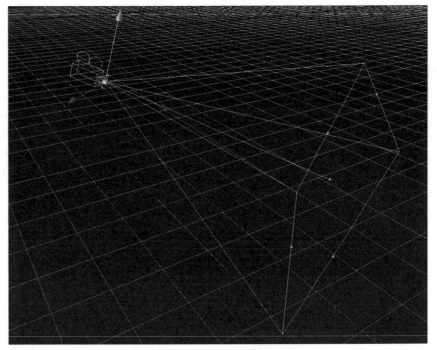

FIGURE 11.1   Camera in C4D. The background is black just to help make the screenshot a little clearer.

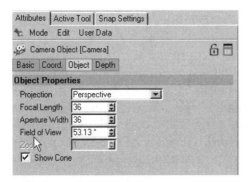

FIGURE 11.2   Attributes Editor for a camera.

FIGURE 11.3   Creating a camera with the top command palette.

Editor Camera, or the view point in which you are viewing your scene. This means that usually it is important that the Perspective view panel is the active view panel when you do create a camera.

When you first create a camera, it does not mean that you are automatically looking through it. In fact, when you first create the camera, it will show up as a big green X in the middle of your view panel. To actually look through this new camera's viewfinder, select Cameras>Camera from the pull-down menus within the view panel.

When you are looking through the camera's viewfinder in one of your view panels, as you use the Camera Move, Camera Scale, and Camera Rotate tools in the top corner of the view panel, the actual camera object will also move, scale, or rotate. Additionally, if you select the camera in the Objects Manager and then move or rotate the object in any of the view panels, you will see the updated point of view within the view panel representing the camera's viewfinder.

Remember that a camera object is just like any other object within the 3D space. You can animate its position, scale, rotation, or a host of other parameters.

One last note on cameras: notice that in the Attributes Editor there is a section called Depth. This allows you to activate the post-rendering effect of Depth of Field. We will talk more of this a little later in the chapter; but just remember that this is where you must activate this effect in the camera.

RENDERING

Rendering is the process of C4D taking all the modeling, texturing, lighting, and animation information, and "painting" it, complete with shadows, highlights, reflections, etc. Throughout the course of the book, we've done several test renderings to get a quick idea of how our work has been looking. However, manipulating the Rendering settings is an art form in itself, and can present a good project at its best. Conversely, rendering is one of the slowest parts of most animation projects; so mastering the art of the Rendering settings can save hours in rendering time, allowing you to move quicker on your project and produce better projects through more in-depth revision.

R8 AND ADVANCED RENDER

New to R8's module-based system is the ability to take or leave the module Advanced Render. In this chapter, we are going to talk about some things that are common to C4D with or without Advanced Render. But for the most part, we are going to assume that you have Advanced Render. If you're serious about a good range of rendering styles and effects, you undoubtedly have this powerful module anyway.

RENDERING TOOLS

There are three main buttons allowing you to access the various rendering options. All three are located in the top command palette (Figure 11.4). To start with, we'll look at the Rendering Settings button (far right) as it determines how the other two tools will work.

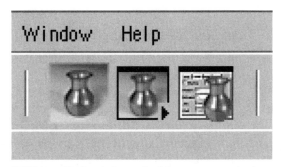

FIGURE 11.4   The Rendering tools of the top command palette.

Upon clicking the Rendering Settings button, a dialog box will appear that allows you to define how C4D will interpret the information you've given it thus far. In C4D R8, the settings are broken up into 10 sections available via the section head on the left. The first, the General tab (Figure 11.5), allows you to make general changes to how the scene is rendered. By default, C4D renders using Raytracing. Raytracing is the standard rendering engine of most 3D packages, although C4D's is known for being quite snappy. However, C4D can also render collections of frames just as you see them in your view panel. Notice the little checkbox "Render As Editor." This isn't usually of much use in still work, but in animation it's important, especially with complex scenes, to create quickly done renderings As Editor to get an idea of the true timing of your motion. There are other ways that C4D can produce images, including radiosity and cel-shading, but we will talk of these later in the chapter.

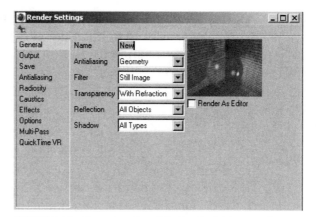

FIGURE 11.5   The General section of the Render Settings window.

When C4D renders, it's dealing with a lot of information and a great many calculations. Literally, it has to analyze all the polygons in the scene and decide how the materials, lights, and setting come together and how this should be drawn. Because of this, the Rendering Settings have been optimized to attempt to provide good quality in very little time. However, sometimes you may not need C4D to calculate all the things it looks for in the rendering process. Or perhaps the default quality just doesn't cut it, and you need C4D to spend a bit more time to provide a little more refined rendering. There are several ways and places to decrease or increase the amount of issues C4D takes time to look at as it renders. You can tell C4D's Renderer to not worry about everything from reflections to shadows. You can tell C4D to be careful in how it handles edges or to just pound them out. Knowing when to ask C4D to do what will determine how much time you spend waiting for C4D to render. To analyze these possibilities, we'll look at the settings here in the General section and see how these options can be manipulated.

GENERAL OPTIONS

The General section provides the means to define the ground rules that C4D will use to render. By default now in R8, C4D renders using raytracing, and so the General area only allows you to define the raytracing attributes (with the exception of turning on the Render As Editor option discussed earlier).

Antialiasing

By default, C4D renders with Antialiasing activated. Antialiasing is the process of creating sub-pixels that keep the edges of objects clean with no jagged edges. Without Antialiasing activated, you can end up with a very stair-like, rough edge.

Figure 11.6 shows a rendering done without Antialiasing activated. Notice the jagged edges along the bent capsule shape. When any of the Antialiasing options are activated, C4D takes extra time to "Oversample" pixels as it renders. With this extra time comes more accurate and smoother renderings, but at a fairly healthy rendering cost. Antialiasing always slows rendering. However, when you work with still images or broadcast animation, some antialiasing can be necessary (Figure 11.6b).

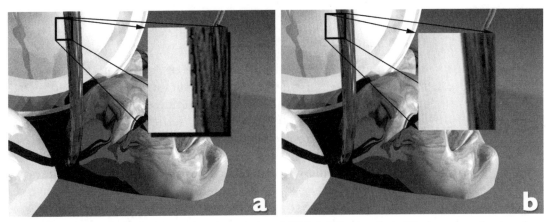

FIGURE 11.6   (a) No Antialiasing and the resultant jagged edges. (b) With Antialiasing activated, the image is rendered much smoother, but at a time cost.

So the key is to know when to use the default Antialiasing and what Oversampling settings to use. Although there are no rock-solid rules, there are some general guidelines that you can count on. First, when you do first-run renderings even of stills, don't bother with the antialiasing, there's no need. For those first renderings, you want C4D to pound out the rendering, giving you accurate color and composition but not worrying about immaculate edges.

Notice that the default setting for Antialiasing is Geometry. Geometry Antialiasing smoothes out the edges of objects when rendered. Best Antialiasing not only smoothes the edges, but it carefully softens areas of high contrast, such as where a shadow is laid across a bright surface. Again, Best Antialiasing produces the best quality images, but also takes some time to render.

Immediately below the Antialiasing option is the ability to use Filters. All of these filters are in reference to the Antialiasing process. In general, the only two of real use are the Still Image and Animation settings. If you are doing a still shot, you want as crisp an image as you can possibly get; Still Image will give you sharp contrast and sharp edges. However, these sharp edges can really wreak havoc when you are animating things. Renders with Still Image as the chosen filter can end up with the dreaded visual "flicker" that often invades 3D work. If your output is indeed animation, use the Animation filter as it will provide much smoother edges and help reduce unwanted flicker.

Transparency, Reflection, and Shadow

Still within the General tab are three options that can speed the rendering process. By default, raytraced images are rendered recognizing and showing objects' Transparency and Reflection properties. Also by default, the Raytracing settings calculate Shadows. However, all of these options can be turned off. Figure 11.07a shows the scene we've been working on with all of these turned on. Figure 11.07b shows Transparency set to None. Suddenly all transparent, glass-like, or alpha-parameterized objects become opaque. You can also use the raytracer to render transparency but not bother to calculate the bend of light as it passes through objects. The Transparency>No Refraction setting can give you a quick view and idea of transparent objects but still save time as the bent light isn't bothered with (Figure 11.7c).

Similarly, Figure 11.8a shows the scene (with Transparency activated again) but Reflection set to None. Figure 11.8b shows the results of setting the Reflection to only worry about the Floor and Sky and not worry about other objects in the scene.

Output

The Output area allows you to define how big, how many frames, and how many frames per second you want C4D to render out for you. Most of these areas are fairly self-explanatory, so we won't go

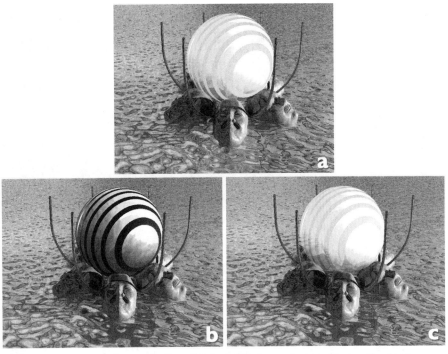

FIGURE 11.7   Various Transparency settings affect how C4D chooses to deal with glass-like objects.

FIGURE 11.8   (a) Reflection>None. (b) Reflection>Floor and Sky Only.

into much depth here (Figure 11.9). There are a few things to re-member, however.

First, remember that the Resolution size becomes very impor-tant as you get ready to output your projects to different media. The

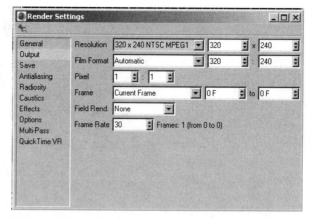

FIGURE 11.9 The Output area of the Render Settings.

default 320 × 240 (pixels) is probably an acceptable setting if you are outputting to the web. However, a 320 × 240 movie file will look either very small on a TV screen or fuzzy and unclear if stretched up to the size you need. If you are using DV-NTSC, note that some programs (such as Apple's Final Cut Pro) use the settings 720 × 480 as an output size—not the 720 × 486 that is the C4D NTSC preset.

Second, remember that you need to do a bit of math if you are creating imagery for print. The resolution settings listed in this section are in the absolute value of number of pixels. So, if you are creating an image that is to appear 4" × 4" in print, and you know that you need 300 dots per inch (dpi), you need to manually enter 1200 × 1200 in the resolution settings. The nice thing is that as C4D will allow you to enter mathematical equations in input fields, some of this work can be done for you. So if you're doing a poster that is 18" × 24" and you are rending the imagery that is to appear there, and your printer tells you that 600dpi is what will work best, then you can enter 18*600 (that's 18" × 600dpi) in one input field and 24*600 in the other. C4D will automatically update these values to 10800 × 14400.

Of course, this is a large number of pixels and it will take C4D quite a while to render this much information. Similarly, if you render out 20 seconds of animation (600 frames) at the wrong resolution, you are really aching for that time back. Take some good time to carefully research exactly what resolution you need and have C4D create it correctly from the start. Although you can fool with images in Photoshop and stretch images in video editing software, the results are always inferior compared with having the output correct to begin with.

Save

The Save area is also a fairly well understood area, as it is a natural way to think for most folks involved with computers. This is where you instruct C4D to save the fruits of its labors. Not only can you tell it to save, but you tell it what format to save it as. Do remember that when you are rendering animation, you *must* give it a place to save; if not, it simply discards each frame as it finishes rendering it.

Also remember that when picking your Format, there are often other settings to refine the format in the Options button next to the Format input line.

Toward the bottom of this area are two areas of interest that are a bit beyond what we are covering in this volume. Alpha Channels is a compositing tool that allows you to ask C4D to create a channel in the image that defines where the objects in your rendering end. This means you can render a logo and then drop this logo into Photoshop or a video editing package and have the black background automatically drop away. This makes for very quick implementation of you 3D monsters into your real-life footage or the ability to work with animation in several layers. Beneath the Alpha Channel option are a few other options to refine how this Alpha Channel is created; be sure to check out the manual about the specifics of these options to render right the first time for your project.

The second is the ability to create an After Effects Project File. This is truly one of the most clever inventions ever developed by the folks at Maxon. When created as an After Effects file, you can seamlessly add new visual elements to many rendered projects in After Effects without having to render the scene anew in C4D. This is more advanced than we want to cover here, but take a look on page 541 of the R8 manual for a nice tutorial showing you the basics of utilizing this powerful advanced feature.

Antialiasing (Refined)

Basically, this area allows you to further refine the Antialiasing settings you chose in the General section. Usually, the need to adjust these is for either very special cases or for minute adjustments of the final output. Chances are, if you are needing to adjust these settings, you are at a level far beyond the scope of this book. However, there are some nice technical explanations in the R8 manual of these settings, so take a look if you feel you need to refine the Antialiasing settings.

Radiosity and Caustics

Here's where things get interesting. Remember that in Chapter 7 (the chapter on lighting) we looked quickly at how to fake radiosity and how to optimize your scene in preparation for radiosity rendering. Please be sure to check out that chapter more closely if you feel that the radiosity look is the look you desire for a project.

Radiosity and Caustics are particulars to the Advanced Rendering module, and although the multitude of settings are indeed important, they are also very technical. Here's a brief run-down of what they are, what they mean, and what to use for most rendering situations.

Radiosity Settings

Let's take a look at some of these settings now.

Radiosity

Radiosity invokes the radiosity engine. This provides beautiful results that closely mimic the real world, but at a considerable expense in rendering time. Use with caution. Remember that you can sometimes fake the radiosity look with raytracing lighting tricks (see Chapter 7).

Stochastic Mode

This is a fairly speedy setting that gives you the classic "Arnold" look. There are several high-profile rendering packages (e.g., Brazil) that make use of this Arnold look, and C4D has it built in. There is definitely a difference in the final rendering between a Stochastic mode rendering and a traditional radiosity image (Figure 11.10); and there is a place for both.

Notice that Stochastic gives a grainy appearance. Although this grain might be part of the "look" for one project, you may want to minimize it in the next. When you choose to use Stochastic Mode, many of the options are disabled in the Rendering settings. How-

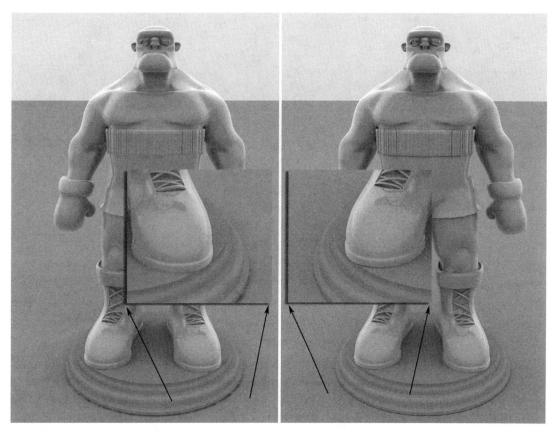

FIGURE 11.10   Comparison between straight up radiosity (left) and Stochastic mode (right). Model by Richard Clark.

ever, Diffuse Depth and Stochastic Samples remain active. The more Stochastic Samples you have, the less grain is apparent in the scene; however, you also have slower renderings. The key is finding the look you want at the rendering time you are willing to take.

Strength

For straight-up radiosity or Stochastic mode, strength determines how strong the radiosity look will be. The often means how bright your scene will render. Typically, I use strength values of over 100% to punch the visual effect up a bit. However, this could also be achieved by adjusting the GI Generate and Received values of individual materials. Figure 11.11 shows the same scene with various rendering strengths. Notice that too high a strength setting can result in overexposed scenes.

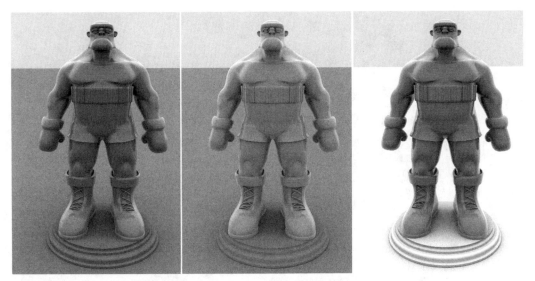

FIGURE 11.11 Identical lighting setups rendered with various Strength settings. Model by Richard Clark.

Accuracy

This defines how accurately the bounced light will calculate. Again, a lower accuracy produces faster render times, while higher values increase quality. The trick is finding the lowest value that gives you the acceptable results. Figure 11.12 shows the same scene rendered twice with two different accurate values. The image on the left uses an accuracy setting of 5% while the one on the right uses an accuracy setting of 70%. Take careful note of where the model intersects the floor.

Prepass Size

You'll probably want to leave this alone most of the time. The Prepass is the rendering pass that calculates "shading points" for the final image. 1/1 is closest to what you see is what you get; lowering this value increases rendering times but quickly diminishes quality.

Diffusion Depth

Imagine Diffusion as how quickly the light radiation disintegrates, or "diffuses." The depth actually calculates the number of times a ray of light is reflected and refracted. Although this value can go as high as 100, the default 3 is usually just right. Be especially wary of

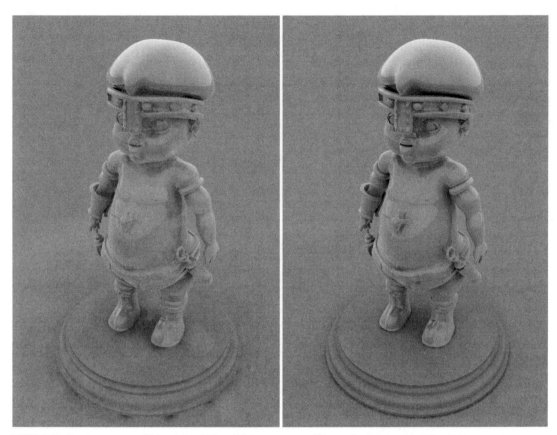

FIGURE 11.12   Varying accuracy (5% on left—70% at right) creates very different final output. Model by AJ Moore.

high values here if you have a complex scene with a lot of surfaces. Each light ray having to bounce 50 times in a complex scene could tie your machine up for weeks.

Stochastic Samples

The theory behind this setting is that as light rays hit a surface (and the renderer is using radiosity), C4D shoots off bounced light from that surface in a dome shape. This value indicates how many rays will be bounced off that impact point. This means that the higher the value, the more light rays will be ultimately bouncing around. So lower values will give you faster rendering times (fewer rays to calculate) but may actually affect how bright your scene is. Usually the default setting of 300 is more than enough. However, if you have some far-recessed corners where light will have to bounce a lot to illuminate them, a slightly higher value may be necessary.

Min and Max Resolutions

This is actually an optimization of the Accuracy setting discussed above. This allows C4D to create higher numbers of shading points where they are needed (for example, where two objects sit upon one another or intersect) and leaves low numbers in open spaces (open walls, floors, etc.). This is a tricky setting as it can really speed up a rendering with the right settings, but make the output look bad with the wrong settings. Again, this largely depends on the nature of your scene and often takes a bit of experimentation and test renderings to get the settings right.

We won't get into the highly technical reasons for settings, but a general rule of thumb is to start out with a fairly low value for your Max resolution. If your rendering appears with dark splotches or abnormal shadows (Figure 11.13a), then gradually increase your Accuracy and Max Resolution settings until the splotches disappear (Figure 11.13b). Remember the appropriate setting is going to be different for every scene.

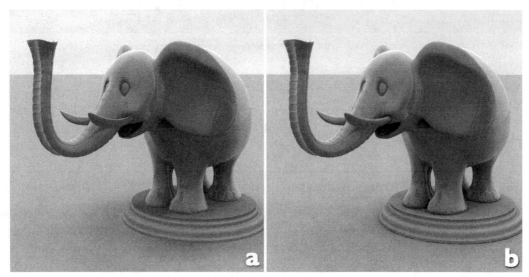

FIGURE 11.13 (a) Low Max Resolution setting creates fairly quick renders, but inappropriate shadows. (b) Higher values create longer render times but ultimately better output. Model by Jenny Barton.

Recompute/Save Solution/Single Animation Solution

These settings are built to help decrease rendering times. This can be especially helpful if you haven't made changes in the scene (such as lighting or different objects). However, generally, you've made changes to your scene, which is why you are re-rendering in the first place. However, when you ultimately work with radiosity in animation, these settings may come in handy. But, with the current speeds of radiosity-based images, animation is usually not feasible; so we won't discuss them much more.

Other Notes

The screen shots that we have looked at in this section were all created by rendering a scene with a Floor object and a Sky object. A light blue texture was applied to both. There was no light source in the scene; the materials themselves were creating all the lighting in the scene.

Remember that Radiosity can indeed use light objects to illuminate a scene (see the tutorial in Chapter 7). However, if you are not using light objects, be sure that you turn off the Auto Light option in the Options section. If you don't, your scene will undoubtedly be washed out with the default flood light that will be used.

Later in this chapter we will look at a couple of tutorials that analyze ways to create radiosity-based images. They are just introductory tutorials, but will show us ways to use images to create lighting, and more impressively, how to use HDRIs to create really nice looking renders.

Caustics

Caustics is the phenomenon of light radiation becoming bent and focused as it passes through transparent materials. Think of what the light looks like on a tabletop as it passes through a glass of water. This is a really powerful ability for C4D to have included; however, it is also highly specialized for transparent objects, and often the results, although beautiful, can be distracting to the story or image at hand. Because of its highly specialized nature, we won't cover it in-depth here; but take a look at the Advanced Render Module manual for details on this feature if you have a shot that needs it.

Effects

Here, effects refers to Post Rendering Effects. These are visual effects added to an image *after* it is done rendering. The benefit of this is that the final image is rendered much faster than if the rendering engine were trying to figure out the physics of, say, a lens flare. The drawback is that as these effects are painted on, they don't show up in things such as reflected surfaces. Remember our discussion (in Chapter 7) of issues such as the Glow parameter of a material? These are functioning along the same benefits and drawbacks.

Additionally, these Post Rendering Effects are the most quickly abused and overused looks in 3D. As soon as a 3D application can do things automatically, artists everywhere use it where it shouldn't be used. Take lens flares for instance. Because 3D applications make them so easily, almost every beginning 3D student creates some projects with a ton of lens flares that are neither a part of the story nor push the visual quality forward. So although we are going to look at the Effects area and the truly impressive collection of Post Rendering Effects in C4D, use them with caution and taste.

By clicking the Effects section of the Rendering Settings window, you can take a look at what effects are already active (Figure 11.14).

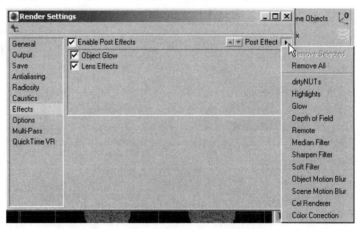

FIGURE 11.14   Post Rendering Effects available in the Effects section of the Render Settings section.

By default, Object Glow (from the Glow channel in materials) and Lens Effects (i.e., lens flares available in the Lens section of the

Attributes Editor for any light object) are activated. You can choose to deactivate them if you wish by just unclicking the checkboxes. Simlarly, when you add any Effects, you can choose to deactivate them in the same way.

Not all of the Effects are created equal. Because of this we won't cover all of them. However there are four effects in particular that are of value to enhancing your renderings: Highlights, Depth of Field, Object and Scene Motion Blur, and Cel Renderer. What follows is a cursory exploration of what these effects are, what they do, and what they look like.

Before we get started, note that you can turn an effect off by unchecking its name in the list of Effects. To activate an effect, select it from the pop-down menu shown in Figure 11.14. For every Effect, when selected in the Effects list, that effect's options are available toward the bottom of the window.

Highlights

This is new to R8, and indeed makes some beautiful images (Figure 11.15). This effect is akin to the lens effects that light sources create, only instead of being created when the camera looks directly into a light source, this results in the sort of artifacts created by cameras when looking at specular highlights that are especially "hot." Because of this, many of the Presets are classified by the kind of camera or the kind of camera lens you are virtually viewing your scene with (Figure 11.16).

Be careful with this effect as it is easy to end up with an image that is more about the highlights than the object with the highlights. Additionally, these effects can tend to "pop" when you are animating an object, so use them with care in animations.

Depth of Field

Real cameras usually have a focal length which determines at what distance from the camera's lens the objects are in focus. One of the ways to tell right away if an image is computer-generated is often the lack of any sort of Depth of Field (objects outside of this focal length being out of focus). Earlier versions of C4D had depth of field capabilities, but these have taken a huge leap forward in R8.

The amount of control you can take over how Depth of Field occurs is amazingly deep. So deep in fact that many of the options

FIGURE 11.15 Highlight Effect. This creates exaggerated highlights that mimic lens effects created through camera lenses. Model by Roger Castro.

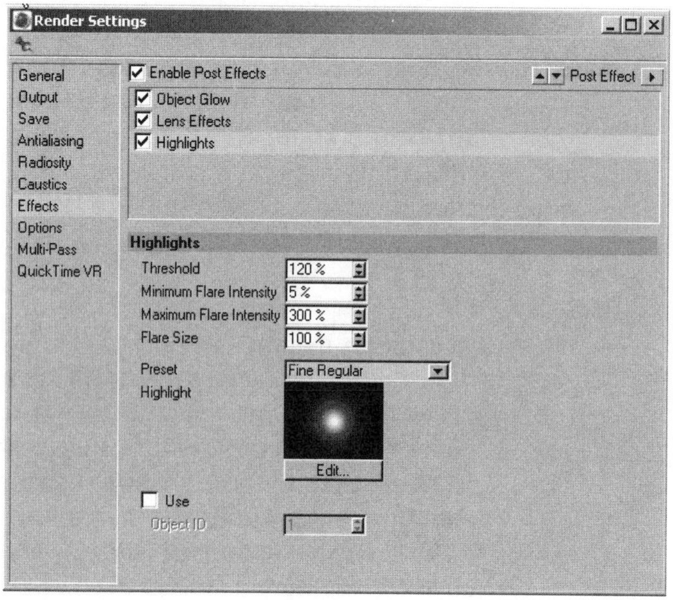

FIGURE 11.16 Settings for the Highlight Effect.

are really more detailed than they need to be for most situations. So what we are going to look at here is the basics of how to use Depth of Field (DOF) and how to get the basic looks to you want.

The first rule to effective DOF is to have a Camera object in your scene. Something that will help in the process is to not just use a Camera object, but to use a Camera With Target (Figure 11.17).

FIGURE 11.17   Creating a Camera With Target.

What this does is create two objects—a Camera object and a Null object called "Camera.Target." The power of this is that the Camera will always point at this Camera.Target. So when you move the Camera.Target, the Camera will turn to look at it. This is a really powerful tool for animation, as it allows you to keep a camera focused right where you want it, and it also is very powerful (and saves tons of time) when working with a scene that is to use DOF.

When you create a Camera With Target, and then select the Camera object in the Objects Manager, look toward the Attributes Editor. In the Depth section of the Camera's attributes, you can control whether this Camera is going to use DOF or not. Of interest to us here is the ability to "Use Target Object." This lets the Camera assume that the focal point (where the image will be most in focus) is the Camera.Target object. This allows for animated DOF that shifts as the Camera.Target object moves, or, as the Camera moves away from the Camera.Target object, the focus remains on the Camera.Target object.

To see how DOF works, consider this example. Figure 11.18 shows a Camera and a Camera.Target object and their relationship to a character. The image at right shows the rendering. Notice that there is no depth of field at all and every part of the image is equally in focus.

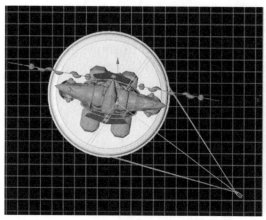 

FIGURE 11.18 Our starting point with a Camera and a Camera.Target object. The Figure at right shows the render with these settings. Model by Benjamin Yumol.

To make use of DOF, we need to do two things. First, we must activate the DOF in the Camera object itself. Do this by selecting the Camera, and then in the Depth section of the Attributes Editor, choosing Rear Blur and/or Front Blur. When you do this, you activate the input fields below that allow you to define Start and End values.

Start and End values have to do with the Start and End of the blurring process. The Start setting indicates the distance from the focal plane (which is right at Camera.Target) where blurring will begin. The End value is the distance from the focal plane where the blur is complete. When you activate Front or Read Blur, your Camera will give you a few extra visual hints in the view panel to indicate the End values.

Figure 11.19 shows our Camera with Front Blur and Rear Blur activated. Extra emphasis is added to this screenshot to point at new planes connected with the camera. The Rear Blur End plane indicates that any further from this plane, the image is completely blurred. From this plane back to the Focal Plane, the image will gradually increase focus. Similarly, the Front Blur plane indicates that from that plane and closer to the Camera, the image is completely blurred; and that from that plane to the Focal Plane, the image gradually becomes more in focus.

Unfortunately, if you really have 0 for the Start value of both Front Blur and Rear Blur, you only have a paper-thin region that is in focus. This is usually undesirable, so you want to add a value for the Start. C4D does not give you a new plane to visually indicate this Start value (regrettably), so you have to visually decide how

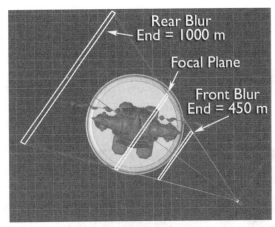

FIGURE 11.19 Adding Front Blur and Rear Blur gives you additional visual clues in your view panel. Model by Benjamin Yumol.

deep you want the blur by guessing the desired depth from the End values visual clues.

The second thing you must do is activate DOF in the Render Settings. First, add the effect from the pop-down menu in the Effects section. Click on Depth of Field from the list of Effects and the available options will appear toward the bottom of the window. Here you can choose how powerful your blur will be (Figure 11.20). The default 5% is subtle—often too subtle—so play with pumping that value up to spice things up.

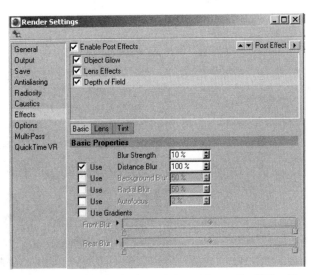

FIGURE 11.20 The Render Settings window with an active DOF and its available options.

To see some illustrations of this in action, take a look at the following screenshot/rendering pairs. Figure 11.21 shows our scene with Rear Blur activated. In this case, the Start value is set at 700m, with the End value set at 1000m. So, as you can see the 1000m mark in the view panel, imagine the Start plane being about 3/4ths of the distance from the Focal Plane to the End Plane. The Render Settings has a Blur Strength at a low 5%.

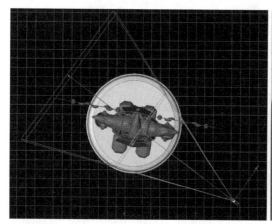 

FIGURE 11.21   Rear DOF with a Blur Strength of 5%. Model by Benjamin Yumol.

To make things a little more dramatic, Figure 11.22 is the same scene with the same Camera settings only with the Blur Strength set at a higher 25% (in the Effects section of the Settings Attributes).

FIGURE 11.22   Rear DOF with a Blur Strength of 25%. Model by Benjamin Yumol.

Of course, there is such a thing as too much of a good thing. Figure 11.23 shows the same scene once again, but with a Blur Strength of 50%. You can see how there begins to be a real disconnect from the areas of focus to those with depth of field.

FIGURE 11.23 Rear DOF with a Blur Strength of 50%. Model by Benjamin Yumol.

Finally, Figure 11.24 shows everything coming together. In this image, Front Blur is activated as well. The Start value is set at 300m and the End value is at 450m. Remember that the Start value for the Rear Blur is set at 700m. So we have a total of 1000 meters

FIGURE 11.24 Front and Rear Blur activated. Blur Strength at 25%. Model by Benjamin Yumol.

(300 in front and 700 behind the Focal Plane) of depth that is in focus. The rest drops out of focus. This works well as it allows our entire head to be in focus. Take a close look at the chest area to see where things begin to blur.

Now there are other options to play with in Depth of Field. In the Lens area, you can create artifacts within blurred regions of the image. You can even color the blurred area in the Tint area. But we've covered the basics that work for most situations. Notice that DOF can give a nice sophistication to images and animations. Give it a try.

Motion Blur

Motion blur is a really powerful effect. When you are watching a movie on your VCR/DVD player, try pressing the Pause button in the middle of some fast-moving action. The result is a very blurred still image. This is because the frames are being captured so slowly that there is considerable motion taking place between frames. The result is a blurred image in any one frame. Our eyes have come to expect this in film and television. In 3D animation, the lens captures every frame by default as a clean pristine image (Figure 11.25a). By activating the Scene Motion Blur effect, you can simulate the effects of real world cameras (Figure 11.25b).

Scene Motion Blur comes with a price, though. In order to create the motion blur, C4D renders the frame several times (as defined by your setting in Scene Motion Blur) and then blends the frames together. It moves each frame slightly ahead of the last, which is what gives the blur. This is nice because everything (including shadows) are blurred, giving you a good effect. Note that when Scene Motion blur is activated and selected in the Effects list, you can define how many x Samples or times the frame is drawn to create the blur. The drawback is that if you are using 16 times Scene Motion Blur, this means each frame must render sixteen times; so your rendering time is automatically increased 16x! If you use higher blur (such as 25 times (Figure 11.25c)), you get more blur, but 25x the rendering time. The only rendering benefit to this is that blurred scenes don't often need any antialiasing. So, if you're using Scene Motion Blur, you can typically turn off all Antialiasing options.

A decent alternative to Scene Motion Blur is the Object Motion Blur effect. This is only activated for objects that have a Motion Blur tag attached to them, created in the Objects Manager by right-clicking (COMMAND-clicking) the object and selecting New Tag> Motion Blur Tag...from the pop-down menu. It is there that you can determine the percent of the Object Motion Blur. When C4D renders the scene when tags have Object Motion Blur attached, it blurs the objects in motion. This renders much more quickly than Scene Motion Blur, but doesn't take into account things such as blurred shadows (Figure 11.25d), or, if the camera is the fastest-moving object and objects are still, there is no blur rendered.

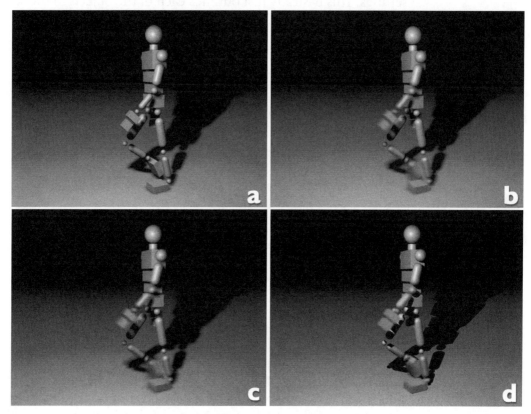

FIGURE 11.25   Various options to Motion Blur. Deciding whether to use the beautiful but time-expensive Scene Motion Blur, or the faster estimation of Object Motion Blur depends upon the nature of your scene.

Cel Renderer

C4D has long had a Cel Renderer-type option. However, R8's is by far the best realization of this powerful idea. Again, as with any other Effect, you add it to the list in the Effects section of the Render Settings. When you select it from the list of Enabled Post Effects, the Basic Properties of this effect will appear at the bottom.

Cel Rendering is a reference to the early days of animation, or current-day traditional animation. Traditional animators draw individual frames that are referred to as cels. A Cel Renderer attempts to make a scene look more hand-drawn, or more like traditional animation. Frankly, most Cel Rendered animations look like a computer still did the rendering, but this can still be very effective and produce some interesting effects.

Figure 11.26 shows the results of the default Basic Properties settings. This basically just outlines each of the objects in the scene.

FIGURE 11.26   Basic Cel Renderer, with just Outline activated.

Figure 11.27 shows the results once the Edges option has been activated. This gives you an idea of how the polygons are broken down in your scene. The result is a really tech-y looking rendering, which can be combined with traditional renderings to make some interesting images. The cover image of this book was created by compositing together a Cel Rendered image with Outline and Edges activated and a traditional rendering.

Figure 11.28 has the Edges option turn off, but the Color option turned on. The image on the left shows the render with Illumination activated, which means that C4D does its best to change the colors of the scene to reflect the lighting setup. The image on the right has Illumination turned off; this gives color to the scene but doesn't attempt to try and work the lighting scheme into the rendering.

FIGURE 11.27   Cel Renderer with Outline and Edges activated.

FIGURE 11.28   Color activated.

Remember that there are several combinations of the above settings that you can use to get a good variety of looks. The new C4D R8's Cel Renderer is quick and makes for some great-looking images. Experiment with them when you need to spice things up in your scene.

Options

The Options section of the Render Settings window is an amazingly complex, diverse, and important collection of settings. For most of your scenes, these settings will not be of any importance and many folks never have to touch them. However, there are some situations in which—without an understanding of these tools—your renderings will be confusing and incorrect.

In addition to correcting specialized problems, the settings in the Options section provide further options for optimizing early renderings. You can choose here to have C4D render the Active Object Only to get a quick idea of a newly added object without having to manually hide all the other objects in a scene. You can choose to have C4D automatically render using the floodlight attached to the camera that we discussed in the Lighting chapter (Chapter 7) if there are no other lights in the scene, using the Auto Light option. Conversely, you can turn this off if you didn't put any lights in the scene and really want it to render without any lights (e.g., glowing eyeballs that are glowing through Luminance and Glow parameters, or when you are creating Radiosity scenes). Within the Options section, you can have C4D create a Log file that gives a report of the settings done for a particular rendering by activating the Log File option. You can also tell C4D whether to carry on rendering if it cannot find a texture as it begins rendering.

The next five input fields—Ray Depth, Reflection Depth, Shadow Depth, Threshold, and Level of Detail (Figure 11.29)—are all very specific ways of instructing C4D how closely to interpret your scene. Ray Depth has to do with how far each ray is allowed to travel through transparent or Alpha Parameterized objects. Figure 11.30a shows the Editor view of several thin cubes with a texture defining the black parts as alpha'd. Figure 11.30b shows what this scene should look like in theory. Figure 11.31 shows what happens at different Ray Depths settings.

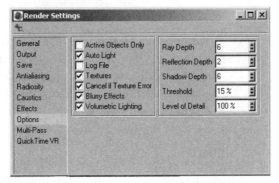

FIGURE 11.29 The Options section of the Render settings.

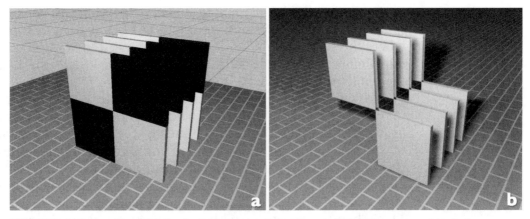

FIGURE 11.30   (a) Scene with multiple levels of objects using Alpha Channels. (b) How the scene ought to look.

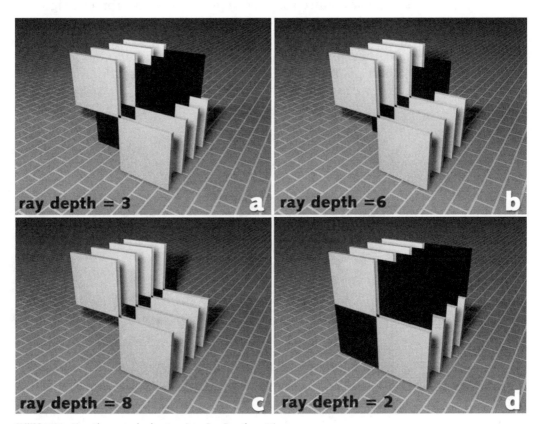

FIGURE 11.31   How the scene looks at various Ray Depths settings.

Typically, the default setting of "6" is sufficient. However, in some situations, if you mysteriously find black regions rendering where the scene should be clear, you may need to adjust this setting. Remember, the deeper the rays needed to calculate, the longer the rendering time.

The next setting is the Reflection Depth setting. Basically, this is in reference to highly reflective objects that are close to each other or whose reflections should be bouncing off each other. In theory, rays of light, or reflections, should continue indefinitely or until they break down because of air or dust. However, infinite reflections can take infinitely long to render; also, too many reflections tend to muddy a scene and make it difficult to decipher. Figure 11.32 shows a scene setup with two mirrors on either sides of a collection of spheres. These mirrors face each other. One mirror's reflection should be picked up by the other mirror, whose reflection should be bounced back again to the other mirror, etc. Figure 11.33 shows three settings for Reflection Depth and how the renderings appear. Notice that when Reflection Depth is 1, the mirror reflects the other mirror, but not the reflection of that other mirror. As the Reflection Depth increases, the number of times you can see the mirror's reflection's reflections increases. Also, as always, as the

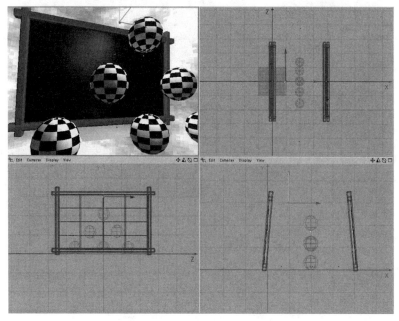

FIGURE 11.32   Reflection Scene setup.

Reflection Depth increases and there is more to calculate, the rendering time increases.

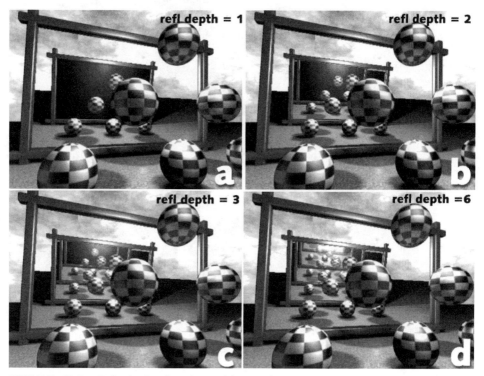

FIGURE 11.33   Various Reflection Depth settings and their results.

The Shadow Depth input field goes hand in hand with the Reflection Depth setting. Notice in Figure 11.34 where the Shadow Depth is set to 1; none of the reflections in the mirrors show shadows. As the Shadow Depth is increased, the number of reflections revealing the shadows increases. (More shadows to calculate, of course, means longer rendering time.)

C4D is smart enough to know that light dissipates as it travels. The rays that it uses to raytrace dissipate as well. It turns out that with issues such as reflection, these rays spend a lot of time to create this nice effect. Essentially, for most scenes, the reflections are a minor issue for the look as a whole. The Threshold setting tells C4D when to just stop worrying about a ray; once it drops below the percentage listed in this field, it stops the ray. Usually, the 15% listed by default works great; however, if your Reflection Parameter for a

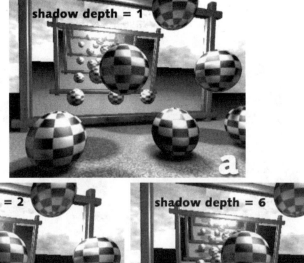

FIGURE 11.34 Shadow Depth illustrations.

material is set below 15% (in cases where you want a very slight re-flection), your scene will render with no reflection at all. To retain those very subtle reflections, decrease the Threshold value (Figure 11.35).

Certain objects in C4D (e.g., Metaballs) allow you to define LOD or Level of Detail. Basically, this determines how finely C4D is going to visually represent the scene or object. This typically trans-lates into a change in the number of polygons that are rendered. A high Level of Detail requires a lot of polygons. The Level of Detail

FIGURE 11.35   (a). Increased Threshold values result in faster rendering but less accurate reflections. (b) Notice the subtle reflections on the tiled floor.

value indicates how objects with variable LOD should be rendered. A value of 100% will render these objects at full detail, and a lower value will change the amount of detail shown for all objects with variable levels of detail.

Multi-Pass

The Multi-Pass option is an illustrator's dream come true. What this area allows you to do is create a multi-layered Photoshop image where things such as the reflection, material color, or caustics are on their own layer. This allows you to tint the reflection, increase the saturation of the material color, or lower the intensity of the caustics from within Photoshop. There is no need to re-render. This makes for very quick and easy updates or tweaks to images that have been rendered at a high resolution (and thus a high rendering time) without the need to re-render.

Figure 11.36 shows a list of the various Multi-Pass channels that can be activated. If you are planning on using your 3D project as a print output, it is not a very time-expensive thing to enable. Even if you don't always end up altering things in Photoshop, the one time that you do makes all the instances where you activated it worthwhile.

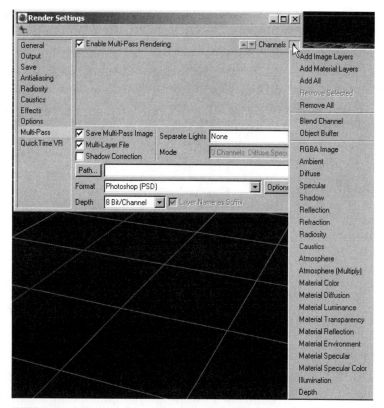

FIGURE 11.36 Multi-Pass and the variety of channels that can be activated for a Multi-Pass rendering.

QUICKTIME VR

Fun and ever so useful, QTVR (Quicktime Virtual Reality) is an Apple invention that has many copy-cat incarnations throughout the online world. Basically, a QTVR is an interactive movie that lets the view either spin around inside a virtual world or spin an object around to view all sides. C4D allows you to build these automatically. Once you have the settings correct, the rendering C4D creates is automatically altered to create the finished QTVR movie; however, there are several points you need to be aware of.

There are two different types of QTVR movies: QTVR Panorama and QTVR Object. If you wish to have a camera that interactively spins around a room, this is a QTVR Panorama movie.

Our room setup with all the necessary settings for a QTVR of the room can be found on the CD-ROM (Tutorials>Chapter 11>Room QTVR).

ON THE CD

To set your scene up to create a QTVR Panorama movie, you need to do four important things. First, set your camera up in about the middle of the room. This way, you can rotate all the way around the room and see the whole thing.

Second, in the Render Settings window, go to the Output section. Here, in the Resolution area, you can choose one of two QTVR resolutions. Yes, these values appear very large. The reason for this is the way C4D creates QTVR Panorama movies is to render a very large image that the viewer pans across. C4D renders this huge image in a way to provide a nice turn-around look (Figure 11.38).

Third, make sure that you go to the Save section and give C4D a place to save the file in the Path section and change the Format to QuickTime VR Panorama. You can choose to use one of the many QT compressions under the Options button.

Finally, in the QuickTime VR section, you can change the angles that the Camera will render from. In general, for QTVR Panoramas, you can leave this alone. Figure 11.37 shows all the settings needed for a QTVR Panorama.

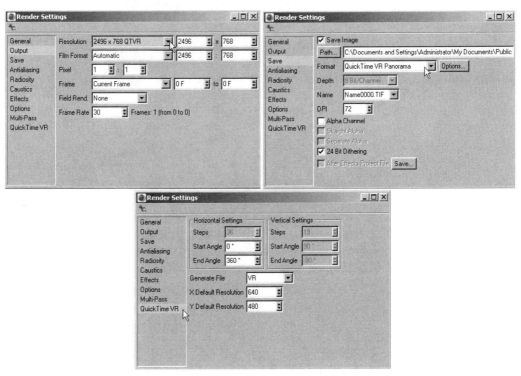

FIGURE 11.37   The Render Settings needed for an effective QTVR Panorama movie.

FIGURE 11.38 The image that C4D actually renders to create the movie.

FIGURE 11.39 Once opened in Quicktime Player, you can interactively maneuver around the room.

The second type of QTVR movie is a QTVR Object. This is the equivalent of looking at an object that you can virtually reach out and spin around to see all sides. Figure 11.40 shows the Render Settings needed to get such a rendering. Note that in the Output, you need to enter the size of the movie as you wish to view it. In the Save section, be sure to change the Format to Quicktime VR Object.

Finally, the QuickTime VR section will allow you to define how many frames you wish to render and from what angles. Each step represents a frame. So the screenshot of Figure 11.40 shows that it will take 36 shots rotating from 0 to 360 degrees horizontally; and that it will repeat this ring 3 times between the vertical angles of –20 to 20 degrees. This means that to create this rendering, C4D will need to render 108 frames (36 × 3). This will create a very smooth rotation when you rotate the QTVR file in the Quicktime player, but it also means that the rendering time could be substantial. Remember, that you can reduce the number of steps, and change the angles you wish to render the object out at.

On the CD-ROM (Tutorials>Chapter 11>QTVR Object), you can find an early version of the character we created in Chapter 5 rendered as a QTVR.

ON THE CD

This was done during the modeling process to provide an idea of how light would play across the surface of the model. Be sure to take a look at the QTVR movie in that same folder for an idea of what kind of output is created.

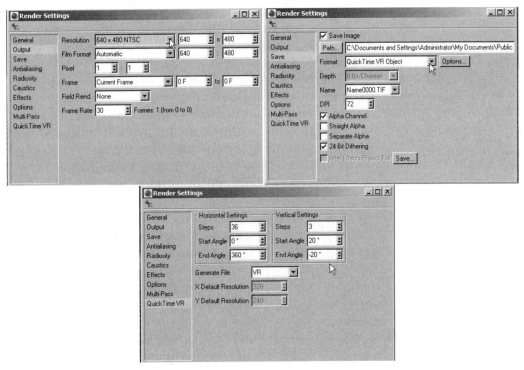

FIGURE 11.40 Render Settings for a QTVR Object.

RUNNING THROUGH THE TABS

The important thing to remember when you render is that there are many options located in the different tabs. Before you send a big project to render for a final time, follow the steps below.

1. Make sure you're rendering using the right Renderer (Raytracer Radiosity).
2. Make sure you've got the *necessary* Antialiasing settings. Don't activate it until you're sure you're going to keep the rendering.
3. Check the Output tab. Make sure
   a. that you're rendering at the right size and
   b. if you're doing an animation, that you have the correct frames selected. It's a terrible feeling to come back from letting your computer render all weekend to find that it did indeed render frame 0, but that was all it rendered when you needed 500 frames of an animation done.
4. If you're dealing with animation, double-check that Format is set to Quicktime or AVI in the Save tab.
5. Again, if you are dealing with animation, ensure that you are indeed saving the animation somewhere as defined by the Path in the Save tab, and that there is room on the disk you are saving it to. You can't suspend a rendering in C4D, so when you are rendering Quicktimes or AVIs, if you run out of room and the rendering stops, you've lost the entire rendering.
6. If you are still unsure about the animation, consider rendering to a series of .tiffs—if you are familiar with NLDVE programs, you can quickly drop this sequence in and render a Quicktime from the stills. The benefit of this is that, if you need to adjust 30 frames in the middle of the animation, you only need to render those 30 frames again and drop them back into the NLDVE, without having to re-render the entire project.
7. Check your Effects tab to make sure all the effects you're using will actually render, and if you want Scene Motion Blur or Object Motion Blur, that it's activated. If you are using Highlights, take a couple of test renderings at different points of your animation to be sure it's giving you the effect you want. And if you're using Cel-Rendering, verify that the appropriate options are checked.
8. Finally, take some good time to optimize your Options tab. Take a series of small still test renderings to see if all of the "Depths" are appropriate.

So there you have a brief overview of the many dark corners of the Render Settings, but it should give you a good idea of where to go to get certain looks or solve rendering problems that may emerge.

The rest of this chapter consists of three short tutorials that outline a radiosity technique, an HDRI technique, and an output to Flash technique. Of course, these are quick tutorials that focus on general concepts and a few tricky settings. To keep things moving quickly, we are going to use models that we created earlier in the book. Be sure to take a look on the CD-ROM for the tutorial files to see what the settings are.

ON THE CD

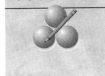

TUTORIAL

11.1 RADIOSITY: USING AN IMAGE AS THE LIGHT SOURCE

Now radiosity is more than just using an image to light the scene. As we discussed earlier, radiosity is the rendering engine that creates the calculation of bounced light. And one of the nicest functions is its ability to render a scene using no light sources at all, but using the implied light sources of an image.

To prepare for this tutorial, open up any of your room files and delete all of the lights in the scene. Since we are going to be lighting this scene using radiosity techniques—and specifically, using an image for the light source—we don't want a bunch of other light sources cluttering up the look.

Secondly, and this is a detail that is often forgotten, open your Render Settings and go to the Options areas and turn off Auto Light. Remember that as you have deleted all your light sources, C4D will automatically put a floodlight over the camera. This Auto (Flood) Light will totally skew all the results we use. So, before you even get started with the rest, make sure this is turned off.

On the CD-ROM, in Tutorials>Chapter 11>Tutorial 11.01>Tex, is a file called EastSideCyc.tif.

ON THE CD

Copy this from the CD-ROM to the Tex folder of your scene. This is a shot of a front yard that we will use to dictate how our scene is lit. In your scene, create a new material in the Materials editor. Turn off all channels but the Luminance. In the Luminance channel, click the Texture button and import EastSideCyc.tif as the image map. This will indicate that this material will be exuding light radiation.

Click the Illumination channel. Here we want to tell this material that it is to have some rather special settings. Specifically, because it will be the only light source, we want it to generate quite a bit of GI. So enter 1500 as the value for Generate under Global Illumination. Usually, you wouldn't want such a high value, especially when you have a scene *with* light sources. But in this case—as this *is* the light source—it's appropriate.

Now we need to create a cyclorama. In theatre, the cyclorama, or cyc, is the backdrop that sits at the far end of the stage that implies further things happening off in the distance. In 3D, we can use this outside of windows or doors in the same way we used backing flats in earlier tutorials. What we will do is create geometry just outside of the windows, that we will apply our newly created texture to, that will serve two purposes. First, when we look out the window, we see this front-yard scene. Secondly, it will act as the light coming into the windows to illuminate that scene.

To create this cyc, we will use a Bezier NURBS. As we want the light to be coming in from several angles including up high and down low, we can bend our cyc with a Bezier NURBS. Figure 11.41 shows the Bezier NURBS object resized quite large outside the room. Figure 11.42 shows the new material created earlier applied to this surface.

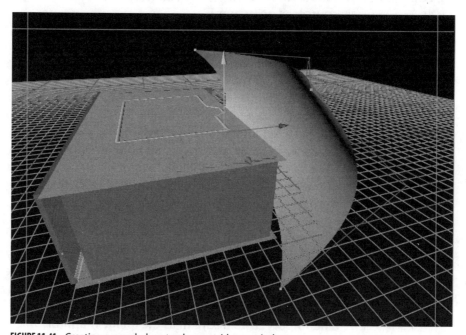

FIGURE 11.41　Creating a rounded cyc to place outside our window.

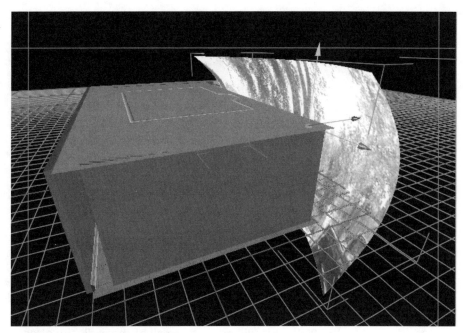

FIGURE 11.42   Cyc with material applied.

Finally, we will refine one more material for a second. The majority of the visible surfaces of this room are the walls textured with the material Tan Walls. Open this material, and in the Illumination area, turn the Generate GI value up to 500. This allows for some extra light to be bounced around the room. It will help the room look more like it does when it is lit during the day.

Now for some test renders. By default, C4D's Radiosity settings are high enough for a final render. Unfortunately, when you are setting up scenes such as this, the correct values for Generate GI and other things need to be tweaked. So, you don't want to wait for the really high-quality radiosity rendering to take place. Also, in this scene, we have a particularly complex collection of polygons right in the middle of the room which we should hide to get a good idea of the look of our scene.

So, start out by hiding the Dinner Table, the Chairs, and all the things sitting on the table by clicking the bottom gray dot on each in the Objects Manager (Figure 11.43).

Next, open the Render Settings and go to the Radiosity section. Here we want to make a few alterations to get a good idea of the general lighting setup. First, change the Accuracy to something like 20%. (We don't need perfect accuracy for this type of rendering.) Also, reduce the

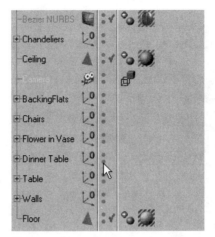

FIGURE 11.43 Hiding the high poly-count chairs and table for test renders.

Stochastic Samples to something low, such as 60. Finally, to pump up the effect of the bounced light a bit more, change the Strength setting to 500%. This will exaggerate all of the radiosity effect and further emphasize the daylight look (Figure 11.44).

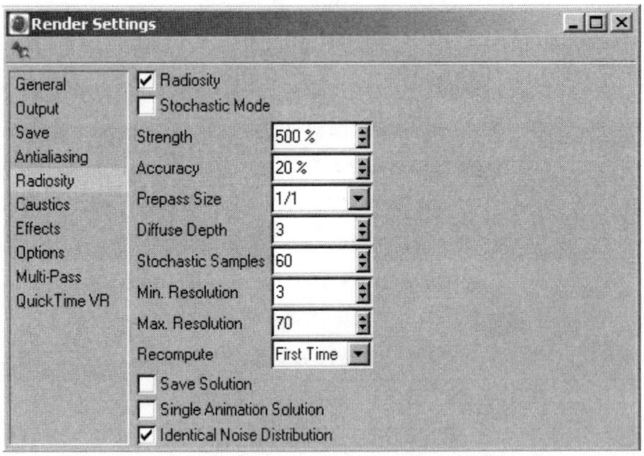

FIGURE 11.44 The Render Settings area with suggested "rough-draft" settings.

The rendering that these settings produce is not exactly the most beautiful thing in the world. In fact, it will be fairly ugly (Figure 11.45). But it gives us a good idea of how our settings are working for illumination purposes. In fact, Figure 11.45 is a screenshot of the rendering still in-progress. No need to wait for the finished rendering as even after the prepass, you can get a good idea of how your lighting is working out.

FIGURE 11.45   Rendering with low setting to give a good idea of lighting settings.

If you like what you see, turn up the Accuracy setting to 70%, and turn up the Stochastic Samples to 300 or so. Take another test rendering (Figure 11.46).

If you are pleased with this, unhide your table and chair and render away. If, with these new settings, you feel you need to make some adjustments (e.g, the scene is too bright), make the adjustments (change the Radiosity Strength) and render.

Again, this is a fairly time-consuming process, and not for the faint of heart or time-strapped. However, the results are indeed beautiful with light that is slightly tinted. It produces some amazing images (Figure 11.47).

FIGURE 11.46 High quality Accuracy and Stochastic Samples to provide a more detailed look at what the scene will render.

FIGURE 11.47 Final Radiosity-rendered images using a cyc as the lighting instrument.

11.2 HDRI

HDRI stands for High-Dynamics Range Image. We won't go into a lot of detail of what these images are, but they can contain more information than the standard digitized image. Most computer images contain brightness values of between 0 and 255. An HDRI has brightness values in the millions. This doesn't mean much when you are just looking at such an image, but in the hands of a powerful renderer, this added information can do great things. In C4D R8.1, you can make use of HDRI to create great image quality.

When you see a specular highlight in "real" life; you are actually looking at a semi-reflective surface reflecting a light source. Raytracing attempts to simulate this effect by drawing on specular highlights. HDRI images allow the renderer (either Raytracing or Radiosity) to create highlights via the Reflection channel—much closer to the "real" world.

Not just any image is an HDRI. You can create HDRIs with a program called HDR Shop available at *http://www.debevec.org/HDRShop/*. This software will assist you in infusing the added information needed for an HDRI. In this tutorial, we won't be going into this; instead, we will use some that are already constructed and freely available online.

But before we download them, take a look at the CD-ROM.

ON THE CD

Included in Tutorials>Chapter 11>Tutorial 11.02 is a .c4d file that is a stripped-down version of the room file. In this file, most of the walls and ceiling have been deleted. This allows the two spheres in the scene to provide the lighting (and subsequent reflections and highlights) for the scene.

When constructing your own scene, there are several things you'll want to keep in mind. First, remember that HDRI can be used with both Raytracing and Radiosity. However, the best images are created with Radiosity by letting the HDRI image also create the image-based lighting for the scene. Secondly, remember that to do this, you need to create a sphere or sky object that will have a material (created with HDRIs) that will provide this lighting. Finally, remember that you'll need to adjust most of your materials. The Specular channel no longer should be activated, but the Reflection channel should. Even if the Reflection channel is extremely low in intensity, it should still be activated to allow for the highlights the HDRIs will create.

If you would like to construct the scene yourself, open one of your room files from earlier tutorials and again make sure that all the lights have been deleted. Also make sure that the Render Settings has the Auto Light deactivated in the Options section. Delete walls and ceilings that may get in the way of the environment that you are going to create with a sphere. Finally, go through and work with materials that are going to be affected by the HDRI-based image to turn off their Specular channels and turn on their Reflections. If you would like, you could also use the .c4d file (Tutorial 11-02-01) on the CD-ROM.

The Web site *http://www.debevec.org/Probes/* is a fantastic site containing several HDRI as both probe images and vertical crosses. These are basically just a couple of different ways to map an image to a surface that will be reflected. For this tutorial, just go to the site and download any of the probe images. They look like a distorted globe. Make sure you download the .hdr file and save it to your Tex file associated with your room file.

When HDRI first emerged as a C4D tool, the biggest problem was getting these HDRIs to map correctly to a sky object, or a large sphere. Now with 8.1, there is a great utility Plugins>Advanced Render>Convert HDR Probe…that will take these HDRIs and convert them into a file that is usable on a sphere or sky object. Once your .hdr file is downloaded (and placed within your Tex folder), select Plugins>Advanced Render>Convert HDR Probe… and then select your .hdr file. After a second of calculation, your Picture View will show up with the results of the utility. Also, in your Tex folder, your .hdr file will have a companion file with _con attached to it. This new companion file is the converted file you will want to use in your material construction.

Create a new material, and deactivate all channels except the Luminance. Click the Image button in the Texture area and select your _con.hdr image from your Tex folder. Because of the extremely high contrast of these images, sometimes changing the O: setting (the O stands for Offset) to something like 15% will help blur the image just a bit and give you better rendered results.

Now create a sphere that completely surround your scene. Apply this newly created material to the sphere. Finally, set up your Render Settings to look something like Figure 11.48. And take a render.

Remember you can also use Stochastic mode and even Raytracing. Notice that you get nice soft highlights created from the implied light sources within the HDRI image.

Figure 11.49 shows three renderings (be sure to check these out in color on the CD-ROM) that use three different HDRIs. Notice that not only the entire color balance of each shots is altered, but the highlights on the bowls are subtle, and very realistic. All three of these scenes are also included on the CD-ROM for your dissection.

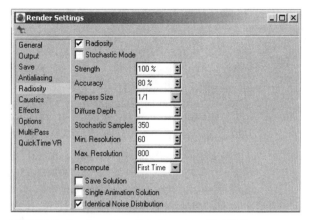

FIGURE 11.48   Render settings for a file set up with HDRI images.

FIGURE 11.49   HDRIs were used for all three of these renderings.

11.3 FLASH OUTPUT VIA FLASHEX

One of the holy grails of 3D has been the ability to output your work as a Web-conscious, Web-sized file. Most animations—regardless of codecs used—are still fairly large files and tend to eventually degrade image and sound quality. Macromedia's Flash has long been a deliverer of vector-based web content. Because it is vector-based, the file sizes are extremely small, but motion and dynamic content is easily added. Unfortunately, output by C4D or any 3D application is raster- (not vector-) based, and so does not easily fit into Flash's strategy or output without significantly increasing the size.

New to R8 is a free plug-in called FlashEx. In theory, this is a really nice little package that allows you to export your 3D projects as Flash files. C4D actually renders your file as a vector-based output. In reality, it doesn't look too bad. There are still some problems—it is not as seamless as you may like, and it doesn't create the absolute smallest file sizes—but the results are still encouraging.

To use the FlashEx rendering engine, you actually don't use the Render Settings at all. Instead go to Plugins>Cinema4D>FlashEX V2.... This will open a window similar to Figure 11.50. This interface give you the opportunity to decide how C4D will output the Flash content of your scene.

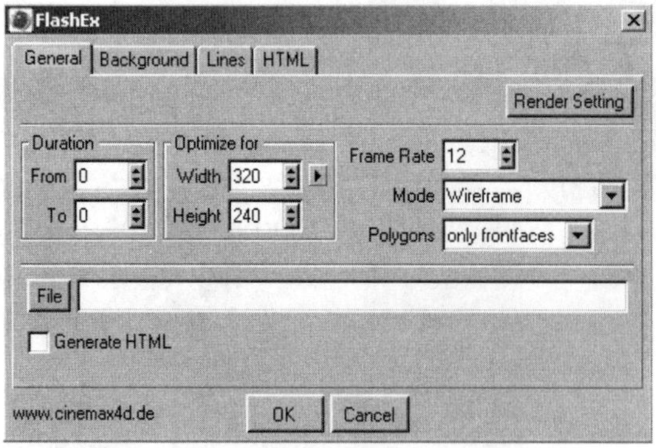

FIGURE 11.50 The FlashEx plug-in interface.

Notice that here you can define everything from how many frames you wish to render (Duration) to how large you want to create the output (Optimize for) to the Frame Rate, to where you want to save the output (File). Or, you can just hit the Render Settings button and all the settings you have set up already in the Render Settings window will be transferred into this plug-in.

There are also several additional tabs to this interface including Background, Lines, and HTML. Each of these allows you to further define or refine how you wish the output to look. As most of these are self-explanatory, we will leave it at just pointing them out. However, Figure 11.51 and 11.52 are a collection of Flash outputs that show the results of various settings.

FIGURE 11.51   Single frame output of the FlashEx plug-in.

solid - 2.73kb   outline - 2.76kb   hidden line - 48.8kb

FIGURE 11.52   Still more single frame outputs of the FlashEx plug-in.

Finally, it should be noted that although C4D will now export your movie as a .swf (Flash's native output), you can often still get slightly smaller file sizes by importing your .swf output into Flash and exporting again.

One note on potential problems: if you render your file using FlashEx and find strange holes in your results, this often means that the Normals of some of your polygons are facing the wrong way. A polygon's Normal is essentially the side of the polygons that C4D recognizes as the front. If a polygon is backward, C4D thinks "Oh, this is the back of the polygon, so I won't show it." This causes the holes. If you see this happening, switch to Polygon mode and select the polygons in the offending area, then use Structure>Align Normals to get all the normals in the area to agree, and then Structure>Reverse Normals if necessary to make sure that your Normals are facing outward.

CONCLUSION

So there you have it: the rundown of C4D's rendering process and tools. Remember that every 3D application has its own default "look." Don't allow all of your own work to always have the C4D look; make sure you are taking control and making C4D paint your creations as you want them presented. Remember that rendering is a time-intensive process but experimentation is still very necessary to show your work off right. Don't short-change your work by failing to plan enough time in for rendering. If you have the time to develop the right look for your project, you (and your client) will be happier with the unique and specialized results.

XPRESSO

by Donovan Keith

http://www.donovankeith.com

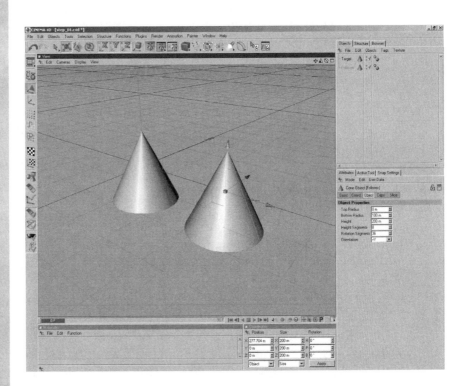

INTRODUCTION

Xpresso is a new tool in Cinema 4D R8 that provides a visual "node-based" interface for creating expressions. Expressions change elements in your scene based on the motion or properties of another element in your scene. The goal of adding expressions to your scene is to minimize the number of objects and settings you need to manipulate in order to get the results you want. So if there is something in your scene that has a cause/effect relationship with something else in your scene, such as a ball rolling because it moves from point A to point B, an expression could save you the work of manually keying the rotation.

In past versions of Cinema 4D, expressions were created by programming in a language called C.O.F.F.E.E. This was, and still is, a very good way to make complicated expressions. However, writing in a programming language can be a very intimidating and difficult thing to do, especially for those with little or no previous programming experience. Xpresso was created in order to simplify the process of making custom expressions, especially for beginners. It provides a visual interface for creating expressions. Instead of writing lines of code to link elements in a scene, all you have to do is drag a "wire" between any two properties that you want a relationship between.

Expressions can greatly simplify how you work with a scene. If there is any part of your current workflow that annoys you or you wish you could simplify, it is probably possible to create an expression that does what you want. The use of custom expressions can change Cinema 4D from a general 3D package to a tool that is custom-tailored to your current project or the way you want to work. Effects and animation studios constantly use expressions to overcome problems or limitations in their 3D software.

The goal of this chapter is to give you a working knowledge of Xpresso. The focus will not be so much on re-creating specific expressions (although this will occur) as it will be on teaching you the skills necessary to plan and build working expressions that are useful for your daily work in Cinema 4D. For this reason, there will not be an exhaustive overview of every aspect of Xpresso; that is the job of the manual. Instead, this chapter will cover the most widely-used aspects of Xpresso and the thought process behind building Xpressions.

THE ANATOMY OF AN XPRESSION

Xpresso expressions create complex relationships between objects by adding and linking together a number of simple parts. An expression that centers an object between two targets would resemble Figure 12.1. You might notice that it looks a little bit like a logic flow-chart. This is because, in essence, Xpresso expressions are visual representations of logic.

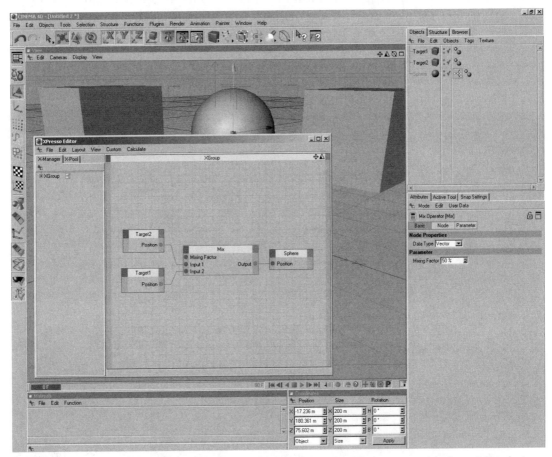

FIGURE 12.1   A quick example of an Xpresso xpression that centers an object between two targets. It looks much like a logic flowchart.

An Xpresso expression has a number of basic parts: *Nodes*, *input/output ports*, and *wires*. A good understanding of these parts and how they relate to each other is crucial when building your own expressions. The basic flow of an expression goes something like the following:

A node gets some value from the scene, such as the rotation of an object named "Target." This node's output, the rotation of "Target," is then sent to the input of another node. This node then performs a calculation on the rotation of "Target," perhaps doubling its value. This doubled rotation value can then be routed to the input of another node that sets this doubled rotation for an object named "Follower." Now the rotation of "Target" controls the rotation of "Follower." In fact, "Follower's" rotation will be exactly double that of "Target."

An expression that does just this would look similar to what you see in Figure 12.2.

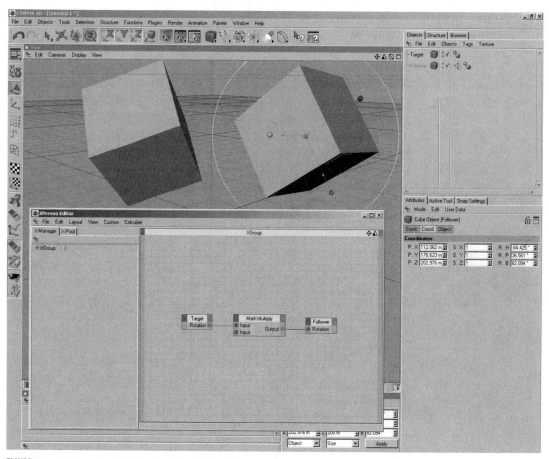

FIGURE 12.2 An Xpression that doubles the rotation of a target object.

Nodes

Nodes (Figure 12.3) are the basic units of all Xpresso expressions. They retrieve and/or change information about objects and settings in a scene or in other nodes. The Object node, for example, allows one to retrieve and change the current position of an object in your scene. Another example, the Mix node, will take two values (perhaps the positions of two objects) and mix between them based on a mixing factor (50% would result in the position of a point centered between the two objects).

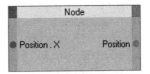

FIGURE 12.3   A Node within Xpresso.

There are many different nodes, each serving a different purpose. However, they break down into three basic categories: *General Nodes* that retrieve or change scene information, *Calculation Nodes* that manipulate or change the information provided by other nodes, and *Logic Nodes* that decide which calculations to perform based on certain states in the scene.

Input and Output Ports

By themselves, nodes are essentially useless. The real power of node-based expressions stems from your ability to link nodes together in a logical fashion. A subpart of all nodes is something called a *port*. A port is basically a place that information either enters (input) or leaves (output) a node. Information first enters a node through an input. The node then processes it, performing some mathematical or logical operation on the data. Finally it leaves the node through an output port to be further processed by other nodes. The "object node," a type of General Node, has a number of input and output ports, including position, scale, rotation, and anything else that can be edited about a given object in the Active Manager.

Ports can be of different *types*. In this case, "types" refers to the kind of information that a port is capable of working with. Ports are "typed" because there are many mathematical and other operations that are impossible to perform unless you are working with data of a given type. For example, how would you multiply an object by the number 2? It can't be done. You might multiply the position, scale, and rotation by two. But how do you multiply an object's name by two, and why would you ever want to affect an object's position, scale, rotation, and name all at the same time by the same amount? Limiting ports to certain data types makes calculations predictable and easy to understand.

There are a number of different data types—*Boolean*, *Integer*, *Real*, *Vector*, and many others. There are two possible values for a Boolean port, true or false (1 or 0). For this reason, Boolean ports are most often found in logic nodes. Integers represent the standard counting numbers: 0, 1, 2, 3, 4, etc. Integer ports are found on nodes where the order and amount of information is important. An example of a use for integers would be to store the number of points in an object or the index of a given point. Real value ports are quite versatile. Real numbers represent both positive and negative decimal numbers. These are quite useful for working with data that requires lots of precision like percentages, user inputs, lengths, and distances. Vector ports are useful for working with data that represent coordinates in space (be it Cartesian space or RGB-color space), such as positions, scales, rotations, offsets, and colors.

Figure 12.4 is a screenshot showing just some of the mind-numbing number of ports available for modification in the Light object's node.

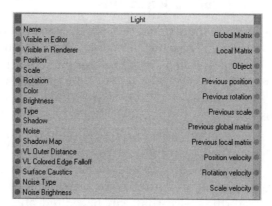

FIGURE 12.4 An illustration of some of the many ports available for a Light object's node.

Probably the most important aspect of any port is whether it is an input or an output. An input port takes information from other nodes for processing. An output port spits out the processed information for use by other nodes. By default, the blue boxes on the left of a node are the inputs and the red nodes on the right are outputs. The color and position of input and output ports can be changed by altering your preferences, but for now just keep them the way they are by default.

T U T O R I A L

12.1 LINKING THE ROTATION OF TWO OBJECTS

In this section, you will learn how to connect together the basic elements of an Xpresso expression. This expression will link together the rotations of two objects in your scenes. Among other things, this expression can be used to force both of a character's eyes to point in the same direction, preventing your character from going cross-eyed.

STEP 1: GETTING STARTED

Before we can build the Xpression, we need to first set up the scene. Start by creating a new scene (File>New Scene). Next, add two Cone Primitive objects to your scene. Name the first cone "Target" and name the second cone "Follower." Now move "Follower" so that there is a difference in position between them. You should see something similar to Figure 12.5.

STEP 2: ADDING THE XPRESSO TAG

Before you can start building an Xpression by adding nodes and connecting wires, you must first add and select an Xpresso Tag to an object in your scene. Which object you add the Xpression to in your scene really depends on personal preference to a great extent. Typically, you should add the Xpresso tag to the object that is being most directly affected by the Xpression. However, you can modify any object/property of your scene regardless of where the Xpresso tag is placed.

In the case of our current project, we could place the Xpresso tag on one of two objects: "Target" or "Follower." The "Follower" object's rotation will be controlled by the "Target" object's rotation. If we wanted to have multiple objects controlled by a single target, it makes the most sense to add the Xpresso tag to "Follower." This way, there will be at most one Xpresso tag on any given object. If we placed a new Xpresso tag on "Target" for every object we wanted to be controlled by "Target,"

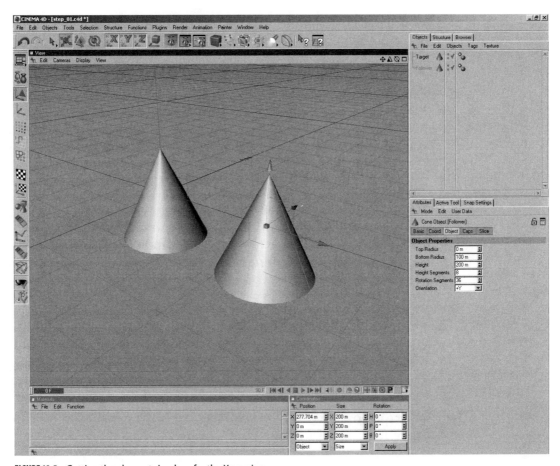

FIGURE 12.5 Getting the elements in place for the Xpression.

we could very easily end up with 20 tags that looked more or less identical.

To add an Xpresso Tag to "Follower," first select "Follower." Then, in the Objects Manager, select File>New Expression>Xpresso Expression. A new tag will appear on "Follower" and a window called the Xpresso Editor will open. Your screen should resemble Figure 12.6.

The Xpresso Editor is where you will be doing most of your work when you are working with Xpresso expressions. It is a sort of schematic view of all the parts in your expression. The part of the Xpresso Editor that looks like a piece of gray graphing paper and is labeled "XGroup" is where you add and connect the nodes in your expression. In the upper right hand corner of the XGroup are two buttons for navigation that function the same way as those found in the view ports and Picture Viewer.

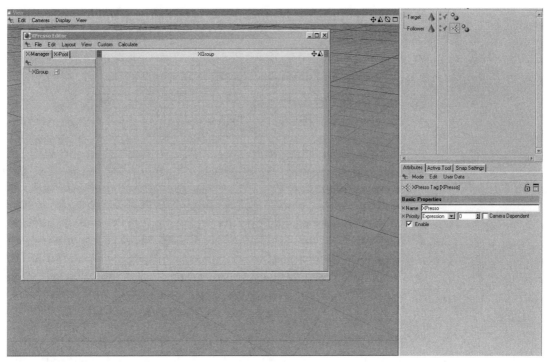

FIGURE 12.6   The Xpresso Editor after an Xpresso tag has been placed.

STEP 3: ADDING THE NODES

In order to link the rotations of "Target" and "Follower," we must first add the nodes that represent those two objects. The process for doing this is quite simple. Let's first add the node for "Target" to the Xpresso Editor. To do this, click and drag "Target" from the Objects Manager to the middle of the Gray grid in the Xpresso Editor. A box labeled "Target" should appear in the Xpresso Editor; this is the "Target" Node. Next click and drag "Follower" from the Objects Manager to the Xpresso Editor. Release the mouse over part of the grid to the right of the "Target" node. We do this so that the nodes don't overlap. Xpresso Editor should now have the two nodes available for creating relationships.

You can move and resize nodes in order to make them more aesthetically pleasing and easy to read. To move a node, simply click and drag on its title bar (where the name of the node is printed). To resize a node, click and drag on any of its edges or corners. You have to be very exact when trying to manipulate the corners or a node, especially the upper corners. This is because there is only about a 2x2 pixel area to click

on. If you want to quickly make a node as small as possible, simply double-click on the node's title bar. This will minimize the node.

STEP 4: ADDING THE PORTS

Now that we have nodes in our expression that represent the objects in
our scene, we need to specify which properties of these objects we want
to modify. Adding input and output ports to our nodes accomplishes
this. If you want to change an object's property, you must add an input
port that represents this property to that object's node. In this example,
we want to modify the rotation of "Follower" based on the rotation of
"Target." To do this we need to add a Rotation input port to "Follower" so
that its rotation can be modified. To add an input port to a node, click on
the blue box in the upper left of the "Follower" node, a drop-down menu
will appear. In it will be a list of all the possible input ports you can add to
the "Follower" node. Select Coordinates>Rotation>Rotation. The text
"Rotation" should appear just to the right of a new blue dot on the left-
hand side of the node. You have just added a Rotation input port to a
node.

Now, we want the rotation of "Follower" to be controlled by the rotation of "Target." We need to feed the rotation from "Target" to the Rotation input port on the "Follower" node. To do this, we need to add a
Rotation output port to "Target" so that we have access to its rotation. To
do this, click on the red box in the upper right corner of "Target" and select Coordinates>Rotation>Rotation from the dropdown menu. You
now have all the ports you need to complete the Xpression. Figure 12.7
shows what your nodes should look like.

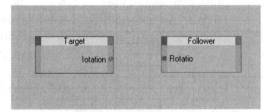

FIGURE 12.7   Two nodes with Rotation ports added as the
output of Target and the input of Follower.

STEP 5: CONNECTING THE NODES

Now that we have all of the nodes and ports set up, we can connect
them together. To connect them, drag a "wire" from an output port on

one node to an input port on another node that is of the same type. To connect the rotations of our two objects, all we have to do is wire them together. To do this, click and drag from the Rotation output port (red circle) on "Target" to the Rotation input port on "Follower" (blue circle). The nodes are now connected to each other.

To see the results of your efforts, select the "Target" object and rotate it. You should see "Follower" copy the rotation of "Target" exactly. See Figure 12.8 to see what your Xpression should look like.

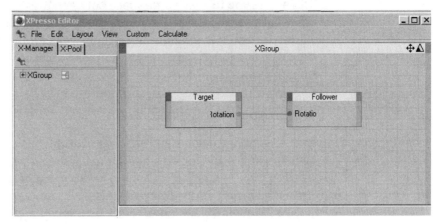

FIGURE 12.8   The completed Xpression.

SUMMARY

Congratulations! You have completed your first Xpression. Using what you've learned here, you should be able to directly link together the parameters of any two objects. Very simple two-node expressions similar to this are actually what you will end up using a lot of the time when you are working in Cinema 4D. They are very useful for rigging characters (linking rotations of bones in a tail or fingers) and building parent/child-like relationships outside of hierarchies.

ON THE CD

If you would like to see each of the steps of this tutorial within C4D, be sure and check the CD-ROM (Tutorials/Chapter12/Tutorial 01) for the .c4d files.

12.2 COPYING THE GLOBAL POSITION OF TWO OBJECTS WITH AN OFFSET

An expression that is quite useful for a number of tasks is one that copies the global position of a target object that is then given to a follower object. You already know the basics of building this expression; you did it in Tutorial 12.1. Simply add ports for Global Position (Coordinates>Global Position>Global Position) instead of ports for Rotation. However, this expression can be made dramatically more useful with the simple addition of the ability to add an offset to the position of the target object. This allows you to keep some space between the target and the follower while still copying the same overall motion. This expression is quite useful in character animation and other applications. One possible use would be to allow a character to pick up an object that is outside of its hierarchy.

PLANNING THE EXPRESSION

In this section, we will start by going over the basics of planning an expression and using logic to get the result you want. The first thing you need to do when planning how to build an expression is to decide exactly what you want it to do. In this case, we want the expression to have a follower object move to the position of a target object. We also want to be able to offset the target and follower positions by a user-definable amount on all three *xyz* axes.

The next step is to determine what information you will need to get from the scene and the user in order for your expression to function. All expressions need you to get data at some point and then set/change data. In Tutorial 12.1, the data that we were getting and setting was the local rotation of two objects. If we did not set data, there would not be a visible change in the scene, and if we did not get data, there would be no basis for the change. In this case, we need to get the Global Position of the target object and the amount the user wants the follower to be offset from the target. We also need to set the Global Position of the follower object.

After you have figured out what data you are going to get from the scene and what you're going to change with it, you need to decide how you want to modify the input data. Here, we simply want to add the user-specified offset to the target object's position. Finally, we make a step-by-step breakdown for the expression:

1. *Get* the target object's Global Position.
2. *Get* the offset amount from the user.

3. ***Add*** the offset to the target object's position.
4. ***Set*** the follower object's Global position to the target + offset position.

SCENE SETUP

Now that we have a plan for our expression, all we really need to do is implement it. First we'll put a scene together for the expression to work with. Start by adding two cubes. Name one "Target" and the other "Follower." Then add an Xpresso tag to "Target" (in the Objects Manager, New Expression>Xpresso Expression).

STEP 1: GET TARGET OBJECT'S GLOBAL POSITION

Start by dragging the "Target" object from the Objects Manager to the Xpresso Editor. Next we need to add an output port to the "Target" node so that we can get its global position. To do this, click on the red box in the upper right corner of the node. Choose: Coordinates>Global Position>Global Position from the dropdown menu. We now have access to the Target object's Global Position (Figure 12.9).

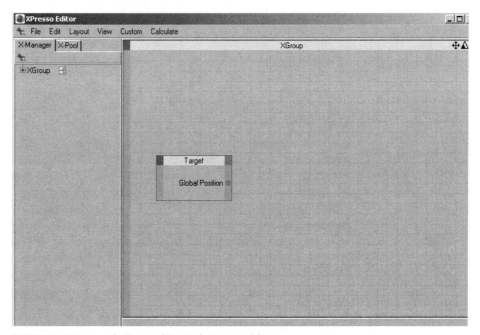

FIGURE 12.9   Setting up the Target object in the Xpresso Editor.

STEP 2: GET THE OFFSET AMOUNT FROM THE USER

There are a number of ways for users to interact with values that an Xpresso expression uses. They can change the Position, Scale, and/or Rotation of a Null object, change values in the Active Manager for a node directly, or use User Data fields to feed values to Xpresso. User Data fields are the most elegant solution in that they add sliders directly to the Cinema Interface. However, they are somewhat difficult to set up. Modifying the values in a node directly is actually quite easy, especially when there are only a few values that the user needs to change. Modifying a Null object is difficult at best; more than anything, it is a legacy from the days of programming in Cinema 4D before the advent of Xpresso and the Active Manager.

For this expression, we will allow the user to enter data—the amount of offset—directly into a node in the Xpresso Expression. The easiest way to do this is to create what is called a Constant node. Basically, a Constant node acts as a storage container for a value specified by the user, it does not change. To add a Constant node, right-click in the Xpresso Editor and choose: New Node>Xpresso>General>Constant from the drop-down menu. You should now have a new node labeled Constant. It already has an output port, so there is no need to create one. With this node, we can get the amount of offset from the user.

Currently, the data type of the Constant node is set to Real (decimal numbers, if you'll recall). However, a single decimal place number cannot represent offsets, or the difference in the position of two points in 3D space. To adequately represent an offset in space, we need three values. We now have two options: we can create two more Constant nodes each representing one axis of the *xyz* offset or we can simply change the type of the Constant node from Real to Vector (a data type that stores three real values together). To change the data type of the Constant node, simply select the Constant node in the Xpresso Editor and then change the Data Type value for the node in the Active Manager from Real to Vector. In the Active Manager, you should now see three input fields to the right of the text "Value." When you're done, your view should look like Figure 12.10.

STEP 3: ADD THE OFFSET TO THE TARGET OBJECT'S POSITION

To modify any data or to perform any calculation in Xpresso, a node must be used. In order to add together the Target object's position and the offset, we will need to use a Math node. The Math node has two input ports and one output port. The Math node will take the two values

FIGURE 12.10   Two nodes getting all the necessary info; including the new Constant node to allow for Vector input.

it gets from the inputs and then perform a simple mathematical calculation between them. It then returns the result of this calculation through its output port.

Start by adding a Math node to the Xpresso Editor. You can do this by right-clicking where you want to place it in the Editor and then selecting New Node>Xpresso>Calculate>Math. You should now have a new Math node. Now we need to change its properties so that it does what we need it to. First, make sure that the operation it is performing is addition (we want to add the offset to the target position). To do this, select the Math node and then ensure that the Function value in the Active Manager is set to "Add." Then change the Data Type of the node to Vector so that it can properly deal with the values we need to add together.

Now that the node is configured, we simply need to connect it with the other nodes in our expression. Drag a wire (click-drag) from the Target Global Position output port to one of the Input ports on the Math node. Then drag a wire from the Constant node's output port to the remaining input port on the Math node. Your expression should now look like the one in Figure 12.11.

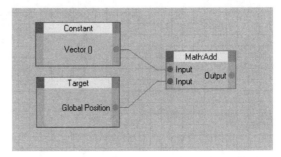

FIGURE 12.11   Adding together the position and the offset by creating wires between the Math node and the Constant and Target nodes.

STEP 4: SET FOLLOWER OBJECT'S POSITION

The last step is to set the position of the Follower object to that of the target plus the positional offset. To do this, drag and drop the Follower object from the Objects Manager into the Xpresso Editor. Then add a Global Position input port to the Follower node by clicking on the blue box in the upper-left corner of the node and selecting Coordinates> Global Position>Global Position from the drop-down menu. Finally, drag a wire from the output of the Math node to the new Global Position input port on the Follower node. The completed expression should look like Figure 12.12.

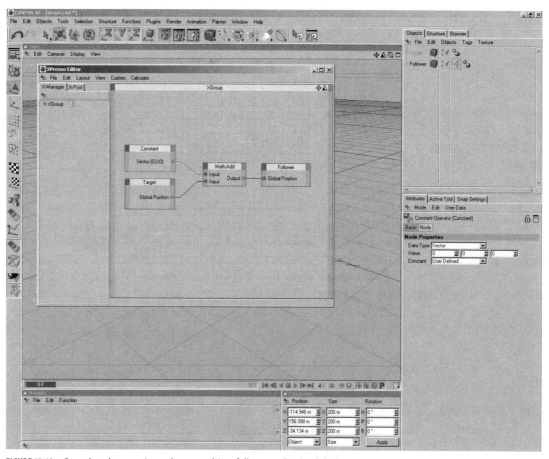

FIGURE 12.12 Completed expression to have an object follow another in global space.

SUMMARY

You have just created a very useful expression. To see this, start by moving the target object around. At the moment it looks like there is only one cube in the scene. This is where the offset feature we built in will come in handy. Open up the expression, select the Constant node and then change the *xyz* values for the Constant in the Active Manager. Try typing in 200, 200, 200. Now the Follower cube will stay fixed on the corner of the Target cube. This expression is very useful if you want a character to pick up and set down an object that is outside of its hierarchy. By animating the "enable" property of the Xpresso Expression tag in the Active Manager, you can control whether or not the expression actually affects your scene. In order to animate the example of a character picking something up, start by having "enable" turned off. Keyframe the starting position of the object you want the character to pick up. Then when you want your character to pick up the object, switch enable to on and set another keyframe. Your character can now easily pick up and set down objects.

This expression can also be easily adapted to many other situations. Simply change the Global Position ports to Rotation and you have a different expression entirely. Also, try changing the function of the Math node from addition to multiplication; you can very easily create an expression that distributes the rotation of a simple 3-bone spine to that of a much more complex, smoother bending 15-bone spine. Again, to get a better idea of this expression (if you need it), be sure to check out the .c4d files on the CD-ROM (Tutorials/Chapter12/Tutorial 02).

ON THE CD

TUTORIAL

12.3 KEEPING AN OBJECT ABOVE THE FLOOR

One of the most common problems faced by character animators is that their character's feet sometimes sink below the ground plane. This often results in feet slipping during walk cycles and it can destroy the "illusion of life" that animators strive to create. Xpresso provides us with the tools to prevent objects, namely a character's feet, from slipping through the floor plane.

PLANNING THE EXPRESSION

The goal of this expression is to prevent an object from passing below the floor plane. Before creating an expression to resolve the problem, we must first define the problem. Our problem only exists when the base of our character's feet is lower than the position of the floor plane. This is a pretty good definition of our problem, but it needs to be more exact. When the base of a character's foot is lower on the global y-axis than the level of the floor plane on the global y-axis, it appears that the floor is not solid.

Next, we have to decide what the expression must do to fix the problem. What we need it to do is keep the foot object above the floor object. This can be more exactly defined as not letting the y-position of the foot object become less than the y-position of the floor object. Now that we have defined the problem and its solution in relatively plain English, we need to translate it into a logical description that we can build with Xpresso.

In Xpresso, there are a number of logic nodes. These nodes allow the expression to do one thing if a scene is in a certain state or do something else if the scene is not in that state. When using a written plan, these logic nodes can be represented with the words *if* and *else*. These statements are structured something like: **If** [something] is occurring/true, then do this. **Else**, or otherwise, do this.

The two nodes most useful for dealing with these sorts of logical statements are *Comparison* and *Condition*. The Comparison node takes two values as inputs. It then compares them, using one of a number of operators (less than, greater than, equal to, not equal to, etc.) and returns 1 (true) or 0 (false) depending on whether or not the statement: **input 1 [operator] input 2** is true. For example:

< 2 would return 1/true because 1 is less than 2.
< 1 would return 0 /false because 2 is not less than 1.
!= 4 would return 1/true because 3 is not equal to 4.
<= 2 would return 1/true because 2 is less than or equal to 2.

The Condition node will take a number of inputs: a switch and an input for each possible state the switch can be. This is useful if you want an expression to do one thing if a given state is true and something different if something else is true. It is especially useful for switching between two options based on the result of a comparison node.

Now that we have the language to represent logic and know that it is possible to represent this logic with Xpresso (using the Comparison and Condition nodes) we can begin to plan our expression to keep feet above the floor. Once again, let us restate when our problem occurs and what we should do about it: When the foot y-position is less than (<) the floor y-position, the foot object should be moved up to the level of the floor. If the foot is above the position of the floor, we don't need to do anything, as it is not a problem. One thing to remember is that most times, the axis of a foot object is not actually at the base of the foot, so it is important that the user can specify an offset from the floor. Now lets do a complete breakdown for what the expression needs to do, step-by-step:

1. **Get** the global *y*-positions of both the floor and the foot objects. Also, **get** the amount of offset the user wants from the floor.
2. **Add** the user-specified offset to the floor's position. This basically adds an imaginary floor plane above the actual floor plane.
3. **Compare** the foot's *y*-position and the *y*-position of the floor plus the offset. This is done to establish whether the foot is below the floor.
4. **If** the *y*-position of the foot is less than that of the floor, **set** the *y*-position of the foot to that of the floor. This will move the foot up to the position of the floor.

SCENE SETUP

Create a new scene. Add a floor object and a sphere. The sphere will represent the foot in our scene. Rename "Sphere" to "Foot." Now add an Xpresso Expression tag to the "Foot" object.

STEP 1: GET THE INFO

We want to get the *y*-positions of the two objects in our scene. To do this, we need to have them represented in the Xpresso editor. From the Objects Manager, drag the floor and the "Foot" into the Xpresso Editor. You should now have two nodes. Add a "Global Position.Y" output port to each node by clicking on the red square in the upper-right corner of each node and selecting Coordinates>Global Position>Global Position.Y from the drop-down menu. By choosing Global Position instead of just Position from the drop-down, we now have access to the position of the object unaffected by hierarchy (it is the same result you would get from changing Object to World space in the Coordinates Manager).

We also need to get the amount the foot is naturally offset from the floor. To do this, add a Constant node by right-clicking in the Xpresso editor and selecting New Node>Xpresso>General>Constant from the drop-down menu. By default, the value stored in the Constant node is 0. Click on the Constant node and—in the Active Manager—change the value from 0 to 100. The radius of the sphere representing the foot is 100; this way the sphere will not penetrate the floor (Figure 12.13).

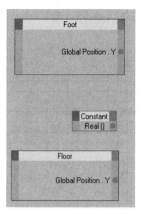

FIGURE 12.13 Setting up the scene by creating a Constant note to get the data for the height of the foot from the floor.

STEP 2: ADD THE FLOOR POSITION AND THE OFFSET

Next, we wanted to add the *y*-Position of the floor object and the user-specified offset. This is done so that any calculations that occur in the future will be based on the height of the "virtual" floor that we don't want the axis of our foot object to go through. To add the two values together, we need to add a Math node. To do this, right-click in the Xpresso editor and choose New Node>Xpresso>Calculate>Math. Ensure that the function is set to Add in the Active Manager and that the data type is Real. To actually perform the addition, all we have to do is wire the nodes together. Drag a wire from the Constant's output port to the first input port of the Math node. Next, drag a wire from the Floor node's Global Position.Y output port to the second input port on the Math node (Figure 12.14).

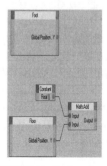

FIGURE 12.14 Performing the addition using a Math node.

STEP 3: COMPARE THE POSITIONS

Now that we have the position of the foot and the position of the virtual floor plane, we need to determine if the foot is below the floor, so we need to add a Comparison node. To do this, right-click in the Xpresso Editor and choose New Node>Xpresso>Logic>Compare. The Comparison node takes two inputs and places them in an inequality (a mathematical statement where there is a value on the left and the right of an operator/function). Depending on whether or not the inequality is true, the node will output either 1 (true), or 0 (false). What we want to test is whether the foot's position is less than the floor's position.

To perform this comparison, start by selecting the Comparison node. Next, change its function in the Active Manager from equality (==) to less than (<). Now, drag a wire from the output from the Foot node (its y-position) to the first input on the Comparison node. Finally, drag a wire from the output of the Math node (floor position plus the offset) to the second input on the Comparison node. You have just constructed the inequality:

Foot y-Position < (Floor y-Position + Offset).

The results of all this connecting is shown in Figure 12.15.

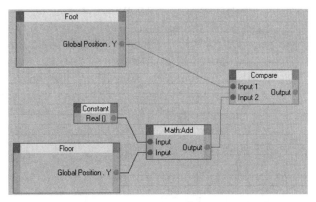

FIGURE 12.15   Creating the inequality equation by connecting nodes within the Xpression Editor.

STEP 4: IF THE FOOT IS BELOW THE FLOOR...

Now that we have performed a comparison to see whether or not the foot is below the floor, we need to do something useful with that information. Through the use of the Condition node, we can set the position of the foot to that of the floor, if the foot is below the floor. To do this, add a Condition node to the Xpresso Editor by right-clicking and choosing New Node>Xpresso>Logic>Condition. The Condition node by default has 3 input ports. The top-most port is the switch port; this value input into this port determines which of the other input ports to use/output. If the value put into the switch port is 0, it will return the first of the "input" ports. If the value put into the switch port is 1, it will return the second of the "input" ports.

The Comparison node will return one of two values: 0 if the foot is above the floor (inequality is false), and 1 if the foot is below the floor (inequality is true). Thus it makes sense to connect the output of the Comparison node to the switch input port of the Condition node. This way the Condition node can switch between one of two values based on the result of the Comparison node (the Condition node will switch based on whether or not the foot is below the floor). Next, we need to connect values to the two remaining input ports on the Condition node. The Condition node returns the first input if the switch input (result of the Comparison node) is false (foot is above the floor). For this reason, you should drag a wire from the Foot's y-Position output port into the first "input" input port on the Condition node. Because there is only one input left on the Condition node, it seems reasonable to connect it to the result of the Addition node (floor + offset); drag a wire between these ports to make the connection.

The Condition node will now output the position of the foot object if the foot is above the floor. It will also output the position of the floor plus the offset when the foot is below the floor. The last step is to plug in these possible outputs where they belong, the Global Position.Y input port of the foot object. To do this, drag the foot object from the Object Manager into the Xpresso Editor, add a Global Position.Y input port to the new node, and finally drag a wire from the output of the Condition node to the input of the new Foot node (Figure 12.16).

SUMMARY

Try moving the sphere (or foot) around in the scene. It should stay firmly above the floor plane. This example introduced some new and important concepts that you will use in most of the more complex expressions you create. The use of the Comparison and Condition nodes allow you to create logic-based expressions. Objects can be manipulated in a number of different ways, based on their current state. A good understanding of the logic nodes will make working with Xpresso significantly easier.

As this is a more complicated expression than covered earlier, make sure and take a look at the .c4d files if your expression didn't emerge

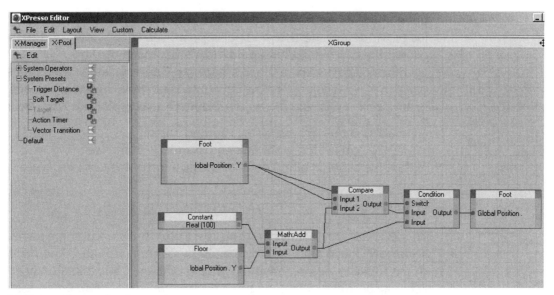

FIGURE 12.16   The completed expression.

ON THE CD

with the desired results. They can be found on the CD-ROM in Tutorials/Chapter12/Tutorial 03.

TUTORIAL

12.4 CONTROLLING SPLINES/POINTS WITH OBJECTS

Manipulating points in splines and polygon objects can be quite useful. Simulating the hanging behavior of ropes, mathematically based morphs, and deformations are all possible. In this tutorial, you will learn the basics of working with points. After completing this expression, you will have a way to manipulate the points in a spline based on the positions of controller objects.

PLANNING THE EXPRESSION

An expression that controls the points of an object is actually pretty simple in concept. You get the point that you want, then manipulate it, and finally set its position to the new position. There are only a couple things that make this process a bit slower, you can't simply click on a point in the editor view and then drag it into the Xpresso Editor to get a Point node. You have to specify which object the point belongs to, and which point in the object it is. The points are accessed/differentiated by their index. To determine the index of a point, select the point and then choose the command View>Jump Next Selection in the Structure Manager (nested beneath the Objects Manager). The point index is the number in the far left column of the highlighted row. Now that we are clearer on how points work in Xpresso, we should be able to plan our Xpression:

1. Get the Global Position of the Control object.
2. Get the object the point belongs to and the point itself.
3. Set the position of the point to the position of the Control object.

Scene Setup

To manipulate the points of an object, we need two things, some points and a controller object. Start by drawing a spline curve with 2-3 points; it doesn't have to look like anything in particular. Next, add a small cube to act as a controller object. Name the cube "Controller." Add an Xpresso tag to the cube, this way if we want to use more controller objects in the future, all we have to do is copy the tag from one controller to another.

Step 1: Get the Global Position of the Control Object

Start by opening the Xpresso Editor for the expression on the Control object if you haven't already. Then drag the controller object into the Xpresso editor. Add a Global Position output port to the new node (Coordinates>Global Position>Global Position). The scene should look somewhat like Figure 12.17.

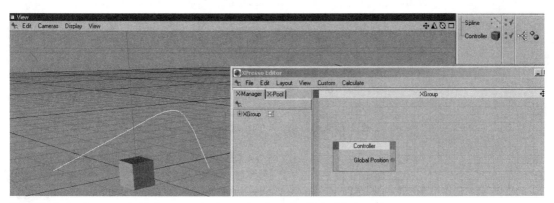

FIGURE 12.17   Getting started with the expression by getting the controller's global position.

STEP 2: GET THE POINT

Before accessing an object's points, we must first have a node to represent the object in the Xpresso editor. To do this, drag the spline object from the Objects Manager into the Xpresso Editor. Next, we need to add a Point node so that we can manipulate the points. To do this, right click in the Xpresso Editor and select New Node>Xpresso>General>Point. A new node labeled "point" should appear in your view. Observe that there are two available inputs: Object, and Point Index. The Object port should be wired to the object whose points you want to access. The Point Index refers to which point you want to access. Just to make things easy, we will be manipulating the first point in the spline, point 0. You can adjust which point is being accessed. Feeding a value from another node into the Point Index port can do this. Or you can select the Point node and change the Point Index value in the Active Manager.

The Object port on the Point node needs to be wired to an output port from another node of the data type Object. Conveniently enough, the Controller object node has Object listed in its list of possible output ports. Add an Object output port to the Controller node by clicking on the red box in the upper-right corner of the node and choosing Object from the drop-down menu. Now drag a wire from the Object output port to the Object input port on the Point node (Figure 12.18).

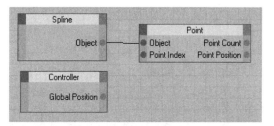

FIGURE 12.18   Getting the Point.

STEP 3: SET THE POINT POSITION

Now all that remains is to set the position of the point to that of the Controller object. To do this, add a Point Position input port to the Point node. This port will change the position of the point indicated by the Point Index port. Now, drag a wire from the Global Position port on the Controller node to the Input Position port on the Point node (Figure 12.19).

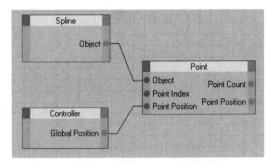

FIGURE 12.19 Expression setup to change the point.

SUMMARY

Move the Controller object, and watch as the shape of the spline updates so that it stays connected with the Controller object. This expression can be used to easily animate the points of a spline. PLA (Point Level Animation) can be difficult to work with and doesn't allow independent animation of each point. Try copying the Controller object and changing the value for Point Index in the Point node. As an exercise, create an expression that will move objects based on the positions of points in a spline. For examples of these exercises, be sure to check out the Tutorial files on the CD-ROM (Tutorials/Chapter12/Tutorial 04).

ON THE CD

BUILDING BLOCKS

Although the tutorials in the previous sections are quite useful and cover a lot of information, it is unnecessary to use large portions of Xpresso in a well-planned expression. In order to adequately cover the aspects of Xpresso that you will be using in most of your expressions, it is necessary to break from the exercise-based teaching model. The goal of this section is to introduce you to all of the commonly used and easily misunderstood parts of Xpresso so that you will be able to build expressions on your own.

UNDERSTANDING VECTORS

Understanding what exactly a vector is and how to use it is almost necessary knowledge for Xpresso programming. Vectors allow you to determine point normals, center objects between others, perform point deformations, and many other things. A vector is made of 3 components (*x*, *y*, and *z*), one for each axis. Essentially the components of a vector act as a set of directions that tell you how to go from one point to another. The value of each of the components represent how far one has to travel along each axis to get to the point in space the vector is describing. The vector (2,–5,10) is saying to move 2 units over on the *x*-axis, 5 units down (the minus sign indicates travel in the opposite direction of the axis) on the *y*-axis, and 10 units back on the *z*-axis.

Basic math is quite useful for working with vectors. However, visualizing and understanding the effects of math on vectors can be somewhat difficult. When trying to understand vectors, it really helps to think of them as arrows that have a direction (determined by the relative size of the components) and a length (determined by the overall size of the components). These arrows are basically paths that can be traveled (Figure 12.20).

FIGURE 12.20   A basic vector.

When you add two vectors together, you are essentially taking one vector and putting it on the tip of the other. The result of the addition is the vector going from the base of the first vector and extending to the tip of the second vector. Vector addition is useful if you are trying to offset a point in space (Figure 12.21).

The result of a vector subtraction is a vector describing the path from the tip of one vector to the tip of the other. Whether this is a trip from vector *a* to vector *b* or vice versa is determined by the order of the subtraction. To get the vector describing the path from point *a* to point *b*, you would subtract point *a* from point *b*. This is

FIGURE 12.21 Vector addition.

useful for determining how to move from one point in space to another (Figure 12.22).

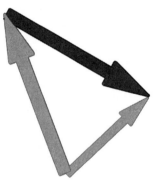

FIGURE 12.22 Vector subtraction.

Multiplying a vector with a real/decimal number will essentially scale the length of the vector by the real number (Figure 12.23). The direction does not change because each of the components of the vector is scaled equally. This is quite useful if you want to scale up the difference in positions of two vectors. Dividing a vector by a real number will also scale it in a similar (but opposite) way.

Multiplying a vector with a vector (also called the Cross Product of two vectors) will give you a vector that is perpendicular to the two vectors you are multiplying. Use the Cross Product node in order to perform this operation. It is useful for constructing the normal of a plane that is defined by two vectors (the Polygon node does this for you automatically by outputting a normal vector).

FIGURE 12.23   Vector real multiplication.

Unit vectors, or normal vectors, are vectors that are used to describe only rotation. They are one unit long. This makes them especially well-suited to storing rotations because when they are multiplied with real numbers, the direction stays the same but the vectors become length of the real number they are multiplied by. You can convert a vector to a normal vector by using the Universal Adapter node.

By using these basic mathematical functions on vectors, you can do almost any kind of point manipulation you would ever want to do. You can move points out along their normals (point position + (normal*distance)) or move them with an offset (point position + offset vector), among other things.

LOGIC

There are a number of logic nodes in Xpresso. There is a fair amount of overlap in their functionality. Essentially, the use of logic nodes allows you to program expressions that do one thing in one situation and do something entirely different in another situation. Tutorial 12.3 gave a good example of the possibilities that logic nodes allow you. Probably the two of the most useful logic nodes are the Comparison and Condition nodes. The Comparison node allows you to evaluate whether or a not an inequality is true. The Condition node will switch between node structures/branches depending on its input. Combining these nodes allows you to prevent unnecessary or impossible calculations (e.g., division by 0).

If the Comparison node does not afford enough control with just one operator, it is possible to join multiple Comparison nodes using Bool nodes. Bool nodes are nodes that take Boolean values (0 and 1) as inputs and then do a test of Boolean logic on the inputs, which results in a value of 0 (false) or 1 (true). An example of the combination of two Comparison nodes and a Bool node would be the following:

(10 < A)	&&	(A < 50)
Comparison	Bool	Comparison

This would only return true if A was above 10 and below 50.

ITERATOR NODES

Iterator nodes allow you to go through and operate on a list of elements very quickly and automatically. Instead of adding nodes to move every point in an object individually, you can use an iteration node to execute the same nodes over and over again automatically. Essentially iteration nodes start at one place, be it a number or place in a hierarchy, and end in another after going through every single step between the start and the destination. Try plugging an iteration node into the Point Index port of a Point node; you can now change every point in the object using the same collection of nodes.

These nodes are useful if you want to operate on large lists of anything. If you want to build a deformer with Xpresso, you will definitely need to use an iterator node. Or if you want to fix a large number of objects to the surface of another object, you can use a hierarchy iterator node. A good understanding of iterator nodes is indispensable.

TIPS & TRICKS

Set Driver, Set Driven

A lot of what Xpresso is useful for (direct connection of parameters) can easily be achieved with the Set Driver, Set Driven commands. When learning Xpresso, it is important to build up all of the nodes and connections yourself. However, once you understand Xpresso, you can and should do what takes the least amount of time, yet still yields the result you want. In many cases, this means using the Set Driver, Set Driven commands. Don't think that because the parameters you want to link aren't positions or other coordinates that you can't use Set Driver, Set Driven. In fact, it is possible to link any two animatable parameters using these commands. A great use is driving a morph based on the rotation of a bone; this is an elegant way of having a bicep automatically flex as the arm bends. For more information on these commands, reference the manual.

Commenting

Commenting your Xpressions is invaluable. By adding descriptions of what each part of an Xpresso expression is doing, you will greatly add to your ability to understand it when you are creating it and especially when you are editing it in the future. To add a comment, right-click in the Xpresso Editor and select New Node>Xpresso> General>Remark.

Keep Your Wires Clean

There is nothing more frustrating than working with an expression where you don't know exactly what is going on. One thing that often makes the flow of an expression difficult to follow is crossing wires. Whenever possible, arrange your nodes so that there are direct lines between nodes that cross each other as little as possible. Sometimes it helps to have multiple copies of the same node—if you can't see where a wire is coming from it's very difficult to determine what it is doing and why it is doing it. One last thing is to attempt to clump or group your nodes together into larger blocks of logic.

Plan. Plan. Plan.

Coming up with a clear plan for every step of your expression will save you hours of head-scratching. The more time you spend planning an expression, the less time you will spend working on it overall. To come up with a good plan, you should:

1. Define the problem you want the expression to solve.
2. Define exactly what you want the expression to do.
3. Decide what information you will be getting and setting.
4. Draw any sketches or look up any formulas you will need to properly modify the data.
5. Break down what you need to do into simple steps.

WHERE TO GO FROM HERE

This chapter was only a very brief introduction to Xpresso. It was meant to give you some confidence and a better understanding of how Xpressions are planned and built. With the knowledge you now have, you should be able to create a number of very useful expressions for your day-to-day work. It is very rare for most expressions you create to expand beyond just a few nodes. There are, of course, cases where Xpressions can become very complex, but these are typically created for interesting and unusual situations.

CONCLUSION

If you would like to know more about Xpresso, the Cinema 4D manual is actually a great reference for what nodes do and how to use them. Maxon's Plugin Café website *(http://www.plugincafe.com)* also offers tutorials, downloads, and a support forum for Xpresso. More and more users are also putting Xpresso tutorials and example files online. There is no one source that will give you all the information you need for a given project; look everywhere. At times, the number of nodes and possible combinations can seem overwhelming. Don't be discouraged. Look them up as you need them. If you don't know how to approach a problem, break it up into smaller sub-problems and solve each of them individually.

Have fun!

ABOUT THE CD-ROM

Often, as you read through books, magazines, or tutorials, the screenshots included are just not enough. Sometimes, you need to be able to really look closely at the images and illustrations in full color and really full screen. For this reason, all of the screen shots included in this volume are also included on the CD-ROM, in the Images folder. The chapters on Rendering and Textures especially require you to look at the color images on the CD-ROM.

But sometimes screenshots just don't do the trick either. To help make sure that these tutorials make sense, the finished C4D files are included on the CD-ROM. Open them up, tear them apart, and take a look at how the process works.

The CD-ROM is often a forgotten resource. Be sure to take advantage of the important details contained there.

The CD-ROM is broken down into two main sections:

Images—Here you will find all the images of the book as large, full-color files. They are saved as .jpg's so you should be able to open them on almost any computer. If you are reading through the book and one of the figures doesn't quite do it for you, or is unclear, be sure to take a look here.

Tutorials—Within this folder, you will find all the C4D files used to create the tutorials in this volume. Sometimes the best way to learn from a project is to be able to break the file down and look at what settings are set to what. The tutorials for each chapter are broken down into their own folders, and each chapter folder has separate folders for each individual tutorial. If you don't need to access these—great. But be sure to grab them if you need them.

RECOMMENDED SYSTEM REQUIREMENTS

Mac

G3 Processor
256 MB Ram
200 MB Hard-Drive Space
16 MB Video Card
QuickTime 6.0 or higher
Cinema 4D R8

PC

PIII Processor
256 MB RAM
200 MB Hard-Drive Space
32 MB Video Card
QuickTime 6.0 or higher
Cinema 4D R8

INDEX